FAVORITE BRAND NAME

Treasury of
CHRISTMAS

Publications International, Ltd.

Favorite Brand Name Recipes at www.fbnr.com

Pictured on the front cover *(clockwise from top right):* Chocolate Crinkle Cookies *(page 463),* Pinwheels *(page 426),* Kringle's Cutouts *(page 435),* Herb Sauced Vegetables *(page 237),* Festive Green Beans *(page 232)* and Roast Turkey with Pan Gravy *(page 160).*

Pictured on the back cover *(clockwise from top):* Holiday Stollen *(page 264),* Chicken with Brandied Fruit Sauce *(page 174)* and Christmas Ornament Cookies *(page 428).*

ISBN: 0-7853-7605-4

Library of Congress Control Number: 2002104415

Manufactured in China.

8 7 6 5 4 3 2 1

Microwave Cooking: Microwave ovens vary in wattage. The microwave cooking times given in this publication are approximate. Use the cooking times as guidelines and check for doneness before adding more time. Consult manufacturer's instructions for suitable microwave-safe cooking dishes.

Contents

TREASURY OF CHRISTMAS

Bright Beginnings

TO HOLIDAY COOKING

Cooking takes on special joy during the Christmas season. Open houses, intimate dinners, casual gatherings and cookie exchanges all call for the finest holiday foods. Christmas is also a time for remembering special neighbors, teachers, coworkers and friends with tasty homemade gifts from your kitchen. In *Treasury of Christmas* you'll find festive recipes for tempting appetizers, savory side dishes, noteworthy main courses, dazzling desserts and irresistible cookies and confections. Make this holiday cooking season your most enjoyable and rewarding ever with the delicious recipes in this wonderful collection.

HOLIDAY ENTERTAINING HOW–TOS

Planning is the most important step for successful holiday entertaining. Following are helpful ways to get started.
• Putting your ideas down on paper is the first step. Doing this helps avoid chaos later on.
• Building a party around the Christmas theme helps coordinate all aspects of the affair. You may want to plan your get-together around holiday activities, such as tree trimming, caroling or sledding. Or coordinate a party to follow an outing to the ballet or theater.
• Keep your budget in mind when deciding on your entertaining style, number of guests, menu selections and party supplies.
• If this will be one of your first company meals, keep it on the small side. It is easier to cook and serve for eight to ten people than for twenty.
• If you are planning a sit-down dinner, do not invite more people than you can comfortably seat at your table. Similarly, for casual get-togethers, do not invite more people than your entertainment area can easily accommodate. Guests may become uncomfortable if they are crowded.
• Not all entertaining requires a full meal. Consider inviting family and friends over for desserts or light snacks.
• Many guests like to contribute to the festivities by bringing a side dish, dessert, appetizer or wine. Be sure to have some recommendations ready so that if you are asked, you may offer suggestions for foods that will complement the rest of the meal.

PLANNING FESTIVE MENUS

Whether you're planning a Christmas dinner with the relatives or a holiday open house, these guidelines for selecting a menu will make the foods you serve more inviting.
• Select the entrée first, then plan the other dishes around it.

• Not every item on the menu needs to be a showstopper. Select one or two involved recipes and let the remainder be foods that are purchased or are easy to prepare.

• Eye appeal is an important consideration when planning a meal. Select foods with a variety of colors. Green or orange vegetables, red cranberry relish or multi-colored salad all add visual interest. A monochromatic meal is not only visually uninteresting, but is usually perceived as less flavorful.

• Pick foods that offer a variety of textures. Crisp-tender broccoli, creamy mashed potatoes and crunchy fruit all complement the firm, chewy texture of meats.

• A balanced meal offers contrasting flavors. The tart flavor of cranberries and the mild flavor of turkey make a perfect combination.

• Choose side dishes with different shapes and sizes. Whole-berry cranberry relish served alongside peas and Brussels sprouts would not be as interesting with a meal as whole-berry cranberry relish served alongside broccoli spears and diagonally sliced carrots.

• When selecting recipes, choose several that can be made ahead of time. This will leave you more time for visiting with your guests.

• Make sure you have enough serving dishes and utensils for the foods you plan to serve. Borrow dishes or utensils from relatives or friends before the party day, if needed.

• Review the recipes you plan to make, then prepare a comprehensive grocery list. Remember to place any special orders well in advance. Nonperishable items can be purchased weeks ahead. More perishable items should be purchased close to the day of your event. Preparing an organized shopping list will prevent those stressful last-minute dashes to the supermarket.

Come for Cocktails

• For a cocktail party or open house where appetizers are the main event, plan a variety of snacks and spreads, including some that are hearty and filling.

• Prepare a balance of hot and cold appetizers that provides a range of flavors and textures, from spicy and rich to light and refreshing.

• Keep in mind that at a large party where seating is limited, guests appreciate finger food and bite-sized portions with not-too-drippy sauces.

• Remember that the longer the occasion lasts, the more your guests will eat. Plan on a minimum of ten to twelve servings per person for a cocktail party.

• When serving appetizers before a meal, one or two selections should be ample, allowing five to seven servings per person.

MASTERING MEAT AND POULTRY

Selecting the main course is an important first step in the planning of any meal, especially one for the holidays. To please family and friends, consider holiday meal traditions and food preferences. As the host, evaluate your entertaining style (casual to formal) and your monetary and time budgets. When preparing meat and poultry, follow recipe directions closely and make note of the following helpful tips.

• Recommended refrigerator storage time for unopened, prepackaged fresh cuts of meat is generally two to three days; for ground meats, one to two days.

• To prepare beef, pork, lamb or veal roasts, place meat, fat side up, on a rack in a shallow, open roasting pan. Insert a meat thermometer into the thickest part, not resting in fat or on bone. Roasts are usually cooked uncovered in a 325°F oven.

• Standard final temperatures for roast beef, lamb and veal are 140°F for rare, 160°F for medium and 170°F for well done. Pork temperatures should reach 160°F. Fully cooked hams can be warmed to 120° to 140°F. Smoked hams that must be cooked before eating should reach 160°F.

• Thaw frozen poultry in the refrigerator in its original wrapper. Allow 24 hours thawing time for every five pounds. Fresh poultry should be used within two days of purchase.

• Mix stuffing ingredients and stuff the bird immediately before putting it in the oven. Stuff lightly—do not pack.

• To determine when a whole chicken or turkey is cooked and ready to eat, use a meat thermometer inserted in the meatiest part of the thigh, away from bone or fat. For turkey and chicken the thigh temperature should be 180°F; breast temperature 170°F.

• Bone-in chicken pieces are thoroughly cooked when you can insert a fork with ease and the juices run clear, not pink. Boneless chicken pieces are done when the centers are no longer pink.

• The temperatures given in recipes for removing meat and poultry from the oven are 5° to 10°F lower than the standard final temperatures. This is because the temperature continues to rise during the stand time.

• Before serving, allow enough time for cooking the meat, stand time and carving.

The Art of Carving

One of the more formidable tasks when preparing a large meal is carving the roast or bird. To help you carve the main attraction like a pro, follow these general meat preparation guidelines and the special carving instructions for some of the holiday's most popular entrées.

General Guidelines

• After roasting, a stand time of 10 to 20 minutes is recommended for large cuts of meat, such as roasts and turkeys. Stand time allows the meat to finish cooking. It is also easier to carve after standing. If meat is carved right after being removed from the oven, it loses more of its flavorful juices.

• Unless you are planning on carving at the table, place the meat on a large cutting board with a well at one end to hold the juice. (Or, place a cutting board inside a baking sheet. The juice will collect in the baking sheet.) Use a long, sharp carving knife to slice and a long-handled meat fork to steady the meat.

Boneless Cuts

Boneless beef, pork and lamb roasts and boneless hams are easy to carve. Hold the meat steady with a long-handled meat fork. With the knife held perpendicular to the cutting board, cut across the grain into thin, uniform slices. Cut the slices between ¼ and ½ inch thick (illustration 1).

For a thinner cut of meat, such as a beef brisket, follow the preceding directions, but slice the meat diagonally across the grain. This will give a meat slice with a larger surface area.

Standing Beef Rib Roast

For added stability, cut a wedge-shaped slice from the large end of the roast so that the meat will sit flat on the cutting board. Insert a long-handled meat fork below the top rib. Slice across the top of the roast toward the rib bone. This roast can be sliced between ½ and ¾ inch thick (illustration 2).

With the tip of the knife, cut along the rib bone to release the slice of meat (illustration 3).

To remove the meat slice, slide the knife blade under the cut slice of meat. Holding it steady with a meat fork, lift the slice and place it on a platter (illustration 4).

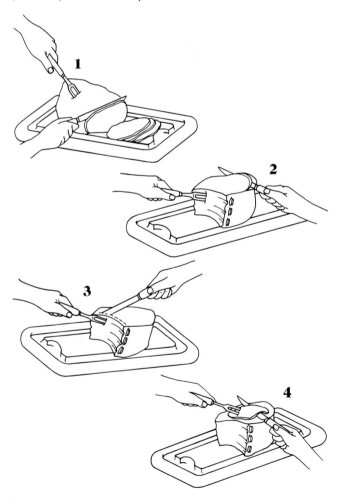

Bone-In Leg of Lamb

For stability, place the roast on its side on the cutting board with the shank bone facing away from you. Cut two or three lengthwise slices from the section of the meat facing you. This will allow the meat to sit flat on the cutting board (illustration 5).

Turn the roast up so that it sits on the cut area. Hold the roast steady with a long-handled meat fork inserted into the meat opposite the shank bone. Holding the knife perpendicular to the cutting board and starting by the shank bone, cut across the grain into uniform, thin slices. Cut the slices between ¼ and ½ inch thick (illustration 6).

When you reach the aitch bone, release the slices by cutting under them along the leg bone (illustration 7). This same technique can be used when carving ham.

Roast Turkey

To remove the leg, hold the drumstick and cut the skin with a carving knife between the thigh and the body of the turkey to the joint. Pull the leg away from the body of the turkey and cut through the joint at the backbone (illustration 8).

To separate the drumstick from the thigh, place the leg on the cutting board skin side up. Cut through at the joint (illustration 9).

At this point, the drumstick may be served as it is or cut into slices. To slice the drumstick, hold the drumstick at an angle, bony side up. Cut down into ¼-inch slices. Rotate the drumstick as you cut. Remove and discard the large tendons (illustration 10).

To cut the thigh into slices, turn the thigh skin side down. Cut along the length of the bone, then turn skin side up and cut the meat across the grain (illustration 11).

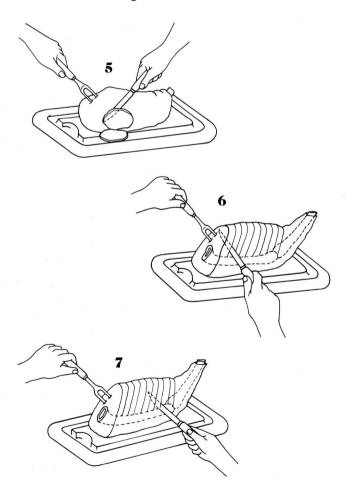

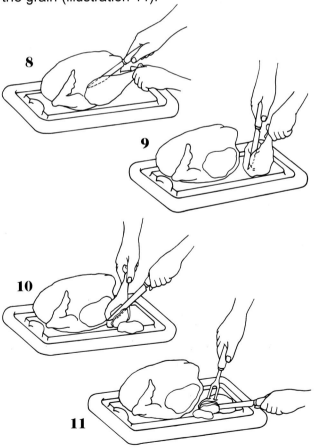

To remove the wings, insert a long-handled meat fork into the turkey to hold it steady. Cut down between the wing and the body of the turkey with a carving knife. Pull the wing out and cut through the joint (illustration 12).

To remove the breast meat, insert a long-handled meat fork into the turkey to hold it steady. At the base of the breast meat, make a horizontal cut across the breast to the bone. Cut the slices with straight, even strokes down to the horizontal cut. At that point, the slices will fall free (illustration 13).

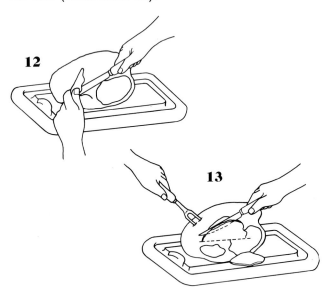

SEAFOOD SAVVY

The vast variety of seafood available makes preparing exceptional seafood entrées and appetizers easier than ever. You and your guests will find delicious, nutritious fish and shellfish perfect holiday fare. Following are helpful purchasing and cooking guidelines for successfully preparing the catch of the day.

Purchasing Guidelines

• When buying fresh whole fish, look for bright, clear, protruding eyes and moist, shiny skin. The gills should be red or pink and the flesh firm and elastic. A fresh fish has a fresh, slightly oceanlike, mild odor. If there is a distinctly fishy, sour smell, do not buy it.
• When purchasing fresh fish fillets and steaks, look for cuts with moist flesh that is free from discoloration and skin that is shiny and resilient. If the fillet or steak has an off odor, do not buy it.
• All fresh shellfish should have a fresh, mild, sea-breeze odor. Fresh lobsters and crabs should be purchased live and as close to the time of cooking as possible. Shrimp should feel firm to the touch. Hard-shell clams, mussels and oysters should have tightly closed shells or snap tightly closed when tapped. Freshly shucked oysters are usually creamy white, although the color varies with the variety, and should be surrounded by a clear, slightly milky white or light gray liquid. Freshly shucked clams should be plump, moist and shiny.

Cooking Tips

• Before cooking fish, rinse it under cold running water and pat it dry with paper towels. Fish cooks quickly, so be careful not to overcook it (this makes the fish tough and destroys flavor). Fish is done cooking when the flesh turns opaque and begins to flake easily when tested with a fork.
• When cooking clams, mussels and oysters in the shell, the shell should open. Remove them as they open. Discard any that do not open.
• Shucked shellfish, such as clams, mussels and oysters, become opaque when cooked, and the edges of the oysters will start to curl.
• Raw shrimp turn pink and opaque. Scallops turn milky white or opaque and firm.

BAKING BASICS FOR THE CHRISTMAS KITCHEN

Let the tantalizing aromas of homebaked breads, cakes and pies fill your kitchen during the Christmas season. Ensure successful holiday baking by practicing good cooking techniques.

Getting Started

• Read the entire recipe before beginning your baking to make sure you have all the necessary ingredients and utensils.
• Use the ingredients called for in the recipe. Do not assume that butter, shortening and margarine are interchangeable.

• Adjust oven racks and preheat the oven. Check oven temperature for accuracy with an oven thermometer.
• Do any necessary food preparation before making the recipe (e.g., separating eggs, slicing fruit, toasting nuts, melting chocolate).
• Measure all the ingredients accurately and assemble them in the order in which they are called for in the recipe.
• Use the pan size specified in the recipe. Prepare the pan according to the recipe directions.
• Follow recipe directions and baking times exactly. Check for doneness using the test given in the recipe.

Tips for Melting Chocolate

• Make sure the utensils used for melting chocolate are completely dry. Moisture causes chocolate to become stiff and grainy. If this happens, add ½ teaspoon shortening (not butter) for each ounce of chocolate and stir until smooth. Chocolate scorches easily, and once scorched it cannot be used. Follow one of these three methods for successful melting:

Direct Heat: Place the chocolate in a heavy saucepan and melt over very low heat, stirring constantly. Remove the chocolate from heat as soon as it is melted. Be sure to watch the chocolate carefully because it is easily scorched when using this method.

Double Boiler: This is the safest method because it prevents scorching. Place the chocolate in the top of a double boiler or in a bowl over hot, not boiling, water and stir until smooth. (Make sure that the water remains just below a simmer and is one inch below the bottom of the top pan or bowl.) Be careful that no steam or water gets into the chocolate.

Microwave Oven: Place an unwrapped 1-ounce square or 1 cup of chips in a small microwavable bowl. Microwave on HIGH (100% power) 1 to 1½ minutes, stirring after 1 minute. Stir the chocolate at 30-second intervals until smooth. Be sure to stir microwaved chocolate since it may retain its original shape even after melting.

FILLING THE CHRISTMAS COOKIE JAR

With Santa's arrival, it's time to fill the cookie jar. Adults and kids alike enjoy baking cookies for the yuletide season. Whether you choose to make old-world favorites or quick and easy treats, these tips for preparing, baking and storing your cookies will be helpful.

Preparation Tips

• For cutout cookies, chill cookie dough before rolling for easier handling. Remove only enough dough from the refrigerator to work with at one time.
• For shaped or drop cookies, dough should be portioned in uniform size and shape on cookie sheet.
• Space mounds of dough about 2 inches apart on cookie sheet to allow for spreading unless the recipe directs otherwise.
• Use the pan size called for in the recipe for baking brownies and bar cookies. Substituting a different pan will affect the cookies' cooking time and texture.

Baking Tips

• The best cookie sheets to use are those with no sides or only one or two short sides. These sheets allow the heat to circulate easily during baking and promote even browning.
• For even baking and browning, place only one cookie sheet at a time in the center of the oven. If the cookies begin to brown unevenly, rotate the cookie sheet from front to back halfway through the baking time.
• When baking more than one sheet of cookies at a time, rotate the two sheets from top to bottom and bottom to top halfway through the baking time.
• For best results, use shortening or a nonstick cooking spray to grease cookie sheets. Or, line the cookie sheets with parchment paper.
• Allow cookie sheets to cool between batches, as the dough will spread too quickly if placed on a hot cookie sheet.
• To avoid overbaking the cookies, check them at the minimum baking time. If more time is needed, watch carefully to make sure the cookies don't burn. It is usually better to slightly underbake cookies than to overbake them.

Storing Tips

• Unbaked cookie dough can usually be refrigerated up to one week or frozen up to six weeks before using. Rolls of dough should be sealed tightly in plastic wrap; other doughs should be stored in airtight containers. Label dough with baking information for convenience.

• Store soft and crisp cookies separately at room temperature to prevent changes in texture and flavor. Keep soft cookies in airtight containers. If they begin to dry out, add a piece of apple or bread to the container to help them retain moisture. If crisp cookies become soggy, heat undecorated cookies in a 300°F oven for 3 to 5 minutes or until crisp.

• Store cookies with glazes, icings and fragile decorations in single layers between sheets of waxed paper. Bar cookies and brownies may be stored in their own baking pans; cover with foil or plastic wrap when cool.

• As a rule, crisp cookies freeze better than soft, moist cookies. Rich, buttery bar cookies and brownies are an exception to this rule since they freeze extremely well. Baked cookies can be frozen in airtight containers or plastic food storage bags up to three months. Meringue-based cookies do not freeze well and chocolate-dipped cookies may discolor if frozen. Thaw frozen cookies and brownies, unwrapped, at room temperature.

CANDY MAKING—STEPS TO SWEET SUCCESS

An abundance of irresistible treats is a delicious sign of the Christmas season. Candies are fun to make and a satisfying indulgence for the sweet tooth. The following are tips to ensure successful candy making.

Getting Started

• Read recipes thoroughly before starting. Have all equipment ready and ingredients measured before you begin cooking.

• Do not try to double or halve candy recipes or use ingredient substitutions unless alternates are listed.

• Humidity will affect the preparation of many candies so it's best to choose dry days for candy making.

• Use a heavy saucepan with a flat bottom to prevent candy from scorching during cooking. Pan size is important; pans should be large enough to prevent syrups from boiling and foaming over the rim.

• Using a candy thermometer is the most accurate way to tell the temperature of boiling syrup. Before each use, verify your candy thermometer's accuracy by checking its reading in boiling water. Water normally boils at 212°F at sea level. If the thermometer does not read 212°F, you may not live at sea level or the thermometer may be slightly off. To adjust the temperature given in a recipe, add or subtract the difference from 212°F as needed. For example, if your thermometer reads 210°F in boiling water and the recipe temperature is 240°F, cook the candy to 238°F, or two degrees less than the temperature stated in the recipe.

Cooking Tips

• When making candy, it is necessary to prevent large sugar crystals from forming because they cause candy to become grainy. To prevent large crystals, sugar should be completely dissolved and crystals should be washed down from the side of the pan before a candy thermometer is placed in the pan. To wash down the crystals, use a pastry brush dipped in hot water to gently brush the crystals down into the syrup. Dip the brush frequently in hot water to clean off the bristles.

• It is important to cook candy to the proper temperature. Attach the candy thermometer to the side of the pan after washing down sugar crystals, making sure the thermometer does not touch the bottom of the pan. Be sure the thermometer bulb is completely covered with boiling syrup, not just foam. Read the thermometer at eye level.

• If a candy thermometer is not available, use the cold water test.

Cold Water Test for Candy

Place a small amount of the hot syrup in a cup of cold (but not iced) water. Using your fingers, remove the cooled syrup. If the syrup has not reached the desired ball or thread stage, continue cooking the candy and test again.

Soft-ball stage (234° to 240°F): The syrup can be rolled into a soft ball that flattens when removed from water (photo 1).

Firm-ball stage (244° to 248°F): The syrup can be rolled into a firm ball that does not flatten immediately when removed from water (photo 2).

Hard-ball stage (250° to 266°F): The syrup can be rolled into a firm ball that gives some resistance when pressed (photo 3).

Soft-crack stage (270° to 290°F): The syrup can be stretched into threads that are hard but elastic (photo 4).

Hard-crack stage (300° to 310°F): The syrup forms threads that are thin, hard and brittle and can easily be snapped in half (photo 5).

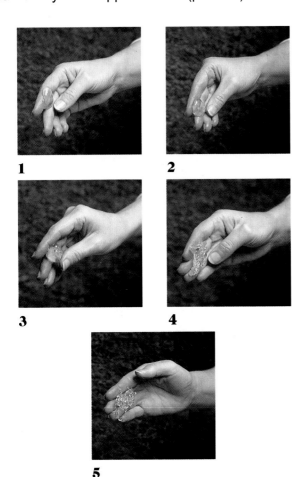

TASTY GIFTS—ALWAYS IN GOOD TASTE

Giving a homemade gift from your kitchen is a beautiful way to express warm holiday wishes. And the yuletide season is the perfect time to help a holiday hostess by contributing a favorite appetizer or luscious dessert to the party menu. Here are some tips for festive food gift-giving.

• Buttery cookies, gooey confections, savory breads and fresh-from-the-oven cakes are obvious gift choices. But don't forget homemade soups, heavenly dessert sauces and crispy snack mixes.

• Be sure to label your gifts of food. People like to know what they're eating. Also include any special storage, serving or reheating directions. Some cooks like to include a copy of their recipe, too.

• Festive packaging adds holiday spirit to your homemade specialties. Use baskets, boxes, tins, jars and gift bags as containers. Disposable plates, cups and bakeware come in many delightful holiday designs. Plastic food containers, coffee cans and berry baskets can be recycled into clever packaging.

• It's fun to pair your gifts of food with complementary items: a bottle of wine with your favorite homemade cheese spread, a new wooden bread board with a crusty loaf of homebaked bread or a brightly patterned set of oven mitts with a cheery tin of decorated Christmas cookies.

Mailing Gifts of Food

When sending edible holiday greetings, proper food selection and packaging is important. Moist quick breads and sturdy cookies are ideal choices for mailing, as are many non-fragile confections, such as fudge and caramels. It's best to prepare food just before packing and mailing, and to choose a speedy method of shipment. Foods should be completely cooled before wrapping. For cookies, leave bars uncut and wrap individual cookies in pairs, back-to-back. Use sturdy gift containers and crumpled waxed paper for cushioning. Place containers in sturdy boxes with bubble wrap, foam packing pieces, crumpled tissue or unseasoned, unbuttered popcorn.

FRENCH-STYLE PIZZA BITES

2 tablespoons olive oil
1 medium onion, thinly sliced
1 medium red bell pepper, cut into
   3-inch-long strips
2 cloves garlic, minced
⅓ cup pitted ripe olives, cut into thin wedges
1 can (10 ounces) refrigerated pizza crust
   dough
¾ cup (3 ounces) finely shredded Swiss or
   Gruyère cheese

Position oven rack to lowest position. Preheat oven to 425°F. Heat oil in medium skillet over medium heat. Add onion, bell pepper and garlic. Cook and stir 5 minutes or until vegetables are crisp-tender. Stir in olives. Remove from heat; set aside. Pat dough into 16×12-inch rectangle on greased large cookie sheet. Arrange vegetables over dough. Sprinkle with cheese. Bake 10 minutes. With long spatula, loosen crust from cookie sheet. Slide crust onto oven rack. Bake 3 to 5 minutes more or until golden brown.

Slide cookie sheet under crust; remove crust from rack. Transfer to cutting board. Cut dough crosswise into eight 1¾-inch-wide strips. Cut dough diagonally into ten 2-inch-wide strips, making diamond pieces. Serve immediately.

Makes about 24 servings

TORTELLONI WREATH WITH PESTO DIP

1 (9-ounce) package DIGIORNO® Mushroom Tortelloni
1 (9-ounce) package DIGIORNO® Hot Red Pepper Tortelloni
1 (8-ounce) container PHILADELPHIA BRAND® Soft Cream Cheese
1 (7-ounce) package DIGIORNO® Pesto Sauce
1 teaspoon lemon juice
Green and red pepper chunks
Pitted ripe olives

• Add both packages of pasta to 4 quarts boiling water. Boil gently, uncovered, 6 minutes, stirring frequently. Drain; rinse with cold water.

• Mix cream cheese, sauce and juice. Place in small bowl.

• Place bowl in middle of round serving platter. Arrange pasta, peppers and olives around bowl for dipping.   *Makes 24 servings*

PREP TIME: 10 minutes
COOK TIME: 6 minutes

MARINATED MUSHROOMS

1 pint whole, uniformly sized, small white button mushroom caps, washed
½ cup olive oil
3 tablespoons tarragon vinegar
¼ cup finely chopped parsley
1 tablespoon Dijon-style mustard
3 cloves garlic, finely chopped
1 teaspoon sugar
¾ teaspoon dried tarragon leaves, crushed
½ teaspoon salt
Freshly ground black pepper

Fill 16-ounce jar with mushrooms. Process remaining ingredients in food processor or combine in small bowl with wire whisk. Pour dressing into jar to cover mushrooms completely. Seal jar and marinate overnight at room temperature to blend flavors. Store up to 1 week in refrigerator. Bring to room temperature before serving.

Makes about 6 servings or
3 cups mushrooms

Tortelloni Wreath with Pesto Dip

SPINACH–CHEESE APPETIZERS

¼ cup olive oil
½ cup chopped onion
2 eggs
16 ounces crumbled feta cheese
3 packages (10 ounces each) frozen chopped spinach, thawed and well drained
½ cup minced fresh parsley
1 teaspoon dried oregano leaves, crushed *or* 2 tablespoons fresh oregano, chopped
Freshly grated nutmeg
Salt and black pepper
1 package (16 ounces) frozen phyllo dough, thawed
2 cups margarine, melted

Preheat oven to 375°F. Heat oil over medium-high heat in small skillet. Add onion; cook and stir until translucent. Beat eggs in large bowl; stir in onion, feta cheese, spinach, parsley and oregano. Season with nutmeg, salt and pepper.

Remove phyllo from package; unroll and place on large sheet of waxed paper. Fold phyllo crosswise into thirds. Use scissors to cut along folds into thirds. Cover phyllo with large sheet of plastic wrap and damp clean kitchen towel. Lay 1 strip of phyllo at a time on a flat surface and brush with melted margarine. Fold strip in half lengthwise; brush with margarine again. Place rounded teaspoonful of spinach filling on 1 end of strip; fold over one corner to make triangle. Continue folding end to end, as you would fold a flag, keeping edges straight. Brush top with margarine. Repeat process until all filling is used. Place triangles in a single layer, seam side down, on ungreased baking sheet. Bake 20 minutes or until lightly browned. Serve warm. *Makes 5 dozen appetizers*

Spinach-Cheese Appetizers

LITTLE CHRISTMAS PIZZAS

⅓ cup olive oil
1 tablespoon TABASCO® pepper sauce
2 large cloves garlic, minced
1 teaspoon dried rosemary, crushed
1 (16-ounce) package hot roll mix with yeast packet
1¼ cups hot water*
    All-purpose flour
TOPPINGS
1 large tomato, diced
¼ cup crumbled goat cheese
2 tablespoons chopped fresh parsley
½ cup shredded mozzarella cheese
½ cup sliced pitted green olives
⅓ cup roasted red pepper strips
½ cup chopped artichoke hearts
½ cup cherry tomatoes, sliced into wedges
⅓ cup sliced green onions

In small bowl, combine olive oil, TABASCO sauce, garlic and rosemary. In large bowl, combine hot roll mix, yeast packet, hot water and 2 tablespoons of the TABASCO mixture; stir until dough pulls away from side of bowl. Turn dough onto lightly floured surface; shape dough into a ball. Knead until smooth, adding additional flour as necessary.

Preheat oven to 425°F. Cut dough into quarters; cut each quarter into 10 equal pieces. Roll each piece into a ball. On large cookie sheet, press each ball into 2-inch round. Brush each with remaining TABASCO mixture. Arrange approximately 2 teaspoons toppings on each dough round. Bake 12 minutes or until dough is lightly browned and puffed.

Makes 40 appetizer servings

*Check hot roll mix package directions for temperature of water.

Little Christmas Pizzas, Party Polenta Stars

PARTY POLENTA STARS

    3 cups water
    2 tablespoons butter or margarine,
        divided
    ¾ teaspoon salt
    1 cup yellow cornmeal
    ½ cup grated Parmesan cheese
    1 teaspoon TABASCO® pepper sauce
    1 tablespoon olive oil
        Spicy Tomato Salsa (recipe follows)

Grease jelly-roll pan; set aside. In 2-quart saucepan over high heat, bring water, 1 tablespoon of the butter and salt to a boil. Reduce heat to low; slowly add cornmeal in a thin stream, stirring constantly. Continue to cook, stirring constantly until mixture thickens, about 5 to 10 minutes. Remove from heat; stir in cheese and TABASCO sauce.

Spread cooked cornmeal mixture in prepared jelly-roll pan to a thickness of ½ inch. Refrigerate, uncovered, for 30 minutes.

With a 2½-inch star-shaped cookie cutter, cut cooled polenta mixture into stars. In 12-inch skillet over medium-high heat, heat oil and remaining tablespoon of butter. Add polenta stars; cook 2 minutes on each side or until lightly browned, turning carefully. Repeat with remaining stars, adding oil and butter if necessary. Serve polenta stars with Spicy Tomato Salsa.   *Makes 18 stars*

SPICY TOMATO SALSA
    8 ounces ripe fresh tomatoes, finely
        diced (about 1 cup)
    3 tablespoons minced green onions
    1 tablespoon minced cilantro
    1½ teaspoons freshly squeezed lemon juice
    ½ teaspoon TABASCO® pepper sauce
    ½ garlic clove, minced
    ¼ teaspoon ground cumin
    ⅛ teaspoon salt

Mix all ingredients in small bowl. Cover and refrigerate 1 to 2 hours to blend flavors.
                    Makes about 1 cup

BAKED ARTICHOKE SQUARES

    ½ cup plus 3 tablespoons CRISCO® Oil,
        divided
    1 cup chopped mushrooms
    ¼ cup thinly sliced celery
    1 clove garlic, minced
    1 can (14 ounces) artichoke hearts,
        drained, chopped
    ⅓ cup chopped green onions
    ½ teaspoon dried marjoram, crushed
    ¼ teaspoon dried oregano, crushed
    ¼ teaspoon ground red pepper
    1 cup (4 ounces) shredded Cheddar
        cheese
    1 cup (4 ounces) shredded Monterey
        Jack cheese
    2 eggs, slightly beaten
    1½ cups all-purpose flour
    ½ teaspoon salt
    ¼ cup milk

Heat 3 tablespoons of the Crisco oil in medium skillet over medium-high heat. Cook and stir mushrooms, celery and garlic in hot oil until celery is tender. Remove from heat. Stir in artichoke hearts, onions, marjoram, oregano and ground red pepper. Add cheeses and eggs; mix well. Set aside.

Combine flour and salt in medium bowl. Blend remaining ½ cup Crisco oil and the milk in small bowl. Add to flour mixture. Stir with fork until mixture forms a ball. Press dough in bottom and 1½ inches up sides of 13×9×2-inch pan. Bake in preheated 350°F oven 10 minutes. Spread artichoke mixture on baked crust. Continue baking about 20 minutes more or until center is set. Cool slightly. Cut into 24 squares. Serve warm.   *Makes 24 appetizers*

NEUFTY CUPS

2 (18×14-inch) sheets phyllo dough, thawed according to package directions
2 tablespoons butter
1 package (6 ounces) FLEUR DE LAIT® Neufchâtel® cheese, Garden Vegetables variety

Preheat oven to 350°F. Cover phyllo with damp cloth.

Melt butter; brush a small amount onto sides and bottoms of 12 miniature muffin pan cups.

Cut phyllo into 36 (3¼-inch) squares. Place 1 phyllo square into each muffin pan cup with corners pointing upward. Lightly brush phyllo with butter. Top each with another phyllo square, alternating corners; brush with butter. Repeat once more, alternating corners, so that there are 3 phyllo squares arranged in each cup.

Brush all edges of phyllo lightly with melted butter. Bake 8 to 10 minutes or until golden. Remove shells to wire racks; cool completely. Fill with Fleur de Lait®; garnish as desired.

Makes 12 appetizers

CHEDDAR CHEESE PUFFS

PUFFS
1 cup water
6 tablespoons butter, cut into pieces
1 teaspoon salt
    Dash pepper
    Dash ground nutmeg (optional)
1 cup all-purpose flour
5 large eggs, divided
1 cup plus 3 tablespoons finely shredded Cheddar or Swiss cheese, divided
FILLING
1 (11-ounce) jar NEWMAN'S OWN® All Natural Salsa
12 ounces cream cheese, softened

Preheat oven to 425°F. In heavy 2-quart saucepan, bring water, butter, salt, pepper and nutmeg to a full boil over medium heat. Remove from heat. With wooden spoon, beat in flour all at once. (If mixture does not form a ball and leave the sides of pan clean, return to medium heat and beat vigorously for 1 to 2 minutes.) Remove from heat and beat in 4 eggs, 1 at a time, until each egg is thoroughly blended. Beat in 1 cup cheese. Place mixture in pastry bag with ½-inch-diameter round tip. Pipe 1-inch rounds 2 inches apart on 2 greased baking sheets. Beat remaining egg. Brush tops of puffs with beaten egg and sprinkle with remaining 3 tablespoons cheese. Bake 20 to 25 minutes or until golden and crisp; turn off oven. Pierce each puff with knife and return to cooling oven for 10 minutes to dry out. Remove and cool.

Drain approximately ¼ cup liquid from salsa (reserve liquid for another use, if desired). Mix drained salsa with cream cheese. Cut tops off puffs; spoon filling into puffs. Replace tops.

Makes 36 appetizers

Neufty Cups

Elegant Antipasto

ELEGANT ANTIPASTO

   1 jar (16 ounces) mild cherry peppers
   1 package (9 ounces) frozen artichoke
       hearts, cooked and drained
   ½ pound asparagus spears, cooked
   ½ cup pitted ripe olives
   1 medium red onion, cut into wedges
   1 green bell pepper, cut into triangles
   1 red bell pepper, cut into triangles
   1 bottle (8 ounces) KRAFT® House
       Italian with Olive Oil Blend Dressing
   1 wedge (4 ounces) KRAFT® Natural
       Parmesan Cheese, shredded and
       divided
   1 package (8 ounces) OSCAR MAYER®
       Sliced Hard Salami

• Arrange vegetables in rows in 13×9-inch
glass baking dish.

• Pour dressing and ⅓ cup cheese over
vegetables; cover. Refrigerate 1 to 2 hours.

• Drain vegetables, reserving marinade.
Arrange vegetables and salami on serving
platter. Drizzle with marinade; top with
remaining cheese.   *Makes 6 servings*

VARIATION: Substitute mushrooms, green
beans, cherry tomatoes or broccoli flowerets
for any of the vegetables listed.

PREP TIME: 20 minutes plus refrigerating

MINI MISTLETOE TURNOVERS

   1 envelope LIPTON® Recipe Secrets®
       Onion Soup Mix
   2 eggs, beaten
   1 package (10 ounces) frozen chopped
       spinach, cooked and drained
   2 cups (16 ounces) ricotta or creamed
       cottage cheese
   1 scant cup (about 3 ounces) shredded
       mozzarella cheese
   3 packages (8 ounces each) refrigerated
       crescent rolls

Preheat oven to 375°F.

In large bowl, combine onion soup mix, eggs,
spinach and cheeses.

Separate crescent rolls according to package
directions; cut each triangle in half (to make 2
smaller triangles) and flatten slightly. Place 1
tablespoon cheese mixture on center of each
triangle; fold over and seal edges tightly with
fork. Place on ungreased baking sheet; bake
15 minutes or until golden brown.
            Makes 48 turnovers

FREEZING/REHEATING DIRECTIONS:
Tightly wrap turnovers in heavy-duty foil;
freeze. To reheat, unwrap and bake as directed
for 8 minutes or until heated through.

FESTIVE STUFFED DATES

> 1 box (8 ounces) DOLE® Whole Pitted
>   Dates
> 1 package (3 ounces) reduced fat cream
>   cheese, softened
> ¼ cup powdered sugar
> 1 tablespoon grated peel of 1 DOLE®
>   Orange

• Make slit in center of each date. Combine cream cheese, powdered sugar and orange peel. Fill centers of dates with cream cheese mixture. Refrigerate.

• Dust with additional powdered sugar just before serving, if desired.

Makes about 27 stuffed dates

PREP TIME: 25 minutes

BRUSCHETTA

> 1 can (14½ ounces) DEL MONTE®
>   Italian Style Stewed Tomatoes
> 1 to 2 cloves garlic, crushed
> 2 tablespoons chopped fresh basil *or*
>   ½ teaspoon dried basil
> 1 baguette (6 inches) French bread, cut
>   into ½-inch slices
> 1 tablespoon olive oil

Drain tomatoes, reserving liquid. In small saucepan, boil reserved liquid with garlic, 5 to 6 minutes, stirring occasionally. Remove from heat. Chop tomatoes; combine with garlic mixture and basil. Brush bread with oil. Broil until golden. Top with tomato mixture; serve immediately. Garnish with basil leaves, if desired.   *Makes 6 appetizer servings*

STUFFED MUSHROOMS

> 1 package (6 ounces) STOVE TOP®
>   Stuffing Mix for Chicken
> 24 large mushrooms (about 1½ pounds)
> ¼ cup (½ stick) PARKAY® Spread Sticks
> ¼ cup *each* finely chopped red and green
>   pepper
> 3 tablespoons PARKAY® Spread Sticks,
>   melted

Prepare stuffing mix as directed on package, omitting margarine. Remove stems from mushrooms; chop stems. Melt ¼ cup spread in large skillet on medium heat. Add mushroom caps; cook and stir until lightly browned. Arrange in shallow baking pan. Cook and stir chopped mushroom stems and peppers in skillet until tender; stir into prepared stuffing. Spoon into mushroom caps; drizzle with 3 tablespoons melted spread. Place under preheated broiler, 3 to 4 inches from heat, 5 minutes or until heated through.

Makes 12 appetizer servings

Bruschetta

EASY VEGETABLE SQUARES

- 2 (8-ounce) cans refrigerated crescent rolls (16 rolls)
- 1 (8-ounce) package cream cheese, softened
- 1 (3-ounce) package cream cheese, softened
- ⅓ cup mayonnaise or salad dressing
- 1 teaspoon dried dill weed
- 1 teaspoon buttermilk salad dressing mix (¼ of 0.4-ounce package)
- 3 cups desired toppings (suggestions follow)
- 1 cup shredded Wisconsin Cheddar, Mozzarella, or Monterey Jack cheese

For crust, unroll crescent rolls and pat into 15½×10½×2-inch baking pan. Bake according to package directions. Cool.

Meanwhile, in a small mixing bowl stir together cream cheese, mayonnaise, dill weed and salad dressing mix. Spread evenly over cooled crust. Sprinkle with desired toppings and shredded Cheddar, Mozzarella or Monterey Jack cheese. Cut into squares.

Makes 32 appetizer servings

TOPPING SUGGESTIONS: finely chopped broccoli, cauliflower or green pepper; seeded and chopped tomato; thinly sliced green onions, black olives or celery; *or* shredded carrots.

PREP TIME: 20 minutes

Favorite recipe from **Wisconsin Milk Marketing Board**

MINI SAUSAGE QUICHES

- ½ cup butter or margarine, softened
- 3 ounces cream cheese, softened
- 1 cup all-purpose flour
- ½ pound BOB EVANS FARMS® Italian roll sausage
- 1 cup (4 ounces) shredded Swiss cheese
- 1 tablespoon snipped fresh chives
- 2 eggs
- 1 cup half-and-half
- ¼ teaspoon salt
  Dash cayenne pepper

Beat butter and cream cheese in medium bowl until creamy. Blend in flour; refrigerate 1 hour. Roll into 24 (1-inch) balls; press each into mini-muffin cup. Preheat oven to 375°F. To prepare filling, crumble sausage into small skillet. Cook over medium heat until browned, stirring occasionally. Drain off any drippings. Sprinkle evenly into pastry shells in muffin cups; sprinkle with Swiss cheese and chives. Whisk eggs, half-and-half, salt and cayenne until blended; pour over sausage in pastry shells. Bake 20 to 30 minutes or until set. Remove from pans. Serve hot. Refrigerate leftovers.

Makes 24 appetizers

SERVING SUGGESTION: Use standard 2½-inch muffin cups to make larger individual quiches. Serve for breakfast.

Mini Sausage Quiches

MINIATURE TERIYAKI PORK KABOBS

**1 pound boneless pork, cut into
    4×1×½-inch strips**
**1 small green bell pepper, cut into
    1×¼×¼-inch strips**
**1 can (11 ounces) mandarin oranges,
    drained**
¼ cup teriyaki sauce
1 tablespoon honey
1 tablespoon vinegar
⅛ teaspoon garlic powder

Soak 24 (8-inch) bamboo skewers in water 10 minutes. Thread 1 pepper strip, then pork strips accordion-style with mandarin oranges on skewers. Place 1 pepper strip on end of each skewer. Arrange skewers on broiler pan.

*Top plate: Miniature Teriyaki Pork Kabobs,
Appetizer Ham Logs; Bottom plate: Rumaki,
Ham-Wrapped Oysters*

For sauce, combine teriyaki sauce, honey, vinegar and garlic powder in small bowl; mix well. Brush sauce over kabobs. Broil, 6 inches from heat, about 15 minutes or until pork is done, turning and basting with sauce occasionally.   *Makes about 24 appetizers*

*Favorite recipe from **National Pork Producers Council***

APPETIZER HAM LOGS

2 cups ground ham
1 egg, beaten
¼ teaspoon pepper
¼ cup seasoned fine dry bread crumbs
½ cup horseradish sauce
1 tablespoon prepared mustard
⅛ teaspoon celery salt
    Vegetable oil for frying
    Pimiento strips

Combine ham, egg and pepper in medium bowl; mix well. Shape into 1-inch logs or balls. Roll in bread crumbs. Refrigerate, covered, 1 hour.

To make mustard sauce, combine horseradish sauce, mustard and celery salt in small bowl until well blended. Refrigerate, covered, until serving time.

Heat 3 inches oil in heavy, large saucepan over medium-high heat until oil is 365°F; adjust heat to maintain temperature. Fry ham logs, a few at a time, 2 to 3 minutes or until golden. Drain on paper towels. Garnish with pimiento strips. Serve with mustard sauce.

Makes about 24 appetizers

*Favorite recipe from **National Pork Producers Council***

RUMAKI

16 slices bacon
1 pound chicken livers, cut into quarters
1 can (8 ounces) sliced water chestnuts, drained
⅓ cup soy sauce
2 tablespoons packed brown sugar
1 tablespoon Dijon-style mustard

Cut bacon slices in half crosswise. Wrap ½ slice bacon around piece of chicken liver and water chestnut slice. Secure with wooden pick. (Reserve any remaining water chestnut slices for another use.) Arrange on broiler pan. Combine soy sauce, brown sugar and mustard in small bowl. Brush over bacon rolls. Broil, 6 inches from heat, 15 to 20 minutes or until bacon is crisp and chicken livers are done, turning and brushing with soy sauce mixture occasionally. *Makes about 32 appetizers*

*Favorite recipe from **National Pork Producers Council***

HAM−WRAPPED OYSTERS

3 tablespoons prepared horseradish
½ pound ham, cut into 3×1×¼-inch strips
2 dozen fresh oysters, shucked
3 tablespoons butter or margarine, melted
1 tablespoon lemon juice
¼ teaspoon garlic powder

Spread horseradish on 1 side of each ham strip. Place 1 oyster on each ham strip; roll up and secure with wooden pick. Arrange on broiler pan. Combine butter, lemon juice and garlic powder in small cup. Brush each ham roll with some of the lemon butter. Broil, 5 inches from heat, 10 to 15 minutes or until edges of oysters curl, brushing occasionally with the remaining lemon butter. *Makes 24 appetizers*

*Favorite recipe from **National Pork Producers Council***

EASY SAUSAGE EMPANADAS

1 (15-ounce) package refrigerated pie crusts (2 crusts)
¼ pound bulk pork sausage
2 tablespoons finely chopped onion
⅛ teaspoon garlic powder
⅛ teaspoon ground cumin
⅛ teaspoon dried oregano, crushed
1 tablespoon chopped pimiento-stuffed olives
1 tablespoon chopped raisins
1 egg, separated

Let pie crusts stand at room temperature for 20 minutes or according to package directions. Crumble sausage into medium skillet. Add onion, garlic powder, cumin and oregano; cook over medium-high heat until sausage is no longer pink. Drain drippings. Stir in olives and raisins. Beat egg yolk slightly; stir into sausage mixture, mixing well. Carefully unfold crusts. Cut into desired shapes using 3-inch cookie cutters. Place about 2 teaspoons of the sausage filling on each of half the cutouts. Top with remaining cutouts. Moisten fingers with water and pinch dough to seal edges. Beat egg white slightly; gently brush over tops of empanadas. Bake in a 425°F oven 15 to 18 minutes or until golden brown. *Makes 12 appetizer servings*

PREP TIME: 25 minutes
COOK TIME: 15 minutes

*Favorite recipe from **National Pork Producers Council***

LAMB MEATBALLS WITH TOMATO MINT DIP

3 cups cold water
1½ cups fine bulgur
2 pounds ground American lamb
1 cup minced fresh parsley
2 medium onions, minced
1 tablespoon salt
½ teaspoon ground black pepper
½ teaspoon ground allspice
½ teaspoon ground cinnamon
½ teaspoon ground nutmeg
¼ to ½ teaspoon ground red pepper
    (to taste)
1 piece fresh ginger, about 2×1-inch,
    peeled and minced
1 cup ice water

In medium bowl, pour cold water over bulgur to cover; let soak about 10 minutes. Drain and place in fine-meshed strainer; squeeze out water.

In large bowl, knead lamb with parsley, onions, seasonings and ginger. Add bulgur; knead well. Add ice water to keep mixture smooth. Shape teaspoonfuls meat mixture into bite-sized meatballs. Place on ungreased jelly-roll pan. Bake in preheated 375°F oven 20 minutes.

Place meatballs in serving bowl; keep warm. Serve hot with Tomato Mint Dip.
Makes 10 dozen meatballs

TOMATO MINT DIP
2 cans (15 ounces each) tomato sauce
    with tomato bits
1½ teaspoons ground allspice
1 teaspoon dried mint

In small saucepan, heat all ingredients about 5 minutes to blend flavors.

*Favorite recipe from **American Lamb Council***

BEEF KUSHISASHI

½ cup KIKKOMAN® Soy Sauce
¼ cup chopped green onions and tops
2 tablespoons sugar
1 tablespoon vegetable oil
1½ teaspoons cornstarch
1 clove garlic, pressed
1 teaspoon grated fresh ginger root
2½ pounds boneless beef sirloin steak

Blend soy sauce, green onions, sugar, oil, cornstarch, garlic and ginger in small saucepan. Simmer, stirring constantly, until thickened, about 1 minute; cool. Cover and set aside. Slice beef into ⅛-inch-thick strips about 4 inches long and 1 inch wide. Thread onto bamboo or metal skewers keeping meat as flat as possible; brush both sides of beef with sauce. Place skewers on rack of broiler pan; broil to desired degree of doneness.
Makes 10 to 12 appetizer servings

BROILED PEPPERONI BITES

1 package (3 ounces) thinly sliced
    pepperoni
15 slices French bread, cut ¼ inch thick
1 cup (4 ounces) shredded mozzarella
    cheese
2 tablespoons minced green onion

Arrange bread slices on foil-lined 15×10-inch jelly-roll pan. Broil bread about 4 inches from heat until lightly toasted. Sprinkle half the cheese and half the onion evenly on bread slices; top with pepperoni. Sprinkle remaining cheese and onion evenly over pepperoni. Broil 1 minute or until cheese melts.
Makes 15 appetizers

PREP TIME: 10 minutes
COOK TIME: 2 minutes

*Favorite recipe from **National Live Stock & Meat Board***

CHERRY GLAZED SMOKIES

1 package (16 ounces) cocktail smoked sausage links*
⅔ cup cherry preserves
1 teaspoon coarsely ground black pepper

Heat sausage, preserves and pepper in medium saucepan over medium heat until heated through, stirring occasionally. Serve hot with wooden toothpicks.

Makes 48 appetizers

*One pound smoked sausage links, cut into 1-inch pieces, may be substituted for the cocktail smoked sausage links.

Favorite recipe from **National Live Stock & Meat Board**

SPICY CHEESE AND CAPPICOLA APPETIZERS

4 ounces thinly sliced ham cappicola
3 ounces Neufchâtel or reduced fat cream cheese, softened
2 teaspoons spicy brown mustard
½ teaspoon prepared horseradish, undrained
12 bread sticks, each 6 inches long

Combine Neufchâtel cheese, mustard and horseradish. Spread equal amount of cheese mixture evenly on each cappicola slice; wrap each slice around 1 bread stick.

Makes 1 dozen appetizers

PREP TIME: 10 minutes

Favorite recipe from **National Live Stock & Meat Board**

Top to bottom: Spicy Cheese and Cappicola Appetizers, Broiled Pepperoni Bites, Cherry Glazed Smokies

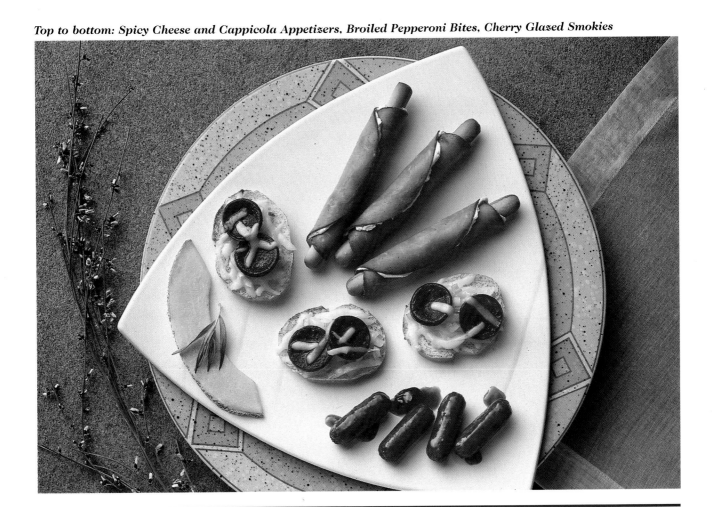

SAUSAGE FILLED WONTONS

1 pound BOB EVANS FARMS® Original
    Recipe roll sausage
¼ cup chopped onion
½ cup (2 ounces) shredded American
    cheese
3 ounces cream cheese
½ teaspoon dried marjoram leaves
¼ teaspoon dried tarragon leaves
30 wonton wrappers
    Vegetable oil
    Dipping sauce, such as plum sauce or
      sweet and sour sauce (optional)

To prepare filling, crumble sausage into large skillet. Add onion. Cook over medium heat until sausage is browned, stirring occasionally. Remove from heat; drain off any drippings. Stir in next 4 ingredients. Mix until cheeses melt. Lightly dampen 1 wrapper by dipping your finger in water and wiping all the edges, making ¼-inch border around square. (To keep wonton wrappers from drying, cover remaining wrappers with damp kitchen towel while working.) Place rounded teaspoonful sausage mixture in the middle of wrapper. Fold wrapper over filling to form triangle, sealing edges and removing any air bubbles. Repeat with remaining wrappers and filling.

Heat 4 inches oil in deep fryer or heavy large saucepan to 350°F; fry wontons, a few at a time, until golden brown. Remove with slotted spoon; drain on paper towels. Reheat oil between batches. Serve hot with dipping sauce, if desired. Refrigerate leftovers.

Makes 30 appetizers

SWEET AND SOUR MEATBALLS

1½ pounds lean ground beef
1 cup fresh bread crumbs (2 slices)
1 egg, slightly beaten
4 teaspoons WYLER'S® or STEERO®
    Beef-Flavor Instant Bouillon
1⅓ cups BAMA® Apricot Preserves
2 tablespoons REALEMON® Lemon Juice
    from Concentrate

In large bowl, combine meat, crumbs, egg and *2 teaspoons* bouillon; mix well. Shape into 1¼-inch meatballs. In large skillet, brown meatballs. Remove from pan; pour off fat. In same skillet, combine preserves, ReaLemon® brand and remaining *2 teaspoons* bouillon. Over low heat, cook and stir 10 minutes. Add meatballs; simmer, uncovered, 10 minutes. Garnish with parsley, if desired. Refrigerate leftovers.   *Makes about 4 dozen meatballs*

SAUSAGE CHEESE PUFFS

1 pound BOB EVANS FARMS® Original
    Recipe roll sausage
2½ cups (10 ounces) grated sharp Cheddar
    cheese
2 cups biscuit mix
½ cup water
1 teaspoon baking powder

Preheat oven to 350°F. Combine ingredients in large bowl until blended. Shape into 1-inch balls. Place on baking sheets. Bake about 25 minutes or until golden brown. Serve hot. Refrigerate leftovers.

Makes about 60 appetizers

Sausage Filled Wontons

Beef with Walnuts and Kiwi

BEEF WITH WALNUTS AND KIWI

> **4 ounces** sliced rare roast beef, cut into **12** uniform pieces
> **¼ cup** finely chopped walnuts, toasted
> **1 tablespoon** *each* fresh lemon juice, olive oil, wine vinegar and snipped dill
> **1** small clove garlic, crushed
> **¼ teaspoon** freshly ground black pepper
> Dash salt
> **12** slices French bread, ¼ inch thick
> **2** kiwi, peeled, cut into **12** slices
> Pimiento, cut into small star shapes

Place roast beef slices in glass dish; sprinkle with walnuts. Combine lemon juice, oil, vinegar, dill, garlic, pepper and salt. Pour over beef and walnuts, lifting meat to coat. Cover and marinate 30 minutes. Drain marinade. To assemble, arrange one piece beef with walnuts on bread round. Top with kiwi slice; garnish with pimiento.   *Makes 12 appetizer servings*

PREP/MARINATING TIME: 40 minutes
ASSEMBLING TIME: 10 minutes

*Favorite recipe from **National Live Stock & Meat Board***

HOLIDAY APPETIZER QUICHE

CRUST
  2 cups all-purpose flour
  1 teaspoon salt
  ¾ BUTTER FLAVOR* CRISCO® Stick *or*
    ¾ cup BUTTER FLAVOR CRISCO
    all-vegetable shortening
  5 tablespoons cold water
FILLING
  2 cups (8 ounces) shredded Swiss cheese
  ⅔ cup chopped ham, crumbled cooked
    sausage, diced pepperoni or
    crumbled cooked bacon
  ¾ cup thinly sliced green onions
    (including tops)
  ¼ cup snipped fresh parsley
  1 jar (4 ounces) diced pimientos, well
    drained
  5 eggs
  1 cup whipping cream
  1 cup half-and-half
  1 teaspoon salt
  ¼ teaspoon pepper

1. Heat oven to 400°F.

2. For crust, combine flour and salt in medium bowl. Cut in shortening using pastry blender (or 2 knives) until all flour is blended in to form pea-size chunks. Sprinkle with water, 1 tablespoon at a time. Toss lightly with fork until dough forms ball.

3. Roll out dough to fit 15×10-inch jelly-roll pan. Place dough in greased pan, folding edges under. Flute edges. Prick crust with fork.

4. For filling, sprinkle cheese, ham, onions, parsley and pimientos evenly over crust. Beat eggs, cream, half-and-half, salt and pepper in medium bowl. Pour over filled crust.

5. Bake at 400°F for 25 to 30 minutes or until set. Cool 5 to 10 minutes. Cut into 2×1½-inch pieces. Serve warm.

Makes about 50 appetizers

NOTE: Crust may bubble during baking and need to be pricked with fork again.

*Butter Flavor Crisco® is artificially flavored.

ORANGE MAPLE SAUSAGE BALLS

  1 pound BOB EVANS FARMS® Original
    Recipe roll sausage
  1 small onion, finely chopped
  1 small red or yellow bell pepper, finely
    chopped
  1 egg
  2 tablespoons uncooked wheat farina
    cereal
  ½ cup maple syrup or maple-flavored
    syrup
  3 to 5 tablespoons frozen orange juice
    concentrate to taste, slightly thawed

Combine first 5 ingredients in large bowl until well blended. Shape into ¾-inch balls. Cook in large skillet over medium-high heat until browned on all sides and no longer pink in centers. Drain off any drippings. Add syrup and orange juice concentrate to sausage balls. Cook and stir over medium heat 2 to 3 minutes or until thick, bubbly syrup forms. Serve hot. Refrigerate leftovers.

Makes about 24 appetizers

SERVING SUGGESTIONS: Serve on party picks with sautéed mushrooms and water chestnuts. These meatballs also make an excellent breakfast item; serve with small pancakes.

POTATO WRAPS

4 small new potatoes (1½-inch diameter each)
½ teaspoon LAWRY'S® Seasoned Salt
½ teaspoon LAWRY'S® Seasoned Pepper
¼ teaspoon crushed bay leaves
8 slices bacon, cut in half crosswise

Preheat oven to 400°F. Wash potatoes and cut into quarters. Sprinkle each with a mixture of Seasoned Salt, Seasoned Pepper and bay leaves. Wrap 1 bacon piece around each potato piece. Sprinkle with any remaining seasonings. Place in baking dish and bake uncovered 20 minutes or until bacon is crispy and potatoes are cooked through. Drain on paper towels. Serve with sour cream and chives, if desired.   *Makes 16 appetizers*

MARIACHI DRUMSTICKS

1¼ cups crushed plain tortilla chips
1 package (1.25 ounces) LAWRY'S® Taco Seasoning Mix
18 to 20 chicken drumettes
Salsa

Preheat oven to 350°F. In large plastic bag, combine tortilla chips with Taco Seasoning Mix. Dampen chicken with water and shake off excess. Place a few pieces at a time in plastic bag; shake thoroughly to coat with chips. Arrange chicken in greased shallow baking pan; bake uncovered 30 minutes or until chicken is crispy. Serve with salsa for dipping.
Makes 18 to 20 drumettes

MINI TURKEY EMPANADAS

1 pound ground turkey
1 cup chopped onion
½ cup chopped green pepper
1 clove garlic, minced
1 can (16 ounces) tomatoes, drained and crushed
1 tablespoon dried parsley
1 teaspoon *each* dried cilantro and cumin seed
½ teaspoon *each* dried oregano and red pepper flakes
⅛ teaspoon black pepper
2 packages (15 ounces each) refrigerated pie crusts
Nonstick cooking spray

1. In large nonstick skillet, over medium-high heat, sauté turkey, onion, green pepper and garlic 5 to 6 minutes or until turkey is no longer pink and vegetables are tender. Stir in tomatoes, parsley, cilantro, cumin, oregano, pepper flakes and black pepper. Reduce heat to medium and cook 10 to 15 minutes, stirring constantly, or until any liquid is evaporated. Remove skillet from heat and cool.

2. Using 3-inch round biscuit cutter, cut 12 rounds from each pie crust, rerolling remaining crust to yield 48 rounds.

3. Spoon heaping teaspoonful of filling in center of each round. Fold each pastry in half and pinch edges together to seal. Place mini empanadas on two 15×10-inch cookie sheets lightly coated with nonstick cooking spray. Bake at 400°F 15 to 20 minutes or until mini empanadas are golden brown.
Makes 48 empanadas

Favorite recipe from **National Turkey Federation**

Potato Wraps, Mariachi Drumsticks

SMOKED TURKEY ROLL-UPS

2 packages (4 ounces each) herb-flavored
   soft spreadable cheese
4 flour (8-inch diameter) tortillas*
2 packages (6 ounces each) smoked
   turkey breast slices
2 green onions, sliced lengthwise into
   quarters
   Whole, pickled red cherry peppers
   (optional)

1. Divide one package of cheese equally and spread over tortillas. Divide turkey slices equally and layer over cheese, overlapping turkey slices slightly to cover tortillas. Divide remaining package of cheese equally and spread over turkey slices.

2. At one edge of each tortilla, place 2 quarters of green onion. Roll up tortillas, jelly-roll style. Place turkey tortilla roll-ups, seam side down, in resealable plastic bag; refrigerate several hours or overnight.

3. To serve, cut each turkey tortilla roll-up crosswise into ½-inch slices to form pinwheels. If desired, arrange pinwheels on serving plate and garnish with cherry peppers in center.
Makes 56 appetizer servings

*To keep flour tortillas soft while preparing turkey roll-ups, cover with a slightly damp cloth.

Favorite recipe from **National Turkey Federation**

Smoked Turkey Roll-Ups

TENDER CHICKEN PARTY DIPPERS

1 package (12 ounces) PERDUE DONE IT!® Breaded Chicken Breast Nuggets (18 per package)
Tangy Mustard Dip or Creole Dip (recipes follow)

Following package directions, warm nuggets in conventional oven or heat in microwave. Serve with Tangy Mustard Dip or Creole Dip.

Makes 8 to 10 appetizer servings

TANGY MUSTARD DIP

1 cup mayonnaise
3 tablespoons Dijon mustard
1 teaspoon grated orange peel
1 tablespoon orange juice

In small bowl, combine all ingredients until well blended. Serve immediately or refrigerate until ready to serve.

Makes about 1¼ cups (enough for 1 package nuggets)

CREOLE DIP

⅔ cup bottled chili sauce
1 tablespoon prepared horseradish (optional)
1 tablespoon Worcestershire sauce
1 tablespoon chopped parsley
1 tablespoon minced green onion
1 tablespoon minced celery

In small bowl, combine all ingredients. If time allows, let stand at room temperature 1 hour for flavors to blend.

Makes about 1 cup (enough for 1 package nuggets)

CRUNCHY MEXICAN TURKEY TIDBITS

1 pound ground turkey
1 egg, beaten
2 garlic cloves, minced
¼ cup *each* finely chopped onion and dry bread crumbs
1 teaspoon chili powder
½ teaspoon cumin
4 ounces tortilla chips, finely crushed
Nonstick cooking spray
¾ cup nonfat sour cream
½ cup salsa

1. In medium bowl combine turkey, egg, garlic, onion, bread crumbs, chili powder and cumin; shape into approximately 36 (¾-inch) balls.

2. Place crushed chips on plate. Roll each meatball in chips, coating thoroughly. On 15×10×1-inch baking pan lightly coated with nonstick cooking spray, arrange meatballs. Bake at 350°F 20 minutes or until meat is no longer pink in center.

3. In small bowl combine sour cream and salsa. Use as dip for meatballs.

Makes 36 meatballs

*Favorite recipe from **National Turkey Federation***

GINGERED CHICKEN POT STICKERS

3 cups finely shredded cabbage
1 egg white, lightly beaten
1 tablespoon light soy sauce
¼ teaspoon crushed red pepper
1 tablespoon minced fresh ginger
4 green onions with tops, finely chopped
¼ pound ground chicken breast, cooked and drained
24 wonton wrappers, at room temperature
   Cornstarch
½ cup water
1 tablespoon oyster sauce
½ teaspoon honey
⅛ teaspoon crushed red pepper
2 teaspoons grated lemon peel
1 tablespoon peanut oil

Steam cabbage 5 minutes, then cool to room temperature. Squeeze out any excess moisture; set aside. To prepare filling, combine egg white, soy sauce, ¼ teaspoon red pepper, ginger and green onions in large bowl; blend well. Stir in cabbage and chicken.

To prepare pot stickers, place 1 tablespoon filling in center of 1 wonton wrapper. Gather edges around filling, pressing firmly at top to seal. Repeat with remaining wrappers and filling. Place pot stickers on large baking sheet dusted with cornstarch. Refrigerate 1 hour or until cold. Meanwhile, to prepare sauce, combine remaining ingredients except oil in small bowl; mix well. Set aside.

Heat oil in large nonstick skillet over high heat. Add pot stickers and cook until bottoms are golden brown. Pour sauce over top. Cover and cook 3 minutes. Uncover and cook until all liquid is absorbed. Serve warm on tray as finger food or on small plates with chopsticks as first course.   *Makes 8 appetizer servings*

DEVILED SHRIMP

Devil Sauce (recipe follows)
2 eggs, lightly beaten
¼ teaspoon salt
¼ teaspoon TABASCO® pepper sauce
1 quart vegetable oil
1 pound raw shrimp, peeled and cleaned
1 cup dry bread crumbs

Prepare Devil Sauce; set aside. In shallow dish stir together eggs, salt and TABASCO sauce until well blended. Pour oil into heavy 3-quart saucepan or deep-fat fryer, filling no more than ⅓ full. Heat oil over medium heat to 375°F. Dip shrimp into egg mixture, then into bread crumbs; shake off excess. Carefully add shrimp to oil, a few at a time. Cook 1 to 2 minutes or until golden. Drain on paper towels. Just before serving, drizzle Devil Sauce over shrimp.
     Makes 4 to 6 appetizer servings

DEVIL SAUCE

2 tablespoons butter or margarine
1 small onion, finely chopped
1 clove garlic, minced
1½ teaspoons dry mustard
½ cup beef consommé
2 tablespoons Worcestershire sauce
2 tablespoons dry white wine
¼ teaspoon TABASCO® pepper sauce
¼ cup lemon juice

In 1-quart saucepan melt butter over medium heat; add onion and garlic. Stirring frequently, cook 3 minutes or until tender. Blend in mustard. Gradually stir in consommé, Worcestershire sauce, wine and TABASCO sauce until well blended. Bring to a boil and simmer 5 minutes. Stir in lemon juice. Serve warm over shrimp or use as a dip.
     Makes about 1¼ cups

Gingered Chicken Pot Stickers

TINY SEAFOOD TOSTADAS WITH BLACK BEAN DIP

  Nonstick cooking spray
  4 (8-inch) whole wheat or flour tortillas
  1 cup Black Bean Dip (recipe follows)
  1 cup shredded fresh spinach
  ¾ cup tiny cooked or canned shrimp
  ¾ cup salsa
  ½ cup (2 ounces) shredded reduced fat
    Monterey Jack cheese
  ¼ cup light sour cream

Preheat oven to 350°F. Spray cooking spray on baking sheet. Cut tortillas with 2½-inch round cookie cutter to make 32 rounds.* Place tortilla rounds evenly on prepared baking sheet. Lightly spray tortilla rounds with cooking spray and bake 10 minutes. Turn over and spray again; bake 3 minutes more. Meanwhile, prepare Black Bean Dip.

To prepare tostadas, spread each toasted tortilla round with 1½ teaspoons Black Bean Dip. Layer each with 1½ teaspoons shredded spinach, 1 teaspoon shrimp, 1 teaspoon salsa, a sprinkle of cheese and a dab of sour cream. Garnish with thin green chili strips or fresh cilantro, if desired. Serve immediately.
Makes 8 appetizer servings

*Tortillas may be cut with cookie cutters into other festive shapes.

BLACK BEAN DIP
  1 can (15 ounces) black beans,
    undrained
  1 teaspoon chili powder
  ¼ teaspoon salt
  ¼ teaspoon black pepper
  ¼ teaspoon ground cumin
  2 drops hot pepper sauce
  ¾ cup minced white onion
  2 cloves garlic, minced
  1 can (4 ounces) chopped green chilies,
    drained

Drain beans, reserving 2 tablespoons liquid. Combine drained beans, reserved liquid, chili powder, salt, black pepper, cumin and hot pepper sauce in blender or food processor; process until smooth.

Combine onion and garlic in nonstick skillet or saucepan; cover and cook over low heat until onion is soft and translucent. Uncover and cook until slightly browned. Add chilies and cook 3 minutes more. Add bean mixture and mix well.
Makes about 1½ cups

NOTE: Black Bean Dip can be served (hot or cold) as a dip for tortilla chips or cut-up fresh vegetables.

CRAB-STUFFED MUSHROOMS

  12 large fresh mushrooms
  ¼ cup margarine or butter
  2 tablespoons finely chopped onion
  1 to 4 cloves garlic, finely chopped
  1 tablespoon chopped parsley
  ¼ cup plain dry bread crumbs or cracker
    crumbs
  1 (6-ounce) can HARRIS® or ORLEANS®
    Crab Meat, drained
    Seafood seasonings or seasoned salt, to
    taste

Preheat oven to 350°F. Remove stems from mushrooms and finely chop. In large skillet, lightly brown mushroom caps in margarine; place in 8- or 9-inch square baking dish. In same skillet, cook chopped mushrooms, onion, garlic and parsley until lightly browned. Stir in crumbs, crab meat and seafood seasonings; fill mushroom caps with crab meat mixture. Bake 8 to 10 minutes or until hot. Serve immediately. Refrigerate leftovers.   *Makes 12 appetizers*

Top to bottom: Black Bean Dip, Tiny Seafood Tostadas with Black Bean Dip

Blue Crab Stuffed Tomatoes

BLUE CRAB STUFFED TOMATOES

½ pound blue crabmeat
10 plum tomatoes
½ cup finely chopped celery
⅓ cup plain low fat yogurt
2 tablespoons minced green onion
2 tablespoons finely chopped red bell
    pepper
½ teaspoon lemon juice
¼ teaspoon salt
⅛ teaspoon black pepper

Remove any shell or cartilage from crabmeat.

Cut tomatoes in half lengthwise. Carefully scoop out centers of tomatoes; discard pulp. Invert on paper towels.

Combine crabmeat, celery, yogurt, onion, red pepper, lemon juice, salt and black pepper. Mix well.

Fill tomato halves with crab mixture. Refrigerate 2 hours.   *Makes 20 appetizers*

*Favorite recipe from **Florida Department of Agriculture and Consumer Services Bureau of Seafood and Aquaculture***

COCONUT SHRIMP

1 pound large raw shrimp, peeled and
    deveined with tails on (about 20)
½ cup COCO LOPEZ® Cream of Coconut
3 tablespoons cornstarch
1 tablespoon REALEMON® Lemon Juice
    from Concentrate
1 teaspoon Worcestershire sauce
    Additional cornstarch
⅔ cup flaked coconut
½ cup fresh bread crumbs (1 slice)
    Vegetable oil
    Sweet & Spicy Dipping Sauce (recipe
    follows)

In medium bowl, combine cream of coconut, *3 tablespoons* cornstarch, ReaLemon® brand and Worcestershire; mix until smooth. Coat shrimp with cornstarch. Dip into cream of coconut batter; drain on wire rack. Coat with flaked coconut, then bread crumbs. Place on baking sheet. Cover; refrigerate 1 hour or overnight. Into deep, hot oil (375°F), drop shrimp, one at a time; fry a few shrimp at a time until golden brown. Drain on paper towels. Serve with Sweet & Spicy Dipping Sauce. Refrigerate leftovers.

Makes about 20 appetizers

TIP: Recipe can be doubled. If doubling and using medium shrimp, use 1⅔ cups flaked coconut and 1 cup fresh bread crumbs.

SWEET & SPICY DIPPING SAUCE
    ⅓ cup COCO LOPEZ® Cream of Coconut
    ⅓ cup BENNETT'S® Chili Sauce
    1 tablespoon REALEMON® Lemon Juice
        from Concentrate
    2 teaspoons soy sauce
    1 teaspoon Worcestershire sauce
    ½ to 1 teaspoon prepared horseradish
    ½ teaspoon hot pepper sauce

In small bowl, combine ingredients; mix well. Cover; refrigerate 4 hours or overnight. Serve chilled or at room temperature with Coconut Shrimp. Refrigerate leftovers.

Makes about ¾ cup

SAVORY SHRIMP CHEESE CUPS

¼ pound peeled cooked shrimp, finely chopped *or* 1 (4¼-ounce) can ORLEANS® Shrimp, drained and soaked as label directs

1 (8-ounce) package cream cheese, softened

¼ cup BENNETT'S® Cocktail Sauce

⅛ teaspoon *each* basil leaves, garlic powder, marjoram leaves, oregano leaves and thyme leaves

1 (8-ounce) can refrigerated crescent dinner rolls

Additional BENNETT'S® Cocktail Sauce

Preheat oven to 375°F. In small mixer bowl, beat cream cheese, ¼ cup cocktail sauce and seasonings until smooth. Stir in shrimp. Unroll crescent roll dough; separate into 4 rectangles. Firmly press perforations together to seal. Cut each rectangle lengthwise, then crosswise into 4 pieces; press onto bottoms and ½ inch up sides of muffin cups. Spoon 1 rounded tablespoon cheese mixture into each prepared muffin cup. Bake 10 minutes or until hot. Let stand 5 minutes; remove from pan. Serve warm with additional Bennett's® Cocktail Sauce; garnish as desired. Refrigerate leftovers.

Makes 16 appetizers

Savory Shrimp Cheese Cups

SHRIMP CRESCENTS

- 1 can (14 ounces) artichoke hearts, drained and chopped
- 1 can (4 ounces) diced green chilies, drained
- 1 cup grated Parmesan cheese
- ¼ cup mayonnaise
- ¼ teaspoon ground red pepper
- ¼ teaspoon garlic powder
- 2 cans (8 ounces each) refrigerated crescent dinner rolls
- 32 cooked small shrimp, peeled and deveined

In medium bowl, combine all ingredients except crescent rolls and shrimp. Mix well; set aside.

Unroll crescent rolls and cut each triangle in half lengthwise, forming 32 triangles. Stretch dough to shape and flatten.

Spoon rounded tablespoon of artichoke mixture onto each triangle; place 1 shrimp on top. Roll up, starting at wide end, and place on well-greased baking sheet. (At this point, crescents may be refrigerated until ready to bake and serve.)

Bake at 375°F 12 to 15 minutes or until golden brown. Serve warm.   *Makes 32 appetizers*

*Favorite recipe from **Florida Department of Agriculture and Consumer Services Bureau of Seafood and Aquaculture***

Stone Crab Claws with Honey-Mustard Sauce

STONE CRAB CLAWS WITH HONEY–MUSTARD SAUCE

- 2½ pounds stone crab claws, cooked, cracked
- 1 cup mayonnaise
- ⅓ cup half-and-half or light cream
- 2 tablespoons honey
- 2 tablespoons prepared mustard
- 1 teaspoon ground coriander
- Cocktail sauce (optional)

Arrange cracked claws on serving plate.

Combine remaining ingredients except cocktail sauce; stir until well blended. Serve sauces with stone crab claws.

Makes 3 servings crab claws and 1½ cups sauce

*Favorite recipe from **Florida Department of Agriculture and Consumer Services Bureau of Seafood and Aquaculture***

BAKED VEGETABLE & SEAFOOD WONTONS

**1 envelope LIPTON® Recipe Secrets®
Vegetable Soup Mix**
1 container (15 ounces) ricotta cheese
½ pound imitation crabmeat, chopped
¼ teaspoon garlic powder
⅛ teaspoon pepper
**40 refrigerated or thawed frozen wonton
wrappers**
1 tablespoon olive or vegetable oil

Preheat oven to 350°F. In medium bowl, combine vegetable soup mix, ricotta cheese, crabmeat, garlic powder and pepper. Place 1 tablespoon ricotta mixture on center of each wonton. Brush edges with water; fold corners into centers. Press to seal. Place on lightly greased cookie sheet; brush with oil. Bake 25 minutes or until crisp and golden brown, turning once. *Makes 40 wontons*

NOTE: Cover filled wontons with damp cloth until ready to bake, then brush with oil.

VARIATION: Use 1½ cups chopped cooked shrimp in place of crabmeat.

GARLIC & HERB DIP

1 cup sour cream
¼ cup mayonnaise
2 tablespoons chopped green onion
1 teaspoon dried basil, crushed
½ teaspoon dried tarragon, crushed
1 clove garlic, minced
¼ teaspoon salt
¼ teaspoon black pepper
**Assorted fresh vegetable dippers or
pita chips**

Combine all ingredients except dippers in medium bowl until blended. Cover; refrigerate several hours or overnight. Serve with dippers. *Makes about 1¼ cups*

Baked Vegetable & Seafood Wontons

FRENCH ONION DIP

2 cups sour cream
½ cup HELLMANN'S® or BEST FOODS®
Real or Light Mayonnaise or Low Fat
Cholesterol Free Mayonnaise
Dressing
1 package (1.9 ounces) KNORR® French
Onion Soup and Recipe Mix

In medium bowl combine sour cream, mayonnaise and soup mix. Cover; chill. Serve with fresh vegetables or potato chips. Garnish as desired. *Makes about 2½ cups*

CUCUMBER DILL DIP

1 package (8 ounces) reduced fat cream
cheese, softened
1 cup HELLMANN'S® or BEST FOODS®
Real or Light Mayonnaise or Low Fat
Cholesterol Free Mayonnaise
Dressing
2 medium cucumbers, peeled, seeded
and chopped
2 tablespoons sliced green onions
1 tablespoon lemon juice
2 teaspoons snipped fresh dill *or*
½ teaspoon dried dill weed
½ teaspoon hot pepper sauce

In medium bowl beat cream cheese until smooth. Stir in mayonnaise, cucumbers, green onions, lemon juice, dill and hot pepper sauce. Cover; chill. Serve with fresh vegetables, crackers or chips. Garnish as desired.
Makes about 2½ cups

SPINACH DIP

1 package (10 ounces) frozen chopped
spinach, thawed and drained
1 container (16 ounces) sour cream
1 cup HELLMANN'S® or BEST FOODS®
Real or Light Mayonnaise or Low Fat
Cholesterol Free Mayonnaise
Dressing
1 package (1.4 ounces) KNORR®
Vegetable Soup and Recipe Mix
1 can (8 ounces) water chestnuts,
drained and chopped (optional)
3 green onions, chopped

In medium bowl combine spinach, sour cream, mayonnaise, soup mix, water chestnuts and green onions. Cover; chill. Serve with fresh vegetables, crackers or chips. Garnish as desired. *Makes about 3 cups*

SPICY DIJON DIP

1 (8-ounce) package cream cheese,
softened
¼ cup GREY POUPON® Dijon or Country
Dijon Mustard
¼ cup dairy sour cream
1 tablespoon finely chopped green onions
1 (4¼-ounce) can tiny shrimp, drained
***or* ½ cup cooked shrimp, chopped**
Sliced green onions for garnish
Assorted cut-up vegetables

In small bowl, with electric mixer at medium speed, blend cream cheese, mustard, sour cream and chopped onions; stir in shrimp. Cover; refrigerate at least 2 hours. Garnish with sliced onions; serve as a dip with vegetables.
Makes 1½ cups

Left to right: French Onion Dip,
Cucumber Dill Dip, Spinach Dip

TACO DIP

12 ounces cream cheese, softened
½ cup dairy sour cream
2 teaspoons chili powder
1½ teaspoons ground cumin
⅛ teaspoon ground red pepper
½ cup salsa
2 cups shredded lettuce or lettuce leaves
1 cup (4 ounces) shredded Wisconsin
    Cheddar cheese
1 cup (4 ounces) shredded Wisconsin
    Monterey Jack cheese
½ cup diced plum tomatoes
⅓ cup sliced green onions
¼ cup sliced ripe olives
¼ cup sliced pimiento-stuffed green olives
    Tortilla chips and blue corn chips

Combine cream cheese, sour cream, chili powder, cumin and red pepper in large bowl; mix until well blended. Stir in salsa. Spread onto 10-inch serving platter lined with lettuce. Top with cheeses, tomatoes, green onions and olives. Serve with chips.

Makes 10 appetizer servings

Favorite recipe from **Wisconsin Milk Marketing Board**

PICANTE VEGETABLE DIP

⅔ cup sour cream or reduced-fat sour
    cream
½ cup picante sauce
⅓ cup mayonnaise or reduced-fat
    mayonnaise
¼ cup finely chopped green or red bell
    pepper
2 tablespoons finely chopped green onion
¾ teaspoon garlic salt
    Assorted fresh vegetable dippers or
    tortilla chips

Combine all ingredients in medium bowl until well blended. Cover; refrigerate several hours or overnight to allow flavors to blend.

Makes about 1⅔ cups

SPINACH−PARMESAN DIP

1 cup MIRACLE WHIP® Salad Dressing
1 cup BREAKSTONE'S® Sour Cream
1 package (10 ounces) frozen chopped
    spinach, thawed, well drained
½ cup (2 ounces) KRAFT® 100% Natural
    Grated Parmesan Cheese
1 can (8 ounces) water chestnuts,
    drained, chopped
⅛ teaspoon ground red pepper

• Mix all ingredients until well blended. Refrigerate. Serve with assorted crackers.

Makes 4 cups

PREP TIME: 5 minutes plus refrigerating

CLAM DIP

1 package (3 ounces) cream cheese,
    softened
1 cup dairy sour cream
1 can (6½ ounces) minced clams
½ teaspoon LAWRY'S® Seasoned Salt
    Dash LAWRY'S® Seasoned Pepper
2 teaspoons lemon juice
1½ teaspoons Worcestershire sauce

In medium bowl, blend cream cheese and sour cream. Drain clams and reserve 1 tablespoon clam juice. Add to sour cream mixture. Add remaining ingredients and blend well.

Makes 1½ cups

PRESENTATION: Serve with crisp raw vegetables and Johannisberg Riesling.

HINT: For a thinner dip, add more clam juice.

Taco Dip

THREE MUSHROOM RATATOUILLE

- 1 package (3½ ounces) fresh shiitake mushrooms*
- 1 tablespoon olive oil
- 1 large onion, chopped
- 4 cloves garlic, minced
- 1 package (8 ounces) button mushrooms, chopped
- 1 package (6 ounces) crimini mushrooms, chopped
- 1 cup chicken broth
- 1 small tomato, chopped
- 2 tablespoons chopped parsley
- 2 tablespoons grated Parmesan cheese
- 3 pita breads (6 inches each)

Remove stems from shiitake mushrooms; discard stems. Chop caps. Heat oil in large skillet over medium heat until hot. Add onion and garlic. Cook 5 minutes, stirring occasionally. Add all 3 types of mushrooms. Cook 5 minutes more, stirring often. Add chicken broth. Bring to a boil. Cook about 10 minutes or until liquid is absorbed. Remove from heat. Stir in tomato, parsley and cheese. Spoon into bowl.

Meanwhile, preheat broiler. Split each pita bread horizontally in half. Stack halves; cut the stack into 6 wedges. Arrange wedges in single layer on baking sheet. Broil 4 inches from heat 1 to 3 minutes or until wedges are toasted. Serve toasted pita bread triangles with warm dip. Garnish, if desired.

Makes about 2¼ cups

*Or, substitute 1 ounce dried black Chinese mushrooms. Place dried mushrooms in small bowl; cover with warm water. Soak 20 minutes to soften. Drain; squeeze out excess moisture.

MEXICAN TURKEY DIP

- 1 pound ground turkey
- 1 package (1¼ ounces) reduced-sodium taco seasoning mix
  Nonstick cooking spray
- 1 cup salsa
- 3 ounces reduced fat cream cheese, softened
- ½ cup nonfat sour cream
- 1 cup grated reduced fat Cheddar cheese
- 2 tablespoons *each* minced green onion and sliced black olives
- 24 no-salt corn chips

1. In large nonstick skillet, over medium-high heat, sauté turkey 5 to 6 minutes or until turkey is no longer pink; drain. Stir in seasoning mix.

2. Spread turkey mixture in 9-inch square baking dish lightly coated with nonstick cooking spray. Top turkey mixture with salsa.

3. In small bowl combine cream cheese and sour cream. Spread mixture over salsa and sprinkle Cheddar cheese over top. Bake at 350°F 25 minutes or until bubbly.

4. Garnish with green onion and olives and serve with chips. *Makes 24 servings*

*Favorite recipe from **National Turkey Federation***

Three Mushroom Ratatouille

HOT BROCCOLI DIP

1 (1½-pound) round sourdough bread
    loaf
½ cup finely chopped celery
½ cup chopped red pepper
¼ cup finely chopped onion
2 tablespoons PARKAY® Spread Sticks
1 pound VELVEETA® Pasteurized
    Process Cheese Spread, cubed
1 (10-ounce) package frozen chopped
    broccoli, thawed, drained
¼ teaspoon dried rosemary leaves,
    crushed

Cut slice from top of bread loaf; remove center, leaving 1-inch shell. Cut removed bread into bite-size pieces. Cover shell with top. Place on cookie sheet with bread pieces. Bake at 350°F, 15 minutes or until hot. In large skillet, sauté celery, pepper and onion in spread. Reduce heat to low. Add process cheese spread; stir until melted. Stir in remaining ingredients; heat thoroughly, stirring constantly. Spoon into bread loaf. Serve hot with toasted bread pieces and vegetable dippers.   *Makes 6 to 8 servings*

PREP TIME: 15 minutes
BAKE TIME: 15 minutes

Hot Broccoli Dip

MICROWAVE DIRECTIONS: Prepare bread loaf as directed. Combine celery, pepper, onion and spread in 2-quart microwave-safe bowl. Microwave on HIGH 1 minute. Add remaining ingredients; microwave on HIGH 5 to 6 minutes or until hot, stirring after 3 minutes. Spoon into bread loaf. Serve hot with toasted bread pieces and vegetable dippers.

PINEAPPLE–ALMOND CHEESE SPREAD

2 cans (8 ounces each) DOLE® Crushed
    Pineapple
1 package (8 ounces) cream cheese,
    softened
4 cups (16 ounces) shredded sharp
    Cheddar cheese
½ cup mayonnaise
1 tablespoon soy sauce
1 cup DOLE® Chopped Natural Almonds,
    toasted
½ cup finely chopped DOLE® Green Bell
    Pepper
¼ cup minced green onions or chives
    DOLE® Celery stalks or assorted
    breads

• Drain pineapple. In large bowl, beat cream cheese until smooth; beat in Cheddar cheese, mayonnaise and soy sauce until smooth. Stir in pineapple, almonds, green pepper and onions. Refrigerate, covered. Use to stuff celery stalks or serve as spread with assorted breads. Serve at room temperature.   *Makes 4 cups*

Zesty Seafood Vegetable Spread

ZESTY SEAFOOD VEGETABLE SPREAD

2 (8-ounce) packages cream cheese, softened
1 (8-ounce) container BORDEN® or MEADOW GOLD® Sour Cream
1 (1.7-ounce) package MRS. GRASS® Homestyle Vegetable Recipe, Soup & Dip Mix
¾ cup BENNETT'S® Cocktail or Hot Seafood Sauce, chilled
1 (6-ounce) can ORLEANS® or HARRIS® Fancy White Crab Meat, rinsed, drained and chilled *or* 1 (4¼-ounce) can ORLEANS® Shrimp, rinsed and soaked as label directs

In large mixer bowl, beat cream cheese until fluffy; beat in sour cream and dip mix. On serving plate, spread cheese mixture into 8-inch circle. Chill at least 1 hour. Just before serving, top with cocktail sauce, then crab meat. Garnish as desired. Serve with assorted crackers. Refrigerate leftovers.

Makes 12 servings

TANGY WISCONSIN BLUE CHEESE WHIP

1 cup whipping cream
½ cup finely crumbled Wisconsin Blue cheese (2 ounces)
1 teaspoon dried basil, crushed
¼ teaspoon garlic salt
½ cup almonds, toasted and chopped
Assorted vegetable or fruit dippers

In small mixer bowl combine whipping cream, Blue cheese, basil, and garlic salt. Beat with electric mixer on medium speed until slightly thickened. Gently fold in chopped almonds. Serve with vegetable or fruit dippers. (Dip can be made ahead and chilled, covered, up to 2 hours.) *Makes about 2 cups*

*Favorite recipe from **Wisconsin Milk Marketing Board***

FRESH TOMATO EGGPLANT SPREAD

- 1 medium eggplant
- 2 large ripe tomatoes, seeded and chopped
- 1 cup minced zucchini
- ¼ cup chopped green onions with tops
- 2 tablespoons red wine vinegar
- 1 tablespoon olive oil
- 1 teaspoon honey
- 1 clove garlic, minced
- 1 tablespoon minced fresh basil
- 2 teaspoons minced fresh oregano
- 1 teaspoon minced fresh thyme
- ⅛ teaspoon ground black pepper
- ¼ cup pine nuts or slivered almonds
- 32 melba toast rounds

Preheat oven to 375°F. Poke holes in surface of eggplant with fork. Bake 20 to 25 minutes or until tender. Cool completely; peel and mince. Place in colander; press to release excess water.

Combine eggplant with tomatoes, zucchini, green onions, vinegar, oil, honey, garlic, basil, oregano, thyme and black pepper in large bowl. Mix well. Refrigerate 2 hours to allow flavors to blend. Stir in pine nuts just before serving. Serve with melba toast rounds.

Makes 8 servings

HOLIDAY PATE

- 1 (8-ounce) package JONES® Braunschweiger
- 1 (3-ounce) package cream cheese, softened
- 1 tablespoon finely chopped onion
- 1 tablespoon Worcestershire sauce
- 1 to 2 tablespoons dry sherry
- ¼ to ½ teaspoon ground nutmeg
  Dash of hot pepper sauce

Blend all ingredients and serve with crackers or cocktail bread. *Makes about 1¼ cups*

BLACK OLIVE TAPANADE

- 1 can (6 ounces) pitted ripe olives, drained
- ¼ cup chopped red pepper
- 3 tablespoons olive oil
- 1 tablespoon lemon juice
- 1½ teaspoons dried oregano leaves
- ½ teaspoon minced garlic
- ½ cup (3 ounces) crumbled ATHENOS® Feta Natural Cheese

• Place all ingredients except cheese in blender or food processor container fitted with steel blade; cover. Process until smooth. Stir in cheese.

• Refrigerate several hours or overnight.

• Serve with crackers or French bread chunks. Sprinkle with additional feta cheese, if desired.
Makes 1½ cups

PREP TIME: 15 minutes plus refrigerating

WHIPPED FETA WITH HERBS

- 1 cup (6 ounces) crumbled ATHENOS® Feta Natural Cheese
- 2 tablespoons sour cream
- ½ teaspoon lemon juice
- ¼ teaspoon *each* dried oregano and basil leaves, crushed *or* 2 teaspoons *each* chopped fresh oregano and basil
  Freshly ground black pepper

• Blend all ingredients except pepper in blender or food processor container until smooth. Refrigerate 1 hour. Season with pepper. Serve with pita bread wedges or crackers.
Makes about ½ cup

PREP TIME: 15 minutes plus refrigerating

Fresh Tomato Eggplant Spread

CHEESE PINE CONES

2 cups (8 ounces) shredded Swiss cheese
½ cup butter or margarine, softened
3 tablespoons milk
2 tablespoons dry sherry or milk
⅛ teaspoon ground red pepper
1 cup finely chopped blanched almonds
¾ cup slivered blanched almonds
¾ cup sliced almonds
½ cup whole almonds
   Fresh rosemary sprigs
   Assorted crackers

Beat cheese, butter, milk, sherry and red pepper in medium bowl until smooth; stir in chopped almonds.

Divide mixture into 3 equal portions; shape into tapered ovals to resemble pine cones. Insert slivered, sliced and whole almonds into cones. Cover; refrigerate 2 to 3 hours or until firm.

Arrange Cheese Pine Cones on wooden board or serving plate. Garnish tops with rosemary. Serve with assorted crackers.
Makes 12 to 16 appetizer servings

PESTO CHEESE WREATH

Parsley-Basil Pesto* (page 55)
3 packages (8 ounces each) cream
   cheese, softened
½ cup mayonnaise
¼ cup whipping cream or half-and-half
1 teaspoon sugar
1 teaspoon onion salt
⅓ cup chopped roasted red peppers** or
   pimiento, drained
   Pimiento strips and Italian flat leaf
   parsley leaves (optional)
   Assorted crackers and cut-up
   vegetables

Clockwise from top right: Holiday Appetizer Puffs (page 65), Pesto Cheese Wreath, Cheese Pine Cones

Prepare Parsley-Basil Pesto; set aside. Beat cream cheese and mayonnaise in medium bowl until smooth; beat in whipping cream, sugar and onion salt.

Line 5-cup ring mold with plastic wrap. Spoon half the cheese mixture into prepared mold; spread evenly. Spread Parsley-Basil Pesto evenly over cheese mixture; top with chopped red peppers. Spoon remaining cheese mixture over peppers; spread evenly. Cover; refrigerate until cheese mixture is firm, 8 hours or overnight.

Uncover mold; invert onto serving plate. Carefully remove plastic wrap. Smooth top and sides of wreath with spatula. Garnish with pimiento strips and parsley leaves, if desired. Serve with assorted crackers and vegetables.
Makes 16 to 24 appetizer servings

*½ cup purchased pesto may be substituted for Parsley-Basil Pesto.

**Look for roasted red peppers packed in cans or jars in the Italian food section of the supermarket.

PARSLEY–BASIL PESTO
   2 cups fresh parsley leaves
   ¼ cup pine nuts or slivered almonds
   2 tablespoons grated Parmesan cheese
   2 cloves garlic, peeled
   1 tablespoon dried basil leaves, crushed
   ¼ teaspoon salt
   2 tablespoons olive or vegetable oil

Process all ingredients except oil in food processor or blender until finely chopped. With machine running, add oil gradually, processing until mixture is smooth.   *Makes about ½ cup*

CLAM CHEESE BALL

   1 (8-ounce) package cream cheese, softened
   1 (6½-ounce) can SNOW'S® or DOXSEE® Minced Clams, well drained
   ½ teaspoon pepper
   ½ teaspoon garlic powder
   ¼ cup grated Parmesan cheese
   1 tablespoon chopped parsley

In small mixer bowl, beat cream cheese until fluffy. Stir in clams, pepper and garlic powder. Cover; chill about 1 hour. Shape into ball. In small bowl, combine Parmesan cheese and parsley. Roll ball in Parmesan cheese mixture. Cover; chill several hours to blend flavors. Garnish as desired. Serve with assorted crackers. Refrigerate leftovers.
Makes one 3-inch cheese ball

SPICY TURKEY HAM SPREAD

   1 pound turkey ham, cut into chunks
   ¼ cup chopped onion
   ¼ cup Dijon-style mustard
   4 teaspoons Worcestershire sauce
   ¼ teaspoon cayenne pepper

1. In food processor fitted with metal blade, process ham, onion, mustard, Worcestershire sauce and cayenne pepper until smooth.

2. To serve, spoon mixture into red or green bell pepper halves, accompanied with melba toast rounds, if desired.   *Makes 2 cups*

*Favorite recipe from **National Turkey Federation***

Preheat oven to 350°F. To toast walnuts, place on baking sheet. Bake 8 to 10 minutes or until golden brown, stirring frequently; cool. Process walnuts in food processor using on/off pulsing action until walnuts are ground, but not pasty. Remove from food processor; set aside.

Process cream cheese, pesto and feta cheese in food processor until smooth. Spread ¾ cup cheese mixture on waxed paper and form 4-inch log. Wrap waxed paper around cheese log. Repeat with remaining cheese mixture. Refrigerate logs at least 4 hours, until well chilled. Roll each chilled log to form 5-inch log.

Combine walnuts and pepper. Roll 1 log in nut mixture to coat. Combine carrot and parsley. Roll remaining log in carrot mixture to coat. Serve immediately or wrap and refrigerate up to a day before serving. Thinly slice log and serve with crackers. Garnish, if desired.

Makes 2 logs

Pesto-Cheese Logs

PESTO–CHEESE LOGS

⅓ cup walnuts
1 package (8 ounces) cream cheese, softened
⅓ cup prepared pesto sauce
⅓ cup crumbled feta cheese
2 teaspoons cracked black pepper
2 tablespoons finely shredded carrot
2 tablespoons chopped fresh parsley
  Assorted crackers
  Carrot slivers, parsley and fresh thyme for garnish

CHEDDAR CHEESE SPREAD

3 ounces *each* white Cheddar, yellow Cheddar and cream cheese, cut into small pieces
6 green onions, white parts only, finely chopped
2 tablespoons butter or margarine, softened
2 tablespoons dry sherry
1 teaspoon Worcestershire sauce
1 teaspoon Dijon-style mustard
¼ teaspoon salt (optional)
  Dash hot pepper sauce (optional)
2 tablespoons finely chopped chives
  Assorted crackers

Place all ingredients except chives and crackers in food processor or blender; process until smooth. Add chives; pulse to mix in. Cover; refrigerate. Allow spread to soften at room temperature before serving. Serve with crackers. *Makes about 2 cups spread*

BACON AND TWO ONION CHEESECAKE

6 slices bacon, diced
1 large sweet onion, chopped
1 clove garlic, minced
1 container (15 ounces) SARGENTO®
 Light Ricotta Cheese
½ cup half-and-half
2 tablespoons flour
½ teaspoon salt
¼ teaspoon cayenne pepper
2 eggs
½ cup thinly sliced green onions

In 10-inch skillet, cook bacon until crisp; remove to paper towels with slotted spoon. Cook sweet onion and garlic in drippings until tender, about 6 minutes. Drain in strainer; discard bacon drippings. In bowl of electric mixer, combine ricotta cheese, half-and-half, flour, salt and pepper; blend until smooth. Add eggs, one at a time; blend until smooth. Reserve 3 tablespoons of the bacon for garnish. Stir remaining bacon, cooked onion mixture and green onions into ricotta mixture. Lightly grease sides of 8- or 9-inch springform pan; pour batter into pan. Bake at 350°F 40 minutes or until center is just set. Remove to wire cooling rack; cool to room temperature. Remove side of pan. Garnish with reserved bacon; serve with assorted crackers.

Makes 10 appetizer servings

FRUITY CHEESE SPREAD

1 package (8 ounces) cream cheese, softened
1 teaspoon grated orange peel
¾ teaspoon almond extract
½ teaspoon ground ginger
1½ cups RALSTON® brand Fruit Muesli with Cranberries, crushed to 1 cup, divided
 Apple and pear slices
 Crackers and cookies

Combine cream cheese, orange peel, almond extract and ginger; beat until smooth. Place ½ cup cereal in serving dish; spoon cheese mixture on top. Refrigerate 2 to 3 hours. Just before serving, sprinkle remaining ½ cup cereal over cheese spread. Serve with apple and pear slices, crackers and cookies.

Makes 16 servings

SAVORY PEPPER–HERB CHEESECAKE

CRUST
1¼ cups fresh dark rye or pumpernickel bread crumbs (about 2 slices, processed in blender or food processor)
3 tablespoons melted margarine
FILLING
1 container (15 ounces) SARGENTO® Light Ricotta Cheese
½ cup half-and-half
2 tablespoons flour
2 eggs
⅓ cup chopped mixed fresh herbs (such as parsley, basil, mint, tarragon, rosemary, thyme and oregano)
¼ cup chopped fresh chives or green onion tops
1½ teaspoons finely grated lemon peel
¾ teaspoon salt
½ teaspoon cracked black pepper

Lightly grease sides of 8- or 9-inch springform pan. Combine crust ingredients; press evenly over bottom of pan. Chill while preparing filling. In bowl of electric mixer, combine ricotta cheese, half-and-half and flour; blend until smooth. Add eggs, one at a time; blend until smooth. Blend in fresh herbs, chives, lemon peel, salt and pepper. Pour into crust; bake at 350°F 30 to 35 minutes or until center is just set. Remove to wire cooling rack; cool to room temperature. Remove side of pan. Cut into wedges to serve.

Makes 10 appetizer servings

HOT ARTICHOKE SPREAD

1 cup MIRACLE WHIP® Salad Dressing
1 cup (4 ounces) KRAFT® 100% Grated Parmesan Cheese
1 (14-ounce) can artichoke hearts, drained, chopped
1 (4-ounce) can chopped green chilies, drained
1 garlic clove, minced
2 tablespoons green onion slices
2 tablespoons chopped tomato

• Preheat oven to 350°F.

• Mix all ingredients except onion and tomato until well blended.

• Spoon into shallow ovenproof dish or 9-inch pie plate.

• Bake 20 to 25 minutes or until lightly browned. Sprinkle with onion and tomato. Serve with toasted bread cutouts.

Makes 2 cups

PREP TIME: 10 minutes
COOK TIME: 25 minutes

WARM HERB CHEESE SPREAD

3 (8-ounce) packages cream cheese, softened
¼ cup BORDEN® or MEADOW GOLD® Milk
¼ cup REALEMON® Lemon Juice from Concentrate
½ teaspoon *each* dried basil, marjoram, oregano and thyme leaves
¼ teaspoon garlic powder
½ pound cooked shrimp, chopped (1½ cups) (optional)

Preheat oven to 350°F. In large mixer bowl, beat cream cheese just until smooth. Gradually beat in milk then ReaLemon® brand and seasonings. Add shrimp if desired. Spoon into 9-inch quiche dish or pie plate. Cover; bake 15 minutes or until hot. Garnish as desired. Serve warm with crackers, breadsticks and assorted fresh vegetables. Refrigerate leftovers.

Makes about 4 cups

MICROWAVE DIRECTIONS: Prepare cheese mixture as above; spoon into 8- or 9-inch glass pie plate. Cook on 50% power (MEDIUM) 5 to 6 minutes or until hot. Stir before serving. Proceed as above.

MARINATED SHRIMP & VEGETABLES

1 pound raw medium shrimp, peeled, deveined and cooked
1 cup fresh cauliflowerets
4 ounces small whole fresh mushrooms
1 cup sliced zucchini
1 large green bell pepper, seeded and cut into squares
1 large red bell pepper, seeded and cut into squares
¾ cup REALEMON® Lemon Juice from Concentrate
1 tablespoon chopped green onion
2 teaspoons sugar
1 teaspoon salt
¼ to ½ teaspoon dried dill weed
5 drops hot pepper sauce
¾ cup vegetable oil

Place shrimp, cauliflower, mushrooms, zucchini and bell peppers in large shallow dish. In small bowl or jar, combine all remaining ingredients except oil; mix well. Add oil; whisk or shake well. Pour over shrimp mixture. Cover; chill 6 hours or overnight, stirring occasionally. Garnish as desired. Refrigerate leftovers.

Makes 6 to 8 servings

Hot Artichoke Spread

SEOUL ROLLED BEEF WITH VEGETABLES

4 thin slices beef top round steak, trimmed
2 medium carrots, peeled and halved
2 medium parsnips, peeled and halved
8 small green beans, halved lengthwise
4 tablespoons vegetable oil, divided
1 can (13¾ ounces) beef broth, divided
1 piece fresh ginger (about 1½ inches long), peeled and cut into 6 (¼-inch-thick) slices
¼ teaspoon ground red pepper
1 tablespoon rice wine or dry sherry
1 tablespoon soy sauce
1 teaspoon sugar
1 teaspoon cornstarch
1 teaspoon sesame oil

Cut each beef slice crosswise into 2 pieces (about 4 to 5 inches in length). Cut carrots and parsnips lengthwise into pencil-thick strips. Place ⅛ of carrots, ⅛ of parsnips and 2 green bean halves on each piece of beef along one short end. Starting with short end, roll up beef, jelly-roll style, to enclose vegetables; secure with short bamboo or metal skewer. Repeat with remaining beef and vegetables.

Heat wok over high heat 1 minute or until hot. Drizzle 2 tablespoons vegetable oil into wok; add 4 beef rolls. Cook rolls 2½ to 3 minutes until browned on all sides, turning occasionally. Transfer to bowl; set aside. Reheat wok and repeat with remaining 2 tablespoons vegetable oil and 4 beef rolls. Return all rolls to wok. Add 1 cup broth, ginger and red pepper. Cover and bring to a boil. Reduce heat to low and simmer rolls 1 hour or until beef is fork-tender, turning rolls to cook evenly. Add more broth if it evaporates.

Seoul Rolled Beef with Vegetables

Transfer cooked rolls to cutting board; set aside. Pour cooking liquid from wok into glass measuring cup. Discard ginger. Add enough broth or water to make ⅔ cup liquid; return to wok and bring to a boil. Meanwhile, combine rice wine, soy sauce, sugar, cornstarch and sesame oil in small bowl; mix well and add to wok. Cook and stir until liquid boils and thickens. Pour sauce into small bowl.

Remove skewers from beef rolls. Cut rolls in half diagonally at sharp angle. Arrange on lettuce-lined platter.

Makes 8 appetizer servings

POLENTA TRIANGLES

1 cup coarse yellow cornmeal
1 envelope LIPTON® Recipe Secrets®
    Onion or Golden Onion Soup Mix
3 cups cold water
1 can (4 ounces) mild chopped green
    chilies, drained
½ cup whole kernel corn
⅓ cup finely chopped roasted red peppers
½ cup shredded sharp Cheddar cheese
    (about 2 ounces)

In 3-quart microwave-safe casserole, combine cornmeal, onion soup mix and water. Microwave covered at HIGH (Full Power) 20 minutes, stirring every 5 minutes (mixture will be thick). Stir in chilies, corn and roasted red peppers. Spread into lightly greased 9-inch square baking pan; sprinkle with cheese. Let stand 20 minutes or until firm; cut into triangles. Serve at room temperature or microwave at HIGH 30 seconds or until warm.

Makes about 30 appetizers

CONVENTIONAL DIRECTIONS: In 3-quart saucepan, bring 3 cups water to a boil. With wire whisk, stir in cornmeal, then onion soup mix. Simmer uncovered, stirring constantly, 25 minutes or until thickened. Stir in chilies, corn and roasted red peppers. Spread into pan and proceed as above. Serve at room temperature or heat in oven at 350°F for 5 minutes or until warm.

Polenta Triangles

OYSTERS ROMANO

12 oysters, shucked and on the half shell
2 slices bacon, cut into 1-inch pieces
½ cup Italian-seasoned dry bread crumbs
2 tablespoons butter or margarine, melted
½ teaspoon garlic salt
6 tablespoons grated Romano, Parmesan or provolone cheese
Fresh chives for garnish

Preheat oven to 375°F. Place shells with oysters on baking sheet. Top each oyster with 1 piece bacon. Bake 10 minutes or until bacon is crisp. Meanwhile, combine bread crumbs, butter and garlic salt in small bowl. Spoon mixture over oysters; top with cheese. Bake 5 to 10 minutes or until cheese melts. Serve immediately. Garnish with chives, if desired.

Makes 4 appetizer servings

GREEK-STYLE SAUSAGE ROLL

1 pound bulk pork sausage
¼ cup finely chopped onion
1 (10-ounce) package frozen chopped spinach, thawed and drained
¼ pound feta cheese, crumbled
¼ cup finely chopped parsley
⅛ teaspoon white pepper
1 egg, beaten
10 sheets frozen phyllo dough (17×13-inch rectangles), thawed
½ cup butter or margarine, melted

In large skillet, cook sausage and onion over medium-high heat until sausage is done and onion is tender, stirring occasionally. Drain. Stir in spinach, feta cheese, parsley, white pepper and egg. Set aside.

Preheat oven to 350°F. Unfold phyllo dough. Spread 1 sheet flat; top with another sheet of phyllo. Gently brush with some of melted butter.

Top with remaining sheets of phyllo, brushing each with butter. Reserve 1 tablespoon butter for top of pastry.

Spread sausage-spinach mixture lengthwise over bottom third of layered phyllo dough to within 2 inches of ends. Fold ends over. Carefully roll up phyllo. Place roll, seam side down, on lightly greased baking sheet; brush with reserved 1 tablespoon butter. Bake 30 to 35 minutes or until golden. To serve, cut into slices. *Makes 16 appetizer servings*

PREP TIME: 30 minutes
COOK TIME: 30 minutes

*Favorite recipe from **National Pork Producers Council***

FESTIVE PEPPER MEDLEY À LA GRECQUE

1 green bell pepper, cut into thin strips
1 yellow bell pepper, cut into thin strips
1 red bell pepper, cut into thin strips
3 tablespoons olive or vegetable oil
1 tablespoon water
2 teaspoons balsamic or red wine vinegar
1 tablespoon chopped fresh oregano *or* 1 teaspoon dried oregano
Salt and black pepper to taste
¾ cup chopped walnuts
¼ cup olives (Greek or Niçoise)
¼ cup crumbled feta cheese (optional)
Radicchio or spinach leaves for garnish

Arrange bell peppers in microwavable serving dish. In small bowl, combine oil, water, vinegar, oregano, salt and black pepper; pour over bell peppers. Sprinkle with walnuts. Microwave at HIGH (100% power) 5 minutes or until peppers are cooked. Top with olives and cheese. Serve warm or at room temperature. Garnish with radicchio leaves, if desired.

Makes 4 to 6 servings

*Favorite recipe from **Walnut Marketing Board***

Oysters Romano

Cheese Twists, Deviled Mixed Nuts

CHEESE TWISTS

1 cup all-purpose flour
½ teaspoon baking soda
½ teaspoon dry mustard
½ teaspoon salt
⅛ teaspoon ground red pepper (cayenne)
¾ cup grated Parmesan cheese, divided
½ cup butter or margarine, softened
3 egg yolks
2 teaspoons water
1 egg white, slightly beaten
1 tablespoon sesame seeds (optional)

Combine flour, baking soda, mustard, salt and red pepper in large bowl. Reserve 1 tablespoon cheese; stir remaining cheese into flour mixture. Cut in butter with pastry blender or 2 knives until mixture resembles fine crumbs. Add egg yolks and water, mixing until dough forms. Shape into a ball; flatten and wrap in plastic wrap. Refrigerate 2 hours or until firm.

Preheat oven to 400°F. Grease two cookie sheets. Roll out dough on lightly floured surface into 12-inch square (about ⅛ inch thick). Brush surface lightly with egg white and sprinkle with remaining 1 tablespoon cheese and sesame seeds, if desired. Cut dough in half. Cut each half crosswise into ¼-inch strips. Twist 2 strips together. Repeat with remaining strips. Place 1 inch apart on prepared cookie sheets.

Bake 6 to 8 minutes or until light golden brown. Remove from cookie sheets and cool completely on wire racks. Store in airtight container. *Makes about 48 twists*

VARIATION: Prepare dough and cut as directed. Place ¾ of strips on cookie sheets. Form rings with remaining strips; seal edges. Place on cookie sheets. Bake and cool as directed. To serve, arrange 3 to 4 strips to form small stack. Insert stack into ring. Repeat with remaining strips.

DEVILED MIXED NUTS

3 tablespoons vegetable oil
2 cups assorted unsalted nuts, such as peanuts, almonds, Brazil nuts or walnuts
2 tablespoons sugar
1 teaspoon paprika
½ teaspoon ground chili powder
½ teaspoon curry powder
½ teaspoon ground cumin
½ teaspoon ground coriander
½ teaspoon ground black pepper
¼ teaspoon salt

Heat oil in large skillet over medium heat; cook and stir nuts in hot oil 2 to 3 minutes or until browned. Combine remaining ingredients in small bowl; sprinkle over nuts. Stir to coat evenly. Heat 1 to 2 minutes more. Drain nuts on wire rack lined with paper towels. Serve warm.

Makes 6 to 8 servings or 2 cups nuts

CAJUN–SPICED WALNUTS

Nonstick vegetable cooking spray
2 egg whites, slightly beaten
1 tablespoon garlic salt
2 teaspoons ground cayenne pepper
2 teaspoons mixed dried herbs
2 teaspoons paprika
4 cups (1 pound) walnut halves and pieces

Coat large, shallow baking pan with nonstick vegetable cooking spray. Mix egg whites with spices. Stir in walnuts and coat thoroughly. Spread in prepared pan. Bake in 350°F oven 15 to 18 minutes or until dry and crisp. Cool completely before serving. *Makes 4 cups*

MICROWAVE DIRECTIONS: Prepare ingredients as above. Spread one quarter prepared walnuts in microwavable dish. Microwave on HIGH for 2 to 3 minutes or until dry and crisp. Cool completely. Repeat with remaining walnuts.

NOTE: Cajun-Spiced Walnuts are best if made at least one day ahead. (Flavors intensify overnight.) Store in sealed container.

*Favorite recipe from **Walnut Marketing Board***

HOLIDAY APPETIZER PUFFS

1 sheet frozen puff pastry, thawed (½ of 17¼-ounce package)
2 tablespoons olive or vegetable oil
Toppings: grated Parmesan cheese, sesame seeds, poppy seeds, dried dill weed, dried basil leaves, paprika, drained capers, pimiento-stuffed green olive slices

Preheat oven to 425°F. Roll pastry on lightly floured surface to 13-inch square. Cut into shapes with cookie cutters (simple-shaped cutters work best). Place on ungreased baking sheets.

Brush cut-outs lightly with oil. Decorate with desired toppings.

Bake 6 to 8 minutes or until golden. Serve warm or at room temperature.

Makes about 1½ dozen appetizers

TRADITIONAL CHEX® BRAND PARTY MIX

¼ cup margarine or butter
4½ teaspoons Worcestershire sauce
1¼ teaspoons seasoned salt
8 cups of your favorite CHEX® brand
    cereal (Corn, Rice and/or Wheat)
1 cup mixed nuts
1 cup pretzel sticks

1. Melt margarine in open roasting pan in preheated 250°F oven. Stir in seasonings.

2. Gradually add cereals, nuts and pretzels; stir to coat evenly.

3. Bake 1 hour, stirring every 15 minutes. Spread on absorbent paper to cool. Store in airtight container.   *Makes 10 cups*

MICROWAVE DIRECTIONS:

1. Melt margarine in large microwave-safe bowl on HIGH 1 minute. Stir in seasonings.

2. Gradually add cereals, nuts and pretzels; stir to coat evenly.

3. Microwave on HIGH 5 to 6 minutes, stirring thoroughly every 2 minutes. While stirring, make sure to scrape sides and bottom of bowl. Spread on absorbent paper to cool. Store in airtight container.

Traditional Chex® Brand Party Mix

CHEESY SUN CRISPS

    2 cups (8 ounces) shredded Cheddar
        cheese
    ½ cup grated Parmesan cheese
    ½ cup sunflower oil margarine, softened
    3 tablespoons water
    1 cup all-purpose flour
    ¼ teaspoon salt (optional)
    1 cup uncooked quick oats
    ⅔ cup roasted, salted sunflower seeds

Beat cheeses, margarine and water in bowl
until blended. Mix in flour and salt. Stir in oats
and sunflower seeds until combined. Shape
into 12-inch-long roll; wrap securely. Refrigerate
about 4 hours or up to 1 week.

Preheat oven to 400°F. Lightly grease cookie
sheets. Cut roll into ⅛- to ¼-inch slices; flatten
each slice slightly. Place on prepared cookie
sheets. Bake 8 to 10 minutes or until edges are
light golden brown. Remove immediately; cool
on wire rack.   *Makes 4 to 5 dozen crackers*

*Favorite recipe from **National Sunflower Association***

PARTY MIX

    2 cups shredded wheat
    1 cup puffed wheat cereal
    1 cup toasted oat cereal
    1 cup small thin pretzels
    ½ cup unsalted peanuts or mixed nuts
    3 tablespoons vegetable oil
    1½ teaspoons Worcestershire sauce
    ½ teaspoon LAWRY'S® Garlic Powder
        with Parsley

In large bowl, combine all cereals, pretzels
and nuts. In separate bowl, combine oil,
Worcestershire sauce and Garlic Powder with
Parsley. Pour over cereal mixture and toss to
coat all dry ingredients well. Spread out evenly
on a cookie sheet. Bake in 250°F. oven for 40
minutes, stirring every 15 minutes. Serve warm
or cooled.   *Makes 15 (⅓-cup) servings*

Cheesy Sun Crisps

Merry

SOUPS & SALADS

TOMATO FRENCH ONION SOUP

    4 medium onions, chopped
    2 tablespoons butter or margarine
    1 can (14½ ounces) DEL MONTE® Italian
        Recipe Stewed Tomatoes
    2 cups water
    1 can (10½ ounces) condensed beef consommé
    ¼ cup dry sherry
    4 slices toasted French bread
    1½ cups shredded Swiss cheese
    ¼ cup grated Parmesan cheese

In large saucepan, cook onions in butter about 10 minutes. Drain tomatoes, reserving liquid. Chop tomatoes. Add tomatoes, reserved liquid, water, consommé and sherry to onions. Bring to a boil, skimming off foam. Reduce heat and simmer 10 minutes. Place soup in four broilerproof bowls; top with bread and cheeses. Broil until cheese is melted and golden.

Makes 4 (1¼-cup) servings

HEARTY MINESTRONE GRATINÉ

1 cup diced celery
1 cup diced zucchini
1 can (28 ounces) tomatoes with liquid,
   chopped
2 cups water
2 teaspoons sugar
1 teaspoon dried Italian herb seasoning
1 can (15 ounces) garbanzo beans,
   drained
4 (½-inch) slices French bread, toasted
1 cup (4 ounces) SARGENTO® Preferred
   Light® Fancy Shredded Mozzarella
   Cheese
2 tablespoons SARGENTO® Grated
   Parmesan Cheese
   Freshly chopped parsley

Spray large saucepan or Dutch oven with nonstick cooking spray. Over medium heat, sauté celery and zucchini until tender. Add tomatoes, water, sugar and herb seasoning. Simmer, uncovered, 15 to 20 minutes. Add garbanzo beans and heat an additional 10 minutes. Meanwhile, heat broiler. Place toasted French bread on broiler pan. Top with mozzarella cheese. Broil until cheese melts. Ladle soup into bowls and top with French bread. Sprinkle Parmesan cheese over each bowl and garnish with parsley. Serve immediately. *Makes 4 servings*

Hearty Minestrone Gratiné, Marinated Vegetable Spinach Salad (page 94)

RED BEAN SOUP

1 pound dried red kidney beans
1 sprig thyme
1 sprig parsley
2 tablespoons butter or margarine
1 small onion, finely chopped
4 carrots, peeled and chopped
2 ribs celery, chopped
1½ quarts water
1 pound smoked ham hocks
1 bay leaf
3 cloves garlic, finely chopped
½ teaspoon salt
¼ teaspoon black pepper
2 tablespoons fresh lemon juice
Sour cream for garnish
"Holly leaf" and "berry" cutouts, made from green and red bell peppers (optional)

Soak beans in 1 quart water in large bowl 6 hours or overnight. Drain, rinse and set aside. Tie together thyme and parsley sprigs with thread; set aside.

Heat butter in heavy, large stockpot over medium-high heat until melted and bubbly. Cook and stir onion in hot butter 3 minutes or until onion is softened. Add carrots and celery; cook and stir 5 minutes or until browned. Add 1½ quarts water, beans, ham hocks, bay leaf, garlic and reserved thyme and parsley sprigs. Bring to a boil over high heat. Reduce heat to low. Cover; simmer 1¼ to 1½ hours or until beans are softened. Discard bones from ham hocks, thyme and parsley sprigs and bay leaf. Stir in salt and pepper.

Process soup in batches in food processor or blender until smooth. Return to stockpot. Heat to simmering; stir in lemon juice and season to taste with additional salt and pepper. Ladle into bowls. Garnish with dollops of sour cream (or pipe sour cream in decorative design) and green pepper "holly leaves" and red pepper "berries," if desired. *Makes 6 servings*

BLACK BEAN SOUP: Substitute dried black beans for the red kidney beans. Proceed as directed, simmering soup 1½ to 2 hours or until beans are tender. Add 4 to 5 tablespoons dry sherry, to taste, just before serving.

CRANBERRY BEAN SOUP: Substitute dried cranberry beans for the red kidney beans. Proceed as directed, simmering soup 2 to 2¼ hours or until beans are tender. (Cranberry beans can be found in specialty food stores. They are the color of cranberries but taste like kidney beans.)

WISCONSIN CHEESE 'N' BEER SOUP

2 tablespoons butter or margarine
2 tablespoons all-purpose flour
1 envelope LIPTON® Recipe Secrets® Golden Onion Soup Mix
3 cups milk
1 teaspoon Worcestershire sauce
1 cup shredded Cheddar cheese (about 4 ounces)
½ cup beer
1 teaspoon prepared mustard

In medium saucepan, melt butter over medium heat. Add flour and cook, stirring constantly, 3 minutes or until bubbling. Stir in golden onion soup mix thoroughly blended with milk and Worcestershire sauce. Bring just to the boiling point, then simmer, stirring occasionally, 10 minutes. Stir in remaining ingredients and simmer, stirring constantly, 5 minutes or until cheese is melted. Garnish, if desired, with additional cheese, chopped red pepper and parsley. *Makes about 4 (1-cup) servings*

BUTTERNUT BISQUE

1 medium butternut squash (about 1½ pounds)
1 teaspoon margarine or butter
1 large onion, coarsely chopped (1 cup)
2 cans (about 14 ounces each) reduced-sodium or regular chicken broth, divided
½ teaspoon ground nutmeg or freshly grated nutmeg
⅛ teaspoon ground white pepper
   Plain nonfat yogurt and chives for garnish

Peel squash; cut flesh into ½-inch pieces. Set aside. Melt margarine in large saucepan over medium heat. Add onion. Cook and stir 3 minutes. Add squash and 1 can broth. Bring to a boil over high heat. Reduce heat to low. Cover and simmer 20 minutes or until squash is very tender.

Process squash mixture, in 2 batches, in food processor until smooth. Return soup to saucepan; add remaining can of broth, nutmeg and pepper. Simmer, uncovered, 5 minutes, stirring occasionally.*

Ladle soup into soup bowls. Place yogurt in pastry bag fitted with round decorating tip. Pipe yogurt onto soup in decorative design. Garnish with chives, if desired.

Makes about 5 cups, 6 servings

*At this point, soup may be covered and refrigerated up to 2 days before serving. Reheat over medium heat, stirring occasionally.

CREAM OF BUTTERNUT SOUP: Add ½ cup whipping cream or half-and-half with second can of broth. Proceed as directed.

EASY CURRIED CORN CHOWDER

1 can (16 ounces) California cling peach slices in juice or extra light syrup
½ pound bacon, cut into 1-inch pieces
1 onion, thinly sliced
½ cup *each* chopped celery, red bell pepper and green bell pepper
¼ cup all-purpose flour
2 teaspoons curry powder
1 package (10 ounces) frozen corn, thawed
1 large potato, cut into 1-inch cubes
2 (13¾-ounce) cans chicken broth
1 bay leaf
1 cup half-and-half

Drain peaches; cut slices in half and set aside. Cook bacon until crisp in large saucepan over medium heat; remove from pan and drain on paper towels. Reserve. Drain drippings from pan, reserving 2 tablespoons. Cook onion in reserved drippings about 8 minutes or until golden brown.

Stir in celery, bell peppers, flour and curry powder; cook 1 minute. Stir in corn, potato, chicken broth and bay leaf. Bring to a boil, stirring frequently. Cover and simmer 20 minutes or until potatoes are tender. Remove from heat. Remove and discard bay leaf; stir in half-and-half and reserved peaches. Ladle soup into serving bowls. Top with reserved crisp bacon just before serving.

Makes 6 servings

*Favorite recipe from **Canned Fruit Promotion Service***

Butternut Bisque

CARROT CREAM SOUP

¼ cup butter or margarine
¼ cup chopped onion
¼ teaspoon LAWRY'S® Seasoned Salt
½ teaspoon LAWRY'S® Garlic Powder
    with Parsley
2 cups chopped carrots
½ cup all-purpose flour
4½ cups chicken broth
¼ cup whipping cream
    Chopped fresh parsley for garnish

In large saucepan, melt butter and sauté onion, Seasoned Salt and Garlic Powder with Parsley. Add carrots and cook 5 minutes. Stir in flour; blend well. Stirring constantly, add chicken broth; blend well. Bring to a boil; reduce heat, cover and simmer 30 minutes, stirring occasionally. In blender or food processor, purée carrot mixture; return to pan. Stir in cream; heat thoroughly.   *Makes 4 servings*

PRESENTATION: Serve warm soup topped with a sprinkling of parsley. Warm French bread or crackers are welcome accompaniments.

CARROT & CORIANDER SOUP

4 tablespoons butter or margarine
4 cups grated carrots (about 1 pound)
1 cup finely chopped onion
3 cups chicken broth
2 tablespoons fresh lemon juice
1½ teaspoons ground coriander
1½ teaspoons ground cumin
1 clove garlic, finely chopped
2 tablespoons finely chopped fresh
    coriander (cilantro)
Salt and pepper

Heat butter in medium saucepan over medium-high heat until melted and bubbly. Cook and stir carrots and onion in hot butter 5 minutes or until onion begins to soften. Add broth, lemon juice, ground coriander, cumin and garlic. Bring to a boil over high heat. Reduce heat to low. Cover; simmer 25 to 30 minutes or until vegetables are soft.

Process soup in batches in food processor or blender until smooth. Stir in fresh coriander. Season to taste with salt and pepper. Serve immediately *or* cool and store up to 1 week in refrigerator. Reheat before serving.
Makes 4 to 6 servings

EASY TOMATO CHEESE BISQUE

1 can (10¾ ounces) condensed Cheddar
    cheese soup
2 cups water
1 cup tomato juice
1 tablespoon PARKAY® Spread Sticks
1 tablespoon freeze-dried chopped chives
    (optional)
½ teaspoon salt
½ teaspoon sugar
½ teaspoon dry mustard
½ teaspoon Worcestershire sauce
1 cup MINUTE® Rice, uncooked
¾ cup milk, light cream or evaporated
    milk

Mix soup, water and juice in large saucepan. Add spread, chives, salt, sugar, mustard and Worcestershire sauce. Bring to a boil over medium heat. Stir in rice and milk. Reduce heat; cover and simmer 10 minutes, stirring occasionally. Garnish with additional chopped chives or popcorn, if desired.
Makes 5½ cups or 7 servings

Left to right: Italian Vegetable Soup (page 81), Broccoli Cheese Soup

BROCCOLI CHEESE SOUP

½ cup chopped onion
¼ cup margarine or butter
¼ cup unsifted flour
3 cups water
2 (10-ounce) packages frozen chopped
    broccoli, thawed and well drained
4 teaspoons WYLER'S® or STEERO®
    Chicken-Flavor Instant Bouillon *or*
    4 Chicken-Flavor Bouillon Cubes
1 teaspoon Worcestershire sauce
3 cups (12 ounces) shredded Cheddar
    cheese
2 cups (1 pint) BORDEN® or MEADOW
    GOLD® Coffee Cream or Half-and-
    Half

In large kettle or Dutch oven, cook onion in margarine until tender; stir in flour until smooth. Gradually add water, then broccoli, bouillon and Worcestershire. Over medium heat, cook and stir until thickened and broccoli is tender, about 10 minutes. Add cheese and cream. Cook and stir until cheese melts and soup is hot (*do not boil*). Refrigerate leftovers.

Makes about 2 quarts

TIP: 6 cups (about 1¼ pounds) chopped fresh broccoli may be substituted for frozen broccoli.

MICROWAVE DIRECTIONS: In 3- to 4-quart microwavable round baking dish, combine onion and margarine; cook covered on 100% power (HIGH) 2 to 3 minutes or until onion is tender. Stir in flour. Gradually stir in water, then broccoli, bouillon and Worcestershire. Cook covered on 100% power (HIGH) 10 to 12 minutes or until mixture is thickened and broccoli is tender. Add cheese and cream; mix well. Cook covered on 100% power (HIGH) 2 to 4 minutes or until heated through.

PUMPKIN ALMOND BISQUE IN A PUMPKIN SHELL

 1 medium-size pumpkin
 3 cups chicken broth, divided
 2 tablespoons butter or margarine
 3 tablespoons chopped celery
 3 tablespoons chopped onion
 2 tablespoons almond paste
 1 tablespoon tomato paste
 1½ cups half-and-half
 3 tablespoons almond-flavored liqueur
 1 teaspoon ground nutmeg
 1 teaspoon black pepper
    Salt to taste
    Toasted Pumpkin Seeds (recipe
    follows)

Cut slice from top of pumpkin. Scoop out seeds and fibers; reserve. Scoop out flesh, leaving shell that can be used for serving. Simmer pumpkin flesh in small amount of the chicken broth until tender. Place cooked pumpkin in food processor or blender container; process until smooth. (There should be 2 cups of pumpkin purée.) Leave purée in food processor.

Melt butter in heavy stockpot. Add celery and onion; cook over low heat 5 minutes. Add celery mixture, almond paste and tomato paste to pumpkin purée; process until smooth. Return contents of food processor to stockpot; add remaining broth and simmer over low heat, 30 minutes. Stir in half-and-half and cook until heated through. Stir in liqueur, nutmeg, pepper and salt. Pour into reserved pumpkin shell. Garnish with Toasted Pumpkin Seeds.

Makes about 8 servings

TOASTED PUMPKIN SEEDS: Preheat oven to 275°F. Carefully separate reserved seeds from fibers. Wash, drain and dry seeds on paper towels. In small bowl, coat seeds with small amount of vegetable oil. Add 2 tablespoons Worcestershire sauce and ½ teaspoon ground red pepper; toss to mix thoroughly. Spread seasoned seeds in single layer on baking sheet. Bake, stirring occasionally, until golden brown.

FRENCH ONION SOUP

 3 medium onions, thinly sliced and
    separated into rings
 2 tablespoons unsalted butter
 1 package (1 ounce) LAWRY'S® Au Jus
    Gravy Mix
 3 cups water
 4 thin slices sourdough French bread
    Unsalted butter, softened
 4 slices Swiss or Gruyère cheese

In large skillet, sauté onions in 2 tablespoons butter until golden. In small bowl, combine Au Jus Gravy Mix and water; add to onions. Bring to a boil. Reduce heat to low; cover and simmer 15 minutes, stirring occasionally. Broil bread on one side until lightly toasted. Turn bread slices over; spread with softened butter. Top with cheese; broil until cheese melts.

Makes 4 servings

PRESENTATION: To serve, pour soup into tureen or individual bowls. Top each serving with toast.

HINT: If using individual, ovenproof bowls, pour soup into bowls; top each with untoasted bread slice. Top with cheese. Place under broiler just until cheese is melted.

Pumpkin Almond Bisque in a Pumpkin Shell

QUICK GARDEN CHEESE SOUP

1 cup sliced celery
1 cup chopped onion
2 tablespoons margarine or butter
⅔ cup unsifted flour
4 cups water
2 tablespoons WYLER'S® or STEERO®
    Chicken-Flavor Instant Bouillon *or*
    6 Chicken-Flavor Bouillon Cubes
¼ teaspoon pepper
2 cups frozen broccoli, cauliflower and
    carrot combination
1 cup frozen hash brown potatoes
3 cups BORDEN® or MEADOW GOLD®
    Milk or Half-and-Half
2½ cups (10 ounces) shredded Cheddar
    cheese

In large kettle or Dutch oven, cook celery and onion in margarine until tender; stir in flour until smooth. Gradually add water then bouillon, pepper and vegetables; bring to a boil. Reduce heat; cover and simmer 15 minutes. Add milk and cheese. Cook and stir until cheese melts and soup is hot *(do not boil)*. Garnish as desired. Refrigerate leftovers.

Makes about 2 quarts

Top to bottom; Italian-Style Chili (page 80), Quick Garden Cheese Soup

UPSIDE–DOWN ONION SOUP

3 medium onions, thinly sliced
2 tablespoons vegetable oil
1 cup 1½×¼-inch carrot strips
1 cup diced zucchini
1 tomato, diced (optional)
6 cups chicken broth
1½ cups water
1 teaspoon salt or to taste
¼ teaspoon ground pepper
2 tablespoons chopped parsley
8 KAVLI® Crispbreads, Thick or Muesli
2 cups shredded JARLSBERG or
    NOKKELOST Cheese (or
    combination)

Cook onions in oil in large saucepan or Dutch oven over medium heat, stirring often, 15 minutes or until tender and just beginning to brown. Add carrots, zucchini, tomato, broth, water, salt and pepper. Bring to a boil. Cover and simmer 15 minutes or until vegetables are tender.* Stir in parsley.

To serve, crumble crispbreads into bite-sized pieces into each of 8 ovenproof soup bowls or 12-ounce custard cups. Sprinkle ¼ cup cheese over each. Just before serving, place bowls under preheated broiler until cheese is melted and bubbly. Ladle hot soup into bowls and serve.

Makes 8 servings

*Soup can be prepared ahead to this point and reheated just before serving.

*Favorite recipe from **Norseland, Inc.***

PAPPA AL POMODORO ALLA PAPA NEWMAN (BREAD AND TOMATO SOUP)

¾ cup olive oil plus extra for drizzling on
    soup, divided
3 large cloves garlic, smashed
1 teaspoon dried sage
12 ounces stale Italian or French bread,
    thinly sliced, crusts removed (about
    30 slices), divided
1 jar NEWMAN'S OWN® Bombolina
    Sauce (about 3 cups)
4 cups chicken broth
½ teaspoon hot red pepper flakes
½ teaspoon freshly ground black pepper
    Freshly grated Parmesan cheese

1. In large skillet, heat ¼ cup of the oil over medium heat. Add garlic and sage and cook, stirring frequently, 1 to 2 minutes. Remove garlic from oil. Add one third of the bread slices and cook, turning once, until golden brown on both sides, 2 to 3 minutes per side. Remove from heat; repeat with remaining oil and bread.

2. In large heavy saucepan, heat Bombolina Sauce and chicken broth over medium-high heat to boiling. Reduce heat to low. Add red pepper flakes, black pepper and bread; simmer, covered, 30 minutes. Remove from heat and let stand 30 minutes to 1 hour. Ladle into soup bowls. Drizzle lightly with olive oil and sprinkle with Parmesan cheese.

Makes 6 to 8 servings

COUNTRY ITALIAN SOUP

1 tablespoon oil
½ pound boneless beef, cut into 1-inch
    cubes
1 can (14½ ounces) whole peeled
    tomatoes, undrained and chopped
1 envelope LIPTON® Recipe Secrets®
    Onion or Beefy Mushroom Soup Mix
3 cups water
1 medium onion, cut into chunks
1 large stalk celery, cut into 1-inch
    pieces
½ cup sliced carrot
1 cup cut green beans
1 can (16 ounces) chick peas or
    garbanzos, rinsed and drained
½ cup sliced zucchini
¼ cup uncooked elbow macaroni
¼ teaspoon dried oregano

In large saucepan or stockpot, heat oil and brown beef over medium-high heat. Add tomatoes, then onion soup mix blended with water. Simmer uncovered, stirring occasionally, 30 minutes. Add onion, celery, carrot and green beans. Simmer uncovered, stirring occasionally, 30 minutes. Stir in remaining ingredients and simmer uncovered, stirring occasionally, an additional 15 minutes or until vegetables and macaroni are tender. Serve with grated Parmesan cheese, if desired.

Makes about 8 (1-cup) servings

Miami Heat Chili

In Dutch oven or large saucepot, heat 2 teaspoons oil until hot. Add meat, a few pieces at a time; cook and stir until browned on all sides. Remove meat from Dutch oven; repeat until all meat is browned. Set aside. Heat remaining 3 teaspoons oil until hot. Add chili powder, cumin, garlic, oregano, paprika, and red and black peppers; cook and stir 1 minute. Remove from heat. Stir in tomato sauce, beer, water and reserved meat; bring to a boil. Reduce heat and simmer, covered, until meat is tender, about 2 hours, stirring occasionally. Serve with cooked pinto beans, chopped onions, jalapeño peppers and grated Cheddar cheese, if desired.   *Makes 4 to 6 servings*

Favorite recipe from **American Spice Trade Association**

MIAMI HEAT CHILI

  5 teaspoons vegetable oil, divided
  1 pound round steak, cut into 1-inch
     cubes
  1 pound boneless chuck steak, cut into
     1-inch cubes
  3 tablespoons chili powder
  1 tablespoon ground cumin
  1 tablespoon instant minced garlic
  ½ teaspoon oregano leaves, crushed
  ½ teaspoon paprika
  ⅛ teaspoon ground red pepper
  ⅛ teaspoon ground black pepper
  1 can (15 ounces) tomato sauce
  1 can (12 ounces) beer
1½ cups water

ITALIAN-STYLE CHILI

  1 pound lean ground beef
  ¾ cup chopped onion
  1 (26-ounce) jar CLASSICO® Di Napoli
     (Tomato & Basil) Pasta Sauce
1½ cups water
  1 (14½-ounce) can whole tomatoes,
     undrained and broken up
  1 (4-ounce) can sliced mushrooms,
     drained
  2 ounces sliced pepperoni (⅓ cup)
  1 tablespoon WYLER'S® or STEERO®
     Beef-Flavor Instant Bouillon *or*
     3 Beef-Flavor Bouillon Cubes
  1 tablespoon chili powder
  2 teaspoons sugar

In large kettle or Dutch oven, brown meat with onion; pour off fat. Add remaining ingredients; bring to a boil. Reduce heat; simmer uncovered 30 minutes, stirring occasionally. Garnish as desired. Refrigerate leftovers.

Makes about 2 quarts

ITALIAN VEGETABLE SOUP

1 pound bulk Italian sausage
2 cups chopped onion
2 cloves garlic, finely chopped
7 cups water
4 medium carrots, pared and sliced
1 (28-ounce) can whole tomatoes,
    undrained and broken up
2 tablespoons WYLER'S® or STEERO®
    Beef-Flavor Instant Bouillon *or*
    6 Beef-Flavor Bouillon Cubes
1 teaspoon Italian seasoning
¼ teaspoon pepper
1½ cups coarsely chopped zucchini
1 (15-ounce) can garbanzo beans,
    drained
1 cup uncooked CREAMETTE® Rotini or
    Elbow Macaroni

In large kettle or Dutch oven, brown sausage, onion and garlic; pour off fat. Add water, carrots, tomatoes, bouillon, Italian seasoning and pepper; bring to a boil. Reduce heat; cover and simmer 30 minutes. Add zucchini, beans and rotini. Cook 15 to 20 minutes or until rotini is tender, stirring occasionally. Refrigerate leftovers. *Makes about 2½ quarts*

HEAD–'EM–OFF–AT–THE– PASS WHITE CHILI

½ cup fresh or frozen chopped onions
1 tablespoon olive oil
1½ cups chopped cooked chicken *or*
    2 (5-ounce) cans chopped chicken
½ cup chicken broth
2 (15-ounce) cans cannellini beans,
    undrained
1 teaspoon dried oregano
½ teaspoon celery salt
1 (11-ounce) jar NEWMAN'S OWN®
    Bandito Salsa*, divided
1½ cups shredded mozzarella cheese,
    divided

In 2-quart saucepan, cook and stir onions in olive oil until translucent. Add chopped chicken, mixing thoroughly, then add chicken broth. Stir in cannellini beans, oregano, celery salt and ½ cup salsa. Simmer over medium heat 10 minutes, gently stirring occasionally. Just before serving, stir in 1 cup mozzarella cheese. Divide among serving bowls and top each with a portion of remaining mozzarella cheese and salsa. *Makes 4 servings*

*Choose a flavor (mild, medium or hot) that suits your taste.

CREAMY DIJON TURKEY SOUP

1 cup *each* chopped celery and thinly
    sliced onions
3 tablespoons margarine
1 large garlic clove, minced
3 tablespoons flour
½ teaspoon salt
¼ teaspoon white pepper
4 cups skim milk
¼ cup Dijon mustard
2 teaspoons reduced sodium chicken
    bouillon granules
2 cups cubed cooked turkey (½ to
    ¾-inch cubes)
French bread (optional)

1. In 3-quart saucepan, over medium-high heat, sauté celery and onions in margarine 5 to 6 minutes or until celery is tender and onions are golden brown. Add garlic and sauté 1 to 2 minutes. Stir in flour, salt and pepper and cook 1 to 2 minutes. Remove pan from heat and slowly add milk, stirring constantly.

2. Return pan to medium-high heat. Stir in mustard and bouillon; cook and stir 5 to 8 minutes or until mixture is thickened and bubbly. Stir in turkey and heat 1 to 2 minutes. Serve with sliced French bread.

Makes 6 servings

*Favorite recipe from **National Turkey Federation***

SHRIMP BISQUE

1 pound medium raw shrimp, peeled and
    deveined
¼ cup butter or margarine
2 large green onions, sliced
1 large clove garlic, minced
¼ cup all-purpose flour
1 cup Fish Stock (page 208) or canned
    chicken broth
3 cups half-and-half
½ teaspoon salt
½ teaspoon grated lemon peel
    Dash ground red pepper
2 tablespoons white wine (optional)
    Quartered lemon slices, green onion
       slivers and whole shrimp for garnish
       (optional)

Coarsely chop shrimp into ½-inch pieces. Melt butter in large saucepan over medium heat. Cook and stir shrimp, onions and garlic in butter until shrimp turns pink and opaque. Remove from heat. Blend in flour. Cook and stir just until bubbly. Stir in Fish Stock and cook until bubbly. Cook 2 minutes, stirring constantly. Remove from heat. Process soup in small batches in food processor or blender until smooth. Return soup to saucepan. Stir in half-and-half, salt, lemon peel, red pepper and wine. Heat through. Garnish, if desired.

Makes 4 servings

Shrimp Bisque

CHILI SOUP JARLSBERG

    1 pound beef round steak, cut into small
        cubes
    2 tablespoons vegetable oil
    2 cans (14 ounces each) ready-to-serve
        beef broth
    1 can (15 ounces) dark red kidney beans
    1 can (14½ ounces) tomatoes, chopped,
        undrained
    1 medium green bell pepper, chopped
    1 medium red bell pepper, chopped
    1 large onion, chopped
    1 large clove garlic, minced
    3¼ teaspoons chili powder, divided
    ¼ teaspoon ground cumin
    1½ cups (6 ounces) shredded JARLSBERG
        Cheese, divided
    ¼ cup butter or margarine, softened
    1 small clove garlic, minced
    12 KAVLI® Norwegian Crispbreads

Brown beef in hot oil in large, deep saucepan over medium-high heat. Add broth. Bring to a boil over high heat. Reduce heat to low. Cover and simmer 1 hour. Add beans, tomatoes, peppers, onion, large garlic clove, 3 teaspoons chili powder and cumin. Simmer, covered, 30 minutes. Gradually blend in ½ cup Jarlsberg cheese. Heat just until cheese melts.

Blend butter, small garlic clove and remaining ¼ teaspoon chili powder in small bowl. Spread on crispbreads; arrange on cookie sheet. Bake in preheated 375°F oven several minutes or until butter is melted. Sprinkle with ½ cup Jarlsberg cheese. Bake just until cheese is melted.

Ladle soup into bowls. Garnish with remaining ½ cup Jarlsberg cheese. Serve with crispbreads. *Makes 6 servings*

*Favorite recipe from **Norseland, Inc.***

VEGETABLE MEAT STEW

    2 tablespoons all-purpose flour
    1½ teaspoons salt
    1 teaspoon ACCENT® Flavor Enhancer
    ⅛ teaspoon pepper
    1 pound beef stew meat
    3 tablespoons vegetable oil
    ¼ cup chopped onion
    3 cups water
    1 clove garlic, minced
    1 bay leaf
    1 teaspoon dried thyme, crushed
    4 small potatoes, pared, cubed
    4 carrots, chopped *or* 12 mini carrots,
        pared
    1 cup frozen peas, thawed
    ½ cup PET® Evaporated Milk

Combine flour, salt, ACCENT® Flavor Enhancer and pepper in shallow dish. Dredge meat in flour mixture; reserve excess flour mixture. Brown meat in hot oil in Dutch oven over medium-high heat. Sprinkle any remaining flour mixture over meat. Toss to coat meat. Add onion; cook until onion is limp. Add water, garlic, bay leaf and thyme. Bring to a boil over high heat. Reduce heat to low. Cover and simmer 1 hour. Add potatoes, carrots and additional water if needed. Simmer, covered, 15 minutes. Add peas; simmer, covered, 10 minutes or until vegetables are tender. Stir in evaporated milk; heat through. *Do not boil.* Remove bay leaf before serving.
Makes 6 servings

KALEIDOSCOPE CHOWDER

3 cups water
3 large potatoes, peeled and diced
1 (26-ounce) jar NEWMAN'S OWN®
   Diavolo Sauce
2 large carrots, peeled and thinly sliced
1½ to 2 pounds assorted seafood, such as
   fish fillets, bay scallops, shrimp or
   clams
½ cup dry white wine
2 cups shredded fresh spinach leaves
1 yellow bell pepper, seeded and diced
   Freshly grated Parmesan cheese

In large stockpot, bring water to a boil. Add potatoes; cook 5 minutes. Stir in Diavolo Sauce and carrots. Bring to a boil; reduce heat and simmer 5 minutes.

Cut fish fillets into bite-size pieces. Peel and devein shrimp. Add seafood and wine to soup. Cook over medium-high heat, stirring often, until fish is opaque, 3 to 4 minutes. Add spinach and pepper; cover. Remove from heat and let stand until spinach and pepper are heated through, about 2 minutes. Serve with Parmesan cheese.   *Makes 4 servings*

NOTE: This chowder is also excellent with diced cooked chicken breast.

QUICK AND ZESTY VEGETABLE SOUP

1 pound lean ground beef
½ cup chopped onion
   Salt and pepper
2 cans (14½ ounces each) DEL MONTE®
   Italian Style Stewed Tomatoes
2 cans (13¾ ounces each) beef broth
1 can (17 ounces) DEL MONTE® Mixed
   Vegetables
½ cup uncooked medium egg noodles
½ teaspoon dried oregano

In large pot, brown meat with onion. Cook until onion is tender; drain. Season to taste with salt and pepper. Stir in remaining ingredients. Bring to boil; reduce heat. Cover and simmer 15 minutes or until noodles are tender.
        Makes 8 servings

PREP TIME: 5 minutes
COOK TIME: 15 minutes

BULGUR CHILI

1 cup chopped onion
½ cup chopped celery
4 teaspoons sugar
2 tablespoons chili powder
1 tablespoon dried oregano
1 teaspoon ground cumin
1 teaspoon black pepper
2 teaspoons vegetable oil
⅔ cup uncooked bulgur
1½ cups water
1 (14-ounce) can black beans, rinsed and
   drained *or* 2 cups cooked black beans
1 (14-ounce) can cannellini or navy
   beans, rinsed and drained *or* 2 cups
   cooked cannellini or navy beans
1 (28-ounce) can tomatoes, crushed or
   stewed

In 3- to 4-quart saucepan, sauté onion, celery, sugar and spices in oil 5 minutes. Stir in bulgur and water. Simmer, covered, over low heat 10 minutes, stirring occasionally. Add beans and tomatoes. Simmer, covered, over low heat 15 to 20 minutes, stirring occasionally. Serve in warmed bowls.   *Makes 4 servings*

*Favorite recipe from **The Sugar Association, Inc.***

Kaleidoscope Chowder

Cobb Salad

COBB SALAD

4 skinless boneless chicken breast
halves, cooked, cooled
⅔ cup vegetable oil
⅓ cup HEINZ® Distilled White or Apple
Cider Vinegar
1 clove garlic, minced
2 teaspoons dried dill weed
1½ teaspoons granulated sugar
½ teaspoon salt
¼ teaspoon black pepper
8 cups torn salad greens, chilled
1 large tomato, diced
1 medium green bell pepper, diced
1 small red onion, chopped
¾ cup crumbled blue cheese
6 slices bacon, cooked, crumbled
1 hard-cooked egg, chopped

Shred chicken into bite-size pieces. For
dressing, in jar, combine oil, vinegar, garlic, dill,
sugar, salt and black pepper; cover and shake
vigorously. Pour ½ cup dressing over chicken;
toss well to coat. Toss greens with remaining
dressing. Line each of 4 large individual salad
bowls with greens; mound chicken mixture in
center. Arrange mounds of tomato, green
pepper, onion, cheese, bacon and egg around
chicken. *Makes 4 servings*

HOLIDAY SPLIT PEAS VINAIGRETTE

4 cups green or yellow split peas, washed
2 quarts water
3 pounds cooked smoked sausage, sliced
12 medium (4 pounds) onions, finely
chopped and steamed or sautéed
2 cups olive oil
¾ cup vinegar
1½ cups chopped fresh parsley
⅓ cup German hot or coarse mustard
Sugar to taste
Salt and white pepper to taste
12 medium (4 pounds) tomatoes or red
bell peppers, coarsely chopped and
sautéed

1. Combine split peas and water in stockpot.
Bring to a boil; reduce heat and simmer 20
minutes or until peas are tender.

2. Remove from heat; drain, if necessary. Stir
in sausage and onions. Keep warm.

3. Blend together oil, vinegar, parsley, mustard,
sugar, salt and pepper.

4. Pour oil mixture over split pea mixture;
blend.

5. Gently stir in tomatoes. Serve immediately
as warm salad or cassoulet. Cover and
refrigerate several hours for chilled salad.
Makes 24 (1½-cup) servings

*Favorite recipe from **USA Dry Pea & Lentil Council***

SMOKED TURKEY & PEPPER PASTA SALAD

¾ cup MIRACLE WHIP® Salad Dressing
1 tablespoon Dijon mustard
½ teaspoon dried thyme leaves
8 ounces fettucini, cooked, drained
1 cup (8 ounces) diced LOUIS RICH®
    Smoked Boneless Turkey Breast
¾ cup zucchini slices, cut into halves
½ cup red bell pepper strips
½ cup yellow bell pepper strips
    Salt and black pepper

Mix salad dressing, mustard and thyme until well blended. Add pasta, turkey and vegetables; mix lightly. Season with salt and black pepper to taste. Chill. Add additional dressing before serving, if desired.

Makes about 6 servings

PREP TIME: 15 minutes plus chilling

Smoked Turkey & Pepper Pasta Salad

SEA BREEZE FISH SALAD

1 pound firm white fish fillets (red
    snapper, sea bass or orange roughy),
    about 1 inch thick
1¾ cups water
1 tablespoon grated lemon peel
6 tablespoons lemon juice, divided
3 tablespoons KIKKOMAN® Lite Soy
    Sauce, divided
6 ounces fresh snow peas, trimmed and
    cut diagonally into 1-inch pieces
2 tablespoons vegetable oil
1 tablespoon minced onion
½ teaspoon dried thyme, crumbled
¼ teaspoon sugar
½ medium cantaloupe, chunked
1 tablespoon minced fresh cilantro or
    parsley

Cut fish into 1-inch cubes. Combine water, lemon peel, 4 tablespoons lemon juice and 1 tablespoon lite soy sauce in large skillet. Heat only until mixture starts to simmer. Add fish; simmer, uncovered, 3 minutes, or until fish flakes easily when tested with fork. Remove fish with slotted spoon to plate. Cool slightly; cover and refrigerate 1 hour or until thoroughly chilled. Meanwhile, cook snow peas in boiling water 2 minutes, or until tender-crisp; cool under cold water and drain thoroughly. Chill. Measure remaining 2 tablespoons lemon juice and 2 tablespoons lite soy sauce, oil, onion, thyme and sugar into jar with screw-top lid; cover and shake well. Combine snow peas, cantaloupe and cilantro in large bowl; add dressing and toss to coat all ingredients. Add fish and gently stir to combine. Serve immediately.

Makes 4 servings

CRISP AND CRUNCHY TURKEY SALAD

1 cup (8 ounces) plain low fat yogurt
3 tablespoons mayonnaise
2 teaspoons Dijon-style mustard
1 clove garlic, minced
½ teaspoon salt
   Freshly ground black pepper to taste
1½ cups chopped cooked turkey
2 cups shredded red cabbage
2 cups fresh bean sprouts
¼ pound fresh snow peas, trimmed
¾ cup celery slices
½ cup sliced almonds, toasted
¼ cup chopped red onion
   Fresh spinach leaves
2 hard-cooked eggs, peeled and sliced,
   for garnish

Combine yogurt, mayonnaise, mustard, garlic and seasonings in large bowl. Add turkey, cabbage, bean sprouts, snow peas, celery, almonds and onion; mix lightly. Serve in spinach-lined salad bowl or on spinach-covered salad plates. Garnish with eggs.

Makes 4 servings

SALMON PLATTER SALAD

1 can (15½ ounces) salmon
1 pound asparagus
2 tablespoons oil
2 tablespoons lemon juice
¼ teaspoon dry mustard
¼ teaspoon salt
   Dash pepper
   Salad greens
   Tomato wedges
   Cucumber slices
   Pimiento strips
   Radish roses
½ cup dairy sour cream
1 teaspoon dried dill weed

Chill can of salmon. Cook asparagus in boiling salted water until just tender. Drain and place in shallow glass container. Combine oil, lemon juice, mustard, salt and pepper. Pour over asparagus. Marinate for 1 hour. Drain, reserving marinade. Drain salmon and remove from can in one piece. Place salmon and asparagus on platter lined with greens. Garnish with tomato wedges, cucumber slices, pimiento strips and radish roses. Combine reserved marinade with sour cream. Blend in dill weed. Season with additional salt and pepper to taste. Serve with salad. *Makes 4 to 6 servings*

*Favorite recipe from **Alaska Seafood Marketing Institute***

CONFETTI CHICKEN SALAD

¼ cup white vinegar
3 tablespoons Chef Paul Prudhomme's
   POULTRY MAGIC®
1 teaspoon ground allspice
½ teaspoon ground bay leaf
½ teaspoon salt
1 cup vegetable oil
4 cups cooked rice
12 ounces cooked chicken, cut into bite-
   size pieces
2 cups small broccoli florets
2 cups chopped fresh tomatoes
1 cup shredded carrots
½ cup chopped onion
½ cup chopped celery
   Lettuce leaves

Make dressing by combining vinegar, Poultry Magic®, allspice, bay leaf and salt in food processor. Process until well mixed. With motor running, add oil in slow steady stream until incorporated and dressing is thick and creamy. Combine remaining measured ingredients in a large mixing bowl. Mix well. Stir in dressing. To serve, line 6 serving plates with lettuce leaves. Divide salad into portions. Mound each portion of salad onto center of lettuce leaf.

Makes 6 servings

Crisp and Crunchy Turkey Salad

SWEET AND SOUR CHICKEN SALAD

½ cup HEINZ® Chili Sauce
⅓ cup apple juice
1 tablespoon HEINZ® Distilled White
    Vinegar
2 teaspoons cornstarch
2 teaspoons granulated sugar
2 cups cubed cooked chicken
1 can (8 ounces) sliced water chestnuts,
    drained
1 small zucchini, halved lengthwise,
    sliced (about 1 cup)
1 medium-size red apple, cut into
    chunks
¾ cup sliced celery
    Leaf lettuce
    Apple wedges
1 cup chow mein noodles

In 1-quart saucepan, combine chili sauce, apple juice, vinegar, cornstarch and sugar. Bring to a boil over medium heat, stirring constantly. Boil 1 minute or until thickened and clear; cool slightly.

In medium bowl, combine chicken, water chestnuts, zucchini, apple chunks and celery. Pour warm dressing over chicken mixture; mix well.

Line individual plates with lettuce; arrange apple wedges on lettuce. Spoon chicken mixture on top. Sprinkle with chow mein noodles.   *Makes 4 servings*

Sweet and Sour Chicken Salad

Tarragon-Tanged Shrimp and Orange Salad

TARRAGON-TANGED SHRIMP AND ORANGE SALAD

     12 ounces cooked, shelled and deveined shrimp
      2 cups cooked brown rice*
      2 cups torn romaine lettuce leaves
    1½ cups orange sections
      1 cup halved cherry tomatoes
      ½ cup sliced red onion
      ⅓ cup Orange Tarragon Dressing (recipe follows)

In large serving bowl place shrimp, rice, romaine, orange sections, cherry tomatoes and red onion. Just before serving toss with Orange Tarragon Dressing.

Makes 4 (2-cup) servings

*1 cup uncooked instant brown rice will yield 2 cups cooked rice.

ORANGE TARRAGON DRESSING

      3 tablespoons frozen orange juice concentrate
      2 tablespoons cider vinegar
      1 tablespoon olive oil
      1 teaspoon garlic powder
      ¾ teaspoon tarragon leaves, crushed
      ½ teaspoon salt
      ¼ teaspoon ground black pepper

In small bowl using a wire whisk, whisk all ingredients until combined.   *Makes ⅓ cup*

Favorite recipe from **American Spice Trade Association**

TURKEY WALDORF SALAD

      ⅔ cup HELLMANN'S® or BEST FOODS® Real or Light Mayonnaise or Low Fat Cholesterol Free Mayonnaise Dressing
      2 tablespoons lemon juice
      ½ teaspoon salt
      ¼ teaspoon freshly ground pepper
      2 cups diced cooked turkey or chicken
      2 red apples, cored and diced
      ⅔ cup sliced celery
      ½ cup chopped walnuts

In large bowl combine mayonnaise, lemon juice, salt and pepper. Add turkey, apples and celery; toss to coat well. Cover; chill. Just before serving, sprinkle with walnuts.

Makes about 4 to 6 servings

Mediterranean Phyllo Twists with Grapes and Cheese

MEDITERRANEAN PHYLLO TWISTS WITH GRAPES AND CHEESE

6 sheets phyllo dough
2 tablespoons olive oil, divided
5 to 6 ounces goat cheese
2 tablespoons chopped fresh basil
⅛ teaspoon medium-grind pepper
2 cups California seedless grapes
3 quarts mixed greens
   Mustard Vinaigrette (recipe follows)
12 small California grape clusters

Cut each sheet of phyllo dough into 4 equal (about 6½×8½-inch) pieces and keep under a damp, clean towel to prevent drying. Working with 4 pieces at a time, brush each with oil and stack, alternating directions with each piece to enable the complete covering of filling. Portion ⅙ of cheese in center of dough. Combine basil and pepper; mix well. Top cheese with 1 teaspoon basil mixture and ⅓ cup grapes. Carefully gather dough to enclose filling, twisting dough at top to form small bundle. Brush lightly with oil to prevent drying. Place on greased baking sheet. Repeat with remaining ingredients. Bake at 400°F 10 minutes or until thoroughly heated. Toss mixed greens with Mustard Vinaigrette. Serve each phyllo packet on bed of mixed greens; garnish with grape clusters. *Makes 6 servings*

MUSTARD VINAIGRETTE: Combine 3 tablespoons balsamic vinegar, 1 tablespoon *each* olive oil and chopped parsley, 1 teaspoon Dijon-style mustard, ½ teaspoon *each* sugar and salt and ¼ teaspoon pepper. Makes ⅓ cup.

*Favorite recipe from **California Table Grape Commission***

3–GREEN SALAD WITH CRANBERRY VINAIGRETTE

1 head red leaf lettuce
1 head romaine
1 pound (or bag) fresh spinach
1 cup bottled oil and vinegar dressing
½ cup ground cranberries
1 teaspoon tarragon
1 clove garlic, crushed
   Red cabbage slivers, cut paper thin, for garnish
   Bean sprouts for garnish

Clean greens, removing tough stems or ribs and tearing into bite-sized pieces. Combine greens in large bowl; cover and refrigerate. Mix dressing, cranberries, tarragon and garlic in a covered jar. Allow to steep for at least 2 hours, then toss with greens. Garnish with cabbage and sprouts. *Makes 6 servings*

*Favorite recipe from **Perdue® Farms***

MANDARIN ORANGE AND RED ONION SALAD

- **1 cup BLUE DIAMOND® Sliced Natural Almonds**
- **1 tablespoon butter**
- **2 tablespoons lemon juice**
- **1 teaspoon Dijon mustard**
- **½ teaspoon sugar**
- **½ teaspoon salt**
- **¼ teaspoon white pepper**
- **½ cup vegetable oil**
- **1 head romaine lettuce, torn into pieces**
- **1 can (11 ounces) mandarin orange segments, drained**
- **1 small red onion, thinly sliced, rings separated**

Sauté almonds in butter until golden; reserve. Combine next 5 ingredients. Whisk in oil. Combine lettuce, oranges, onion and almonds. Toss with dressing.   *Makes 4 to 6 servings*

FRESH SPINACH SALAD WITH RED WINE VINAIGRETTE DRESSING

- **½ pound spinach leaves, torn into pieces**
- **2 hard-cooked eggs, peeled and chopped**
- **6 bacon slices, cooked and crumbled**
- **2 cups sliced fresh mushrooms**
- **¾ cup LAWRY'S® Red Wine Vinaigrette with Cabernet Sauvignon Dressing**

In large salad bowl, gently toss together all ingredients except dressing; chill. Toss with dressing just before serving.

Makes 6 servings

PRESENTATION: Serve on chilled salad plates with chilled forks, if desired.

Mandarin Orange and Red Onion Salad

WINTER PEAR AND STILTON SALAD

⅓ cup extra virgin olive oil
1½ tablespoons sherry wine vinegar or white wine vinegar
1 tablespoon Dijon-style mustard
4 teaspoons honey
¼ teaspoon salt
2 ripe Bosc, Bartlett or Anjou pears
Lemon juice (optional)
5 cups washed and torn assorted gourmet mixed salad greens, such as oakleaf, frisee, watercress, radicchio, arugula or escarole
2 cups washed and torn Boston or Bibb lettuce leaves
6 ounces Stilton or Gorgonzola cheese, crumbled
Freshly ground black pepper

Place oil, vinegar, mustard, honey and salt in small bowl. Whisk together until combined. Cover and refrigerate up to 2 days.

Quarter and core pears; cut into ½-inch pieces. To help prevent discoloration, brush pear pieces with lemon juice, if desired. Combine greens, pears, cheese and dressing in large bowl. Toss lightly to coat; sprinkle with pepper.

Makes 6 to 8 servings

MARINATED VEGETABLE SPINACH SALAD

Mustard Tarragon Marinade (recipe follows)
8 ounces fresh mushrooms, quartered
2 slices purple onion, separated into rings
16 cherry tomatoes, halved
4 cups fresh spinach leaves, washed and stems removed
3 slices (3 ounces) SARGENTO® Preferred Light® Sliced Mozzarella Cheese, cut into julienne strips
Freshly ground black pepper

Prepare Mustard Tarragon Marinade. Place mushrooms, onion and tomatoes in bowl. Toss with marinade and let stand 15 minutes. Meanwhile, wash and dry spinach leaves. Arrange on 4 individual serving plates. Divide marinated vegetables among plates and top each salad with ¼ of the cheese. Serve with freshly ground pepper, if desired.

Makes 4 servings

MUSTARD TARRAGON MARINADE

3 tablespoons red wine vinegar
1 tablespoon Dijon mustard
1½ teaspoons dried tarragon
2 tablespoons olive oil

Combine first three ingredients. Slowly whisk oil into mixture until slightly thickened.

Makes ⅓ cup

Winter Pear and Stilton Salad

SALAD PRIMAVERA

6 cups romaine lettuce, washed and torn
    into bite-sized pieces
1 package (9 ounces) frozen artichoke
    hearts, thawed, drained and cut into
    bite-sized pieces
1 cup chopped watercress
1 orange, peeled, separated into
    segments and cut into halves
½ cup chopped red bell pepper
¼ cup chopped green onions with tops
    Citrus-Caper Dressing (recipe follows)
2 tablespoons freshly grated Parmesan
    cheese

Combine lettuce, artichoke hearts, watercress,
orange segments, bell pepper and green
onions in large bowl. Prepare Citrus-Caper
Dressing. Add dressing to lettuce mixture. Mix
well. Sprinkle with Parmesan cheese before
serving.   *Makes 8 servings*

Salad Primavera

CITRUS–CAPER DRESSING

⅓ cup orange juice
¼ cup white wine vinegar
2 tablespoons chopped fresh parsley
1 tablespoon minced capers
2 teaspoons Dijon mustard
1 teaspoon sugar
1 teaspoon minced fresh garlic
¼ teaspoon ground black pepper
¼ teaspoon olive oil

Combine all ingredients in jar or bottle with
tight-fitting lid; shake well. Refrigerate until
ready to serve. Shake well before using.
                    Makes ½ cup dressing

GARDEN GREENS WITH FENNEL DRESSING

DRESSING
½ teaspoon unflavored gelatin
2 tablespoons cold water
¼ cup boiling water
½ teaspoon salt
½ teaspoon sugar
¼ teaspoon dry mustard
⅛ teaspoon black pepper
¼ teaspoon anise extract or ground
    fennel seeds
1 tablespoon fresh lemon juice
¼ cup raspberry or wine vinegar
1¼ teaspoons walnut or canola oil
SALAD
1 head (10 ounces) Bibb lettuce, washed
    and torn into bite-sized pieces
1 head (10 ounces) radicchio, washed
    and torn into bite-sized pieces
1 bunch (3 ounces) arugula, washed and
    torn into bite-sized pieces
1 cup mâche or spinach leaves, washed
    and torn into bite-sized pieces
1 fennel bulb (8 ounces), finely chopped
    (reserve fern for garnish)
1 tablespoon pine nuts, toasted

To prepare dressing, sprinkle gelatin over cold water in small bowl; let stand 1 minute to soften. Add boiling water; stir 2 minutes or until gelatin is completely dissolved. Add salt and sugar; stir until sugar is completely dissolved. Add all remaining dressing ingredients except oil; mix well. Slowly whisk in oil until well blended. Cover and refrigerate 2 hours or overnight. Mix well before using.

To prepare salad, place all salad ingredients except pine nuts in large bowl. Add dressing; toss until all leaves glisten. Divide salad among 6 chilled salad plates. Top each salad with ½ teaspoon pine nuts. Garnish with sprig of fennel fern, if desired.   *Makes 6 servings*

ENSALADA DE NOCHE BUENA (CHRISTMAS EVE SALAD)

1 head iceberg lettuce, shredded
3 oranges, peeled and sectioned
2 firm bananas, sliced crosswise ¼ inch thick
1 large apple, unpeeled, cored and chopped
1 cup pineapple chunks, drained
1 cup sliced canned beets
   Seeds of 1 pomegranate *or* ¼ cup canned whole-berry cranberry sauce
½ cup coarsely chopped toasted peanuts (not dry roasted)
   Vinaigrette Dressing (page 117)

On large platter, top shredded lettuce with fruit and beets. Sprinkle with pomegranate seeds and nuts. Serve with Vinaigrette Dressing.
          Makes 10 servings

Favorite recipe from **Lawry's**

Garden Greens with Fennel Dressing

MIXED GREENS WITH RASPBERRY VINAIGRETTE

½ cup walnut pieces
⅓ cup vegetable oil
2½ tablespoons raspberry vinegar
1 tablespoon chopped shallot
½ teaspoon salt
½ teaspoon sugar
2 cups washed and torn Romaine lettuce leaves
2 cups washed and torn spinach leaves
2 cups washed and torn red leaf lettuce leaves
1 cup halved red seedless grapes

Preheat oven to 350°F. To toast walnuts, spread in single layer on baking sheet. Bake 6 to 8 minutes or until lightly golden brown, stirring frequently; cool. Coarsely chop; set aside.

Place oil, vinegar, shallot, salt and sugar in small bowl or small jar with lid. Whisk together or cover and shake jar until mixed. Cover; refrigerate up to 1 week. Combine greens, grapes and chopped walnuts in large bowl. Just before serving, add dressing; toss well to coat.

Makes 6 to 8 servings

CHEESY WALDORF SALAD

⅓ cup mayonnaise or reduced-fat mayonnaise
1 tablespoon honey
1 tablespoon cider vinegar
4 small or 3 large apples
4 ounces Provolone cheese
2 ribs celery, thinly sliced
½ cup walnuts or pecans, toasted and chopped, divided
Red leaf lettuce leaves

Combine mayonnaise, honey and vinegar in large bowl until blended. Core apples; cut enough into ½-inch pieces to equal 4 cups. Cut cheese into cubes. Add apples, cheese, celery and ¼ cup walnuts; stir to coat. At this point the salad may be refrigerated, covered with plastic wrap, up to 8 hours. To serve, line individual salad plates with lettuce, then top with salad. Sprinkle remaining ¼ cup walnuts over each serving. *Makes 6 to 8 servings*

CREAMY ITALIAN PASTA SALAD

1 cup HELLMANN'S® or BEST FOODS® Real or Light Mayonnaise or Low Fat Cholesterol Free Mayonnaise Dressing
2 tablespoons red wine vinegar
1 clove garlic, minced
1 tablespoon chopped fresh basil *or* 1 teaspoon dried basil
1 teaspoon salt
¼ teaspoon freshly ground black pepper
1½ cups twist or spiral pasta, cooked, rinsed with cold water and drained
1 cup quartered cherry tomatoes
½ cup coarsely chopped green pepper
½ cup slivered pitted ripe olives

In large bowl combine mayonnaise, vinegar, garlic, basil, salt and pepper. Stir in pasta, cherry tomatoes, green pepper and olives. Cover; chill. *Makes about 6 servings*

Mixed Greens with Raspberry Vinaigrette

BEET AND PEAR SALAD

- 1 can (16 ounces) DEL MONTE® Bartlett Pear Halves
- 1 can (16 ounces) DEL MONTE® Sliced Beets, drained
- ½ cup thinly sliced red onion, separated into rings
- 2 tablespoons vegetable oil
- 1 tablespoon white wine vinegar
- ⅓ cup crumbled blue cheese
  Lettuce leaves (optional)

Drain pears reserving 1 tablespoon syrup. Cut pears in half lengthwise. Place pears, beets and onion in medium bowl. Whisk together oil, vinegar and reserved syrup. Pour over salad; toss gently. Just before serving, add cheese and toss. Serve on bed of lettuce leaves, if desired.   *Makes 4 to 6 servings*

TOTAL TIME: 10 minutes

WARM TOMATO–POTATO SALAD

- 3 medium (about 1 pound) tomatoes
- 1 pound small red-skinned potatoes, quartered
- 3 slices bacon, cut into ½-inch pieces
- ¼ cup chopped onion
- 1½ teaspoons sugar
- ½ teaspoon flour
- 1 teaspoon salt
- ⅛ teaspoon ground black pepper
- 1 tablespoon cider vinegar
- ¼ cup water
- 1 cup fresh or frozen sugar snap peas

Beet and Pear Salad

Use tomatoes held at room temperature until fully ripe. Core tomatoes; cut into large chunks (about 3 cups). Set aside. In large saucepan cook potatoes in enough water to cover until tender, 10 to 15 minutes; drain. Set aside. Meanwhile, in large skillet cook bacon, stirring occasionally, until crisp, 3 to 5 minutes. Using a slotted spoon, transfer bacon to paper towel to drain. Remove all but 1 tablespoon drippings from skillet; stir in onion. Cook, stirring occasionally, until tender, 5 to 7 minutes. Add sugar, flour, salt and pepper, stirring until smooth. Stir in vinegar, ¼ cup water and sugar snap peas; cook and stir until mixture boils and thickens slightly, 1 to 2 minutes. Stir in reserved potatoes and bacon. Add reserved tomatoes, tossing to coat. Place potato mixture on large serving plate. *Makes 6 servings, 5 cups*

Favorite recipe from **Florida Tomato Committee**

Wild Rice & Pepper Salad

TANGY VEGETABLE SALAD

  2 cups small broccoli flowerets
  1 cup finely shredded red cabbage
  ¾ cup diced red bell pepper
  1 medium carrot, shredded (about
      ½ cup)
  ½ cup bottled ranch salad dressing
  2 teaspoons prepared horseradish

Combine broccoli, cabbage, bell pepper and carrot in large bowl; toss to mix. Combine salad dressing and horseradish, then pour over salad; toss to coat. Cover with plastic wrap. Refrigerate until ready to serve.

Makes 3 cups

WILD RICE & PEPPER SALAD

  1 (6-ounce) package long-grain & wild rice
  ½ cup MIRACLE WHIP® Salad Dressing
  2 tablespoons olive oil
  ½ teaspoon black pepper
  ¼ teaspoon grated lemon peel
  1 cup chopped red pepper
  1 cup chopped yellow pepper
  ¼ cup 1-inch green onion pieces

Prepare rice as directed on package, omitting margarine. Cool. Combine salad dressing, oil, black pepper and peel; mix well. Add remaining ingredients; mix lightly. Serve at room temperature or chilled. *Makes 6 servings*

PREP TIME: 35 minutes

VARIATION: Substitute MIRACLE WHIP® LIGHT Reduced Calorie Salad Dressing for regular Salad Dressing.

Christmas Cabbage Slaw

CHRISTMAS CABBAGE SLAW

2 cups finely shredded green cabbage
2 cups finely shredded red cabbage
1 cup jicama strips
¼ cup diced green bell pepper
¼ cup thinly sliced green onions with tops
¼ cup vegetable oil
¼ cup lime juice
¾ teaspoon salt
⅛ teaspoon freshly ground black pepper
2 tablespoons coarsely chopped cilantro leaves

Combine cabbages, jicama, bell pepper and onions in large bowl. Whisk oil, lime juice, salt and black pepper in small bowl until well blended. Stir in cilantro. Pour over cabbage mixture; toss lightly. Cover; refrigerate 2 to 6 hours for flavors to blend.

Makes 4 to 6 servings

ROASTED TOMATO AND MOZZARELLA PASTA SALAD

3 cups (8 ounces) rotelle (corkscrew) pasta, uncooked
Roasted Fresh Tomatoes (page 103)
1 cup coarsely chopped green bell pepper
4 ounces mozzarella cheese, cut into ½-inch cubes
¼ cup chopped sweet red onion
½ teaspoon salt
¼ teaspoon ground black pepper
⅓ cup bottled red wine vinaigrette salad dressing

Cook pasta according to package directions; rinse and drain. Place in large bowl. Cut Roasted Fresh Tomatoes into chunks; add to pasta along with green pepper, mozzarella cheese, onion, salt and black pepper. Add salad dressing; toss to coat. Serve garnished with basil leaves, if desired.

Makes 4 servings, 8 cups

ROASTED FRESH TOMATOES

6 large tomatoes (about 3 pounds)
2 tablespoons vegetable oil
½ teaspoon dried basil leaves, crushed
¼ teaspoon dried thyme leaves, crushed
¼ teaspoon salt
¼ teaspoon ground black pepper

Preheat oven to 425°F. Use tomatoes held at room temperature until fully ripe. Core tomatoes; cut in half horizontally. Gently squeeze to remove seeds. Place, cut side up, on rack in broiler pan; set aside. In small bowl combine oil, basil, thyme, salt and black pepper; brush over cut sides of tomatoes. Place tomatoes cut side down. Bake until well browned, about 30 minutes. Remove tomato skins, if desired.

Makes 4 to 6 servings, 3 cups

NOTE: Recipe also may be served hot, warm or chilled as a side dish.

*Favorite recipe from **Florida Tomato Committee***

Roasted Tomato and Mozzarella Pasta Salad

APPLE & DRIED CHERRY CHUTNEY

3 tablespoons vegetable oil
1½ cups chopped red onions
1 tablespoon minced fresh ginger
¼ teaspoon red pepper flakes
⅓ cup dried cherries
1 tablespoon packed dark brown sugar
¼ teaspoon salt
1 cup water
1 Granny Smith apple, cored and finely chopped
1 teaspoon cornstarch, dissolved in 1 tablespoon water
1 teaspoon balsamic vinegar

In large skillet, heat oil over medium heat. Add onions, ginger and pepper flakes; cook and stir 5 minutes. Add dried cherries, brown sugar and salt. Stir in water; cover and cook over medium heat 5 minutes.

Add apple to onion mixture. Cover; cook 6 to 8 minutes or until apple is tender. Stir cornstarch mixture into apple-onion mixture and cook over high heat, stirring constantly, until mixture is thickened and appears glazed, about 1 minute. Remove from heat; stir in vinegar. Cool before serving or storing. Chutney can be refrigerated for one week or frozen for one month.

Makes 2 cups

*Favorite recipe from **Washington Apple Commission***

SWEET POTATO SALAD

2 pounds sweet potatoes, peeled and cubed
2 tablespoons lemon juice
1 cup HELLMANN'S® or BEST FOODS® Real or Light Mayonnaise or Low Fat Cholesterol Free Mayonnaise Dressing
1 teaspoon grated orange peel
2 tablespoons orange juice
1 tablespoon honey
1 teaspoon chopped fresh ginger
¼ teaspoon salt
⅛ teaspoon nutmeg
1 cup coarsely chopped pecans
1 cup sliced celery
⅓ cup chopped pitted dates
Lettuce leaves
1 can (11 ounces) mandarin orange segments, drained

Sweet Potato Salad

In medium saucepan cook potatoes 8 to 10 minutes in boiling, salted water just until tender. *(Do not overcook.)* Drain. Toss with lemon juice. In large bowl combine mayonnaise, orange peel, orange juice, honey, ginger, salt and nutmeg. Stir in warm potatoes, pecans, celery and dates. Cover; chill. To serve, spoon salad onto lettuce-lined platter. Arrange orange segments around salad. Garnish as desired.

Makes 6 servings

CRANBERRY AND RED PEPPER RELISH

2 medium red bell peppers, roasted, peeled, seeded and cut into 1-inch pieces*
1 cup fresh cranberries, rinsed and drained
1 green onion, cut into 1-inch pieces
3 tablespoons fresh cilantro leaves
2 tablespoons fresh orange juice
½ teaspoon grated lime peel
½ cup sugar
⅛ teaspoon salt

1. In food processor fitted with steel blade, process peppers, cranberries, onion, cilantro, orange juice and lime peel until coarsely chopped.

2. In medium-size bowl combine cranberry mixture, sugar and salt. Cover and refrigerate 1 or more hours to allow flavors to mix.

Makes 1½ cups

*To roast bell peppers, place peppers under broiler, turning frequently, until slightly scorched on all sides. Place broiled peppers in a paper bag; close bag and set aside five minutes. Remove blistered skins from peppers.

*Favorite recipe from **National Turkey Federation***

Spicy California Apricot Chutney

SPICY CALIFORNIA APRICOT CHUTNEY

  2 teaspoons olive oil
½ cup chopped onion
  1 jalapeño pepper, minced
  2 teaspoons minced fresh ginger
  2 teaspoons minced garlic
  1 tablespoon dark brown sugar
½ teaspoon ground cinnamon
¼ teaspoon dry mustard
⅛ teaspoon ground cloves
½ cup apple cider vinegar
¼ cup water
¼ cup currants
  2 (17-ounce) cans California apricot
      halves, well drained and cut into
      ½-inch slices

In large skillet, heat oil. Add onion, pepper, ginger and garlic; cook, covered, over medium heat until soft, about 5 minutes. Combine brown sugar, cinnamon, mustard and cloves. Uncover skillet; add brown sugar mixture and remaining ingredients. Simmer, uncovered, 25 minutes or until most of the liquid has evaporated. Remove to heatproof glass container; let cool completely. Cover and refrigerate. Serve chutney at room temperature with poultry, pork or lamb.   *Makes 1½ cups*

Favorite recipe from **California Apricot Advisory Board**

AMBROSIA

  1 can (20 ounces) DOLE® Pineapple
      Chunks
  1 can (11 ounces) DOLE® Mandarin
      Orange Segments
  1 firm, large DOLE® Banana, sliced
      (optional)
1½ cups DOLE® Seedless Grapes
  1 cup miniature marshmallows
  1 cup flaked coconut
½ cup pecan halves or coarsely chopped
      nuts
  1 cup dairy sour cream or plain yogurt
  1 tablespoon brown sugar

• Drain pineapple and orange segments. In large bowl, combine pineapple, orange segments, banana, grapes, marshmallows, coconut and nuts.

• In 1-quart measure, combine sour cream and brown sugar. Stir into fruit mixture. Refrigerate, covered, 1 hour or overnight.

Makes 4 servings

CRANBERRY–APPLE CHUTNEY

1¼ cups granulated sugar
½ cup water
1 package (12 ounces) fresh or frozen cranberries (about 3½ cups)
2 medium Granny Smith apples, cut into ¼-inch pieces (2 cups)
1 medium onion, chopped
½ cup golden raisins
½ cup packed light brown sugar
¼ cup cider vinegar
1 teaspoon ground cinnamon
1 teaspoon ground ginger
⅛ teaspoon ground cloves
⅛ teaspoon ground allspice
½ cup walnuts or pecans, toasted and chopped (optional)

Combine granulated sugar and water in heavy 2-quart saucepan. Bring to a boil over high heat. Boil gently 3 minutes. Add cranberries, apples, onion, raisins, brown sugar, vinegar, cinnamon, ginger, cloves and allspice.

Bring to a boil over high heat. Reduce heat to medium. Simmer, uncovered, 20 to 25 minutes or until mixture is very thick, stirring occasionally. Cool; stir in walnuts. Cover and refrigerate up to 2 weeks before serving.

Makes about 3½ cups without walnuts or 4 cups with walnuts

NOTE: This chutney makes a wonderful appetizer when spooned over cream cheese spread on melba rounds.

CLASSIC WALDORF SALAD

½ cup HELLMANN'S® or BEST FOODS® Real or Light Mayonnaise or Low Fat Cholesterol Free Mayonnaise Dressing
1 tablespoon sugar
1 tablespoon lemon juice
⅛ teaspoon salt
3 medium-size red apples, cored and diced
1 cup sliced celery
½ cup chopped walnuts

In medium bowl combine mayonnaise, sugar, lemon juice and salt. Add apples and celery; toss to coat well. Cover; chill. Just before serving, sprinkle with walnuts.

Makes about 8 servings

WINTER FRUIT MOLD

2 cups boiling water
1 package (8-serving size) *or* 2 packages (4-serving size) JELL-O® Brand Lemon Flavor Gelatin
1 cup grape or orange juice
½ cup cold water
1½ cups fresh fruit (halved seedless grapes, diced pears and apples)

Stir boiling water into gelatin in large bowl 2 minutes or until completely dissolved. Stir in juice and cold water. Refrigerate until thickened (spoon drawn through gelatin leaves definite impression). Stir in fruit; spoon into 5-cup mold. Refrigerate 4 hours or until firm. Unmold.

Makes 10 servings

Cranberry-Apple Chutney

GINGER PINEAPPLE MOLD

1 can (20 ounces) pineapple chunks in
   juice*
1½ cups boiling water
1 package (8-serving size) *or* 2 packages
   (4-serving size) JELL-O® Brand Lime
   or Apricot Flavor Gelatin
1 cup ginger ale or cold water
¼ teaspoon ground ginger

Drain pineapple, reserving juice. Stir boiling
water into gelatin in large bowl 2 minutes or
until completely dissolved. Stir in reserved
juice, ginger ale and ginger. Refrigerate about
1¼ hours or until slightly thickened (mixture
should be consistency of unbeaten egg
whites).

Arrange some of the pineapple chunks in
6-cup ring mold or 9×5-inch loaf pan; top with
1 cup of the slightly thickened gelatin.
Refrigerate about 10 minutes or until set but
not firm (sticks to finger when touched and
moves to the side when pan is tilted). Stir
remaining pineapple into remaining gelatin;
spoon into mold. Refrigerate 4 hours or until
firm. Unmold. Garnish as desired. Serve as
dessert or salad.   *Makes 10 servings*

*Or use 1 can (20 ounces) pineapple slices in
juice; reserve 4 slices for garnish and dice
remaining slices.

NOTE: Arrangement of pineapple may be
omitted; fold all pineapple into thickened
gelatin.

Ginger Pineapple Mold

Spiced Cranberry-Orange Mold

SPICED CRANBERRY–ORANGE MOLD

1 bag (12 ounces) fresh cranberries*
½ cup sugar*
1½ cups boiling water
1 package (8-serving size) *or* 2 packages (4-serving size) JELL-O® Brand Cranberry, Orange or Lemon Flavor Gelatin
¼ teaspoon salt (optional)
1 cup cold water*
1 tablespoon lemon juice
¼ teaspoon ground cinnamon
⅛ teaspoon ground cloves
1 orange, sectioned, diced
½ cup chopped nuts

Finely chop cranberries in food processor; mix with sugar. Set aside.

Stir boiling water into combined gelatin and salt in large bowl 2 minutes or until gelatin is completely dissolved. Stir in cold water, lemon juice, cinnamon and cloves. Refrigerate about 1½ hours or until thickened (spoon drawn through gelatin leaves a definite impression).

Stir in cranberries, orange and nuts. Spoon into 5-cup mold that has been lightly sprayed with no-stick cooking spray.

Refrigerate about 4 hours or until firm. Unmold. Garnish as desired. Store leftover gelatin mold in refrigerator.   *Makes 10 servings*

*Or use 1 can (16 ounces) whole berry cranberry sauce; omit sugar and reduce cold water to ½ cup.

HOLIDAY FRUIT SALAD

3 packages (3 ounces each) strawberry flavor gelatin
3 cups boiling water
2 ripe DOLE® Bananas
1 package (16 ounces) frozen strawberries
1 can (20 ounces) DOLE® Crushed Pineapple
1 package (8 ounces) cream cheese, softened
1 cup dairy sour cream or plain yogurt
¼ cup sugar
Crisp DOLE® Lettuce leaves

• In large bowl, dissolve gelatin in boiling water. Slice bananas into gelatin mixture. Add frozen strawberries and undrained pineapple. Reserve half of the mixture at room temperature. Pour remaining mixture into 13×9-inch pan. Refrigerate 1 hour or until firm.

• In mixer bowl, beat cream cheese with sour cream and sugar; spread over chilled layer. Gently spoon reserved gelatin mixture on top. Refrigerate until firm, about 2 hours.

• Cut into squares; serve on lettuce-lined salad plates. Garnish with additional pineapple and mint leaves, if desired.   *Makes 12 servings*

ORANGE–BERRY SALAD

½ cup prepared HIDDEN VALLEY
    RANCH® Original Ranch® salad
    dressing
2 tablespoons orange juice
1 teaspoon grated orange peel
½ cup heavy cream, whipped
1 (11-ounce) can mandarin orange
    segments
2 (3-ounce) packages strawberry- or
    raspberry-flavored gelatin
1 (16-ounce) can whole-berry cranberry
    sauce
½ cup walnut pieces
    Mint sprigs
    Whole fresh strawberries and
    raspberries

In large bowl, whisk together salad dressing, orange juice and peel. Fold in whipped cream; cover and refrigerate. Drain oranges, reserving juice. Add water to juice to measure 3 cups; pour into large saucepan and bring to a boil. Remove from heat. Stir in gelatin until dissolved. Cover and refrigerate until partially set. Fold orange segments, cranberry sauce and walnuts into gelatin. Pour into lightly oiled 6-cup ring mold. Cover and refrigerate until firm; unmold. Garnish with mint, fresh strawberries and raspberries. Serve with chilled dressing. *Makes 8 servings*

RIBBON SQUARES

1 package (4-serving size) JELL-O®
    Brand Lemon Flavor Gelatin
1 package (4-serving size) JELL-O®
    Brand Gelatin, any red flavor
1 package (4-serving size) JELL-O®
    Brand Lime Flavor Gelatin
3 cups boiling water, divided
1 package (8 ounces) PHILADELPHIA
    BRAND® Cream Cheese, softened
1 can (8¼ ounces) crushed pineapple in
    syrup
1 cup thawed COOL WHIP® Whipped
    Topping*
½ cup KRAFT® Real Mayonnaise
1½ cups cold water, divided

Dissolve each flavor of gelatin separately in 1 cup of the boiling water. Gradually add lemon gelatin to cream cheese, mixing until well blended. Stir in pineapple with syrup. Refrigerate about 1¼ hours or until slightly thickened (mixture should be consistency of unbeaten egg whites). Blend in whipped topping and mayonnaise. Refrigerate until thickened (spoon drawn through mixture leaves definite impression).

Meanwhile, add ¾ cup of the cold water to red gelatin. Pour into 9-inch square pan. Refrigerate about 2 hours or until set but not firm. Add the remaining ¾ cup cold water to lime gelatin. Refrigerate about 1¼ hours or until slightly thickened (gelatin should be consistency of unbeaten egg whites).

Spoon lemon gelatin mixture over red gelatin layer in pan. Refrigerate until set but not firm (sticks to finger when touched and moves to side when pan is tilted). Top with lime gelatin. Refrigerate 4 hours or until firm. Unmold. Cut into squares. Garnish with drained, canned, sliced pineapple and celery leaves, if desired. *Makes 16 servings*

*Or use 1 cup prepared DREAM WHIP® Whipped Topping.

Orange-Berry Salad

HOLIDAY WALDORF SALAD

1½ cups boiling water
1 package (8-serving size) *or* 2 packages
   (4-serving size) JELL-O® Brand
   Strawberry Flavor Gelatin
1 tablespoon lemon juice
1 cup cold water
   Ice cubes
1 medium red apple, diced
½ cup halved seedless grapes
½ cup thinly sliced celery
½ cup chopped walnuts
1 cup KRAFT® Real Mayonnaise

Stir boiling water into gelatin in large bowl 2 minutes or until completely dissolved. Stir in lemon juice. Mix cold water and ice cubes to make 2½ cups. Add to gelatin, stirring until slightly thickened. Remove any remaining ice. Refrigerate about 10 minutes or until thickened (spoon drawn through gelatin leaves definite impression).

Stir apple, grapes, celery and walnuts into gelatin. Measure 1 cup gelatin mixture and set aside. Pour remaining gelatin mixture into 8-cup serving bowl. Refrigerate until set but not firm (sticks to finger when touched and moves to side when bowl is tilted).

Blend mayonnaise into reserved 1 cup gelatin mixture. Spoon over fruited layer. Refrigerate 3 hours or until firm. Garnish with apple slices and grapes, if desired.

Makes about 14 servings

APPLESAUCE CRANBERRY MOLD

2 envelopes unflavored gelatin
½ cup orange or cranberry juice
½ cup boiling water
1 can or jar (16 ounces) whole-berry
   cranberry sauce
1 cup applesauce
1 apple, cored and cut up
1 cup diced celery
½ cup chopped walnuts
1 orange, peeled and diced
2 tablespoons grated orange peel

Soften gelatin in juice. Add boiling water and stir to dissolve; cool. Mix all other ingredients; add to gelatin mixture. Pour into a greased 2-quart mold and refrigerate several hours. Unmold.   *Makes 6 to 8 servings*

Favorite recipe from **New York Apple Association, Inc.**

PINEAPPLE LIME MOLD

1 can (20 ounces) DOLE® Pineapple
   Chunks
2 packages (3 ounces each) lime gelatin
2 cups boiling water
1 cup dairy sour cream
½ cup chopped walnuts
½ cup chopped celery

• Drain pineapple, reserving syrup. Dissolve gelatin in boiling water. Add sour cream and reserved syrup. Chill until slightly thickened. Stir in pineapple, walnuts and celery. Pour into 7-cup mold. Chill until set. Unmold.

Makes 8 servings

CHRISTMAS RIBBON

5 cups boiling water, divided
1   package (8-serving size) *or* 2 packages
(4-serving size) JELL-O® Brand
Strawberry Flavor Gelatin
⅔ cup BREYER'S® or KNUDSEN® Sour
Cream*, divided
1   package (8-serving size) *or* 2 packages
(4-serving size) JELL-O® Brand Lime
Flavor Gelatin

Stir 2½ cups of the boiling water into
strawberry flavor gelatin in large bowl 2
minutes or until completely dissolved. Pour
1½ cups into 6-cup ring mold. Refrigerate
about 30 minutes or until set but not firm
(should stick to finger when touched and
mound). Refrigerate remaining gelatin in bowl
until slightly thickened. Gradually stir in ⅓ cup
of the sour cream; spoon over gelatin in mold.
Refrigerate about 15 minutes or until set but
not firm.

Repeat with lime flavor gelatin, remaining
2½ cups boiling water and ⅓ cup sour cream,
refrigerating dissolved gelatin before measuring
and pouring into mold. Refrigerate 2 hours or
until firm. Unmold.

Makes about 12 servings

*Or use BREYER'S® or KNUDSEN® Plain or
Vanilla Yogurt.

Christmas Ribbon

RASPBERRY–LEMON GELATIN SALAD

> 1 (10-ounce) package frozen raspberries, thawed
> Cold water
> 1 package (4-serving size) JELL-O® Brand Raspberry Flavor Gelatin
> 1 envelope unflavored gelatin
> ½ cup lemon juice
> 1 package (4-serving size) JELL-O® Brand Lemon Flavor Instant Pudding and Pie Filling
> 2 cups cold milk
> 1 cup MIRACLE WHIP® Salad Dressing

Drain raspberries, reserving liquid. Add enough water to reserved liquid to measure ¾ cup; set aside. Bring 1 cup water to boil. Gradually add to raspberry gelatin, stirring until dissolved. Stir in reserved raspberry liquid. Cover; chill until thickened but not set. Fold in raspberries. Pour into 1½-quart clear serving bowl. Cover; chill until almost set. Combine unflavored gelatin and juice in small saucepan; let stand 1 minute. Stir over low heat until gelatin is dissolved. Cool. Combine pudding mix and milk; mix as directed on package for pudding. Stir in salad dressing. Gradually add gelatin mixture, mixing until well blended. Pour over raspberry layer; cover. Chill until firm.   *Makes 8 to 10 servings*

PREP TIME: 1½ hours plus final chilling

STRAWBERRY MIRACLE MOLD

> 1½ cups boiling water
> 2 packages (4-serving size) JELL-O® Brand Strawberry Flavor Gelatin
> 1¾ cups cold water
> ½ cup MIRACLE WHIP® Salad Dressing
> Assorted fruit

Stir boiling water into gelatin in medium bowl 2 minutes or until dissolved. Stir in cold water. Gradually whisk gelatin into salad dressing in large bowl until well blended.

Pour into 1-quart mold or glass serving bowl that has been lightly sprayed with no-stick cooking spray. Refrigerate until firm. Unmold onto serving plate; serve with fruit.
Makes 4 to 6 servings

PREP TIME: 10 minutes plus refrigerating

CRANBERRY HOLIDAY RING

> 2¼ cups water, divided
> 1 package (4-serving size) JELL-O® Brand Strawberry Flavor Gelatin
> 1 (10½-ounce) package frozen cranberry-orange relish, thawed
> 1 (8-ounce) can crushed pineapple
> 1 package (4-serving size) JELL-O® Brand Lemon Flavor Gelatin
> 2 cups KRAFT® Miniature Marshmallows
> ½ cup MIRACLE WHIP® Salad Dressing
> 1 cup whipping cream, whipped

Bring 1 cup water to boil. Gradually add to strawberry gelatin, stirring until dissolved. Add cranberry-orange relish; mix well. Pour into lightly oiled 6½-cup ring mold; cover. Chill until almost set. Drain pineapple, reserving liquid. Bring remaining 1¼ cups water to boil. Gradually add to lemon gelatin, stirring until dissolved. Add marshmallows; stir until melted. Add reserved pineapple liquid; cover. Chill until partially set. Add salad dressing and pineapple to marshmallow mixture. Fold in whipped cream; pour over strawberry layer. Cover; chill until firm. Unmold. Garnish as desired.
Makes 12 servings

PREP TIME: 1½ hours plus final chilling

VARIATION: Substitute 12×8-inch dish for ring mold. Do not unmold.

Strawberry Miracle Mold

Cherry Waldorf Gelatin

MICROWAVE OR ROASTED BELL PEPPER DRESSING

   1 green or red bell pepper
   ½ cup buttermilk
   2 teaspoons sugar
   1 teaspoon chopped fresh parsley
      (optional)
   ¾ teaspoon lemon juice
   ¼ teaspoon paprika
   ⅛ teaspoon salt
   ⅛ teaspoon black pepper
   ⅛ teaspoon onion powder

Microwave bell pepper on HIGH (100% power) 5 minutes or until tender. (Or roast pepper in 375°F oven 20 to 25 minutes or until tender.) Cut bell pepper in half and remove seeds. Pat dry with paper towel. In blender or food processor blend all ingredients thoroughly. Chill. Serve over green salad.

Makes 6 servings

Favorite recipe from **The Sugar Association, Inc.**

CHERRY WALDORF GELATIN

   2 cups boiling water
   1 (6-ounce) package cherry flavor gelatin
   1 cup cold water
   ¼ cup REALEMON® Lemon Juice from
      Concentrate
   1½ cups chopped apples
   1 cup chopped celery
   ½ cup chopped walnuts or pecans
      Lettuce leaves
      Apple slices and celery leaves
      (optional)

In medium bowl, pour boiling water over gelatin; stir until dissolved. Add cold water and ReaLemon® brand; chill until partially set. Fold in apples, celery and nuts. Pour into lightly oiled 6-cup mold or 9-inch square baking pan. Chill until set, 4 to 6 hours or overnight. Serve on lettuce. Garnish with apple and celery leaves, if desired.   *Makes 8 to 10 servings*

SOUTHWEST SALSA DRESSING

   ⅔ cup mild salsa*
   2 tablespoons plain nonfat yogurt
   4 teaspoons sugar
   2 teaspoons chopped cilantro (optional)

In small bowl, stir all ingredients together. (Or, for a smoother dressing, process ingredients in food processor.) Chill or serve immediately over green salad, chicken or turkey salad, taco salad or seafood salad.   *Makes 4 servings*

*For a spicier dressing, use medium or hot salsa.

Favorite recipe from **The Sugar Association, Inc.**

VINAIGRETTE DRESSING

¼ cup red wine vinegar
1 tablespoon water
1 tablespoon lemon juice
1 teaspoon sugar
½ teaspoon LAWRY'S® Seasoned Pepper
½ teaspoon dried basil
½ teaspoon LAWRY'S® Seasoned Salt
½ teaspoon LAWRY'S® Garlic Salt
¼ teaspoon paprika
¼ teaspoon dry mustard
¼ teaspoon dried tarragon
¼ teaspoon celery seed
⅔ cup vegetable oil

In container with stopper or lid, combine vinegar, water, lemon juice, sugar and seasonings; blend or shake well. Add oil; blend or shake again. For best flavor, refrigerate several hours before serving.

Makes about 1 cup

CANTALOUPE DRESSING

1 cup cubed cantaloupe*
½ cup vanilla low-fat yogurt
4 teaspoons sugar

In blender or food processor blend all ingredients thoroughly. Chill or serve immediately over fruit salad.

Makes 6 servings

*For a tangier dressing, substitute 1 kiwifruit for cantaloupe. Cut kiwifruit in half and scoop out fruit with a spoon. Proceed as directed. Serve immediately. For a thicker dressing, substitute 1 cup peeled cubed pear for cantaloupe. Proceed as directed. Chill or serve immediately over fruit salad.

*Favorite recipe from **The Sugar Association, Inc.***

ORIENTAL GINGER DRESSING

½ cup pineapple juice
2 tablespoons cider vinegar
1 tablespoon sugar
1 tablespoon soy sauce
1 teaspoon grated fresh ginger
½ teaspoon sesame oil

Combine all ingredients in a jar. Cover and shake vigorously. (Or combine ingredients in food processor.) Chill or serve over green salad, chicken salad or pasta salad.

Makes 4 servings

*Favorite recipe from **The Sugar Association, Inc.***

PARMESAN CURRY DRESSING

½ cup plain nonfat yogurt
½ cup buttermilk
1 tablespoon Parmesan cheese
1½ teaspoons sugar
1 teaspoon capers
¼ teaspoon pepper
⅛ teaspoon onion powder
⅛ teaspoon curry powder

In blender or food processor blend all ingredients. Chill or serve immediately over green salad. *Makes 6 servings*

*Favorite recipe from **The Sugar Association, Inc.***

PEPPERED BEEF TIP ROAST WITH CORN PUDDING

1 (3½- to 5-pound) beef tip roast
2 teaspoons *each* cracked black pepper and
dry mustard
½ teaspoon *each* ground allspice and ground
red pepper
1 large clove garlic, minced
1 teaspoon vegetable oil
Corn Pudding (page 233)

Preheat oven to 325°F. Combine black pepper, mustard, allspice, ground red pepper and garlic; stir in oil to form paste.

Spread mixture evenly on surface of beef tip roast. Place roast, fat side up, on rack in open roasting pan. Insert meat thermometer so bulb is centered in thickest part of roast. *Do not add water. Do not cover.* Roast to desired doneness, allowing 30 to 35 minutes per pound. Meanwhile, prepare Corn Pudding. Remove roast when meat thermometer registers 155°F for medium. Allow roast to stand 15 to 20 minutes in a warm place before carving. Roast will continue to rise about 5°F in temperature to reach 160°F. Serve carved roast with Corn Pudding.   *Makes 3 to 4 servings per pound*

*Favorite recipe from **National Live Stock & Meat Board***

118

PRIME RIB WITH YORKSHIRE PUDDING AND HORSERADISH SAUCE

3 cloves garlic, minced
1 teaspoon freshly ground black pepper
1 (3-rib) standing beef roast, trimmed*
    (about 6 to 7 pounds)
    Yorkshire Pudding (recipe follows)
    Horseradish Sauce (recipe follows)

Preheat oven to 450°F. Combine garlic and pepper; rub over roast. Place roast, bone side down, (the bones take the place of a meat rack) in shallow roasting pan. Insert meat thermometer in thickest part of roast, not touching bone or fat. Roast 15 minutes.

Reduce oven temperature to 325°F. Roast 20 minutes per pound or until internal temperature is 120° to 130°F for rare, 135° to 145°F for medium. Meanwhile, prepare Yorkshire Pudding and Horseradish Sauce.

When roast has reached desired temperature, transfer to cutting board; tent with foil. Immediately after roast has been removed from oven, *increase oven temperature to 450°F.* Let roast stand in warm place 20 to 30 minutes to allow for easier carving. Temperature of roast will continue to rise about 10°F during stand time. Reserve ¼ cup drippings from roasting pan. Carve roast. Serve with Yorkshire Pudding and Horseradish Sauce.

Makes 6 to 8 servings

*Ask meat retailer to remove the chine bone for easier carving. Fat should be trimmed to ¼-inch thickness.

YORKSHIRE PUDDING

1 cup milk
2 eggs
½ teaspoon salt
1 cup all-purpose flour
¼ cup reserved drippings from roast or
    unsalted butter

Process milk, eggs and salt in food processor or blender 15 seconds. Add flour; process 2 minutes. Let batter stand in food processor at room temperature 30 minutes to 1 hour. Pour drippings into 9-inch square baking pan. Place in 450°F oven 5 minutes. Process batter another 10 seconds; pour into hot drippings. *Do not stir.* Immediately return pan to oven. Bake 20 minutes. Reduce oven temperature to 350°F; bake 10 minutes or until pudding is golden brown and puffed. Cut into squares.

Makes 6 to 8 servings

HORSERADISH SAUCE

1 cup whipping cream
⅓ cup prepared horseradish, undrained
2 teaspoons balsamic or red wine vinegar
1 teaspoon dry mustard
¼ teaspoon sugar
⅛ teaspoon salt

Beat cream until soft peaks form. *Do not overbeat.* Combine horseradish, vinegar, mustard, sugar and salt in medium bowl. Fold whipped cream into horseradish mixture. Cover and refrigerate at least 1 hour. Sauce may be made up to 8 hours before serving.

Makes 1½ cups

*Prime Rib with Yorkshire Pudding
and Horseradish Sauce*

HOLIDAY BEEF STEAKS WITH VEGETABLE SAUTÉ AND HOT MUSTARD SAUCE

Boneless beef top loin steaks, cut
    1 inch thick
½ cup plain yogurt
 1 teaspoon cornstarch
¼ cup condensed beef broth
 2 teaspoons coarse-grained mustard
 1 teaspoon *each* prepared grated
    horseradish and Dijon-style mustard
¼ teaspoon sugar
½ teaspoon lemon pepper
 1 package (16 ounces) frozen whole
    green beans
 1 cup quartered large mushrooms
 1 tablespoon butter
¼ cup water

Place yogurt and cornstarch in medium saucepan and stir until blended. Stir in beef broth, coarse-grained mustard, horseradish, Dijon-style mustard and sugar; reserve. Press an equal amount of lemon pepper into surface of boneless beef top loin steaks. Place steaks on rack in broiler pan so surface of steaks is 3 to 4 inches from heat. Broil steaks about 15 minutes for rare; 20 minutes for medium, turning once. Meanwhile, cook beans and mushrooms in butter in large frying pan over medium heat 6 minutes, stirring occasionally. Add water; cover and continue cooking 6 to 8 minutes, stirring occasionally until beans are tender. Cook reserved sauce over medium-low heat 5 minutes, stirring until sauce is slightly thickened. Serve steaks and vegetables with sauce. *Makes 6 servings*

PREP TIME: 15 minutes
COOK TIME: 15 minutes

NOTE: A boneless beef top loin steak will yield four 3-ounce cooked servings per pound.

Favorite recipe from **National Live Stock & Meat Board**

*Holiday Beef Steaks with Vegetable Sauté
and Hot Mustard Sauce*

RIB EYE ROAST AND OVEN BROWNED VEGETABLES WITH EASY SAVORY SAUCE

1 (4-pound) boneless beef rib eye roast (small end)
2 tablespoons minced fresh rosemary leaves *or* 2 teaspoons dried rosemary leaves, crushed
4 cloves garlic, crushed
1 teaspoon *each* dry mustard, salt and cracked black pepper
2 tablespoons vegetable oil
3 medium baking potatoes (about 1 pound), peeled and quartered
4 small onions (about ¾ pound), peeled and cut in half
2 large sweet potatoes (about 1 pound), peeled, halved and cut into quarters
Easy Savory Sauce (recipe follows)

Combine rosemary, garlic, mustard, salt and pepper. Rub half of herb mixture evenly over surface of beef roast. Add oil to remaining herb mixture. Place vegetables in large bowl; add herb-oil mixture, tossing to coat evenly. Place roast, fat side up, on rack in shallow roasting pan. Insert meat thermometer so bulb is centered in thickest part of roast but not resting in fat. Arrange coated vegetables around roast. Do not add water. Do not cover.

Roast in 350°F oven to desired degree of doneness. For roast, allow 20 to 22 minutes per pound for rare or medium. Remove roast when meat thermometer registers 135°F for rare; 155°F for medium. Cook vegetables 1½ hours or until tender. Place roast on carving board; return vegetables to oven if longer cooking is necessary. Tent roast with foil and let stand 15 minutes before carving. Roasts should continue to rise about 5°F in temperature to 140°F for rare; 160°F for medium. Meanwhile, prepare Easy Savory Sauce. Carve roast into slices. Serve with vegetables and sauce.

Makes 8 servings

NOTE: A boneless beef rib eye roast will yield three 3-ounce cooked servings per pound.

EASY SAVORY SAUCE
1½ teaspoons dry mustard
1 teaspoon water
1 jar (12 ounces) prepared brown gravy*
¼ cup currant jelly

Combine mustard and water in small saucepan, stirring to dissolve mustard. Stir in brown gravy and currant jelly. Cook over medium heat about 5 minutes or until mixture is bubbly and jelly is melted, stirring occasionally.

Makes 2 cups

*One can (13¾ ounces) ready-to-serve beef broth may be substituted for prepared brown gravy. In small saucepan, combine beef broth and 2 tablespoons cornstarch, mixing well. Cook over medium-high heat 3 minutes or until slightly thickened, stirring occasionally. Use as directed for sauce.

PREP TIME: 10 minutes
COOK TIME: 1 hour 30 minutes

*Favorite recipe from **National Live Stock & Meat Board***

Rib Eye Roast and Oven Browned Vegetables with Easy Savory Sauce

OVEN-BAKED BOURGUIGNONNE

**2 pounds boneless beef chuck, cut into
    1-inch cubes**
¼ cup all-purpose flour
1⅓ cups sliced carrots
**1 can (14½ ounces) whole peeled
    tomatoes, undrained and chopped**
1 bay leaf
**1 envelope LIPTON® Recipe Secrets®
    Onion or Beefy Onion Soup Mix**
½ cup dry red wine
1 cup fresh or canned sliced mushrooms
**1 package (8 ounces) medium or broad
    egg noodles**

Preheat oven to 400°F. In 2-quart casserole,
toss beef with flour. Bake uncovered 20
minutes. Add carrots, tomatoes and bay leaf,
then onion soup mix blended with wine. Bake
covered 1½ hours or until beef is tender. Add
mushrooms and bake covered an additional 10
minutes. Remove bay leaf.

Meanwhile, cook noodles according to package
directions. To serve, spoon bourguignonne over
noodles.   *Makes about 8 servings*

MICROWAVE DIRECTIONS: Toss beef with
flour; set aside. In 2-quart casserole, combine
tomatoes, bay leaf and onion soup mix blended
with wine. Heat covered at HIGH (full power)
7 minutes, stirring once. Add beef and carrots.
Heat covered at DEFROST (30% power),
stirring occasionally, 1¼ hours. Add
mushrooms and heat covered at DEFROST
30 minutes or until beef is tender. Remove bay
leaf. Let stand covered 5 minutes. Cook
noodles and serve as above.

FREEZING/REHEATING DIRECTIONS:
Bourguignonne can be baked, then frozen.
Simply wrap covered casserole in heavy-duty
aluminum foil; freeze. To reheat, unwrap and
bake covered at 400°F, stirring occasionally to
separate beef and vegetables, 1 hour. OR,
microwave at HIGH (full power), stirring
occasionally, 20 minutes or until heated
through. Let stand covered 5 minutes.

CHRISTMAS TWO-RIB BEEF ROAST

1 (3-pound) 2-rib beef roast, trimmed
**1 teaspoon *each* dried sage, thyme and
    kosher or sea salt**

Preheat oven to 325°F. Place roast, bone side
down, on rack in open roasting pan. Rub
surface with herbs and salt. Do not add water.
Do not cover. Insert meat thermometer in
thickest part, not touching fat or bone. Roast to
desired doneness (about 27 to 30 minutes per
pound for medium). Remove roast when meat
thermometer registers 155°F. Allow roast to
stand tented with foil 10 to 20 minutes before
carving. (Roast temperature will continue to
rise about 5°F.)   *Makes 4 to 6 servings*

PREP TIME: 5 minutes
COOK TIME: 1 to 1½ hours

*Favorite recipe from **California Beef Council***

BRISKET OF BEEF

1 whole well-trimmed beef brisket (about 5 pounds)
4 cloves garlic, minced
½ teaspoon freshly ground black pepper
2 large onions, cut into ¼-inch-thick slices and separated into rings
1 bottle (12 ounces) chili sauce
¾ cup beef broth, beer or water
2 tablespoons Worcestershire sauce
1 tablespoon packed brown sugar

Preheat oven to 350°F. Place brisket, fat side up, in shallow roasting pan. Spread garlic evenly over brisket; sprinkle with pepper. Arrange onions over brisket. Combine chili sauce, broth, Worcestershire sauce and sugar; pour over brisket and onions. Cover with heavy-duty foil or roasting pan lid.

Roast 2 hours. Turn brisket over; stir onions into sauce and spoon over brisket. Cover; roast 1 to 2 hours more or until fork-tender. Transfer brisket to cutting board. Tent with foil; let stand 10 minutes.*

Stir juices in roasting pan. Spoon off and discard fat from juices. (Juices may be thinned to desired consistency with water or thickened by simmering, uncovered, in saucepan.) Carve brisket across grain into thin slices. Spoon juices over brisket.   *Makes 10 to 12 servings*

*At this point, brisket may be covered and refrigerated up to 1 day before serving. To reheat brisket, cut diagonally into thin slices. Place brisket slices and juice in large skillet. Cover and cook over medium-low heat until heated through.

VARIATION: If desired, stir red boiling potatoes or cut carrots, parsnips or turnips into juices during last hour of cooking time.

Brisket of Beef

PEPPERED BEEF TENDERLOIN ROAST

1 (3- to 4-pound) beef tenderloin, fat trimmed
5 cloves garlic, finely chopped
2 tablespoons finely chopped fresh rosemary
1 tablespoon green peppercorns in brine, drained and finely chopped
1 teaspoon freshly ground black pepper
1 teaspoon salt
2 tablespoons olive oil or vegetable oil
1¼ cups beef stock

Place beef on sheet of plastic wrap. Combine remaining ingredients except oil and beef stock; rub over roast. Wrap tightly and refrigerate at least 4 hours and no longer than 48 hours. Return to room temperature before cooking.

Preheat oven to 425°F. In large ovenproof skillet or roasting pan, heat oil over medium-high heat. Place roast in skillet; brown on all sides (about 4 minutes per side). Carefully lift roast with large carving fork and place roasting rack in skillet under roast. Do not cover. Insert meat thermometer in thickest part of roast. Roast until meat thermometer registers 155°F. (Roast temperature will usually increase about 5°F after removal from oven.) Remove to cutting board and let rest in warm place 15 minutes before carving. Place skillet with pan drippings over high heat until hot. Stir in beef stock. Cook, stirring occasionally, until reduced to about ¾ cup. Strain and serve in sauce pitcher. *Makes 10 to 12 servings*

*Favorite recipe from **California Beef Council***

EASY BEEF STROGANOFF

2 tablespoons oil
2 teaspoons finely chopped garlic
½ pound boneless sirloin steak, cut into thin strips
¼ cup dry red wine
2 teaspoons Worcestershire sauce
1¼ cups water
½ cup milk
2 tablespoons butter or margarine
1 package LIPTON® Noodles & Sauce— Stroganoff
½ cup pearl onions

In large skillet, heat oil and cook garlic over medium heat 30 seconds. Add beef and cook over medium-high heat 1 minute or until almost done. Add wine and Worcestershire sauce and cook 30 seconds; remove beef. Into skillet, stir water, milk, butter and noodles & stroganoff sauce. Bring to the boiling point, then continue boiling, stirring occasionally, 7 minutes. Stir in onions and beef, then cook 2 minutes or until noodles are tender. Garnish, if desired, with chopped parsley and paprika.
Makes about 2 servings

NOTE: This recipe is also delicious with Lipton® Noodles & Sauce—Beef Flavor.

Peppered Beef Tenderloin Roast, Baked Mini Acorn Squash with Peas and Onions (page 222)

MARVELOUS MARINATED LONDON BROIL

½ cup HELLMANN'S® or BEST FOODS®
Real or Light Mayonnaise
⅓ cup soy sauce
¼ cup lemon juice
2 tablespoons prepared mustard
1 clove garlic, minced or pressed
½ teaspoon ground ginger
¼ teaspoon freshly ground pepper
1 beef top round steak (3 pounds),
2 inches thick

In large shallow dish combine mayonnaise, soy sauce, lemon juice, mustard, garlic, ginger and pepper. Add steak, turning to coat. Cover; marinate in refrigerator several hours or overnight. Grill or broil about 6 inches from heat, turning once, 25 to 30 minutes or until desired doneness. To serve, slice diagonally across grain. *Makes 6 to 8 servings*

HOLIDAY BEEF TIP ROAST

1 (3½- to 5-pound) beef tip roast
1 tablespoon minced fresh ginger
1 large clove garlic, minced
½ teaspoon pepper

Preheat oven to 325°F. Combine ginger, garlic and pepper; rub evenly over surface of beef tip roast. Place roast, fat side up, on rack in open roasting pan. Insert meat thermometer so bulb is centered in thickest part of roast. *Do not add water. Do not cover.*

Roast to desired degree of doneness, allowing 35 to 40 minutes per pound.

Remove roast from oven when meat thermometer registers 155°F (medium). Let roast stand 15 to 20 minutes in warm place before carving.
Makes 3 to 4 servings per pound

Favorite recipe from **National Live Stock & Meat Board**

SPICY CHINESE TORTILLAS

2 tablespoons soy sauce
4 teaspoons sugar
1 tablespoon catsup
1 tablespoon Worcestershire sauce
4 cloves garlic, minced
¼ teaspoon crushed red pepper*
½ pound lean beef, cut into thin strips
1 teaspoon vegetable oil
3 cups thinly sliced green cabbage
2 carrots, peeled and sliced
1 cup well-drained, thawed frozen spinach
2 green onions, sliced
12 tortillas, warmed

In small bowl mix soy sauce, sugar, catsup and Worcestershire sauce; set aside. In large skillet sauté garlic, red pepper and beef in oil 5 minutes. Add cabbage, carrots, spinach, onions and reserved soy sauce mixture. Cook covered until vegetables are tender, about 10 minutes. Divide a quarter of the mixture among three tortillas; wrap. Repeat with remaining mixture and tortillas. *Makes 4 servings*

*This is a spicy dish. If less spice is desired, reduce or eliminate the crushed red pepper.

Favorite recipe from **The Sugar Association, Inc.**

SPICY–SWEET BRISKET

4 to 5 pounds beef brisket, well trimmed
3 carrots, cut into 2-inch pieces
3 onions, thinly sliced
1 pound fresh whole mushrooms
1 rib celery, cut into 2-inch pieces
1 (26-ounce) jar NEWMAN'S OWN®
Diavolo Sauce
½ cup water
½ cup packed brown sugar
1 tablespoon garlic powder
½ teaspoon ground black pepper

Heat oven to 350°F. Brown meat in large ungreased skillet. Remove to large Dutch oven. Add vegetables to meat. In separate bowl, combine diavolo sauce, water and brown sugar; pour over meat. Sprinkle with garlic powder and black pepper.

Cover tightly and bake 3 hours. Remove cover; bake 30 minutes more or until meat is fork-tender and slightly browned. Refrigerate meat and sauce mixture overnight to allow flavors to blend. Cut meat in thin slices across the grain. Reheat meat slices and sauce mixture in covered skillet over medium-low heat.

Makes 12 servings

OVERNIGHT CORNBREAD CASSEROLE

1 package (8 ounces) cornbread stuffing mix (about 3½ cups)
2 cups frozen mixed vegetables (any mixture), slightly thawed
1½ cups (about 8 ounces) cubed cooked ham
3 eggs, lightly beaten
2 cups milk
¼ teaspoon salt
¼ teaspoon ground black pepper
½ cup shredded Cheddar cheese

In a 12×8×2-inch microwavable baking dish, stir together stuffing mix, vegetables and ham. In a medium bowl combine eggs, milk, salt and black pepper. Pour over cornbread mixture. Cover with plastic wrap; refrigerate overnight or at least 5 hours. Remove plastic wrap; cover with waxed paper. Microwave on HIGH (100% power) for 6 minutes; rotate ¼ turn. Microwave on MEDIUM-HIGH (80% power) until a knife inserted 1 inch from the center comes out clean, 7 to 9 minutes. Sprinkle with cheese. Let stand, covered, for 10 minutes. Stir gently before serving. *Makes 4 to 6 servings*

Favorite recipe from **National Dairy Board**

Overnight Cornbread Casserole

CROWN PORK ROAST WITH CRANBERRY STUFFING

1 (5- to 6-pound) pork rib crown roast
    (14 to 16 ribs)
1 cup chopped celery
1 cup chopped onion
½ cup margarine or butter
1 (16-ounce) can whole berry cranberry
    sauce
2 teaspoons WYLER'S® or STEERO®
    Chicken-Flavor Instant Bouillon *or*
    2 Chicken-Flavor Bouillon Cubes
1 (16-ounce) package herb-seasoned
    stuffing mix
1 cup chopped pecans
2 cups water

Place roast, rib ends down, in shallow roasting pan. Roast in preheated 325°F oven for 2½ hours. Meanwhile, in large skillet, cook and stir celery and onion in margarine until tender. In small saucepan, cook and stir cranberry sauce and bouillon until bouillon dissolves. In large bowl, combine all remaining ingredients; add celery and cranberry mixtures. Mix well. Remove roast from oven and turn rib ends up. Cover bone tips with foil to prevent overbrowning. Spoon stuffing into center of roast. Place any remaining stuffing in greased baking dish. Roast pork 45 to 60 minutes longer or until meat thermometer registers 160° to 170°F. Bake remaining stuffing, covered, during last 30 minutes of roasting time or until hot. Refrigerate leftovers.   *Makes 12 servings*

PORK CHOPS WITH SHALLOT STUFFING

6 tablespoons olive oil, divided
1½ cups minced shallots (about 1 pound)*
1 rounded tablespoon dried oregano
    leaves *or* 4 tablespoons chopped
    fresh oregano
1 cup white wine or chicken broth
2 cups (8 ounces) shredded GJETOST
    Cheese
8 (¾- to 1-inch-thick) loin pork chops
    with bone, pockets slit for stuffing
    (about 3½ to 4 pounds)
¼ cup flour

In 2 tablespoons olive oil, cook shallots and oregano, stirring until shallots are softened. Add wine and cook 5 minutes or until liquid is reduced by half.

Remove from heat and stir in cheese. Stuff mixture into pockets of pork chops, dividing mixture evenly. Secure with wooden picks, if desired. Dredge chops lightly in flour.

Heat 2 tablespoons oil in each of 2 large, heavy skillets. Cook chops over medium-high heat 4 minutes on first side. Reduce heat to medium. Turn chops and cook second side 6 minutes or until done. If stuffing comes out of chop, tuck back in with spatula.

Makes 8 servings

*Mincing may be done in food processor. Pulse on and off to achieve a coarse texture, not a purée.

SERVING SUGGESTION: Serve with noodles or brown rice, green beans and crusty rolls.

*Favorite recipe from **Norseland, Inc.***

Crown Pork Roast with Cranberry Stuffing

Creamy Ham and Noodle Dinner

CREAMY HAM AND NOODLE DINNER

¼ cup all-purpose flour
4 cups milk
1½ teaspoons dried dill weed, crushed
1½ teaspoons Dijon-style mustard
2 tablespoons butter
1 cup diced carrots
1 teaspoon minced garlic
1 pound ham, cubed*
1 package (16 ounces) wide egg noodles,
    cooked according to package
    directions
1 package (10 ounces) frozen green peas,
    thawed

In a small bowl combine flour and a small amount of milk until smooth. Add remaining milk, dill and mustard; set aside. In a large saucepan over medium heat melt butter. Add carrots and garlic; cook, stirring occasionally until crisp-tender. Stir in reserved milk mixture;

bring to a boil, stirring constantly, until mixture thickens. Cook and stir 1 minute. Stir in ham, noodles and peas. Cook and stir until heated through. *Makes 8 servings*

*Purchase unsliced ham at the deli counter.

*Favorite recipe from **National Dairy Board***

MEDITERRANEAN BLACK BEAN & RICE SKILLET

2 tablespoons olive oil
1 pound lean boneless pork or chicken,
    cubed
1 cup chopped onion
4 cloves garlic, minced
1 cup chopped fresh or canned tomatoes
½ cup dry red wine
⅓ cup chopped prunes or chopped raisins
3 cups water
1 (8-ounce) package FARMHOUSE®
    Spanish Black Beans & Rice
1 teaspoon dried thyme leaves
⅛ teaspoon cayenne pepper
⅓ cup chopped red bell pepper
1 cup frozen peas, thawed
2 tablespoons chopped fresh parsley
1 tablespoon lime or lemon juice
    Salt and black pepper to taste

In large skillet, heat olive oil. Brown meat in oil until no longer pink. Add onion and garlic; sauté until tender. Add tomatoes, wine and prunes. Bring to a boil. Cook until liquid has evaporated. Add water; bring to a boil. Add beans & rice, contents of seasoning packet, thyme leaves and cayenne pepper. Reduce heat; cover and simmer 20 minutes. Add red bell pepper; cook 5 minutes longer or until liquid is absorbed. Stir in peas, parsley and lime juice. Season to taste with salt and black pepper. *Makes approximately 6 servings*

HONEY GLAZED HAM

   2 (8-ounce) fully-cooked ham steaks
   ¼ cup honey
   3 tablespoons water
   1½ teaspoons dry mustard
   ½ teaspoon ground ginger
   ¼ teaspoon ground cloves

Pan-fry or broil ham steaks until lightly browned and thoroughly heated. Remove ham from skillet or broiler pan. Combine honey, water and spices; add to pan drippings and bring to a boil. Simmer 1 to 2 minutes. Brush over ham. Serve ham with remaining sauce.

Makes 4 servings

Favorite recipe from **National Honey Board**

PORK TENDERLOIN DIANE

   1 pound pork tenderloin, cut into 8
      crosswise pieces
   2 teaspoons lemon pepper
   2 tablespoons butter
   2 tablespoons lemon juice
   1 tablespoon Worcestershire sauce
   1 teaspoon Dijon-style mustard
   1 tablespoon minced fresh parsley or
      chives

Pound each tenderloin slice with meat mallet to 1-inch thickness; sprinkle with lemon pepper. Heat butter in heavy skillet; cook tenderloin medallions 3 to 4 minutes on each side or until fork-tender. Remove medallions to serving platter; keep warm. Add lemon juice, Worcestershire sauce and mustard to pan juices in skillet. Cook until heated through. Pour sauce over medallions and sprinkle with parsley; serve. *Makes 4 servings*

Favorite recipe from **National Pork Producers Council**

Honey Glazed Ham

GLAZED ROAST PORK LOIN WITH CRANBERRY STUFFING

1¼ cups chopped fresh or partially thawed
    frozen cranberries
2 teaspoons sugar
½ cup butter or margarine
1 cup chopped onion
1 package (8 ounces) herb-seasoned
    stuffing mix
1 cup chicken broth
½ cup peeled and diced orange
1 egg, beaten
½ teaspoon grated orange peel
1 (2½- to 3-pound) boneless center cut
    loin pork roast
¼ cup currant jelly
1 tablespoon cranberry liqueur, cassis or
    cranberry juice

Toss cranberries with sugar in small bowl; set aside. Melt butter in saucepan over medium heat until foamy. Add onion; cook and stir until tender. Remove from heat. Combine stuffing mix, broth, orange, egg and orange peel. Add cranberry mixture and onion; toss lightly.

Preheat oven to 325°F. To butterfly roast, cut lengthwise down roast almost to, but not through bottom. Open like a book. Cover roast with plastic wrap; pound with flat side of meat mallet. Remove plastic wrap; spread roast with stuffing. Tie roast with cotton string at 2-inch intervals. Place leftover stuffing in covered casserole; bake with roast during last 45 minutes of cooking time. Place roast on meat rack in foil-lined roasting pan. Insert meat thermometer in center of stuffing. Roast 30 minutes per pound until temperature registers 155°F.

Combine jelly and liqueur. Brush half of mixture over roast after first 45 minutes in oven. Roast 30 minutes more; brush with remaining jelly mixture. Transfer roast to cutting board; tent with foil. Let stand 10 to 15 minutes. Carve roast crosswise; serve with stuffing.

Makes 8 to 10 servings

PEACH–GLAZED VIRGINIA HAM

GLAZED HAM
1 (8-pound) smoked Virginia ham
½ cup peach preserves
1 tablespoon coarse-grained mustard
¾ teaspoon TABASCO® pepper sauce
⅛ teaspoon ground cloves
PEACH–CORN PICCALILLI
3 large ripe peaches
1 tablespoon vegetable oil
1 medium red bell pepper, diced
¼ cup sliced green onions
1 (17-ounce) can corn, drained
2 tablespoons brown sugar
2 tablespoons cider vinegar
1 teaspoon TABASCO® pepper sauce
¼ teaspoon salt

Heat oven to 325°F. Remove skin from ham; trim off any excess fat. Score fat ¼ inch deep in 1-inch diamonds. Place ham, fat side up, in roasting pan. Insert meat thermometer into thickest part of ham, not touching the bone. Bake 1½ hours until thermometer reaches 135°F.

For glaze, in bowl, mix peach preserves, mustard, TABASCO sauce and cloves. Remove ham from oven, maintaining oven temperature; brush with glaze. Bake 20 minutes or until the temperature reaches 160°F.

Meanwhile, prepare Peach-Corn Piccalilli. Cut peaches in half and remove pits. Chop two of the peach halves; set aside. In 2-quart saucepan heat oil over medium heat. Add red pepper and green onions. Cook 3 minutes, stirring frequently. Add corn, brown sugar, vinegar, TABASCO sauce and salt. Heat to boiling; stir in chopped peaches. Reduce heat to low; cover and simmer 5 minutes or until peaches are just tender.

To serve, arrange ham on a large platter. Fill remaining peach halves with Peach-Corn Piccalilli and arrange around ham on platter.

Makes 8 to 12 servings

Glazed Roast Pork Loin with Cranberry Stuffing

BAKED HAM WITH SWEET AND SPICY GLAZE

**1 (8-pound) bone-in smoked half ham
Sweet and Spicy Glaze (recipe follows)**

Preheat oven to 325°F. Place ham, fat side up, on rack in roasting pan. Insert meat thermometer with bulb in thickest part away from fat or bone. Roast ham in oven about 3 hours.

Prepare Sweet and Spicy Glaze. Remove ham from oven; do not turn oven off. Generously brush glaze over ham; return to oven 30 minutes longer or until meat thermometer registers internal temperature of 160°F. Remove ham from oven and brush with glaze. Let ham stand about 20 minutes before slicing.

Makes 8 to 10 servings

SWEET AND SPICY GLAZE

**¾ cup packed brown sugar
⅓ cup cider vinegar
¼ cup golden raisins
1 can (8¾ ounces) sliced peaches in heavy syrup, drained, chopped, syrup reserved
1 tablespoon cornstarch
¼ cup orange juice
1 can (8¼ ounces) crushed pineapple in syrup, undrained
1 tablespoon grated orange peel
1 clove garlic, crushed
½ teaspoon crushed red pepper flakes
½ teaspoon grated fresh ginger**

Combine brown sugar, vinegar, raisins and peach syrup in medium saucepan. Bring to a boil over high heat; reduce to low and simmer 8 to 10 minutes. In small bowl, dissolve cornstarch in orange juice; add to brown sugar mixture. Add remaining ingredients; mix well. Cook over medium heat, stirring constantly, until mixture boils and thickens. Remove from heat.

Makes about 2 cups

HOPPING JOHN

**1 tablespoon vegetable oil
3 slices bacon, chopped
1 cup ¼-inch smoked ham cubes
½ cup finely chopped onion
1 tablespoon finely minced garlic
½ cup diced red bell pepper
1 tablespoon chopped fresh parsley
1 cup FARMHOUSE® Natural Long Grain White Rice
2 cups canned chicken broth
1½ teaspoons dried thyme leaves
½ teaspoon rubbed sage
½ teaspoon salt
¼ teaspoon ground red pepper
⅛ teaspoon ground black pepper
1 bay leaf
1 (15-ounce) can black eyed peas, drained**

Heat oil in medium saucepan. Add bacon; cook over medium heat until bacon is crisp. Add ham, onion and garlic; sauté until onion is softened and translucent. Add bell pepper and parsley; sauté 1 minute. Add rice; stir to coat well. Add broth, thyme, sage, salt, ground red pepper, black pepper and bay leaf. Bring to a boil. Reduce heat; cover and simmer 20 to 25 minutes or until liquid is absorbed. Stir in black eyed peas. Remove bay leaf.

Makes approximately 6 (1-cup) servings

Baked Ham with Sweet and Spicy Glaze

Roasted Pork with Apricots and Sweet Spices

ROASTED PORK WITH APRICOTS AND SWEET SPICES

1 cup plus 2 tablespoons low-sodium chicken broth, divided
1 tablespoon ground cinnamon
½ teaspoon ground cloves
⅛ teaspoon ground cumin
1½ pounds boneless pork loin, rolled and tied
2 teaspoons olive oil, divided
¼ cup chopped onion
1 teaspoon minced garlic
1 cup orange juice
¼ cup water
1 tablespoon Worcestershire sauce
½ cup julienned California dried apricot halves
¼ cup sliced almonds, toasted
1 teaspoon grated orange peel
2 tablespoons chopped cilantro
Salt and pepper to taste

Combine 2 tablespoons chicken broth with cinnamon, cloves and cumin. Rub marinade mixture over pork; cover and refrigerate 4 hours or overnight. (Reserve any remaining marinade mixture.)

Preheat oven to 350°F. Heat 1 teaspoon oil in skillet over high heat; brown pork on all sides. Remove pork to roasting pan. Roast in preheated oven until internal temperature of pork reaches 155°F, about 40 minutes. Transfer pork to cutting board; tent with foil. Let stand 10 minutes.

In same skillet, over medium heat, heat remaining 1 teaspoon oil; cook and stir onion and garlic until tender. Add reserved marinade mixture, juice, remaining 1 cup chicken broth, water and Worcestershire sauce. Bring to a boil; reduce heat and simmer 10 minutes. Add apricots; simmer 5 minutes. Stir in almonds and orange peel; remove from heat. Stir in cilantro; season with salt and pepper. Serve apricot mixture over sliced, roasted pork.

Makes 6 servings

*Favorite recipe from **California Apricot Advisory Board***

STRAWBERRY GLAZED HAM

1 (5- to 7-pound) fully-cooked smoked butt or shank-half ham
1½ cups SMUCKER'S® Simply Fruit Strawberry
⅓ cup prepared mustard
¼ cup lemon juice

Trim skin from ham. With sharp knife, score fat surface, making uniform diagonal cuts about ⅛ inch deep and ¾ inch apart. Place ham, fat side up, on a rack in a shallow roasting pan; bake in 325°F oven 1¾ to 2½ hours. Meanwhile, in a small saucepan, combine fruit spread, mustard and lemon juice; cook over low heat, stirring, until blended. During last 20 minutes of baking time, brush ham with about ½ cup strawberry glaze. Let ham stand 10 minutes for easier slicing. Heat remaining glaze and serve as a sauce for the ham.

Makes 8 to 10 servings

APRICOT AND NUT GLAZED HAM

1 (3- to 4-pound) boneless fully cooked
  smoked ham half
½ cup plus 1 teaspoon water
1 teaspoon dry mustard
½ cup apricot preserves
¼ cup chopped pecans
¼ teaspoon ground cloves
  Canned apricot halves and Boston
  lettuce leaves, for garnish

Do not preheat oven. Place smoked ham half (straight from refrigerator) on rack in shallow roasting pan. Add ½ cup water. Insert meat thermometer into thickest part of ham. Cover pan tightly with aluminum foil, leaving thermometer dial exposed. Place in 325°F oven and roast until thermometer registers 135°F, about 19 to 23 minutes per pound.

Meanwhile, stir mustard into 1 teaspoon water; combine with apricot preserves, pecans and cloves. Remove aluminum foil and spread glaze over ham 15 minutes before end of roasting time. When finished roasting, allow ham to stand, covered, about 10 minutes or until thermometer registers 140°F. Garnish with apricot halves and lettuce leaves, if desired.
  Makes 4 to 5 (3-ounce) servings per pound

PREP TIME: 10 minutes
COOK TIME: 1 to 1½ hours

Favorite recipe from **National Live Stock & Meat Board**

JONES HAM QUICHE

1 cup short strips JONES® Ham
⅓ cup short red bell pepper strips
⅓ cup chopped asparagus
⅓ cup sliced leek
1 cup (4 ounces) shredded Swiss cheese
2 tablespoons all-purpose flour
3 eggs, slightly beaten
2⅓ cups half-and-half or whipping cream
1 (9-inch) pie crust, unbaked

Combine ham, pepper, asparagus, leek, cheese and flour; toss lightly. Gently mix eggs and half-and-half. Add ham mixture to egg mixture, mixing lightly.

Pour mixture into pastry-lined 9-inch quiche dish or pie pan. Bake 10 minutes at 425°F; reduce heat to 325°F. Continue baking 20 minutes or until done.   *Makes 6 to 8 servings*

Apricot and Nut Glazed Ham

HONEY SESAME TENDERLOIN

1 pound whole pork tenderloin
½ cup soy sauce
2 cloves garlic, minced
1 tablespoon grated fresh ginger
1 tablespoon sesame oil
¼ cup honey
2 tablespoons packed brown sugar
4 tablespoons sesame seeds

Combine soy sauce, garlic, ginger and sesame oil. Place tenderloin in resealable plastic food storage bag; pour in soy sauce mixture. Marinate 2 hours or overnight in refrigerator. Preheat oven to 375°F. Remove pork from marinade; pat dry with paper towel. Mix honey and brown sugar on plate. Place sesame seeds on another plate. Roll pork in honey mixture; roll in sesame seeds. Roast in shallow pan 20 to 30 minutes or until meat thermometer inserted in thickest part registers 160°F. Serve immediately. *Makes 4 servings*

*Favorite recipe from **National Pork Producers Council***

FESTIVE HAM GLAZE

½ cup apricot or peach preserves
½ cup light or dark corn syrup
2 tablespoons packed brown sugar
¼ teaspoon ground ginger

Combine all ingredients in medium saucepan. Cook over low heat until melted and smooth, stirring constantly. Brush on ham frequently during last 30 minutes of cooking.
Makes enough glaze for 5- to 7-pound ham

Honey Sesame Tenderloin

Festive Ham Glaze

HOLIDAY BAKED HAM

    1 bone-in smoked ham (8½ pounds)
    1 can (20 ounces) DOLE® Sliced
        Pineapple in Syrup or Juice
    1 cup apricot preserves
    1 teaspoon dry mustard
   ½ teaspoon ground allspice
       Whole cloves
       Maraschino cherries

• Preheat oven to 325°F. Remove rind from ham. Place ham on rack in open roasting pan, fat side up. Insert meat thermometer with bulb in thickest part away from fat or bone. Roast ham in oven about 3 hours.

• Drain pineapple; reserve syrup. In small saucepan, combine syrup, preserves, mustard and allspice. Bring to boil; continue boiling, stirring occasionally, 10 minutes. Remove ham from oven, but keep oven hot. Stud ham with cloves; brush with glaze. Using wooden picks, secure pineapple and cherries to ham. Brush again with glaze. Return ham to oven. Roast 30 minutes longer or until thermometer registers 160°F (about 25 minutes per pound total cooking time). Brush with glaze 15 minutes before done. Let ham stand 20 minutes before slicing. *Makes 8 to 10 servings*

HOLIDAY PORK ROAST

    1 tablespoon minced fresh ginger
    2 cloves garlic, minced
    1 teaspoon dried sage leaves, crushed
   ¼ teaspoon salt
    1 (5- to 7-pound) pork loin roast
   ⅓ cup apple jelly
   ½ teaspoon TABASCO® pepper sauce
    2 medium carrots, sliced
    2 medium onions, sliced
  1¾ cups water, divided
    1 teaspoon browning and seasoning
       sauce

Preheat oven to 325°F. Combine ginger, garlic, sage and salt; rub over pork. Place in shallow roasting pan. Roast pork 1½ hours. Remove from oven; score meat in diamond pattern.

Combine jelly and TABASCO sauce; spread generously over roast. Arrange carrots and onions around meat; add 1 cup water. Roast 1 hour until meat thermometer registers 170°F. Remove roast to serving platter; keep warm.

Skim fat from drippings in pan; discard fat. Place vegetables and drippings in food processor or blender; process until puréed. Return purée to roasting pan. Stir in remaining ¾ cup water and browning sauce; heat. Serve sauce with roast. *Makes 6 to 8 servings*

PORK CHOPS WITH APPLES AND BOURBON

4 boneless pork loin chops, cut 1 inch thick, fat trimmed
1 clove garlic, halved lengthwise
Pinch dried sage
2 tablespoons margarine or butter
¼ teaspoon TABASCO® pepper sauce
1 teaspoon fresh lemon juice
½ cup chopped onion
1 medium apple (preferably Granny Smith), peeled, cored and diced
⅓ cup bourbon or apple cider

Pat pork chops dry with paper towel. Rub both sides of chops with cut sides of garlic. Sprinkle with sage. In large skillet over medium-high heat, combine margarine and TABASCO sauce; heat until mixture sizzles. Add chops; cook 12 to 14 minutes, turning once, or until chops are golden brown on both sides and cooked through. Remove from pan; sprinkle with lemon juice and keep warm.

Add onion to skillet; cook and stir over medium heat 1 minute. Stir in apple; cook 1 minute longer. Add bourbon; cook, stirring, 1 minute. Spoon sauce over pork chops; serve immediately. *Makes 4 servings*

SPICY SICHUAN PORK STEW

2 pounds boneless pork shoulder (Boston butt)
¼ cup all-purpose flour
2 tablespoons vegetable oil
1¾ cups water, divided
¼ cup KIKKOMAN® Soy Sauce
3 tablespoons dry sherry
2 cloves garlic, pressed
1 teaspoon minced fresh ginger root
½ teaspoon crushed red pepper
¼ teaspoon fennel seed, crushed
8 green onions and tops, cut into 1-inch lengths, separating whites from tops
2 large carrots, cut into chunks
Hot cooked rice

Cut pork into 1-inch cubes. Coat in flour; reserve 2 tablespoons remaining flour. Heat oil in Dutch oven or large pan over medium-high heat; brown pork on all sides in hot oil. Add 1½ cups water, soy sauce, sherry, garlic, ginger, red pepper, fennel and white parts of green onions. Cover pan; bring to boil. Reduce heat and simmer 30 minutes. Add carrots; simmer, covered, 30 minutes longer, or until pork and carrots are tender. Meanwhile, combine reserved flour and remaining ¼ cup water; set aside. Stir green onion tops into pork mixture; simmer 1 minute. Add flour mixture; bring to boil. Cook and stir until mixture is slightly thickened. Serve over rice.

Makes 6 servings

Spicy Sichuan Pork Stew

142

GLAZED PORK TENDERLOIN

**2 whole well-trimmed pork tenderloins
(about 1½ pounds total)**
**½ cup currant jelly or canned jellied
cranberry sauce**
**1 tablespoon bottled grated horseradish,
drained**
½ cup chicken broth
**¼ cup Rhine or other sweet white wine
Salt and pepper to taste (optional)**

Preheat oven to 325°F. Place tenderloins on meat rack in shallow roasting pan. Combine jelly and horseradish in microwavable dish or small saucepan. Heat at HIGH 1 minute or over low heat on rangetop until jelly is melted; stir well. Brush half of mixture over tenderloins. Roast 30 minutes; turn tenderloins over. Brush with remaining jelly mixture. Continue to roast 30 to 40 minutes depending on thickness of tenderloins or until meat thermometer registers 160°F.*

Transfer tenderloins to cutting board; tent with foil. Let stand 10 minutes. Remove meat rack from roasting pan. Pour broth and wine into pan. Place over burners; cook over medium-high heat, stirring frequently and scraping up any browned bits, 4 to 5 minutes or until sauce is reduced to ½ cup. Strain sauce; season to taste with salt and pepper. Carve tenderloins into thin slices. Serve with sauce.

Makes 6 servings

*The most accurate way to measure the internal temperature of pork tenderloin is with an instant-read thermometer. Do not leave the thermometer in the tenderloin during roasting since it is not ovenproof.

Glazed Pork Tenderloin

FRUITED WINTER PORK CHOPS

  1 medium DOLE® Fresh Pineapple
  4 (1-inch-thick) pork chops, trimmed
 16 DOLE® Pitted Prunes
    Salt and pepper to taste
  1 teaspoon vegetable oil
  ⅓ cup minced onion
    Orange Herb Sauce (recipe follows)
  1 DOLE® Orange, peeled and sliced
  4 DOLE® Green Onions, sliced

• Twist crown from pineapple. Cut pineapple in half lengthwise. Refrigerate half for another use. Cut fruit from shell, then cut crosswise into slices. Cut fruit into large chunks; set aside.

• Cut slit in side of each pork chop. Stuff each with 2 prunes. Cut remaining prunes into thirds. Season pork chops with salt and pepper. In large nonstick skillet, brown chops in oil. Add cut prunes and onion. Cover, reduce heat and cook 8 minutes. Add Orange Herb Sauce. Cook, stirring, until sauce boils and thickens. Add reserved pineapple, orange and green onions. Heat through.   *Makes 4 servings*

ORANGE HERB SAUCE
  ½ cup frozen DOLE® Pineapple Orange
       Juice concentrate, thawed
  ¼ cup water
  2 tablespoons white wine vinegar
  1 tablespoon grated orange peel
  1 teaspoon *each* dried basil and mint
       leaves
  1 teaspoon chili powder
  1 teaspoon cornstarch
  2 large cloves garlic, pressed

Combine all ingredients. Stir until blended.
                    Makes about 1 cup

Fruited Winter Pork Chop

PORK CHOPS WITH ALMOND PLUM SAUCE

1 cup water
6 tablespoons lemon juice
6 tablespoons soy sauce
4 cloves garlic, chopped finely
1½ teaspoons cornstarch
½ teaspoon white pepper
¼ teaspoon salt
    Pinch cayenne
4 pork chops, about 1 inch thick
1 tablespoon vegetable oil
⅔ cup plum jam
¼ cup BLUE DIAMOND® Sliced Natural
    Almonds, lightly toasted
¼ cup sliced green onion tops, for
    garnish

Combine first 8 ingredients. Marinate pork chops in mixture in refrigerator 1 hour or overnight. Remove pork chops, reserving marinade. Sauté pork chops in oil over high heat 2 to 3 minutes on each side or until golden brown. Remove and reserve. Add marinade and plum jam to pan. Cook over medium heat until mixture thickens and coats the back of a spoon, about 5 minutes. Return pork chops to pan in single layer. Simmer, covered, 5 to 7 minutes. Remove cover and continue cooking 3 to 4 minutes or until pork chops are just cooked through and tender. To serve, remove chops to serving plate; sprinkle 1 tablespoon almonds over each chop. Pour sauce over and sprinkle each chop with 1 tablespoon sliced green onion tops.

Makes 4 servings

LEMON–GINGER–PRUNE–VEAL ROLL

1 cup chopped prunes
1 tablespoon finely shredded lemon peel
1 tablespoon grated fresh ginger
1 (4- to 4½-pound) boneless veal breast
½ teaspoon salt
2 teaspoons vegetable oil
⅔ cup Madeira wine
⅓ cup water
    Lemon wedges

In small bowl, combine prunes, lemon peel and ginger. Unroll boneless veal breast; trim fat. Sprinkle evenly with salt. Distribute prune mixture evenly over surface. Roll up veal breast; tie securely with string. Heat oil in Dutch oven just large enough to hold veal. Brown veal on all sides. Drain excess fat if necessary. Add Madeira and water to pan; cover tightly. Cook in 325°F oven until tender, 2 to 2½ hours. Transfer veal to warm platter; let stand. Skim fat from pan juices. Place Dutch oven over direct heat. Bring pan juices to a boil and cook until reduced by half. Slice veal roll; discard strings. Spoon sauce over each serving. Garnish with lemon wedges.

Makes 10 servings

Favorite recipe from **National Live Stock & Meat Board**

Pork Chops with Almond Plum Sauce

Veal in Gingered Sweet Bell Pepper Sauce

VEAL IN GINGERED SWEET BELL PEPPER SAUCE

1 teaspoon olive oil
¾ pound veal cutlets, thinly sliced
½ cup skim milk
1 tablespoon finely chopped fresh tarragon
2 teaspoons crushed capers
1 jar (7 ounces) roasted red peppers, drained
1 tablespoon lemon juice
½ teaspoon grated fresh ginger
½ teaspoon ground black pepper
Capers and fresh tarragon for garnish (optional)

Heat oil in medium saucepan over high heat. Add veal; lightly brown both sides. Reduce heat to medium. Add milk, chopped tarragon and crushed capers. Cook, uncovered, 5 minutes or until veal is fork-tender and milk evaporates.

Place roasted peppers, lemon juice, ginger and black pepper in food processor or blender; process until smooth. Set aside.

Remove veal from pan with slotted spoon; place in serving dish. Spoon roasted pepper sauce over veal. Garnish with capers and fresh tarragon, if desired. *Makes 4 servings*

VEAL RIB ROAST WITH CRANBERRY-PORT SAUCE

   1 (4- to 5-pound) veal rib roast (cap removed)
1¼ cups fresh bread crumbs
   3 tablespoons minced fresh parsley
   2 tablespoons butter, melted
1¼ teaspoons dried marjoram leaves, crushed
   2 medium cloves garlic, minced
   2 tablespoons Dijon-style mustard
   ⅓ cup ruby port wine
   1 can (16 ounces) whole-berry cranberry sauce

Place veal rib roast, rib ends down, in shallow roasting pan. Insert meat thermometer so bulb is centered in thickest part, not touching bone or fat. *Do not add water; do not cover.*

Roast until meat thermometer registers 150°F for medium. Allow approximately 25 to 27 minutes per pound for medium. Approximately 30 minutes before end of cooking time, combine bread crumbs, parsley, butter, marjoram and garlic; set aside.

Remove roast from oven. Spread top surface evenly with mustard. Cover top of roast with crumb mixture, patting firmly into place. Return roast to oven; roast until meat thermometer registers 155°F, about 25 minutes. *Do not overcook.* Remove roast from roasting pan; let stand 15 minutes in warm place before carving.

Meanwhile, skim and discard fat from drippings, if necessary. Add wine to drippings in roasting pan, stirring to scrape browned bits from bottom. Stir in cranberry sauce. On rangetop, cook cranberry-port mixture over medium-high heat, stirring frequently, until mixture is thickened, about 10 minutes.

Trim excess fat and remove backbone from roast. Carve roast; serve with cranberry-port sauce. *Makes 8 to 10 servings*

NOTE: Ask meat retailer to loosen the chine, or backbone, by sawing across the rib bones. When roasting is finished, the backbone can be removed easily by running the carving knife along the edge of the roast before the meat is placed on the platter to be carved.

PREP TIME: 15 minutes
COOK TIME: 1 hour 45 minutes to 2 hours 15 minutes

*Favorite recipe from **National Live Stock & Meat Board***

VEAL FRICASSEE

   3 pounds lean boneless veal, cut into 1½-inch cubes
   2 tablespoons oil
   2 teaspoons paprika
   1 teaspoon salt
   ¼ teaspoon pepper
   2 cups water
   ½ pound mushrooms, quartered
   2 cups thickly sliced celery
   3 tablespoons all-purpose flour
   ½ cup light cream or half-and-half
   1 cup shredded GJETOST Cheese
   ¼ cup chopped parsley
   Hot cooked rice

In 12-inch skillet or Dutch oven, brown veal in oil. Add paprika, salt, pepper and water. Cover and simmer 1 hour. Add vegetables and simmer 15 minutes, stirring occasionally.

Blend flour and cream. Stir into sauce and cook, stirring, until thickened and smooth. Gradually stir in cheese. Add parsley; stir gently to combine. Serve over rice.
Makes 6 to 8 servings

*Favorite recipe from **Norseland, Inc.***

ROAST LEG OF LAMB

3 tablespoons coarse-grained mustard
2 cloves garlic, minced*
1½ teaspoons dried rosemary leaves,
    crushed
½ teaspoon freshly ground black pepper
1 leg of lamb, well trimmed, boned,
    rolled and tied (about 4 pounds)
    Mint jelly (optional)

Preheat oven to 400°F. Combine mustard, garlic, rosemary and pepper. Rub mustard mixture over surface of lamb.** Place roast on meat rack in shallow, foil-lined roasting pan. Insert meat thermometer in thickest part of roast. Roast 15 minutes. *Reduce oven temperature to 325°F; roast 20 minutes per pound until roast registers 150°F for medium.*

Transfer roast to cutting board; tent with foil. Let stand 10 minutes before carving. Temperature will continue to rise 5° to 10°F during stand time.

Cut strings; discard. Carve roast into thin slices; serve with mint jelly, if desired.
                    Makes 6 to 8 servings

*For more intense garlic flavor inside the meat, cut garlic into slivers. Cut small pockets at random intervals throughout roast with tip of sharp knife; insert garlic slivers.

**At this point lamb may be covered and refrigerated up to 24 hours before roasting.

HORSERADISH–HERB–CRUSTED LEG OF LAMB

1 (6-pound) leg of lamb
2 cups fresh white bread crumbs
⅓ cup chopped parsley
3 cloves garlic, minced
1½ teaspoons dried rosemary leaves
1 teaspoon dried thyme leaves
½ cup BLUE BONNET® Spread, melted
⅓ cup GREY POUPON® Specialty
    Mustard: Horseradish

Preheat oven to 350°F. Remove fat from lamb with sharp knife. Place on rack in roasting pan. Bake 1 hour. Remove from oven; cool 10 to 15 minutes.

Combine crumbs, parsley, garlic, rosemary and thyme; blend in spread. Spread top and sides of lamb with mustard. Press crumb mixture evenly and firmly into mustard. Lightly cover with foil. Bake 30 minutes. Remove foil; bake 30 to 45 minutes more or until meat thermometer registers internal temperature of 140° to 160°F, depending on desired doneness. Remove from oven and let stand 10 minutes before slicing.   *Makes 10 servings*

Roast Leg of Lamb

LEG OF LAMB WITH APRICOT STUFFING

1 (6-ounce) package dried apricots, snipped
¼ cup apple juice
¼ cup wild rice, rinsed and drained
1½ cups chicken broth
½ cup long-grain rice
¼ cup chutney
¼ cup sliced green onions
2 teaspoons dried basil leaves
½ teaspoon lemon pepper
3 to 3½ pounds American leg of lamb, shank half, boned and butterflied
¼ teaspoon salt
¼ teaspoon ground black pepper

In bowl, combine apricots and apple juice; cover and let stand 20 minutes, stirring occasionally. In saucepan, combine wild rice and broth. Bring to a boil; reduce heat. Cover and simmer 40 minutes. Add long-grain rice. Cover and simmer 15 minutes more. Remove from heat. Let stand, covered, 5 minutes. Stir in apricot mixture, chutney (cut up any large chutney pieces), green onions, basil and lemon pepper.

Trim any fat from lamb. With boned side up, pound meat evenly with a meat mallet to rectangle measuring 20 × 4 inches. Sprinkle lightly with salt and pepper. Spread rice mixture over meat. Roll up, starting with a narrow end; tie securely. Place roast on end, spiral side up, on a rack in a shallow roasting pan. Cover exposed rice mixture with a small piece of foil. Roast at 325°F for 1¾ hours, or to medium doneness (150° to 160°F). Remove from oven. Let stand about 10 minutes. Remove strings; cut into wedges to serve.

Makes 12 servings

*Favorite recipe from **American Lamb Council***

RACK OF LAMB WITH DIJON–MUSTARD SAUCE

1 rack of lamb (3 pounds), all visible fat removed
1 cup finely chopped fresh parsley
½ cup Dijon-style mustard
½ cup soft whole wheat bread crumbs
1 tablespoon chopped fresh rosemary *or* 2 teaspoons dried rosemary
1 teaspoon minced garlic
Fresh rosemary, lemon slices and lemon peel strips (optional)

Preheat oven to 500°F. Place lamb in large baking pan. Combine parsley, mustard, bread crumbs, rosemary and garlic in small bowl. Spread evenly over top of lamb. Place in center of oven; cook 7 minutes for medium-rare. *Turn off oven but do not open door for at least 30 minutes.* Serve 2 to 3 chops on each plate, depending on size and total number of chops. Garnish with additional fresh rosemary, lemon slices and lemon peel strips, if desired.

Makes 6 servings

Rack of Lamb with Dijon-Mustard Sauce

Lamb Rib Roast Dijon

LAMB RIB ROAST DIJON

 1 (6-rib) lamb rib roast (about 1½ to
    1¾ pounds)
 1 tablespoon Dijon-style mustard
 ⅓ cup soft bread crumbs
 ½ teaspoon dried basil leaves, crushed
    Dash garlic powder
    Lemon slices (optional)
    Italian parsley (optional)

Trim fat from lamb rib roast; spread roast with mustard. Combine bread crumbs, basil and garlic powder; press mixture into mustard. Place roast, fat side up, on rack in shallow roasting pan.

Insert meat thermometer into thickest part of roast, not touching bone or fat. Do not add water. Do not cover. Roast in 375°F oven to desired degree of doneness. Allow 35 to 40 minutes for medium. Remove roast when meat thermometer registers 155°F. Cover roast with aluminum foil tent and allow to stand 15 to 20 minutes before carving. Roast will continue to rise approximately 5°F in temperature to reach 160°F for medium. Garnish with lemon and parsley, if desired. *Makes 2 servings*

*Favorite recipe from **National Live Stock & Meat Board***

PINWHEEL MEAT LOAF

½ cup milk
1½ cups crustless Italian or French bread
    cubes
1½ pounds ground beef
½ pound sweet Italian sausage, removed
    from casings and crumbled
2 eggs, slightly beaten
2 tablespoons finely chopped parsley
1 tablespoon finely chopped garlic
1 teaspoon salt
½ teaspoon pepper
2 cups water
1 tablespoon butter or margarine
1 package LIPTON® Rice & Sauce—
    Cajun-Style
2 packages (10 ounces each) frozen
    chopped spinach, thawed and
    squeezed dry

In bowl, pour milk over bread cubes; mash until bread is soaked. Combine bread mixture with ground beef, sausage, eggs, parsley, garlic, salt and pepper. Place on 12-inch square sheet of aluminum foil moistened with water. Cover with 12×14-inch sheet of waxed paper moistened with water. Using hands or rolling pin, press meat mixture into 12-inch square. Refrigerate 2 hours or until well chilled.

In medium saucepan, bring water, butter and rice & Cajun-style sauce to a boil. Continue boiling over medium heat, stirring occasionally, 10 minutes or until rice is tender. Refrigerate 2 hours or until well chilled.

Preheat oven to 350°F. Remove waxed paper from ground beef mixture. If desired, season spinach with additional salt and pepper. Spread spinach over ground beef mixture leaving 1-inch border. Spread rice evenly over spinach. Roll jelly-roll style, starting at long end and using foil as a guide, removing foil while rolling; seal edges tightly. In 13×9-inch baking pan, place meat loaf seam side down. Bake 1 hour or until done. Let stand 15 minutes before serving. Cut into 1-inch slices.

Makes about 8 servings

QUICK SHEPHERD'S PIE

1 pound lean ground beef
½ cup seasoned dry bread crumbs
½ cup finely chopped onion
1 egg, lightly beaten
2 tablespoons water
1 tablespoon Worcestershire sauce
¼ teaspoon ground black pepper
2 cups hot prepared instant mashed
    potatoes
1½ cups (8 ounces) sharp Cheddar cheese,
    cut into ¼-inch cubes
1 cup mixed frozen peas and carrots,
    cooked

Preheat oven to 400°F. In a medium bowl place beef, bread crumbs, onion, egg, water, Worcestershire sauce and black pepper; mix with hands until combined. In a 9-inch pie plate press meat mixture over bottom and up sides to the rim, forming a shell. Bake until meat is brown and firm, about 15 minutes. Remove from oven; pour off excess fat. Set shell aside. *Reduce oven temperature to 350°F.* In a medium bowl stir together potatoes, cheese and peas and carrots. Spoon into reserved meat shell. Bake until heated through and cheese begins to melt, 10 to 15 minutes.

Makes 4 to 6 servings

*Favorite recipe from **National Dairy Board***

Quick Shepherd's Pie

ZESTY ZUCCHINI LASAGNA

    1 pound ground beef
    1 package (1.5 ounces) LAWRY'S®
        Original-Style Spaghetti Sauce
        Spices & Seasonings
    1 can (6 ounces) tomato paste
 1¾ cups water
    2 tablespoons butter or margarine
    ½ teaspoon basil leaves
    ⅛ teaspoon thyme leaves
    2 cups ricotta cheese
    1 egg, slightly beaten
    4 medium zucchini, thinly sliced
        lengthwise
    1 cup shredded mozzarella cheese (about
        4 ounces)

Preheat oven to 350°F. In medium saucepan, brown ground beef until no longer pink; drain. Stir in Spaghetti Sauce Spices & Seasonings, tomato paste, water, butter, basil and thyme. Bring to a boil, then simmer uncovered 10 minutes. In small bowl, combine ricotta cheese with egg; set aside. In medium saucepan, bring 1 quart water to a boil. Add zucchini and cook 2 minutes; remove and rinse under cold running water. In 12×8-inch casserole, layer half the zucchini, ricotta mixture and meat sauce. Repeat layers. Top with mozzarella cheese and bake uncovered 30 minutes or until cheese is melted.   *Makes about 6 servings*

SAUSAGE "BRUNCH" CASSEROLE

    6 slices white bread
    2 (12 ounce) packages JONES® All-
        Natural Roll Sausage *or* 1½ pounds
        JONES® Ham, diced
    1 can (8 ounces) chopped mushrooms
    1 pound (16 ounces) Cheddar cheese,
        grated
    6 eggs
    2 cups light cream or milk

Zesty Zucchini Lasagna

Tear bread into bite-size pieces and place in 13×9-inch baking dish. Crumble sausage; cook and drain. Spread over bread. Add mushrooms and top with Cheddar cheese.

Beat eggs; add light cream. Mix well and pour over casserole. Bake uncovered at 350°F 30 to 45 minutes. *Makes 6 to 8 servings*

JONES SAUSAGE AND WILD RICE

  1 cup wild rice
  1 (12-ounce) package JONES® All-
    Natural Sausage Links
  1 medium onion, chopped
  1 rib celery, sliced
  1 (10¾-ounce) can condensed cream of
    mushroom soup
  1 (4-ounce) can sliced mushrooms,
    drained
  ½ cup dry white wine

Prepare wild rice according to package directions, omitting salt; do not overcook. Prepare sausage links according to package directions in large skillet; do not overcook. Drain well, leaving 1 tablespoon of fat in pan. Cool sausages slightly and cut into bite-size pieces.

In same pan, sauté onion and celery. Add soup, cooked rice, sausage pieces, mushrooms and wine, stirring carefully to mix. Place in well-greased 12×9-inch baking dish and bake at 350°F 30 minutes. *Makes 6 servings*

SWEET & SOUR MEATBALLS

  1½ pounds lean ground beef
    1 (8-ounce) can water chestnuts, drained
      and chopped
    2 eggs, slightly beaten
  ⅓ cup plain dry bread crumbs
    4 teaspoons WYLER'S® or STEERO®
      Beef-Flavor Instant Bouillon
    1 tablespoon Worcestershire sauce
    1 cup water
  ½ cup firmly packed light brown sugar
  ½ cup REALEMON® Lemon Juice from
      Concentrate
  ¼ cup ketchup
    2 tablespoons cornstarch
  ¼ teaspoon salt
    1 cup coarsely chopped red and green
      bell peppers
    Hot cooked rice

In large bowl, combine meat, water chestnuts, eggs, crumbs, bouillon and Worcestershire; mix well. Shape into 1¼-inch meatballs. In large skillet, brown meatballs. Remove from pan; pour off fat. In same skillet, combine remaining ingredients except peppers and rice; mix well. Over medium heat, cook and stir until sauce thickens. Reduce heat. Add meatballs; simmer uncovered 10 minutes. Add peppers; heat through. Serve with rice. Garnish with parsley, if desired. Refrigerate leftovers.

Makes 6 to 8 servings

COUNTRY RICE & BEANS WITH CHICKEN & SAUSAGE

  8 ounces boneless, skinless chicken breasts, cut into strips
  8 ounces smoked sausage, sliced
  ¼ cup coarsely chopped onion
  1 tablespoon butter or margarine
  3 cups water
  1 (8-ounce) package FARMHOUSE® Red Beans & Rice
  ¼ cup sliced green pepper
  ¼ cup sliced celery

In large saucepan, sauté chicken, sausage and onion in butter 5 to 7 minutes or until chicken is no longer pink. Add water, beans & rice, contents of seasoning packet, green pepper and celery. Bring to a boil; cover. Reduce heat and simmer 20 to 25 minutes or until liquid is absorbed. *Makes 6 servings*

ITALIAN STUFFED SHELLS

  24 CREAMETTE® Jumbo Macaroni Shells, cooked and drained
  1 pound lean ground beef
  ⅔ cup chopped onion
  1 clove garlic, chopped
  2 cups boiling water
  1 (12-ounce) can tomato paste
  1 tablespoon WYLER'S® Beef-Flavor Instant Bouillon *or* 3 Beef-Flavor Bouillon Cubes
  1½ teaspoons oregano leaves
  1 (16-ounce) container BORDEN® or MEADOW GOLD® Cottage Cheese
  2 cups (8 ounces) shredded Mozzarella cheese
  ½ cup grated Parmesan cheese
  1 egg

In large skillet, brown beef, onion and garlic; pour off fat. Stir in water, tomato paste, bouillon and oregano; simmer 30 minutes. In medium bowl, combine cottage cheese, *1 cup* Mozzarella, grated Parmesan and egg; mix well. Stuff shells with cheese mixture; arrange in individual ramekins or 13×9-inch baking dish. Pour sauce over shells; cover. Bake in preheated 350°F. oven 30 minutes. Uncover; sprinkle with remaining *1 cup* Mozzarella. Bake 3 minutes longer. Refrigerate leftovers.
Makes 6 to 8 servings

MEAT LOAF ITALIANO

  1 egg, beaten
  1½ pounds ground beef
  1 (8-ounce) can pizza sauce
  ¾ cup (3 ounces) VELVEETA® Shredded Pasteurized Process Cheese Food
  ¾ cup old-fashioned or quick oats, uncooked
  ¼ cup cold water
  ½ teaspoon dried oregano leaves, crushed

In large bowl, combine all ingredients except ¼ cup sauce; mix lightly. Shape into loaf in 10×6-inch baking dish. Bake at 350°F, 1 hour. Top with remaining sauce. Let stand 10 minutes before serving. *Makes 6 servings*

PREP TIME: 10 minutes
BAKE TIME: 60 minutes plus standing

Country Rice & Beans with Chicken & Sausage

Splendid

POULTRY

ROAST TURKEY WITH PAN GRAVY

> **1 fresh or thawed frozen turkey (12 to 14 pounds), reserve giblets and neck**
> **Sausage-Cornbread Stuffing (page 256) or prepared stuffing (optional)**
> **2 cloves garlic, minced**
> **½ cup butter, melted**
> **Turkey Broth with Giblets (page 162)**
> **1 cup dry white wine or vermouth**
> **3 tablespoons all-purpose flour**
> **Salt and black pepper**

Preheat oven to 450°F. Rinse turkey; pat dry with paper towels. Prepare stuffing, if desired. Stuff body and neck cavities loosely with stuffing, if desired. Fold skin over openings and close with skewers. Tie legs together with cotton string or tuck through skin flap, if provided. Tuck wings under turkey. Place turkey on meat rack in shallow roasting pan. Stir garlic into butter. Insert meat thermometer in thickest part of thigh not touching bone. Brush ⅓ of butter mixture evenly over turkey. Place turkey in oven; turn temperature down to 325°F. Roast

continued on page 162

Roast Turkey with Pan Gravy, continued

18 to 20 minutes per pound for unstuffed turkey or 22 to 24 minutes per pound for stuffed turkey, brushing with butter mixture after 1 hour and then after 1½ hours. Baste with pan juices every hour of roasting. (Total roasting time should be 4 to 5 hours.) If turkey is overbrowning, tent with foil. Cook until internal temperature reaches 180°F and legs move easily in sockets. While turkey is roasting, prepare Turkey Broth with Giblets.

Transfer turkey to cutting board; tent with foil. Let stand 15 minutes while preparing gravy. Pour off and reserve juices from roasting pan. To deglaze pan, pour wine into pan. Place over burners and cook over medium-high heat; scrape up browned bits and stir constantly 2 to 3 minutes or until mixture has reduced by about half.

Spoon off ⅓ cup fat from pan drippings; discard remaining fat.* Place ⅓ cup fat in large saucepan. Add flour; cook over medium heat 1 minute, stirring constantly. Slowly stir in 3 cups Turkey Broth, defatted turkey drippings and deglazed wine mixture from roasting pan. Cook over medium heat 10 minutes, stirring occasionally. Stir in reserved chopped giblets; heat through. Season with salt and pepper to taste.

Makes 12 servings and 3½ cups gravy

*Or, substitute ⅓ cup butter or margarine for turkey fat.

CREAMY TURKEY GRAVY: Stir in 1 cup heavy cream with giblets; proceed as recipe directs. Makes 4½ cups gravy.

TURKEY BROTH WITH GIBLETS

Reserved giblets and neck from turkey (discard liver or reserve for another use)
4 cups water
1 can (13¾ ounces) chicken broth
1 medium onion, cut into quarters
2 medium carrots, coarsely chopped
4 large parsley sprigs
1 bay leaf
1 teaspoon dried thyme leaves, crushed
10 whole black peppercorns

For broth, combine giblets and neck, water and chicken broth in 3-quart saucepan. Bring to a boil over high heat; skim off foam. Stir in onion, carrots, parsley, bay leaf, thyme and peppercorns. Reduce heat to low. Simmer, uncovered, 1½ to 2 hours, stirring occasionally. (If liquid evaporates too quickly, add additional ½ cup water.) Cool to room temperature.

Strain broth; set aside. If broth measures less than 3 cups, add water to equal 3 cups liquid. If broth measures more than 3 cups, bring to a boil and heat until liquid is reduced to 3 cups. Remove meat from neck and chop giblets finely; set aside. Broth may be prepared up to 1 day before serving. Cover giblets and broth separately and refrigerate. *Makes 3 cups*

TURKEY BREAST PROVENÇAL WITH VEGETABLES

1 cup turkey or chicken bouillon
¼ cup white wine
¼ cup lemon juice
1 head garlic, cloves separated, unpeeled
1 bag (10 ounces) frozen onions
2 teaspoons dried rosemary, crushed
1 teaspoon dried thyme leaves, crushed
½ teaspoon salt
¼ teaspoon fennel seeds
¼ teaspoon ground black pepper
6 plum tomatoes, quartered
1 package (9 ounces) frozen artichoke hearts, slightly thawed
1 package (10 ounces) frozen asparagus spears, slightly thawed
1 can (3¼ ounces) pitted ripe olives, drained
1 bone-in (4½-pound) turkey breast

1. Preheat oven to 325°F. In 13×9-inch baking pan combine bouillon, wine, lemon juice, garlic, onions, rosemary, thyme, salt, fennel seeds and black pepper. Cover pan with foil; bake 20 minutes.

2. Remove pan from oven. Add tomatoes, artichoke hearts, asparagus and olives. Place turkey breast on top of vegetables. Cover and bake 1 hour. Remove foil and bake 1 hour or until meat thermometer inserted in thickest part of breast registers 170°F. Baste turkey and vegetables frequently with pan juices.

3. Remove turkey and vegetables to serving platter. Reserve 6 cloves of garlic and pan juices.

4. Remove skin from reserved garlic. Combine garlic with pan juices in food processor; process 30 to 60 seconds until mixture is smooth.

5. Serve sauce with turkey and vegetables.
Makes 12 servings

*Favorite recipe from **National Turkey Federation***

Turkey Breast Provençal with Vegetables

163

ROASTED TURKEY WITH SAVORY CRANBERRY STUFFING

1 cup chopped celery
1 cup chopped onion
½ cup margarine or butter
1 (16-ounce) can whole-berry cranberry sauce
2 tablespoons WYLER'S® or STEERO® Chicken-Flavor Instant Bouillon *or* 6 Chicken-Flavor Bouillon Cubes
12 cups dry bread cubes (about 16 slices bread)
1 cup chopped pecans
2 teaspoons poultry seasoning
1 teaspoon rubbed sage
3 cups hot water
1 (12- to 14-pound) turkey, thawed if frozen
Vegetable oil
Rich Turkey Gravy (recipe follows)

In large skillet, cook celery and onion in margarine until tender; add cranberry sauce and bouillon. Cook and stir until bouillon dissolves. In large bowl, combine bread cubes, pecans, seasonings and water; add cranberry mixture. Mix well.

Preheat oven to 325°F. Remove neck and giblets from turkey cavities. Rinse turkey; drain well. Stuff neck and body cavities lightly with stuffing. (Place extra stuffing in greased baking dish. Cover baking dish; refrigerate.) Turn wings back to hold neck skin in place. Place turkey, breast side up, on flat rack in open pan. Insert meat thermometer into thickest part of thigh next to body, not touching bone. Brush skin with oil. Place turkey in oven and roast about 4 hours. (Bake extra stuffing with turkey during last 40 minutes or until hot.) When skin is golden brown, shield breast loosely with foil to prevent overbrowning. Check for doneness; thigh temperature should be 180° to 185°F. Let turkey stand 15 to 20 minutes before carving. Serve with Rich Turkey Gravy. Refrigerate leftovers. *Makes 10 to 12 servings*

RICH TURKEY GRAVY: In medium skillet, stir ¼ to ⅓ cup flour into ¼ cup pan drippings; cook and stir until dark brown. Stir in 2 cups hot water and 2 teaspoons WYLER'S® or STEERO® Chicken-Flavor Instant Bouillon or 2 Chicken-Flavor Bouillon Cubes; cook and stir until thickened and bouillon is dissolved. Refrigerate leftovers. Makes about 1½ cups.

TURKEY EN CROÛTE

1 (5-pound) boneless turkey
1 pound fresh mushrooms, chopped
½ cup sliced green onions
2 cloves garlic, minced
¼ cup butter, melted
2 tablespoons dry sherry
¼ cup seasoned dry bread crumbs
2 eggs, divided
½ (17¼-ounce) package frozen puff pastry, thawed

Roast turkey at 350°F for 1 hour until internal temperature on meat thermometer registers 165°F. Cool slightly; remove netting, if present.

Cook mushrooms, onions and garlic in butter until liquid is absorbed. Stir in sherry, bread crumbs and 1 beaten egg. Cut turkey into 1-inch diagonal slices, cutting only ¾ of the way through meat; fill slices with mushroom mixture.

Roll out pastry large enough to enclose turkey. Place turkey, top side down, in center of pastry; wrap pastry around turkey, sealing edges with water. Place enclosed turkey, seam side down, on baking sheet; brush with remaining 1 beaten egg. Prick surface with fork. Bake at 350°F for 1 hour until golden brown; let stand 10 minutes. To serve, cut straight across into slices.
Makes 10 to 12 servings

Favorite recipe from **National Turkey Federation**

Roasted Turkey with Savory Cranberry Stuffing

TURKEY BREAST WITH SOUTHWESTERN CORN BREAD DRESSING

5 cups coarsely crumbled corn bread
4 English muffins, coarsely crumbled
3 mild green chilies, roasted, peeled, seeded and chopped
1 red bell pepper, roasted, peeled, seeded and chopped
¾ cup pine nuts, toasted
1 tablespoon chopped fresh cilantro
1 tablespoon chopped fresh parsley
1½ teaspoons chopped fresh basil *or* 1 teaspoon dried basil leaves
1½ teaspoons chopped fresh thyme *or* 1 teaspoon dried thyme leaves
1½ teaspoons chopped fresh oregano *or* 1 teaspoon dried oregano leaves
1 pound Italian turkey sausage
3 cups chopped celery
1 cup chopped onion
2 to 4 tablespoons turkey broth or water
1 bone-in turkey breast (5 to 6 pounds)
2 tablespoons minced garlic
½ cup chopped fresh cilantro
Nonstick cooking spray

1. In large bowl combine corn bread, muffins, chilies, red pepper, pine nuts, 1 tablespoon cilantro, parsley, basil, thyme and oregano; set aside.

2. In large skillet, over medium-high heat, sauté turkey sausage, celery and onion 8 to 10 minutes or until sausage is no longer pink and vegetables are tender. Combine turkey sausage mixture with cornbread mixture. Add broth or water if mixture is too dry; set aside.

3. Loosen skin on both sides of turkey breast, being careful not to tear skin, leaving it connected at breast bone. Spread 1 tablespoon garlic under loosened skin over each breast half. Repeat procedure, spreading ¼ cup cilantro over each breast half.

4. Place turkey breast in 13×9×2-inch roasting pan lightly coated with nonstick cooking spray. Spoon half of stuffing mixture under breast cavity. Spoon remaining stuffing into 2-quart casserole lightly coated with nonstick cooking spray; set aside. Roast turkey breast, uncovered, at 325°F, for 2 to 2½ hours or until meat thermometer registers 170°F in deepest portion of breast. Bake remaining stuffing, uncovered, along with turkey breast during last 45 minutes.   *Makes 12 servings*

Favorite recipe from **National Turkey Federation**

ROAST STUFFED TURKEY

2 packages (6 ounces each) STOVE TOP® Stuffing Mix, any variety
½ cup (1 stick) butter or margarine, cut into pieces
3 cups hot water
1 (8- to 12-pound) turkey

Prepare stuffing by placing contents of vegetable/seasoning packets and butter in a large bowl. Add hot water; stir just to partially melt butter. Add stuffing crumbs. Stir just to moisten. *Do not stuff bird until ready to roast.*

Rinse turkey with cold water; pat dry. Do not rub cavities with salt. Lightly stuff neck and body cavities with prepared stuffing. Close openings with skewer and string. Place turkey, breast side up, in roasting pan. Roast at 325°F for 3 to 4 hours or as directed on poultry wrapper. Bake any remaining stuffing at 325°F for 30 minutes. Cover the baking dish for moist stuffing. If drier stuffing is desired, bake uncovered.   *Makes 8 to 10 servings*

Stuffed Chicken with Apple Glaze

STUFFED CHICKEN WITH APPLE GLAZE

1 broiler-fryer chicken (3½ to 4 pounds)
½ teaspoon salt
¼ teaspoon pepper
2 tablespoons vegetable oil
1 package (6 ounces) chicken-flavored stuffing mix, plus ingredients to prepare mix
1 cup chopped apple
¼ cup chopped walnuts
¼ cup raisins
¼ cup thinly sliced celery
½ teaspoon grated lemon peel
½ cup apple jelly
1 tablespoon lemon juice
½ teaspoon ground cinnamon

Preheat oven to 350°F. Sprinkle inside of chicken with salt and pepper; rub outside with oil.

Prepare stuffing mix in large bowl according to package directions. Add apple, walnuts, raisins, celery and lemon peel; mix thoroughly. Stuff body cavity loosely with stuffing.* Place chicken in baking pan. Cover loosely with aluminum foil; roast 1 hour.

Meanwhile, combine jelly, lemon juice and cinnamon in small saucepan. Simmer over low heat 3 minutes or until blended. Remove foil from chicken; brush with jelly glaze. Roast chicken, uncovered, brushing frequently with jelly glaze, 30 minutes or until meat thermometer inserted into thickest part of thigh registers 185°F and juices run clear. Let chicken stand 15 minutes before carving.

Makes 4 servings

*Bake any leftover stuffing in covered casserole alongside chicken until heated through.

*Favorite recipe from **Delmarva Poultry Industry, Inc.***

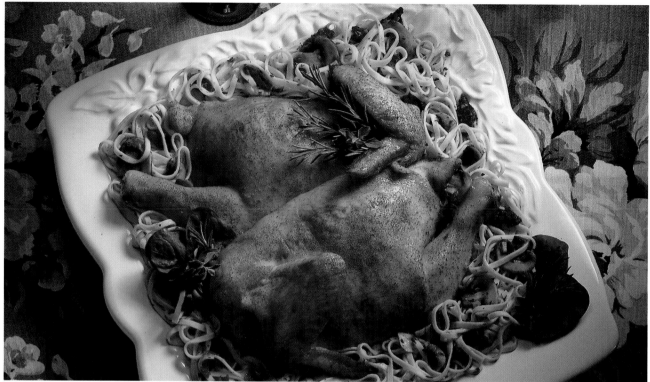

Ricotta-Stuffed Chicken with Sun-Dried Tomato Linguine

RICOTTA-STUFFED CHICKEN WITH SUN-DRIED TOMATO LINGUINE

1 broiler-fryer chicken (3 pounds)
1 cup reduced fat ricotta cheese
1 cup chopped fresh spinach leaves
4 cloves garlic, minced
2 teaspoons dried basil leaves
2 teaspoons minced fresh parsley
1 teaspoon dried oregano leaves
¼ teaspoon salt
   Nonstick olive oil cooking spray
   Paprika
   Sun-Dried Tomato Linguine (page 169)

Preheat oven to 375°F. Split chicken in half, cutting through breast bone. Press down on chicken with palm of hand so that chicken will lie flat. Loosen skin over top of chicken using fingers and sharp paring knife; do not loosen skin over wings and drumsticks.

Combine ricotta cheese, spinach, garlic, basil, parsley, oregano and salt in small bowl. Stuff mixture under skin of chicken using small rubber spatula or spoon. Place chicken in roasting pan. Spray top of chicken lightly with cooking spray; sprinkle with paprika. Bake about 1 hour 15 minutes or until chicken is no longer pink in center and juices run clear. Serve with Sun-Dried Tomato Linguine. Garnish as desired. *Makes 6 servings*

SUN-DRIED TOMATO LINGUINE

6 sun-dried tomato halves, not packed in oil
Hot water
Nonstick olive oil cooking spray
1 cup sliced mushrooms
3 cloves garlic, minced
1 tablespoon minced fresh parsley
¾ teaspoon dried rosemary
1 can (15 ounces) low sodium chicken broth, defatted
2 tablespoons cornstarch
¼ cup cold water
1 package (9 ounces) linguine, cooked in salted water, drained, hot

Place sun-dried tomatoes in small bowl; pour hot water over to cover. Let stand 10 to 15 minutes or until tomatoes are soft. Drain well; cut tomatoes into quarters. Spray medium nonstick skillet with cooking spray; heat over medium heat until hot. Add mushrooms and garlic; cook and stir about 5 minutes or until tender. Add sun-dried tomatoes, parsley and rosemary; cook and stir 1 minute.

Stir chicken broth into vegetable mixture; heat to a boil. Combine cornstarch and cold water in small bowl; stir into chicken broth mixture. Boil 1 to 2 minutes, stirring constantly. Pour mixture over linguine; toss.   *Makes 6 servings*

SPICY ORANGE ROASTER WITH CORNBREAD, BACON AND PECAN STUFFING

1 PERDUE® Oven Stuffer® Roaster (5 to 8 pounds)
¼ cup chicken broth or water
2 tablespoons dry sherry wine
¼ cup butter or margarine
3 cups cornbread stuffing mix
¼ pound cooked bacon slices, crumbled
¼ cup coarsely chopped pecans
Spicy Orange Baste (recipe follows)
Orange Sherry Gravy (recipe follows)

Remove giblets and reserve for gravy. Rinse roaster; pat dry with paper towel. In saucepan, bring broth, sherry and butter to a boil; stir in stuffing mix. Add bacon and pecans. Stuff roaster; close cavity with skewers or string. Tie legs together and fold wings back.

Place roaster in roasting pan. Roast at 350°F for 2 to 2¾ hours. After 1 hour, brush with Spicy Orange Baste; repeat occasionally. Roaster is done when Bird-Watcher® thermometer pops up and juices are clear. Remove to platter. Allow to rest 10 minutes. Serve with Orange Sherry Gravy.
    Makes 6 servings

SPICY ORANGE BASTE

3 tablespoons orange juice
3 tablespoons lemon juice
2 tablespoons vegetable oil
1 tablespoon grated orange peel
½ teaspoon ground ginger
½ teaspoon salt
⅛ teaspoon freshly ground pepper

Combine all ingredients in small bowl.

ORANGE SHERRY GRAVY

Oven Stuffer® Roaster giblets, except liver
4 cups water
¼ cup dry sherry wine
3 tablespoons cornstarch
¼ teaspoon freshly ground pepper
1 tablespoon orange marmalade

While roaster is cooking, simmer giblets, uncovered, in water in saucepan until 2 cups of liquid remain. Strain and reserve liquid.

When roaster is done, pour off all but 2 tablespoons pan juices. Combine sherry and cornstarch; add to pan with reserved liquid from giblets and pepper. Bring to a boil; simmer until thickened, stirring constantly. Stir in marmalade. Serve with roaster.

WINE AND HERB ROASTER WITH HAM AND OYSTER STUFFING

1 PERDUE® Oven Stuffer® Roaster (5 to 8 pounds)
   Salt
½ teaspoon pepper
¼ cup butter or margarine
¼ cup chopped onion
 2 tablespoons chopped celery
½ cup water
 6 cooked oysters, diced
 3 cups herb stuffing mix (4 ounces)
½ cup diced lean ham
   Wine and Herb Baste (recipe follows)
   Madeira Gravy (recipe follows)

Remove giblets and reserve for gravy. Rinse roaster, if desired; pat dry with paper towel. Season with salt and pepper. In medium skillet, melt butter and sauté onion and celery 5 minutes. Mix in water, oysters, stuffing mix and ham. Stuff roaster and close cavity with skewers or string. Tie legs together and fold wings back.

Place roaster in large roasting pan. Roast at 350°F for 2 to 2¾ hours. After 1 hour, brush with Wine and Herb Baste; repeat occasionally. Roaster is done when Bird-Watcher® thermometer pops up and juices are clear when thigh is pierced. Remove to serving platter and allow to rest 10 minutes while preparing gravy. Serve with Madeira Gravy.

Makes 6 servings

WINE AND HERB BASTE
¼ cup butter
 1 clove garlic, minced
 1 tablespoon chopped fresh parsley
 1 teaspoon dried thyme leaves
½ teaspoon dried rosemary leaves, crumbled
¼ cup dry red wine

Combine all ingredients in small saucepan over low heat, stirring until butter is melted.

MADEIRA GRAVY
   Oven Stuffer® Roaster giblets, except liver
 4 cups water
½ cup Madeira wine
¼ cup flour

While roaster is cooking, place giblets in small saucepan with water and simmer, uncovered, until 2 cups liquid remain. Strain and reserve liquid.

When roaster is done, pour off all but 2 tablespoons drippings. Add reserved liquid from giblets to pan and stir to remove brown bits from bottom of pan. Combine wine and flour to make a smooth paste. Add to pan and cook over medium heat, whisking frequently, until gravy is thickened. Serve with roaster.

HOT & SPICY ARROZ CON POLLO

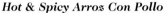

2 tablespoons vegetable oil
1 medium onion, chopped
1 can (14½ ounces) whole tomatoes
1 can (13¾ ounces) chicken broth
1¼ cups long-grain rice
1 teaspoon salt
   Pinch saffron threads (optional)
1 jar (4 ounces) chopped pimientos,
   drained
½ cup sliced pitted ripe olives
1 package (10 ounces) frozen peas,
   thawed
1 package (12 ounces) PERDUE DONE
   IT!® Hot & Spicy Wings (about
   12 wings)
   Water (optional)

In large deep skillet or Dutch oven over medium-high heat, heat oil. Add onion; cook 3 to 5 minutes or until tender. Stir in tomatoes with their liquid, broth, rice, salt and saffron; bring to a boil. Reduce heat to low; cover and simmer 10 minutes. Stir in pimientos, olives and peas; gently stir in chicken wings. Cover and cook 10 to 15 minutes longer or until all liquid is absorbed, rice is tender and wings are heated through; add ¼ to ½ cup water if mixture becomes too dry. Serve hot.

Makes 4 servings

NOTE: For a larger crowd, recipe may be doubled using PERDUE DONE IT!® Hot & Spicy Wings Party Tray *(24 ounces)*. Double other ingredients and cook in large Dutch oven.

Hot & Spicy Arroz Con Pollo

COUNTRY CAPTAIN JARLSBERG

3½ pounds chicken pieces
1 tablespoon butter or margarine
1 teaspoon salt
¼ teaspoon black pepper
1 small green bell pepper, cut into strips
1 small red bell pepper, cut into strips
2 tablespoons oil
1 large tomato, chopped
1 medium clove garlic, minced
1 teaspoon curry powder
¼ teaspoon ground cumin
1½ cups chicken broth, divided
1 tablespoon cornstarch
¼ cup toasted slivered almonds
¼ cup currants
1½ cups shredded JARLSBERG Cheese

Arrange chicken in shallow baking dish. Dot with butter. Season with salt and black pepper. Bake at 350°F 45 minutes or until tender.

Meanwhile, in large saucepan, sauté bell peppers in oil until just tender. Add tomato, garlic, curry, cumin and 1¼ cups chicken broth. Simmer 10 minutes, stirring occasionally.

Blend cornstarch and remaining ¼ cup chicken broth. Gradually stir into sauce and cook, stirring, until mixture is thickened and smooth. Add almonds and currants. Pour over chicken. Top with cheese. Bake an additional 10 minutes.   *Makes 6 servings*

*Favorite recipe from **Norseland, Inc.***

Classic Chicken Curry with Winter Fruit and Walnuts

CLASSIC CHICKEN CURRY WITH WINTER FRUIT AND WALNUTS

¼ cup butter
2 cloves garlic, minced
1 tablespoon curry powder
1 teaspoon paprika
¼ teaspoon ground red pepper (optional)
1 tablespoon cornstarch
1 cup chicken broth
6 chicken breast halves, skinned and boned
2 pears, cored and thickly sliced
¾ cup chopped walnuts
½ cup chopped green onions
¼ cup fresh cranberries or currants
    Hot cooked rice or couscous (optional)

MICROWAVE DIRECTIONS: Microwave butter in uncovered 3-quart glass casserole dish 2 minutes at HIGH (100% power). Stir in garlic and spices; microwave 3 minutes. Mix cornstarch with broth and add to garlic mixture; stir. Arrange chicken breast halves in single layer in sauce with thickest pieces toward side of dish. Cover and microwave 6 to 8 minutes, rotating chicken pieces every 2 minutes. Stir in remaining ingredients. Cover and microwave 6 to 8 minutes or until chicken is cooked through. Arrange chicken and pears on serving platter. Pour remaining sauce over chicken; serve with rice or couscous, if desired.

Makes 4 to 6 servings

*Favorite recipe from **Walnut Marketing Board***

LOUISIANA CHICKEN

4 chicken breast halves, skinned and boned
2 cans (14½ ounces each) DEL MONTE® Cajun Recipe Stewed Tomatoes
2 tablespoons cornstarch
4 slices Monterey Jack cheese
Parsley
Hot cooked rice (optional)

Place chicken in baking dish. Cover and bake at 375°F, 30 to 35 minutes; drain. Combine tomatoes and cornstarch in saucepan; stir to dissolve cornstarch. Cook, stirring constantly, until thickened. Remove chicken from baking dish. Pour all but 1 cup sauce into dish. Arrange chicken over sauce in dish; top with remaining sauce. Place 1 slice cheese on each piece of chicken. Bake until cheese melts. Garnish with parsley. Serve with hot cooked rice, if desired.

Makes 4 servings

CHICKEN VERMOUTH WITH ARTICHOKES

½ teaspoon salt, divided
⅛ teaspoon black pepper
2 tablespoons olive oil
½ medium red pepper, cut into thin strips
2 whole broiler-fryer chicken breasts, halved, boned, skinned
2 cloves garlic, minced
1 package (9 ounces) frozen artichoke hearts
½ cup chicken broth
¼ cup dry vermouth
1 tablespoon lemon juice
½ teaspoon dried marjoram

Sprinkle ¼ teaspoon salt and black pepper over chicken. In skillet, place oil and heat to medium-high temperature. Add red pepper strips and cook, stirring, about 2 to 3 minutes or until tender. Remove to small bowl. To drippings in same skillet, add chicken and cook, turning, about 6 minutes or until browned on both sides. Add garlic and cook 1 minute or until translucent. Add artichoke hearts, broth, vermouth, lemon juice, marjoram and remaining ¼ teaspoon salt. Bring to a boil; reduce heat. Cover and cook about 10 minutes or until chicken and artichokes are fork-tender. Arrange chicken and artichokes on serving platter. Top with pan juices. Garnish with red pepper strips.

Makes 4 servings

*Favorite recipe from **Delmarva Poultry Industry, Inc.***

CHICKEN WITH BRANDIED FRUIT SAUCE

4 broiler-fryer chicken breast halves, boned, skinned
½ teaspoon salt
¼ teaspoon ground nutmeg
2 tablespoons butter or margarine
1 tablespoon cornstarch
¼ teaspoon ground red pepper
Juice of 1 *each* orange, lemon and lime
⅓ cup orange marmalade
2 tablespoons brandy
1 cup red seedless grapes, halved

With meat mallet or similar flattening utensil, pound chicken to ½-inch thickness. Sprinkle salt and nutmeg over chicken. In skillet, place butter and heat to medium-high temperature. Add chicken and cook, turning, about 8 minutes or until chicken is browned and fork-tender. In small bowl, mix cornstarch and red pepper. Stir in orange, lemon and lime juices; set aside. Remove chicken to serving platter. To juices remaining in same skillet, add marmalade and heat until melted. Stir in juice mixture and cook, stirring, until mixture boils and thickens. Add brandy and grapes. Return chicken to pan; spoon sauce over chicken. Cook over low heat 5 minutes.

Makes 4 servings

*Favorite recipe from **Delmarva Poultry Industry, Inc.***

CHICKEN TANDOORI WITH JARLSBERG LITE

8 ounces (1 cup) plain yogurt
1 tablespoon minced garlic (3 to 4 cloves)
2 teaspoons fresh thyme *or* 1 teaspoon dried thyme leaves
2 teaspoons paprika
2 teaspoons ground cumin
Pinch ground cloves (optional)
4 boneless skinless chicken breast halves, flattened to ¼ inch (about 1½ pounds)
¼ cup seasoned dry bread crumbs
1 cup (4 ounces) shredded JARLSBERG LITE Cheese

Mix first six ingredients in large glass bowl; reserve ¼ cup. Add chicken to bowl, turning to coat evenly. Marinate in refrigerator 2 hours.

Remove chicken from yogurt mixture; discard yogurt mixture. Mix reserved ¼ cup yogurt mixture, bread crumbs and cheese. Spread one quarter of the cheese mixture on each chicken breast. Roll up from pointed end and secure with wooden picks.

Broil on rack of broiler pan, 10 to 12 inches from heat source, 12 to 15 minutes or until done, turning after 5 minutes.

Makes 4 servings

SERVING SUGGESTION: Serve with brown rice and vinegared cucumbers. Garnish with lemon slices and cilantro, if desired.

*Favorite recipe from **Norseland, Inc.***

Chicken with Brandied Fruit Sauce

DRESSED CHICKEN BREASTS WITH ANGEL HAIR PASTA

1 cup prepared HIDDEN VALLEY RANCH® Original Ranch® salad dressing
⅓ cup Dijon-style mustard
4 whole chicken breasts, halved, skinned, boned and pounded thin
½ cup butter or margarine
⅓ cup dry white wine
10 ounces angel hair pasta, cooked and drained
Chopped parsley

In small bowl, whisk together salad dressing and mustard; set aside. In medium skillet, sauté chicken in butter until browned; transfer to dish. Keep warm. Pour wine into skillet; cook over medium-high heat, scraping up any browned bits from bottom of skillet, about 5 minutes. Whisk in dressing mixture; blend well. Serve chicken with sauce over pasta; sprinkle with parsley. *Makes 8 servings*

CHICKEN–ASPARAGUS MARSALA

4 broiler-fryer chicken breast halves, boned, skinned
2 tablespoons butter or margarine
1 tablespoon vegetable oil
1 package (10 ounces) frozen asparagus spears, partially thawed, cut diagonally into 2-inch pieces
½ pound small mushrooms
¼ cup Marsala wine
¼ cup water
½ teaspoon salt
⅛ teaspoon pepper
1 tablespoon chopped fresh parsley

Dressed Chicken Breasts with Angel Hair Pasta

With meat mallet or similar flattening utensil, pound chicken to ¼-inch thickness. In skillet, place butter and oil; heat to medium-high temperature. Add chicken and cook, turning, about 5 minutes or until browned. Remove chicken; set aside. To drippings remaining in same skillet, add asparagus and mushrooms; cook, stirring, about 3 minutes. Return chicken to pan; add wine, water, salt and pepper. Bring to a boil; boil 2 minutes to reduce liquid. Reduce heat, cover and simmer about 3 minutes or until chicken and vegetables are tender. Arrange chicken on platter; spoon vegetable sauce over chicken. Sprinkle with chopped parsley. *Makes 4 servings*

Favorite recipe from **Delmarva Poultry Industry, Inc.**

CHICKEN WELLINGTON

6 large boneless skinless chicken breast halves (about 6 ounces each)
¾ teaspoon salt, divided
¼ teaspoon freshly ground black pepper, divided
¼ cup butter or margarine, divided
12 ounces mushrooms (button or crimini), finely chopped
½ cup finely chopped shallots or onion
2 tablespoons port wine or cognac
1 tablespoon fresh thyme leaves *or* 1 teaspoon dried thyme leaves, crushed
1 package (17¼ ounces) frozen puff pastry, thawed
1 egg, separated
1 tablespoon country-style Dijon-style mustard
1 teaspoon milk

Sprinkle chicken with ¼ teaspoon salt and ⅛ teaspoon pepper. Melt 2 tablespoons butter in skillet over medium heat. Cook 3 chicken breasts 6 minutes or until golden brown, turning once. Transfer to plate. Cook remaining chicken; cool slightly.

Melt remaining 2 tablespoons butter in skillet over medium heat. Add mushrooms and shallots. Cook and stir 5 minutes or until mushrooms release their liquid. Add wine, thyme, remaining ½ teaspoon salt and ⅛ teaspoon pepper; simmer 10 minutes or until liquid evaporates, stirring often. Cool.

Roll out each pastry sheet to 15×12-inch rectangle. Cut each into 3 (12×5-inch) rectangles. Cut small amount of pastry from corners to use as decoration, if desired. Brush beaten egg white over pastry rectangles. Place 1 cooled chicken breast on one side of each pastry rectangle. Spread ½ teaspoon mustard over each chicken breast, then spread with ¼ cup mushroom mixture. Fold pastry over chicken. Fold edge of bottom dough over top; press edges to seal. Place on *ungreased* baking sheet. Brush combined egg yolk and milk over pastry; top with pastry scraps cut into decorative shapes, if desired. Brush decorations. Cover loosely with plastic wrap. Refrigerate until cold, 1 to 4 hours.

Preheat oven to 400°F. Remove plastic wrap. Bake chicken 25 to 30 minutes or until deep golden brown and chicken is 160°F. Garnish, if desired. *Makes 6 servings*

Chicken Wellington

ALMOND BUTTER CHICKEN

4 boneless skinless chicken breast halves
(about 1¼ pounds)
2 tablespoons all-purpose flour
½ teaspoon salt
½ teaspoon pepper
1 egg, beaten
1 package (2¼ ounces) sliced almonds
¼ cup butter
Orange Sauce (recipe follows)

Place each chicken breast half between 2 pieces of plastic wrap. Pound to ¼-inch thickness. Coat chicken with flour. Sprinkle with salt and pepper. Dip one side of each chicken breast into egg; press with almonds. Melt butter in large skillet over medium-high heat. Cook chicken, almond side down, 3 to 5 minutes or until almonds are toasted; turn chicken over. Reduce heat to medium-low; cook 10 to 12 minutes or until chicken is tender and juices run clear. Serve, almond side up, with Orange Sauce. Garnish as desired.

Makes 4 servings

ORANGE SAUCE

1 tablespoon brown sugar
2 teaspoons cornstarch
Juice of 1 orange (about ½ cup)
2 tablespoons butter
1 teaspoon grated orange peel

Combine brown sugar and cornstarch in saucepan. Add juice, butter and orange peel. Cook over medium heat, stirring constantly, until thickened.

Makes ⅔ cup

*Favorite recipe from **Wisconsin Milk Marketing Board***

PECAN TURKEY SAUTÉ WITH WARM CRANBERRY SAUCE

½ cup unseasoned dry bread crumbs
¼ cup ground pecans
½ teaspoon LAWRY'S® Garlic Powder
with Parsley
½ teaspoon LAWRY'S® Seasoned Salt
1 pound turkey cutlets
3 eggs, beaten
3 tablespoons butter or margarine
1 can (8 ounces) jellied cranberry sauce
or whole-berry cranberry sauce
⅓ cup French salad dressing
3 tablespoons water
2 tablespoons chopped green onion

In pie plate, combine bread crumbs, pecans and seasonings; mix well. Dip each turkey cutlet in eggs, then coat both sides with crumb mixture. In large skillet, melt butter and brown turkey cutlets 5 minutes on each side or until cooked through. In small saucepan, combine cranberry sauce, salad dressing, water and onion; blend well. Gently heat until warmed through, about 5 minutes. Spoon warm cranberry sauce over cutlets.

Makes 4 servings

PRESENTATION: Serve with mashed potatoes or stuffing.

Almond Butter Chicken

CHICKEN WITH ARTICHOKES AND MUSHROOMS

    4 whole broiler-fryer chicken breasts,
        halved, boned, skinned
    ¾ teaspoon salt, divided
    ¼ cup butter or margarine, divided
    ½ pound fresh mushrooms, sliced
    ¼ cup chopped green onions
    3 cloves garlic, minced
    1 package (9 ounces) frozen artichoke
        hearts, thawed, drained, cut in half
    ⅓ cup chicken broth
    ½ teaspoon dried thyme, crumbled
    ¼ teaspoon ground red pepper
    ⅓ cup dry white wine
    2 teaspoons cornstarch
        Fresh herbs for garnish

With meat mallet or similar flattening utensil, pound chicken to ¼-inch thickness. Sprinkle ½ teaspoon salt over chicken. In large skillet melt 2 tablespoons butter over medium-high heat. Add chicken, 4 pieces at a time, and cook, turning, about 6 minutes or until browned on both sides. Remove chicken; set aside. To drippings in same skillet, add remaining 2 tablespoons butter and melt over medium heat. Add mushrooms, onions and garlic. Cook, stirring frequently, about 4 minutes or until vegetables are tender. Add artichoke hearts, broth, remaining ¼ teaspoon salt, thyme and red pepper; stir to mix well. In small dish, mix wine and cornstarch. Stir into vegetable mixture and cook, stirring, until slightly thickened. Return chicken to pan, spooning sauce over chicken. Cover and cook about 3 minutes or until chicken is fork-tender and heated through. Garnish with fresh herbs.   *Makes 8 servings*

*Favorite recipe from **Delmarva Poultry Industry, Inc.***

Chicken with Artichokes and Mushrooms

PÂTÉ STUFFED CHICKEN BREASTS WITH SOUR CREAM

    1 (8-ounce) package JONES® Chub
        Braunschweiger
    8 boneless skinless chicken breast halves
    1 (10¾-ounce) can condensed cream of
        celery soup
    3 cups sour cream
    ½ teaspoon curry powder
    ½ teaspoon paprika
        Hot cooked rice or mashed potatoes

Cut braunschweiger chub in half crosswise and then cut each half into quarters lengthwise to make 8 strips. Cut pocket in each chicken breast and insert 1 strip in each pocket. Place chicken in 13×9-inch baking pan.

Blend together soup, sour cream, curry powder and paprika; pour over chicken. Cover tightly and bake at 275°F 2 hours. Uncover and continue baking 30 minutes. Serve with hot cooked rice or mashed potatoes, if desired.
Makes 8 servings

APPLE BRANDY CHICKEN

> 3 whole chicken breasts, halved, boned
>   and skinned
> 3 tablespoons butter
> ⅓ cup Calvados or other apple brandy
> ½ cup minced shallots
> 1 tablespoon minced parsley
> ⅛ teaspoon dried thyme
>   LAWRY'S® Seasoned Salt to taste
>   LAWRY'S® Seasoned Pepper to taste
> 6 tablespoons apple cider
> 6 tablespoons whipping cream

In large skillet, brown chicken in butter and continue cooking, over low heat and uncovered, 15 minutes. Add Calvados to skillet and ignite. When flame subsides, add shallots, parsley, thyme, Seasoned Salt, Seasoned Pepper and apple cider. Bring to a boil; reduce heat, cover and simmer about 20 minutes or until chicken is tender. Remove chicken to serving platter and keep warm. Gradually add cream to skillet; heat but do not boil. Season to taste. Pour some of sauce over chicken. Serve remaining sauce in separate bowl.

Makes 4 to 6 servings

CIDER-GLAZED CORNISH HENS

> 6 PERDUE® fresh Cornish Hens (about
>   1½ pounds each)
>   Salt
>   Freshly ground pepper
> 1 quart apple cider or juice
> 1 cinnamon stick
> 2 tablespoons unsalted butter
> 2 tablespoons honey
> 1 tablespoon Dijon-style mustard
> 1 tablespoon red wine vinegar

Preheat oven to 375°F. Wash hens and pat dry with paper towel. Season inside and out with salt and pepper. Tie legs together and fold wings back. For glaze, place cider and cinnamon stick in medium saucepan; boil until volume is reduced to 1 cup. Remove cinnamon stick and stir in butter, honey, mustard and vinegar. Boil until thick, syrupy and translucent.

Place hens in shallow roasting pan. Roast hens, brushing occasionally with glaze, 55 to 60 minutes or until golden and tender.

Makes 6 to 12 servings

BRAISED DUCKLING AND PEARS

> 1 (4- to 5-pound) frozen duckling,
>   thawed and quartered
> 1 can (16 ounces) pear halves in heavy
>   syrup
> ⅓ cup KIKKOMAN® Stir-Fry Sauce
> 1 cinnamon stick, about 3 inches long

Wash duckling quarters; dry thoroughly with paper towels. Heat large skillet or Dutch oven over medium heat. Add duckling; brown slowly on both sides, about 15 minutes, or until golden. Meanwhile, drain pears; reserve all syrup. Remove ¼ cup pear syrup and combine with stir-fry sauce; set aside. Drain off fat from pan. Pour syrup mixture over duckling; add cinnamon stick. Cover and simmer 40 minutes or until tender, turning quarters over once. Remove duckling to serving platter; keep warm. Remove and discard cinnamon stick. Pour drippings into measuring cup; skim off fat. Combine ½ cup drippings with 2 tablespoons reserved pear syrup; return to pan with pears. Gently bring to boil and cook until pears are heated through, stirring occasionally. Serve duckling with pears and sauce.

Makes 3 to 4 servings

GLAZED CORNISH HENS

**6 fresh or thawed frozen Rock Cornish
   game hens (1¼ to 1½ pounds each)***
1 small onion, cut into 6 wedges
1 lemon, cut into 6 wedges
**2 tablespoons butter, softened
   Salt (optional)**
½ cup apricot preserves
1 tablespoon lemon juice
1 teaspoon shredded lemon peel

Preheat oven to 350°F. Wash hens inside and out with cold running water; pat dry with paper towels. Place 1 onion wedge and 1 lemon wedge in cavity of each hen. Tuck wings under hens. Tie legs together with cotton string. Place hens on meat rack in shallow roasting pan. Spread butter evenly over hens; sprinkle with salt. Roast 45 minutes.

Meanwhile, combine apricot preserves, lemon juice and lemon peel. Brush half of mixture over hens; roast 15 minutes. Brush hens with remaining preserve mixture; roast 15 minutes more or until hens are glazed, juices run clear when hens are pierced with long-handled fork and internal temperature is 180°F.** Cut string with scissors; discard. Remove onion and lemon wedges from cavities; discard.

Makes 6 servings

*A 1¼- to 1½-pound Rock Cornish game hen should take 1 to 2 days to thaw in the refrigerator. *Do not thaw at room temperature.*

**Since Rock Cornish game hens are so small, the most accurate way to measure internal temperature is with an instant-read thermometer, which has a narrower stem than a standard meat thermometer. Insert thermometer in fleshy part of thigh. Do not leave the thermometer in the hen during roasting since the thermometer is not ovenproof.

ROASTED DUCKLING WITH ORANGE & PLUM SAUCE

1 (3-pound) duckling
1 medium orange, halved
1 medium onion, halved
**½ cup WISH-BONE® Deluxe French or
   Lite French-Style Dressing**
½ cup orange juice
2 tablespoons brown sugar
1 teaspoon grated orange peel (optional)
¼ teaspoon ground cinnamon
⅛ teaspoon ground cloves
⅛ teaspoon ground nutmeg
½ cup chopped onion
1 teaspoon finely chopped garlic
1 tablespoon butter or margarine
2 tablespoons brandy
**2 medium plums, pitted and cut into
   wedges**
**2 small oranges, peeled, sectioned and
   seeded**

Preheat oven to 400°F. Stuff duckling with orange and onion halves. Close cavity with skewers or wooden toothpicks; tie legs together with string. With pin or fork, pierce skin. Place duckling, breast side up, on rack in roasting pan. Roast 40 minutes, turning duckling every 10 minutes.

Meanwhile, in small bowl, blend deluxe French dressing, orange juice, sugar, orange peel, cinnamon, cloves and nutmeg. Pour ½ of the dressing mixture over duckling; loosely cover with heavy-duty aluminum foil. Continue roasting, basting occasionally, 30 minutes or until meat thermometer reaches 185°F. Remove to serving platter and keep warm.

Meanwhile, in medium saucepan cook chopped onion and garlic in butter over medium heat 5 minutes or until onion is tender, stirring occasionally. Add brandy, plums and orange sections. Cook, stirring occasionally, 5 minutes. Stir in remaining dressing mixture and heat through. Serve with duckling.

Makes about 2 servings

Glazed Cornish Hen

CORNISH HENS WITH OYSTER STUFFING MOUNT VERNON

4 PERDUE® fresh Cornish Hens (about
    1½ pounds each)
    Salt and ground pepper
4 tablespoons butter or margarine,
    divided
6 oysters, shucked, coarsely chopped
    and strained through a fine sieve or
    coffee filter (reserve oyster liquor),
    divided
    Pinch ground mace
¼ teaspoon dried thyme leaves, crushed
¼ cup chopped onion
2 to 3 slices day-old bread, cubed
2 tablespoons dry sherry, divided
1 tablespoon lemon juice
    Sherried Pan Gravy (page 185)
    Spiced or brandied fruit (optional)

Preheat oven to 350°F. Rinse hens; pat dry
with paper towel. Season inside and out with
salt and pepper.

In medium skillet over medium heat, melt 2
tablespoons butter with ½ cup oyster liquor,
mace and thyme. Add onion; cook 5 minutes
until onion is tender and liquid is reduced to
about ⅓ cup.

In medium bowl, toss onion mixture, oysters,
bread cubes, ¼ teaspoon salt, ⅛ teaspoon
pepper, 1 tablespoon sherry and lemon juice.
Spoon oyster stuffing loosely into hens. Tie
legs together and fold back wings. Place hens
in shallow roasting pan.

Cornish Hens with Oyster Stuffing Mount Vernon

In small saucepan, melt remaining 2 tablespoons butter; combine with remaining 1 tablespoon sherry and baste hens with mixture. Roast hens, basting occasionally, about 1 hour and 15 minutes or until juices run clear with no hint of pink when thigh is pierced. Remove hens from roasting pan, cut strings, place on serving platter and keep warm. Reserve 2 tablespoons pan juices for gravy. Prepare gravy.

If desired, serve hens garnished with spiced or brandied fruit. Serve with Sherried Pan Gravy.

Makes 4 servings

SHERRIED PAN GRAVY
    2 tablespoons reserved pan juices
    2 tablespoons all-purpose flour
    2 cups chicken broth or stock
    4 tablespoons dry sherry

After removing hens, place roasting pan containing reserved pan juices over medium heat; add flour to pan and cook 2 minutes, stirring and scraping bottom to incorporate browned bits. Stir in chicken broth and sherry; simmer, stirring constantly, 2 minutes longer. Strain gravy into sauceboat.

Makes about 2 cups

Swiss Chicken Quiche

SWISS CHICKEN QUICHE

    1 (9-inch) unbaked pastry shell, pricked
    2 cups cubed cooked chicken or turkey
    1 cup (4 ounces) shredded Swiss cheese
    2 tablespoons flour
    1 tablespoon WYLER'S® or STEERO®
        Chicken-Flavor Instant Bouillon
    1 cup BORDEN® or MEADOW GOLD®
        Milk
    3 eggs, well beaten
    ¼ cup chopped onion
    2 tablespoons chopped green bell pepper
    2 tablespoons chopped pimiento

Preheat oven to 425°F. Bake pastry shell 8 minutes; remove from oven. *Reduce oven temperature to 350°F.* In medium bowl, toss cheese with flour and bouillon; add all remaining ingredients. Mix well. Pour into prepared pastry shell. Bake 40 to 45 minutes or until set. Let stand 10 minutes before serving. Garnish as desired. Refrigerate leftovers.

Makes one 9-inch quiche

CAJUN CORNISH HENS

    4 ounces hot smoked sausage, chopped
    ½ cup long grain white rice
    1 can (14½ ounces) DEL MONTE® Cajun
        Recipe Stewed Tomatoes
    ½ cup sliced green onions
    ¼ cup chopped green pepper
    1 clove garlic, minced
    ¼ teaspoon dried thyme leaves
    4 (20 ounces each) rock Cornish hens
    1 tablespoon butter, melted

Brown sausage in saucepan. Stir in rice; cook 2 minutes. Add tomatoes, onions, pepper, garlic and thyme. Bring to boil. Cover; simmer 20 minutes (rice will be firm). Rinse hens; drain well. Stuff with rice mixture. Place breast side up on rack in shallow pan. Brush with butter. Bake at 375°F 1 hour or until done.

Makes 4 servings

Sweet Potato Turkey Pie

SWEET POTATO TURKEY PIE

    1 can (24 ounces) sweet potatoes,
        drained
    2 tablespoons margarine, melted
    ¼ teaspoon pumpkin pie spice
        Nonstick vegetable cooking spray
    2 cups cubed cooked turkey (½- to
        ¾-inch cubes)
    1 can (10¾ ounces) reduced fat and
        sodium condensed cream of
        mushroom soup
    1 package (9 ounces) frozen French-style
        green beans, thawed and drained
    1 can (2 ounces) mushroom stems and
        pieces, drained
    ½ teaspoon *each* salt and pepper
    2 tablespoons crushed canned French
        fried onion rings
    1 can (8 ounces) cranberry sauce
        (optional)

1. In medium bowl mash sweet potatoes, margarine and pumpkin pie spice until smooth. Spray 9-inch pie plate with cooking spray. Line pie plate with potato mixture to form a "pie shell"; set aside.

2. In medium bowl combine turkey, soup, beans, mushrooms, salt and pepper. Pour mixture into prepared shell. Sprinkle onions over top. Bake at 350°F for 30 minutes or until hot. Serve with cranberry sauce, if desired.

Makes 6 servings

Favorite recipe from **National Turkey Federation**

TURKEY TETRAZZINI

⅔ cup MIRACLE WHIP® Salad Dressing
⅓ cup flour
½ teaspoon celery salt
    Dash of pepper
2 cups milk
7 ounces spaghetti, broken into thirds,
    cooked, drained
2 cups chopped cooked turkey or
    chicken
¾ cup (3 ounces) KRAFT 100% Grated
    Parmesan Cheese, divided
1 (4-ounce) can mushrooms, drained
2 tablespoons chopped pimiento
    (optional)
2 cups fresh bread cubes
3 tablespoons PARKAY® Spread Sticks,
    melted

Combine salad dressing, flour and seasonings in medium saucepan. Gradually add milk. Cook, stirring constantly, over low heat until thickened. Add spaghetti, turkey, ½ cup of the cheese, mushrooms and pimiento; mix lightly. Spoon into 2-quart casserole. Toss bread cubes with melted spread and remaining ¼ cup cheese; top casserole. Bake at 350°F, 30 minutes or until lightly browned.

Makes 6 servings

PREP TIME: 30 minutes
BAKE TIME: 30 minutes

MAKE AHEAD: Prepare as directed except for topping with bread cubes and baking. Cover; chill. When ready to bake, toss bread cubes with melted spread and remaining ¼ cup cheese. Top casserole; cover with foil. Bake at 350°F, 25 minutes. Uncover; continue baking 30 minutes or until lightly browned.

MICROWAVE DIRECTIONS: Reduce spread to 2 tablespoons. Microwave spread in 2-quart microwave-safe casserole on HIGH 30 seconds or until melted. Add bread cubes; toss. Microwave on HIGH 3½ to 4½ minutes or until crisp, stirring after 2 minutes. Remove from casserole; set aside. Combine salad dressing, flour and seasonings in same casserole; gradually add milk. Microwave on HIGH 5 to 6 minutes or until thickened, stirring after each minute. Stir in spaghetti, turkey, ½ cup of the cheese, mushrooms and pimiento; mix lightly. Cover; microwave on HIGH 8 to 10 minutes or until thoroughly heated, stirring after 5 minutes. Stir; top with bread cubes. Sprinkle with remaining ¼ cup cheese. Let stand 5 minutes.

SPEEDY ZITI

1 pound ziti, mostaccioli or other
    medium pasta shape, uncooked
2 teaspoons butter or margarine
1 medium onion, chopped
1 tablespoon Dijon mustard
2 tablespoons all-purpose flour
2 cups low-sodium chicken broth
¼ cup lemon juice
1 (10-ounce) package frozen peas,
    thawed and drained
¼ cup chopped fresh parsley
12 ounces chopped cooked chicken
    Salt and pepper to taste

Prepare pasta according to package directions. While pasta is cooking, melt butter over medium heat in large skillet. Add onion and cook 3 minutes. Stir in Dijon mustard and flour. Very gradually whisk in chicken broth. Bring broth to a boil and stir in lemon juice, peas and parsley.

When pasta is done, drain well. Toss pasta and chicken with sauce; season to taste with salt and pepper. *Makes 4 servings*

*Favorite recipe from **National Pasta Association***

MILANESE CHICKEN & RICE SKILLET

- 1 pound boneless skinless chicken breasts, thinly sliced
- 2 tablespoons olive or vegetable oil
- 1 cup sliced green onions
- ¼ cup *each* chopped green and red bell pepper
- 2 to 3 cloves garlic, minced
- 1 teaspoon dried oregano leaves
- 1 (14½-ounce) can diced tomatoes, undrained
- 1 (13¾-ounce) can chicken broth
- ¼ teaspoon ground black pepper
- 1 cup FARMHOUSE® Natural Long Grain White Rice
- ½ cup small pitted ripe olives
- ⅓ cup frozen peas, thawed
- ¼ cup grated Parmesan cheese
- 2 tablespoons chopped fresh basil *or* 2 teaspoons dried basil leaves
- 2 tablespoons chopped fresh parsley *or* 2 teaspoons parsley flakes

In large skillet, sauté chicken in oil until no longer pink in center. Add green onions, bell peppers, garlic and oregano; stir to coat. Add tomatoes, chicken broth and black pepper; bring to a boil. Stir in rice. Cover; reduce heat and cook 20 minutes or until most of the liquid is absorbed. Stir in olives, peas, cheese, basil and parsley.   *Makes 4 servings, 8 cups*

TURKEY LOAF WITH DRIED TOMATOES AND JARLSBERG

- 1 (½-ounce) package dried mushrooms
- 12 pieces (about 1½ ounces) sun-dried tomatoes, chopped
- 2 cups dry white wine or chicken broth
- 1 tablespoon dried thyme leaves *or* 3 tablespoons chopped fresh thyme
- ½ cup toasted pignoli (pine nuts) or chopped walnuts (optional)
- 1 cup seasoned bread crumbs
- 2 egg whites
- 2½ pounds ground turkey
- 2½ to 3 cups (10 to 12 ounces) shredded JARLSBERG LITE Cheese, divided

Microwave first 4 ingredients on HIGH 6 minutes; let stand 2 minutes. (OR bring first 4 ingredients to a boil and simmer, covered, 10 minutes. Let stand 5 minutes.) Allow to cool.

Preheat oven to 350°F. Combine vegetable mixture with nuts, crumbs, egg whites, turkey and 2 to 2½ cups of the cheese. On baking sheet lined with foil and sprayed with nonstick cooking spray, form a 12×5-inch rectangular loaf. (Recipe can be made ahead to this point and refrigerated. Baking time may need to be increased.)

Bake 55 to 60 minutes.＊ Sprinkle top with remaining ½ cup cheese. Bake 8 to 10 minutes longer or until cheese is melted. Let stand approximately 15 minutes before serving. Serve with baked potatoes and homemade red coleslaw or green salad.   *Makes 8 servings*

＊If loaf is thick, check middle to test for doneness.

Favorite recipe from **Norseland, Inc.**

Milanese Chicken & Rice Skillet

CHEESY CHICKEN TETRAZZINI

2 whole chicken breasts, boned, skinned and cut into 1-inch pieces (about 1½ pounds)
2 tablespoons butter or margarine
1½ cups sliced mushrooms
1 small red pepper, cut into julienne strips
½ cup sliced green onions
¼ cup all-purpose flour
1¾ cups chicken broth
1 cup light cream or half-and-half
2 tablespoons dry sherry
½ teaspoon salt
¼ teaspoon black pepper
¼ teaspoon dried thyme leaves, crushed
1 package (8 ounces) tri-color rotelle pasta, cooked until just tender and drained
¼ cup freshly grated Parmesan cheese
2 tablespoons chopped fresh parsley
1 cup shredded NOKKELOST or JARLSBERG Cheese

In skillet, brown chicken in butter. Add mushrooms and brown. Add red pepper and green onions; cook several minutes, stirring occasionally. Stir in flour and cook several minutes until blended. Gradually blend in chicken broth, cream and sherry. Cook, stirring, until thickened and smooth. Season with salt, pepper and thyme. Toss sauce with pasta, Parmesan cheese and parsley. Spoon into 1½-quart baking dish. Bake at 350°F. for 30 minutes. Top with cheese. Bake until cheese is melted.   *Makes 6 servings*

Favorite recipe from **Norseland, Inc.**

Turkey Picadillo

TURKEY PICADILLO

2 tablespoons instant minced onion
1 teaspoon instant minced garlic
2 tablespoons water
1 pound ground turkey
1 teaspoon ground cumin
¾ teaspoon salt
½ teaspoon ground black pepper
¼ teaspoon ground red pepper
¼ teaspoon ground allspice
1 tablespoon olive oil
1 can (8 ounces) tomato sauce
¼ cup sliced pimiento-stuffed green olives
¼ cup golden or dark seedless raisins
12 large Boston or iceberg lettuce leaves

Combine onion, garlic and water; let stand 10 minutes to soften. In medium bowl combine turkey, cumin, salt, black and red peppers and allspice. In large nonstick skillet heat oil until hot. Add onion mixture; cook, stirring occasionally, about 3 minutes. Add turkey mixture; cook, stirring to break up turkey, until turkey is no longer pink. Stir in tomato sauce, olives and raisins; cook, stirring occasionally, until most of the liquid has evaporated, 3 to 4 minutes. To serve, place about ¼ cup turkey mixture in each lettuce leaf; roll up lettuce, folding in sides to enclose filling. Serve with rice, if desired.   *Makes 4 servings, 12 rolls*

*Favorite recipe from **American Spice Trade Association***

SWEET CHICKEN RISOTTO

¾ pound boneless skinless chicken
    breasts, thinly sliced
¾ cup chopped onion
1 tablespoon vegetable oil
2 cups uncooked instant brown rice
4 cups chicken broth *or* 2 (13¾ ounces
    each) cans chicken broth
1 tablespoon prepared horseradish
4 teaspoons sugar
1 medium green bell pepper, seeded and
    sliced
1 medium red bell pepper, seeded and
    sliced
1 can (14 ounces) black beans, rinsed
    and drained *or* 2 cups cooked black
    beans
¼ cup grated Parmesan cheese

In large skillet (3 to 4 quarts), sauté chicken and onion in oil 5 minutes. Add rice, chicken broth, horseradish and sugar. Simmer, covered, 15 minutes or until rice is tender (there should be extra liquid). Add peppers and black beans. Simmer 5 minutes. Sprinkle with Parmesan cheese before serving.   *Makes 4 servings*

*Favorite recipe from **The Sugar Association, Inc.***

THAI PUMPKIN SATAY

1 cup LIBBY'S® Solid Pack Pumpkin
⅔ cup milk
⅓ cup peanut butter
⅓ cup chopped green onions
2 cloves garlic
2 tablespoons chopped cilantro
2 tablespoons lime juice
2 teaspoons granulated sugar
1 tablespoon soy sauce
¼ teaspoon salt
⅛ to ¼ teaspoon cayenne pepper
1 pound (about 4) boneless skinless
    chicken breast halves, cut into
    5×½-inch strips
1 medium red bell pepper, cut into
    1-inch pieces (1 cup)
1 bunch green onions, cut into 1-inch
    pieces, white part only
Hot cooked rice

COMBINE pumpkin, milk, peanut butter, *chopped* green onions, garlic, cilantro, lime juice, sugar, soy sauce, salt and cayenne pepper in blender or food processor; blend thoroughly. Combine ½ *cup* satay sauce with chicken in medium bowl; cover. Refrigerate 1 hour. Remove chicken from marinade; discard marinade.

PLACE chicken, red pepper and green onion pieces alternately on skewers. Broil or barbecue 10 minutes or until chicken is no longer pink in center, turning once halfway through cooking. Serve over rice with remaining satay sauce.   *Makes 4 servings*

WALNUT TURKEY HASH

> **4 cups boneless skinless cooked turkey chunks**
> **2 medium baked potatoes, cubed**
> **3 tablespoons butter or margarine**
> **1 cup California walnut pieces**
> **½ cup sliced green onions**
> **1 teaspoon rubbed sage**
> **1 teaspoon dried thyme leaves, crushed**
> **1 cup turkey gravy**
> **Salt and pepper to taste**
> **⅓ cup chopped parsley**

Combine turkey and potatoes in food processor. Process until coarsely chopped; set aside. Melt butter in large skillet. Add walnuts; toss over medium-low heat until golden brown. Remove with slotted spoon; set aside. Add onions, sage and thyme to skillet. Cook and stir 2 minutes. Add turkey mixture and gravy. Cook and stir until heated through. Add reserved walnuts, salt and pepper. Spoon onto serving platter; sprinkle with parsley.

Makes 4 to 6 servings

*Favorite recipe from **Walnut Marketing Board***

TURKEY CRANBERRY LOAF WEDGES

> **1 (12-ounce) container cranberry-orange sauce**
> **1½ pounds ground fresh turkey**
> **1½ cups fresh bread crumbs (3 slices)**
> **¼ cup REALEMON® Lemon Juice from Concentrate**
> **1 egg**
> **1 tablespoon WYLER'S® or STEERO® Chicken-Flavor Instant Bouillon *or* 3 Chicken-Flavor Bouillon Cubes**
> **1 to 2 teaspoons poultry seasoning**

Preheat oven to 350°F. Reserve ½ cup cranberry-orange sauce.

In large bowl, combine remaining ingredients; mix well. Press into 9-inch pie plate.

Bake 50 minutes or until set. Top with reserved cranberry-orange sauce. Let stand 5 minutes before serving. Cut into wedges; garnish as desired. Refrigerate leftovers.

Makes 6 servings

QUICK TURKEY TORTELLONI

> **1 (10-ounce) package DIGIORNO® Alfredo or Four Cheese Sauce**
> **1 (10-ounce) package frozen chopped broccoli, thawed, drained *or* 2 cups broccoli flowerets, cooked tender-crisp**
> **½ pound cooked turkey, cut into strips (about 1½ cups)**
> **1 (2½-ounce) jar sliced mushrooms, drained (optional)**
> **1 (9-ounce) package DIGIORNO® Mushroom or Mozzarella Garlic Tortelloni, cooked, drained**
> **Toasted sliced almonds (optional)**

• Mix sauce, broccoli, turkey and mushrooms in saucepan; heat thoroughly.

• Serve over pasta. Top with almonds.

Makes 3 to 4 servings

PREP TIME: 5 minutes
COOK TIME: 10 minutes

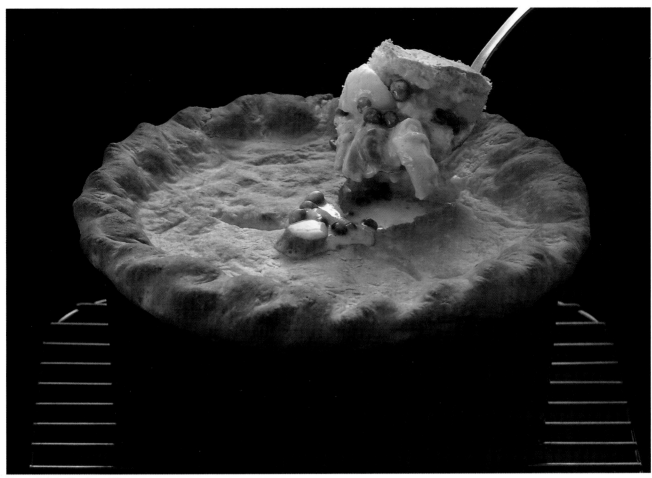

Deep-Dish Turkey Pie

DEEP-DISH TURKEY PIE

3 cups cubed cooked turkey or chicken
1 cup sliced cooked carrots
1 cup cubed cooked potatoes
1 cup frozen green peas, thawed
6 tablespoons margarine or butter
⅓ cup unsifted flour
2 tablespoons WYLER'S® or STEERO®
    Chicken-Flavor Instant Bouillon *or*
    6 Chicken-Flavor Bouillon Cubes
¼ teaspoon pepper
4 cups BORDEN® or MEADOW GOLD®
    Milk
2¼ cups biscuit baking mix

Preheat oven to 375°F. In large saucepan, melt margarine; stir in flour, bouillon and pepper. Over medium heat, gradually add milk; cook and stir until bouillon dissolves and mixture thickens. Add remaining ingredients except biscuit mix; mix well. Pour into 2½-quart baking dish. Prepare biscuit mix according to package directions for rolled biscuits. Roll out to cover dish; cut slashes in center of dough. Place on top of dish; crimp edges. Bake 40 minutes or until golden. Refrigerate leftovers.

Makes 6 servings

CURRIED TURKEY DINNER

1 package (10 ounces) frozen broccoli
spears, cooked and drained
2 cups cubed cooked turkey
1 can (10½ ounces) reduced-sodium
cream of mushroom soup
¼ cup reduced-calorie mayonnaise
1½ teaspoons lemon juice
1 teaspoon curry powder
1 cup seasoned croutons

1. Preheat oven to 350°F.

2. In 8-inch square baking dish arrange
broccoli; top with turkey.

3. In small bowl combine soup, mayonnaise,
lemon juice and curry powder. Pour over turkey
and top with croutons.

4. Bake 20 to 25 minutes or until bubbly.
Makes 4 servings

*Favorite recipe from **National Turkey Federation***

HERBED CHICKEN AND BROCCOLI

10 ounces boneless skinless chicken
breasts, sliced into ½-inch strips
1 teaspoon Italian herb seasoning
1 cup *undiluted* CARNATION® Lite
Evaporated Skimmed Milk
2 tablespoons all-purpose flour
1 clove garlic, crushed
¼ teaspoon salt (optional)
⅛ teaspoon white pepper
½ cup (2 ounces) shredded, reduced-fat
Swiss cheese
1 package (10 ounces) frozen broccoli
spears, thawed, drained and cut into
bite-size pieces
Paprika

Curried Turkey Dinner

Sprinkle chicken with Italian seasoning. Pound between sheets of plastic wrap. Spray nonstick skillet with nonstick cooking spray. Sauté chicken strips just until no longer pink. Keep warm. In small saucepan, whisk small amount of evaporated skimmed milk into flour. Stir in remaining milk, garlic, salt and pepper. Cook over medium heat, stirring constantly, until mixture just comes to a boil and thickens. Add cheese; stir until melted. Spray 10×6×2-inch baking dish with nonstick cooking spray. Spread about ¼ cup sauce in bottom of dish. Arrange broccoli over sauce; top with chicken pieces. Pour *remaining* sauce over top. Sprinkle with paprika. Cover. Bake in preheated 350°F oven 20 to 25 minutes or until heated through.

Makes 4 servings

TASTY TURKEY POT PIE

½ cup MIRACLE WHIP® Salad Dressing
2 tablespoons flour
1 teaspoon instant chicken bouillon
⅛ teaspoon pepper
¾ cup milk
1½ cups chopped cooked turkey or chicken
1 (10-ounce) package frozen mixed vegetables, thawed, drained
1 (4-ounce) can refrigerated quick crescent dinner rolls

Combine salad dressing, flour, bouillon and pepper in medium saucepan. Gradually add milk. Cook, stirring constantly, over low heat until thickened. Add turkey and vegetables; heat thoroughly, stirring occasionally. Spoon into 8-inch square baking dish. Unroll dough into two rectangles. Press perforations together to seal. Place rectangles side-by-side to form square; press edges together to form seam. Cover turkey mixture with dough. Bake at 375°F, 15 to 20 minutes or until browned.

Makes 4 to 6 servings

PREP TIME: 15 minutes
BAKE TIME: 20 minutes

VARIATIONS: Combine 1 egg, beaten, and 1 tablespoon cold water, mixing until well blended. Brush dough with egg mixture just before baking.

Substitute 1 chicken bouillon cube for instant chicken bouillon.

Substitute 10×6-inch baking dish for 8-inch square baking dish.

Substitute 12×8-inch baking dish for 8-inch square dish. Double all ingredients. Assemble recipe as directed, using three dough rectangles to form top crust. Decorate crust with cut-outs from remaining rectangle. Bake as directed.

MICROWAVE TIP: To prepare sauce, combine salad dressing, flour, bouillon and pepper in 1-quart microwave-safe measure or bowl; gradually add milk. Microwave on HIGH 4 to 5 minutes or until thickened, stirring after each minute.

CHICKEN AND VEGGIE LASAGNA

Tomato-Herb Sauce (recipe follows)
Nonstick olive oil cooking spray
1½ cups thinly sliced zucchini
1 cup thinly sliced carrots
3 cups torn fresh spinach leaves
½ teaspoon salt
1 container (15 ounces) fat free ricotta
   cheese
½ cup grated Parmesan cheese
9 lasagna noodles, cooked and drained
2 cups (8 ounces) reduced fat shredded
   mozzarella cheese

Prepare Tomato-Herb Sauce. Preheat oven to 350°F. Spray large nonstick skillet with cooking spray; heat over medium heat until hot. Add zucchini and carrots; cook and stir about 5 minutes or until almost tender. Remove from heat; stir in spinach and salt.

Combine ricotta and Parmesan cheese in small bowl. Spread 1⅔ cups Tomato-Herb Sauce on bottom of 13×9-inch baking pan. Top with 3 noodles. Spoon half the ricotta cheese mixture over noodles; spread lightly with spatula. Spoon half the zucchini mixture over ricotta cheese mixture; sprinkle with 1 cup mozzarella cheese. Repeat layers; place remaining 3 noodles on top.

Spread remaining Tomato-Herb Sauce over noodles. Cover with aluminum foil; bake 1 hour or until sauce is bubbly. Let stand 5 to 10 minutes; cut into rectangles. Garnish as desired. *Makes 12 servings*

TOMATO–HERB SAUCE

Nonstick olive oil cooking spray
1½ cups chopped onions (about 2
   medium)
4 cloves garlic, minced
1 tablespoon dried basil leaves
1 teaspoon dried oregano leaves
½ teaspoon dried tarragon leaves
¼ teaspoon dried thyme leaves
2½ pounds ripe tomatoes, peeled, cut into
   wedges
1 pound ground chicken, cooked,
   crumbled and drained
¾ cup water
¼ cup no-salt-added tomato paste
½ teaspoon salt
½ teaspoon pepper

Spray large nonstick skillet with cooking spray; heat over medium heat until hot. Add onions, garlic, basil, oregano, tarragon and thyme; cook and stir about 5 minutes or until onions are tender.

Add tomatoes, chicken, water and tomato paste; heat to a boil. Reduce heat to low and simmer, uncovered, about 20 minutes or until sauce is reduced to 5 cups. Stir in salt and pepper. *Makes 5 cups*

Chicken and Veggie Lasagna

Seafood TREASURES

BAKED STUFFED SNAPPER

1 red snapper (1½ pounds)
2 cups hot cooked rice
1 can (4 ounces) sliced mushrooms, drained
½ cup diced water chestnuts
¼ cup thinly sliced green onions
¼ cup diced pimiento
2 tablespoons chopped parsley
1 tablespoon finely shredded lemon peel
½ teaspoon salt
⅛ teaspoon ground black pepper
1 tablespoon margarine, melted

Preheat oven to 400°F. Clean and butterfly fish. Combine rice, mushrooms, water chestnuts, onions, pimiento, parsley, lemon peel, salt and pepper; toss lightly. Fill cavity of fish with rice mixture; close with wooden toothpicks soaked in water. Place fish in 13×9-inch baking dish coated with nonstick cooking spray; brush fish with margarine. Bake 18 to 20 minutes or until fish flakes easily when tested with fork. Wrap any remaining rice in foil and bake in oven with fish. *Makes 4 servings*

Favorite recipe from **USA Rice Council**

Baked Salmon with Almonds and Lime-Parsley Sauce

In food processor or blender, combine garlic, egg yolk, lime juice, cumin, ¼ teaspoon salt and pinch of pepper. With machine running, slowly pour in vegetable oil and 1½ teaspoons olive oil. (To prepare by hand, beat egg yolk until thick and lemon colored. Beat in garlic, lime juice, cumin, ¼ teaspoon salt and pinch of pepper. Combine vegetable oil and 1½ teaspoons olive oil. Whisking constantly, add oil one drop at a time until mixture begins to thicken. Pour remaining oil in a thin, steady stream, whisking constantly.) Mixture will resemble mayonnaise. Fold in chopped parsley. Place salmon in baking dish. Brush with remaining 3 teaspoons olive oil; season with salt and pepper. Spread lime-parsley sauce down center of each fillet. Top with almonds. Bake at 400°F for 8 to 12 minutes or until fish is just firm. *Makes 4 to 6 servings*

BAKED SALMON WITH ALMONDS AND LIME–PARSLEY SAUCE

 1 large clove garlic, finely chopped
 1 egg yolk
 1 teaspoon lime juice
 ½ teaspoon cumin
  Salt
  White pepper
 ½ cup vegetable oil
4½ teaspoons olive oil, divided
 6 tablespoons chopped parsley
 4 salmon fillets, about 6 ounces each
 ¾ cup BLUE DIAMOND® Sliced Natural Almonds, lightly toasted

BROILED RAINBOW TROUT WITH HERB MAYONNAISE

 6 tablespoons regular or light mayonnaise
 1 clove garlic, minced
 1 tablespoon lemon juice
  Herbs to taste
  Dash pepper
 4 CLEAR SPRINGS® Brand Idaho Rainbow Trout fillets (4 ounces each)

Combine mayonnaise, garlic, lemon juice, herbs and pepper in bowl; mix well. Place trout, skin side down, on rack of broiler pan. Top each fillet with ¼ of mayonnaise mixture. Broil 4 inches from heat source for about 3 to 5 minutes or until fish flakes with a fork and topping is bubbly. *Makes 2 to 4 servings*

SOLEFUL ROULETTES

  1 package (6 ounces) long-grain and wild
      rice mix
  1 package (3 ounces) cream cheese,
      softened
  2 tablespoons milk
32 medium fresh spinach leaves, washed
  4 sole fillets (about 1 pound)
     Salt and coarsely ground black pepper
¼ cup dry white wine
½ cup water

Cook rice mix according to package directions.
Place 2 cups cooked rice in large bowl.
(Refrigerate remaining rice for another use.)
Combine cream cheese and milk in medium
bowl. Stir into rice; set aside.

Place spinach in heatproof bowl. Pour very hot
water (not boiling) over spinach to wilt leaves
slightly. Rinse sole and pat dry with paper
towels. Sprinkle both sides of each fillet with
salt and pepper. Cover each fillet with spinach
leaves. Divide rice mixture evenly and spread
over top of each spinach-lined fillet. To roll
fillets, begin with thin end of fillet, roll up and
secure with wooden toothpicks.

Combine wine and water in large, heavy
saucepan. Stand fillets upright on rolled edges
in saucepan; cover. Simmer over low heat 10
minutes or until fish flakes easily when tested
with fork. *(Do not boil. This will cause fish to
break apart.)*   *Makes 4 servings*

Soleful Roulette

MAHI-MAHI WITH FRESH PINEAPPLE SALSA

1½ cups diced fresh pineapple
¼ cup finely chopped red bell pepper
¼ cup finely chopped green bell pepper
2 tablespoons chopped fresh cilantro
2 tablespoons fresh lime juice, divided
½ teaspoon crushed red pepper flakes
½ teaspoon grated lime peel
   Nonstick cooking spray
4 mahi-mahi fillets (4 ounces each)
1 tablespoon olive oil
½ teaspoon ground white pepper

To prepare Pineapple Salsa, combine pineapple, red and green peppers, cilantro, 1 tablespoon lime juice, red pepper flakes and lime peel in medium bowl.

Preheat broiler. Spray rack of broiler pan with cooking spray. Rinse mahi-mahi and pat dry with paper towels. Place mahi-mahi on rack. Combine remaining 1 tablespoon lime juice and olive oil; brush on mahi-mahi.

Broil, 4 inches from heat, 2 minutes. Turn and brush second side with olive oil mixture; sprinkle with white pepper. Continue to broil 2 minutes or until mahi-mahi flakes easily when tested with fork. Serve with Pineapple Salsa.

Makes 4 servings

NOTE: Pineapple Salsa may be prepared 1 to 2 days ahead and refrigerated.

TROUT WITH APPLES AND TOASTED HAZELNUTS

⅓ cup whole hazelnuts
5 tablespoons butter or margarine, divided
1 large Red Delicious apple, cored and cut into 16 wedges
2 butterflied rainbow trout fillets (about 8 ounces each)
   Salt and black pepper
3 tablespoons all-purpose flour
1 tablespoon lemon juice
1 tablespoon snipped fresh chives
   Lemon slices and fresh chives for garnish

Preheat oven to 350°F. To toast hazelnuts, spread in single layer on baking sheet. Bake 8 to 10 minutes or until skins split.

Wrap hazelnuts in kitchen towel; set aside 5 minutes to cool slightly. Rub nuts in towel to remove as much of the papery skins as possible. Process hazelnuts in food processor until coarsely chopped; set aside.

Melt 3 tablespoons butter in medium skillet over medium-high heat. Add apple; cook 4 to 5 minutes or until crisp-tender. Remove from skillet with slotted spoon; set aside.

Rinse trout and pat dry with paper towels. Sprinkle fish with salt and pepper, then coat in flour. Place fish in skillet. Cook 4 minutes or until golden and fish flakes easily when tested with fork, turning halfway through cooking time. Return apple to skillet. Reduce heat to low and keep warm.

Melt remaining 2 tablespoons butter in small saucepan over low heat. Stir in lemon juice, chives and hazelnuts. Drizzle fish and apple with hazelnut mixture. Garnish, if desired.

Makes 2 servings

Mahi-Mahi with Fresh Pineapple Salsa

GRILLED SWORDFISH À L'ORANGE

4 swordfish, halibut or shark steaks (about 1½ pounds)
1 orange
¾ cup orange juice
1 tablespoon lemon juice
1 tablespoon sesame oil
1 tablespoon soy sauce
1 teaspoon cornstarch
 Salt and black pepper to taste

Rinse swordfish and pat dry with paper towels. Grate enough orange peel to measure 1 teaspoon; set aside. Peel orange and cut into sections; set aside. Combine orange juice, lemon juice, oil and soy sauce in small bowl. Pour half of orange juice mixture into shallow glass dish. Add ½ teaspoon grated orange peel to orange juice mixture. Place fish in dish; turn to coat in mixture. Cover and allow to marinate in refrigerator for at least 1 hour.

Place remaining half of orange juice mixture in small saucepan. Stir in cornstarch and remaining ½ teaspoon orange peel. Heat over medium-high heat, stirring constantly, 3 to 5 minutes or until sauce thickens; set aside.

Remove fish from marinade; discard remaining marinade. Lightly sprinkle fish with salt and pepper. Grill over medium coals 3 to 4 minutes per side or until fish is opaque and flakes easily when tested with fork. Top with reserved orange sections and orange sauce. Serve immediately. *Makes 4 servings*

Grilled Swordfish à l'Orange

SALMON EN PAPILLOTE

¾ cup water
1 teaspoon extra virgin olive oil
¼ teaspoon salt
⅛ teaspoon black pepper
½ cup uncooked couscous
    Parchment paper
1 small yellow squash, cut into julienned
    strips (1 cup)
½ pound fresh salmon fillet, bones
    removed and cut into 2 pieces
½ cup peeled and diced plum tomatoes
2 teaspoons *each* chopped fresh dill and
    chopped fresh tarragon, divided *or*
    ¼ teaspoon *each* dried dill weed and
    dried tarragon leaves, divided
2 teaspoons *each* chopped fresh chives
    and chopped fresh parsley, divided
1 egg, beaten
    Dilled Wine Sauce (recipe follows)

Preheat oven to 350°F. To prepare couscous, combine water, oil, salt and black pepper in small saucepan with tight-fitting lid. Bring to a boil. Add couscous and mix well. Cover and remove from heat. Let stand 5 minutes or until all liquid is absorbed.

Cut parchment paper into two 12-inch squares. Fold in half diagonally and cut into half-heart shapes. Unfold hearts and spoon ½ cup couscous on one side of each heart. Top each with ½ cup squash, 1 piece salmon, ¼ cup tomato and 1 teaspoon *each* dill, tarragon, chives and parsley. To seal packages, brush outer edges of hearts with beaten egg. Fold over again, making half-heart shapes; press edges together, crimping tightly with fingers. Place packages on ungreased baking sheet; bake 14 minutes. Meanwhile, prepare Dilled Wine Sauce.

To serve, place each package on large plate and cut an "X" in top. Fold corners back and drizzle sauce over each serving. Garnish with edible flowers, such as pansies, violets or nasturtiums, if desired.   *Makes 2 servings*

DILLED WINE SAUCE

1½ cups finely chopped onions
½ cup chopped fresh dill *or* 1 tablespoon
    dried dill weed
¼ cup chopped fresh tarragon *or*
    1½ teaspoons dried tarragon leaves
1 clove garlic, peeled and quartered
½ cup dry white wine
2 teaspoons extra virgin olive oil

Combine all ingredients except oil in blender or food processor; process until smooth. Pour dill mixture into small saucepan and bring to a boil over medium heat. Reduce heat to low; simmer until reduced by half. Strain sauce into small bowl, pressing all liquid through strainer with back of spoon. Slowly whisk in oil until smooth and well blended.   *Makes ½ cup*

Salmon en Papillote

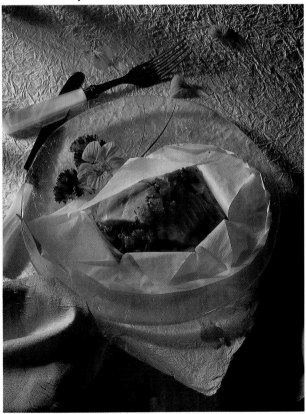

TUNA WITH PEPPERCORNS ON A BED OF GREENS

    4 tuna steaks (about 1½ pounds)
      Salt
    2 teaspoons coarsely ground black
      pepper
    1 tablespoon butter or margarine
    1 large onion, thinly sliced
    ¼ cup dry white wine
    ½ pound fresh kale or spinach, washed
    1 tablespoon olive oil
    ½ teaspoon sugar
    ¼ teaspoon black pepper
   12 julienne strips carrot
      Lemon slices and purple kale for
      garnish

Preheat oven to 325°F. Rinse tuna and pat dry with paper towels. Lightly sprinkle fish with salt, then press coarsely ground pepper into both sides of steaks; set aside.

Melt butter in large skillet over medium heat. Add onion; cook and stir 5 minutes or until crisp-tender. Add wine and remove from heat. Spread onion mixture on bottom of 13×9-inch glass baking dish. Top with fish. Bake 15 minutes. Spoon liquid over fish and bake 15 minutes more or until fish flakes easily when tested with fork.

Tuna with Peppercorns on a Bed of Greens

Meanwhile, trim away tough stems from kale; cut leaves into 1-inch strips. Heat oil in medium skillet over medium-high heat. Add kale, sugar and black pepper. Cook and stir 2 to 3 minutes or until tender. Place kale on plates. Top with fish and onion mixture. Top fish with carrot strips. Garnish, if desired. Serve immediately.
Makes 4 servings

BLACKENED SNAPPER WITH RED ONION SALSA

      Cajun Seasoning Mix (recipe follows)
      Red Onion Salsa (page 207)
    4 red snapper fillets (about 6 ounces
      each)
    2 tablespoons butter

Prepare Cajun Seasoning Mix and Red Onion Salsa; set aside. Rinse red snapper and pat dry with paper towels. Sprinkle with Cajun Seasoning Mix. Heat large, heavy skillet over high heat until very hot. Add butter and swirl skillet to coat bottom. When butter no longer bubbles, place fish in pan. Cook fish 6 to 8 minutes or until surface is very brown and fish flakes easily when tested with fork, turning halfway through cooking. Serve with Red Onion Salsa. *Makes 4 servings*

CAJUN SEASONING MIX
    2 tablespoons salt
    1 tablespoon paprika
   1½ teaspoons garlic powder
    1 teaspoon onion powder
    1 teaspoon ground red pepper
    ½ teaspoon ground white pepper
    ½ teaspoon ground black pepper
    ½ teaspoon dried thyme leaves, crushed
    ½ teaspoon dried oregano leaves, crushed

Combine all ingredients in small bowl.
Makes about ½ cup

RED ONION SALSA

    1 tablespoon vegetable oil
    1 large red onion, chopped
    1 clove garlic, minced
  ½ cup Fish Stock (page 208) or chicken
      broth
  ¼ cup dry red wine or red wine vinegar
  ¼ teaspoon dried thyme leaves, crushed
    Salt and ground black pepper to taste

Heat oil in small saucepan over medium-high heat. Add onion; cover and cook 5 minutes. Add garlic; cook 1 minute. Add remaining ingredients. Cover and cook about 10 minutes. Uncover and cook until liquid reduces to ¼ cup.

Makes about 1 cup

SAUMON AU FOUR (BAKED SALMON)

    5 tablespoons butter, divided
 1½ pounds salmon steaks
  15 frozen artichoke hearts, cooked, halved
    Juice of 1 large lemon
    Salt and pepper
   1 (4-ounce) package ALOUETTE® Garlic
      & Spices Cheese
   1 teaspoon dried basil leaves, crushed

Preheat oven to 375°F. Grease casserole dish with 1 tablespoon butter. Arrange salmon steaks and artichoke hearts in dish; sprinkle with lemon juice. Melt remaining 4 tablespoons butter; pour over salmon and artichokes. Season with salt and pepper.

Spread Alouette® generously over salmon and artichokes; sprinkle with basil. Bake about 20 minutes or until fish flakes easily when tested with fork and cheese is melted.

Makes 4 servings

*Favorite recipe from **Bongrain Cheese U.S.A.***

Blackened Snapper with Red Onion Salsa

POACHED SALMON WITH TARRAGON CREAM SAUCE

2 tablespoons butter or margarine
3 tablespoons minced shallot
1 clove garlic, minced
1 cup dry white wine, divided
½ cup clam juice
½ cup heavy cream
1 tablespoon chopped fresh parsley
½ teaspoon dried tarragon leaves, crushed
2 salmon steaks, 1 inch thick (about 8 ounces each)
Fish Stock (recipe follows), clam juice or water
Fresh tarragon for garnish

To make Tarragon Cream Sauce, melt butter in medium saucepan over medium heat. Add shallot and garlic; reduce heat to low and cook 5 minutes or until shallot is tender. Add ½ cup wine and clam juice. Bring to a simmer. Simmer 10 minutes or until sauce is reduced to ½ cup. Add heavy cream and simmer 5 minutes or until sauce is reduced by half. (The sauce should heavily coat the back of a metal spoon.) Stir in parsley and dried tarragon; keep warm over very low heat.

Rinse salmon and pat dry with paper towels. Place steaks in saucepan just large enough to hold them. Add remaining ½ cup wine and enough Fish Stock to barely cover fish. Bring liquid to a simmer over medium heat. *(Do not boil. This will cause fish to break apart.)* Adjust heat, if necessary, to keep liquid at a simmer. Simmer 10 minutes or until center is no longer red and fish flakes easily when tested with fork. Remove fish with slotted spatula; transfer to serving plates. Top fish with Tarragon Cream Sauce. Garnish, if desired.

Makes 2 servings

FISH STOCK

1¾ pounds fish skeletons and heads from lean fish, such as red snapper, cod, halibut or flounder
2 medium onions, cut into wedges
3 ribs celery, cut into 2-inch pieces
10 cups cold water
2 slices lemon
¾ teaspoon dried thyme leaves, crushed
8 black peppercorns
3 fresh parsley sprigs
1 bay leaf
1 clove garlic

Rinse fish; cut out gills and discard. Combine fish skeletons and heads, onions and celery in stockpot or Dutch oven. Add remaining ingredients. Bring to a boil over high heat. Reduce heat to medium-low; simmer, uncovered, 30 minutes, skimming foam that rises to the surface. Remove stock from heat and cool slightly. Strain stock through large sieve or colander lined with several layers of dampened cheesecloth, removing all bones, vegetables and seasonings; discard. Use immediately or refrigerate in tightly covered container up to 2 days or freeze stock in freezer containers for several months.

Makes about 10 cups

Poached Salmon with Tarragon Cream Sauce

SEAFOOD LASAGNA WITH SPAGHETTI SQUASH AND BROCCOLI

- 1 tablespoon olive oil
- 1 cup minced shallots
- 16 small mushrooms, cut in half
- 1 tablespoon minced garlic (2 to 4 cloves)
- 1 teaspoon dried thyme leaves
- 3 tablespoons flour
- 2 cups dry white wine or chicken broth
- 1 cup bottled clam juice
- ¼ teaspoon freshly ground nutmeg
  Ground pepper to taste
- 1½ pounds cooked seafood mixture of firm-textured fish (such as salmon) and scallops, cut into bite-sized pieces, divided
- 6 lasagna noodles, cooked and drained
- 4 ounces (1½ to 2 cups) stuffing mix
- 1 (10-ounce) package frozen chopped broccoli, thawed
- 1 pound JARLSBERG LITE Cheese, shredded
- 3 cups cooked spaghetti squash

Heat oil in large skillet over medium-high heat. Sauté shallots, mushrooms, garlic and thyme in oil 4 minutes or until shallots begin to brown. Add flour; cook, stirring constantly, 2 to 3 minutes. Add wine, clam juice, nutmeg and pepper. Boil 3 minutes to thicken and reduce liquid. Add fish pieces and simmer 3 minutes. Add scallops; remove skillet from heat and set aside.

Arrange 3 lasagna noodles on bottom of 3½-quart, rectangular baking dish. Evenly sprinkle with stuffing mix. Reserve 1 cup sauce mixture; spoon remaining sauce mixture over stuffing mix. Cover evenly with broccoli, ⅔ of cheese and 2 cups spaghetti squash. Cover with remaining lasagna noodles, cheese, reserved sauce mixture and remaining spaghetti squash. Press down firmly.* Cover tightly with tented foil and bake at 350°F, 45 to 50 minutes or until heated through. *Makes 10 to 12 servings*

*Recipe can be made ahead up to this point and refrigerated. Bring to room temperature before baking.

TIP: To cook spaghetti squash, pierce in several places and place on baking sheet in 350°F oven for 1 hour or until tender when pierced with knife. When squash is cool, cut in half, scoop out seeds and remove strands with two forks. Squash may be prepared ahead and refrigerated until needed.

*Favorite recipe from **Norseland, Inc.***

CHESAPEAKE CRAB CAKES

- 1 pound backfin crabmeat
- ½ cup soft bread crumbs
- 1 tablespoon minced onion
- 1 tablespoon finely chopped green bell pepper
- 1 tablespoon chopped fresh parsley
- ¼ cup mayonnaise
- 1 egg
- 2 teaspoons white wine Worcestershire sauce
- 2 teaspoons lemon juice
- 1 teaspoon prepared mustard
- ½ teaspoon salt
- ¼ teaspoon ground white pepper
  Vegetable oil for frying (optional)
  Tartar Sauce (page 211)

Pick out and discard any shell or cartilage from crabmeat. Flake with fork. Place crabmeat in medium bowl. Add bread crumbs, onion, bell pepper and parsley; set aside.

Mix remaining ingredients except oil and Tartar Sauce in small bowl. Stir well to combine. Pour mayonnaise mixture over crabmeat mixture. Gently mix so large lumps will not be broken. Shape mixture into 6 large (¾-inch-thick) cakes or 36 bite-sized cakes.

TO PAN-FRY CRAB CAKES:

Pour enough oil into 12-inch skillet to cover bottom. Heat oil over medium-high heat until hot. Add crab cakes; fry 10 minutes for large cakes and 6 minutes for bite-sized cakes or until cakes are lightly browned on bottom. Using spatula, carefully turn halfway through cooking without breaking cakes.

TO BROIL CRAB CAKES:

Preheat broiler. Place crab cakes on broiler pan. Broil 4 to 6 inches below heat 10 minutes for large cakes and 6 minutes for bite-sized cakes or until cakes are lightly browned on surface, turning halfway through cooking.

Makes 6 servings

TARTAR SAUCE

- **1 cup mayonnaise**
- **2 tablespoons chopped cornichons or dill relish**
- **1 clove garlic, minced**
- **1 teaspoon fresh lemon juice**
- **1 teaspoon prepared horseradish**
- **2 to 3 dashes ground red pepper**
- **3 tablespoons sun-dried tomatoes packed in oil (optional)**

Combine mayonnaise, cornichons, garlic, lemon juice, horseradish and red pepper in small bowl. Drain sun-dried tomatoes and pat dry with paper towels. Slice tomatoes lengthwise into thin strips and cut in half. Fold tomatoes into mayonnaise mixture.

Makes about 1 cup

SERVING SUGGESTIONS: Serve large crab cakes on plates or as sandwiches with round buns. Serve bite-sized cakes on plates or with toothpicks as appetizers. Accompany with Tartar Sauce.

Chesapeake Crab Cake

CAJUN CHRISTMAS GUMBO

10 to 12 chicken thighs (4 to 5 pounds)
¼ cup olive or vegetable oil
1 cup chopped onion
½ cup chopped green bell pepper
⅓ cup all-purpose flour
2 cloves garlic, crushed
1 can (28 ounces) whole peeled tomatoes
2 cups chicken broth or water
½ teaspoon crushed red pepper flakes
½ teaspoon dried thyme leaves, crushed
1 bay leaf
½ package (10 ounces) frozen sliced okra
24 ounces Surimi Seafood, crab flavored, chunk or flake style
½ pint standard oysters
½ cup fresh parsley, finely chopped
Hot cooked white rice

Preheat oven to 350°F. Place chicken thighs in single layer in shallow baking pan. Bake 45 to 50 minutes or until chicken is no longer pink and juices run clear.

Meanwhile, heat oil in Dutch oven. Add onion and bell pepper; cook over medium-low heat 10 minutes or until onion is translucent, stirring occasionally. Stir in flour; reduce heat to low. Cook 5 minutes, stirring occasionally. Add garlic, tomatoes, chicken broth, red pepper, thyme and bay leaf. Cook, uncovered, stirring constantly, until slightly thickened. Cover; cook over low heat 30 minutes, stirring occasionally to prevent sticking.

Add cooked chicken with pan juices and okra to vegetable mixture. Increase heat to medium-low; simmer 15 to 20 minutes. Stir in Surimi Seafood, oysters and parsley; cook 5 to 10 minutes or until seafood is heated through and oysters begin to curl. Remove and discard bay leaf. Pour gumbo into soup tureen or serving bowl. Ladle gumbo over rice in soup bowls to serve. *Makes 10 to 12 servings*

Favorite recipe from **National Fisheries Institute**

SEAFOOD OVER ANGEL HAIR PASTA

¼ cup WISH-BONE® Italian Dressing*
¼ cup chopped shallots or onion
1 cup thinly sliced carrots
4 ounces snow peas, thinly sliced (about 1 cup)
1 cup chicken broth
¼ cup dry sherry
½ pound uncooked medium shrimp, cleaned (keep tails on)
½ pound sea scallops
8 mussels, well scrubbed
¼ cup whipping or heavy cream
2 tablespoons all-purpose flour
Salt and pepper to taste
8 ounces angel hair pasta or capellini, cooked and drained
Freshly ground black pepper and grated Parmesan cheese (optional)

In 12-inch skillet, heat Italian dressing and cook shallots over medium-high heat 2 minutes. Add carrots and snow peas and cook 2 minutes. Add broth, then sherry. Bring to a boil; add shrimp, scallops and mussels. Simmer covered 3 minutes or until seafood is done and mussel shells open. (Discard any unopened shells.) Stir in cream blended with flour and cook over medium heat, stirring occasionally, 2 minutes or until sauce is slightly thickened. Stir in salt and pepper. Serve over hot pasta and sprinkle, if desired, with freshly ground pepper and grated Parmesan cheese. *Makes about 4 servings*

*Also terrific with Wish-Bone® Robusto Italian, Italian & Cheese, Herbal Italian, Blended Italian, Classic Dijon Vinaigrette, Olive Oil Vinaigrette or Lite Classic Dijon Vinaigrette Dressing.

Cajun Christmas Gumbo

EASY PAELLA

1 medium onion, cut into halves and
　　chopped
1 large red or green bell pepper, sliced
1 clove garlic, minced
2 tablespoons vegetable oil
1 can (16 ounces) tomatoes with juice,
　　cut up
1 package (9 ounces) frozen artichoke
　　hearts, cut into quarters
½ cup dry white wine
½ teaspoon dried thyme, crushed
¼ teaspoon salt
⅛ teaspoon saffron or turmeric
2 cups cooked rice
1 cup frozen peas
½ pound large shrimp, peeled and
　　deveined
1 can (6 ounces) STARKIST® Tuna,
　　drained and broken into chunks

In a large skillet sauté onion, bell pepper and
garlic in oil for 3 minutes. Stir in tomatoes with
juice, artichoke hearts, wine and seasonings.
Bring to a boil; reduce heat. Simmer for 10
minutes. Stir in rice, peas, shrimp and tuna.
Cook for 3 to 5 minutes more or until shrimp
turn pink and mixture is heated.

Makes 4 servings

PREP TIME: 30 minutes

Easy Paella

CRAB & SHRIMP QUICHE

1 (9-inch) unbaked pastry shell
6 slices BORDEN® Process American
Cheese Food
2 tablespoons sliced green onion
2 tablespoons chopped pimiento
1 tablespoon flour
1 (6-ounce) can ORLEANS® or HARRIS®
Crabmeat, drained
1 (4¼-ounce) can ORLEANS® Shrimp,
drained and soaked as label directs
1½ cups BORDEN® or MEADOW GOLD®
Half-and-Half
3 eggs, beaten

Place rack in lowest position in oven; preheat oven to 425°F. Cut *4 slices* cheese food into pieces. In large bowl, toss cheese food pieces, onion and pimiento with flour. Add remaining ingredients except pastry shell and cheese food slices. Pour into pastry shell. Bake 20 minutes. Reduce oven temperature to 325°F; bake 20 minutes longer or until set. Arrange remaining *2 slices* cheese food on top of quiche. Let stand 10 minutes before serving. Garnish as desired. Refrigerate leftovers.

Makes one 9-inch quiche

Boiled Whole Lobster with Burned Butter Sauce

BOILED WHOLE LOBSTER WITH BURNED BUTTER SAUCE

½ cup butter
2 tablespoons chopped fresh parsley
1 tablespoon cider vinegar
1 tablespoon capers
2 live lobsters*

Fill 8-quart stockpot with enough water to cover lobsters. Cover stockpot; bring water to a boil over high heat. Meanwhile, to make Burned Butter Sauce, melt butter in medium saucepan over medium heat. Cook and stir butter until it turns dark chocolate brown. Remove from heat. Add parsley, vinegar and capers. Pour into 2 individual ramekins; set aside.

Holding each lobster by its back, submerge head first into boiling water. Cover and continue to heat. When water returns to a boil, cook lobsters from 10 to 18 minutes, according to size:

1 pound—10 minutes
1¼ pounds—12 minutes
1½ pounds—15 minutes
2 pounds—18 minutes

Transfer to 2 large serving platters. Remove bands restraining claws. Cut through underside of shells with kitchen shears and loosen meat from shells. Provide nutcrackers and seafood forks. Serve lobsters with Burned Butter Sauce.

Makes 2 servings

*Purchase live lobsters as close to time of cooking as possible. Store in refrigerator.

SEAFOOD PAELLA

1 tablespoon olive oil
4 cloves garlic, minced
4½ cups finely chopped onions
2 cups uncooked long-grain white rice
2 cups clam juice
2 cups dry white wine
3 tablespoons fresh lemon juice
½ teaspoon paprika
¼ cup boiling water
½ teaspoon saffron or ground turmeric
1½ cups peeled and diced plum tomatoes
½ cup chopped fresh parsley
1 jar (8 ounces) roasted red peppers, drained, thinly sliced and divided
1 pound bay scallops
1½ cups frozen peas, thawed
10 clams, scrubbed
10 mussels, scrubbed
20 large shrimp (1 pound), shelled and deveined

Preheat oven to 375°F. Heat oil in large ovenproof skillet or paella pan over medium-low heat until hot. Add garlic and cook just until garlic sizzles. Add onions and rice; cook and stir 10 minutes or until onions are soft. Stir in clam juice, wine, lemon juice and paprika; mix well.

Combine boiling water and saffron in small bowl; stir until saffron is dissolved. Stir into onion mixture. Stir in tomatoes, parsley and half the red peppers. Bring to a boil over medium heat. Remove from heat; cover. Place on lowest shelf of oven. Bake 1 hour or until all liquid is absorbed.

Remove from oven; stir in scallops and peas. *Turn oven off;* return paella to oven. Steam clams and mussels 4 to 6 minutes, removing each as shells open. (Discard any unopened clams or mussels.) Steam shrimp 2 to 3 minutes *just* until shrimp turn pink and opaque. Remove paella from oven and arrange clams, mussels and shrimp on top. Garnish with remaining red pepper.   *Makes 10 servings*

SHRIMP PASTA MEDLEY

¼ cup (½ stick) PARKAY® Spread Sticks
1 clove garlic, minced
12 ounces medium shrimp, cleaned
1 cup half-and-half
1 cup pea pods, cut in half diagonally
1 red bell pepper, cut into strips
¼ cup dry white wine
¼ teaspoon crushed red pepper
8 ounces linguine, cooked, drained
1 wedge (4 ounces) KRAFT® Natural Parmesan Cheese, shredded, divided

• Melt spread in large skillet on medium heat. Add garlic; cook and stir until lightly browned.

• Stir in shrimp, half-and-half, pea pods, bell pepper, wine and crushed red pepper. Simmer 3 to 5 minutes or until shrimp turn pink.

• Pour sauce mixture over hot linguine. Sprinkle with ¾ cup of the cheese; toss to coat. Serve with remaining ¼ cup cheese.
Makes 4 servings

PREP TIME: 10 minutes
COOKING TIME: 10 minutes

VARIATION: Substitute 1½ cups chopped cooked chicken for shrimp.

Seafood Paella

Yuletide

VEGETABLES & SIDES

ORANGE–GLAZED CARROTS

1 pound fresh or thawed frozen baby carrots
⅓ cup orange marmalade
2 tablespoons butter
2 teaspoons Dijon-style mustard
½ teaspoon grated fresh ginger

To cook carrots, heat 1 inch lightly salted water in 2-quart saucepan over high heat to a boil; immediately add carrots. Return to a boil. Reduce heat to low. Cover and simmer 10 to 12 minutes for fresh carrots (8 to 10 minutes for frozen carrots) or until crisp-tender. Drain well; return carrots to pan. Stir in marmalade, butter, mustard and ginger. Simmer, uncovered, over medium heat 3 minutes or until carrots are glazed, stirring occasionally.* *Makes 6 servings*

*At this point, carrots may be transferred to a microwavable casserole dish with lid. Cover and refrigerate up to 8 hours before serving. To reheat, microwave at HIGH (100% power) 4 to 5 minutes or until hot.

Hot & Spicy Glazed Carrots

HOT & SPICY GLAZED CARROTS

> **2 tablespoons vegetable oil**
> **2 dried red chili peppers**
> **1 pound carrots, peeled and cut diagonally into ⅛-inch slices**
> **¼ cup KIKKOMAN® Teriyaki Baste & Glaze**

Heat oil in hot wok or large skillet over high heat. Add peppers and stir-fry until darkened; remove and discard. Add carrots; reduce heat to medium. Stirfry 4 minutes or until tender-crisp. Stir in teriyaki baste & glaze and cook until carrots are glazed. Serve immediately.

Makes 4 servings

LEMON−GLAZED CARROTS AND RUTABAGA

> **4 to 5 medium carrots (about 12 ounces)**
> **1 small rutabaga (about 12 ounces)**
> **½ cup water**
> **2 tablespoons butter**
> **1 tablespoon *each* brown sugar and lemon juice**
> **½ teaspoon grated lemon peel**
> **¼ teaspoon *each* dill weed and salt**

Cut carrots and rutabaga into julienne strips about 3 inches long. Place carrots, rutabaga and water in medium saucepan; cover and cook over medium heat 13 to 15 minutes. Meanwhile, heat butter, brown sugar, lemon juice, lemon peel, dill weed and salt in small saucepan over medium heat, 2 to 3 minutes. Add to vegetables and continue cooking 3 to 4 minutes, stirring occasionally or until vegetables are glazed and tender.

Makes 8 servings

*Favorite recipe from **National Live Stock & Meat Board***

MICROWAVE GLAZED CARROTS, APPLES AND PEPPERS

> **2 cups thin carrot slices, cut diagonally**
> **1 cup green bell pepper chunks, cut into ½-inch pieces**
> **3 tablespoons water**
> **1½ cups thinly sliced peeled apples**
> **¼ cup light brown sugar**
> **1 teaspoon cornstarch**
> **½ teaspoon ground cinnamon**
> **2 teaspoons margarine**

Combine carrots, bell peppers and water in 1-quart microwavable dish. Cook, covered, on HIGH 3 minutes or until carrots are crisp-tender; drain. Gently toss apples with vegetable mixture. In small mixing bowl, combine brown sugar, cornstarch and cinnamon; cut in margarine. Sprinkle over vegetable mixture. Cover and microwave on HIGH 3 minutes. Gently toss mixture to coat vegetables and apples with sauce; cook, uncovered, 2 to 3 minutes or until sauce thickens.

Makes 5 (½-cup) servings

*Favorite recipe from **The Sugar Association, Inc.***

CARROTS AU GRATIN

    5 tablespoons margarine or butter, divided
1½ cups KELLOGG'S CORN FLAKES® cereal, crushed to ¾ cup
    ⅓ cup chopped onion
    3 tablespoons all-purpose flour
    1 teaspoon salt
    ⅛ teaspoon pepper
1½ cups milk
    1 cup (4 ounces) shredded American cheese
    4 cups sliced carrots, cooked and drained (about 1½ pounds)
    1 tablespoon dried parsley flakes

1. Melt 2 tablespoons margarine. Combine with crushed Kellogg's Corn Flakes cereal; set aside.

2. Melt remaining 3 tablespoons margarine in large saucepan over low heat. Add onion. Cook, stirring frequently, until onion is softened, but not browned. Stir in flour, salt and pepper. Add milk gradually, stirring until smooth. Increase heat to medium and cook until mixture is bubbly and thickened, stirring constantly. Add cheese, stirring until melted. Remove from heat.

3. Stir in carrots and parsley flakes. Spoon mixture into greased 1½-quart glass baking dish. Sprinkle cereal mixture evenly over top.

4. Bake at 350°F about 20 minutes or until thoroughly heated and bubbly. Remove from oven. Let stand about 5 minutes before serving. *Makes 8 servings*

ZUCCHINI AND CARROT FRITTERS

1¾ cups grated zucchini
    ½ teaspoon salt
1¾ cups grated carrots
    2 tablespoons butter or margarine
    3 eggs, beaten
    ½ cup grated Parmesan cheese
    ⅓ cup flour
    1 tablespoon dill weed
    Salt and pepper
    Vegetable oil
    Butter

Mix zucchini and ½ teaspoon salt; let stand 15 minutes. Drain.

Meanwhile, in large skillet, lightly sauté carrots in 2 tablespoons butter. Stir in drained zucchini, eggs, cheese, flour and dill weed. Season with salt and pepper. Spread in greased 13×9-inch baking pan. Bake in preheated 350°F oven 20 to 25 minutes. Brush top with oil and broil until lightly browned. Cut into squares (or cut into rounds using 3-inch fluted biscuit cutter). Serve with butter. *Makes 6 servings*

VARIATION: Prepare mixture as directed. Do not bake. Drop large spoonfuls mixture into hot vegetable oil in large skillet. Fry until golden brown.

Favorite recipe from **Perdue® Farms**

BROCCOLI WITH RED PEPPER AND SHALLOTS

2 bunches fresh broccoli (about 2¼ pounds)
2 teaspoons margarine or butter
1 large red bell pepper, cut into short thin strips
3 large shallots (3 ounces) *or* 1 small onion, thinly sliced
½ teaspoon salt
¼ teaspoon freshly ground black pepper
¼ cup sliced almonds, toasted (optional)

Trim off leaves and tough ends of broccoli stalks. Cut broccoli into flowerets. Peel stalks, then cut into 1-inch pieces. To cook broccoli, heat 2 quarts lightly salted water in 3-quart saucepan over high heat to a boil. Add broccoli and boil, uncovered, 3 to 5 minutes or until bright green and tender. Drain broccoli in colander. Rinse under cold water; drain thoroughly.

Melt margarine in 12-inch nonstick skillet over medium heat. Add bell pepper and shallots. Cook 3 minutes, stirring occasionally. Add broccoli. Cook 4 to 6 minutes, stirring occasionally. Sprinkle with salt and black pepper; mix well. Garnish with almonds, if desired.   *Makes 6 cups, 6 to 8 servings*

CHEESY BROCCOLI 'N' MUSHROOM BAKE

2 (10-ounce) packages frozen broccoli spears, thawed
1 (10¾-ounce) can condensed cream of mushroom soup
½ cup MIRACLE WHIP® Salad Dressing
½ cup milk
1 cup (4 ounces) KRAFT® Natural Shredded Cheddar Cheese
½ cup coarsely crushed croutons

Preheat oven to 350°F. Arrange broccoli in 12×8-inch baking dish. Whisk together soup, salad dressing and milk. Pour over broccoli. Sprinkle with cheese and croutons. Bake 30 to 35 minutes or until heated through. Garnish as desired.   *Makes 6 to 8 servings*

PREP TIME: 10 minutes
BAKE TIME: 30 to 35 minutes

BAKED MINI ACORN SQUASH WITH PEAS AND ONIONS

12 mini acorn squash* (or 1 per person)
6 cups frozen peas with pearl onions

Cut 1-inch slit on each side of squash. Preheat oven to 425°F. Bake squash 30 to 40 minutes or until tender. Meanwhile, cook peas and onions until tender; let cool. To serve, remove tops and seeds from squash; spoon about ½ cup peas and onions into each squash.
       Makes 12 servings

*Mini pumpkins may be substituted if mini acorn squash are not available.

*Favorite recipe from **California Beef Council***

Broccoli with Red Pepper and Shallots

GLAZED STIR-FRY HOLIDAY VEGETABLES

2 tablespoons sugar
½ teaspoon grated lemon peel
3 tablespoons fresh lemon juice
1 tablespoon low sodium soy sauce
2 teaspoons cornstarch
½ cup water
4 teaspoons vegetable oil
3 cups fresh broccoli florets
1 medium red bell pepper, cut into 1-inch pieces
1 cup peeled, julienne-cut jicama
Lemon zest (slivers of lemon peel)

In small bowl combine sugar, lemon peel, lemon juice, soy sauce and cornstarch. Stir in water; set aside. Heat oil in large nonstick skillet. Add broccoli and pepper; stir-fry over high heat 2 minutes. (If needed, add more oil to skillet.) Add jicama and continue cooking 1 to 2 minutes or until vegetables are crisp-tender. Pour lemon mixture over vegetables and continue cooking just until glaze thickens. Toss vegetables to coat thoroughly with glaze. Garnish with lemon zest.

Makes 6 (½-cup) servings

*Favorite recipe from **The Sugar Association, Inc.***

BROCCOLI TIMBALES

1 pound fresh broccoli
3 eggs
1 cup heavy cream
1 tablespoon lemon juice
¼ teaspoon salt
Dash pepper
4 cups boiling water
Chopped tomato and green onion top pieces for garnish

Generously butter six 6-ounce ramekins or custard cups; set in 13×9-inch baking pan. Preheat oven to 375°F.

Trim off leaves and tough ends of broccoli stalks. Cut broccoli into flowerets; set aside. Peel stalks with vegetable peeler. Cut into 1-inch pieces, then cut each piece lengthwise in half. Bring ½ inch of water in medium saucepan to a boil over high heat. Reduce heat to medium-low; add broccoli stem pieces. Cover; simmer about 10 minutes or until fork-tender. Transfer cooked stems with slotted spoon to food processor or blender. Add flowerets to same pan. Cover; simmer about 5 minutes or until flowerets turn bright green. Remove flowerets with slotted spoon to cutting board.

Add eggs to stem pieces in food processor; process until smooth. Add cream; pulse to blend. Add lemon juice, salt and pepper; pulse once. Set aside 6 small flowerets for garnish. Chop remaining flowerets; add to food processor. Pulse several times to blend.

Divide mixture evenly into prepared ramekins. Add boiling water to pan so water comes halfway up sides of ramekins. Bake 25 to 30 minutes or until knife inserted in center comes out clean. Top with reserved flowerets. Garnish, if desired. Let stand 5 minutes. Serve in ramekins. *Makes 6 side-dish servings*

Broccoli Timbales

SWISS VEGETABLE MEDLEY

1 bag (16 ounces) frozen vegetable
  combination (broccoli, carrots,
  cauliflower), thawed and drained
1 can (10¾ ounces) condensed cream of
  mushroom soup
1 cup (4 ounces) shredded Swiss cheese,
  divided
⅓ cup sour cream
¼ teaspoon ground black pepper
1 jar (4 ounces) diced pimiento, drained
  (optional)
1 can (2.8 ounces) FRENCH'S® French
  Fried Onions, divided

Preheat oven to 350°F. In large bowl, combine
vegetables, soup, ½ cup cheese, sour cream,
pepper, pimiento and ½ can French Fried
Onions. Pour into shallow 1-quart casserole.
Bake, covered, 30 minutes or until vegetables
are done. Sprinkle remaining cheese and
onions in diagonal rows across top; bake,
uncovered, 5 minutes or until onions are golden
brown.   *Makes 6 servings*

PREP TIME: 5 minutes

MICROWAVE DIRECTIONS: Prepare
vegetable mixture as above; pour into shallow
1-quart microwave-safe casserole. Cook,
covered, on HIGH 8 to 10 minutes or until
vegetables are done. Stir vegetables halfway
through cooking time. Top with remaining
cheese and onions as above; cook, uncovered,
1 minute or until cheese melts. Let stand 5
minutes.

HARVEST VEGETABLE SCALLOP

4 medium carrots, thinly sliced (about
  2 cups)
1 package (10 ounces) frozen chopped
  broccoli, thawed and drained
1 can (2.8 ounces) FRENCH'S® French
  Fried Onions
5 small red potatoes, sliced ⅛ inch thick
  (about 2 cups)
1 jar (8 ounces) pasteurized processed
  cheese spread
¼ cup milk
  Ground black pepper
  Seasoned salt

Preheat oven to 375°F. In 12×8-inch baking
dish, combine carrots, broccoli and ½ can
French Fried Onions. Tuck potato slices into
vegetable mixture at an angle. Dot vegetables
evenly with cheese spread. Pour milk over
vegetables; sprinkle with seasonings as
desired. Bake, covered, 30 minutes or until
vegetables are tender. Top with remaining
onions; bake, uncovered, 3 minutes or until
onions are golden brown.   *Makes 6 servings*

Harvest Vegetable Scallop

226

CRUMB-TOPPED SNOWBALL

1 large head cauliflower (about 1¼ pounds)
¼ cup butter or margarine
1 cup fresh bread crumbs (about 2 slices)
2 green onions, thinly sliced
2 eggs, hard cooked and finely chopped
2 tablespoons lemon juice

Remove and discard leaves and stem from cauliflower. Cut around core with paring knife, being careful not to separate flowerets from head; remove and discard core. Rinse.

Pour 1 inch of water into large saucepan. Place cauliflower in water, stem side down; cover. Bring to a boil over high heat; reduce heat to low. Simmer 10 to 12 minutes or until crisp-tender; drain. Place cauliflower in 8-inch square baking dish. Preheat oven to 375°F. Melt butter over medium heat in small skillet. Stir in bread crumbs and onions; cook until crumbs are lightly browned. Stir in eggs and lemon juice. Press crumb mixture evenly over top of cauliflower. Place any extra crumb mixture in baking dish. Bake 10 minutes or until crumb mixture is crispy and lightly browned. Garnish, if desired. Serve immediately.

Makes 6 side-dish servings

Crumb-Topped Snowball

Savory Lemon Vegetables

SAVORY LEMON VEGETABLES

6 slices bacon, cooked and crumbled,
    reserving ¼ cup drippings
1 pound carrots, pared and sliced
1 medium head cauliflower, core
    removed
1 cup finely chopped onion
½ cup REALEMON® Lemon Juice from
    Concentrate
½ cup water
4 teaspoons sugar
1 teaspoon salt
1 teaspoon dried thyme leaves
    Chopped parsley

In large saucepan, cook carrots and cauliflower in small amount of water until tender. Meanwhile, in medium skillet, cook onion in reserved drippings. Add ReaLemon® brand, ½ cup water, sugar, salt and thyme; bring to a boil. Drain vegetables; arrange on serving dish. Pour warm sauce over vegetables. Garnish with bacon and parsley.   *Makes 8 servings*

MICROWAVE DIRECTIONS: On large microwavable platter with rim, arrange carrots and cauliflower. Cover with plastic wrap; cook on HIGH (100% power) 14 to 16 minutes. In 1-quart glass measure, cook reserved bacon drippings and onion on HIGH 1 minute. Add ReaLemon® brand, water, sugar, salt and thyme. Cook on HIGH 5½ to 6 minutes or until sauce boils. Proceed as directed.

NEW YEAR'S DAY BLACK-EYED PEAS

½ pound dried black-eyed peas, sorted
    and rinsed
4 cups water
⅓ cup FILIPPO BERIO® Extra Virgin
    Olive Oil
1 small onion, chopped
2 tablespoons wine vinegar
1 clove garlic, minced
½ teaspoon pepper
1 large bay leaf
⅛ teaspoon dried thyme leaves, crushed
    Hot cooked rice (optional)

1. Place peas and water in medium saucepan; bring to a boil over high heat.

2. Reduce heat; stir in olive oil, onion, vinegar, garlic, pepper, bay leaf and thyme. Cover; simmer 1 hour or until peas are tender. Drain peas; remove and discard bay leaf. Serve with rice, if desired.   *Makes 4 servings*

VARIATION: For cold salad, prepare peas as directed in step 1. Stir in *only* the bay leaf; cover and simmer 1 hour or until peas are tender. Drain peas; remove and discard bay leaf. Add onion, garlic, pepper and thyme. In small bowl, whisk together olive oil and vinegar. Pour over pea mixture; stir to combine. Cover; refrigerate at least 2 hours before serving.

PREP TIME: 10 minutes
COOK TIME: 1 hour
CHILL TIME: 2 hours (salad only)

ARABIAN VEGETABLE MEDLEY

2 pounds eggplant, unpeeled, cut into
 1½-inch cubes
2 tablespoons olive oil, divided
4 cups sliced onions
2 teaspoons minced garlic
1 teaspoon salt
½ teaspoon *each* ground cinnamon and
 black pepper
2 cans (16 ounces each) tomatoes,
 undrained and coarsely chopped
1 can (16 ounces) chick peas, rinsed and
 drained

1. In large nonstick skillet, over medium-high heat, sauté eggplant in 1 tablespoon oil 10 to 12 minutes or until lightly browned and crisp-tender. Remove eggplant from pan; set aside.

2. In same skillet, over medium-high heat, sauté onions in remaining 1 tablespoon oil 6 to 8 minutes or until lightly browned and tender. Stir in garlic, salt, cinnamon and pepper and cook 2 to 3 minutes.

3. Stir in eggplant, tomatoes and chick peas; bring to a boil. Reduce heat to low; cover and simmer 30 minutes or until eggplant is tender. Remove cover and cook 15 minutes or until most of liquid is absorbed.

Makes 16 servings

*Favorite recipe from **National Turkey Federation***

SAVORY ONION TART

Pastry for 9-inch single-crust pie
¼ cup WISH-BONE® Italian Dressing
2 tablespoons butter or margarine
2 large onions, thinly sliced
1 cup shredded fontina or Gruyère
 cheese (about 4 ounces)
2 eggs
½ cup whipping or heavy cream
2 teaspoons finely chopped fresh sage
 leaves or ½ teaspoon dried sage
 leaves, crushed
1 teaspoon dried marjoram leaves,
 crushed
⅛ teaspoon pepper

Preheat oven to 425°F. Roll pastry into 10-inch circle. Press into 9-inch tart pan and crimp edges tightly. Pierce bottom and side with fork. Bake 8 minutes or until lightly golden. Remove to wire rack and cool completely.

Meanwhile, in large skillet, heat Italian dressing and butter over medium heat. Add onions; cook, stirring occasionally, 15 minutes or until onions are tender. Fill prepared tart shell with cheese, then onion mixture. In small bowl, beat eggs, cream, sage, marjoram and pepper; slowly pour over onion mixture. Bake 35 minutes or until golden. To serve, cut into wedges. *Makes about 8 servings*

ORIGINAL GREEN BEAN CASSEROLE

2 cans (16 ounces each) cut green beans, drained, *or* 2 packages (9 ounces each) frozen cut green beans, cooked and drained

¾ cup milk

1 can (10¾ ounces) condensed cream of mushroom soup

⅛ teaspoon ground black pepper

1 can (2.8 ounces) FRENCH'S® French Fried Onions, divided

Preheat oven to 350°F. In medium bowl, combine beans, milk, soup, pepper and *½ can* French Fried Onions; pour into 1½-quart casserole. Bake, uncovered, 30 minutes or until heated through. Top with remaining onions; bake, uncovered, 5 minutes or until onions are golden brown.   *Makes 6 servings*

PREP TIME: 5 minutes

MICROWAVE DIRECTIONS: Prepare green bean mixture as above; pour into 1½-quart microwave-safe casserole. Cook, covered, on HIGH 8 to 10 minutes or until heated through. Stir beans halfway through cooking time. Top with remaining onions; cook, uncovered, 1 minute. Let stand 5 minutes.

Original Green Bean Casserole, Swiss Vegetable Medley (page 226)

GREEN BEAN BUNDLES

8 ounces haricot vert beans or other tiny, young green beans
1 yellow squash, about 1½ inches in diameter
1 tablespoon olive oil
1 clove garlic, minced
¼ teaspoon dried tarragon leaves, crushed
Salt and pepper

Place beans in colander; rinse well. Snap off stem end from each bean; arrange beans in 8 stacks, about 10 to 12 beans per stack. Cut eight ½-inch-thick slices of squash; hollow out with spoon to within ¼ inch of rind. Thread bean stacks through squash pieces as if each piece were a napkin ring.

Place steamer basket in large stockpot or saucepan; add 1 inch of water. (Water should not touch bottom of basket.) Place bean bundles in basket. Cover. Bring to a boil over high heat; steam 4 minutes or until beans are bright green and crisp-tender. Add water, as necessary, to prevent pan from boiling dry.

Meanwhile, heat oil in small skillet over medium-high heat. Cook and stir garlic and tarragon in hot oil until garlic is soft but not brown. Transfer bean bundles to warm serving plate and pour garlic oil over top. Season to taste with salt and pepper. Garnish, if desired. Serve immediately.

Makes 8 side-dish servings

Green Bean Bundles

Green Bean Almond Rice

GREEN BEAN ALMOND RICE

- 1 tablespoon butter or margarine
- ½ cup slivered almonds
- ½ cup chopped onion
- ⅓ cup chopped red bell pepper
- 3 cups cooked brown rice (cooked in beef broth)
- 1 package (10 ounces) frozen French-style green beans, thawed
- ⅛ to ¼ teaspoon ground white pepper
- ¼ teaspoon dried tarragon leaves, crushed

Melt butter in large skillet over medium-high heat. Add almonds; stir until lightly browned. Add onion and bell pepper; cook 2 minutes or until tender. Add rice, beans, white pepper, and tarragon. Stir until thoroughly heated.

Makes 8 servings

*Favorite recipe from **USA Rice Council***

FESTIVE GREEN BEANS

- 1 tablespoon olive oil
- 1 tablespoon butter or margarine
- 3 medium leeks, well rinsed and sliced
- 2 large red bell peppers, seeded and cut into thin strips
- 2 pounds green beans, trimmed
- 1 large garlic clove, minced
- 1½ teaspoons salt
- 1 teaspoon TABASCO® pepper sauce
- 1 teaspoon grated lemon peel
- ¼ cup sliced natural almonds, toasted

In 12-inch skillet over medium heat, heat oil and butter; add leeks. Cook 5 minutes, stirring occasionally. Add red peppers; cook 5 minutes longer or until vegetables are tender.

Meanwhile, steam green beans 5 minutes or until crisp-tender. Add beans, garlic, salt, TABASCO sauce and lemon peel to skillet; toss to mix well. Sprinkle with toasted almonds.

Makes 8 servings

DOUBLE ONION QUICHE

    3 cups thinly sliced yellow onions
    3 tablespoons butter or margarine
    1 cup thinly sliced green onions
    3 eggs
    1 cup heavy cream
    ½ cup grated Parmesan cheese
    ¼ teaspoon hot pepper sauce
    1 package (1 ounce) HIDDEN VALLEY
        RANCH® Milk Recipe Original
        Ranch® salad dressing mix
    1 (9-inch) deep-dish pastry shell, baked
        and cooled
       Fresh oregano sprig

Preheat oven to 350°F. In medium skillet, sauté yellow onions in butter, stirring occasionally, about 10 minutes. Add green onions and cook 5 minutes longer. Remove from heat and let cool.

In large bowl, whisk eggs until frothy. Whisk in cream, cheese, pepper sauce and salad dressing mix. Stir in onion mixture. Pour egg and onion mixture into baked and cooled pastry shell. Bake until top is browned and knife inserted in center comes out clean, 35 to 40 minutes. Cool on wire rack 10 minutes before slicing. Garnish with oregano.

Makes 8 servings

CORN PUDDING

    1 bag (20 ounces) frozen whole kernel
        corn, thawed
    1 small onion, quartered
    2 cups milk
    2 eggs, beaten
    1 package (8½ ounces) corn muffin mix
    ½ teaspoon salt
    1 cup shredded Cheddar cheese
    1 cup thinly sliced romaine lettuce
    ½ cup julienned radishes

Preheat oven to 325°F. Combine corn and onion in food processor; cover and process using on/off pulse until corn is broken but not puréed, scraping side of bowl as necessary. Add milk and eggs; pulse until just blended. Add muffin mix and salt; pulse only until mixed. Pour mixture into greased 11¾×7½-inch baking dish. Bake 45 to 50 minutes or until outside crust is golden brown. Sprinkle pudding with cheese; place under broiler 3 to 4 inches from heat. Broil until cheese is melted and top is crusty. To serve, top with romaine lettuce and radishes. *Makes 8 to 10 servings*

*Favorite recipe from **National Live Stock & Meat Board***

CINNAMON APPLE RINGS

    3 large cooking apples
    ¼ cup lemon juice
    1 cup water
    ½ cup sugar
    ¼ cup red cinnamon candies

Peel and core apples; cut crosswise into ½-inch-thick rings. Toss with lemon juice to prevent discoloration. Combine water, sugar and candies in large saucepan. Bring to a boil, stirring until sugar and candies are dissolved. Add apple rings and simmer until just tender, about 15 minutes. Let cool in liquid. Drain.

Makes 4 servings

*Favorite recipe from **Perdue® Farms***

BRUSSELS SPROUTS IN MUSTARD SAUCE

1½ pounds fresh Brussels sprouts*
1 tablespoon butter or margarine
⅓ cup chopped shallots or onion
⅓ cup half-and-half
1 tablespoon plus 1½ teaspoons tarragon Dijon-style mustard or Dusseldorf mustard**
¼ teaspoon salt
⅛ teaspoon freshly ground black pepper or ground nutmeg
1½ tablespoons shredded Parmesan cheese (optional)

Cut stem from each Brussels sprout and pull off outer bruised leaves. Cut an "X" deep into the stem end of each Brussels sprout with paring knife. If some Brussels sprouts are larger than others, cut large Brussels sprouts lengthwise into halves. Bring 2 quarts salted water to a boil in saucepan large enough to allow Brussels sprouts to fit in a single layer. Add Brussels sprouts; return to a boil. Boil, uncovered, 7 to 10 minutes or until almost tender when pierced with fork. Drain in colander. Rinse under cold water to stop cooking; drain thoroughly.

Melt butter in same saucepan over medium heat. Add shallots; cook 3 minutes, stirring occasionally. Add half-and-half, mustard, salt and pepper. Simmer 1 minute or until thickened. Add drained Brussels sprouts; heat about 1 minute or until heated through, tossing gently with sauce. Sprinkle with cheese.

Makes 4 cups, 6 to 8 servings

*Or, substitute 2 (10-ounce) packages frozen Brussels sprouts for fresh Brussels sprouts. Cook according to package directions; drain and rinse as directed.

**Or, substitute 1 tablespoon plus 1½ teaspoons Dijon-style mustard *and* ½ teaspoon dried tarragon leaves, crushed, for tarragon Dijon-style mustard.

NOTE: Recipe may be prepared in advance except for sprinkling with cheese. Cover and refrigerate up to 8 hours before serving. Reheat in saucepan over low heat. Or, place in covered microwavable dish and reheat in microwave oven at HIGH (100% power) about 3 minutes or until hot. Sprinkle with cheese.

EASY SPINACH SOUFFLÉ

½ cup HELLMANN'S® or BEST FOODS® Real or Light Mayonnaise or Low Fat Cholesterol Free Mayonnaise Dressing
¼ cup flour
2 tablespoons grated onion
¾ teaspoon salt
¼ teaspoon ground nutmeg
¼ teaspoon freshly ground pepper
1 cup milk
1 package (10 ounces) frozen chopped spinach, thawed and well drained on paper towels
4 eggs, separated
¼ teaspoon cream of tartar

Preheat oven to 400°F. Grease 2-quart soufflé dish. In 3-quart saucepan combine mayonnaise, flour, onion, salt, nutmeg and pepper. Stirring constantly, cook over medium heat 1 minute. Gradually stir in milk until smooth. Stirring constantly, cook until thickened. Remove from heat. Stir in spinach. Beat in egg yolks. In small bowl with mixer at high speed, beat egg whites with cream of tartar until stiff peaks form. Gently fold into spinach mixture. Spoon into prepared dish. Place on lowest rack of oven. *Immediately reduce oven temperature to 375°F.* Bake 40 minutes or until top is puffed and golden brown. Serve immediately. *Makes 4 to 6 servings*

Brussels Sprouts in Mustard Sauce

SPINACH CHEESE TORTA

3 medium corn muffins, crumbled (about 2½ cups crumbs)
3 tablespoons butter or margarine, melted
3 teaspoons chopped fresh basil leaves, divided
Salt and pepper to taste
1 tablespoon olive or vegetable oil
2 teaspoons finely chopped garlic
1 package (10 ounces) frozen chopped spinach, thawed and squeezed dry
1 cup ricotta cheese
¼ cup grated Parmesan cheese
1 egg, slightly beaten
1 package LIPTON® Rice & Sauce–Cheddar Broccoli
1½ cups shredded mozzarella cheese (about 6 ounces), divided

Preheat oven to 400°F. In medium bowl, thoroughly combine corn muffin crumbs, butter, 2 teaspoons basil, salt and pepper. Press into bottom and ½ inch up sides of 9-inch springform or square baking pan. Bake 12 minutes; cool on wire rack.

In medium saucepan, heat oil and cook garlic over medium heat 30 seconds. Add spinach and cook over medium heat, stirring constantly, 2 minutes or until heated through; add salt and pepper. Stir in ricotta cheese, Parmesan cheese, egg and remaining 1 teaspoon basil; set aside.

Prepare rice & Cheddar broccoli sauce according to package directions. Into prepared pan, layer ¾ cup mozzarella cheese, rice mixture, spinach mixture and remaining ¾ cup mozzarella cheese. *Decrease oven temperature to 375°F.* Bake 30 minutes or until set. Remove sides of springform pan. Garnish as desired. Serve warm or cool.

Makes about 8 servings

VARIATION: Substitute ½ teaspoon dried basil leaves in crust and 1 teaspoon dried basil leaves in filling for fresh basil.

SPINACH SQUARES

1 (10-ounce) package frozen chopped spinach, cooked, well drained
⅓ cup chopped onion
⅓ cup chopped red pepper
½ pound VELVEETA® Pasteurized Process Cheese Spread, cubed
2 cups cooked rice
3 eggs, beaten
⅛ teaspoon pepper

In large bowl, combine ingredients; spoon into greased 10×6-inch baking dish. Bake at 350°F, 25 minutes. Let stand 5 minutes before serving. Cut into squares. *Makes 8 to 10 servings*

PREP TIME: 10 minutes
BAKE TIME: 25 minutes plus standing

CREAMED SPINACH À LA LAWRY'S

4 bacon slices, finely chopped
1 cup finely chopped onion
¼ cup all-purpose flour
2 teaspoons LAWRY'S® Seasoned Salt
½ teaspoon LAWRY'S® Seasoned Pepper
½ teaspoon LAWRY'S® Garlic Powder with Parsley
1½ to 2 cups milk
2 packages (10 ounces each) frozen spinach, cooked and drained

In large skillet, fry bacon until almost crisp. Add onion to bacon and cook until onion is tender, about 10 minutes. Remove from heat. Add flour, Seasoned Salt, Seasoned Pepper and Garlic Powder with Parsley to skillet; blend thoroughly. Gradually add milk, starting with 1½ cups; cook and stir over low heat until thickened. Add spinach and mix thoroughly. If mixture is too thick, stir in additional milk.

Makes 8 servings

Skillet Zucchini

SKILLET ZUCCHINI

   3 cups sliced zucchini
2½ cups sliced mushrooms
   1 medium red bell pepper, cut into strips
   2 tablespoons olive or vegetable oil
   1 cup (4 ounces) KRAFT® 100%
      Shredded Parmesan Cheese

• Cook and stir zucchini, mushrooms and pepper in oil over medium-high heat 5 to 6 minutes or until vegetables are crisp-tender.

• Remove from heat. Sprinkle with Parmesan cheese; cover. Let stand 2 minutes before serving. *Makes 4 servings*

PREP TIME: 10 minutes
COOK TIME: 8 minutes

HOMESTEAD SUCCOTASH

  ¼ pound bacon, diced
   1 cup chopped onion
  ½ teaspoon dried thyme leaves
   1 can (17 ounces) DEL MONTE® Whole
      Kernel Golden Sweet Corn, drained
   1 can (17 ounces) DEL MONTE® Green
      Lima Beans, drained

In skillet, cook bacon until crisp; drain. Add onion and thyme; cook until onion is tender. Stir in vegetables and heat through.
Makes 6 to 8 servings

TOTAL TIME: 13 minutes

MICROWAVE DIRECTIONS: In shallow 1-quart microwavable dish, cook bacon on HIGH 6 minutes or until crisp; drain. Add onion and thyme; cover and cook on HIGH 2 to 3 minutes or until onion is tender. Add vegetables. Cover and cook on HIGH 3 to 4 minutes or until heated through.

HERB SAUCED VEGETABLES

   3 cups fresh vegetables, such as broccoli
      flowerets, cauliflowerets, sliced
      yellow squash, green beans, carrots
      and snow peas
   1 cup chicken broth
  ½ cup prepared HIDDEN VALLEY
      RANCH® Original Ranch® salad
      dressing
  ¼ cup chopped fresh parsley

In large saucepan, steam vegetables separately over boiling chicken broth until crisp-tender, about 5 minutes for each batch. Transfer to heated serving dish. Warm salad dressing and spoon over vegetables. Sprinkle with parsley. *Makes 4 servings*

LOW-CALORIE MASHED POTATOES

2 pounds medium red boiling potatoes, peeled and cut into chunks
4 large cloves garlic, peeled
¾ cup cultured buttermilk (1½% fat)
½ teaspoon salt
¼ teaspoon freshly ground black pepper
2 tablespoons chopped chives for garnish

Place potatoes and garlic in large saucepan. Add enough water to cover; bring to a boil over high heat. Reduce heat to medium. Simmer, uncovered, 20 to 30 minutes or until potatoes are fork-tender; drain.

Place potatoes and garlic in medium bowl. Mash with potato masher or beat with electric mixer at medium speed until smooth.* Add buttermilk, salt and pepper. Stir with fork until just combined. Garnish, if desired.

Makes 4 cups, 8 servings

*For a smoother texture, force potatoes through potato ricer or food mill into medium bowl. Proceed as directed.

BUTTERY MASHED POTATOES: Prepare as directed except add 1 tablespoon butter or margarine along with buttermilk, salt and pepper.

CHEESY MASHED POTATOES AND TURNIPS

2 pounds all-purpose potatoes, peeled
1 pound turnips, peeled
¼ cup milk
½ cup shredded Cheddar cheese
¼ cup butter or margarine
1 teaspoon TABASCO® pepper sauce
½ teaspoon salt

In large saucepan over high heat, combine potatoes and turnips with enough water to cover. Bring to a boil and reduce heat to low; cover and simmer 25 to 30 minutes or until vegetables are tender. Drain. Return vegetables to saucepan; heat over high heat for a few seconds to eliminate any excess moisture, shaking saucepan to prevent sticking.

In small saucepan over medium heat, bring milk to a simmer. In large bowl, mash vegetables. Stir in warmed milk, Cheddar cheese, butter, TABASCO sauce and salt.

Makes 8 servings

NOTE: Potatoes may be made up to 2 days in advance and reheated in microwave or double boiler above simmering water.

GOLDEN MASHED POTATOES

2½ cups cubed cooked potatoes, mashed
3 tablespoons milk
2 tablespoons PARKAY® Spread Sticks
1 tablespoon chopped fresh chives
½ pound VELVEETA® Pasteurized Process Cheese Spread, cubed, divided
¼ cup (1 ounce) KRAFT® 100% Grated Parmesan Cheese

Combine potatoes, milk, spread sticks and chives; beat until fluffy. Stir in half of the process cheese spread. Spoon into 1-quart casserole; sprinkle with Parmesan cheese. Bake at 350°F, 20 to 25 minutes or until thoroughly heated. Top with remaining process cheese spread; continue baking until process cheese spread begins to melt.

Makes 4 to 6 servings

PREP TIME: 20 minutes
BAKE TIME: 30 minutes

Low-Calorie Mashed Potatoes

CINNAMON APPLE SWEET POTATOES

    4 medium sweet potatoes
1½ cups finely chopped apples
    ½ cup orange juice
    ¼ cup sugar
1½ teaspoons cornstarch
    ½ teaspoon ground cinnamon
    ½ teaspoon grated orange peel

Prick potatoes with fork. Place on paper towels and microwave on HIGH 10 to 13 minutes or until tender, turning halfway through cooking. Set aside. In microwavable bowl, combine remaining ingredients. Cover and cook on HIGH 3 minutes; stir. Cook uncovered on HIGH 1½ to 2½ minutes or until sauce is thickened. Slit sweet potatoes and spoon sauce over each. *Makes 4 servings*

*Favorite recipe from **The Sugar Association, Inc.***

Glazed Stir-Fry Holiday Vegetables (page 224), Cinnamon Apple Sweet Potatoes

HOT SWEET POTATOES

    4 small (4 ounces each) sweet potatoes
    2 tablespoons margarine or unsalted butter, softened
    ½ teaspoon TABASCO® pepper sauce
    ¼ teaspoon dried savory leaves, crushed

In large saucepan cover potatoes with water. Cover and cook over high heat 20 to 25 minutes or until potatoes are tender. Drain potatoes and cut in half lengthwise.

Preheat broiler. In small bowl, combine margarine and TABASCO sauce. Spread ¾ teaspoon margarine mixture over cut side of each potato half. Season each with pinch of savory. Place on foil-lined broiler pan and broil, watching carefully, about 5 minutes or until lightly browned. Serve hot.
Makes 4 servings

BAKED APPLE & SWEET POTATO CASSEROLE

    6 sweet potatoes
    3 apples
    2 tablespoons butter, divided
    ½ cup orange juice
    ¼ cup packed dark brown sugar
    ⅛ teaspoon ground cinnamon
    ⅛ teaspoon ground allspice
    ¼ cup rum

Preheat oven to 350°F. Boil or steam potatoes until tender. Remove skin and cut lengthwise into slices. Peel and core apples; slice into rings. Grease 9×6-inch baking dish with 1 tablespoon butter; alternate potato and apple layers until dish is filled. Pour combined orange juice, sugar, spices, rum and remaining 1 tablespoon butter, melted, over potato mixture. Bake 30 minutes or until potatoes are brown and shiny and liquid is absorbed.
Makes 6 servings

*Favorite recipe from **Michigan Apple Committee***

SWEET POTATO GRATIN

3 pounds sweet potatoes (about 5 large)
½ cup butter or margarine, divided
¼ cup plus 2 tablespoons packed light brown sugar, divided
2 eggs
⅔ cup orange juice
2 teaspoons ground cinnamon, divided
½ teaspoon salt
¼ teaspoon ground nutmeg
⅓ cup all-purpose flour
¼ cup uncooked old-fashioned oats
⅓ cup chopped pecans or walnuts

Bake sweet potatoes until tender in preheated 350°F oven 1 hour. Or, pierce sweet potatoes several times with fork and place on microwavable plate. Microwave at HIGH (100% power) 16 to 18 minutes, rotating and turning over after 9 minutes. Let stand 5 minutes. While sweet potatoes are hot, cut lengthwise into halves. Scrape hot pulp from skins into large bowl. Beat ¼ cup butter and 2 tablespoons sugar into sweet potatoes with electric mixer at medium speed until butter is melted. Beat in eggs, orange juice, 1½ teaspoons cinnamon, salt and nutmeg, scraping down side of bowl once. Beat until smooth. Pour mixture into 1½-quart baking dish; smooth top.

For topping, combine flour, oats, remaining ¼ cup sugar and ½ teaspoon cinnamon in medium bowl. Cut in remaining ¼ cup butter with pastry blender or 2 knives until mixture becomes coarse crumbs. Stir in pecans. Sprinkle topping evenly over sweet potatoes.*

Preheat oven to 350°F. Bake 25 to 30 minutes or until sweet potatoes are heated through. For a crisper topping, broil 5 inches from heat 2 to 3 minutes or until golden brown. Garnish, if desired. *Makes 6 to 8 servings*

*At this point, Sweet Potato Gratin may be covered and refrigerated up to 1 day. Let stand at room temperature 1 hour before baking.

Sweet Potato Gratin

MAPLE GLAZED SWEET POTATOES

1½ pounds sweet potatoes or yams,
    cooked, peeled and quartered
½ cup CARY'S®, MAPLE ORCHARDS® or
    MACDONALD'S™ Pure Maple Syrup
½ cup orange juice
3 tablespoons margarine or butter,
    melted
1 tablespoon cornstarch
1 teaspoon grated orange peel

Preheat oven to 350°F. Arrange sweet potatoes
in 1½-quart shallow baking dish. Combine
remaining ingredients; pour over potatoes.
Bake 40 minutes or until hot and sauce is
thickened, basting frequently. Refrigerate
leftovers.   *Makes 6 to 8 servings*

SAUCY SKILLET POTATOES

1 tablespoon MAZOLA® Margarine
1 cup chopped onion
½ cup HELLMANN'S® or BEST FOODS®
    Real or Light Mayonnaise or Low Fat
    Cholesterol Free Mayonnaise
    Dressing
⅓ cup cider vinegar
1 tablespoon sugar
1 teaspoon salt
¼ teaspoon freshly ground pepper
4 medium potatoes, cooked, peeled and
    sliced
1 tablespoon chopped parsley
1 tablespoon crumbled cooked bacon or
    real bacon bits

In large skillet, melt margarine over medium
heat. Add onion; cook 2 to 3 minutes or until
tender-crisp. Stir in mayonnaise, vinegar, sugar,
salt and pepper. Add potatoes; cook, stirring
constantly, 2 minutes or until hot (do not boil).
Sprinkle with parsley and bacon.
    Makes 6 to 8 servings

POTATO LATKES

2 large or 3 medium baking (russet)
    potatoes (about 1¾ pounds), peeled
1 large onion (8 ounces)
2 eggs
¼ cup matzo meal
¾ teaspoon salt
¼ teaspoon freshly ground black pepper
2 tablespoons vegetable oil, divided
    Applesauce (optional)
    Sour cream (optional)

Shred potatoes and onion with shredding disc
of food processor or shred by hand using
grater. Place potato mixture in large bowl. Add
eggs, matzo meal, salt and pepper; mix well.

Heat 1 tablespoon oil in large nonstick skillet
over medium-low heat until hot. Drop potato
mixture by level ¼ cupfuls into skillet. Use back
of spatula to flatten potato mixture into 3½-inch
patties, about ½ inch thick. Cook about 4
minutes per side or until golden brown. Transfer
to ovenproof platter lined with paper towels.

Keep warm in 200°F oven while preparing
remaining latkes. Add remaining 1 tablespoon
oil to skillet as needed. Serve warm with
applesauce or sour cream. Garnish as desired.
    Makes about 18 latkes

Potato Latkes

Sherried Mushroom Rice

Melt spread in medium skillet on medium heat. Add garlic; cook and stir 1 minute. Add mushrooms and red pepper; cook and stir 2 minutes.

Add broth, water, sherry, onion flakes and salt. Bring to boil.

Stir in rice; cover. Remove from heat. Let stand 5 minutes or until liquid is absorbed. Stir. Sprinkle with cheese and parsley.

Makes 6 servings

MICROWAVE DIRECTIONS: Mix spread, cut into pieces, garlic, mushrooms and red pepper in 2-quart microwavable casserole. Cover. Microwave on HIGH 2 to 3 minutes. Stir in rice, broth, water, sherry, onion flakes and salt. Cover. Microwave on HIGH 4 minutes; stir. Microwave on HIGH 2 to 3 minutes; stir. Let stand 5 minutes or until liquid is absorbed. Sprinkle with cheese and parsley.

SHERRIED MUSHROOM RICE

2 tablespoons PARKAY® Spread Sticks or butter
1 clove garlic, minced
2 cups sliced mushrooms
¼ cup chopped red pepper
1 cup chicken broth
¼ cup water
¼ cup dry sherry or water
2 teaspoons onion flakes
¼ teaspoon salt
1½ cups MINUTE® Original Instant Enriched Rice, uncooked
2 tablespoons KRAFT® 100% Grated Parmesan Cheese
1 tablespoon chopped fresh parsley *or* 1 teaspoon parsley flakes

FESTIVE RICE

¼ cup oil
2¼ cups MINUTE® Original Instant Enriched Rice, uncooked
1 medium green pepper, chopped*
1 envelope GOOD SEASONS® Italian or Mild Italian Salad Dressing Mix
2¼ cups water
2 tablespoons chopped pimiento or fresh parsley

Heat oil in large skillet on medium heat. Add rice and pepper; cook and stir 2 minutes.

Sprinkle with salad dressing mix. Stir in water; cover. Bring to boil.

Remove from heat. Let stand 5 minutes or until liquid is absorbed. Stir in pimiento.

Makes 6 servings

*Or use ½ medium green pepper, chopped, and ½ cup grated carrot.

FRUITED RICE PILAF

2½ cups water
1 cup uncooked rice
2 tablespoons butter or margarine
1 medium tomato, chopped
⅓ cup minced dried apples
¼ cup minced dried apricots
¼ cup sliced green onions
¾ teaspoon LAWRY'S® Seasoned Salt
¼ teaspoon LAWRY'S® Garlic Powder
    with Parsley
3 tablespoons sliced almonds

In 2-quart saucepan, bring water to a boil; add rice and butter. Return to a boil. Reduce heat; cover and simmer 15 minutes. Add remaining ingredients except almonds; cook 5 to 10 minutes longer or until rice is tender. Stir in almonds. Garnish with apple slices and celery leaves, if desired.   *Makes 4 servings*

PRESENTATION: Serve with baked pork chops, roasted meats or poultry.

HINT: For variety and added flavor, add ¼ teaspoon curry powder to cooked rice.

ORANGE WILD RICE

¾ cup wild rice, rinsed well
1 small onion, chopped
2 tablespoons margarine
    Juice of 1 medium orange plus chicken
        broth to equal 1¼ cups
    Finely grated peel of 1 small orange
½ teaspoon LAWRY'S® Seasoned Pepper
¼ teaspoon LAWRY'S® Garlic Powder
    with Parsley
1 package (10 ounces) frozen peas,
    thawed
⅓ cup chopped pecans
    Mandarin orange sections for garnish

In large saucepan, sauté rice and onion in margarine, stirring frequently. Add combined orange juice and broth, orange peel, Seasoned Pepper and Garlic Powder with Parsley. Bring to a boil; reduce heat, cover and simmer 35 minutes or until liquid is almost absorbed. Stir in peas and pecans; simmer 3 to 5 minutes longer. Garnish with Mandarin orange sections.
          Makes 4 to 6 servings

PRESENTATION: Serve with roast pork.

Fruited Rice Pilaf

HOLIDAY HARVEST RICE

2 tablespoons margarine
1½ cups MAHATMA®, CAROLINA®,
    RIVER® or WATER MAID® Rice
½ teaspoon salt
2 cups unsweetened apple juice
1 cup cranberry juice
2 tablespoons fresh lemon juice
1 tablespoon chopped raisins
2 teaspoons light brown sugar
½ teaspoon ground cinnamon
2 small tart apples, peeled, cored and
    chopped
½ cup chopped green onions

In saucepan, over medium heat, melt
margarine. Stir in rice and salt, stirring to coat
rice. Add juices, raisins, sugar and cinnamon.
Bring to a boil. Cover and simmer 20 minutes.
Stir in apples and green onions.

Makes 6 to 8 servings

APRICOT AND WALNUT BROWN RICE STUFFING

½ cup chopped onion
½ cup chopped celery
1 teaspoon margarine
3 cups cooked brown rice
⅔ cup coarsely chopped dried apricots
¼ cup coarsely chopped walnuts
¼ cup raisins, plumped
2 tablespoons snipped parsley
½ teaspoon dried thyme leaves
¼ teaspoon salt
¼ teaspoon rubbed sage
¼ teaspoon ground black pepper
½ cup chicken broth

Cook onion and celery in margarine in large
skillet over medium-high heat until tender-crisp.
Add rice, apricots, walnuts, raisins, parsley,
thyme, salt, sage, pepper and broth; transfer to
2-quart baking dish. Bake in covered baking
dish at 375°F for 15 to 20 minutes. (Stuffing
may be baked inside poultry.)

Makes 6 servings

TIP: To plump raisins, cover with 1 cup boiling
water. Let stand 1 to 2 minutes; drain.

Favorite recipe from **USA Rice Council**

HERBED RICE

¾ cup uncooked long-grain white rice
¼ cup uncooked wild rice
1 chicken-flavor bouillon cube
2 tablespoons butter
1 cup finely chopped celery
¼ cup finely chopped onion
2½ teaspoons LAWRY'S® Pinch of Herbs
½ teaspoon LAWRY'S® Seasoned Salt
¼ teaspoon LAWRY'S® Seasoned Pepper
½ pound fresh mushrooms, sliced

Cook each rice separately according to
package directions, except omitting salt and
adding bouillon cube to water for white rice. In
large skillet, melt butter; sauté celery and onion
until tender. Add Pinch of Herbs, Seasoned
Salt, Seasoned Pepper and mushrooms; sauté
until mushrooms are tender. Add rice and toss.

*Makes 6 side-dish servings or
enough stuffing for 10-pound turkey*

PRESENTATION: Serve with broiled chicken,
fish or beef.

Holiday Harvest Rice

HOLIDAY GRAPE DRESSING

1 cup brown rice
2 tablespoons olive oil
½ cup *each* chopped onion and sliced celery
½ cup *each* chopped rehydrated shiitake* and white mushrooms
2 cups chicken broth
½ teaspoon *each* dried thyme and oregano leaves, crushed
⅛ teaspoon coarsely ground pepper
2 cups California grapes**
½ cup chopped macadamia nuts or almonds
2 tablespoons chopped parsley

Cook and stir rice in oil until browned; remove from skillet and set aside. Cook and stir onion and celery in skillet. Stir in mushrooms, broth, rice and seasonings. Simmer, covered, 25 to 30 minutes or until rice is cooked and liquid is absorbed. Stir in grapes, nuts and parsley; cook about 2 minutes longer or until grapes are thoroughly heated.   *Makes 6 servings*

PREPARATION TIME: About 45 minutes

*To rehydrate shiitake mushrooms, cover with warm water and let stand 10 to 14 minutes before slicing.

**Red, green, or blue/black grapes or a combination may be used. Seed grapes if necessary.

*Favorite recipe from **California Table Grape Commission***

Holiday Grape Dressing

PINE NUT DRESSING

  1 bag SUCCESS® White or Brown Rice
  1 tablespoon reduced-calorie margarine
  ½ cup chopped onion
  ½ cup chopped celery
  ½ cup low sodium chicken broth
  ¼ cup pine nuts, toasted
  1 tablespoon chopped fresh parsley
  ¾ teaspoon poultry seasoning
  ¼ teaspoon celery salt
  ¼ teaspoon pepper

Prepare rice according to package directions.

Melt margarine in large saucepan over medium heat. Add onion and celery; cook and stir until crisp-tender. Stir in rice and remaining ingredients. Reduce heat to low; simmer 10 minutes, stirring occasionally.

Makes 6 servings

SUCCESS WALDORF DRESSING

  1 box SUCCESS® Long Grain & Wild
     Rice Mix
  3 slices bacon
  ½ cup chopped celery
  1 medium red apple, chopped
  1 medium green apple, chopped
  ½ cup chopped walnuts
  ½ cup raisins
  2 tablespoons honey
  2 tablespoons lemon juice

Prepare rice mix according to package directions. Meanwhile, fry bacon in large skillet until crisp. Remove bacon; crumble. Set aside. Add celery to skillet; sauté until tender. Add all remaining ingredients except rice and bacon. Fold in cooked rice. Top with reserved bacon.

Makes 4 to 6 servings

Pine Nut Dressing

WILD RICE MUSHROOM STUFFING

½ cup uncooked wild rice
  Day-old French bread (about 4 ounces)
½ cup butter or margarine
1 large onion, chopped
1 clove garlic, minced
3 cups sliced fresh mushrooms*
½ teaspoon rubbed sage
½ teaspoon dried thyme leaves, crushed
½ teaspoon salt
¼ teaspoon freshly ground black pepper
1 cup chicken broth
½ cup coarsely chopped pecans
  Thyme sprigs for garnish

Rinse and cook rice according to package directions; set aside. Cut enough bread into ½-inch cubes to measure 4 cups. Spread in single layer on baking sheet. Broil 5 to 6 inches from heat 4 minutes or until lightly toasted, stirring after 2 minutes; set aside.

Melt butter in large skillet over medium heat. Add onion and garlic. Cook and stir 3 minutes. Add mushrooms; cook 3 minutes, stirring occasionally. Add sage, dried thyme leaves, salt and pepper. Add cooked rice; cook 2 minutes, stirring occasionally. Stir in broth. Add pecans and toasted bread cubes; toss lightly.

Transfer to 1½-quart casserole.** Preheat oven to 325°F. Cover casserole with lid or foil. Bake 40 minutes or until heated through. Garnish, if desired. *Makes 6 to 8 servings*

*Or, substitute 1½ cups sliced fresh shiitake mushrooms for 1½ cups fresh mushrooms.

**At this point, Wild Rice Mushroom Stuffing may be covered and refrigerated up to 8 hours before baking. Bake 50 minutes or until heated through.

JONES® FANCY HOLIDAY STUFFING

2 packages (12 ounces each) JONES®
  All-Natural Roll Sausage
¾ cup (1½ sticks) unsalted butter
3 medium onions, coarsely chopped
2 cups chopped celery, including tops
¾ (1-pound) loaf day-old white bread
  with crusts, torn into small pieces
2 eggs, lightly beaten
1 (10-ounce) package frozen chopped
  spinach, thawed and squeezed dry
1 (8-ounce) can whole water chestnuts,
  drained and coarsely chopped *or*
  1 apple, chopped
½ cup chopped fresh parsley
1 tablespoon plus 1½ teaspoons poultry
  seasoning
2 teaspoons salt or to taste
1½ teaspoons freshly ground pepper

Crumble sausage into large skillet. Cook and stir sausage over medium-high heat until cooked through (no longer pink but not dry), about 5 to 8 minutes. Transfer sausage and drippings, if desired (there will be less than 2 tablespoons) to large mixing bowl.

Melt butter in same skillet over medium heat. Sauté onions in butter until tender. Add celery and continue cooking 2 to 3 minutes. Add onion mixture to sausage. Add remaining ingredients, mixing thoroughly but gently. Use to stuff turkey loosely just before roasting. Place any remaining stuffing in greased baking dish. Bake in 325°F oven 30 minutes or until thoroughly heated.
*Makes enough stuffing for
12- to 16-pound turkey*

VARIATION: Substitute a mixture of dried tarragon, thyme and sage, proportioned as desired to equal 1 tablespoon plus 1½ teaspoons, for poultry seasoning.

Wild Rice Mushroom Stuffing

APPLE & HERB STUFFING

    2 cups sliced celery
1½ cups chopped onions
    ½ cup margarine or butter
1¾ cups hot water
    1 tablespoon WYLER'S® or STEERO®
        Chicken-Flavor Instant Bouillon *or*
        3 Chicken-Flavor Bouillon Cubes
12 cups dry bread cubes (about 16 slices
        bread)
    3 cups coarsely chopped apples
    1 cup toasted slivered almonds
    1 tablespoon chopped parsley
    2 teaspoons poultry seasoning
    ¼ teaspoon rubbed sage
        Rich Turkey Gravy (page 164,
        optional)

In large skillet, cook celery and onions in margarine until tender. Add water and bouillon; cook until bouillon dissolves. In large bowl, combine remaining ingredients except Rich Turkey Gravy; add bouillon mixture. Mix well. Loosely stuff turkey just before roasting. Place remaining stuffing in greased baking dish. Bake at 350°F for 30 minutes or until hot. Serve with Rich Turkey Gravy, if desired. Refrigerate leftovers.   *Makes about 2½ quarts*

"LITE" APRICOT STUFFING

    1 cup sliced celery
    ¾ cup chopped onion
1½ cups turkey broth or reduced-sodium
        chicken bouillon
16 slices reduced-calorie bread, cubed and
        dried
    2 tablespoons parsley flakes
1½ teaspoons poultry seasoning
    ½ teaspoon salt
    2 egg whites
    ¼ cup dried apricots, chopped

In small saucepan, over medium-high heat, combine celery, onion and turkey broth; bring to a boil. Reduce heat to low; cover and simmer 5 minutes or until vegetables are tender. In large bowl, combine celery mixture, bread cubes, parsley, poultry seasoning, salt, egg whites and apricots. Spoon into lightly greased 2-quart casserole; cover. Bake at 350°F 30 minutes or until heated through.   *Makes 8 servings*

Favorite recipe from **National Turkey Federation**

CRANBERRY–RAISIN STUFFING

12 slices cinnamon-raisin bread, toasted
    ½ cup butter or margarine
2½ cups chopped onions
    1 teaspoon rubbed sage
    1 bag (12 ounces) fresh or partially
        thawed frozen cranberries, washed,
        picked through, coarsely chopped
    ¼ cup sugar
    ¼ to ½ cup chicken broth*

Cut toast into ½-inch cubes. Place in large bowl; set aside. Melt butter in large skillet; add onions. Cook and stir until tender (about 10 minutes). Add sage; cook 1 minute more. In medium bowl, toss cranberries with sugar; set aside. Add onion mixture and sugared cranberries to bread cubes; mix well. Pour ¼ cup chicken broth over bread cube mixture; mix until evenly moistened. Stuff body and neck of turkey and cook according to instructions given with turkey.   *Makes 7½ cups stuffing*

*If cooking stuffing outside of turkey, use ½ cup chicken broth and bake, covered, at 350°F for 45 minutes or until heated through.

Cranberry-Raisin Stuffing

RAISIN ALMOND STUFFING

**1 package (6 ounces) STOVE TOP®
Stuffing Mix, any flavor**
1⅔ cups water*
½ cup raisins
¼ cup (½ stick) margarine or butter
½ cup slivered almonds

Mix contents of vegetable/seasoning packet, water, raisins and margarine in medium saucepan.

Bring to boil. Reduce heat to low; cover and simmer 5 minutes.

Stir in stuffing crumbs and almonds; cover. Remove from heat. Let stand 5 minutes. Fluff with fork.   *Makes 6 servings*

*For moister stuffing, increase water by 2 tablespoons. For less moist stuffing, decrease water by 2 tablespoons.

EASY OYSTER DRESSING

**1 teaspoon WYLER'S® or STEERO®
Chicken-Flavor Instant Bouillon**
½ cup boiling water
½ cup chopped celery
½ cup margarine or butter
**1 (8-ounce) package herb-seasoned
stuffing mix**
**1 (8-ounce) can ORLEANS® Whole
Oysters, undrained**

Preheat oven to 350°F. Dissolve bouillon in water; set aside. In small skillet, cook celery in margarine until tender. In large bowl, combine all ingredients; mix well. Turn into buttered 1½-quart baking dish. Cover; bake 35 minutes or until hot. Refrigerate leftovers.

Makes 6 to 8 servings

HERBED MUSHROOM STUFFING

1 pound fresh mushrooms, sliced (about 4 cups)
2 cups sliced celery
1½ cups chopped onions
½ cup margarine or butter
½ cup water
5 teaspoons WYLER'S® or STEERO® Chicken-Flavor Instant Bouillon *or* 5 Chicken-Flavor Bouillon Cubes
12 cups dry bread cubes (about 14 slices bread)
1 (8-ounce) can sliced water chestnuts, drained and coarsely chopped
1 tablespoon chopped parsley
2 teaspoons poultry seasoning
¼ teaspoon rubbed sage
¼ teaspoon pepper
Rich Turkey Gravy (page 164, optional)

In large nonstick skillet, cook mushrooms, celery and onions in margarine until tender. Add water and bouillon; heat until bouillon dissolves.

In large bowl, combine bread cubes, water chestnuts, parsley, poultry seasoning, sage and pepper; add bouillon mixture. Mix well. Use to stuff turkey loosely just before roasting, if desired. Place remaining stuffing in greased baking dish; cover. Bake at 350°F for 30 minutes or until hot. Serve with Rich Turkey Gravy, if desired. Refrigerate leftovers.

Makes 10 to 12 servings

Herbed Mushroom Stuffing

GOURMET SAUSAGE STUFFING

2 pounds BOB EVANS FARMS® Original Recipe roll sausage
8 cups fresh bread cubes, dried or toasted
1 cup condensed beef broth
2 cups finely chopped celery leaves
2 cups slivered blanched almonds, toasted
1 cup chopped onion
1 cup thinly sliced fresh mushrooms
¼ cup chopped green bell pepper
¼ cup finely chopped fresh parsley
¼ cup snipped fresh chives
1 tablespoon salt
¼ teaspoon *each* black pepper, ground mace, rubbed sage, dried thyme leaves, ground nutmeg and dried marjoram leaves
4 whole eggs
¼ cup half-and-half
Canned chicken broth or turkey pan drippings (optional)

Crumble sausage into large skillet. Cook over low heat until well browned, stirring occasionally. Stir in bread cubes. (Bread will absorb excess drippings.) Transfer to large bowl. Add beef broth to same skillet, stirring to pick up any browned bits. Add to sausage mixture. Add celery leaves, almonds, onion, mushrooms, green pepper and seasonings to sausage mixture. Beat eggs in small bowl; stir in half-and-half. Add to sausage mixture; toss lightly to combine. Use to stuff turkey loosely just before roasting. Or, place stuffing in greased 13×9-inch baking dish. Add chicken broth, pan drippings or both for added moisture, if desired. Bake in 350°F oven 30 to 45 minutes. Leftover stuffing should be removed from bird and stored in refrigerator separately. Reheat thoroughly before serving.

Makes enough stuffing for 12- to 15-pound turkey, 10 side-dish servings

SAVORY CORN BREAD STUFFING

1 pound fresh mushrooms, sliced (about 4 cups)
1 cup chopped celery
¾ cup chopped onion
½ cup margarine or butter
4 teaspoons WYLER'S® or STEERO® Chicken-Flavor Instant Bouillon *or* 4 Chicken-Flavor Bouillon Cubes
1⅔ cups boiling water
1 pound bulk sausage, browned and drained
1 (16-ounce) package corn bread stuffing mix
1½ teaspoons poultry seasoning

In large skillet, cook mushrooms, celery and onion in margarine until tender. In large bowl, dissolve bouillon in water. Add sausage, mushroom mixture and remaining ingredients; mix well. Loosely stuff turkey just before roasting. Place remaining stuffing in greased baking dish. Bake at 350°F for 30 minutes or until hot. Refrigerate leftovers.

Makes about 3 quarts

SAUSAGE-CORNBREAD STUFFING

**8 ounces bulk pork sausage (regular or
      spicy)**
½ cup butter or margarine
2 medium onions, chopped
2 cloves garlic, minced
2 teaspoons dried sage
1 teaspoon poultry seasoning
**1 package (16 ounces) prepared dry
      cornbread crumbs**
¾ to 1¼ cups chicken broth
      Sage leaves for garnish

Brown sausage in large skillet over medium-
high heat until no longer pink, stirring to
separate meat. Drain sausage on paper towels;
set aside. Wipe skillet with paper towels to
remove grease. Melt butter in same skillet over
medium heat until foamy. Cook and stir onions
and garlic in butter 10 minutes or until onions
are softened. Stir in dried sage and poultry
seasoning; cook 1 minute more.

Combine cornbread crumbs, sausage and
onion mixture in large bowl. *If stuffing is to be
cooked in turkey,* drizzle ¾ cup broth over
stuffing; toss lightly until evenly moistened.
Stuff body and neck cavities loosely with
stuffing. Stuffing may be prepared up to 1 day
before using. *Do not stuff turkey until just
before ready to roast.* Roast according to
directions given on page 160 or according to
instructions with turkey. *If stuffing is to be
cooked separately,* drizzle 1¼ cups broth over
stuffing; toss stuffing lightly until evenly
moistened. Transfer to 3-quart casserole.

Preheat oven to 350°F. Bake 45 minutes (55 to
60 minutes if refrigerated) or until heated
through. For drier stuffing, uncover during last
15 minutes of baking. Garnish, if desired.

Makes 12 cups stuffing

TURKEY PAN GRAVY

Pan drippings from roasted turkey
6 tablespoons all-purpose flour
**4 cups turkey broth, chicken broth, milk
      or water**
LAWRY'S® Seasoned Salt
LAWRY'S® Seasoned Pepper

Pour drippings from turkey into bowl, leaving
browned particles on bottom of roasting pan.
Let fat rise to top of drippings; skim off fat,
reserving 6 tablespoons. Reserve remaining
drippings for part of the liquid for gravy, if
desired. Return reserved fat to roasting pan.
Place roasting pan over low heat; blend in flour
and cook, stirring constantly, until bubbly. Add
liquid, which should be cool, all at once. Cook,
stirring constantly with wire whisk, until
thickened. Continue cooking over low heat
about 5 minutes, stirring constantly. Season to
taste with Seasoned Salt and Seasoned
Pepper.   *Makes about 4 cups*

CREAMED HORSERADISH

1 cup whipping cream
**1 ounce fresh horseradish root, peeled
      and finely grated *or* 1 tablespoon
      prepared horseradish**
1 teaspoon LAWRY'S® Seasoned Salt
2 to 3 drops hot pepper sauce

In medium bowl, whip cream until soft peaks
form. Gradually add horseradish, Seasoned
Salt and hot pepper sauce to taste. Continue
whipping until very stiff. Refrigerate.

Makes 2 cups

PRESENTATION: Serve with prime rib or
roast beef.

Sausage-Cornbread Stuffing

Harvest Sausage Stuffing

HARVEST SAUSAGE STUFFING

1 pound bulk sausage
2 cups chopped celery
8 ounces fresh mushrooms, sliced (about 2 cups)
1½ cups chopped onions
4 teaspoons WYLER'S® or STEERO® Chicken-Flavor Instant Bouillon *or* 4 Chicken-Flavor Bouillon Cubes
1 to 1½ cups boiling water
2 (7-ounce) packages herb-seasoned stuffing mix
1⅓ cups (½ jar) NONE SUCH® Ready-to-Use Mincemeat
1 (8-ounce) can sliced water chestnuts, drained and coarsely chopped
2 teaspoons poultry seasoning

In large skillet, brown sausage; pour off fat. Add celery, mushrooms and onions; cook until onions are tender. Add bouillon and water to sausage mixture; bring to a boil. In large bowl, combine remaining ingredients with sausage mixture; mix well. Use to stuff turkey loosely just before roasting. Place remaining stuffing in 2-quart greased baking dish; cover. Bake at 350°F for 45 minutes or until hot. Refrigerate leftovers. *Makes about 3 quarts*

GOURMET GRITS

½ pound **BOB EVANS FARMS®** Italian
  roll sausage
3 cups water
1 cup uncooked white grits
½ (10-ounce) package frozen chopped
  spinach, thawed and squeezed dry
¼ cup grated Parmesan cheese
¼ cup chopped sun-dried tomatoes
¼ cup olive oil
1 clove garlic, chopped

Crumble sausage into medium skillet. Cook over medium heat until browned, stirring occasionally. Drain off any drippings; set aside. Bring water to a rapid boil in large saucepan. While stirring, add grits in steady stream until mixture thickens into smooth paste. Reduce heat to low; simmer 5 to 7 minutes, stirring frequently to prevent sticking. Stir in sausage, spinach, cheese and tomatoes. Pour into greased 9×5-inch loaf pan. Refrigerate until cool and firm.

Unmold; slice into ½-inch-thick slices. Heat oil in large skillet over medium-high heat until hot. Add garlic; cook and stir 30 seconds or until soft. Add grit slices, 4 to 5 at a time, and cook until golden brown on both sides. Repeat with remaining slices. Serve hot. Refrigerate leftovers. *Makes 4 to 6 side-dish servings*

SERVING SUGGESTION: Melt thinly sliced mozzarella cheese on top of each browned slice. Top slices with warm tomato or spaghetti sauce and serve as a side dish with chicken.

YORKSHIRE PUDDING

2 eggs
1 cup all-purpose flour
½ teaspoon salt
¾ cup milk
¼ cup water
1 package (1 ounce) **LAWRY'S®**
  Seasoning Blend for Au Jus Gravy
1½ cups water
½ cup port wine
  Dash **LAWRY'S®** Seasoned Pepper
  Vegetable oil

In medium bowl, beat eggs with electric mixer until frothy. Reduce speed and gradually add flour and salt, beating until smooth. Slowly add milk and ¼ cup water, beating until blended. Increase speed to high and continue beating 10 minutes. Let stand 1 hour. In medium saucepan, prepare Seasoning Blend for Au Jus Gravy with 1½ cups water, wine and Seasoned Pepper according to package directions. Set aside. Preheat oven to 400°F. Coat 5-inch ovenproof omelet pan with oil and place in oven. When pan is very hot, remove and pour off excess oil. Add 1 tablespoon Au Jus Gravy mixture and ½ cup batter to pan. Bake 20 to 30 minutes or until puffed and brown. Remove pudding and wrap in foil. Keep warm. Repeat with remaining batter.
 Makes 4 Yorkshire Puddings, 8 servings

PRESENTATION: Cut each pudding into quarters and serve with prime rib or roast beef. Serve remaining Au Jus Gravy over meat.

HINT: To make ahead, wrap each cooked pudding in foil; refrigerate. When ready to serve, reheat wrapped puddings individually in warm oven.

FLASH PRIMAVERA

1 pound mostaccioli, ziti or other
  medium pasta shape, uncooked
1 head broccoli or cauliflower, cut into
  small florets
1 tablespoon cornstarch
¼ cup water
1 (13¾-ounce) can low sodium chicken
  broth
3 cloves garlic, minced
1 (10-ounce) package frozen mixed
  vegetables
1 (10-ounce) package frozen chopped
  spinach, thawed
  Salt and pepper
1 cup grated Parmesan cheese

Prepare pasta according to package directions; 3 minutes before pasta is done, stir in broccoli. Drain pasta and vegetables; transfer to large bowl. Set aside and keep warm.

Meanwhile, in small bowl dissolve cornstarch in water; set aside. Simmer broth and garlic in large saucepan over medium heat 3 minutes. Whisk in cornstarch mixture. Stir in mixed vegetables and spinach; cook until hot, about 5 minutes. Toss sauce and vegetables with pasta. Season to taste with salt and pepper; sprinkle with Parmesan cheese.

Makes 6 servings

Favorite recipe from **National Pasta Association**

Flash Primavera

SPINACH–STUFFED MANICOTTI

8 manicotti shells, cooked and drained
1½ teaspoons olive oil
1 teaspoon minced fresh garlic
1½ cups canned or fresh tomatoes, chopped
1 teaspoon dried rosemary leaves, crushed
1 teaspoon dried sage leaves, crushed
1 teaspoon dried oregano leaves, crushed
1 teaspoon dried thyme leaves, crushed
1 package (10 ounces) frozen chopped spinach, cooked, drained and squeezed dry
4 ounces ricotta cheese
1 slice whole wheat bread, torn into coarse crumbs
2 egg whites, slightly beaten

Preheat oven to 350°F. Heat oil in small saucepan over medium heat. Add garlic; cook and stir until lightly browned. Stir in tomatoes, rosemary, sage, oregano and thyme. Reduce heat to low; simmer 10 minutes, stirring occasionally.

Combine spinach, cheese and bread crumbs in medium bowl. Fold in egg whites. Stuff manicotti with spinach mixture. Spoon ⅓ of the sauce into 13×9-inch baking dish. Arrange manicotti over sauce; cover with remaining sauce. Cover with foil. Bake 30 minutes or until hot and bubbly. Garnish as desired.

Makes 4 servings

*Favorite recipe from **National Pasta Association***

Spinach-Stuffed Manicotti

PASTA WITH FRESH VEGETABLES IN GARLIC SAUCE

3 medium carrots
2 small zucchini
¼ cup butter or margarine
1 large onion, chopped
4 cloves garlic, minced
½ cup chicken broth
½ cup heavy cream
½ teaspoon salt
½ teaspoon dried tarragon leaves, crushed
¼ teaspoon pepper
2 cups hot, cooked, drained pasta (fettuccine, ziti or shells)

Cut carrots and zucchini lengthwise into thin slices with vegetable peeler. Bring 1 inch water to a boil in medium saucepan; add carrots and zucchini. Cook until crisp-tender. Remove from saucepan and drain; set aside. Melt butter in same saucepan over medium heat. Add onion and garlic; cook until tender. Gradually stir in broth, cream and seasonings; simmer 5 minutes or until sauce is slightly thickened. Add vegetables; heat thoroughly, stirring occasionally. Add vegetables and sauce to hot cooked pasta; toss lightly.   *Makes 4 servings*

PASTA ROLL-UPS

1 package (1.5 ounces) LAWRY'S® Original-Style Spaghetti Sauce Spices & Seasonings
1 can (6 ounces) tomato paste
2¼ cups water
2 tablespoons butter or vegetable oil
2 cups cottage cheese or ricotta cheese
1 cup (4 ounces) shredded mozzarella cheese
¼ cup grated Parmesan cheese
2 eggs, lightly beaten
½ to 1 teaspoon LAWRY'S® Garlic Salt
½ teaspoon dried basil, crushed (optional)
8 ounces lasagna noodles, cooked and drained

In medium saucepan, prepare Spaghetti Sauce Spices & Seasonings according to package directions using tomato paste, water and butter. In large bowl, combine remaining ingredients except noodles; blend well. Spread ¼ cup cheese mixture on entire length of each lasagna noodle; roll up. Place noodles, seam side down, in microwave-safe baking dish. Cover with vented plastic wrap and microwave on HIGH 6 to 7 minutes or until cheese begins to melt. Pour sauce over rolls and microwave on HIGH 1 minute longer, if necessary, to heat sauce.   *Makes 6 servings*

PRESENTATION: Sprinkle with additional grated Parmesan cheese. Garnish with fresh basil leaves.

HINT: For quick microwavable meals, wrap prepared rolls individually and freeze. Sauce may be frozen in ¼-cup servings.

Pasta with Fresh Vegetables in Garlic Sauce

Mrs. Claus's

BREADS

HOLIDAY STOLLEN

1½ cups unsalted butter, softened
4 egg yolks
½ cup granulated sugar
1 teaspoon salt
Grated peel from 1 lemon and 1 orange
1 teaspoon vanilla
2½ cups hot milk (120° to 130°F)
8 to 8½ cups all-purpose flour, divided
2 packages active dry yeast
½ cup *each* golden raisins, candied orange
    peel, candied lemon peel, chopped candied
    red cherries, chopped candied green
    cherries and chopped almonds
1 egg, beaten
Powdered sugar

In large mixer bowl, beat butter, egg yolks, granulated sugar, salt, lemon peel, orange peel and vanilla until light and fluffy. Slowly add milk; mix thoroughly. Add 2 cups flour and yeast; mix well. When mixture is smooth, add enough remaining flour, ½ cup at a time, until dough forms and can be lifted out of bowl. Lightly flour work surface; knead dough until smooth and elastic, about 10 minutes. Mix raisins, candied orange and lemon peels, cherries and almonds in medium bowl; knead fruit mixture into dough.

continued on page 266

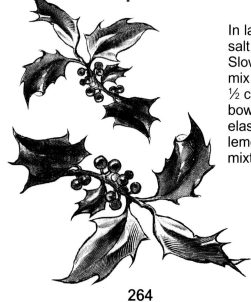

Holiday Stollen, continued

Place dough in greased bowl, cover with plastic wrap and let rise in warm place until doubled in bulk, about 1 hour.

Grease 2 large baking sheets. Turn dough out onto floured work surface. Divide dough in half. Place one half back in bowl; cover and set aside. Cut remaining half into thirds. Roll each third into 12-inch rope. Place on prepared baking sheet. Braid ropes together. Repeat procedure with remaining dough.

Brush beaten egg on braids. Let braids stand at room temperature until doubled in bulk, about 1 hour.

Preheat oven to 350°F. Bake braids until golden brown and sound hollow when tapped, about 45 minutes. Remove to wire rack to cool. Sprinkle with powdered sugar before serving.

Makes 2 braided loaves

Chocolate Walnut Coffee Rings

CHOCOLATE WALNUT COFFEE RINGS

6½ to 7 cups all-purpose flour, divided
½ cup granulated sugar
1½ teaspoons salt
1½ teaspoons ground cinnamon
2 packages active dry yeast
1 cup butter or margarine
1 cup milk
½ cup water
2 eggs
2 egg yolks
2 cups (12-ounce package) NESTLÉ® Toll House® Semi-Sweet Chocolate Morsels
1 cup chopped walnuts
⅓ cup packed brown sugar
Vegetable oil
Glaze (recipe page 267)

In large mixer bowl, combine *2 cups* flour, granulated sugar, salt, cinnamon and yeast. In small saucepan over low heat, warm butter, milk and water until very warm (120° to 130°F). On low speed of electric mixer, gradually beat milk mixture into dry ingredients; beat for 2 minutes. Add eggs, egg yolks and *1 cup* flour. Beat on high speed for 2 minutes. Stir in about *2½ cups* flour to make a stiff dough. Cover; let stand for 20 minutes.

In medium bowl, combine morsels, walnuts and brown sugar. Sprinkle work surface with *½ cup* flour. Turn dough onto work surface; sprinkle with additional *½ cup* flour. Knead for 2 to 3 minutes; cut dough in half. On floured surface, roll out one dough half into 16×10-inch rectangle. Sprinkle one half morsel mixture to within ½ inch of edges. Starting at wide end, roll up jelly-roll fashion; pinch seam to seal. Place, seam side down, on large greased baking sheet, joining ends to from a circle. Cut outside edge at 1-inch intervals, two thirds of way through. Turn each slice on its side to overlap. Brush with oil; cover with plastic wrap.

Repeat with remaining dough and filling. Chill for 2 to 24 hours. Let coffee rings stand uncovered at room temperature for 10 minutes. Bake in preheated 375°F oven for 25 to 30 minutes or until golden. Remove from baking sheets; cool on wire racks. Drizzle with Glaze.

Makes 2 coffee rings

GLAZE: In small bowl, combine 1 cup powdered sugar, 5 to 6 teaspoons milk, ½ teaspoon vanilla extract and dash ground cinnamon; blend until smooth.

APPLE CINNAMON COFFEE RING

SWEET DOUGH
- **1 package active dry yeast**
- **¼ cup warm water (110° to 115°F)**
- **1 cup milk**
- **⅓ cup sugar**
- **⅓ cup butter or margarine**
- **½ teaspoon salt**
- **2 eggs**
- **4½ to 5 cups all-purpose flour**

APPLE CINNAMON FILLING
- **3 tablespoons butter, divided**
- **1 cup thinly sliced Golden Delicious apples**
- **½ cup chopped pecans**
- **½ cup firmly packed brown sugar**
- **1 teaspoon ground cinnamon**
- **1 teaspoon grated orange peel**

GLAZE
- **¾ cup confectioners' sugar**
- **1 tablespoon orange juice**

1. To make Sweet Dough, in small bowl, dissolve yeast in water; set aside until foamy. Meanwhile, heat milk in small saucepan; add sugar, butter and salt. Cool to warm (110°F). In large bowl, combine milk mixture, yeast mixture, eggs and flour, stirring until soft dough forms. Turn out onto lightly floured surface and knead dough 5 minutes or until elastic. Wash, dry, and oil same large bowl; place dough in bowl, cover, and let rise in warm place about 1 hour.

2. Meanwhile, prepare Apple Cinnamon Filling. In skillet, melt 1 tablespoon butter; add apples and sauté until soft. Remove from heat and add pecans, brown sugar, cinnamon and orange peel, mixing well. Set aside.

3. When dough has risen, roll out on lightly floured surface to an 11×9-inch rectangle. Brush with remaining 2 tablespoons melted butter and top with apple mixture, leaving ½-inch border at edges. Fold dough in thirds lengthwise to make 11×3-inch roll. Cut crosswise into 12 equal pieces. Arrange pieces, cut side up, in greased 9-inch springform pan, forming a ring. Cover and let rise 40 minutes.

4. Heat oven to 325°F. Bake coffee ring 30 to 35 minutes or until golden. Cool on wire rack. Remove side of pan. To make Glaze, in small bowl, mix confectioners' sugar and orange juice. Drizzle Glaze over coffee ring and serve.

Makes 12 servings

*Favorite recipe from **Washington Apple Commission***

CINNAMON TWISTS

ROLLS
- 1 package DUNCAN HINES® Cinnamon Muffin Mix, divided
- 2 cups all-purpose flour
- 1 package (¼ ounce) quick-rise yeast
- 1 egg, slightly beaten
- 1 cup hot water (120° to 130°F)
- 2 tablespoons butter or margarine, melted
- 1 egg white, slightly beaten
- 1 teaspoon water

TOPPING
- 1½ cups confectioners sugar
- 2½ tablespoons milk

1. Grease 2 large baking sheets.

2. For rolls, combine muffin mix, flour and yeast in large bowl; set aside.

3. Combine contents of swirl packet from Mix, egg, hot water and melted butter in medium bowl. Stir until thoroughly blended. Pour into flour mixture; stir until thoroughly blended. Invert onto well-floured surface; let rest for 10 minutes. Knead for 10 minutes or until smooth, adding flour as necessary. Divide dough in half. Cut and shape 24 small ropes from each half. Braid 3 ropes to form small twist and place on greased baking sheet. (Or, join ends of twists to form circles.) Combine egg white and 1 teaspoon water in small bowl. Brush each twist with egg white mixture and sprinkle with contents of topping packet from Mix. Allow twists to rise 1 hour or until doubled in size.

4. Preheat oven to 375°F.

5. Bake at 375°F for 17 to 20 minutes or until deep golden brown. Remove to cooling racks.

6. For topping, combine confectioners sugar and milk in small bowl. Stir until smooth. Drizzle over warm rolls. Serve warm or cool completely.

Makes 16 rolls

YEASTY CINNAMON LOAVES

- 1 package DUNCAN HINES® Cinnamon Muffin Mix, divided
- 5 cups all-purpose flour
- 2 packages (¼ ounce each) quick-rise yeast
- 2 eggs, slightly beaten
- ¼ cup plus 2 tablespoons butter or margarine, melted, divided
- 2½ cups hot water (120° to 130°F), divided
- Sifted confectioners sugar (optional)

1. Grease two 9×5×3-inch loaf pans.

2. Combine muffin mix, contents of crumb topping from Mix, flour and yeast in large bowl; set aside.

3. Combine contents of swirl packet from Mix, eggs, ¼ cup melted butter and ½ cup hot water in medium bowl. Stir well. Add remaining 2 cups hot water and stir until thoroughly blended. Add liquid ingredients to flour mixture; stir until thoroughly blended. Invert onto well-floured surface; let rest for 10 minutes. Knead for 10 minutes or until smooth, adding flour as necessary. Divide dough in half. Divide each half into 3 sections. Roll each section into 10-inch rope. Braid 3 ropes. Fold ends under. Place in greased pan. Repeat with remaining dough. Let rise 1 hour or until doubled in size.

4. Preheat oven to 375°F.

5. Bake at 375°F for 30 to 35 minutes or until bread is deep golden brown and sounds hollow when tapped. Brush with remaining 2 tablespoons melted butter. Cool in pans 5 minutes. Remove bread from pans to cooling racks. Cool completely. Sprinkle with confectioners sugar, if desired.

Makes 2 loaves

NOTE: You may also braid loaves and bake free-form on greased baking sheets for 26 to 30 minutes.

Top to bottom: Yeasty Cinnamon Loaf, Cinnamon Twists

HONEY WHEAT BROWN-AND-SERVE ROLLS

2 packages active dry yeast
1 teaspoon sugar
¾ cup warm water (105° to 115°F)
2 cups whole wheat flour
2 to 3 cups all-purpose flour, divided
¼ cup vegetable shortening
¼ cup honey
1 teaspoon salt
1 egg

Sprinkle yeast and sugar over warm water in small bowl; stir until yeast is dissolved. Let stand 5 minutes until mixture is bubbly. Combine whole wheat flour and 2 cups all-purpose flour in medium bowl. Measure 1½ cups flour mixture into large bowl. Add yeast mixture, shortening, honey, salt and egg. Beat with electric mixer at low speed until smooth, scraping down side of bowl once. Increase mixer speed to medium; beat 2 minutes, scraping down side of bowl once. Reduce speed to low; beat in 1 cup flour mixture. Increase mixer speed to medium; beat 2 minutes, scraping down side of bowl once. Stir in remaining flour mixture and enough additional all-purpose flour (about ¼ cup) with wooden spoon to make a soft dough.

Turn dough out onto lightly floured surface. Knead 8 to 10 minutes or until smooth and elastic, adding more flour to prevent sticking, if necessary. Shape dough into a ball; place in large greased bowl. Turn once to grease surface. Cover with clean kitchen towel. Let rise in warm place (80° to 85°F) about 1½ hours or until doubled in bulk. Punch down dough. Turn dough onto lightly floured surface. Knead dough several turns to remove all large air bubbles; cover and let rest 15 minutes. Meanwhile, grease 24 muffin cups.

Honey Wheat Brown-and-Serve Rolls

Divide dough into 24 pieces. Cut each piece into thirds. Roll each third into a ball. Place 3 balls in each muffin cup. Cover and let rise in warm place about 30 minutes until doubled in bulk.

Preheat oven to 275°F.* Bake 20 to 25 minutes or until rolls are set but not brown. Immediately remove rolls from muffin cups and cool completely on wire racks. Store in resealable plastic food storage bags in refrigerator or freezer.

To bake rolls, thaw rolls if frozen. Preheat oven to 400°F. Grease large jelly-roll pan. Place rolls on pan. Bake 8 to 10 minutes or until golden brown. *Makes 24 rolls*

*To bake rolls immediately, preheat oven to 375°F. Bake 15 to 20 minutes or until golden brown. Immediately remove from pan. Serve warm.

NUT–FILLED CHRISTMAS WREATH

2 tablespoons warm water (105° to 115°F)
1 package active dry yeast
3 tablespoons sugar, divided
2 eggs
¼ cup butter or margarine, melted, cooled
3 tablespoons milk
¾ teaspoon salt
½ teaspoon ground cardamom
2½ to 3 cups all-purpose flour, divided
Cherry-Nut Filling (recipe follows)
Almond Icing (recipe follows)

In large bowl, combine water, yeast and 1 tablespoon sugar; stir to dissolve yeast. Let stand until bubbly, about 5 minutes. Add remaining 2 tablespoons sugar, eggs, butter, milk, salt and cardamom; mix well. Stir in 1½ cups flour until smooth. Stir in enough remaining flour to make dough easy to handle. Turn out onto lightly floured surface. Knead 10 minutes or until dough is smooth and elastic, adding as much remaining flour as needed to prevent sticking. Shape dough into ball. Place in large, lightly greased bowl; turn dough once to grease surface. Cover with waxed paper; let rise in warm place (85°F) until doubled, about 1 hour. Meanwhile, prepare Cherry-Nut Filling.

Punch dough down. Roll out dough on floured surface into 24×9-inch rectangle. Sprinkle Cherry-Nut Filling over dough to within 1 inch of edges. Roll up dough, jelly-roll style, beginning on 24-inch side; pinch seam to seal. Using sharp knife, cut roll in half lengthwise; turn each half cut side up. Carefully twist halves together, keeping cut sides up to expose filling. Place dough on greased cookie sheet; shape into a ring. Pinch ends together to seal. Cover; let stand in warm place until almost doubled, about 45 minutes. Bake in preheated 375°F oven 20 minutes or until evenly browned. Remove bread from cookie sheet to wire rack; cool slightly. Prepare Almond Icing; drizzle over warm bread. Serve warm or at room temperature. *Makes 1 bread ring*

CHERRY–NUT FILLING: In medium bowl, combine ¾ cup chopped nuts (hazelnuts, almonds, walnuts or pecans), ¼ cup *each* all-purpose flour, chopped candied red cherries, chopped candied green cherries and softened butter or margarine, 2 tablespoons brown sugar and ½ teaspoon almond extract; mix well.

ALMOND ICING: In small bowl, combine 1 cup sifted powdered sugar, 1 to 2 tablespoons milk and ¼ teaspoon almond extract; blend until smooth.

APRICOT DATE COFFEE CAKES

1 cup warm milk (105° to 115°F)
2 packages active dry yeast
1 cup butter, softened
½ cup granulated sugar
2 eggs, slightly beaten
1 teaspoon salt
1 teaspoon ground cardamom
5 to 5½ cups all-purpose flour
1 cup prepared apricot filling
½ cup chopped dates
2 cups sifted powdered sugar
3 tablespoons light cream or half-and-half
½ teaspoon vanilla
¼ teaspoon almond extract

In large bowl, combine milk and yeast; stir to dissolve yeast. Stir in next 5 ingredients and 2 cups flour; beat until smooth. Stir in enough remaining flour to make dough easy to handle. Turn out onto lightly floured surface. Knead 10 minutes or until dough is smooth and elastic; add as much remaining flour as needed to prevent sticking. Shape into ball. Place in large, buttered bowl; turn once to coat surface. Cover with waxed paper; let rise in warm place until doubled, about 1½ hours. In small bowl, combine apricot filling and dates; set aside.

Punch dough down; divide into 3 pieces. Roll out one piece on lightly floured surface into 12×10-inch rectangle. Spoon ⅓ apricot mixture down center third of dough. Fold long sides over filling to center; pinch to seal. Pinch ends of rectangle to seal. Place dough, seam side down, on buttered baking sheet. With scissors, snip 1-inch-wide strips almost to center on both long sides of coffee cake. Turn each strip on its side. Repeat with remaining dough and filling. Cover; let rise in warm place until doubled, about 30 minutes. Bake in preheated 375°F oven about 18 minutes or until golden brown. Remove to wire racks to cool. In small bowl, combine remaining ingredients; mix well. Drizzle over cakes.   *Makes 3 coffee cakes*

Favorite recipe from **American Dairy Association**

WHOLESOME WHEAT BREAD

5½ to 6 cups whole wheat flour
2 packages active dry yeast
1 teaspoon salt
1 teaspoon ground cinnamon
1 cup KARO® Dark Corn Syrup
1 cup water
½ cup HELLMANN'S® or BEST FOODS® Real or Light Mayonnaise or Low Fat Cholesterol Free Mayonnaise Dressing
2 eggs

In large mixer bowl, combine 2 cups flour, yeast, salt and cinnamon. In medium saucepan, combine corn syrup, water and mayonnaise; heat mixture over medium heat, stirring occasionally, until very warm (120° to 130°F). Pour hot mixture into flour mixture; beat at medium speed 2 minutes. Reduce speed to low; beat in additional 2 cups flour and the eggs until well mixed. Beat at medium speed 2 minutes. By hand, stir in enough remaining flour to make dough easy to handle. Turn out onto lightly floured surface. Knead 10 minutes or until dough is smooth and elastic, adding as much remaining flour as needed to prevent sticking. Shape dough into a ball. Place in large, greased bowl; turn dough once to grease surface. Cover with towel; let rise in warm place (85°F) until doubled, about 1 hour.

Punch dough down; divide in half. Cover; let rest 10 minutes. Shape each half into 8×4-inch oval. Place on greased, floured large baking sheet. Cut 3 slashes, ¼ inch deep, in top of each loaf. Cover; let rise in warm place until doubled, about 1½ hours. Bake in preheated 350°F oven 30 to 40 minutes or until loaves are browned and sound hollow when tapped. Immediately remove from baking sheet to wire racks to cool.   *Makes 2 loaves*

Clockwise from top right: Apple-Cranberry Muffins (page 296), Wholesome Wheat Bread, Nut-Filled Christmas Wreath (page 271)

PEPPER-CHEESE BREAD

5½ to 6 cups all-purpose flour
2 packages active dry yeast
1 cup milk
⅔ cup butter, cut into small pieces
1 tablespoon sugar
1 to 2 teaspoons coarsely ground black
  pepper
1 teaspoon salt
4 eggs
2 cups (8 ounces) shredded sharp
  Wisconsin Cheddar cheese
1¼ cups unseasoned mashed potatoes

In large mixer bowl combine 2 cups flour and yeast. In small saucepan combine milk, butter, sugar, pepper and salt. Cook and stir until warm (115° to 120°F) and butter is almost melted. Add to flour mixture. Add eggs. Beat with electric mixer on low speed for 30 seconds, scraping side of bowl. Beat on high speed for 3 minutes. Stir in Cheddar cheese, mashed potatoes and as much remaining flour as can be mixed in with a spoon.

Turn out onto lightly floured surface. Knead 6 to 8 minutes or until dough is smooth and elastic, adding as much remaining flour as needed to make a moderately stiff dough. Shape into a ball. Place in greased bowl; turn once to grease surface. Cover; let rise in warm place (80° to 85°F) until double (about 1 hour).

Punch down dough; turn out onto lightly floured surface. Divide dough into 6 pieces. Cover; let rest 10 minutes. Roll each piece into 16-inch-long rope. On greased baking sheet braid 3 ropes together. Repeat on second greased baking sheet with remaining ropes. Cover; let rise in warm place until nearly doubled (about 30 minutes).

Preheat oven to 375°F. Bake 35 to 40 minutes or until golden brown, covering with foil the last 15 minutes of baking to prevent overbrowning. Remove from baking sheets; cool.

Makes 2 braids

PREP TIME: 50 minutes plus rising

Favorite recipe from **Wisconsin Milk Marketing Board**

Pepper-Cheese Bread

TOMATO AND CHEESE FOCACCIA

1 package active dry yeast
¾ cup warm water (105° to 115°F)
2 cups all-purpose flour
½ teaspoon salt
¼ cup olive oil, divided
1 teaspoon Italian seasoning
8 oil-packed, sun-dried tomatoes, well
    drained
½ cup (2 ounces) shredded provolone
    cheese
¼ cup (1 ounce) freshly grated Parmesan
    cheese

Dissolve yeast in warm water; let stand 5 minutes. Combine flour and salt in work bowl of food processor.* Stir in yeast mixture and 3 tablespoons oil. Process until ingredients form a ball. Process 1 minute more. Turn out onto lightly floured surface. Knead about 2 minutes or until smooth and elastic. Place dough in oiled bowl; turn once to oil dough surface. Cover with clean kitchen towel. Let rise in warm place about 30 minutes or until doubled in bulk.

Punch dough down. Let rest 5 minutes. Press dough into oiled 10-inch cake pan, deep-dish pizza pan or springform pan. Brush with remaining 1 tablespoon oil. Sprinkle with Italian seasoning. Press sun-dried tomatoes around side of bread, about 1 inch from edge. Sprinkle with cheeses. Cover and let rise in warm place 15 minutes.

Preheat oven to 425°F. Bake 20 to 25 minutes or until golden brown. Cool completely in pan on wire rack. Carefully remove bread from pan before serving.   *Makes 1 (10-inch) bread*

*If mixing dough by hand, combine flour and salt in large bowl. Stir in yeast mixture and 3 tablespoons oil until ingredients form a ball. Turn out onto lightly floured surface and knead about 10 minutes or until smooth and elastic. Proceed as directed.

SAVORY BUBBLE CHEESE BREAD

6 to 7 cups flour, divided
2 tablespoons sugar
4 teaspoons instant minced onion
2 teaspoons salt
2 packages active dry yeast
½ teaspoon caraway seeds
1¾ cups milk
½ cup water
3 tablespoons butter or margarine
1 teaspoon TABASCO® pepper sauce
2 cups (8 ounces) shredded sharp
    Cheddar cheese, divided
1 egg, lightly beaten

In large bowl of electric mixer combine 2½ cups flour, sugar, onion, salt, yeast and caraway seeds. In small saucepan combine milk, water and butter. Heat milk mixture until very warm (120° to 130°F.); stir in TABASCO sauce.

With mixer at medium speed gradually add milk mixture to dry ingredients; beat 2 minutes. Add 1 cup flour. Beat at high speed 2 minutes. With wooden spoon stir in 1½ cups cheese and enough flour to make a stiff dough. Turn dough out onto lightly floured surface. Knead 8 to 10 minutes or until dough is smooth and elastic, adding as much remaining flour as needed to prevent sticking. Place dough in large greased bowl and turn once to grease surface. Cover with towel; let rise in warm place (90° to 100°F.) 1 hour or until doubled in bulk.

Punch dough down. Divide dough into 16 equal pieces; shape each piece into a ball. Place half the balls in well-greased 10-inch tube pan. Sprinkle with remaining ½ cup cheese. Arrange remaining balls on top. Cover with towel; let rise in warm place 45 minutes or until doubled in bulk. Preheat oven to 375°F. Brush dough with egg. Bake 40 to 50 minutes or until golden brown. Remove from pan. Cool completely on wire rack.   *Makes 1 (10-inch) round loaf*

CHALLAH

      2 packages active dry yeast
      2 tablespoons sugar
   1½ cups warm water (110° to 115°F)
      7 to 7½ cups all-purpose flour, divided
      ¼ cup butter or margarine, softened
      1 teaspoon salt
      3 eggs
      1 egg, separated
      1 tablespoon water

Sprinkle yeast and sugar over 1½ cups warm water in small bowl; stir until yeast is dissolved. Let stand until bubbly, about 5 minutes.

Beat yeast mixture, 2 cups flour, butter and salt in large bowl with electric mixer at low speed. Increase mixer speed to medium; beat 2 minutes. Beat in eggs, egg white and 1¼ cups flour at low speed. Increase mixer speed to medium; beat 2 minutes. Stir in enough additional flour (about 2½ cups) with wooden spoon to make a soft dough. Turn dough out onto well-floured surface. Knead 5 minutes or until smooth and elastic, adding more flour to prevent sticking, if necessary. Shape dough into ball; place in large greased bowl. Turn to grease surface. Cover; let rise in warm place about 1½ hours or until doubled in bulk.

Punch down dough. Turn dough onto lightly floured surface. Knead several turns. Cover and let rest 15 minutes. Grease 1 large cookie sheet. Divide dough into 3 pieces. Cut 1 piece into thirds. Roll each third into 16-inch-long rope. Place ropes side by side and braid; pinch both ends to seal. Place on prepared cookie sheet. Repeat with second dough piece for another loaf, placing braids at least 5 inches apart on cookie sheet.

For top parts of loaves, cut remaining piece of dough in half; cut each half into thirds. Roll each third into 17-inch-long rope. Place 3 ropes side by side and braid; pinch both ends to seal. Carefully place small braid on top of large braid, stretching top braid if necessary. Tuck ends of top braid under bottom braid. Repeat with remaining dough. Cover; let rise in warm place about 1 hour or until doubled in bulk.

Preheat oven to 375°F. Beat 1 tablespoon water into reserved egg yolk. Brush top and sides of each loaf with egg mixture. Bake 35 minutes or until bread is browned and loaves sound hollow when tapped with finger. Remove immediately from baking sheet and cool completely on wire racks.   *Makes 2 loaves*

HEALTHY PECAN BREAD

      5 cups all-purpose flour, divided
      2 cups whole wheat flour
      ½ cup wheat germ
      1 cup pecan halves, chopped
      2 teaspoons salt
      2 packages FLEISCHMANN'S® RapidRise
         Yeast
      1 cup water
      1 cup plain yogurt
      ⅓ cup honey
      ¼ cup margarine or butter
      2 eggs, at room temperature

Set aside 1 cup all-purpose flour. In large bowl, mix remaining 4 cups all-purpose flour, whole wheat flour, wheat germ, pecans, salt and yeast. In saucepan, over low heat, heat water, yogurt, honey and margarine until very warm (125° to 130°F); stir into dry mixture. Mix in eggs and only enough reserved flour to make soft dough. On lightly floured surface, knead until smooth and elastic, about 8 to 10 minutes. Cover; let rest 10 minutes.

Divide dough in half; shape each half into smooth ball. Place in two greased 8-inch round cake pans. Cover; let rise in warm (80° to 85°F) place until doubled in size, about 1 hour and 15 minutes.

Preheat oven to 375°F. Bake 35 to 40 minutes or until golden brown. Remove from pans; cool on wire racks.   *Makes 2 loaves*

*Favorite recipe from **Pecan Marketing Board***

Challah

CLASSIC BRAN DINNER ROLLS

1 cup NABISCO® 100% Bran™
1 cup milk
½ cup plus 1 tablespoon water
½ cup margarine
4 to 4½ cups all-purpose flour
2 packages FLEISCHMANN'S® RapidRise Yeast
⅓ cup sugar
¾ teaspoon salt
3 eggs
  Poppy, caraway or sesame seed (optional)

Heat bran, milk, ½ cup water and margarine in medium saucepan until very warm (125° to 130°F); let stand 5 minutes.

Meanwhile, in large bowl, combine 2 cups flour, undissolved yeast, sugar and salt. Stir warm bran mixture into dry ingredients. Mix in 2 eggs and enough remaining flour to make a soft dough. Grease top of dough. Cover tightly with plastic wrap; refrigerate 2 to 24 hours.

Punch dough down. On lightly floured surface, divide dough in half. Shape as desired (see Shaping Ideas, page 279).

Classic Bran Dinner Rolls

Place rolls about 2 inches apart on greased baking sheets. Cover; let rise in warm place (70° to 80°F) until doubled in size, 20 to 30 minutes.

Beat remaining egg with remaining 1 tablespoon water; brush on rolls. If desired, sprinkle with seed. Bake at 375°F for 15 minutes or until golden brown. Remove from sheets; cool on wire racks.

Makes 1 to 2 dozen rolls

SHAPING IDEAS

Crescents: Roll each half to 14-inch circle; cut each into 12 pie-shaped wedges. Roll up each wedge tightly from wide end. Curve ends slightly to form crescent.

Knots: Divide each half into 12 equal pieces; roll each into 9-inch rope. Loosely tie each rope once.

Coils: Divide each half into 12 equal pieces; roll each into 9-inch rope. Coil each rope, tucking end under coil.

Twists: Divide each half into 12 equal pieces; roll each into 12-inch rope. Fold each rope in half and twist together. Pinch ends to seal.

Sandwich Rolls: Divide each half into 6 equal pieces. Roll each piece into 5-inch round. Roll up tightly as for jelly roll. Pinch seam and ends to seal. Place on greased baking sheets, about 2 inches apart. After rising and brushing with egg wash, carefully make 3 diagonal slashes with sharp knife on each roll. If desired, sprinkle with seed. Bake as directed.

ONION DILL BREAD

2 cups bread flour
1 cup whole wheat flour
½ cup instant non-fat dry milk
½ teaspoon salt
1 package active dry yeast
2 tablespoons sugar
1¼ cups water (110° to 115°F)
1 cup KELLOGG'S® ALL-BRAN® cereal
2 egg whites
¼ cup reduced-calorie margarine
¼ cup chopped green onions
¼ cup chopped red onion
1 tablespoon dill weed
1 tablespoon skim milk
2 tablespoons finely chopped onion

1. Stir together flours, dry milk and salt.

2. In large electric mixer bowl, combine yeast, sugar and water. Stir in Kellogg's All-Bran cereal; let stand 2 minutes or until cereal is soft.

3. Add egg whites, margarine and half the flour mixture. Beat at medium speed for 2 minutes or about 200 strokes by hand.

4. Mix in green onions, red onion and dill weed. Stir in remaining flour mixture by hand to form stiff, sticky dough. Cover lightly. Let rise in warm place until double in volume (about 1 hour).

5. Stir down dough to original volume. Spoon dough into 2-quart round casserole dish or 9¼×5¼×2¾-inch loaf pan coated with nonstick cooking spray. Brush surface with milk and sprinkle evenly with 2 tablespoons chopped onion.

6. Bake at 350°F about 55 minutes or until loaf is golden brown and sounds hollow when lightly tapped. Place on wire rack; cool.

Makes 1 loaf

SPICY MINCEMEAT BREAD

6 tablespoons butter or margarine, softened
1 cup packed light brown sugar
2 eggs
1 teaspoon vanilla
2½ cups all-purpose flour
1½ teaspoons baking soda
1 teaspoon ground cinnamon
¾ teaspoon baking powder
½ teaspoon ground nutmeg
¼ teaspoon salt
¾ cup sour cream
1 cup prepared mincemeat
¾ cup chopped pecans

Preheat oven to 350°F. Grease 9×5-inch loaf pan.*

Beat butter and brown sugar in large bowl with electric mixer on medium speed until light and fluffy. Beat in eggs and vanilla until blended. Combine flour, baking soda, cinnamon, baking powder, nutmeg and salt. Add flour mixture to butter mixture on low speed alternately with sour cream, beginning and ending with flour mixture. Mix well after each addition. Stir in mincemeat and pecans on low speed until blended. Spoon into prepared pan.

Bake 55 to 60 minutes or until wooden toothpick inserted in center comes out clean. Cool in pan 15 minutes. Remove from pan and cool completely on wire rack. Store tightly wrapped in plastic wrap at room temperature.

Makes 1 loaf

*Bread may also be baked in four 5½×3-inch greased mini-loaf pans. Prepare batter as directed. Bake at 350°F for 45 to 50 minutes or until wooden toothpick inserted in centers comes out clean. Proceed as directed.

LEMON CRANBERRY LOAVES

1¼ cups finely chopped fresh cranberries
½ cup finely chopped walnuts
¼ cup granulated sugar
1 package DUNCAN HINES® Moist Deluxe Lemon Supreme Cake Mix
1 package (3 ounces) cream cheese, softened
¾ cup milk
4 eggs
Confectioners sugar

Preheat oven to 350°F. Grease and flour two 8½×4½-inch loaf pans.

Stir together cranberries, walnuts and granulated sugar in large bowl; set aside.

Combine cake mix, cream cheese and milk in large bowl. Beat at medium speed with electric mixer for 2 minutes. Add eggs, 1 at a time, beating for an additional 2 minutes. Fold in cranberry mixture. Pour into pans. Bake at 350°F for 45 to 50 minutes or until toothpick inserted in centers comes out clean. Cool in pans 15 minutes. Loosen loaves from pans. Invert onto cooling rack. Turn right side up. Cool completely. Dust with confectioners sugar.

Makes 24 slices

Lemon Cranberry Loaf

WALNUT CHEDDAR APPLE BREAD

½ cup butter or margarine, softened
1 cup packed light brown sugar
2 eggs
1 teaspoon vanilla
2 cups all-purpose flour
2 teaspoons baking powder
1 teaspoon baking soda
¼ teaspoon salt
1 cup sour cream
¼ cup milk
1 cup (4 ounces) shredded Cheddar
    cheese
1 cup diced dried apple
½ cup coarsely chopped walnuts

Preheat oven to 350°F. Grease 9×5-inch
loaf pan.

Beat butter and sugar in large bowl with electric mixer on medium speed until light and fluffy. Beat in eggs and vanilla until blended. Combine flour, baking powder, baking soda and salt in small bowl. Add flour mixture to butter mixture on low speed alternately with sour cream and milk, beginning and ending with flour mixture. Mix well after each addition. Stir in cheese, apple and walnuts on low speed until blended. Spoon into prepared pan.

Bake 50 to 55 minutes or until wooden toothpick inserted in center comes out clean. Cool in pan 15 minutes. Remove from pan and cool completely on wire rack. Store tightly wrapped in plastic wrap at room temperature.

Makes 1 loaf

Walnut Cheddar Apple Bread

PIÑA COLADA BREAD

    2½ cups flour
    ½ cup sugar
    2 teaspoons baking powder
    ½ teaspoon baking soda
    ½ teaspoon salt
    2 eggs
    ½ cup KARO® Light Corn Syrup
    ⅓ cup MAZOLA® Corn Oil
    ¼ cup rum
    1 can (8 ounces) crushed pineapple in
        unsweetened juice, undrained
    1 cup flaked coconut

Preheat oven to 350°F. Grease and flour
9×5×3-inch loaf pan.

In medium bowl, combine flour, sugar, baking
powder, baking soda and salt. In large bowl,
with mixer at medium speed, beat eggs, corn
syrup, corn oil and rum until blended. Gradually
stir in flour mixture just until moistened. Stir in
pineapple with juice and coconut. Pour into
prepared pan.

Bake 60 to 65 minutes or until toothpick
inserted in center comes out clean. Cool in pan
10 minutes. Remove from pan; cool on wire
rack.   *Makes 1 loaf*

PEANUT BUTTER BREAD

    2 cups flour
    ½ cup sugar
    2 teaspoons baking powder
    ½ teaspoon baking soda
    ½ teaspoon salt
    1 cup SKIPPY SUPER CHUNK® or
        Creamy Peanut Butter
    ½ cup KARO® Light or Dark Corn Syrup
    2 eggs
    1 cup milk

Preheat oven to 350°F. Grease and flour
9×5×3-inch loaf pan.

In medium bowl, combine flour, sugar, baking
powder, baking soda and salt. In large bowl,
with mixer at medium speed, beat peanut
butter and corn syrup until smooth. Beat in
eggs, 1 at a time. Gradually beat in milk. Stir in
flour mixture just until moistened. Pour into
prepared pan.

Bake 50 to 55 minutes or until wooden
toothpick inserted in center comes out clean.
Cool in pan 10 minutes. Remove from pan; cool
on wire rack.   *Makes 1 loaf*

BANANA NUT BREAD

    2 extra-ripe, large DOLE® Bananas,
        peeled and cut into chunks
    ⅓ cup butter
    ⅔ cup sugar
    2 eggs
    2 cups all-purpose flour
    2 teaspoons baking powder
    ½ teaspoon baking soda
    ½ cup buttermilk
    ¾ cup chopped nuts

• Purée bananas in blender (1¼ cups). Cream
butter and sugar until light and fluffy. Beat in
bananas and eggs. Combine flour, baking
powder and baking soda. Add dry ingredients
to banana mixture alternately in thirds with
buttermilk, blending well after each addition.
Stir in nuts.

• Pour into greased 9×5-inch loaf pan. Bake in
350°F oven 50 to 60 minutes or until wooden
toothpick inserted in center comes out clean.
Cool in pan on wire rack 10 minutes. Remove
from pan and cool completely.   *Makes 1 loaf*

CRANBERRY RAISIN NUT BREAD

1½ cups all-purpose flour
¾ cup packed light brown sugar
1½ teaspoons baking powder
½ teaspoon baking soda
½ teaspoon ground cinnamon
½ teaspoon ground nutmeg
1 cup halved fresh or frozen cranberries
½ cup golden raisins
½ cup coarsely chopped pecans
1 tablespoon grated orange peel
2 eggs
¾ cup milk
3 tablespoons butter or margarine, melted
1 teaspoon vanilla extract
Cranberry-Orange Spread (recipe follows), optional

Preheat oven to 350°F. Grease 8½×4½-inch loaf pan.

Combine flour, brown sugar, baking powder, baking soda, cinnamon and nutmeg in large bowl. Stir in cranberries, raisins, pecans and orange peel. Mix eggs, milk, melted butter and vanilla in small bowl until combined; stir into flour mixture just until moistened. Spoon into prepared pan.

Bake 55 to 60 minutes or until wooden toothpick inserted in center comes out clean. Cool in pan 15 minutes. Remove from pan and cool completely on wire rack. Store tightly wrapped in plastic wrap at room temperature. Serve slices with Cranberry-Orange Spread, if desired.   *Makes 1 loaf*

CRANBERRY–ORANGE SPREAD

1 package (8 ounces) cream cheese, softened
1 package (3 ounces) cream cheese, softened
1 container (12 ounces) cranberry-orange sauce
¾ cup chopped pecans

Combine cream cheese and cranberry-orange sauce in small bowl. Stir with spoon until blended. Stir in pecans. Store in refrigerator.
Makes about 3 cups spread

STREUSEL LEMON BREAD

½ cup finely chopped nuts
¼ cup firmly packed light brown sugar
½ teaspoon ground nutmeg
2 cups unsifted flour
1 teaspoon baking powder
½ teaspoon baking soda
1¼ cups granulated sugar
½ cup margarine or butter, softened
3 eggs
½ cup REALEMON® Lemon Juice from Concentrate
½ cup BORDEN® or MEADOW GOLD® Milk

Preheat oven to 350°F. In small bowl, combine nuts, brown sugar and nutmeg; set aside. Stir together flour, baking powder and baking soda; set aside. In large mixer bowl, beat granulated sugar and margarine until fluffy. Add eggs, 1 at a time; beat well. Gradually beat in ReaLemon® brand. Add milk alternately with flour mixture; stir well. Spoon half of batter into greased and floured 9×5-inch loaf pan. Sprinkle half of nut mixture over batter; top with remaining batter, spreading to pan edge. Top with remaining nut mixture. Bake 50 to 55 minutes or until wooden pick inserted near center comes out clean. Cool 15 minutes; remove from pan. Cool completely. Store tightly wrapped.
Makes 1 loaf

Cranberry Raisin Nut Bread

CHERRY EGGNOG QUICK BREAD

2½ cups all-purpose flour
¾ cup sugar
1 tablespoon baking powder
½ teaspoon ground nutmeg
1¼ cups prepared dairy eggnog
6 tablespoons butter or margarine, melted and cooled
2 eggs, slightly beaten
1 teaspoon vanilla
½ cup chopped pecans
½ cup chopped candied red cherries

Preheat oven to 350°F. Grease three 5½×3-inch mini-loaf pans.

Combine flour, sugar, baking powder and nutmeg in large bowl. Stir eggnog, melted butter, eggs and vanilla in medium bowl until well blended. Add eggnog mixture to flour mixture. Mix just until all ingredients are moistened. Stir in pecans and cherries. Spoon into prepared pans.

Bake 35 to 40 minutes or until wooden toothpick inserted in centers comes out clean. Cool in pans 15 minutes. Remove from pans and cool completely on wire rack. Store tightly wrapped in plastic wrap at room temperature.
Makes 3 mini loaves

Cherry Eggnog Quick Bread

GOLDEN APPLE BOSTON BROWN BREAD

¼ cup butter or margarine, softened
⅓ cup honey
⅓ cup light molasses
1 cup whole wheat flour
1 cup rye flour
1 cup yellow cornmeal
2 teaspoons baking soda
½ teaspoon salt
2 cups buttermilk
2 cups (2 medium) coarsely chopped
  Golden Delicious apples

In large bowl, cream butter, honey and molasses. In medium bowl, combine flours, cornmeal, baking soda and salt. Add flour mixture to butter mixture alternately with buttermilk, mixing well after each addition. Stir in apples. Pour batter into 2 greased 8½×4½×2½-inch loaf pans. Bake in preheated 350°F oven 1 hour or until wooden pick inserted near centers comes out clean. Let cool in pans on wire racks 10 minutes. Loosen edges; remove from pans. Cool slightly on wire racks; serve warm.   *Makes 2 loaves*

VARIATION: To steam brown bread, divide batter evenly between 2 greased 1-pound coffee cans, filling cans about three-fourths full. Cover tops of cans with aluminum foil; tie foil to cans with string. Place rack in large kettle; add boiling water to depth of 1 inch. Place cans on rack; cover kettle. Steam over low heat 3 hours or until wooden pick inserted near centers comes out clean. If necessary, add more boiling water to kettle during steaming. Cool as above.

Favorite recipe from **Washington Apple Commission**

CHOCOLATE POPOVERS

¾ cup plus 2 tablespoons all-purpose
  flour
¼ cup granulated sugar
2 tablespoons unsweetened cocoa
  powder
¼ teaspoon salt
4 eggs
1 cup milk
2 tablespoons butter or margarine,
  melted
½ teaspoon vanilla
  Powdered sugar

Position rack in lower third of oven. Preheat oven to 375°F. Grease 6-cup popover pan or 6 (6-ounce) custard cups. Set custard cups in jelly-roll pan. Sift flour, granulated sugar, cocoa and salt into medium bowl; set aside. Beat eggs in large bowl with electric mixer at low speed 1 minute. Beat in milk, butter and vanilla. Beat in flour mixture until smooth. Pour batter into prepared pan. Bake 50 minutes. Immediately remove popovers to wire rack. Generously sprinkle powdered sugar over popovers. Serve immediately.
            Makes 6 popovers

Chocolate Popovers

TEDDY BEAR GIFT BREAD

Teddy bear baking pan
1½ cups all-purpose flour
¾ cup granulated sugar
½ cup whole wheat flour
½ cup packed brown sugar
1 tablespoon baking powder
1 teaspoon pumpkin pie spice
½ teaspoon salt
½ teaspoon ground cinnamon
¼ teaspoon ground ginger
¼ teaspoon baking soda
1 egg, beaten
1 cup lowfat milk
4½ teaspoons vegetable oil
Candy for decorating

Preheat oven to 350°F. Generously grease baking pan. In food processor or large bowl, combine all dry ingredients. Add egg, milk and oil. Mix just until blended. Spoon batter into prepared pan. Bake 20 to 25 minutes or until toothpick inserted in center comes out clean. Cool completely in pan. Remove from pan onto serving platter.

Use candy to decorate, such as jelly beans for eyes and buttons, nonpareil for nose, red shoestring licorice for mouth and black shoestring licorice for bow tie.

Makes 1 bread loaf

*Favorite recipe from **The Sugar Association, Inc.***

ORANGE MARMALADE BREAD

3 cups all-purpose flour
4 teaspoons baking powder
1 teaspoon salt
½ cup chopped walnuts
2 eggs, lightly beaten
¾ cup SMUCKER'S® Simply Fruit Orange
    Marmalade
¾ cup milk
¼ cup honey
2 tablespoons vegetable oil

Preheat oven to 350°F. Grease 9×5×3-inch loaf pan. Into large bowl, sift together flour, baking powder and salt. Stir in nuts. In small bowl, combine eggs, marmalade, milk, honey and oil; blend well. Add to flour mixture; stir only until flour is well moistened (batter will be lumpy). Turn batter into prepared pan. Bake 65 to 70 minutes or until lightly browned and wooden toothpick inserted in center comes out clean. Cool in pan on wire rack 10 minutes. Remove from pan; cool completely on rack.

Makes 1 loaf

Orange Marmalade Bread

CRANBERRY PECAN MUFFINS

1¾ cups all-purpose flour
½ cup firmly packed light brown sugar
2½ teaspoons baking powder
½ teaspoon salt
¾ cup milk
¼ cup butter or margarine, melted
1 egg, beaten
1 cup chopped fresh cranberries
⅓ cup chopped pecans
1 teaspoon grated lemon peel

Preheat oven to 400°F. Grease or paper-line 36 (1¾-inch) mini-muffin cups.

Combine flour, brown sugar, baking powder and salt in large bowl. Combine milk, butter and egg in small bowl until blended; stir into flour mixture just until moistened. Fold in cranberries, pecans and lemon peel. Spoon into prepared muffin cups, filling almost full.

Bake 15 to 17 minutes or until wooden toothpick inserted in centers comes out clean. Remove from pans. Cool on wire racks.

Makes 36 mini muffins

NOËL BRAN MUFFINS

1¼ cups whole bran cereal
1 cup milk
1½ cups flour
½ cup firmly packed brown sugar
½ cup shredded carrot
2 teaspoons baking powder
¼ teaspoon salt
¼ teaspoon ground nutmeg
¼ cup butter or margarine, melted
2 eggs
1 cup chopped DEL MONTE® Dried Apricots or Seedless Raisins

Soften bran in milk. In large bowl, blend together flour, sugar, carrot, baking powder, salt and nutmeg. Combine bran mixture, butter and eggs; add to dry ingredients. Stir until flour is moistened. Fold in chopped apricots or raisins. Fill 12 paper-lined or greased 2½-inch muffin-pan cups. Bake at 375°F, 25 to 30 minutes or until golden. Serve warm.

Makes 12 muffins

Cranberry Pecan Muffins

HOLIDAY PUMPKIN–NUT MUFFINS

2½ cups all-purpose flour
1 cup packed light brown sugar
1 tablespoon baking powder
1 teaspoon ground cinnamon
½ teaspoon ground nutmeg
½ teaspoon ground ginger
¼ teaspoon salt
1 cup solid pack pumpkin (not pumpkin pie filling)
¾ cup milk
2 eggs
6 tablespoons butter or margarine, melted
⅔ cup roasted, salted pepitas (pumpkin seeds), divided
½ cup golden raisins

Preheat oven to 400°F. Grease or paper-line 18 (2¾-inch) muffin cups.

Combine flour, brown sugar, baking powder, cinnamon, nutmeg, ginger and salt in large bowl. Stir pumpkin, milk, eggs and melted butter in medium bowl until well blended. Stir pumpkin mixture into flour mixture. Mix just until all ingredients are moistened. Stir in ⅓ cup pepitas and raisins. Spoon into prepared muffin cups, filling ⅔ full. Sprinkle remaining pepitas over muffin batter.

Bake 15 to 18 minutes or until wooden toothpick inserted in centers comes out clean. Cool in pans 10 minutes. Remove from pans and cool completely on wire racks. Store in airtight container.   *Makes 18 muffins*

Holiday Pumpkin-Nut Muffins

SWEET POTATO PECAN MUFFINS

MAZOLA® No Stick cooking spray
1¾ **cups flour**
⅓ **cup sugar**
2 **teaspoons baking powder**
1 **teaspoon ground cinnamon**
½ **teaspoon salt**
⅛ **teaspoon ground nutmeg**
¾ **cup mashed cooked sweet potatoes**
¾ **cup KARO® Dark Corn Syrup**
⅓ **cup MAZOLA® Corn Oil**
2 **eggs**
1 **teaspoon vanilla**
1 **cup chopped pecans**

Preheat oven to 400°F. Spray 12 (2½-inch) muffin pan cups with cooking spray.

In medium bowl, combine flour, sugar, baking powder, cinnamon, salt and nutmeg. In large bowl, with mixer at medium speed, beat sweet potatoes, corn syrup, corn oil, eggs and vanilla until blended. Stir in flour mixture until well blended. Stir in pecans. Spoon into prepared muffin pan cups.

Bake 20 minutes or until lightly browned and firm to the touch. Cool in pan on wire rack 5 minutes; remove from pan.

Makes 12 muffins

Cranberry Pecan Muffins

CRANBERRY PECAN MUFFINS

1½ **cups fresh or frozen cranberries**
¼ **cup light corn syrup**
1 **package DUNCAN HINES® Cinnamon Muffin Mix**
1 **egg**
¾ **cup water or milk**
½ **cup chopped pecans**

1. Preheat oven to 400°F. Place 14 (2½-inch) paper liners in muffin cups. Place cranberries and corn syrup in heavy saucepan. Cook on medium heat, stirring occasionally, until cranberries pop and mixture is slightly thickened. Drain cranberries in strainer; set aside.

2. Empty muffin mix into medium bowl. Break up any lumps. Add egg and water. Stir until moistened, about 50 strokes. Stir in cranberries and pecans. Knead swirl packet from Mix for 10 seconds before opening. Cut off 1 end of swirl packet. Squeeze contents over top of batter. Swirl into batter with knife or spatula. *Do not completely mix in.* Spoon batter into muffin cups (see Tip). Sprinkle with contents of topping packet from Mix. Bake at 400°F for 18 to 22 minutes or until toothpick inserted in centers comes out clean. Cool in pans 5 to 10 minutes. Serve warm or cool completely.

Makes 14 muffins

TIP: Fill an equal number of muffin cups in each muffin pan with batter. For more even baking, fill empty muffin cups with ½ inch of water.

PUMPKIN APPLE STREUSEL MUFFINS

   2½ **cups all-purpose flour**
   2 **cups granulated sugar**
   1 **tablespoon pumpkin pie spice**
   1 **teaspoon baking soda**
   ½ **teaspoon salt**
   2 **eggs, lightly beaten**
   1 **cup LIBBY'S® Solid Pack Pumpkin**
   ½ **cup vegetable oil**
   2 **cups peeled, finely chopped apples**
      Streusel Topping (recipe follows)

In large bowl, combine flour, sugar, pumpkin pie spice, baking soda and salt. In medium bowl, combine eggs, pumpkin and oil. Add liquid ingredients to dry ingredients; stir just until moistened. Stir in apples. Spoon batter into greased or paper-lined muffin cups, filling ¾ full. Sprinkle Streusel Topping over batter. Bake in preheated 350°F. oven for 35 to 40 minutes or until wooden pick inserted in centers comes out clean.

Makes 18 muffins

STREUSEL TOPPING: In small bowl, combine 2 tablespoons all-purpose flour, ¼ cup sugar and ½ teaspoon ground cinnamon. Cut in 4 teaspoons butter until mixture is crumbly.

VARIATION: For 6 giant muffins, follow directions above, increasing baking time to 40 to 45 minutes.

ALMOND CITRUS MUFFINS

   ½ **cup whole natural almonds**
   1¼ **cups all-purpose flour**
   2 **teaspoons baking powder**
   ¼ **teaspoon salt**
   1 **cup shreds of wheat bran cereal**
   ¼ **cup packed brown sugar**
   ¾ **cup milk**
   ¼ **cup orange juice**
   1 **teaspoon grated orange peel**
   1 **egg**
   ¼ **cup vegetable or almond oil**

Spread almonds in single layer on baking sheet. Bake at 350°F, 12 to 15 minutes, stirring occasionally, until lightly toasted. Cool and chop. *Increase oven temperature to 400°F.* In large bowl, combine flour, baking powder and salt. In medium bowl, combine cereal, sugar, milk, orange juice and peel. Let stand 2 minutes or until cereal is softened. Add egg and oil; beat well. Stir in almonds. Add liquid mixture to flour mixture; stir just until moistened. Batter will be lumpy; do not overmix. Spoon batter evenly into 12 greased 2½-inch muffin cups. Bake in preheated 400°F oven 20 minutes or until lightly browned. Remove to wire rack to cool.

Makes 1 dozen muffins

Favorite recipe from **Almond Board of California**

CRANBERRY ORANGE NUT MUFFINS

MAZOLA® No Stick cooking spray
1½ cups flour
½ cup sugar
2 teaspoons baking powder
½ teaspoon salt
2 eggs
½ cup KARO® Light Corn Syrup
½ cup orange juice
¼ cup MAZOLA® Corn Oil
1 teaspoon grated orange peel
1 cup fresh or frozen cranberries, chopped
½ cup chopped walnuts

Preheat oven to 400°F. Spray 12 (2½-inch) muffin pan cups with cooking spray.

In medium bowl, combine flour, sugar, baking powder and salt. In large bowl, combine eggs, corn syrup, orange juice, corn oil and orange peel. Stir in flour mixture until well blended. Stir in cranberries and walnuts. Spoon into prepared muffin pan cups.

Bake 18 to 20 minutes or until lightly browned and firm to the touch. Cool in pan on wire rack 5 minutes; remove from pan.

Makes 12 muffins

BANANA SCOTCH MUFFINS

1 ripe, large DOLE® Banana, peeled and cut into chunks
1 egg, beaten
½ cup sugar
¼ cup milk
¼ cup vegetable oil
1 teaspoon vanilla
1 cup all-purpose flour
1 cup quick-cooking rolled oats
1 teaspoon baking powder
½ teaspoon baking soda
½ teaspoon salt
½ cup butterscotch chips

• Preheat oven to 400°F. Purée banana in blender (⅔ cup). In medium bowl, combine puréed banana, egg, sugar, milk, oil and vanilla.

• In large bowl, combine flour, oats, baking powder, baking soda and salt. Stir banana mixture and butterscotch chips into dry ingredients just until blended.

• Spoon into well-greased 2½-inch muffin cups. Bake 12 to 15 minutes. Remove from pan.

Makes 12 muffins

CARROT–RAISIN BRAN MUFFINS

MAZOLA® No Stick cooking spray
2 cups bran flakes cereal with raisins
⅔ cup buttermilk
½ cup KARO® Dark Corn Syrup
1 cup flour
2 teaspoons baking soda
1 teaspoon ground cinnamon
¼ teaspoon salt
1 egg, slightly beaten
¼ cup sugar
¼ cup MAZOLA® Corn Oil
1 cup shredded carrots

Preheat oven to 400°F. Spray 12 (2½-inch) muffin pan cups with cooking spray.

In large bowl, mix cereal, buttermilk and corn syrup; let stand 5 minutes. In medium bowl, combine flour, baking soda, cinnamon and salt; set aside. Add egg, sugar and corn oil to cereal mixture; mix until blended. Stir in flour mixture until well blended. Stir in carrots. Spoon into prepared muffin pan cups.

Bake 20 minutes or until lightly browned and firm to the touch. Cool in pan on wire rack 5 minutes; remove from pan.

Makes 12 muffins

Clockwise from top: Cranberry Orange Nut Muffins, Carrot-Raisin Bran Muffins, Sweet Potato Pecan Muffins (page 292)

PINEAPPLE CITRUS MUFFINS

⅓ cup honey
¼ cup butter or margarine, softened
1 egg
1 can (8 ounces) DOLE® Crushed Pineapple
1 tablespoon grated orange peel
1 cup all-purpose flour
1 cup whole wheat flour
1½ teaspoons baking powder
¼ teaspoon salt
¼ teaspoon ground nutmeg
1 cup DOLE® Chopped Dates
½ cup chopped walnuts (optional)

• Preheat oven to 375°F. In large mixer bowl, beat together honey and butter 1 minute. Beat in egg, then undrained pineapple and orange peel. In medium bowl, combine remaining ingredients; stir into pineapple mixture until just blended.

Pineapple Citrus Muffins

• Spoon batter into 12 greased muffin cups. Bake in preheated oven 25 minutes or until wooden pick inserted in centers comes out clean. Cool slightly in pan before turning out onto wire rack. Serve warm.

Makes 12 muffins

APPLE–CRANBERRY MUFFINS

1¾ cups plus 2 tablespoons all-purpose flour, divided
½ cup sugar, divided
1½ teaspoons baking powder
½ teaspoon baking soda
½ teaspoon salt
1 egg
¾ cup milk
¾ cup sweetened applesauce
¼ cup butter or margarine, melted
1 cup fresh cranberries, coarsely chopped
½ teaspoon ground cinnamon

In medium bowl, combine 1¾ cups flour, ¼ cup sugar, baking powder, baking soda and salt. In small bowl, combine egg, milk, applesauce and butter; mix well. Add egg mixture to flour mixture; stir just until moistened. Batter will be lumpy; *do not overmix*. In small bowl, toss cranberries with remaining 2 tablespoons flour; fold into batter. Spoon batter evenly into 12 greased 2¾-inch muffin cups. In measuring cup, combine remaining ¼ cup sugar and cinnamon. Sprinkle over tops of muffins. Bake in preheated 400°F oven 20 to 25 minutes or until golden brown. Remove to wire rack to cool. *Makes 1 dozen muffins*

*Favorite recipe from **New York Apple Association, Inc.***

Streusel Raspberry Muffins

STREUSEL RASPBERRY MUFFINS

Pecan Streusel Topping (recipe follows)
1½ cups all-purpose flour
½ cup sugar
2 teaspoons baking powder
½ cup milk
½ cup butter or margarine, melted and
    cooled
1 egg, beaten
1 cup fresh or individually frozen whole
    unsugared raspberries

Preheat oven to 375°F. Grease or paper-line 12 (2½-inch) muffin cups. Prepare Pecan Streusel Topping; set aside.

In large bowl, combine flour, sugar and baking powder. In small bowl, combine milk, butter and egg until blended. Stir into flour mixture just until moistened. Spoon half of batter into muffin cups. Divide raspberries among cups, then top with remaining batter. Sprinkle Pecan Streusel Topping over tops. Bake 25 to 30 minutes or until golden and wooden toothpick inserted in centers comes out clean. Remove from pan. *Makes 12 muffins*

PECAN STREUSEL TOPPING: In small bowl, combine ¼ cup *each* chopped pecans, packed brown sugar and all-purpose flour. Stir in 2 tablespoons melted butter or margarine until mixture resembles moist crumbs.

297

APPLE DATE NUT MUFFINS

1½ cups all-purpose flour
⅔ cup packed brown sugar
½ cup uncooked rolled oats
1 tablespoon baking powder
1 teaspoon ground cinnamon
½ teaspoon salt
⅛ teaspoon ground nutmeg
⅛ teaspoon ground ginger
   Dash ground cloves
1 cup coarsely chopped, peeled apples
½ cup chopped walnuts
½ cup chopped pitted dates
½ cup butter or margarine, melted and
   cooled
¼ cup milk
2 eggs

Preheat oven to 400°F. Grease or paper-line
12 (2½-inch) muffin cups.

Combine flour, brown sugar, oats, baking
powder, cinnamon, salt, nutmeg, ginger and
cloves in large bowl. Mix in apples, nuts and
dates. Combine butter, milk and eggs in small
bowl until blended. Pour into flour mixture,
stirring just until moistened. Spoon evenly into
prepared muffin cups.

Bake 20 to 25 minutes or until wooden
toothpick inserted in centers comes out clean.
Remove from pan.   *Makes 12 muffins*

CRANBERRY ALL-BRAN® MUFFINS

1¼ cups all-purpose flour
½ cup sugar
1 tablespoon baking powder
½ teaspoon pumpkin pie spice
¼ teaspoon salt
1½ cups KELLOGG'S® ALL-BRAN® cereal
1¼ cups skim milk
2 egg whites
¼ cup vegetable oil
1 cup coarsely chopped cranberries
½ cup raisins
1 teaspoon grated orange peel

Stir together flour, sugar, baking powder,
pumpkin pie spice and salt; set aside. Measure
Kellogg's All-Bran cereal and milk into large
mixing bowl; stir to combine. Let stand 2
minutes or until cereal is softened. Add egg
whites and oil; beat well. Stir in cranberries,
raisins and orange peel. Add dry ingredients
to cereal mixture, stirring only until combined.
Divide batter evenly among 12 greased
2½-inch muffin-pan cups. Bake in 400°F oven
about 22 minutes or until lightly browned;
serve hot.   *Makes 12 muffins*

PINEAPPLE CARROT RAISIN MUFFINS

1 cup whole wheat flour
¾ cup all-purpose flour
¼ cup firmly packed brown sugar
1 tablespoon baking powder
¼ teaspoon salt (optional)
1½ cups KELLOGG'S® ALL-BRAN® cereal
1 can (8 ounces) crushed unsweetened
   pineapple, undrained
½ cup unsweetened orange juice
2 egg whites
¼ cup vegetable oil
¾ cup shredded carrots
⅓ cup seedless raisins
   Nonstick vegetable cooking spray

1. Stir together flours, sugar, baking powder and salt. Set aside.

2. In large mixing bowl, combine Kellogg's All-Bran cereal, pineapple including juice and orange juice. Let stand 2 minutes or until cereal is softened. Add egg whites and oil. Beat well. Stir in carrots and raisins.

3. Add flour mixture, stirring only until combined. Portion batter evenly into twelve 2½-inch muffin cups coated with cooking spray.

4. Bake at 400°F about 25 minutes or until lightly browned. Serve warm.

Makes 12 muffins

Bacon Cheese Muffins

MOIST ORANGE MINCE MUFFINS

   2 cups unsifted flour
   ½ cup sugar
   1 tablespoon baking powder
   1 teaspoon salt
   ½ teaspoon baking soda
   1 egg, slightly beaten
   1 (8-ounce) container BORDEN® LITE-
      LINE® or VIVA® Orange Yogurt
   ⅓ cup BORDEN® or MEADOW GOLD®
      Milk
   ⅓ cup vegetable oil
   1 (9-ounce) package NONE SUCH®
      Condensed Mincemeat, finely
      crumbled
   ⅓ cup BAMA® Orange Marmalade, melted
      (optional)

Preheat oven to 400°F. In large bowl, combine dry ingredients. In medium bowl, combine egg, yogurt, milk, oil and mincemeat; mix well. Stir into flour mixture only until moistened. Fill greased or paper-lined muffin cups ¾ full. Bake 20 to 25 minutes or until golden. Immediately remove from pans. Brush warm muffins with marmalade, if desired. Serve warm.

Makes about 1½ dozen muffins

BACON CHEESE MUFFINS

   ½ pound bacon (10 to 12 slices)
      Vegetable oil
   1 egg, beaten
   ¾ cup milk
   1¾ cups all-purpose flour
   ¼ cup sugar
   1 tablespoon baking powder
   1 cup (4 ounces) shredded Wisconsin
      Cheddar cheese
   ½ cup crunchy nutlike cereal nuggets

Preheat oven to 400°F. In large skillet, cook bacon over medium-high heat until crisp. Drain, reserving drippings. If necessary, add oil to drippings to measure ⅓ cup. In small bowl, combine dripping mixture, egg and milk; set aside. Crumble bacon; set aside.

In large bowl, combine flour, sugar and baking powder. Make well in center. Add egg mixture all at once to flour mixture, stirring just until moistened. Batter should be lumpy. Fold in bacon, cheese and cereal. Spoon into greased or paper-lined 2½-inch muffin cups, filling about ¾ full. Bake 15 to 20 minutes or until golden. Remove from pan. Cool on wire rack.

Makes 12 muffins

*Favorite recipe from **Wisconsin Milk Marketing Board***

SOUR CREAM COFFEE CAKE WITH CHOCOLATE AND WALNUTS

¾ cup butter or margarine, softened
1½ cups packed light brown sugar
3 eggs
2 teaspoons vanilla
3 cups all-purpose flour
2 teaspoons baking powder
2 teaspoons ground cinnamon
1½ teaspoons baking soda
½ teaspoon ground nutmeg
¼ teaspoon salt
1½ cups sour cream
½ cup semisweet chocolate chips
½ cup chopped walnuts
    Sifted powdered sugar

Preheat oven to 350°F. Grease and flour 12-cup fluted tube pan or 10-inch tube pan. Beat butter in large bowl with electric mixer on medium speed until creamy. Add brown sugar; beat until light and fluffy. Beat in eggs and vanilla until well blended. Combine flour, baking powder, cinnamon, baking soda, nutmeg and salt in large bowl; add to butter mixture on low speed alternately with sour cream, beginning and ending with flour mixture until well blended. Stir in chocolate and walnuts. Spoon into prepared pan.

Bake 45 to 50 minutes or until wooden toothpick inserted in center comes out clean. Cool in pan on wire rack 15 minutes. Remove from pan to wire rack; cool completely. Store tightly covered at room temperature. Sprinkle with powdered sugar before serving.

Makes 1 (10-inch) coffee cake

CRAN-LEMON COFFEE CAKE

1 package (18.25 ounces) yellow cake
    mix with pudding in the mix
1 cup water
⅓ cup butter or margarine, melted and
    cooled
¼ cup fresh lemon juice
3 eggs
1 tablespoon grated lemon peel
1½ cups coarsely chopped cranberries

Preheat oven to 350°F. Grease and flour 12-inch bundt pan. Beat cake mix, water, butter, lemon juice, eggs and lemon peel in large bowl with electric mixer on low speed 2 minutes. Fold in cranberries. Spread batter evenly in prepared pan.

Bake about 55 minutes or until wooden pick inserted in center comes out clean. Cool on wire rack 10 minutes. Remove from pan; cool on wire rack. Coffee cake may be served warm or at room temperature.

Makes 12 servings

Cran-Lemon Coffee Cake

Cream Cheese Swirl Coffee Cake

Preheat oven to 350°F. In small bowl, beat cheese, confectioners' sugar and ReaLemon® brand until smooth; set aside. Stir together flour, baking powder, baking soda and salt; set aside. In large mixer bowl, beat granulated sugar and margarine until fluffy. Add eggs and vanilla; mix well. Add dry ingredients alternately with sour cream; mix well. Pour half of batter into greased and floured 10-inch tube pan. Spoon cream cheese mixture on top of batter to within ½ inch of pan edge. Spoon remaining batter over filling, spreading to pan edge. Sprinkle with Cinnamon-Nut Topping. Bake 40 to 45 minutes or until wooden pick inserted near center comes out clean. Cool 10 minutes; remove from pan. Serve warm.

Makes one 10-inch cake

CINNAMON–NUT TOPPING: Combine ¼ cup finely chopped nuts, 2 tablespoons granulated sugar and ½ teaspoon ground cinnamon.

CREAM CHEESE SWIRL COFFEE CAKE

- 2 (3-ounce) packages cream cheese, softened
- 2 tablespoons confectioners' sugar
- 2 tablespoons REALEMON® Lemon Juice from Concentrate
- 2 cups unsifted flour
- 1 teaspoon baking powder
- 1 teaspoon baking soda
- ¼ teaspoon salt
- 1 cup granulated sugar
- ½ cup margarine or butter, softened
- 3 eggs
- 1 teaspoon vanilla extract
- 1 (8-ounce) container BORDEN® or MEADOW GOLD® Sour Cream
  Cinnamon-Nut Topping (recipe follows)

CRANBERRY STREUSEL COFFEE CAKE

CAKE BATTER
- 1½ cups flour
- 1½ teaspoons baking powder
- ½ teaspoon salt
- 6 tablespoons (¾ stick) unsalted butter, softened
- ¾ cup granulated sugar
- 2 teaspoons grated orange peel
- 2 eggs
- ½ cup milk

STREUSEL
- ½ cup packed light brown sugar
- ½ cup chopped walnuts
- ¼ cup flour
- 2 tablespoons butter, softened
- ½ teaspoon ground cinnamon

CRANBERRY FILLING
- 1½ cups OCEAN SPRAY® fresh or frozen cranberries
- ¼ cup granulated sugar
- 2 tablespoons orange juice

1. Preheat oven to 350°F. Grease and flour 8-inch square cake pan. Stir together 1½ cups flour, baking powder and salt on piece of waxed paper until well mixed.

2. Beat 6 tablespoons butter, ¾ cup granulated sugar and orange peel in large bowl until light and fluffy. Add eggs, one at a time, beating well after each addition. Stir in flour mixture alternately with milk, beginning and ending with flour. Set batter aside.

3. For streusel, combine all streusel ingredients in small mixing bowl. Mix together with fork until crumbly. Set mixture aside.

4. For cranberry filling, place all filling ingredients in small saucepan. Cook over medium heat, stirring constantly, until berries start to pop. Remove from heat; cool to room temperature.

5. Spread half the coffee cake batter over bottom of prepared pan. Sprinkle with half the streusel mixture; spoon on half the cranberry filling. Cover with remaining batter; top with remaining filling and streusel.

6. Bake 50 to 60 minutes or until toothpick inserted in center comes out clean. Cool on wire rack. Serve warm or at room temperature.

Makes about 9 servings

PREPARATION TIME: 20 minutes

CINNAMON APPLE COFFEE CAKE

1½ cups boiling water
   5 LIPTON® Cinnamon Apple Herbal Tea
      Bags
½ cup confectioners' sugar
 1 cup all-purpose flour
½ cup granulated sugar
 6 tablespoons IMPERIAL® Margarine,
      melted
 1 egg
 1 teaspoon baking powder
¼ teaspoon salt
¼ cup golden raisins
 1 cup chopped apples, divided
½ cup chopped walnuts
½ teaspoon grated lemon peel

Preheat oven to 375°F. In teapot, pour boiling water over cinnamon apple herbal tea bags. Cover and brew 5 minutes. Remove tea bags. In 1-quart saucepan, combine ¾ cup tea and confectioners' sugar. Chill remaining tea at least 10 minutes. Boil tea-sugar mixture over medium-high heat 7 minutes or until thick and syrupy; set aside.

In large bowl, combine chilled tea, flour, granulated sugar, margarine, egg, baking powder and salt. With electric mixer or rotary beater, beat to moisten, then beat at medium speed 2 minutes. Fold in raisins and ½ cup apples. Spread into greased 8-inch round cake pan. Bake 25 minutes or until toothpick inserted in center comes out clean. On wire rack, cool 10 minutes.

In small bowl, combine tea-sugar mixture with remaining ½ cup apples, walnuts and lemon peel. Spoon over warm cake. Garnish, if desired, with apple slices and serve.

Makes about 8 servings

PEACHY CINNAMON COFFEECAKE

1 can (8¼ ounces) juice-pack sliced yellow cling peaches
1 package DUNCAN HINES® Cinnamon Muffin Mix
1 egg

1. Preheat oven to 400°F. Grease 8-inch square or 9-inch round baking pan.

2. Drain peaches, reserving juice. Add water to reserved juice to equal ¾ cup liquid. Chop peaches.

3. Combine muffin mix, egg and ¾ cup peach liquid in medium bowl; fold in peaches. Pour batter into pan. Knead swirl packet 10 seconds before opening. Squeeze contents on top of batter and swirl with knife. Sprinkle topping over batter. Bake at 400°F for 28 to 33 minutes for 8-inch pan (or 20 to 25 minutes for 9-inch pan) or until golden. Serve warm.

Makes 9 servings

Peachy Cinnamon Coffeecake

CHOCOLATE STREUSEL COFFEE CAKE

Chocolate Streusel (recipe follows)
½ cup butter or margarine, softened
1 cup sugar
3 eggs
1 cup dairy sour cream
1 teaspoon vanilla extract
2 cups all-purpose flour
1 teaspoon baking powder
1 teaspoon baking soda
¼ teaspoon salt

Prepare Chocolate Streusel; set aside. Cream butter and sugar in large mixer bowl until light and fluffy. Add eggs; blend well on low speed. Stir in sour cream and vanilla. Combine flour, baking powder, baking soda and salt; add to batter. Blend well.

Sprinkle 1 cup Chocolate Streusel into greased and floured 12-cup Bundt pan. Spread one third of the batter (about 1⅓ cups) in pan; sprinkle with half the remaining streusel (about 1 cup). Repeat layers, ending with batter on top. Bake at 350°F for 50 to 55 minutes or until cake tester comes out clean. Cool 10 minutes; invert onto serving plate. Cool completely.

Makes 12 to 16 servings

CHOCOLATE STREUSEL

¾ cup packed light brown sugar
¼ cup all-purpose flour
¼ cup butter or margarine, softened
¾ cup chopped nuts
¾ cup HERSHEY'S® MINI CHIPS Semi-Sweet Chocolate

Combine brown sugar, flour and butter in medium bowl until crumbly. Stir in nuts and small chocolate chips.

CRANBERRY APPLE STREUSEL COFFEE CAKE

CAKE
2 cups any AUNT JEMIMA® Pancake &
Waffle Mix (see Note)
½ cup granulated sugar
1 (8-ounce) carton sour cream
¾ cup milk
1 egg, beaten
¾ cup chopped cranberries
¾ cup coarsely chopped, peeled apple

STREUSEL
½ cup chopped nuts
¼ cup firmly packed brown sugar
½ teaspoon ground cinnamon
2 tablespoons margarine, melted

GLAZE
¾ cup powdered sugar
1 tablespoon milk
½ teaspoon vanilla

Heat oven to 350°F. Grease 13×9-inch baking
pan. Combine pancake mix and granulated
sugar. Add sour cream, milk and egg; mix just
until dry ingredients are moistened. Spread into
pan; top with cranberries and apple. Combine
Streusel ingredients; mix until crumbly. Sprinkle
over fruit. Bake 30 to 35 minutes or until
wooden pick inserted in center comes out
clean. Combine Glaze ingredients; drizzle over
warm cake. Serve warm. To reheat cooled
cake, microwave each serving at HIGH (100%
power) about 20 seconds.   *Makes 12 servings*

NOTE: AUNT JEMIMA® Buttermilk Complete,
Complete, Original, Whole Wheat or Lite
Buttermilk Complete mixes may be used.

NUTTY COCONUT COFFEECAKE

TOPPING
2 tablespoons butter, melted
⅔ cup flaked coconut
⅓ cup packed dark brown sugar
⅓ cup coarsely chopped nuts (macadamia
nuts, walnuts, almonds or pecans)
2 tablespoons *undiluted* CARNATION®
Evaporated Milk

BATTER
2 cups all-purpose flour
½ cup packed brown sugar
¼ cup granulated sugar
2 teaspoons baking powder
½ teaspoon salt
¼ cup butter
1 cup *undiluted* CARNATION®
Evaporated Milk
1 egg
1 teaspoon vanilla extract

FOR TOPPING:
POUR butter into greased 9-inch round cake
pan. Combine coconut, ⅓ cup brown sugar,
nuts and 2 tablespoons evaporated milk in
small bowl. Sprinkle over butter.

FOR BATTER:
COMBINE flour, ½ cup brown sugar, granulated
sugar, baking powder and salt in bowl. Cut in
butter. Beat 1 cup evaporated milk, egg and
vanilla together in small bowl; stir into flour
mixture just until blended. Pour over nut
mixture.

BAKE in preheated 350°F. oven for 30 to 35
minutes or until wooden pick inserted in center
comes out clean. Cool for 10 minutes on wire
rack. Invert onto serving plate.
Makes 1 (9-inch) round cake

BANANA SPICE COFFEE CAKE

2 extra-ripe, medium DOLE® Bananas, peeled and cut into chunks
½ cup packed brown sugar
1 teaspoon ground cinnamon
¼ teaspoon ground nutmeg
½ cup margarine, divided
¾ cup chopped walnuts
1 cup all-purpose flour
1 cup whole wheat flour
1 teaspoon baking powder
1 teaspoon baking soda
½ teaspoon salt
½ cup granulated sugar
3 eggs
1 teaspoon vanilla
1 cup DOLE® Raisins

• In food processor or blender, purée bananas (1 cup purée). In small bowl, combine brown sugar, cinnamon and nutmeg. Cut in ¼ cup margarine until mixture resembles coarse crumbs. Stir in walnuts; set aside. In small bowl, combine flours, baking powder, baking soda and salt. In large bowl, beat remaining ¼ cup margarine and granulated sugar until light and fluffy. Beat in eggs and vanilla. Add flour mixture to egg mixture alternately with bananas, ending with flour mixture and beating well after each addition. Stir in raisins.

• Spread half the batter in greased and floured 10-inch tube pan. Sprinkle with half the brown sugar mixture. Repeat layers. Bake in preheated 350°F oven 45 to 50 minutes or until wooden pick inserted in center of cake comes out clean. Let cool in pan on wire rack 10 minutes. Loosen edge; remove from pan. Cool completely on wire rack.

Makes 1 (10-inch) coffee cake

CINNAMON-DATE SCONES

¼ cup sugar, divided
¼ teaspoon ground cinnamon
2 cups all-purpose flour
2½ teaspoons baking powder
½ teaspoon salt
5 tablespoons cold butter or margarine
½ cup chopped pitted dates
2 eggs
⅓ cup half-and-half or milk

Preheat oven to 425°F. Combine 2 tablespoons sugar and cinnamon in small bowl; set aside. Combine flour, baking powder, salt and remaining 2 tablespoons sugar in medium bowl. Cut in butter with pastry blender or 2 knives until mixture resembles coarse crumbs. Stir in dates.

Beat eggs in another small bowl with fork. Add half-and-half; beat until well combined. Measure 1 tablespoon mixture into small cup; set aside. Stir remaining egg mixture into flour mixture. Stir until mixture forms soft dough that clings together and forms a ball.

Turn out dough onto well-floured surface. Knead dough gently 10 to 12 times. Roll out dough into 9×6-inch rectangle. Cut rectangle into 6 (3-inch) squares. Cut each square diagonally in half. Place triangles 2 inches apart on *ungreased* baking sheets. Brush with reserved egg mixture; sprinkle with reserved sugar mixture. Bake 10 to 12 minutes or until golden brown. Immediately remove from baking sheets; cool on wire racks 10 minutes. Serve warm.

Makes 12 scones

Cinnamon-Date Scones

PUMPKIN–GINGER SCONES

½ cup sugar, divided
2 cups all-purpose flour
2 teaspoons baking powder
1 teaspoon ground cinnamon
½ teaspoon baking soda
½ teaspoon salt
5 tablespoons butter or margarine, divided
1 egg
½ cup solid pack pumpkin
¼ cup sour cream
½ teaspoon grated fresh ginger *or* 2 tablespoons finely chopped crystallized ginger

Preheat oven to 425°F. Reserve 1 tablespoon sugar. Combine remaining sugar, flour, baking powder, cinnamon, baking soda and salt in large bowl. Cut in 4 tablespoons butter with pastry blender until mixture resembles coarse crumbs. Beat egg in small bowl. Add pumpkin, sour cream and ginger; beat until well combined. Add pumpkin mixture to flour mixture; stir until mixture forms soft dough that leaves side of bowl.

Turn dough out onto well-floured surface. Knead 10 times. Roll dough using floured rolling pin into 9×6-inch rectangle. Cut dough into 6 (3-inch) squares. Cut each square diagonally in half, making 12 triangles. Place triangles, 2 inches apart, on *ungreased* baking sheet. Melt remaining 1 tablespoon butter. Brush tops of triangles with melted butter and sprinkle with reserved sugar. Bake 10 to 12 minutes or until golden brown. Cool 10 minutes on wire racks. Serve warm.

Makes 12 scones

SWEET POTATO BISCUITS

2½ cups all-purpose flour
¼ cup packed brown sugar
1 tablespoon baking powder
¾ teaspoon salt
¾ teaspoon ground cinnamon
¼ teaspoon ground ginger
¼ teaspoon ground allspice
½ cup shortening
½ cup chopped pecans
¾ cup mashed cooked sweet potatoes
½ cup milk

Preheat oven to 450°F. Combine flour, sugar, baking powder, salt, cinnamon, ginger and allspice in medium bowl. Cut in shortening with pastry blender or 2 knives until mixture resembles coarse crumbs. Stir in pecans.

Combine sweet potatoes and milk in medium bowl with wire whisk until smooth. Make well in center of dry ingredients. Add sweet potato mixture; stir until mixture forms a ball.

Turn out dough onto well-floured surface. Knead dough gently 10 to 12 times. Roll or pat dough to ½-inch thickness. Cut out dough with floured 2½-inch biscuit cutter. Place biscuits, 2 inches apart, on *ungreased* large baking sheet. Bake 12 to 14 minutes or until tops and bottoms are golden brown. Serve warm.

Makes about 12 biscuits

Pumpkin-Ginger Scones

Mini Morsel Tea Biscuits

MINI MORSEL TEA BISCUITS

4 cups all-purpose flour
⅓ cup sugar
2 tablespoons baking powder
½ teaspoon salt
½ cup cold butter, cut into small pieces
1 cup (6 ounces) NESTLÉ® Toll House®
   Semi-Sweet Chocolate Mini Morsels
4 eggs, divided
1 cup *undiluted* CARNATION®
   Evaporated Milk
1½ teaspoons vanilla extract
2 tablespoons milk

COMBINE flour, sugar, baking powder and salt in large bowl. With pastry blender or two knives, cut in butter until mixture resembles coarse crumbs. Stir in morsels.

BEAT 3 eggs, evaporated milk and vanilla in medium bowl. Add to flour mixture all at once; stir with fork to form a soft dough. Turn dough onto well-floured surface. Knead 6 to 8 times. Pat dough to ¾-inch thickness. Cut with floured 2½-inch biscuit cutter. Transfer to lightly greased baking sheets. Beat remaining egg and milk in small bowl; brush over biscuits.

BAKE in preheated 400°F. oven for 14 to 16 minutes or until golden brown. Remove to wire racks; serve warm.

Makes about 1½ dozen biscuits

FRENCH BREAKFAST PUFFS

1½ cups unsifted all-purpose flour
½ cup confectioners sugar
1 teaspoon baking powder
1 teaspoon salt
¾ teaspoon ground nutmeg
½ cup milk
½ cup water
¼ cup CRISCO® Oil
1½ teaspoons grated lemon peel
3 eggs
    CRISCO® Oil for frying
    Confectioners sugar

Mix flour, ½ cup confectioners sugar, baking powder, salt and nutmeg in small mixing bowl. Set aside. Combine milk, water, Crisco® oil and lemon peel in medium saucepan. Heat to rolling boil over medium-high heat. Add flour mixture all at once. Beat with wooden spoon until mixture pulls away from sides of pan into a ball. Remove from heat; cool slightly. Add eggs, one at a time, beating after each addition.

Heat 2 to 3 inches Crisco® oil in deep-fryer or large saucepan to 350°F.

Drop dough by tablespoonfuls into hot Crisco® oil. Fry 3 or 4 puffs at a time, 4 to 6 minutes, or until golden brown, turning over several times. Drain on paper towels. Sprinkle top of each puff with confectioners sugar.

Makes 32 puffs

FRUITED SCONES

2 cups unsifted flour
¼ cup sugar
1 tablespoon baking powder
½ teaspoon salt
½ cup cold margarine or butter
1 egg
⅓ cup BORDEN® or MEADOW GOLD® Milk
1 (9-ounce) package NONE SUCH® Condensed Mincemeat, crumbled
1 egg, beaten (optional)

Preheat oven to 400°F. In large bowl, combine flour, sugar, baking powder and salt; cut in margarine until crumbly. Stir in *1 egg,* milk and mincemeat; mix well. On floured surface, knead dough lightly 10 times. Roll out to ½-inch thickness; cut into 2-inch circles. Place 1 inch apart on ungreased baking sheets. For a more golden color, brush with beaten egg, if desired. Bake 10 to 12 minutes or until golden. Serve warm. *Makes about 1½ dozen scones*

French Breakfast Puffs

311

SESAME–ONION TWISTS

2 tablespoons butter or margarine
1½ cups finely chopped onions
¼ teaspoon paprika
1 loaf (16 ounces) frozen bread dough, thawed*
1 egg, beaten
1 tablespoon sesame seeds

Grease large baking sheet; set aside. Melt butter in medium skillet over medium heat until foamy. Add onions and paprika; cook until onions are tender, stirring occasionally. Remove from heat. Spray work surface, such as countertop or cutting board, with nonstick cooking spray. Roll thawed bread dough into 14×12-inch rectangle. If dough gets too elastic or tight, stop rolling and let dough rest. It may be necessary to let dough rest several times when rolling dough into a rectangle.

Spread onion mixture on one side of dough, making 14×6-inch rectangle. Fold dough over onion mixture to make 14×6-inch rectangle. Pinch 14-inch side of dough to seal. Cut dough into 14 strips, each 6×1 inches. Gently twist each strip 2 times and place on prepared sheet. Press both ends of strip down on cookie sheet. Repeat with remaining strips.

Cover with clean kitchen towel. Let twists rise in warm place about 40 minutes or until doubled in bulk. Brush with egg; sprinkle with sesame seeds. Preheat oven to 375°F. Bake 15 to 18 minutes or until golden brown. Serve immediately.   *Makes 14 bread twists*

*To thaw frozen bread dough, place frozen loaf in greased 9×5-inch loaf dish, turning loaf over so that top is greased. Cover with plastic wrap. Let stand at room temperature about 4 to 5 hours or until thawed. Or, place frozen bread loaf in plastic bag and refrigerate overnight until thawed.

LEMON PECAN STICKY ROLLS

½ cup granulated sugar
½ cup firmly packed light brown sugar
¼ cup margarine or butter
¼ cup REALEMON® Lemon Juice from Concentrate
½ teaspoon ground cinnamon
½ cup chopped pecans
2 (8-ounce) cans refrigerated crescent rolls

Preheat oven to 375°F. In small saucepan, combine sugars, margarine, ReaLemon® brand and cinnamon. Bring to a boil; boil 1 minute. Reserving ¼ *cup,* pour remaining lemon mixture into 9-inch round layer cake pan. Sprinkle with nuts. Separate rolls into 8 rectangles; spread with reserved lemon mixture. Roll up jelly-roll fashion, beginning with short side; seal edges. Cut in half. Place rolls, cut side down, in prepared pan. Bake 30 to 35 minutes or until dark golden brown. Loosen sides. Immediately turn onto serving plate; do not remove pan. Let stand 5 minutes; remove pan. Serve warm.   *Makes 16 rolls*

Sesame-Onion Twists

MAPLE FRENCH TOAST

¼ cup CARY'S®, MAPLE ORCHARDS® or
   MACDONALD'S™ Pure Maple Syrup
¼ cup BORDEN® or MEADOW GOLD®
   Milk
2 eggs, beaten
12 (¾-inch) slices French or Italian bread
   Butter
   Maple Butter (recipe follows)

In medium bowl, combine syrup, milk and eggs.
Dip bread into egg mixture. In large greased
skillet, cook bread in butter until golden brown
on both sides. Serve warm with Maple Butter
and additional syrup.   *Makes 4 to 6 servings*

MAPLE BUTTER: In small mixer bowl, beat
½ cup softened unsalted butter and 2
tablespoons CARY'S®, MAPLE ORCHARDS®
or MACDONALD'S™ Pure Maple Syrup until
light and fluffy. Makes about ⅔ cup.

ONION–HERB BAKED BREAD

1 envelope LIPTON® Recipe Secrets®
   Golden Onion Soup Mix
1 medium clove garlic, finely chopped
1 teaspoon dried basil leaves
1 teaspoon dried oregano leaves
⅛ teaspoon pepper
½ cup butter or margarine, softened
1 loaf Italian or French bread (about
   16 inches long), halved lengthwise

Preheat oven to 375°F. In small bowl,
thoroughly blend all ingredients except bread;
generously spread on bread halves. Arrange
bread, cut side up, on baking sheet. Bake 15
minutes or until golden. Serve warm.
                                    Makes 1 loaf

NOTE: Store any remaining spread, covered,
in refrigerator for future use.

Maple French Toast with Maple Butter

QUICKY STICKY BUNS

3 tablespoons packed brown sugar, divided
¼ cup KARO® Light or Dark Corn Syrup
¼ cup coarsely chopped pecans
2 tablespoons MAZOLA® Margarine, softened, divided
1 can (8 ounces) refrigerated crescent rolls
1 teaspoon ground cinnamon

Preheat oven to 350°F. In small bowl combine 2 tablespoons brown sugar, corn syrup, pecans and 1 tablespoon margarine. Spoon about 2 teaspoons mixture into each of 9 (2½-inch) muffin pan cups. Unroll entire crescent roll dough; pinch seams together to form 1 rectangle. Combine remaining 1 tablespoon brown sugar and cinnamon. Spread dough with remaining 1 tablespoon margarine; sprinkle with cinnamon mixture. Roll up from short end. Cut into 9 slices. Place one slice in each prepared muffin pan cup. Bake 25 minutes or until golden brown. Immediately invert pan onto cookie sheet or tray; cool 10 minutes.

Makes 9 buns

PREPARATION TIME: 15 minutes
BAKE TIME: 25 minutes plus cooling

Quicky Sticky Buns

Festive

CAKES & PIES

CHOCOLATE RASPBERRY AVALANCHE CAKE

2 cups all-purpose flour
2 cups granulated sugar
6 tablespoons unsweetened cocoa
1½ teaspoons baking soda
1 teaspoon salt
1 cup hot coffee
¾ BUTTER FLAVOR* CRISCO® Stick *or* ¾ cup BUTTER FLAVOR CRISCO all-vegetable shortening
½ cup milk
3 eggs
¼ cup raspberry-flavored liqueur
Confectioners sugar
1 cup fresh raspberries (optional)

1. Heat oven to 350°F. Grease 10-inch (12-cup) Bundt pan with shortening. Flour lightly. Mix flour, granulated sugar, cocoa, baking soda and salt in large bowl. Add coffee and shortening. Beat with mixer at low speed until moistened. Add milk. Beat at medium speed 1½ minutes. Add eggs, 1 at a time, beating well after each addition. Pour into prepared pan.

2. Bake at 350°F for 40 to 45 minutes or until toothpick inserted in center comes out clean. *Do not overbake.* Cool 10 minutes; remove from pan. Cool on wire rack 10 minutes. Brush top and side with liqueur. Cool completely. Dust with confectioners sugar. Serve with raspberries, if desired.
Makes 1 (10-inch) cake (12 to 16 servings)

SNOWMAN CUPCAKES

1 package (18.5 ounces) yellow or white
 cake mix, plus ingredients to prepare
 mix
2 (16-ounce) containers vanilla frosting
4 cups flaked coconut
15 large marshmallows
15 miniature chocolate-covered peanut
 butter cups, unwrapped
 Decorations: Pretzel sticks and small
 red candies
 Green and red decorating gels

Preheat oven to 350°F. Line 15 regular-size
(2½-inch) muffin pan cups and 15 small (about
1-inch) muffin pan cups with paper muffin cups.
Prepare cake mix according to package
directions. Spoon batter into muffin cups.

Bake 10 to 15 minutes for small cupcakes and
15 to 20 minutes for regular-size cupcakes or
until cupcakes are golden and wooden
toothpick inserted in centers comes out clean.
Cool in pans on wire racks 10 minutes.
Remove from pans to racks; cool completely.
Remove paper liners.

Snowman Cupcakes

For each snowman, frost bottom and side of
1 regular-size cupcake; coat with coconut.
Repeat with 1 small cupcake. Attach small
cupcake to regular-size cupcake with frosting
to form snowman body. Attach marshmallow to
small cupcake with frosting to form snowman
head. Attach inverted peanut butter cup to
marshmallow with frosting to form snowman
hat. Use pretzels for arms and small red
candies for buttons. Pipe face with decorating
gels. Repeat with remaining cupcakes.

Makes 15 snowmen

CARIBBEAN CHRISTMAS RING

3 tablespoons shortening
2½ cups finely chopped California walnuts,
 divided
1 cup all-purpose flour
½ cup whole wheat flour
1 teaspoon baking powder
1 teaspoon baking soda
¾ cup butter, softened
1⅓ cups granulated sugar
3 eggs
1 cup sour cream or plain nonfat yogurt
1 ripe banana, mashed
2 tablespoons orange-flavored liqueur
ORANGE SUGAR GLAZE
1 cup powdered sugar, sifted
2 tablespoons orange juice

Caribbean Christmas Ring

Thoroughly grease 10- to 12-cup microwave-safe Bundt pan with 3 tablespoons shortening; sprinkle with ½ cup chopped walnuts to coat evenly. Sift flours, baking powder and baking soda into small bowl. In large bowl, beat butter and granulated sugar until fluffy; beat in eggs, one at a time. Stir sour cream, banana and liqueur into egg mixture. Fold flour mixture into banana mixture; stir in remaining 2 cups walnuts. Spoon into prepared pan and place on top of microwave-safe bowl in microwave, raising cake to center of oven. Cook at MEDIUM (50% power) 10 minutes. Continue cooking at HIGH (100% power) 5 to 7 minutes or until cake tests done, turning twice. Let cake stand 15 minutes. Turn out onto serving plate. Let cool.

Mix powdered sugar and orange juice until smooth. Pour glaze evenly over cake and serve. *Makes 20 to 24 servings*

Favorite recipe from **Walnut Marketing Board**

WALNUT HOLIDAY CAKE

2 tablespoons dark rum
4 single graham cracker squares
5 eggs, separated
2 cups powdered sugar
1 teaspoon grated orange peel
¼ teaspoon cream of tartar
3½ cups finely ground toasted California
    walnuts
¼ cup grated semisweet chocolate
6 squares (1 ounce each) semisweet
    chocolate
6 tablespoons butter or margarine
1 tablespoon honey
California walnut halves for garnish

Grease 9-inch springform pan. Line bottom with waxed paper; grease waxed paper. In small bowl, pour rum over graham crackers. When crackers are softened, mash with fork. In large bowl, beat egg yolks with electric mixer at medium speed until lemon colored. Add sugar and orange peel; beat at high speed until thickened, about 3 minutes. Beat cracker mixture into yolk mixture. In large mixer bowl using clean beaters, beat egg whites and cream of tartar at high speed until stiff, but not dry, peaks form. Gently fold beaten whites, ground walnuts and grated chocolate into yolk mixture. Pour batter into prepared pan. Bake in preheated 350°F oven 45 to 50 minutes or until toothpick inserted in center comes out clean and small crack appears on surface. Let cool completely in pan on wire rack. Remove side of springform pan. Invert cake onto serving plate; remove bottom of pan and waxed paper. Place strips of waxed paper under edge of cake to cover plate.

In top of double boiler, melt chocolate squares and butter over simmering water, stirring to blend. Stir in honey. Pour chocolate mixture over cake; let stand until slightly cool. Spread over top and side of cake. Remove waxed paper strips. Garnish with walnut halves. When firm, cut into thin wedges.
Makes 16 servings

Favorite recipe from **Walnut Marketing Board**

Winter Wonderland Cake

WINTER WONDERLAND CAKE

1 package DUNCAN HINES® Moist Deluxe Cake Mix (any flavor)
2 containers (16 ounces each) DUNCAN HINES® Creamy Homestyle Vanilla Frosting
Green food coloring
9 ice cream sugar cones
½ cup flaked coconut, finely chopped
Marzipan
Sliced natural almonds
Nonpareil decors

1. Preheat oven to 350°F. Grease and flour 13×9×2-inch baking pan.

2. Prepare, bake and cool cake following package directions for basic recipe.

3. To assemble, place cake on serving plate. Frost sides and top with 1 container Vanilla frosting. Tint remaining container of frosting with green food coloring to desired color; set aside. Break off edges of ice cream cones to form various sized trees. Frost 1 cone with green frosting. Arrange on cake; sprinkle with coconut. Repeat for remaining cones. Form marzipan into bunny shapes. Use almond slices for ears and nonpareil decors for eyes and noses. Arrange as desired. Sprinkle remaining coconut on cake.

Makes 12 to 16 servings

TIP: Marzipan, a cooked mixture of finely ground almonds, sugar and egg whites, is very sweet and pliable. It is available in most supermarkets packaged in cans or in plastic-wrapped logs.

CHRISTMAS TREE POKE CAKE

- **2 baked 9-inch square white cake layers, cooled**
- **1 package (4-serving size) JELL-O® Brand Strawberry Flavor Gelatin**
- **1 package (4-serving size) JELL-O® Brand Lime Flavor Gelatin**
- **2 cups boiling water, divided**
- **1 package (7 ounces) BAKER'S® ANGEL FLAKE® Coconut, divided**
- **Green liquid food coloring**
- **1 tub (12 ounces) COOL WHIP® Whipped Topping, thawed**
- **Gumdrops**
- **Peppermint candies**
- **Red string licorice**

Place cake layers, top sides up, in two clean 9-inch square cake pans. Pierce cakes with large fork at ½-inch intervals.

Dissolve each flavor of gelatin separately in 1 cup of the boiling water. Carefully pour strawberry flavor gelatin over one cake layer and lime flavor gelatin over second cake layer. Refrigerate 4 hours.

Meanwhile, toast ⅓ cup of the coconut; set aside. Tint remaining coconut with green food coloring.

Dip one cake pan in warm water for 10 seconds; unmold. Place right side up on large cutting board. Cut as shown in illustration 1. Arrange pieces as shown in illustration 2. Top with about 1½ cups of the whipped topping. Unmold second cake layer; cut into pieces as shown in illustration 1. Place pieces on first layer. Frost cake with remaining whipped topping.

Sprinkle trunk of tree with toasted coconut. Sprinkle remaining cake with green coconut. Decorate with gumdrops, peppermint candies and string licorice as desired.

Makes 24 servings

Christmas Tree Poke Cake

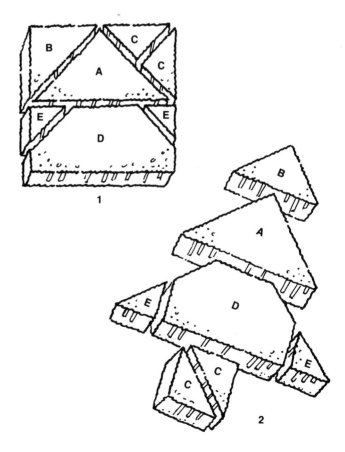

ANGEL CAKE

1 (8-inch) round cake layer
   Creamy White Frosting (recipe follows)
1 to 2 tablespoons milk
5 tablespoons flaked coconut, divided
   Red liquid food coloring
1 teaspoon water
2 small blue or green jelly beans
   Silver edible glitter (optional)

With serrated knife, trim top of cake to form flat surface. Cut cake as shown in diagram 1, using ruler as guide. Position cake pieces on covered cake board as shown in diagram 2, connecting with some of the frosting. Thin 1½ cups frosting with milk, adding 1 teaspoon at a time, until frosting is of thin consistency. Frost entire cake with thinned frosting to seal in crumbs. Frost again with remaining Creamy White Frosting.

Place 4 tablespoons coconut in resealable plastic food storage bag. Combine small amount of food coloring with water in small bowl; add to bag. Seal bag; shake until evenly coated. Toast remaining 1 tablespoon coconut in preheated 350°F oven about 5 minutes or until lightly browned, stirring occasionally.

Sprinkle pink coconut on angel's body and toasted coconut on angel's head for hair. Place jelly beans on face for eyes. Sprinkle glitter over angel's wings, if desired.

Makes 8 to 10 servings

CREAMY WHITE FROSTING

½ cup shortening
6 cups sifted powdered sugar, divided
3 tablespoons milk
2 teaspoons clear vanilla extract
   Additional milk*

Beat shortening in large bowl with electric mixer at medium speed until fluffy. Gradually beat in 3 cups sugar until well blended and smooth. Carefully beat in 3 tablespoons milk and vanilla. Gradually beat in remaining 3 cups sugar, adding more milk, 1 teaspoon at a time, as needed for good spreading consistency. Store in refrigerator.

*Makes enough to fill and frost
2 (8-inch) round cake layers*

*For thinner frosting, use more milk and for thicker frosting use less milk.

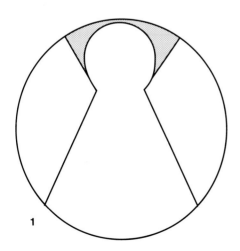

Angel Cake

Merry Christmas Present Cake

MERRY CHRISTMAS PRESENT CAKE

Marzipan (page 504)
Red food coloring
1 package (18.25 ounces) devil's food
  cake mix
1 cup water
½ cup vegetable oil
3 eggs
3 tablespoons unsweetened cocoa
  powder
1 teaspoon vanilla
1 cup mini chocolate chips
⅔ cup finely ground hazelnuts or
  almonds
1 cup whipping cream
2 tablespoons butter or margarine
6 ounces semisweet chocolate, coarsely
  chopped

Prepare Marzipan, tinting with red food coloring; set aside. Preheat oven to 350°F. Grease and flour 13×9-inch baking pan. Combine cake mix, water, oil, eggs, cocoa and vanilla in large bowl. Beat with electric mixer at low speed until blended; beat at medium speed 2 minutes. Mix in chocolate chips and nuts. Pour batter into prepared pan. Bake 50 to 60 minutes or until wooden toothpick inserted in center of cake comes out clean. Cool in pan on wire rack 15 minutes. Remove from pan to wire rack; cool completely.

Bring cream and butter to a simmer in small saucepan; remove from heat. Add chopped chocolate, stirring until melted. Cool to room temperature. Cover; refrigerate until mixture is thick enough to spread, about 1½ hours. Place cake on serving tray. Frost with thickened chocolate mixture. Refrigerate until cake is well chilled, about 2 hours.

Divide Marzipan into 4 equal portions. Roll 1 portion into ½-inch-thick rope. Place rope between sheets of waxed paper and roll into strip 1 inch wide and 16 to 18 inches long (use sharp knife to make edges straight). Lay strip lengthwise down center of cake, continuing down over sides; trim ends to fit. Repeat rolling procedure with second portion of Marzipan; cut crosswise in half. Place strips on cake as shown in diagram 1; trim ends.

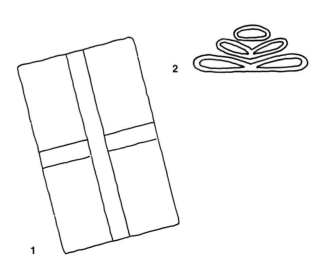

Repeat rolling procedure with third portion of Marzipan, making strip 15 inches long. Fold ends in toward center to make bottom loops of bow as shown in diagram 2; place on cake as shown. Repeat rolling procedure with fourth portion of Marzipan, making one 8-inch strip and one 4-inch strip. Cut 8-inch strip in half crosswise; fold into 2 loops and place on first loop as shown in diagram 2. Fold under ends of 4-inch strip to form loop; place as shown in diagram 2.   *Makes 12 to 16 servings*

JOLLY OLE SAINT NICK CAKE

- **2 packages (18.25 ounces each) yellow cake mix, plus ingredients to prepare mixes**
- **3 containers (16 ounces each) vanilla frosting, divided**
- **2 tablespoons milk**
  Red food coloring
  Chocolate sprinkles
- **2 black licorice drops**
- **1 black licorice whip**
- **1 red candy drop**
- **2 dark brown candy-coated chocolate pieces**
- **7 chocolate nonpareils**

Jolly Ole Saint Nick Cake

Preheat oven to 350°F. Grease and flour one 13×9-inch baking pan and two 8-inch round cake pans. Prepare cake mixes according to package directions. Divide among pans. Bake 35 to 40 minutes or until wooden toothpick inserted in centers comes out clean. Cool in pans on wire racks 10 minutes. Remove from pans; cool completely.

Using diagrams 1 and 2 as guides, cut out pieces. Combine 1 container frosting and milk. Position pieces on 18-inch square cake board or large tray as shown in diagram 3, connecting with some of the thinned frosting. Frost entire cake with remaining thinned frosting.

Frost face area, ball of hat, mittens and boots with some of the frosting from second container, reserving remaining for piping.

Color the third container of frosting with red food coloring. Frost hat, shirt and pants with red frosting, reserving small portion for piping. Using pastry bag, medium star tip and red frosting, pipe design on hat. Using reserved white frosting, pipe beard, cuffs and trim of hat. Decorate with candies.

Makes 14 to 16 servings

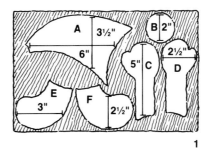

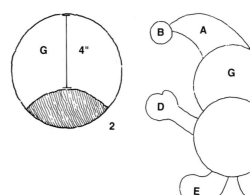

IMPERIAL® SNOWMAN CAKE

¾ cup shortening
1 cup IMPERIAL® Granulated Sugar
½ cup IMPERIAL® Light Brown Sugar,
  packed
1 teaspoon vanilla extract
½ teaspoon coconut-flavored extract
3 eggs
1½ cups all-purpose flour
1½ teaspoons baking powder
½ teaspoon salt
¾ cup milk
  Imperial® Frosting (page 327)
1 (7-ounce) package flaked coconut
  Gumdrops, licorice ropes and candy
    canes

Preheat oven to 350°F. Cream shortening, sugars and extracts. Add eggs; beat well. Combine dry ingredients; add to creamed mixture alternately with milk, ending with milk.

Grease 1 (1½-quart) ovenproof mixing bowl, 2 (3-cup) ovenproof mixing bowls and 1 (6-ounce) ovenproof custard cup. Measure 2 cups batter into large bowl and 1 cup batter into each medium bowl; fill custard cup half full with remaining batter. Bake 50 to 55 minutes for bowls, 20 to 25 minutes for custard cup. Cool cakes in bowls 10 minutes; turn out onto wire racks to cool completely.

Imperial® Snowman Cake

Place largest cake on serving plate, rounded side up. Spread evenly with Imperial® Frosting. Spread small amount of frosting on flat sides of medium cakes and gently press together to form a ball. Center ball on top of frosted largest cake.* Frost side of ball evenly. Place smallest cake on top of ball to form head.* Frost smallest cake evenly. Gently pat coconut over entire snowman. Decorate with gumdrops, licorice ropes and candy canes as desired. Make top hat from black construction paper.
Makes 1 snowman cake

*Secure with wooden toothpicks or drinking straws, if necessary. Before serving, remove and discard any wooden toothpicks or drinking straws.

IMPERIAL® FROSTING

    4 cups IMPERIAL® Powdered Sugar, divided
    5 tablespoons shortening
  1¼ teaspoons vanilla extract
    ½ teaspoon coconut-flavored extract
    ½ teaspoon salt
    5 to 6 tablespoons milk

Cream 1 cup powdered sugar, shortening, extracts and salt. Add milk alternately with remaining 3 cups powdered sugar. Mix until creamy. Add more powdered sugar or milk, if necessary, to make spreading consistency.
Makes about 2 cups

Caramel Fudge Cake

CARAMEL FUDGE CAKE

    1 (18¼- or 18½-ounce) package chocolate cake mix
    1 (14-ounce) package EAGLE™ Brand Caramels, unwrapped
  ½ cup margarine or butter
    1 (14-ounce) can EAGLE® Brand Sweetened Condensed Milk (NOT evaporated milk)
    1 cup coarsely chopped pecans

Preheat oven to 350°F. Prepare cake mix as package directs. Pour *2 cups* batter into greased 13×9-inch baking pan; bake 15 minutes. Meanwhile, in heavy saucepan, over low heat, melt caramels and margarine with sweetened condensed milk, stirring until smooth. Spread evenly over cake; spread remaining cake batter over caramel mixture. Top with nuts. Return cake to oven; bake 30 to 35 minutes longer or until cake springs back when lightly touched. Cool. Garnish as desired.
Makes 1 (13×9-inch) cake

CASSATA

**2 cups (15 ounces) SARGENTO®
Part-Skim Ricotta Cheese**
¼ cup sugar
3 tablespoons orange-flavored liqueur
⅓ cup finely chopped mixed candied fruit
¼ cup chopped almonds
**1¼ cups mini semisweet chocolate chips,
divided**
1 prepared pound cake (10¾ ounces)
**1 teaspoon instant coffee dissolved in
¼ cup boiling water**
**6 tablespoons unsalted butter or
margarine, cut into 8 pieces, chilled**
**Chopped almonds, for garnish
(optional)**

In bowl, combine ricotta cheese, sugar and liqueur; beat until light and fluffy, about 3 minutes. Fold in candied fruit, ¼ cup chopped almonds and ¼ cup chocolate chips. Set aside.

Cut pound cake in half horizontally using sharp serrated knife. Cut each half horizontally in half again. Place top layer of pound cake, top side down, on serving platter. Spread one third ricotta mixture evenly over cake. Repeat procedure twice, using two cake layers and remaining ricotta mixture; stack layers. Top with remaining cake layer; press slightly to compact layers. Cover with plastic wrap; chill at least 2 hours.

Meanwhile, combine remaining 1 cup chocolate chips and coffee in top of double boiler over hot, not boiling, water. Stir constantly until chocolate is melted. Add butter pieces, one at a time, stirring constantly, until all butter is added and melted. Remove from heat; chill to spreading consistency, about 2 to 2½ hours. Spread top and sides of cake with frosting. Garnish top with chopped almonds.

Makes 12 servings

TIP: Cake may be made 1 day in advance, covered with plastic wrap and refrigerated. Let stand at room temperature about 30 minutes before slicing.

Cassata

RIBBON CAKE

CAKE
   **1 package DUNCAN HINES® Moist
      Deluxe White Cake Mix**
   ¼ cup flaked coconut, chopped
   **¼ cup natural pistachio nuts, finely
      chopped**
   Green food coloring
   **¼ cup maraschino cherries, drained,
      finely chopped**
   Red food coloring
FILLING AND FROSTING
   3¼ cups confectioners sugar
   ½ cup CRISCO® all-vegetable shortening
   ⅓ cup water
   ¼ cup powdered non-dairy creamer
   1½ teaspoons vanilla extract
   ¼ teaspoon salt
   Green food coloring
   **½ cup natural pistachio nuts, finely
      chopped**
   ¾ cup cherry jam
   **Whole maraschino cherries with stems,
      for garnish**
   Mint leaves, for garnish

1. Preheat oven to 350°F. Grease and flour three 8-inch square baking pans.

2. For cake, prepare cake mix following package directions for basic recipe. Combine 1¾ cups batter and coconut in small bowl; set aside. Combine 1¾ cups batter, pistachio nuts and 5 drops green food coloring in small bowl; set aside. Combine remaining batter, chopped maraschino cherries and 2 drops red food coloring. Pour batters into separate pans. Bake at 350°F for 18 minutes or until toothpick inserted in centers comes out clean. Cool following package directions. Trim edges of cake.

3. For filling and frosting, combine confectioners sugar, shortening, water, non-dairy creamer, vanilla extract, salt and 5 drops green food coloring in large bowl. Beat for 3 minutes at medium speed with electric mixer. Beat for 5 minutes at high speed. Add more confectioners sugar to thicken or water to thin as needed. Add remaining ½ cup pistachio nuts. Stir until blended.

4. To assemble, spread green and white cake layers with cherry jam. Stack layers. Top with pink layer. Frost sides and top of cake. Garnish with whole maraschino cherries and mint leaves.
Makes 12 to 16 servings

TIP: To save time, use DUNCAN HINES® Creamy Homestyle Vanilla Frosting to frost sides and top of cake. Tint with several drops green food coloring and add pistachio nuts as directed.

Ribbon Cake

Black Forest Cake

BLACK FOREST CAKE

2 cups plus 2 tablespoons all-purpose
    flour
2 cups granulated sugar
¾ cup unsweetened cocoa powder
1½ teaspoons baking powder
¾ teaspoon baking soda
¾ teaspoon salt
3 eggs
1 cup milk
½ cup vegetable oil
1 tablespoon vanilla
    Cherry Topping (page 331)
    Frosting (page 331)

Preheat oven to 350°F. Grease and flour two 9-inch round cake pans. Cover bottoms with waxed paper. Combine dry ingredients in large bowl. Add eggs, milk, oil and vanilla; beat until well blended. Pour evenly into prepared pans. Bake 35 minutes or until wooden toothpick inserted in centers comes out clean. Cool layers in pans on wire racks 10 minutes. Loosen edges and remove to racks to cool completely.

While cake is baking, prepare Cherry Topping and Frosting. With long serrated knife, split each cake layer horizontally in half. Tear one split layer into crumbs; set aside. Reserve 1½ cups Frosting for decorating cake; set aside. Gently brush loose crumbs off top and side of each cake layer with pastry brush or hands.

To assemble, place one cake layer on cake plate. Spread with 1 cup Frosting; top with ¾ cup Cherry Topping. Top with second cake layer; repeat layers of Frosting and Cherry Topping. Top with third cake layer. Frost side of cake with remaining Frosting. Pat reserved crumbs onto Frosting on side of cake. Spoon reserved Frosting into pastry bag fitted with star decorator tip. Pipe around top and bottom edges of cake. Spoon remaining Cherry Topping onto top of cake.

Makes 1 (3-layer) cake

CHERRY TOPPING

> 2 (20-ounce) cans pitted tart cherries,
>   undrained
> 1 cup granulated sugar
> ¼ cup cornstarch
> 1 teaspoon vanilla

Drain cherries, reserving ½ cup juice. Combine reserved juice, cherries, sugar and cornstarch in 2-quart saucepan. Cook over low heat until thickened, stirring constantly. Stir in 1 teaspoon vanilla. Cool before using.

FROSTING

> 3 cups whipping cream
> ⅓ cup powdered sugar

Beat together whipping cream and powdered sugar in chilled medium bowl with electric mixer at high speed until stiff peaks form.

TRIPLE CHOCOLATE CAKE

> ¾ cup butter or margarine, softened
> 1½ cups sugar
> 1 egg
> 1 teaspoon vanilla
> 2 cups all-purpose flour
> ⅔ cup unsweetened cocoa powder
> 2 teaspoons baking soda
> ¼ teaspoon salt
> 1 cup buttermilk
> ¾ cup sour cream
>   Light Ganache Filling (recipe follows)
>   Dark Chocolate Glaze (recipe follows)

Preheat oven to 350°F. Grease and flour two 9-inch round cake pans. Beat butter and sugar in large bowl with electric mixer at medium speed until light and fluffy. Beat in egg and vanilla until blended. Combine flour, cocoa, baking soda and salt in medium bowl. Add flour mixture to butter mixture, alternately with buttermilk and sour cream, beginning and ending with flour mixture. Beat well after each addition. Divide evenly between prepared pans. Bake 30 to 35 minutes or until wooden

toothpick inserted in centers comes out clean. Cool in pans 10 minutes. Remove from pans to wire racks; cool completely.

Meanwhile, prepare Light Ganache Filling. Place one cake layer on serving plate. Spread with Light Ganache Filling. Top with second cake layer. Prepare Dark Chocolate Glaze. Pour over top of cake. Immediately spread glaze over side and top with spatula until smooth. Refrigerate cake at least 30 minutes to set glaze. Garnish as desired. Store tightly covered at room temperature.

Makes 1 (9-inch) layer cake

LIGHT GANACHE FILLING

> 4 squares (1 ounce each) semisweet
>   chocolate
> 1 cup whipping cream
> ½ teaspoon vanilla

Melt chocolate in heavy, small saucepan over low heat, stirring frequently. Pour melted chocolate into small bowl. Wash and dry saucepan. Heat cream in same saucepan over medium heat until hot; *do not boil.* Gradually whisk cream into chocolate. Whisk in vanilla. Let filling stand at room temperature until of spreading consistency. Beat mixture with electric mixer at high speed until light and fluffy.

DARK CHOCOLATE GLAZE

> 8 squares (1 ounce each) semisweet
>   chocolate
> 4 tablespoons butter or margarine
> 1 cup whipping cream

Melt chocolate and butter in heavy, small saucepan over low heat, stirring frequently. Pour melted chocolate mixture into medium bowl. Wash and dry saucepan. Heat cream in same saucepan over medium heat until hot; *do not boil.* Gradually whisk cream into chocolate mixture until slightly thickened.

RICH CHOCOLATE TRUFFLE CAKE

2 packages (8 ounces each) semisweet chocolate (16 squares)
1½ cups butter or margarine
1 cup sugar
½ cup light cream
6 large eggs
2 teaspoons vanilla
Chocolate Curls (recipe follows)
Chocolate Glaze (recipe follows)
Sweetened Whipped Cream (recipe follows)
Mint leaves for garnish

Preheat oven to 350°F. Line bottom of 9-inch springform pan with foil, tucking foil edges under bottom. Attach springform side. Bring foil up around outside of pan. Grease foil-lined bottom and side of pan with butter; set aside.

Heat chocolate, butter, sugar and cream in heavy 2-quart saucepan over low heat until chocolate melts and mixture is smooth, stirring frequently. Remove from heat. Beat eggs and vanilla in large bowl with wire whisk until frothy. Slowly whisk in warm chocolate mixture until well blended. *Do not beat mixture vigorously,* as this will incorporate air into the mixture. Pour batter into prepared pan. Bake 45 minutes or until wooden toothpick inserted about 1 inch from edge comes out clean and center is set. Cool cake completely in pan on wire rack.

Prepare Chocolate Curls; refrigerate. When cake is cool, carefully remove side of springform pan. Leave cake on bottom of pan. Wrap cake in foil. Refrigerate until well chilled, at least 4 hours or overnight.

Prepare Chocolate Glaze. Unwrap cake. Turn upside-down on cake plate; remove bottom of pan. Surround cake with waxed paper strips to catch glaze drippings. Spread top and side of cake with warm glaze using metal spatula. Remove waxed paper after glaze sets.

Prepare Sweetened Whipped Cream. Spoon cream mixture into decorating bag with medium star tip. Pipe cream around edge of cake. Garnish piped cream with Chocolate Curls. Refrigerate until serving. Just before serving, garnish with mint leaves.

Makes 16 to 20 servings

CHOCOLATE CURLS

1 square (1 ounce) chocolate, coarsely chopped
1 teaspoon vegetable shortening

Place chocolate and shortening in 1-cup glass measure. Microwave at HIGH (100% power) about 1 minute or until melted, stirring after 30 seconds of cooking. Pour melted chocolate onto back of baking sheet, marble slab or other heat-resistant flat surface. Quickly spread chocolate in very thin layer with metal spatula. Refrigerate about 10 minutes or until firm, but still pliable. Using small straight-edge metal spatula or paring knife, held at 45° angle, push spatula firmly along baking sheet, under chocolate, so chocolate curls as it is pushed. (If chocolate is too firm to curl, let stand a few minutes at room temperature. Refrigerate again if it becomes too soft.) Using small skewer or toothpick, transfer curls to waxed paper. Store in cool, dry place until ready to use.

CHOCOLATE GLAZE

1 cup semisweet chocolate chips
2 tablespoons butter or margarine
3 tablespoons half-and-half
2 tablespoons light corn syrup

Melt chocolate chips and butter in 1-quart saucepan over low heat, stirring frequently. Remove from heat. Stir in half-and-half and corn syrup. *Makes about 1¼ cups*

SWEETENED WHIPPED CREAM

1 cup heavy cream
2 tablespoons powdered sugar
½ teaspoon vanilla

Beat ingredients in bowl until soft peaks form. Refrigerate. *Makes about 2 cups*

Rich Chocolate Truffle Cake

FESTIVE YULE LOG

CAKE
    5 eggs, room temperature, separated
    ⅔ cup granulated sugar
    2 tablespoons all-purpose flour
    3 tablespoons unsweetened cocoa
        Confectioners' sugar
FILLING
    1 bag (7 ounces) Chocolate RIESEN®
        Caramel Candy, unwrapped
    ¼ cup whipping cream
    2 tablespoons rum
    2 cups whipped topping
    ⅓ cup finely chopped pecans
FROSTING
    6 tablespoons butter or margarine,
        softened
    1 cup confectioners' sugar
    ⅓ cup unsweetened cocoa
    2 to 3 tablespoons milk
    ¼ cup finely chopped pecans

Preheat oven to 350°F. For Cake, in large mixing bowl, beat egg yolks at high speed with electric mixer until light and fluffy. Gradually add granulated sugar, beating until mixture is thick and light colored. On low speed add flour and 3 tablespoons cocoa; mix well. In another mixing bowl, using clean beaters, beat egg whites until soft peaks form. Carefully fold egg whites into chocolate mixture. Spread in 15×10×1-inch greased and waxed-paper-lined jelly-roll pan.

Bake 15 minutes or until cake springs back when lightly touched. Cake will fall slightly as it cools. Let cake cool in pan 15 minutes; loosen edges with knife. Turn cake out onto piece of waxed paper dusted with confectioners' sugar. Carefully remove waxed paper lining. Cover cake with dish towel; cool completely.

For Filling, melt caramels with cream in heavy saucepan, stirring constantly, until smooth. Remove from heat and stir in rum. Cool to room temperature. When cool, fold in whipped topping. Spread over cake and sprinkle with ⅓ cup nuts. Roll up, starting from short end. Place in freezer while preparing frosting.

For Frosting, beat butter until fluffy. Alternately add sugar and ⅓ cup cocoa with milk, beating until frosting is smooth and fluffy. Remove cake from freezer. Slice 1-inch piece of cake roll off end of log. Spread frosting on one side of log and press slice, cut side up, in place. (This will resemble stump of log.) Frost entire cake and stump. Swirl ends of log and flat side of stump to resemble cut section of log. Run tines of fork over length of log to resemble bark. Sprinkle with ¼ cup nuts. Refrigerate at least 2 hours before serving.

Makes 8 to 10 servings

ALMOND CHOCOLATE TORTE WITH RASPBERRY SAUCE

    2½ cups BLUE DIAMOND® Blanched
        Whole Almonds, lightly toasted
    9 squares (1 ounce each) semisweet
        chocolate
    ¼ cup butter
    6 eggs, beaten
    ¾ cup sugar
    2 tablespoons flour
    ¼ cup brandy
        Fudge Glaze (page 335)
        Raspberry Sauce (page 335)

In food processor or blender, process 1 cup almonds until finely ground. Generously grease 9-inch round cake pan; sprinkle with 2 tablespoons ground almonds. In top of double boiler, melt chocolate and butter over simmering water, blending thoroughly; cool slightly. In large bowl, beat eggs and sugar. Gradually beat in chocolate mixture. Add flour, remaining ground almonds and brandy; mix well. Pour batter into prepared pan.

Bake in preheated 350°F oven 25 minutes or until toothpick inserted in center comes out almost clean. Let cool in pan on wire rack 10 minutes. Loosen edge; remove from pan. Cool completely on wire rack.

Prepare Fudge Glaze. Place torte on wire rack over sheet of waxed paper. Pour Fudge Glaze over torte, spreading over top and sides with spatula. Carefully transfer torte to serving plate; let glaze set.

Prepare Raspberry Sauce; set aside. Arrange remaining 1½ cups whole almonds, points toward center, in circle around outer edge of torte. Working towards center, repeat circles, overlapping almonds slightly. To serve, pour small amount of Raspberry Sauce on each serving plate; top with slice of torte.

Makes 10 to 12 servings

FUDGE GLAZE: In small saucepan, combine 6 tablespoons water and 3 tablespoons sugar. Simmer over low heat until sugar dissolves. Stir in 3 squares (1 ounce each) semisweet chocolate and 1 tablespoon brandy. Heat, stirring occasionally, until chocolate melts and glaze coats back of spoon.

RASPBERRY SAUCE: In food processor or blender, purée 2 packages (10 ounces each) thawed frozen raspberries. Strain raspberry purée through a fine sieve to remove seeds. Stir in sugar to taste.

Almond Chocolate Torte with Raspberry Sauce

BÛCHE DE NOËL

¾ cup cake flour
½ teaspoon baking powder
½ teaspoon salt
5 eggs, separated
1 cup granulated sugar, divided
1 teaspoon vanilla
½ cup powdered sugar
1 cup semisweet chocolate chips
¾ cup heavy cream
1 tablespoon rum
   Cocoa Frosting (recipe follows)
   White Chocolate Curls (page 338)
2 teaspoons unsweetened cocoa powder
   (optional)

Preheat oven to 375°F. Grease 15½×10½-inch jelly-roll pan; line pan with waxed paper. Grease waxed paper; set pan aside. Place flour, baking powder and salt in small bowl; stir to combine. Beat egg yolks and ⅔ cup granulated sugar in separate small bowl with electric mixer at high speed about 5 minutes or until thick and lemon colored, scraping down side of bowl once. Beat in vanilla; set aside.

Beat egg whites in clean large bowl using clean beaters with electric mixer at high speed until foamy. Gradually beat in remaining ⅓ cup granulated sugar, 1 tablespoon at a time, until stiff peaks form.

Fold flour mixture into egg yolk mixture. Fold flour/egg yolk mixture into egg white mixture until evenly incorporated. Spread mixture into prepared pan. Bake 12 to 15 minutes or until cake springs back when lightly touched with finger. Meanwhile, lightly sift powdered sugar over clean dish towel.

Loosen warm cake from edges of pan with spatula; invert onto prepared towel. Remove pan; carefully peel off waxed paper. Gently roll up cake in towel from short end, jelly-roll style. Let rolled cake cool completely on wire rack.

For chocolate filling, place chocolate chips and cream in heavy, 1-quart saucepan. Heat over low heat until chocolate is melted, stirring frequently. Pour into small bowl; stir in rum. Cover and refrigerate about 1½ hours or until filling is of spreading consistency, stirring occasionally.

Prepare Cocoa Frosting and White Chocolate Curls; refrigerate until ready to use.

Unroll cake; remove towel. Spread cake with chilled chocolate filling to within ½ inch of edge; reroll cake. Spread Cocoa Frosting over cake roll. Garnish with White Chocolate Curls. Sprinkle with cocoa.   *Makes 12 servings*

COCOA FROSTING

1 cup heavy cream
2 tablespoons unsweetened Dutch-
   processed* cocoa powder, sifted
½ cup powdered sugar, sifted
1 teaspoon vanilla

Beat cream, cocoa, sugar and vanilla with electric mixer at medium speed until soft peaks form. *Do not overbeat.* Refrigerate until ready to use.   *Makes about 2 cups*

*The Dutch-processed, or European-style, cocoa gives this frosting an intense chocolate flavor and a rich color. Other unsweetened cocoas can be substituted, but the flavor may be milder and the color may be lighter.

continued on page 338

Bûche de Noël

Bûche de Noël, continued

WHITE CHOCOLATE CURLS

1 package (8 ounces) white chocolate, coarsely chopped
1 tablespoon vegetable shortening

Place white chocolate and shortening in 2-cup glass measure. Microwave at HIGH (100% power) about 1½ minutes or until melted, stirring after every 30 seconds of cooking. Pour melted white chocolate onto back of baking sheet, marble slab or other heat-resistant flat surface. Quickly spread chocolate into very thin layer with metal spatula. Refrigerate about 10 minutes or until firm, but still pliable. Using small straight-edge metal spatula or paring knife held at 45° angle, push spatula firmly along baking sheet, under chocolate, so chocolate curls as it is pushed. (If chocolate is too firm to curl, let stand a few minutes at room temperature. Refrigerate again if it becomes too soft.) Using small skewer or toothpick, transfer curls to waxed paper. Store in cool, dry place until ready to use.

Chocolate Intensity

CHOCOLATE INTENSITY

CAKE
1 package (8 ounces) NESTLÉ®
Unsweetened Chocolate Baking Bars
1½ cups granulated sugar
½ cup butter, softened
3 eggs
2 teaspoons vanilla extract
⅔ cup all-purpose flour
Sifted powdered sugar (optional)
COFFEE CRÈME ANGLAISE SAUCE
4 egg yolks
⅓ cup granulated sugar
1 tablespoon TASTER'S CHOICE®
Freeze Dried Instant Coffee
1½ cups milk
1 teaspoon vanilla extract

FOR CAKE: In small, heavy saucepan over low heat, melt baking bars, stirring until smooth. Remove from heat; cool to lukewarm. In small mixer bowl, beat granulated sugar, butter, eggs and vanilla for about 4 minutes or until thick and pale yellow. Beat in melted chocolate. Gradually beat in flour. Spread into greased 9-inch springform pan. Bake in preheated 350°F. oven for 25 to 28 minutes. (Wooden pick inserted in center will be moist.) Cool in pan on wire rack for 15 minutes. Remove side of pan; cool completely. Sprinkle with powdered sugar. Cut into 10 to 12 servings. Serve each with 3 to 4 tablespoons sauce.

FOR COFFEE CRÈME ANGLAISE SAUCE:
In small bowl, whisk egg yolks. In medium saucepan, combine sugar and instant coffee; stir in milk. Cook over medium heat, stirring constantly, until mixture comes to a simmer. Remove from heat. Gradually whisk ½ of hot milk mixture into yolks; return to saucepan. Continue cooking, stirring constantly for 3 to 4 minutes or until mixture is slightly thickened. Strain into small bowl; stir in vanilla. Cover with plastic wrap; chill.   *Makes 10 to 12 servings*

ALMOND FUDGE BANANA CAKE

  3 extra-ripe, medium DOLE® Bananas, peeled
1½ cups sugar
  ½ cup margarine, softened
  3 eggs
  3 tablespoons amaretto liqueur *or* ½ to 1 teaspoon almond extract
  1 teaspoon vanilla extract
1⅓ cups all-purpose flour
  ⅓ cup unsweetened cocoa powder
  1 teaspoon baking soda
  ½ teaspoon salt
  ½ cup DOLE® Chopped Almonds, toasted, ground
    Banana Chocolate Glaze (recipe follows)

• Mash bananas; set aside.

• Beat sugar and margarine until light and fluffy. Beat in eggs, liqueur and vanilla.

• Combine dry ingredients. Stir in almonds. Add to sugar mixture alternately with bananas. Beat well.

• Pour batter into greased 10-inch Bundt pan. Bake in preheated 350°F oven 45 to 50 minutes or until toothpick inserted in center comes out almost clean and cake pulls away from side of pan. Cool 10 minutes. Remove cake from pan to wire rack to cool completely. Drizzle glaze over top and down side of cake.
Makes 16 to 20 servings

BANANA CHOCOLATE GLAZE
  1 extra-ripe, small DOLE® Banana, puréed
  1 square (1 ounce) semisweet chocolate, melted

With wire whisk, beat puréed banana into melted chocolate.

Almond Fudge Banana Cake

CHERRY PECAN POUND CAKE

  1 cup butter or margarine, softened
  1 cup sugar
  4 eggs
  1 teaspoon vanilla
  ½ teaspoon almond extract
  ½ teaspoon salt
  ⅛ teaspoon ground nutmeg or mace
1½ cups all-purpose flour
  1 jar (6 ounces) maraschino cherries, drained and chopped
  ¼ cup chopped pecans

In large bowl, beat butter and sugar until light and fluffy. Add eggs, vanilla, almond extract, salt and ground nutmeg; beat until thoroughly blended. Stir in flour, ½ cup at a time, mixing just until blended. Stir in cherries and pecans. Spread batter evenly in greased and floured 9×5×3-inch loaf pan. Bake in preheated 325°F oven 60 to 70 minutes or until toothpick inserted near center comes out clean. Let cool in pan on wire rack 10 minutes. Loosen edges; remove from pan. Cool completely on wire rack.
Makes 1 loaf

*Favorite recipe from **American Egg Board***

CHOCOLATE CREAM–FILLED CAKE ROLL

¾ cup sifted cake flour
¼ cup unsweetened cocoa
½ teaspoon baking powder
¼ teaspoon salt
4 eggs
¾ cup granulated sugar
1 tablespoon water
1 teaspoon vanilla extract
Powdered sugar
Cream Filling (recipe follows)
Chocolate Stars (recipe follows)
Sweetened whipped cream
Fresh raspberries and mint leaves, for garnish (optional)

Preheat oven to 375°F. Grease bottom of 15½×10½×1-inch jelly-roll pan. Line with waxed paper. Grease paper and sides of pan; dust with flour. Combine flour, cocoa, baking powder and salt in small bowl; set aside. Beat eggs in medium bowl with electric mixer at high speed about 5 minutes or until thick and lemon colored. Add granulated sugar, a little at a time, beating well at medium speed; beat until thick and fluffy. Stir in water and vanilla. Fold in flour mixture at low speed until smooth. Spread evenly in prepared pan.

Bake 12 to 15 minutes or until wooden toothpick inserted in center comes out clean. Meanwhile, sprinkle towel with powdered sugar. Loosen cake edges and turn out onto prepared towel. Carefully peel off waxed paper. Roll up cake with towel inside, starting with narrow end. Cool, seam side down, 20 minutes on wire rack.

Meanwhile, prepare Cream Filling and Chocolate Stars. Unroll cake and spread with Cream Filling. Roll up again, without towel. Cover and refrigerate at least 1 hour before serving. Dust with additional powdered sugar before serving. Place star tip in pastry bag; add sweetened whipped cream. Pipe rosettes on top of cake. Place points of Chocolate Stars in rosettes. Garnish with raspberries and mint, if desired. Store tightly covered in refrigerator.

Makes 8 to 10 servings

CREAM FILLING

1 teaspoon unflavored gelatin
¼ cup cold water
1 cup whipping cream
2 tablespoons powdered sugar
1 tablespoon orange-flavored liqueur

Sprinkle gelatin over cold water in small saucepan; let stand 1 minute to soften. Heat over low heat until dissolved, stirring constantly. Cool to room temperature. Beat cream, powdered sugar and liqueur in small chilled bowl with electric mixer at high speed until stiff peaks form. Beat in gelatin mixture at low speed. Cover and refrigerate 5 to 10 minutes.

CHOCOLATE STARS: Melt 2 squares (1 ounce each) semisweet chocolate in heavy small saucepan over low heat, stirring frequently. Pour onto waxed-paper-lined cookie sheet. Spread to ⅛-inch thickness with small metal spatula. Refrigerate about 15 minutes or until firm. Cut out stars with cookie cutter. Carefully lift stars from waxed paper using metal spatula or knife. Refrigerate until ready to use.

Chocolate Cream-Filled Cake Roll

RASPBERRY POUND CAKE

- **1 package DUNCAN HINES® Moist Deluxe Raspberry Cake Mix**
- **1 package (4-serving size) vanilla instant pudding and pie filling mix**
- **4 eggs**
- **1 cup water**
- **⅓ cup CRISCO® Oil or CRISCO® PURITAN® Canola Oil**
- **1 cup miniature semi-sweet chocolate chips**
- **⅔ cup DUNCAN HINES® Creamy Homestyle Chocolate Buttercream Frosting**

1. Preheat oven to 350°F. Grease and flour 10-inch Bundt pan.

2. For cake, combine cake mix, pudding mix, eggs, water and oil in large bowl. Beat at low speed with electric mixer until moistened. Beat at medium speed for 2 minutes. Stir in chocolate chips. Pour into pan. Bake at 350°F for 55 to 60 minutes or until toothpick inserted in center comes out clean. Cool in pan 25 minutes. Invert onto cooling rack. Cool completely.

3. For glaze, place frosting in 1-cup glass measuring cup. Microwave at HIGH (100% power) for 10 to 15 seconds. Stir until smooth. Drizzle over top of cooled cake.

Makes 12 to 16 servings

TIP: Store leftover chocolate buttercream frosting covered in refrigerator. Spread frosting between graham crackers for a quick snack.

CHERRY–PINEAPPLE UPSIDE–DOWN CAKE

- **1¼ cups sifted cake flour**
- **2 teaspoons baking powder**
- **¼ teaspoon salt**
- **½ cup (1 stick) butter or margarine, softened, divided**
- **¾ cup granulated sugar**
- **1 egg**
- **½ cup milk**
- **1 teaspoon vanilla**
- **¾ cup packed brown sugar**
- **1 (20-ounce) can crushed pineapple, well drained**
- **1 (16-ounce) can pitted tart cherries, drained**
- **Fresh mint leaves for garnish**

Preheat oven to 350°F. Combine flour, baking powder and salt in medium bowl; set aside. Beat together ¼ cup butter and granulated sugar in large bowl until light and fluffy. Blend in egg. Add flour mixture alternately with milk, beating well after each addition. Blend in vanilla.

Melt remaining ¼ cup butter in 9-inch ovenproof skillet or 9-inch cake pan. Stir in brown sugar. If necessary, tilt skillet to cover bottom of skillet evenly with brown sugar mixture. Top brown sugar mixture with pineapple. Reserve a few cherries for garnish, if desired. Spoon remaining cherries over pineapple; top with batter. Bake 50 minutes or until wooden toothpick inserted in center comes out clean. Cool cake in pan on wire rack 10 minutes. Loosen edges and turn upside down onto cake plate. Garnish, if desired.

Makes 1 (9-inch) cake

*Favorite recipe from **Illinois State Fair***

Cherry-Pineapple Upside-Down Cake

PUMPKIN JINGLE BARS

¾ cup MIRACLE WHIP® Salad Dressing
1 two-layer spice cake mix
1 (16-ounce) can pumpkin
3 eggs
  Sifted confectioners' sugar
  Vanilla frosting
  Red and green gum drops, sliced

Mix first 4 ingredients in large bowl at medium speed of electric mixer until well blended. Pour into greased 15½×10½×1-inch jelly roll pan. Bake at 350°F, 18 to 20 minutes or until edges pull away from sides of pan. Cool. Sprinkle with sugar. Cut into bars. Decorate with frosting and gum drops.   *Makes about 3 dozen bars*

PREP TIME: 5 minutes
COOK TIME: 20 minutes

JEWELLED FRUITCAKE

2½ cups unsifted flour
1 teaspoon baking soda
2 eggs
1 (27-ounce) jar NONE SUCH® Ready-
  To-Use Mincemeat (Regular or
  Brandy & Rum)
1 (14-ounce) can EAGLE® Brand
  Sweetened Condensed Milk (NOT
  evaporated milk)
1 (8-ounce) container green candied
  cherries, halved (1 cup)
1 (8-ounce) container red candied
  cherries, halved (1 cup)
1 (6-ounce) package dried apricots,
  chopped (1 cup)
1 (6-ounce) container candied pineapple,
  chopped (1 cup)
1½ cups chopped pecans

Pumpkin Jingle Bars

Preheat oven to 300°F. Grease and flour 10-inch tube or fluted tube pan. Combine flour and baking soda. In large bowl, beat eggs. Stir in remaining ingredients; blend in flour mixture. Pour batter into prepared pan. Bake 1 hour and 30 to 40 minutes or until wooden pick inserted near center comes out clean. Cool 10 minutes; remove from pan. Cool completely.

Makes 1 (10-inch) cake

TIP: If desired, glaze with heated corn syrup; garnish with candied fruit and dried apricots.

CHERRY FRUIT CAKE

¾ cup flour
½ teaspoon baking powder
½ teaspoon salt
1 (16-ounce) jar whole maraschino cherries, well drained
8 ounces diced pitted dates
8 ounces candied pineapple chunks
9 ounces pecan halves
3 eggs
1½ ounces rum
¼ cup light corn syrup

Combine flour, baking powder and salt in large mixing bowl; mix well. Add cherries, dates, pineapple and pecans. Toss together until fruits and nuts are coated with flour mixture. Beat eggs and rum until blended. Pour over coated fruit and mix thoroughly. Grease 9×5×3-inch loaf pan; line with parchment paper and grease again. Turn cake mixture into pan, pressing with spatula to pack tightly. Bake at 300°F 1 hour 45 minutes or until wooden pick inserted near center comes out clean. Cool cake in pan 15 minutes. Remove cake from pan; remove paper. Brush with corn syrup while still warm. Cool completely before serving or storing.

Makes 1 cake

*Favorite recipe from **National Cherry Foundation***

GOLDEN APPLE MINCEMEAT CAKE

3 cups flour
4 teaspoons baking powder
1 teaspoon *each* ground allspice and cinnamon
½ teaspoon salt
1½ cups vegetable oil
1½ cups packed brown sugar
2 cups grated Golden Delicious apples
1 cup prepared mincemeat
½ cup chopped pecans
1½ teaspoons vanilla
3 eggs
1 to 2 tablespoons sifted powdered sugar
Hard Sauce (recipe follows, optional)

Preheat oven to 350°F. Combine flour, baking powder, allspice, cinnamon and salt in large bowl; set aside. In large bowl of electric mixer, combine oil and brown sugar; beat well. Add half the flour mixture; mix well. Blend in grated apples, mincemeat, pecans and vanilla. Add remaining flour mixture. Add eggs, 1 at a time; beat well after each addition. Turn into greased 10-inch Bundt pan. Bake 1 hour or until wooden toothpick inserted near center comes out clean. Cool in pan 15 minutes; turn out onto wire rack. When cool, sprinkle with powdered sugar. If desired, cake can be served slightly warm with Hard Sauce.

Makes 16 servings

HARD SAUCE: Beat ½ cup margarine and ⅛ teaspoon salt until light and fluffy. Gradually beat in 1 cup powdered sugar. Stir in 1 tablespoon brandy. Refrigerate 1 hour.

*Favorite recipe from **Washington Apple Commission***

Colonial Apple Cake

COLONIAL APPLE CAKE

2¾ cups unsifted all-purpose flour
  1 teaspoon baking powder
  1 teaspoon ground cinnamon
  ¾ teaspoon salt
  ½ teaspoon baking soda
1¾ cups granulated sugar
1¼ cups CRISCO® Oil
  2 eggs
  ¼ cup milk
  1 teaspoon vanilla
  2 cups chopped peeled apples
  ½ cup chopped dates
  1 teaspoon grated lemon peel
  1 to 2 tablespoons confectioners sugar

Preheat oven to 350°F. Grease and flour 12-cup fluted ring pan. Set aside.

Mix flour, baking powder, cinnamon, salt and baking soda in medium mixing bowl. Set aside. Combine granulated sugar, Crisco® oil, eggs, milk and vanilla in large mixing bowl. Beat with electric mixer at medium speed until blended, scraping bowl constantly. Add dry ingredients. Beat at medium speed 2 minutes longer, scraping bowl frequently. Stir in apples, dates and lemon peel. Pour into prepared pan.

Bake at 350°F, 1 hour to 1 hour 15 minutes or until wooden pick inserted in center comes out clean. Let stand 10 minutes. Invert onto serving plate. Cool slightly. Sift confectioners sugar over cake. Serve warm. Top with whipped cream, if desired. *Makes 1 ring cake*

GLAZED APPLESAUCE SPICE CAKE

¾ cup butter or margarine, softened
1 cup packed light brown sugar
3 eggs
1½ teaspoons vanilla
2¼ cups all-purpose flour
2 teaspoons baking soda
2 teaspoons ground cinnamon
¾ teaspoon ground nutmeg
½ teaspoon ground ginger
¼ teaspoon salt
1½ cups unsweetened applesauce
½ cup milk
⅔ cup chopped walnuts
⅔ cup butterscotch chips
Apple Glaze (recipe follows)

Preheat oven to 350°F. Grease and lightly flour 12-cup Bundt pan or 10-inch tube pan. Beat butter in large bowl with electric mixer at medium speed until creamy. Beat in brown sugar until light and fluffy. Beat in eggs and vanilla until well blended. In medium bowl, combine flour, baking soda, cinnamon, nutmeg, ginger and salt. Add flour mixture to butter mixture at low speed, alternately with applesauce and milk, beginning and ending with flour mixture. Beat well after each addition. Stir in walnuts and butterscotch chips. Spoon into prepared pan.

Bake 45 to 50 minutes until wooden toothpick inserted in center comes out clean. Cool in pan 15 minutes. Remove from pan to wire rack; cool completely. Spoon Apple Glaze over top of cake. Store tightly covered at room temperature.   *Makes 1 (10-inch) round cake*

APPLE GLAZE: Place 1 cup sifted powdered sugar in small bowl. Whisk in 2 to 3 tablespoons apple juice concentrate to form stiff glaze.

HOLIDAY FRUITCAKE

1 cup chopped mixed candied fruit
⅔ cup pitted dates, chopped
½ cup chopped walnuts
¼ cup brandy or orange juice
1 package (6-serving size) JELL-O®
   Vanilla Flavor Instant Pudding & Pie
   Filling
1 package (2-layer size) yellow cake mix
1 cup BREYER'S® or KNUDSEN® Sour
   Cream
⅓ cup vegetable oil
4 eggs
1 tablespoon grated orange peel
⅔ cup milk
   Marzipan Fruits (page 522), optional

Heat oven to 350°F.

Mix fruit, dates, walnuts and brandy in medium bowl. Reserve ⅓ cup pudding mix. Beat cake mix, remaining pudding mix, sour cream, oil, eggs and orange peel in large bowl with electric mixer on low speed just to moisten, scraping sides of bowl often. Beat on medium speed 4 minutes. Stir in fruit mixture. Pour batter into greased and floured 10-inch fluted tube pan.

Bake 45 minutes or until toothpick inserted in center comes out clean. Cool in pan 15 minutes. Remove from pan; cool on wire rack.

Beat reserved ⅓ cup pudding mix and milk in small bowl until smooth. Spoon over top of cake to glaze. Garnish with Marzipan Fruits, if desired.   *Makes 12 servings*

SOUR CREAM POUND CAKE

1 orange
1 cup butter, softened
2¾ cups sugar
1 tablespoon vanilla
6 eggs
3 cups all-purpose flour
½ teaspoon salt
¼ teaspoon baking soda
1 cup sour cream
Citrus Topping (page 349)

Preheat oven to 325°F. Grease 10-inch tube pan. Finely grate colored portion of orange peel. Measure 2 teaspoons orange peel; set aside. Beat butter in large bowl with electric mixer at medium speed until creamy, scraping down side of bowl once. Gradually add sugar, beating until light and fluffy. Beat in vanilla and orange peel. Add eggs, 1 at a time, beating 1 minute after each addition. Combine flour, salt and baking soda in small bowl. Add to butter mixture alternately with sour cream, beginning and ending with flour mixture. Beat well after each addition. Pour into prepared pan. Bake 1 hour and 15 minutes or until cake tester or wooden skewer inserted in center comes out clean.

Meanwhile, prepare Citrus Topping. Spoon over hot cake; cool in pan 15 minutes. Remove from pan to wire rack; cool completely.

Makes 10 to 12 servings

Sour Cream Pound Cake

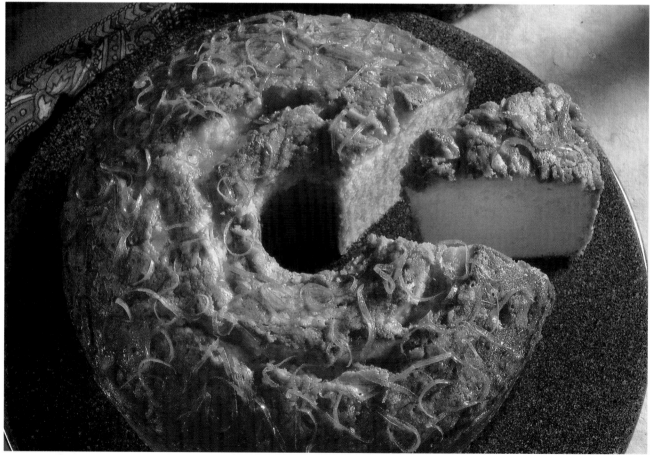

CITRUS TOPPING

    2 oranges
    2 teaspoons salt
    Water
    ½ cup sugar, divided
    ⅓ cup lemon juice
    1 teaspoon vanilla

With citrus zester or vegetable peeler, remove colored peel, not white pith, from oranges. Measure ⅓ cup orange peel. Cut oranges in half. Squeeze juice from oranges into measuring cup or small bowl. Measure ⅓ cup orange juice. Combine orange peel and salt in medium saucepan. Add enough water to cover. Bring to a boil over high heat. Boil 2 minutes. Drain in fine-meshed sieve. Return orange peel to saucepan. Add orange juice and ¼ cup sugar to saucepan. Bring to a boil over high heat. Reduce heat; simmer 10 minutes. Remove from heat. Add remaining ¼ cup sugar, lemon juice and vanilla; stir until smooth.

HOLIDAY NO–FAT FRUIT CAKE

    2 cups dark seedless raisins
    1 cup golden seedless raisins
    1 cup whole red candied cherries
    ¼ cup candied pineapple chunks
    ¼ cup mixed candied fruit
    ¼ cup all-purpose flour
    1 cup MOTT'S® Natural Apple Sauce
1¼ cups packed light brown sugar
    3 tablespoons honey
    8 egg whites
    1 teaspoon vanilla extract
    1 tablespoon freshly grated orange peel
    1 tablespoon freshly grated lemon peel
    2 cups all-purpose flour
    1 teaspoon baking powder
    ½ teaspoon ground nutmeg
    ½ teaspoon ground coriander
    ½ teaspoon ground cardamom
    ½ cup MOTT'S® Apple Juice

1. Preheat oven to 300°F. Spray 9-inch springform pan with cooking spray. Line bottom and side of pan with waxed paper, extending paper at least 1 inch above rim of pan. Spray paper with cooking spray.

2. In medium bowl, combine raisins, cherries, pineapple, candied fruit and ¼ cup flour. Mix well; set aside. In large bowl, combine Mott's® Apple Sauce, brown sugar, honey, egg whites, vanilla and citrus peels; beat thoroughly. In separate large bowl, combine 2 cups flour, baking powder and spices.

3. Add flour mixture to apple sauce mixture, alternating with Mott's® Apple Juice, beating just until blended. Fold in reserved fruit mixture.

4. Spoon into prepared pan; bake 2 hours or until wooden toothpick inserted in center comes out clean and cake is firm to the touch. Remove from oven; place on wire rack to cool completely. Remove cake from pan; peel off paper. *Makes 20 servings*

NOTE: Cake may be wrapped tightly in foil and kept in refrigerator for up to 2 weeks or kept in freezer for up to 2 months.

SPICY GINGERBREAD WITH CINNAMON PEAR SAUCE

      2 cups all-purpose flour
      ½ cup packed light brown sugar
      1 teaspoon baking soda
      1 teaspoon ground ginger
      1 teaspoon ground cinnamon
      ¼ teaspoon ground cloves
      ¼ teaspoon salt
      1 cup light molasses
      ¾ cup buttermilk
      ½ cup butter or margarine, softened
          Cinnamon Pear Sauce (recipe follows)

Preheat oven to 325°F. Grease and lightly flour 9-inch square baking pan.

Combine all ingredients except Cinnamon Pear Sauce in large bowl. Beat with electric mixer at low speed until well blended, scraping side of bowl with rubber spatula frequently. Beat at high speed 2 minutes more. Pour into prepared pan.

Bake 50 to 55 minutes or until wooden toothpick inserted in center comes out clean. Cool in pan on wire rack about 30 minutes. Cut into squares; serve warm with Cinnamon Pear Sauce.
Makes 9 servings

CINNAMON PEAR SAUCE

      2 cans (16 ounces each) pear halves in
          syrup, undrained
      2 tablespoons granulated sugar
      1 teaspoon fresh lemon juice
      ½ teaspoon ground cinnamon

Drain pear halves, reserving ¼ cup syrup. Place pears, reserved syrup, granulated sugar, lemon juice and cinnamon in work bowl of food processor or blender; cover. Process until smooth. Just before serving, place pear sauce in medium saucepan; heat until warm.
Makes 2 cups sauce

LEMON POPPY SEED CAKE

      6 tablespoons margarine, softened
      ½ cup firmly packed light brown sugar
      ½ cup plain low fat yogurt
      1 whole egg
      2 egg whites
      3 teaspoons fresh lemon juice
      1¾ cups all-purpose flour
      1 teaspoon baking powder
      ½ teaspoon baking soda
      ¼ teaspoon salt
      ⅓ cup skim milk
      2 tablespoons poppy seed
      1 tablespoon grated lemon peel
LEMON GLAZE
      1 cup powdered sugar
      2 tablespoons plus 1½ teaspoons lemon
          juice
      ½ teaspoon poppy seed

Preheat oven to 350°F. Grease and flour 6-cup Bundt pan. Beat margarine in large bowl with electric mixer until fluffy. Beat in brown sugar, yogurt, whole egg, egg whites and 3 teaspoons lemon juice. Set aside. Combine flour, baking powder, baking soda and salt in medium bowl. Add flour mixture to margarine mixture alternately with milk, beginning and ending with flour mixture. Mix in 2 tablespoons poppy seed and lemon peel. Pour batter into prepared pan.

Bake about 40 minutes or until cake is golden brown and wooden toothpick inserted in center comes out clean. Cool in pan on wire rack 10 minutes. Remove from pan to wire rack; cool completely.

For Lemon Glaze, mix powdered sugar with 2 tablespoons plus 1½ teaspoons lemon juice until of desired consistency. Spoon glaze over cake and sprinkle with ½ teaspoon poppy seed.
Makes 12 servings

Lemon Poppy Seed Cake

PECAN SPICE CAKE WITH BROWNED BUTTER FROSTING

    1 package (18.25 ounces) moist yellow
      cake mix
    ¾ cup sour cream
    ¾ cup water
    3 eggs
    1 tablespoon grated lemon peel
    1½ teaspoons ground cinnamon
    ½ teaspoon ground nutmeg
    ¼ teaspoon ground allspice
    1 cup chopped pecans
      Browned Butter Frosting (recipe
      follows)
      Additional chopped pecans (optional)

Preheat oven to 350°F. Grease two 9-inch square baking pans. Combine cake mix, sour cream, water, eggs, lemon peel and spices in large bowl with electric mixer at low speed until ingredients are moistened. Beat at high speed 2 minutes, scraping side of bowl frequently. Stir in 1 cup pecans. Divide batter evenly between prepared pans.

Bake 25 to 30 minutes or until wooden toothpick inserted in centers comes out clean. Cool in pans 10 minutes. Remove from pans to wire racks; cool completely. Place one layer on serving plate. Spread with ⅓ of frosting. Top with second layer. Frost sides and top of cake with remaining frosting. Garnish with additional pecans, if desired. Store tightly covered at room temperature.   *Makes 12 to 16 servings*

BROWNED BUTTER FROSTING
    ¾ cup butter
    5½ cups sifted powdered sugar
    1½ teaspoons vanilla
      Dash salt
    8 to 9 tablespoons light cream or
      half-and-half

Heat butter in heavy 1-quart saucepan over medium heat until butter is melted and light amber in color, stirring frequently. Cool butter slightly. Combine browned butter, powdered sugar, vanilla, salt and 8 tablespoons cream in large bowl. Beat with electric mixer at medium speed until smooth and of spreading consistency. Stir in additional 1 tablespoon cream if frosting is too stiff.

GINGERBREAD UPSIDE–DOWN CAKE

    1 can (20 ounces) DOLE® Pineapple
      Slices
    ½ cup margarine, softened, divided
    1 cup packed brown sugar, divided
    10 maraschino cherries
    1 egg
    ½ cup dark molasses
    1½ cups all-purpose flour
    1 teaspoon baking soda
    1 teaspoon ground ginger
    ½ teaspoon ground cinnamon
    ½ teaspoon salt

• Preheat oven to 350°F. Drain pineapple; reserve ½ cup syrup. In 10-inch cast iron skillet, melt ¼ cup margarine. Remove from heat. Add ½ cup brown sugar and stir until blended. Arrange pineapple slices in skillet. Place 1 cherry in center of each slice.

• In large mixer bowl, beat remaining ¼ cup margarine and ½ cup brown sugar until light and fluffy. Beat in egg and molasses. In small bowl, combine flour, baking soda, ginger, cinnamon and salt.

• In small saucepan, bring reserved pineapple syrup to a boil. Add dry ingredients to creamed mixture alternately with hot syrup. Spread evenly over pineapple in skillet. Bake 30 to 40 minutes or until wooden pick inserted in center comes out clean. Let stand in skillet on wire rack 5 minutes. Invert onto serving plate.
    Makes 8 to 10 servings

ORANGE CARROT CAKE

1 cup margarine or butter, softened
1 cup GRANDMA'S® MOLASSES
   Unsulphured
4 eggs
½ cup orange juice
1 cup all-purpose flour
1 cup whole wheat flour
2 teaspoons baking soda
1 teaspoon ground cinnamon
½ teaspoon salt
2 cups shredded carrots
½ cup chopped walnuts

FROSTING

1 package (3 ounces) cream cheese,
   softened
2 tablespoons margarine or butter,
   softened
1½ cups powdered sugar
1 teaspoon grated orange peel

Heat oven to 350°F. Grease two 8- or 9-inch round cake pans. In large bowl, combine margarine, molasses, eggs and orange juice; mix well. Stir in flours, baking soda, cinnamon and salt; mix well. Stir in carrots and walnuts. Pour into prepared pans. Bake at 350°F for 30 to 35 minutes or until toothpick inserted in centers comes out clean. Cool 15 minutes; remove from pans. Cool completely.

In small bowl, combine all frosting ingredients; beat until smooth. Place one layer on serving plate; spread top with frosting. Top with second layer; spread top with frosting. If desired, garnish with additional orange peel and walnuts. *Makes 12 servings*

Orange Carrot Cake

PUMPKIN TART WITH MAPLE CRÈME

1¼ cups all-purpose flour
1 tablespoon granulated sugar
¼ teaspoon salt
⅓ cup cold butter or margarine
3 to 4 tablespoons cold water
1 can (15 ounces) solid-pack pumpkin
    (not pumpkin pie filling)
½ cup maple syrup
⅓ cup packed light brown sugar
¼ cup half-and-half or cream
2 large eggs
1 teaspoon vanilla extract
1 teaspoon ground cinnamon
½ teaspoon ground ginger
⅛ teaspoon ground nutmeg
    Maple Crème (recipe follows)

For pastry, combine flour, granulated sugar and salt in small bowl. Cut in butter with pastry blender or two knives until mixture resembles coarse crumbs. Stir in water, 1 tablespoon at a time, with fork until dough forms a ball. Wrap dough in plastic wrap; refrigerate 30 minutes.

Roll out dough on lightly floured surface with a lightly floured rolling pin into 12-inch circle. Line 10-inch tart pan with removable bottom with dough; trim excess from edge.

Preheat oven to 400°F. For filling, combine pumpkin, maple syrup, brown sugar, half-and-half, eggs, vanilla, cinnamon, ginger and nutmeg in large bowl; stir until well blended. Pour into tart shell.

Bake 20 minutes. Reduce oven temperature to 350°F. Continue baking 30 to 35 minutes or until filling is set. Cool on wire rack. Prepare Maple Crème; dollop on each piece just before serving.   *Makes 8 servings*

Maple Crème: Beat ½ cup whipping cream in large bowl with electric mixer at high speed until soft peaks form. Beat in 4½ teaspoons maple syrup on low speed, then beat in ¼ cup crème fraîche or sour cream. Cover with plastic wrap. Refrigerate until chilled.

DATE–NUT PUMPKIN PIE

CRUST
    1 (9-inch) Classic Crisco® Single Crust
        (page 355)
DATE–NUT LAYER
    1 package (8 ounces) pitted whole dates,
        chopped
    ¾ cup water
    ⅓ cup firmly packed brown sugar
    ¼ cup butter or margarine
    ½ cup chopped walnuts
    ½ teaspoon cinnamon
FILLING
    2 eggs
    1½ cups mashed cooked pumpkin or
        canned solid-pack pumpkin (not
        pumpkin pie filling)
    ½ cup granulated sugar
    ½ cup firmly packed brown sugar
    1 cup evaporated milk
    ½ teaspoon cinnamon
    ½ teaspoon ginger
    ½ teaspoon nutmeg
    ¼ teaspoon salt
    ⅛ teaspoon cloves
GARNISH
    Sweetened whipped cream

1. For crust, prepare Classic Crisco® Single Crust. Do not bake. Reserve dough scraps for cutouts, if desired.✻ Heat oven to 450°F.

2. For date-nut layer, combine dates and water in medium saucepan. Cook on medium heat until mixture comes to a boil and dates have softened. Add ⅓ cup brown sugar and butter. Stir to blend. Remove from heat. Stir in nuts and cinnamon. Cool while preparing filling.

Date-Nut Pumpkin Pie

3. For filling, beat eggs lightly in medium bowl. Add pumpkin, granulated sugar, ½ cup brown sugar, evaporated milk, cinnamon, ginger, nutmeg, salt and cloves. Stir to blend.

4. Spoon date-nut mixture into unbaked pie crust. Pour in filling. Bake at 450°F for 10 minutes. *Reduce oven temperature to 350°F.* Bake 35 minutes or until knife inserted in center comes out clean. Do not overbake. Cool to room temperature before serving.

5. For garnish, spoon whipped cream around outer edge of pie just before serving. Refrigerate leftover pie.   *Makes 1 (9-inch) pie*

*Flute edge or cut small leaves and pumpkins from pastry scraps and press around edge of unbaked pie crust.

CLASSIC CRISCO® SINGLE CRUST
   1⅓ cups all-purpose flour
   ½ teaspoon salt
   ½ CRISCO® Stick *or* ½ cup CRISCO all-vegetable shortening
   3 tablespoons cold water

Spoon flour into measuring cups and level. Combine flour and salt in medium bowl. Cut in shortening using pastry blender (or 2 knives) until all flour is blended to form pea-size chunks. Sprinkle with water, 1 tablespoon at a time. Toss lightly with fork until dough forms a ball. Press dough between hands to form a 5- to 6-inch "pancake." Flour rolling surface and rolling pin lightly. Roll dough into circle. Trim 1 inch larger than upside-down pie plate. Loosen dough carefully. Fold dough into quarters. Unfold and press into pie plate. Fold edge under. Flute.   *Makes 8- to 9-inch single crust*

CLASSIC PUMPKIN PIE WITH CANDIED PECAN TOPPING

CRUST
> 1 (9-inch) Classic Crisco® Single Crust
> (page 355)

FILLING
> 1 can (16 ounces) solid-pack pumpkin
> (not pumpkin pie filling)
> 1 can (12 ounces or 1½ cups)
> evaporated milk
> 2 eggs, lightly beaten
> ½ cup granulated sugar
> ¼ cup firmly packed light brown sugar
> 1 teaspoon cinnamon
> ½ teaspoon salt
> ½ teaspoon ginger
> ¼ teaspoon nutmeg
> ⅛ teaspoon cloves

TOPPING
> ¼ cup granulated sugar
> ¼ cup water
> 2 tablespoons butter or margarine
> 1 cup pecan pieces

1. For crust, prepare according to instructions on page 355. Roll and press crust into 9-inch glass pie plate. Do not bake. Heat oven to 350°F.

2. For filling, combine pumpkin, evaporated milk, eggs, granulated sugar, brown sugar, cinnamon, salt, ginger, nutmeg and cloves in large bowl. Mix well. Pour into unbaked pie crust.

3. Bake at 350°F for 1 hour 10 minutes or until knife inserted in center comes out clean. *Do not overbake.* Cool completely.

4. Grease baking sheet lightly with shortening.

5. For topping, combine granulated sugar and water in small saucepan. Cook and stir on medium heat until sugar dissolves. Increase heat. Bring to a boil. Boil 7 to 8 minutes or until mixture becomes light golden brown, stirring frequently. Stir in butter and nuts. Stir briskly. Spread quickly in thin layer on baking sheet. Cool completely. Break into pieces. Sprinkle around edge of pie. (You might not use all of topping. Cover and store any extra for later use.) Refrigerate leftover pie.

Makes 1 (9-inch) pie (8 servings)

PLUM PUDDING PIE

> ⅓ cup plus 2 tablespoons KAHLÚA®
> ½ cup golden raisins
> ½ cup chopped pitted dates
> ⅓ cup chopped candied cherries
> ½ cup chopped walnuts
> ⅓ cup dark corn syrup
> ½ teaspoon pumpkin pie spice
> ¼ cup butter or margarine, softened
> ¼ cup packed brown sugar
> 2 tablespoons all-purpose flour
> ¼ teaspoon salt
> 2 eggs, slightly beaten
> 1 (9-inch) unbaked pie shell
> 1 cup whipping cream
> Maraschino cherries (optional)

In medium bowl, combine ⅓ cup Kahlúa®, raisins, dates and cherries; mix well. Cover; let stand 1 to 4 hours. Stir in walnuts, corn syrup and spice. In large bowl, cream butter, sugar, flour and salt. Stir in eggs. Add fruit mixture; blend well. Pour into unbaked pie shell. Bake in preheated 350°F oven 35 minutes or until filling is firm and crust is golden. Cool completely on wire rack. When ready to serve, in small bowl, beat whipping cream with remaining 2 tablespoons Kahlúa® just until soft peaks form. Spoon whipped cream into pastry bag fitted with large star tip and pipe decoratively on top. If desired, garnish with maraschino cherries.

Makes 8 servings

Classic Pumpkin Pie with Candied Pecan Topping

TRADITIONAL PUMPKIN PIE

1 (9-inch) unbaked pastry shell
1 (16-ounce) can solid-pack pumpkin
**   (2 cups)**
1 (14-ounce) can EAGLE® Brand
**   Sweetened Condensed Milk (NOT**
**   evaporated milk)**
2 eggs
1 teaspoon ground cinnamon
½ teaspoon ground ginger
½ teaspoon ground nutmeg
½ teaspoon salt

Place rack in lowest position in oven; preheat oven to 425°F. In large mixer bowl, combine all ingredients except pastry shell; mix well. Pour into pastry shell. Bake 15 minutes. *Reduce oven temperature to 350°F;* bake 35 to 40 minutes longer or until knife inserted near edge comes out clean. Cool. Garnish as desired. Refrigerate leftovers.   *Makes 1 (9-inch) pie*

OPTIONAL TOPPINGS

Sour Cream Topping: In medium bowl, combine 1½ cups Borden® or Meadow Gold® Sour Cream, 2 tablespoons sugar and 1 teaspoon vanilla extract. After reducing oven temperature to 350°F and baking pie for 30 minutes, spread topping evenly over pie; bake 10 minutes longer. Garnish as desired.

Traditional Pumpkin Pie

Streusel Topping: In medium bowl, combine ½ cup firmly packed light brown sugar and ½ cup unsifted flour; cut in ¼ cup cold margarine or butter until crumbly. Stir in ¼ cup chopped nuts. After reducing oven temperature to 350°F and baking pie for 30 minutes, spread topping evenly over pie; bake 10 minutes longer.

FESTIVE MINCEMEAT TARTLETS

Pastry for double pie crust
1½ cups prepared mincemeat
½ cup chopped, peeled tart apple
⅓ cup golden raisins
⅓ cup chopped walnuts
3 tablespoons brandy or frozen apple
**   juice concentrate, thawed**
1 tablespoon grated lemon peel

Preheat oven to 400°F. Divide pastry in half. Refrigerate one half. Roll remaining half on lightly floured surface to form 13-inch circle. Cut six 4-inch rounds. Fit each pastry round into 2¾-inch muffin cup. Prick inside of crust with fork; set aside. Repeat with remaining pastry.

Bake unfilled pastry crusts 8 minutes. Meanwhile, combine mincemeat, apple, raisins, walnuts, brandy and lemon peel in medium bowl until well blended. Remove crusts from oven; fill each with rounded tablespoonful of mincemeat mixture. Press lightly into crust with back of spoon.

Bake 18 to 20 minutes more or until crust edges are golden. Cool in pan 5 minutes. Carefully remove from pan to wire rack. Serve warm or cool completely.   *Makes 12 tartlets*

Apple Streusel Mince Pie

APPLE STREUSEL MINCE PIE

  3 all-purpose apples, pared and thinly sliced
  ½ cup plus 3 tablespoons unsifted flour
  2 tablespoons margarine or butter, melted
  1 (9-inch) unbaked pastry shell
  1 jar NONE SUCH® Ready-to-Use Mincemeat (Regular or Brandy & Rum)
  ¼ cup firmly packed light brown sugar
  1 teaspoon ground cinnamon
  ⅓ cup cold margarine or butter
  ¼ cup chopped nuts

In large bowl, toss apples with *3 tablespoons* flour and melted margarine; arrange in pastry shell. Top with mincemeat. In medium bowl, combine remaining *½ cup* flour, sugar and cinnamon; cut in cold margarine until crumbly. Add nuts; sprinkle over mincemeat. Bake in lower half of 425°F oven 10 minutes. *Reduce oven temperature to 375°F;* bake 25 minutes longer or until golden. Cool. Garnish as desired. *Makes 1 (9-inch) pie*

SWEET POTATO CUSTARD PIE

  Pecan Crust (recipe follows)
  3 eggs
  1 can (16 ounces) vacuum-packed sweet potatoes, drained, mashed
  ½ cup packed brown sugar
  1½ teaspoons ground cinnamon
  1 teaspoon ground allspice
  ½ teaspoon salt
  1 can (12 ounces) evaporated milk
  Whipped cream (optional)
  Pecan halves (optional)

Prepare Pecan Crust. In large bowl, beat eggs, sweet potatoes, sugar, spices and salt. In small saucepan, heat evaporated milk over medium heat until hot; gradually stir into sweet potato mixture. Pour into unbaked pie shell. Bake in lower third of preheated 400°F oven 40 to 45 minutes or until knife inserted near center comes out clean. Cool completely on wire rack. If desired, garnish with whipped cream and pecan halves. *Makes 1 (9-inch) pie*

PECAN CRUST
  1½ cups all-purpose flour
  ¼ cup ground pecans
  ½ teaspoon salt
  ½ cup shortening
  1 egg yolk
  4 to 5 tablespoons ice water
  2 teaspoons lemon juice

In large bowl, combine flour, ground pecans and salt. Cut in shortening until mixture resembles coarse crumbs. In small bowl, blend egg yolk, 4 tablespoons water and lemon juice. Add to flour mixture, mixing lightly with fork just until dough sticks together. Add more water, if necessary. Press into ball. Roll out on lightly floured surface into 10-inch circle. Carefully fit into 9-inch pie plate. Trim edge; flute as desired. Prick bottom and side of pastry with fork.

*Favorite recipe from **American Egg Board***

CLASSIC PECAN PIE

3 eggs
1 cup sugar
1 cup KARO® Light or Dark Corn Syrup
2 tablespoons MAZOLA® Margarine, melted
1 teaspoon vanilla
1½ cups pecan halves
  Easy-As-Pie Crust (recipe follows) *or* 1 (9-inch) frozen deep-dish pie crust*

Preheat oven to 350°F. In medium bowl beat eggs slightly. Add sugar, corn syrup, margarine and vanilla; stir until well blended. Stir in pecans. Pour into pie crust. Bake 50 to 55 minutes or until knife inserted halfway between center and edge comes out clean. Cool on wire rack.   *Makes 8 servings*

*To use prepared frozen pie crust, do not thaw crust. Preheat oven and a cookie sheet. Pour filling into frozen crust; bake pie as directed on cookie sheet.

PREP TIME: 10 minutes
BAKE TIME: 55 minutes, plus cooling

CALIFORNIA PECAN PIE: Stir ¼ cup sour cream into eggs until blended.

KENTUCKY BOURBON PECAN PIE: Add up to 2 tablespoons bourbon to filling.

CHOCOLATE PECAN PIE: Reduce sugar to ⅓ cup. Melt 4 squares (1 ounce each) semisweet chocolate with margarine.

EASY–AS–PIE CRUST
1¼ cups flour
⅛ teaspoon salt
½ cup MAZOLA® Margarine
2 tablespoons cold water

In medium bowl mix flour and salt. With pastry blender or 2 knives, cut in margarine until mixture resembles fine crumbs. Sprinkle water over flour mixture while tossing with fork to blend well. Press dough firmly into ball. On lightly floured surface roll out to 12-inch circle. Fit loosely into 9-inch pie plate. Trim and flute edge. Fill and bake according to recipe.
                    Makes 1 (9-inch) pie crust

PREP TIME: 15 minutes

ORANGE PECAN PIE

3 eggs
½ cup GRANDMA'S® MOLASSES Unsulphured
½ cup light corn syrup
¼ cup orange juice
1 teaspoon grated orange peel
1 teaspoon vanilla
1½ cups whole pecans
1 (9-inch) unbaked pie shell

Heat oven to 350°F. In large bowl, beat eggs. Add molasses, corn syrup, orange juice, orange peel and vanilla; beat until well blended. Stir in pecans. Pour into unbaked pie shell. Bake at 350°F. for 40 to 50 minutes or until filling is set. Cool. Serve with whipped cream, if desired.
                    Makes 8 servings

Classic Pecan Pie

CRANBERRY APPLE NUT PIE

    Rich Pie Pastry (recipe follows)
  1 cup sugar
  3 tablespoons all-purpose flour
  ¼ teaspoon salt
  4 cups sliced peeled tart apples (4 large)
  2 cups fresh cranberries
  ½ cup golden raisins
  ½ cup coarsely chopped pecans
  1 tablespoon grated lemon peel
  2 tablespoons butter or margarine
  1 egg, beaten

Preheat oven to 425°F. Divide pie pastry in half. Roll one half on lightly floured surface to form 13-inch circle. Fit into 9-inch pie plate; trim edges. Reroll scraps and cut into decorative shapes, such as holly leaves and berries, for garnish; set aside.

Combine sugar, flour and salt in large bowl. Stir in apples, cranberries, raisins, pecans and lemon peel; toss well. Spoon fruit mixture into unbaked pie crust. Dot with butter. Roll remaining half of pie pastry on lightly floured surface to form 11-inch circle. Place over filling. Trim and seal edges; flute. Cut 3 slits in center of top crust. Moisten pastry cutouts and decorate as desired. Lightly brush top crust with egg.

Bake 35 to 40 minutes or until apples are tender when pierced with a fork and pastry is golden brown. Cool in pan on wire rack. Serve warm or cool completely.

Makes 1 (9-inch) pie

RICH PIE PASTRY
  2 cups all-purpose flour
  ¼ teaspoon salt
  6 tablespoons butter
  6 tablespoons lard
  6 to 8 tablespoons cold water

Combine flour and salt in medium bowl. Cut in butter and lard with pastry blender or 2 knives until mixture resembles coarse crumbs. Sprinkle water, 1 tablespoon at a time, over flour mixture, mixing until flour is moistened. Shape dough into a ball. Roll, fill and bake as recipe directs.
    Makes pastry for 1 (9-inch) double pie crust

NOTE: For single crust, cut recipe in half.

NEW ENGLAND MAPLE APPLE PIE

  1 (9-inch) unbaked pastry shell
  2 pounds all-purpose apples, pared, cored and thinly sliced (about 6 cups)
  ½ cup plus 2 tablespoons unsifted flour
  ½ cup CARY'S®, MAPLE ORCHARDS® or MACDONALD'S™ Pure Maple Syrup
  2 tablespoons margarine or butter, melted
  ¼ cup firmly packed light brown sugar
  1 teaspoon ground cinnamon
  ⅓ cup cold margarine or butter
  ½ cup chopped nuts

Place rack in lowest position in oven; preheat oven to 400°F. In large bowl, combine apples and *2 tablespoons* flour. Combine syrup and melted margarine. Pour over apples; mix well. Turn into pastry shell. In medium bowl, combine remaining *½ cup* flour, sugar and cinnamon; cut in cold margarine until crumbly. Add nuts; sprinkle over apples. Bake 10 minutes. *Reduce oven temperature to 375°F; bake 35 minutes longer or until golden brown. Cool slightly. Serve warm.*

Makes 1 (9-inch) pie

Cranberry Apple Nut Pie

RICE PUDDING PEAR TART

½ (15-ounce) package refrigerated pie
    crust
2 cups dry red wine
1 teaspoon ground cinnamon
2 large pears, peeled, halved, and cored
2 cups cooked rice
2 cups half-and-half
½ cup sugar
2 tablespoons butter or margarine
¼ teaspoon salt
2 eggs, beaten
1 teaspoon vanilla extract
1 tablespoon sugar

Preheat oven to 450°F. Prepare pie crust according to package directions. Place in 10-inch tart pan. Bake 8 to 10 minutes or until lightly browned; set aside. *Reduce oven temperature to 350°F.*

Place wine and cinnamon in 10-inch skillet; bring to a boil. Add pears; reduce heat, cover and poach 10 minutes. Carefully turn pears in liquid; poach 5 to 10 minutes or until tender. Remove from wine; set aside.

Combine rice, half-and-half, ½ cup sugar, butter, and salt in 3-quart saucepan. Cook over medium heat 12 to 15 minutes or until slightly thickened. Gradually stir ¼ of hot rice pudding mixture into eggs; return mixture to saucepan, stirring constantly. Continue to cook 1 to 2 minutes. Stir in vanilla. Pour rice pudding mixture into prepared crust. Place pears, cut sides down, on cutting surface. Cut thin lengthwise slices into each pear one third of the way down from stem end. Fan pears over pudding mixture.

Bake 30 minutes or until pudding is set. Remove from oven; sprinkle with 1 tablespoon sugar. Place tart in oven about 4 to 5 inches from heat; broil 1 to 2 minutes or until top is browned. Cool before serving. Garnish as desired. Tart can be made ahead, if desired.

Makes 1 (10-inch) tart

*Favorite recipe from **USA Rice Council***

Rice Pudding Pear Tart

BRANDIED FRUIT PIE

1 KEEBLER® Ready-Crust® Graham Cracker Pie Crust
2 packages (8 ounces each) mixed, pitted dried fruit
¾ cup plus 1 tablespoon water
¼ cup plus 1 tablespoon brandy or cognac
5 thin lemon slices
¾ cup packed brown sugar
1 teaspoon ground cinnamon
¼ teaspoon ground nutmeg
¼ teaspoon ground cloves
¼ teaspoon salt
½ cup graham cracker crumbs
¼ cup butter or margarine, melted
    Hard sauce or whipped cream (optional)
    Lemon slices for garnish

In medium saucepan, combine dried fruit, ¾ cup of the water, ¼ cup of the brandy and the 5 lemon slices. Simmer over low heat 10 minutes or until liquid is absorbed. Remove and discard lemon slices. Stir in sugar, spices, salt, remaining 1 tablespoon water and remaining 1 tablespoon brandy; pour into pie crust. Sprinkle graham cracker crumbs evenly over top of pie. Drizzle melted butter over crumbs. Bake in preheated 350°F oven 30 minutes. Cool on wire rack. Serve warm or at room temperature. If desired, serve with hard sauce or whipped cream; garnish with lemon slices.

Makes 8 servings

Brandied Fruit Pie

PREMIER WHITE FRUIT TART

    Pastry for single-crust, 9-inch pie
⅓ cup granulated sugar
¼ cup all-purpose flour
3 egg yolks
1 cup milk
1 package (6 ounces) NESTLÉ® Premier
    White Baking Bars, chopped
1 teaspoon vanilla extract
¼ cup apricot jam, warmed
2 kiwifruit, peeled and sliced
1 cup raspberries
    Premier White Leaves (page 367),
    optional

LINE 9-inch tart pan with pastry; trim edges. Prick pastry with fork. Bake in preheated 425°F. oven for 10 to 12 minutes until crust is lightly browned. Cool to room temperature.

COMBINE sugar and flour in small saucepan; stir in egg yolks and milk. Cook over medium heat, stirring constantly, until mixture comes to a boil. Reduce heat. Simmer, stirring constantly, for 3 minutes until mixture is thickened and smooth. Remove from heat.

ADD baking bars and vanilla; stir until smooth. Press plastic wrap directly on surface of filling; chill completely.

REMOVE tart shell from pan. Brush jam over bottom; let stand 5 minutes. Spread with filling. Arrange fruit on top. Chill. Garnish with Premier White Leaves, if desired.

Makes 6 to 8 servings

Premier White Fruit Tart

PREMIER WHITE LEAVES: Wash and dry very well about 6 non-toxic leaves, such as lemon leaves, grape leaves, rose leaves, violet leaves or nasturtium leaves;* set aside.

Melt 4 ounces NESTLÉ® Premier White Baking Bars. Onto the back side of each leaf, spoon or brush melted Premier White mixture about 1⁄16 inch thick. If Premier White mixture runs over edge of leaf, wipe off edge of leaf with fingertip. Place coated leaves on plate or cookie sheet; refrigerate about 30 minutes or until firm. Gently peel leaf from firm Premier White mixture. Arrange white leaves on dessert, as desired.

Makes about 6 large leaves

*These non-toxic leaves are available in florist shops.

PEPPERMINT FUDGE PIE

   1 KEEBLER® Ready Crust® Chocolate Flavored Pie Crust
   1 packaged (6 ounces) semisweet chocolate chips
   2 cups miniature marshmallows
   1⁄4 cup milk or cream
   2 tablespoons chocolate-mint liqueur
   3 cups whipped cream, divided
   2 tablespoons crushed peppermint candies or candy canes

In microwave-safe bowl, combine chocolate chips, marshmallows and milk. Cook at MEDIUM (50% power) 2 to 3 minutes, stirring twice, until smooth. Stir in liqueur. Cool at room temperature. Fold in 1½ cups whipped cream. Spoon into pie shell. Fold crushed candies into remaining 1½ cups whipped cream. Spread over chocolate layer. Cover and freeze until firm, about 3 hours. Pie may be made and frozen several weeks ahead. Remove pie from freezer and slice. Let stand 3 to 5 minutes before serving. Store leftovers in freezer.

Makes 8 servings

CHOCOLATE TRUFFLE TART

CRUST
   2⁄3 cup all-purpose flour
   1⁄2 cup powdered sugar
   1⁄2 cup ground walnuts
   6 tablespoons butter or margarine, softened
   1⁄3 cup NESTLÉ® Toll House® Baking Cocoa
FILLING
   1¼ cups heavy whipping cream
   1⁄4 cup granulated sugar
   2 cups (12-ounce package) NESTLÉ® Toll House® Semi-Sweet Chocolate Morsels
   2 tablespoons seedless raspberry jam Sweetened whipped cream (optional) Fresh raspberries (optional)

FOR CRUST:
BEAT flour, powdered sugar, walnuts, butter and cocoa in large mixer bowl until a soft dough forms. Press dough onto bottom and side of ungreased 9- or 9½-inch fluted tart pan with removable bottom.

BAKE in preheated 350°F. oven for 12 to 14 minutes or until puffed. Cool completely on wire rack.

FOR FILLING:
HEAT cream and granulated sugar in medium saucepan just until boiling, stirring occasionally. Remove from heat. Stir in morsels and jam; let stand for 5 minutes. Whisk until chocolate mixture is smooth. Transfer to small mixer bowl. Cover; chill for 45 to 60 minutes or until mixture is cool and slightly thickened.

BEAT for 20 to 30 seconds, just until color lightens slightly. Spoon into crust. Chill until firm. Remove rim of pan; garnish with whipped cream and raspberries.   *Makes 1 (9-inch) tart*

NOTE: This tart may be made in 9-inch pie plate following above directions.

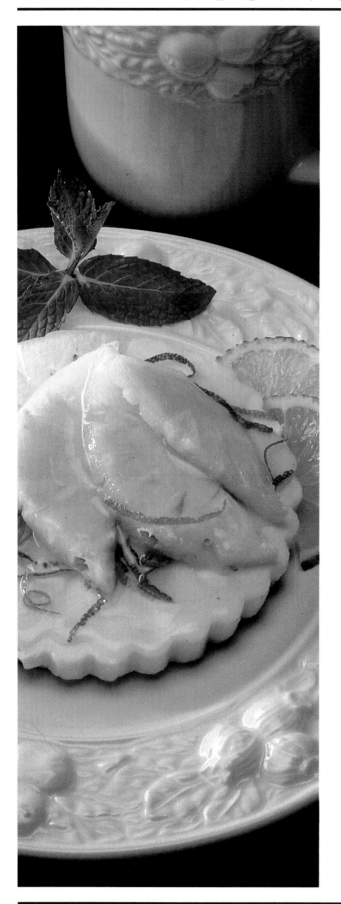

PINEAPPLE LIME TARTLETS

CRUST
    6 to 8 graham crackers
FILLING
    1 envelope unflavored gelatin
    ¼ cup lime juice
    1 carton (8 ounces) lowfat ricotta cheese
    1¼ cups nonfat plain yogurt, divided
    ½ cup sugar
    1 teaspoon coconut extract
    1 teaspoon grated lime peel
PINEAPPLE TOPPING
    1 medium DOLE® Fresh Pineapple
    ¾ cup water
    ¼ cup sugar
    1 tablespoon cornstarch
    1 teaspoon shredded lime peel

• Arrange crackers in 6 (4½-inch) tart pans or 1 (9-inch) tart pan with removable bottoms, breaking crackers to fit.

• Sprinkle gelatin over lime juice in small saucepan; let stand to soften. Stir over low heat until dissolved; cool. Combine ricotta cheese and ¼ cup yogurt in blender until smooth. Pour into bowl. Stir in remaining yogurt, ½ cup sugar, extract and 1 teaspoon grated lime peel. Stir in cooled gelatin. Pour over crackers; refrigerate.

• Twist crown from pineapple. Cut pineapple in half lengthwise. Refrigerate one half for another use. Cut fruit from shell of other half. Cut fruit crosswise into thin slices. Combine water, ¼ cup sugar and cornstarch in saucepan. Cook, stirring, until sauce boils and thickens. Cool. Add pineapple and 1 teaspoon shredded lime peel. Arrange on top of tarts.

Makes 6 servings

Pineapple Lime Tartlets

CHERRY CHEESE PIE

1 (9-inch) graham cracker crumb crust
    or baked pastry shell
1 (8-ounce) package cream cheese,
    softened
1 (14-ounce) can EAGLE® Brand
    Sweetened Condensed Milk (NOT
    evaporated milk)
⅓ cup REALEMON® Lemon Juice from
    Concentrate
1 teaspoon vanilla extract
1 (21-ounce) can cherry pie filling,
    chilled

In large bowl, beat cream cheese until fluffy. Gradually beat in sweetened condensed milk until smooth. Stir in ReaLemon® brand and vanilla. Pour into prepared crust. Chill 3 hours or until set. Top with desired amount of pie filling before serving. Refrigerate leftovers.

Makes 1 (9-inch) pie

TOPPING VARIATIONS
Fresh Fruit: Omit cherry pie filling. Arrange well-drained fresh strawberries, banana slices (dipped in ReaLemon® brand and well drained) and blueberries on top of chilled pie. Just before serving, brush fruit with light corn syrup, if desired.

Ambrosia: Omit cherry pie filling. In small saucepan, combine ½ cup peach *or* apricot preserves, ¼ cup flaked coconut, 2 tablespoons orange juice *or* orange-flavored liqueur and 2 teaspoons cornstarch; cook and stir until thickened. Remove from heat. Arrange fresh orange sections over top of pie; top with coconut mixture. Chill.

Blueberry: Omit cherry pie filling. In medium saucepan, combine ¼ cup sugar and 1 tablespoon cornstarch; mix well. Add ½ cup water, 2 tablespoons ReaLemon® brand, then 2 cups fresh or dry-pack frozen blueberries; mix well. Bring to a boil; reduce heat and simmer 3 minutes or until thickened and clear. Cool 10 minutes. Spread over pie. Chill.

Cranberry: Omit cherry pie filling. In medium saucepan, combine ⅓ cup sugar and 1 tablespoon cornstarch. Add ½ cup plus 2 tablespoons cold water and 2 cups fresh or dry-pack frozen cranberries; mix well. Bring to a boil; reduce heat and simmer 10 minutes, stirring constantly. Cool 15 minutes. Spread over pie. Chill.

Banana Cream Cheese Pie: Omit cherry pie filling. Prepare filling as above. Slice 2 bananas; dip in ReaLemon® brand and drain. Line crust with bananas. Pour filling over bananas; cover. Chill. Before serving, slice 2 bananas; dip in ReaLemon® brand and drain. Garnish top of pie with bananas.

MAPLE CUSTARD PIE

1 (9-inch) unbaked pastry shell
3 eggs
2 cups BORDEN® or MEADOW GOLD®
    Milk
½ cup CARY'S®, MAPLE ORCHARDS® or
    MACDONALD'S™ Pure Maple Syrup
    Maple Whipped Cream (recipe
    follows), optional

Preheat oven to 400°F. Bake pastry shell 5 minutes. Meanwhile, in medium bowl, beat eggs; add remaining ingredients except Maple Whipped Cream. Pour into partially baked pastry shell; reduce oven temperature to 350°F. Bake 45 minutes or until knife inserted near edge comes out clean. Cool. Serve warm or chilled with Maple Whipped Cream, if desired. Refrigerate leftovers.   *Makes 1 (9-inch) pie*

MAPLE WHIPPED CREAM: In small mixer bowl, beat 1 cup (½ pint) BORDEN® or MEADOW GOLD® Whipping Cream and ¼ cup CARY'S®, MAPLE ORCHARDS® or MACDONALD'S™ Pure Maple Syrup until stiff. Refrigerate leftovers. Makes about 2 cups.

GINGER & PEAR TART

30 gingersnap cookies
½ cup chopped pecans
⅓ cup butter, melted
1 cup sour cream
¾ cup half-and-half
1 package (4-serving size) vanilla instant pudding mix
2 tablespoons apricot brandy
4 ripe pears*
⅓ cup packed dark brown sugar
½ teaspoon ground ginger

Preheat oven to 350°F. Combine cookies and pecans in food processor or blender container; process until finely crushed. Combine crumb mixture and butter in medium bowl. Press firmly onto bottom and up side of 10-inch quiche dish or 9-inch pie plate. Bake 7 minutes; cool completely on wire rack.

Combine sour cream and half-and-half in large bowl. Mix until smooth. Whisk in pudding mix. Add apricot brandy. Whisk until smooth. Pour into prepared crust. Cover; refrigerate several hours or overnight.

Just before serving, preheat broiler. Peel pears. Cut into thin slices. Arrange in overlapping circles on top of pudding mixture. Combine brown sugar and ginger in small bowl. Sprinkle evenly over pears. Broil 4 to 6 minutes or until sugar is melted and bubbly. (Watch carefully so sugar does not burn.) Serve immediately.
Makes 6 to 8 servings

*Or, substitute 1 (16-ounce) can pear halves, drained and thinly sliced.

MARGARITA SOUFFLÉ PIE

PRETZEL CRUST
½ cup margarine
1¼ cups finely crushed pretzels
¼ cup sugar
FILLING
½ cup plus 2 tablespoons sugar
½ teaspoon grated lime peel
½ cup fresh lime juice
½ teaspoon salt
4 eggs, beaten
1 envelope unflavored gelatin
¼ cup tequila
¼ cup Triple Sec
3 drops green food coloring
1 container (4 ounces) frozen whipped topping, thawed

1. In 9-inch glass pie plate, melt margarine in microwave oven at HIGH (100% power) 1 to 1½ minutes. Add pretzels and sugar; mix well. Press mixture firmly in bottom and up side of pie plate. Refrigerate crust while preparing filling.

2. In 4-cup glass measure combine sugar, lime peel, lime juice and salt. Cook in microwave oven at HIGH (100% power) 1 to 1½ minutes or until sugar dissolves, stirring once. Slowly add eggs to lime juice mixture, whisking constantly. Cook at HIGH 30 seconds; stir mixture. Continue cooking at HIGH until mixture thickens, stirring every 15 seconds.

3. In 1-cup glass measure sprinkle gelatin over combined tequila and Triple Sec. Let stand 1 minute to soften. Cook gelatin mixture at HIGH 45 seconds or until gelatin dissolves. Add gelatin mixture and food coloring to lime mixture. Refrigerate 1 hour or until mixture is cool and slightly thickened. Fold in whipped topping and pour into prepared pretzel crust. Chill several hours or until set.
Makes 8 servings

*Favorite recipe from **National Turkey Federation***

Ginger & Pear Tart

GRASSHOPPER PIE

2 cups graham cracker crumbs
4 tablespoons unsweetened cocoa
  powder
¼ cup margarine, melted
8 ounces nonfat cream cheese, softened
1 cup 1% low fat milk
2 tablespoons green crème de menthe
  liqueur
2 tablespoons white crème de menthe
  liqueur
1½ teaspoons vanilla
1 container (4 ounces) frozen whipped
  topping, thawed

Spray 9-inch pie plate with nonstick cooking spray. Combine cracker crumbs, cocoa and margarine in medium bowl. Press onto bottom and up side of prepared pie plate. Refrigerate. Beat cream cheese in large bowl with electric mixer until fluffy. *Gradually* beat in milk until smooth. Stir in both liqueurs and vanilla. Fold in whipped topping. Refrigerate 20 minutes or until chilled but not set. Pour into chilled crust. Freeze 4 hours or until set.

Makes 8 servings

MOCHA WALNUT TART

1 (9-inch) unbaked pastry shell
2 (1-ounce) squares unsweetened
  chocolate
¼ cup margarine or butter
1 (14-ounce) can EAGLE® Brand
  Sweetened Condensed Milk (NOT
  evaporated milk)
¼ cup water
2 eggs, well beaten
¼ cup coffee-flavored liqueur
1 teaspoon vanilla extract
⅛ teaspoon salt
1 cup walnuts, toasted and chopped

Preheat oven to 350°F. In medium saucepan, over low heat, melt chocolate and margarine. Stir in sweetened condensed milk, water and eggs; *mix well.* Remove from heat; stir in liqueur, vanilla and salt. Pour into pastry shell; top with walnuts. Bake 40 to 45 minutes or until center is set. Cool. Serve warm or chilled. Garnish as desired. Refrigerate leftovers.

Makes 1 (9-inch) pie

Grasshopper Pie

CREAM CHEESE AND YOGURT TART

Rich Butter Crust (recipe follows)
2 packages (8 ounces each) cream cheese, softened
¼ cup granulated sugar
½ cup vanilla yogurt
1 teaspoon vanilla
Apricots, strawberries and mint leaves for garnish

Prepare and bake Rich Butter Crust; set aside. In small bowl of electric mixer beat cream cheese and sugar until smooth. Add yogurt and vanilla; beat until combined. Pour cream cheese mixture into prepared crust. Refrigerate until firm, about 6 hours. Garnish with sliced apricots, strawberries and mint, if desired.

Makes 8 servings

RICH BUTTER CRUST
1¼ cups all-purpose flour
¼ cup granulated sugar
Pinch salt
⅓ cup butter, cut into chunks
2 tablespoons cold water
1 egg yolk

Add flour, sugar and salt to food processor; mix well. Add butter; process until mixture resembles coarse crumbs. Add water and egg yolk; process just until mixture leaves side of bowl and forms ball.* On square of waxed paper, press mixture into 5-inch disc. Wrap and refrigerate at least 1 hour or up to 2 days.

Preheat oven to 400°F. Working quickly, with dough on lightly floured board or between 2 sheets of waxed paper, roll dough into 12-inch disc. Ease into 10-inch tart pan with removable bottom or 9-inch pie plate. Trim or flute edges; prick bottom with fork. Refrigerate until firm. Bake until golden, about 8 minutes. Cool before filling.

*To prepare dough by hand, place dry ingredients in medium bowl. Cut in butter to resemble coarse crumbs. Add water and egg yolk; mix well until combined.

Favorite recipe from National Dairy Board

CHILEAN FRUIT TART WITH LEMON CURD

Pastry for single-crust, 9-inch pie
⅓ cup butter
3 eggs*
¾ cup sugar
¼ cup lemon juice
2 teaspoons grated lemon peel
1 cup seedless or halved, seeded red or green Chilean grapes
2 cups Chilean winter fruits (blackberries, peach slices, nectarine slices, kiwifruit slices, raspberries)
⅓ cup sweet orange marmalade, melted

Preheat oven to 425°F. Line 9-inch tart pan with pastry; trim and finish edges. Prick generously with fork. Bake about 10 minutes or until golden. Set aside to cool. In top of double boiler over simmering water, melt butter. Whisk in eggs, sugar and lemon juice. Cook, stirring constantly, just until mixture thickens. Stir in lemon peel; remove egg mixture from heat and cool. Spread egg mixture over bottom of baked tart shell. Arrange fruits decoratively over top; brush with marmalade. Refrigerate until serving time. *Makes 6 to 8 servings*

*Use clean, uncracked eggs.

Favorite recipe from Chilean Fresh Fruit Association

Holiday

DESSERTS

FRUITED MERINGUE HEARTS MELBA

       6 egg whites
    ¼ teaspoon cream of tartar
    ¼ teaspoon ground allspice
 1½ cups sugar
       Melba Sauce (page 376)
    **3 cups assorted fruit (melon balls; sliced
          kiwifruit, peaches and strawberries; whole
          blackberries, blueberries, raspberries and
          grapes; pitted cherries)**
       Mint sprigs (optional)

Line large cookie sheet with parchment paper; draw 6 hearts
(3×3 inches) on paper. Beat egg whites in large bowl with
electric mixer until foamy. Add cream of tartar; beat until soft
peaks form. Add allspice. Add sugar, 1 tablespoon at a time,
beating at high speed until stiff peaks form, about 5 minutes.

Preheat oven to 250°F. Spoon meringue into large pastry bag
fitted with medium star tip; pipe heart outlines on parchment
paper. Fill in heart shapes with meringue. Pipe second row on
top of first row of meringue around outside edges of hearts to
form rims. Bake 1 hour or until meringues are firm and crisp to
the touch. Turn off oven; leave meringues in oven with door
closed at least 2 hours.

Prepare Melba Sauce. Set aside. Fill meringue hearts with fruit.
Spoon about ¼ cup sauce onto each dessert plate and place
filled hearts on sauce. Garnish with mint sprig, if desired.
Makes 6 servings

continued on page 376

Fruited Meringue Hearts Melba, continued

MELBA SAUCE

    1 package (16 ounces) frozen
        unsweetened raspberries, thawed,
        drained
    ¼ cup sugar

Place raspberries and sugar in food processor or blender; process until smooth. Strain and discard seeds.   *Makes 1½ cups*

AMBROSIAL FRUIT DESSERT

    1 medium DOLE® Fresh Pineapple
    1 medium DOLE® Orange, peeled, sliced
    1 red DOLE® Apple, cored, sliced
    1 cup seedless DOLE® Grapes
      Fruit Glaze (recipe follows)
    4 teaspoons flaked coconut

• Twist crown from pineapple. Cut pineapple in half lengthwise. Refrigerate one half for another use, such as fruit salad. Cut fruit from shell. Cut fruit crosswise into thin slices.

• Arrange fruits on 4 dessert plates. Drizzle with Fruit Glaze. Sprinkle with coconut.
    Makes 4 servings

FRUIT GLAZE

    ¾ cup DOLE® Pineapple Orange Juice
    2 tablespoons orange marmalade
    1 tablespoon cornstarch
    1 teaspoon rum extract
    2 teaspoons grated lime peel

Combine all ingredients except lime peel in saucepan. Cook, stirring, until sauce boils and thickens. Cool. Stir in lime peel.

MICROWAVE BAKED APPLES WITH RUM RAISIN SAUCE

    4 Rome Beauty apples (7 to 8 ounces
      each)
      Spiced Lemon Baste (recipe follows)
    ½ cup raisins
    3 tablespoons light rum*
    ¾ cup butter or margarine
    ¾ cup sugar
    ⅓ cup half-and-half
    1 egg, beaten
    ¾ teaspoon ground cinnamon
    ¾ teaspoon grated lemon peel

Core apples; peel skin from top third of each apple. Place apples in microwave-safe baking dish or custard cups. Pour Spiced Lemon Baste over apples. Cover with vented plastic wrap. Microwave at HIGH (100% power) 7 to 10 minutes or until apples are tender yet firm, rotating dish ¼ turn and basting apples after 4 minutes. Let stand while preparing sauce.

Microwave raisins and rum, covered, in microwave-safe container at HIGH 1 minute; set aside. Combine butter and sugar in microwave-safe container; microwave at HIGH 1½ minutes or until butter melts. Stir in half-and-half; microwave at HIGH 2 minutes or until just boiling. Stir small amount of hot sugar mixture into egg; return to remaining hot sugar mixture. Microwave at MEDIUM (50% power) 2½ to 3 minutes or until thickened, stirring after every minute. Stir in raisin mixture, cinnamon and lemon peel. Spoon over apples.
    Makes 4 apples and 2½ cups sauce

*3 tablespoons water and ¼ teaspoon rum extract may be substituted for rum.

SPICED LEMON BASTE: Combine ¼ cup water or apple juice, 2 tablespoons lemon juice and ½ teaspoon ground cinnamon; stir to blend. Makes about ⅓ cup.

*Favorite recipe from **Washington Apple Commission***

ALL–AMERICAN PINEAPPLE & FRUIT TRIFLE

1 DOLE® Fresh Pineapple
1 cup frozen sliced peaches, thawed
1 cup frozen strawberries, thawed, sliced
1 cup frozen raspberries, thawed
1 (10-inch) angel food cake
1 package (4-serving size) vanilla flavor sugar free instant pudding and pie filling mix
⅓ cup cream sherry
½ cup thawed frozen whipped topping

• Twist crown from pineapple. Cut pineapple in half lengthwise. Refrigerate one half for another use, such as fruit salad. Cut fruit from shell. Cut fruit into thin wedges. Reserve 3 wedges for garnish; combine remaining pineapple with peaches and berries.

• Cut cake in half. Freeze one half for another use. Tear remaining cake into chunks.

• Prepare mix according to package directions.

• In 2-quart glass serving bowl, arrange half of cake chunks; sprinkle with half of sherry. Top with half each fruit mixture and pudding. Repeat layers. Cover; chill 1 hour or overnight.

• Just before serving, garnish with whipped topping and reserved pineapple wedges.
Makes 8 to 10 servings

All-American Pineapple & Fruit Trifle

PEARS EN CROÛTE (BAKED PEARS IN PASTRY)

2 teaspoons granulated sugar
¼ teaspoon ground cinnamon
1 egg white, slightly beaten
   Cold water
¼ cup golden raisins
¼ cup chopped walnuts
2 tablespoons brown sugar
1 package DUNCAN HINES® Cinnamon
   Muffin Mix
8 small ripe pears
1 cup all-purpose flour
½ BUTTER FLAVOR* CRISCO® Stick or
   ½ cup BUTTER FLAVOR CRISCO
   all-vegetable shortening
   Cinnamon sticks or vanilla beans, for
   garnish
   Caramel flavor topping, at room
   temperature or warmed

1. Preheat oven to 375°F. Grease 13×9×2-inch baking pan.

2. Combine granulated sugar and cinnamon in small bowl; set aside. Combine beaten egg white and 1 teaspoon water in small bowl; set aside.

3. Combine raisins, walnuts, brown sugar, contents of cinnamon swirl packet from Mix and contents of crumb topping packet from Mix in medium bowl; set aside.

4. Core and peel pears; set aside.

5. Combine muffin mix and flour in medium bowl. Cut in shortening with pastry blender or 2 knives until flour is blended to form pea-size chunks. Sprinkle 5 tablespoons *cold* water, 1 tablespoon at a time, over flour mixture. Toss lightly with fork until dough forms ball. Divide in half. Wrap one half with plastic wrap; reserve. Roll remaining dough on well-floured surface to form 13-inch square. Cut square into four 6½-inch squares. Repeat using reserved dough ball.

6. To assemble, fill pear centers with 1½ tablespoons raisin mixture. Cover each pear with square of pastry. Mold with palm of hand to shape, folding corners under pear bottom. Place pears ¾ inch apart in greased pan. Brush with egg white mixture. Sprinkle ¼ teaspoon cinnamon-sugar mixture over each pear.

7. Bake at 375°F for 33 to 35 minutes or until golden brown and pears are tender. Cool in pan for 5 minutes. Remove to serving dish. Insert cinnamon stick or piece of vanilla bean on top of pear to form stem. Drizzle caramel topping over pear, as desired. Serve warm or at room temperature. Refrigerate leftovers.

Makes 8 servings

*Butter Flavor Crisco® is artificially flavored.

QUICK RUMTOPF

1 can (16 ounces) DEL MONTE® Yellow
   Cling Sliced Peaches
1 can (16 ounces) DEL MONTE® Bartlett
   Pear Halves
1 can (15½ ounces) DEL MONTE®
   Pineapple Chunks
1 can (11 ounces) DEL MONTE®
   Mandarin Oranges
1 cup rum
1 cinnamon stick
½ cup DEL MONTE® Seedless Raisins

Drain fruit reserving syrup in medium saucepan. Add rum and cinnamon stick to reserved syrup. Bring to a boil, stirring occasionally. Cool. Layer fruit and raisins in rumtopf pot or large jars. Pour syrup mixture over fruit. Refrigerate. Allow 1 week to mellow. Serve as fruit compote or on ice cream or pound cake.

Makes 2 quarts

Pear en Croûte

CALIFORNIA KIWIFRUIT HOLIDAY FROZEN YOGURT WITH RED RASPBERRY SAUCE

   2 California kiwifruit, peeled and coarsely chopped
   1 tablespoon honey
   1 pint frozen lowfat or nonfat vanilla yogurt, softened
   1 to 2 drops green food coloring (optional)
   1 package (10 ounces) frozen red raspberries in syrup, thawed
   2 tablespoons triple sec or other orange-flavored liqueur
   2 teaspoons cornstarch
   3 California kiwifruit, ends trimmed and sliced lengthwise
   Fresh mint leaves (optional)
   Fresh or frozen whole raspberries (optional)

In food processor or blender, purée chopped kiwifruit; stir in honey. Place in freezer and freeze until slushy (about 45 minutes). In stainless steel bowl, quickly combine softened yogurt, kiwifruit mixture and food coloring; refreeze in bowl. With small ice cream scoop (about 2 tablespoons) form 12 balls frozen yogurt mixture and place on waxed-paper-lined tray; refreeze.

Meanwhile, to make sauce, in food processor or blender purée thawed raspberries. Over saucepan, strain berries through a fine sieve, pressing with back of spoon. Discard seeds. Stir in triple sec and cornstarch. Bring to boil, stirring constantly until slightly thickened. Cool; cover and chill. To assemble, spoon about 2 tablespoons sauce on each of 6 dessert plates or shallow bowls. Arrange kiwifruit slices and frozen yogurt balls on sauce. Garnish with mint and whole raspberries.   *Makes 6 servings*

Favorite recipe from **California Kiwifruit Commission**

California Kiwifruit Holiday Frozen Yogurt with Red Raspberry Sauce

HAZELNUT MERINGUE WITH POACHED PEARS

POACHED PEARS
   3 Bosc pears, peeled and cored
   2 cups NEWMAN'S OWN® Lemonade
   ¾ cup sugar
   1 vanilla bean
   1 cinnamon stick
   Water
MERINGUE
   4 egg whites
1½ cups granulated sugar
   1 teaspoon vanilla
   ½ teaspoon white vinegar
   1 cup (4½ ounces) ground hazelnuts
   1 cup whipping cream, whipped*
   Powdered sugar
   Chocolate Sauce (page 381)

In medium saucepan place pears, lemonade, sugar, vanilla bean and cinnamon stick. Add enough water to cover pears. Bring to a boil and simmer slowly until just tender, 10 to 20 minutes. Let pears cool in liquid. Drain and slice.

Preheat oven to 375°F. Grease and flour two 9-inch springform pans. Line bottom of each pan with parchment paper; grease paper. Beat egg whites until stiff. Gradually add granulated sugar while beating continuously until mixture is very stiff and stands in peaks. Beat in vanilla and vinegar. Fold in ground nuts. Spread in prepared pans, smoothing tops. Bake 30 to 40 minutes. Tops should be crisp but insides should be soft. Remove from pans and cool on wire racks.

At least 3 hours before serving, arrange sliced pears on one meringue; spread with whipped cream. Top with second meringue, flat side up. Sprinkle with powdered sugar. Refrigerate for 3 hours. Serve with Chocolate Sauce.

Makes 6 servings

*Add 1 tablespoon granulated sugar and 1 teaspoon vanilla to whipped cream, if desired.

CHOCOLATE SAUCE
   1 cup light cream
   4 ounces semi-sweet chocolate
   3 tablespoons sugar
   4 egg yolks**
   2 teaspoons vanilla
   2 tablespoons orange-flavored liqueur
      (optional)

In small saucepan heat cream and chocolate over low heat. Meanwhile, beat sugar and yolks until light. Stir into chocolate-cream mixture and stir over low heat for 2 to 3 minutes or until rich and smooth. Do not bring to a boil. Let cool slightly and add flavorings.   *Makes 1½ cups*

**Use clean, uncracked eggs.

COUNTRY HOLIDAY CRISP

   6 cups sliced peeled apples
   ¼ cup orange juice
   2 cups RALSTON® brand Fruit Muesli
      with Cranberries
   ½ cup all-purpose flour
   ⅓ cup sugar
   ¼ cup (½ stick) margarine or butter,
      softened
   1 teaspoon ground cinnamon
      Vanilla ice cream (optional)

Preheat oven to 375°F. In ungreased 2-quart baking dish place apples and orange juice; toss lightly. In medium bowl place cereal, flour, sugar, margarine and cinnamon; blend together. Sprinkle cereal mixture over apples. Bake, covered, 30 to 35 minutes or until apples are tender. Remove cover and bake an additional 10 minutes. Serve with vanilla ice cream, if desired.   *Makes 8 servings*

MICROWAVE DIRECTIONS: In ungreased 2-quart microwave-safe baking dish place apples and orange juice; toss lightly. In medium bowl place cereal, flour, sugar, margarine and cinnamon; blend together. Sprinkle cereal mixture over apples. Microwave on HIGH (100% power) 10 to 12 minutes or until apples are tender. Serve with vanilla ice cream, if desired.

TEMPTING APPLE TRIFLES

½ cup skim milk
1½ teaspoons cornstarch
4½ teaspoons dark brown sugar
1 egg white
½ teaspoon canola oil
½ teaspoon vanilla extract
½ teaspoon rum extract, divided
¼ cup unsweetened apple cider, divided
2 tablespoons raisins
½ teaspoon ground cinnamon
1 cup peeled and chopped Golden
    Delicious apple
1 cup ½-inch angel food cake cubes,
    divided

To prepare custard, combine milk and cornstarch in small, heavy saucepan; stir until cornstarch is completely dissolved. Add brown sugar, egg white and oil; blend well. Slowly bring to a boil over medium-low heat until thickened, stirring constantly with whisk. Remove from heat; stir in vanilla and ¼ teaspoon rum extract. Set aside; cool completely.

Combine 2 tablespoons cider, raisins and cinnamon in medium saucepan; bring to a boil over medium-low heat. Add apple and cook until apple is fork-tender and all liquid has been absorbed, stirring frequently. Remove from heat; set aside to cool.

To assemble, place ¼ cup cake cubes in bottom of 2 small trifle or dessert dishes. Combine remaining 2 tablespoons cider and ¼ teaspoon rum extract in small bowl; mix well. Spoon 1½ teaspoons cider mixture over cake in each dish. Top each with ¼ of custard mixture and ¼ cup cooked apple mixture. Repeat layers. Serve immediately. Garnish with fresh mint, if desired. *Makes 2 servings*

WINTERFRUIT COBBLER

FILLING
2 cups SUN-MAID® Raisins
2 cups fresh or frozen cranberries
¾ cup sugar
2 teaspoons cornstarch
½ teaspoon ground allspice
1 cup orange juice
TOPPING
1 cup all-purpose flour
2 tablespoons sugar
2 teaspoons baking powder
¼ teaspoon salt
¼ cup butter or margarine
½ cup milk
Sugar
Ground cinnamon

TO PREPARE FILLING: In medium saucepan, combine raisins, cranberries, sugar, cornstarch and allspice. Gradually stir in orange juice. Bring to boil over high heat; reduce heat to low and simmer, stirring until cranberries begin to pop and mixture thickens slightly. Pour into shallow 1½-quart baking dish.

TO PREPARE TOPPING: In small bowl, combine flour, sugar, baking powder and salt. Cut in butter until mixture resembles coarse crumbs. Mix in milk lightly with fork. Drop spoonfuls of batter over filling; sprinkle lightly with additional sugar mixed with a little cinnamon. Bake in preheated 400°F oven about 25 minutes or until golden. Serve warm with ice cream or whipping cream.
Makes 6 servings

Tempting Apple Trifles

Rum and Spumoni Layered Torte

RUM AND SPUMONI LAYERED TORTE

**1 package (18 to 19 ounces) moist
    butter recipe yellow cake mix**
3 eggs
½ cup butter or margarine, softened
⅓ cup plus 2 teaspoons rum, divided
⅓ cup water
1 quart spumoni ice cream, softened
1 cup whipping cream
1 tablespoon powdered sugar
    Chopped mixed candied fruit
    **Red and green sugars, for decorating
    (optional)**

Preheat oven to 375°F. Grease and flour 15½×10½×1-inch jelly-roll pan. Combine cake mix, eggs, butter, ⅓ cup rum and water in large bowl. Beat with electric mixer at low speed until moistened. Beat at high speed 4 minutes. Pour evenly into prepared pan.

Bake 20 to 25 minutes or until wooden toothpick inserted in center comes out clean. Cool in pan 10 minutes. Turn out of pan onto wire rack; cool completely.

Cut cake into three 10×5-inch pieces. Place one cake layer on serving plate. Spread with half the softened ice cream. Cover with second cake layer. Spread with remaining ice cream. Place remaining cake layer on top. Gently push down. Wrap cake in plastic wrap and freeze at least 4 hours.

Just before serving, combine cream, powdered sugar and remaining 2 teaspoons rum in small chilled bowl. Beat at high speed with chilled beaters until stiff peaks form. Remove cake from freezer. Spread thin layer of whipped cream mixture over top of cake. Place star tip in pastry bag; fill with remaining whipped cream mixture. Pipe rosettes around outer top edges of cake. Place candied fruit in narrow strip down center of cake. Sprinkle colored sugars over rosettes, if desired. Serve immediately.
Makes 8 to 10 servings

ORANGE–THYME GRANITÀ IN COOKIE CUPS

2½ cups fresh orange juice
½ cup lemon juice
¼ cup sugar
1 teaspoon finely chopped fresh thyme
6 Lemon Anise Cookie Cups (recipe follows)

Combine juices, sugar and thyme in medium bowl; stir until sugar dissolves. Freeze until slightly firm, about 1 hour. Beat with wire whisk to break ice crystals. Repeat freezing and beating process 2 to 3 times until ice is firm and granular. To serve, scoop ½ cup granità into each cookie cup. *Makes 6 servings*

LEMON ANISE COOKIE CUPS

3 tablespoons all-purpose flour
3 tablespoons sugar
2 tablespoons margarine, melted
1 teaspoon grated lemon peel
¼ teaspoon anise extract
1 egg white
Nonstick cooking spray
¼ cup sliced almonds

Preheat oven to 375°F. Combine flour, sugar, margarine, lemon peel, anise extract and egg white in food processor; process until smooth. Spray bottoms of 6 custard cups and 2 baking sheets with nonstick cooking spray. Spread 1 tablespoon batter into 5-inch-diameter circle on baking sheet with rubber spatula. Repeat to make total of 6 circles. Sprinkle 2 teaspoons almonds in center of each.

Bake 3 to 4 minutes or until edges are browned. Place each cookie over bottom of prepared custard cup so almonds face inside. Press cookies against custard cup to form cookie cup. Cool. *Makes 6 cookie cups*

Orange-Thyme Granità in Cookie Cup

MOCHA FRUITY TORTE

1⅓ cups plus ¼ cup sugar, divided
1 cup all-purpose flour
3 tablespoons unsweetened cocoa
1 tablespoon espresso powder or instant coffee
1 teaspoon baking soda
¼ teaspoon salt
½ cup sour cream
½ cup butter or margarine, softened
2 eggs
1 teaspoon vanilla
1 package (3 ounces) cream cheese, softened
1 cup whipping cream
1 can (11 ounces) mandarin orange segments, drained
2 kiwifruit, peeled, halved lengthwise and sliced
3 or 4 strawberries, sliced
1 slice star fruit (optional)

Preheat oven to 350°F. Grease and flour 9-inch round pan. Combine 1⅓ cups sugar, flour, cocoa, espresso powder, baking soda and salt in large bowl. Add sour cream, butter, eggs and vanilla. Beat at low speed until combined. Beat at medium speed 3 minutes or until fluffy. Pour into pan. Bake 40 minutes or until set. Cool in pan on wire rack 10 minutes. Remove from pan; cool on wire rack.

Process cream cheese and remaining ¼ cup sugar in food processor until light and fluffy. Beat whipping cream in bowl until soft peaks form. Beat cream cheese mixture into whipped cream.

To serve, carefully cut cake horizontally in half to make two layers. Place bottom half of cake on plate. Spread with half the filling. Top with remaining cake layer. Spread with remaining filling. Arrange fruit over top.

Makes 10 servings

CINNAMON CRISP PLUM PUDDING

2 cups KEEBLER® Cinnamon Crisp Graham Cracker crumbs (about 15 large crackers)
1¼ teaspoons baking soda
½ teaspoon salt
¼ teaspoon ground ginger
¼ teaspoon ground cloves
½ cup shortening
½ cup packed brown sugar
2 eggs
½ cup water
1 can (16 ounces) purple plums in heavy syrup, drained, pitted and chopped (syrup reserved)
1 cup golden raisins
½ cup chopped walnuts
Plum Sauce (recipe follows)

Stir together Cinnamon Crisp Graham Cracker crumbs, baking soda, salt, ginger and cloves; set aside. Cream shortening with brown sugar until fluffy. Beat in eggs, 1 at a time. Add crumb mixture alternately with water to sugar mixture, beating well after each addition. Stir in chopped plums, raisins and walnuts. If mixture is dry, stir in more water 1 tablespoon at a time. Pour batter into well-greased 5- to 6-cup kugelhopf or Bundt pan. Bake in preheated 375°F oven 40 to 50 minutes or until wooden pick inserted near center comes out clean. Loosen edges of plum pudding; immediately turn out of pan onto serving platter. Spoon Plum Sauce over slices of pudding. *Makes 8 to 10 servings*

PLUM SAUCE: Combine plum syrup (about 1 cup), ¼ cup granulated sugar and 2 tablespoons cornstarch in small saucepan. Cook over medium heat, stirring constantly, until thickened, about 5 minutes. Stir in 1 tablespoon lemon juice or brandy.

Mocha Fruity Torte

Cherry-Topped Icebox Cake

CHERRY–TOPPED ICEBOX CAKE

  20 whole graham crackers, divided
   1 package (6-serving size) JELL-O®
       Vanilla or Chocolate Flavor Instant
       Pudding & Pie Filling
   2 cups cold milk
1¾ cups thawed COOL WHIP® Whipped
       Topping
   2 cans (21 ounces each) cherry pie filling

Line 13×9-inch pan with one third of the graham crackers, breaking crackers, if necessary.

Prepare pudding mix with cold milk as directed on package. Let stand 5 minutes. Gently stir in whipped topping. Spread half the pudding mixture over crackers. Add second layer of crackers; top with remaining pudding mixture. Add third layer of crackers. Top with cherry pie filling. Refrigerate 3 hours.

Makes 12 servings

CHOCOLATE–FROSTED ICEBOX CAKE:
Prepare Cherry-Topped Icebox Cake as directed, substituting ¾ cup ready-to-spread chocolate fudge frosting for the cherry pie filling. Carefully spread frosting over top layer of graham crackers.

CHOCOLATE CREAM TERRINE

2 bags (7 ounces) Chocolate RIESEN®
   Caramel Candy, unwrapped
2 cups whipping cream, divided
2 envelopes unflavored gelatin
2 tablespoons coffee-flavored liqueur
CREAM SAUCE
   1 cup whipping cream
   ¼ cup sugar
   ½ teaspoon vanilla extract
   1 cup sour cream
      Fresh raspberries
      Fresh mint leaves

Grease 8½×4½×2½-inch loaf pan. Cut a piece of waxed paper 16 inches long. Fold in half lengthwise. Place in bottom of pan, allowing excess to hang equally over sides. Grease waxed paper. Set aside. In heavy saucepan, melt caramel candy and ½ cup cream over low heat, stirring constantly, until smooth. In small bowl, sprinkle gelatin over additional ½ cup cream. Let stand 1 minute to soften. Stir into chocolate mixture. Remove from heat; stir until gelatin dissolves. Stir in liqueur. Let cool to room temperature. Whip remaining 1 cup cream until stiff. Fold ⅓ of whipped cream into chocolate mixture; fold in remaining whipped cream. Spoon into prepared pan; cover with foil. Refrigerate overnight.

For Cream Sauce, whip 1 cup cream with sugar and vanilla until soft peaks form; fold into sour cream. Refrigerate until serving time. (Sauce can be made up to 4 hours before serving.)

To unmold terrine, carefully run knife around waxed-paper-lined sides. Place oblong platter over top of pan and invert. Carefully lift pan, holding waxed paper at the same time. Slowly remove waxed paper. Cover with plastic wrap; refrigerate until serving. Slice terrine with knife dipped in water. Serve sliced terrine on dessert plates with dollop of Cream Sauce at side of slice. Top each dollop with raspberry and mint leaf. Serve immediately. *Makes 15 servings*

LEMON MERINGUE TORTE

MERINGUE
   4 egg whites
   ¼ teaspoon cream of tartar
   1 cup sugar
LEMON LAYER
   4 egg yolks
   ½ cup sugar
   ¼ cup fresh lemon juice
      Grated peel of 1 lemon
   1 cup whipping cream
      Candied lemon peel and salad burnet
      (optional)

Preheat oven to 275°F. To prepare meringue, beat egg whites and cream of tartar in medium bowl with electric mixer on medium speed until frothy. Gradually beat in 1 cup sugar on high speed until stiff peaks form. Draw 9-inch circle on heavy brown paper. Place on baking sheet; spread meringue inside circle to form 8- to 9-inch round. Bake 1 hour. *Turn off oven; cool completely in oven.*

Meanwhile, to prepare lemon layer, beat egg yolks in top of double boiler. Stir in ½ cup sugar, juice and grated peel. Place over hot, not boiling, water; cook 5 to 8 minutes or until thickened, stirring constantly. Remove top of double boiler; cover and set aside to cool.

Place cooled meringue on serving plate. Spread with lemon mixture. Refrigerate until set. Just before serving, whip cream and spread over lemon filling. Garnish with candied peel and salad burnet, if desired. Refrigerate leftovers. *Makes 8 servings*

Favorite recipe from **Bob Evans Farms®**

CHOCOLATE/ESPRESSO DREAM LAYERS

½ gallon DREYER'S or EDY'S Chocolate
    Brownie Chunk Frozen Yogurt
1 quart DREYER'S or EDY'S GRAND
    Espresso Chip Ice Cream
½ gallon DREYER'S or EDY'S GRAND
    Mocha Almond Fudge Ice Cream or
    Light Ice Cream
    Chocolate Espresso Sauce (recipe
    follows)

• Slightly soften frozen yogurt and ice creams at room temperature for 10 minutes.

• Press alternating layers of frozen yogurt and ice cream flavors into 6-cup ring mold, fluted mold or springform pan. Freeze until firm (about 30 minutes).

• To unmold, briefly dip mold in hot water to loosen sides, then turn out onto serving plate. Slice and serve with warm Chocolate Espresso Sauce. *Makes 8 servings*

CHOCOLATE ESPRESSO SAUCE

1 cup sugar
½ cup water
2 tablespoons unsalted butter
4 ounces unsweetened chocolate,
    chopped
1 teaspoon instant espresso or coffee
    granules

• Combine sugar, water and butter in heavy saucepan. Bring to a simmer, stirring until sugar dissolves. Remove from heat.

• Add chocolate and coffee. Stir until melted and smooth. *Makes about 1½ cups*

NOTE: Sauce may be made ahead and reheated.

TIRAMISU

2 packages (8 ounces each) cream
    cheese, softened
⅔ cup sugar
¼ cup Marsala wine
2 teaspoons vanilla extract
2 cups whipping cream, whipped
1 cup strong coffee or espresso, chilled
2 tablespoons almond liqueur *or*
    1 teaspoon almond extract
2 packages (3 ounces each) ladyfingers
    (24 ladyfingers)
1 cup HEATH® Bits

In mixing bowl, beat cream cheese and sugar until light. Blend in wine and vanilla. Fold in whipped cream. In small bowl or measuring cup, combine coffee and liqueur. To assemble, split each ladyfinger in half horizontally and vertically. Place four pieces in each of eight footed dessert or wine glasses. Drizzle ladyfingers with coffee mixture. Top with about ¼ cup cream mixture and several teaspoons Heath® Bits. Repeat for two more layers, ending with Heath® Bits. Cover; refrigerate at least 2 hours before serving.
Makes 8 servings

Tiramisu

LINZER TORTE

½ cup whole almonds, toasted
1½ cups all-purpose flour
1 teaspoon ground cinnamon
¼ teaspoon salt
¾ cup granulated sugar
½ cup butter or margarine, softened
½ teaspoon grated lemon peel
1 egg
¾ cup raspberry or apricot jam
Sifted powdered sugar

Process almonds in food processor until ground, but not pasty. Preheat oven to 375°F. Combine flour, almonds, cinnamon and salt in medium bowl; set aside. Beat granulated sugar, butter and lemon peel in large bowl with electric mixer at medium speed about 5 minutes or until light and fluffy, scraping down side of bowl once. Beat in egg until well blended. Beat in flour mixture at low speed until well blended.

Spoon ⅔ of dough onto bottom of 10-inch tart pan with removable bottom. Pat dough evenly over bottom and up side of pan. Spread jam over bottom of dough. Roll remaining ⅓ of dough on lightly floured surface into 10×5-inch rectangle. Cut dough into ten ½-inch-wide strips using pizza wheel or sharp knife.

Arrange 4 or 5 strips of dough lengthwise across jam. Arrange another 4 or 5 strips of dough crosswise across top. Trim and press ends of dough strips into edge of crust. Bake 25 to 35 minutes or until crust is golden brown. Cool completely in pan on wire rack. Remove torte from pan. Sprinkle with powdered sugar. Cut into wedges. Store, tightly covered, at room temperature 1 to 2 days.   *Makes 12 servings*

Linzer Torte

CHARLOTTE RUSSE

2 cups boiling water
**1 package (8-serving size) *or* 2 packages
(4-serving size) JELL-O® Brand
Black Cherry, Orange or Black
Raspberry Flavor Gelatin**
1 quart vanilla ice cream, softened
12 ladyfingers, split*
**COOL WHIP® Whipped Topping,
thawed**

Stir boiling water into gelatin in medium bowl 2
minutes or until dissolved. Spoon in ice cream,
stirring until melted and smooth. Refrigerate
until thickened (or when spoon drawn through
mixture leaves definite impression.)

Meanwhile, trim about 1 inch off one end of
each split ladyfinger. Place ladyfingers, cut
ends down, around side of 8-inch springform
pan. Spoon gelatin mixture into pan.
Refrigerate 4 hours or until firm. Remove side
of pan. Garnish with whipped topping.
Decorate as desired.   *Makes 10 servings*

*Or use thin strips of sponge cake.

PREP TIME: 20 minutes
CHILL TIME: 4 hours

Charlotte Russe

RASPBERRY GIFT BOX

1½ cups boiling water
1 package (8-serving size) *or* 2 packages
   (4-serving size) JELL-O® Brand
   Raspberry Flavor Gelatin
¾ cup cran-raspberry juice
   Ice cubes
1 tub (8 ounces) COOL WHIP® Whipped
   Topping, thawed
   Large green gumdrops
   Sugar
   Frosted cranberries* (optional)
   Raspberry Sauce (recipe follows)

Stir boiling water into gelatin in large bowl 2
minutes or until completely dissolved. Mix juice
and ice cubes to make 1¾ cups. Stir into
gelatin until slightly thickened (consistency of
unbeaten egg whites). Remove any remaining
ice. Stir in whipped topping with wire whisk until
smooth. Pour into 9×5-inch loaf pan.

Refrigerate 4 hours or until firm. Unmold
raspberry loaf onto serving plate.

Place gumdrops in a row on smooth flat
surface or sheet of waxed paper sprinkled with
sugar. Flatten into long strips with rolling pin,
turning frequently to coat with sugar. Cut into
1-inch-wide strips with sharp knife. Place on
raspberry loaf to resemble a ribbon. Cut 7
(3×1-inch) strips; form strips into a bow. Place
bow on ribbon. Garnish with Frosted
Cranberries. Serve with Raspberry Sauce.
Store leftover dessert in refrigerator.
Makes 8 servings

RASPBERRY SAUCE

2 packages (10 ounces each) frozen red
   raspberries, thawed
2 teaspoons cornstarch

Place raspberries in food processor or blender;
cover. Process until smooth; strain to remove
seeds. Combine cornstarch with small amount
of raspberries in medium saucepan; add
remaining raspberries. Bring to boil over
medium heat, stirring constantly; boil 1 minute.
Refrigerate. *Makes 2 cups*

*To frost cranberries, moisten cranberries with
water; shake off excess. Roll in sugar; let stand
on waxed paper until dry.

PREP TIME: 30 minutes
CHILL TIME: 4 hours

CREAMY EGGNOG DESSERT

CRUST
1 package DUNCAN HINES® Moist
   Deluxe Swiss Chocolate Cake Mix
½ cup butter or margarine, melted
½ cup chopped pecans
FILLING
1 package (8 ounces) cream cheese,
   softened
1 cup sugar
1 container (12 ounces) frozen whipped
   topping, thawed and divided
2 packages (4-serving size each) French
   vanilla instant pudding and pie mix
3 cups cold milk
¼ teaspoon rum extract
¼ teaspoon ground nutmeg

1. Preheat oven to 350°F. For crust, combine
cake mix, butter and pecans. Reserve ½ cup
mixture. Press remaining mixture into bottom of
13×9×2-inch pan. Bake at 350°F for 15 to 20
minutes or until surface is firm. Cool. Toast
reserved ½ cup mixture on cookie sheet at
350°F for 3 to 4 minutes, stirring once. Cool
completely. Break lumps with fork to make
small crumbs.

2. For filling, beat cream cheese and sugar
until smooth in large bowl. Stir in 1 cup
whipped topping. Spread over cooled crust.
Refrigerate. Combine pudding mix and milk;
beat 1 minute. Add rum extract and nutmeg.
Spread over cheese layer. Spread remaining
whipped topping over pudding layer. Sprinkle
with reserved crumbs. Refrigerate at least 2
hours. *Makes 12 to 16 servings*

Top to bottom: Eggnog Cheesecake (page 406),
Holiday Fruitcake (page 347), Marzipan
Fruits (page 522), Raspberry Gift Box

DRIED FRUIT AND NOODLE DESSERT

8 ounces dried medium-width egg noodles
1 (8-ounce) package cream cheese, softened
1 cup dairy sour cream
6 tablespoons butter, softened
⅓ cup sugar
3 tablespoons honey
1 teaspoon vanilla extract
5 eggs
2 (6-ounce) packages diced dried mixed fruit
1 tablespoon sugar
½ teaspoon ground cinnamon

Preheat oven to 350°F. Cook noodles according to package directions; rinse, drain and set aside. Meanwhile, beat cream cheese in small mixer bowl until smooth and fluffy. Beat in sour cream, butter, ⅓ cup sugar, honey and vanilla until well blended. Beat in eggs. Combine noodles and dried fruit in large mixing bowl. Stir in cream cheese mixture until all ingredients are well combined. Pour into well-greased 2-quart casserole. Combine 1 tablespoon sugar and cinnamon. Sprinkle over top of noodle mixture. Bake 1 hour or until knife inserted near center comes out clean. Cool on wire rack. Serve warm or at room temperature.

Makes 10 to 12 servings

*Favorite recipe from **American Dairy Association***

Dried Fruit and Noodle Dessert

COLD CHERRY MOUSSE WITH VANILLA SAUCE

1 envelope whipped topping mix
½ cup skim milk
½ teaspoon vanilla extract
2 envelopes unflavored gelatin
½ cup sugar
½ cup cold water
1 package (16 ounces) frozen unsweetened cherries, thawed, undrained and divided
1 tablespoon fresh lemon juice
½ teaspoon almond extract
Vanilla Sauce (recipe follows)

Prepare whipped topping according to package directions using milk and vanilla; set aside. Combine gelatin and sugar in small saucepan; stir in water. Let stand 5 minutes to soften. Heat over low heat until gelatin is completely dissolved. Cool to room temperature. Set aside 1 cup cherries without juice for garnish. Place remaining cherries and juice in blender. Add lemon juice, almond extract and gelatin mixture; process until blended. Fold cherry purée into whipped topping. Pour mixture into Bundt pan or ring mold. Refrigerate 4 hours or overnight until jelled.

To serve, unmold mousse onto large serving plate. Spoon remaining 1 cup cherries into center of mousse. Serve with Vanilla Sauce. Garnish with fresh mint, if desired.

Makes 6 servings

VANILLA SAUCE

4½ teaspoons cherry brandy *or* 1 teaspoon vanilla extract plus ½ teaspoon cherry extract
¾ cup melted vanilla ice milk or low fat ice cream, cooled

Stir brandy into ice milk in small bowl; blend well.

Makes ¾ cup

Cold Cherry Mousse with Vanilla Sauce

CHOCOLATE TRUFFLE LOAF WITH SWEET RASPBERRY SAUCE

   2 cups heavy cream, divided
   3 egg yolks
  16 squares (1 ounce each) semisweet
      chocolate
   ½ cup KARO® Light or Dark Corn Syrup
   ½ cup MAZOLA® Margarine
   ¼ cup confectioners' sugar
   1 teaspoon vanilla
     Sweet Raspberry Sauce (recipe
     follows)

Line 9¼×5¼×2¾-inch loaf pan with plastic wrap. In small bowl mix ½ cup cream with egg yolks. In large saucepan combine chocolate, corn syrup and margarine; stir over medium heat until melted. Add egg mixture. Cook 3 minutes over medium heat, stirring constantly. Cool to room temperature. In small bowl with mixer at medium speed, beat remaining 1½ cups cream, sugar and vanilla until soft peaks form. Gently fold into chocolate mixture just until combined. Pour into prepared pan; cover with plastic wrap. Refrigerate overnight or chill in freezer 3 hours. Slice and serve with Sweet Raspberry Sauce. Garnish with fresh raspberries, if desired.   *Makes 12 servings*

Chocolate Truffle Loaf with Sweet Raspberry Sauce

SWEET RASPBERRY SAUCE: In blender or food processor purée 1 package (10 ounces) frozen raspberries, thawed; strain to remove seeds. Stir in ⅓ cup KARO® Light Corn Syrup.

PREP TIME: 30 minutes, plus chilling

MICROWAVE DIRECTIONS: Prepare pan and egg mixture as above. In 3-quart microwavable bowl mix chocolate, corn syrup and margarine. Microwave on HIGH (100% power) 2 to 2½ minutes or until melted, stirring twice. Stir in egg mixture. Microwave on HIGH 3 minutes, stirring twice. Continue as above.

PUMPKIN GINGERBREAD SURPRISE

   2 tablespoons butter
   ½ (6¼-ounce) bag miniature
      marshmallows
   1 cup gingersnaps
   1 quart DREYER'S or EDY'S GRAND
      Pumpkin Ice Cream*
    Pumpkin pie spice or ground nutmeg

• Melt butter in saucepan over low heat; slowly add marshmallows, stirring constantly until melted.

• Divide gingersnaps among 4 serving bowls or dessert plates; top each serving with 1 scoop Dreyer's or Edy's Grand Pumpkin Ice Cream.

• Spoon marshmallow mixture over ice cream; sprinkle with pumpkin pie spice.
   Makes 4 servings

*Available September through December.

Tiramisu

TIRAMISU

 6 egg yolks
 ½ cup sugar
 ⅓ cup cognac or brandy
 **2 cups (15 ounces) SARGENTO® Old
    Fashioned Ricotta Cheese**
 1 cup whipping cream, whipped
 32 ladyfingers, split in half
 **3 teaspoons instant coffee dissolved in
    ¾ cup boiling water**
 **1 tablespoon unsweetened cocoa
    Chocolate Curls (recipe follows),
    optional**

In top of double boiler, whisk together egg yolks, sugar and cognac. Place pan over simmering water. Cook, whisking constantly, until mixture is thickened, about 2 to 3 minutes. Cool. In large bowl of electric mixer, beat yolk mixture and Ricotta cheese on medium speed until blended. Fold in whipping cream.

Place 32 ladyfinger halves in bottom of 13×9-inch pan, cut side up. Brush with half of coffee; spread with half of Ricotta mixture. Repeat layers. Chill 2 hours. Just before serving, dust with cocoa; cut into squares. Garnish with Chocolate Curls.   *Makes 16 servings*

CHOCOLATE CURLS: Combine ½ cup semisweet chocolate chips and 2 teaspoons shortening in small microwavable bowl. Microwave at HIGH (100% power) 1 minute. Stir until chocolate is melted. Spread evenly in thin layer on small cookie sheet. Cool. Hold small pancake turner upside-down at a 45° angle to cookie sheet. Run pancake turner across chocolate, allowing chocolate to curl.

ALMOND CUSTARD CREAM PUFFS

1 package (3.4 ounces) instant vanilla pudding and pie filling mix
1 cup cold milk
2 teaspoons almond-flavored liqueur *or* ½ teaspoon almond extract
1 cup whipped topping or whipped cream
¾ cup water
⅓ cup butter or margarine
¾ cup all-purpose flour
¼ teaspoon salt
3 eggs
1 can (11 ounces) mandarin orange segments, drained
Powdered sugar

For filling, beat pudding mix and milk in medium bowl with electric mixer at medium speed 2 minutes or until thickened. Stir in liqueur. Fold in whipped topping. Cover with plastic wrap. Refrigerate until ready to fill cream puffs.

For cream puffs, preheat oven to 400°F. Grease baking sheet. Bring water and butter to a boil in medium saucepan over high heat; stir until butter melts. Add flour and salt all at once, stirring vigorously. Continue cooking and stirring until mixture forms a ball. Remove from heat and cool 10 minutes. Add eggs, one at a time, beating vigorously after each addition until mixture is smooth.

Drop heaping tablespoons of batter into 6 mounds, 3 inches apart, on prepared baking sheet. Bake about 35 minutes or until golden brown and puffed. Cool slightly. Cut off tops and remove soft dough from insides. Cool completely on wire rack.

To serve, spoon filling into bottoms of cream puffs. Place oranges on top of filling, then cover with tops. Dust cream puffs with powdered sugar.   *Makes 6 servings*

PUMPKIN CHEESECAKE

Ginger-Walnut Crumb Crust (recipe follows)
3 packages (8 ounces each) cream cheese, softened
½ cup sugar
1 can (16 ounces) pumpkin
3 eggs
1 teaspoon ground cinnamon
½ teaspoon ground ginger
¼ teaspoon ground nutmeg
1 teaspoon grated lemon peel
Whipped cream
Walnut halves
Lemon peel twists

Prepare Ginger-Walnut Crumb Crust; set aside. *Reduce oven temperature to 300°F.*

Beat cream cheese and sugar in large bowl until fluffy. Beat in pumpkin and eggs; mix in spices and grated lemon peel. Pour mixture into crust.

Bake about 1¼ hours or until cheesecake is just set in center. Cool to room temperature on wire rack. Refrigerate until chilled, 3 to 4 hours.

Remove side of pan. Garnish cheesecake with whipped cream, walnut halves and lemon peel twists.   *Makes 14 to 16 servings*

GINGER–WALNUT CRUMB CRUST
1 cup gingersnap crumbs
¾ cup graham cracker crumbs
¼ cup ground walnuts
⅓ cup melted butter or margarine

Mix gingersnap and graham cracker crumbs with walnuts in bottom of 9-inch springform pan; mix in melted butter. Pat mixture evenly on bottom and 1 inch up side of pan. Bake in preheated 350°F oven until light brown, about 8 minutes. Cool on wire rack.

Favorite recipe from **Canned Food Information Council**

Almond Custard Cream Puffs

Peppermint Cheesecake

Lightly grease sides of 8- or 9-inch springform pan. Combine crust ingredients; mix well. Press evenly over bottom of pan. Chill while preparing filling. In bowl of electric mixer, combine Ricotta cheese, sugar, half-and-half, flour, vanilla and salt; beat until smooth. Add eggs, one at a time; beat until smooth. Place candies in heavy plastic bag. Crush with meat mallet or hammer. Reserve ¼ cup large pieces for garnish; stir remaining crushed candies into batter. Pour batter over crust. Bake at 350°F 1 hour or until center is just set. Turn off oven; cool in oven with door propped open 30 minutes. Remove to wire cooling rack; loosen cake from rim of pan with metal spatula. Cool completely; chill at least 4 hours. Just before serving, garnish cake around top edge with reserved crushed candies and mint leaves, if desired.

Makes 8 servings

PEPPERMINT CHEESECAKE

CRUST
- 1¼ cups vanilla wafer crumbs
- 3 tablespoons melted margarine

FILLING
- 4 cups (30 ounces) SARGENTO® Light Ricotta Cheese
- ½ cup sugar
- ½ cup half-and-half
- ¼ cup all-purpose flour
- 1 teaspoon vanilla
- ¼ teaspoon salt
- 3 eggs
- 16 peppermint candies
- Fresh mint leaves (optional)

RASPBERRY PEAR CHEESECAKE

- 1 (10-ounce) package frozen raspberries in syrup, thawed
- 2 teaspoons cornstarch
- 1 (6½- to 8-inch diameter) prepared plain cheesecake
- Canned Pears (page 403)
- Fresh raspberries (optional)
- ½ ounce semi-sweet chocolate
- ½ teaspoon shortening

Combine raspberries in syrup and cornstarch in small saucepan. Stir to dissolve cornstarch. Over medium heat, bring to a boil and cook just until clear and thickened, stirring constantly. Cool for 10 minutes. Spoon ⅓ cup raspberry sauce on top of cheesecake. Cut 3 or 4 Canned Pear halves in half lengthwise. Arrange pears spoke-fashion on top of sauce. Garnish with fresh raspberries, if desired. Melt chocolate with shortening. Drizzle over pears. Cut into wedges and serve with remaining raspberry sauce. *Makes 6 to 8 servings*

CANNED PEARS

- **4 pounds pears**
- **3½ cups water**
- **1¾ cups sugar**
- **3 tablespoons bottled lemon juice**
- **6 KERR® pint jars *or* 3 KERR® quart jars (with bands and lids)**

Peel, core and halve pears lengthwise. In 6- to 8-quart saucepan, combine water, sugar and lemon juice. Over medium-high heat, bring to a boil. Add pears and return to a boil. Remove from heat. Immediately fill jars with pears and syrup, leaving ½-inch headspace. Carefully run a non-metallic utensil down inside of jars to remove trapped air bubbles. Wipe jar tops and threads clean. Place hot lids on jars and screw bands on firmly. Process in boiling water canner 20 minutes for pint jars, 25 minutes for quart jars.   *Makes 6 pints or 3 quarts*

NOTES: For smaller yield, halve ingredients. Processing times and other directions remain the same.

Processing times must be increased for altitudes higher than 1000 feet. For altitudes between 1001-3000 feet, add 5 minutes; 3001-6000 feet, add 10 minutes; 6001-8000 feet, add 15 minutes; 8001-10,000 feet, add 20 minutes.

Raspberry Pear Cheesecake

LOW FAT CHEESECAKE

1 cup whole grain bagel-shaped cereal
½ cup zwieback crumbs
1 cup plus 2 tablespoons sugar, divided
2 tablespoons water
2 teaspoons margarine, melted
3 cups nonfat ricotta cheese
1½ cups reduced fat cream cheese
1 cup low fat sour cream
2 egg whites
3 tablespoons cornstarch
1 tablespoon vanilla
1 teaspoon grated lemon peel
   Blueberry Sauce or Pineapple Sauce
   (recipes follow), optional

Preheat oven to 325°F. Spray 10-inch springform pan with nonstick cooking spray. Combine cereal, zwieback crumbs and 2 tablespoons sugar in food processor or blender; process until fine crumbs form. Gradually add water and margarine; process until moistened. Press crumb mixture onto bottom and up side of prepared pan. Set aside.

Place ricotta cheese in food processor or blender; process about 2 minutes or until smooth. Add cream cheese, remaining 1 cup sugar, sour cream, egg whites, cornstarch, vanilla and lemon peel; process until smooth. Pour batter into prepared crust.

Bake 1 hour or until center is almost set. Turn off oven; leave cheesecake in oven with door closed 30 minutes. Remove from oven; cool completely on wire rack. Remove side of springform pan. Cover cheesecake with plastic wrap; refrigerate at least 4 hours or up to 2 days. Serve with Blueberry Sauce or Pineapple Sauce, if desired. *Makes 12 servings*

BLUEBERRY SAUCE

6 tablespoons blueberry jam
2 tablespoons lemon juice
2 tablespoons water
2 teaspoons cornstarch
1 cup fresh or frozen blueberries,
   thawed, drained
1 teaspoon grated lemon peel

Heat jam and lemon juice in medium saucepan over low heat. Stir together water and cornstarch; add to jam mixture. Cook until slightly thickened and let cool. Stir in blueberries and lemon peel.
Makes 12 (2-tablespoon) servings

PINEAPPLE SAUCE

1 can (8 ounces) crushed pineapple in
   juice, drained (reserve juice)
1 tablespoon plus 1½ teaspoons
   cornstarch
1 tablespoon sugar
2 tablespoons spiced rum *or* 1½
   teaspoons rum extract
½ teaspoon grated lemon or lime peel

Combine reserved pineapple juice and cornstarch in small saucepan; stir in sugar. Heat over medium heat until slightly thickened. Stir in rum; cool. Stir in crushed pineapple and lemon peel.
Makes 12 (2-tablespoon) servings

Low Fat Cheesecake

EGGNOG CHEESECAKE

2 packages (5½ ounces each) chocolate-laced pirouette cookies
⅓ cup graham cracker crumbs
3 tablespoons PARKAY® Spread Sticks, melted
2 packages (8 ounces each) PHILADELPHIA BRAND® Cream Cheese, softened
2 cups canned or dairy eggnog
1 cup milk
2 packages (4-serving size each) JELL-O® French Vanilla or Vanilla Flavor Instant Pudding & Pie Filling
1 tablespoon light rum
⅛ teaspoon ground nutmeg
COOL WHIP® Whipped Topping, thawed (optional)

Cut 1 inch crosswise off each cookie. Crush short pieces; set aside long pieces for garnish.

Combine cookie crumbs, graham cracker crumbs and spread until well mixed. Press firmly into bottom of 9-inch springform pan.

Beat cream cheese in large bowl with electric mixer on medium speed until well blended. Gradually add 1 cup of the eggnog, blending until smooth. Add remaining 1 cup eggnog, milk, pudding mix, rum and nutmeg. Beat until well blended, about 1 minute. Pour into prepared pan. Refrigerate 3 hours or until firm.

Run a small knife or spatula around side of pan to loosen cheesecake; remove side of pan. Press reserved cookie pieces, cut sides down, into side of cake. Garnish with whipped topping and additional cookies, if desired.
Makes 12 servings

CHOCOLATE TURTLE CHEESECAKE

24 chocolate sandwich cookies, ground (about 2¾ cups)
2 tablespoons butter or margarine, melted
2 packages (8 ounces each) cream cheese, softened
⅓ cup sugar
¼ cup sour cream
2 eggs
1 teaspoon vanilla
½ cup prepared caramel sauce
½ cup prepared fudge sauce
½ cup pecan halves

Preheat oven to 350°F. Combine ground cookies and butter in medium bowl; pat evenly on bottom and 1 inch up side of 9-inch springform pan. Place in freezer while preparing filling.

Beat cream cheese in large bowl with electric mixer at medium speed until fluffy. Beat in sugar, sour cream, eggs and vanilla until smooth. Pour mixture into prepared crust.

Bake cheesecake 30 to 35 minutes or until almost set in center. Loosen cheesecake from side of pan by running a spatula between cheesecake and pan. Cool on wire rack. Refrigerate, loosely covered, 8 hours or up to 3 days.

Remove side of springform pan from cheesecake, then place on a serving plate. Drizzle caramel and fudge sauces over cheesecake. Top each serving with 2 or 3 pecan halves.
Makes 12 servings

Chocolate Turtle Cheesecake

Mini Cheesecakes

MINI CHEESECAKES

1½ cups graham cracker or chocolate
    wafer crumbs
¼ cup sugar
¼ cup margarine or butter, melted
3 (8-ounce) packages cream cheese,
    softened
1 (14-ounce) can EAGLE® Brand
    Sweetened Condensed Milk (NOT
    evaporated milk)
3 eggs
2 teaspoons vanilla extract

Preheat oven to 300°F. Combine crumbs, sugar
and margarine; press equal portions onto
bottoms of 24 lightly greased* or paper-lined
muffin cups. In large mixer bowl, beat cream
cheese until fluffy. Gradually beat in sweetened
condensed milk until smooth. Add eggs and
vanilla; mix well. Spoon equal amounts of
mixture (about 3 tablespoons) into prepared
cups. Bake 20 minutes or until cakes spring
back when lightly touched. Cool. Chill. Garnish
as desired. Refrigerate leftovers.

Makes 2 dozen

CHOCOLATE MINI CHEESECAKES: Add 1
(6-ounce) package semi-sweet chocolate chips
(1 cup), melted, to batter; mix well. Proceed as
above. Bake 20 to 25 minutes.

*If greased muffin cups are used, cool baked
cheesecakes. Freeze 15 minutes; remove from
pans. Proceed as above.

MARBLE CHEESECAKE

Graham Crust (recipe follows)
3 packages (8 ounces each) cream cheese, softened
¾ cup sugar
½ cup dairy sour cream
2 teaspoons vanilla extract
3 tablespoons all-purpose flour
3 eggs
¼ cup HERSHEY₂S Cocoa
¼ cup sugar
1 tablespoon vegetable oil
½ teaspoon vanilla extract

Prepare Graham Crust; set aside. Combine cream cheese, ¾ cup sugar, sour cream and 2 teaspoons vanilla in large mixer bowl; beat on medium speed until smooth. Add flour, 1 tablespoon at a time, blending well. Add eggs; beat well. Combine cocoa and ¼ cup sugar in small bowl. Add oil, ½ teaspoon vanilla and 1½ cups of the cream cheese mixture; mix until well blended.

Spoon plain and chocolate mixtures alternately into prepared crust, ending with dollops of chocolate on top; gently swirl with knife or spatula for marbled effect. Bake at 450°F for 10 minutes; without opening oven door, *decrease temperature to 250°F* and continue to bake for 30 minutes. Turn off oven; let cheesecake remain in oven 30 minutes without opening door. Remove from oven; loosen cake from side of pan. Cool completely; chill thoroughly.   *Makes 10 to 12 servings*

GRAHAM CRUST
1 cup graham cracker crumbs
2 tablespoons sugar
¼ cup butter or margarine, melted

Combine graham cracker crumbs, sugar and melted butter. Press mixture onto bottom and ½ inch up side of 9-inch springform pan. Bake at 350°F for 8 to 10 minutes; cool.

Marble Cheesecake

Chilled Raspberry Cheesecake

CHILLED RASPBERRY CHEESECAKE

1½ cups vanilla wafer crumbs (about 45 wafers, crushed)
⅓ cup HERSHEY'S Cocoa
⅓ cup powdered sugar
⅓ cup butter or margarine, melted
1 package (10 ounces) frozen raspberries, thawed
1 envelope unflavored gelatin
½ cup cold water
½ cup boiling water
2 packages (8 ounces each) cream cheese, softened
½ cup granulated sugar
1 teaspoon vanilla extract
3 tablespoons seedless red raspberry preserves
Chocolate Whipped Cream (recipe follows)

Heat oven to 350°F. In medium bowl stir together crumbs, cocoa and powdered sugar; stir in melted butter. Press mixture onto bottom and 1½ inches up side of 9-inch springform pan. Bake 10 minutes; cool completely. Purée and strain raspberries; set aside. In small bowl sprinkle gelatin over cold water; let stand several minutes to soften. Add boiling water; stir until gelatin dissolves completely and mixture is clear. In large mixer bowl beat cream cheese, granulated sugar and vanilla, blending well. Gradually add raspberry purée and gelatin, mixing thoroughly; pour into prepared crust. Refrigerate several hours or overnight; remove rim of pan. Spread raspberry preserves over top. Garnish with Chocolate Whipped Cream. Cover leftovers; refrigerate.
Makes 10 to 12 servings

CHOCOLATE WHIPPED CREAM: In small mixer bowl stir together ½ cup powdered sugar and ¼ cup HERSHEY'S Cocoa. Add 1 cup chilled whipping cream and 1 teaspoon vanilla extract; beat until stiff.

RASPBERRY CHOCOLATE CHEESECAKE

 1 KEEBLER® Chocolate-Flavored Ready-
    Crust Pie Crust
12 ounces cream cheese, softened
½ cup sugar
 1 teaspoon vanilla extract
 2 eggs
½ cup frozen raspberries, well drained

GLAZE

 1 ounce unsweetened chocolate
¼ cup powdered sugar
 1 tablespoon evaporated milk
 2 teaspoons boiling water
 1 teaspoon butter
 1 teaspoon dark corn syrup
½ teaspoon vanilla

Preheat oven to 325°F. Beat cream cheese in large mixer bowl until fluffy; beat in sugar and vanilla. Add eggs, one at a time, beating after each addition until well blended.

Fold in raspberries, reserving a few for garnish. Pour mixture into crust. Bake 30 to 35 minutes. Cool completely; refrigerate.

To make Glaze, combine all ingredients except vanilla in saucepan. Stir constantly over low heat until smooth. Remove from heat; add vanilla. Pour over chilled cheesecake and refrigerate at least 3 hours. Use reserved raspberries for garnish when serving.

Makes 8 servings

HEATH® BAR CHEESECAKE

CRUST

1¾ cups vanilla wafer crumbs
 2 tablespoons sugar
⅓ cup margarine, melted

FILLING

 3 (8-ounce) packages cream cheese,
    softened
 1 cup sugar
 3 eggs
 1 cup sour cream
1½ teaspoons vanilla
 5 (1.2-ounce) HEATH® Bars, crushed

Preheat oven to 350°F. Combine crust ingredients; press into bottom and 1½ inches up side of 9-inch springform pan. Refrigerate.

In large mixer bowl, beat cream cheese with sugar at medium speed until fluffy. Add eggs, 1 at a time, beating well after each addition. Beat in sour cream and vanilla; blend until smooth. Spoon half of filling over prepared crust. Sprinkle half of Heath® Bars over filling; cover with remaining filling. Bake 1 hour or until cheesecake is just firm when pan is tapped gently. Cool completely in pan on wire rack. Sprinkle remaining Heath® Bars over top. Refrigerate until chilled.

Makes 10 to 12 servings

EASY CHOCOLATE CHEESECAKE

1¾ cups chocolate cookie or graham
    cracker crumbs
2 tablespoons sugar
⅓ cup margarine or butter, melted
2 packages (4 ounces each) BAKER'S®
    GERMAN'S® Sweet Chocolate,
    divided
2 eggs
⅔ cup light or dark corn syrup
⅓ cup heavy cream
1½ teaspoons vanilla
2 packages (8 ounces each)
    PHILADELPHIA BRAND® Cream
    Cheese, cut into cubes and softened

Heat oven to 325°F.

Combine cookie crumbs, sugar and margarine
in 9-inch pie plate or springform pan until well
mixed. Press into pie plate or onto bottom and
1¼ inches up side of springform pan.

Microwave 1½ packages (6 ounces) chocolate
in microwavable bowl on HIGH 1½ to 2
minutes, stirring halfway through heating time.
Stir until completely melted. Place eggs, corn
syrup, cream and vanilla in blender container;
cover. Blend until smooth. With blender
running, gradually add cream cheese, blending
until smooth. Blend in melted chocolate. Pour
into crust.

Bake 50 to 55 minutes or until center is almost
set. Cool on wire rack. Cover; refrigerate 3
hours or overnight. Just before serving, melt
remaining ½ package (2 ounces) chocolate and
drizzle over top. Garnish with raspberries, if
desired.   *Makes 8 servings*

WALNUT BROWNIE CHEESECAKE

CRUST
1¼ cups fine chocolate wafer crumbs
    (about 25 cookies, processed in
    blender or food processor)
3 tablespoons melted margarine
FILLING
4 cups (30 ounces) SARGENTO® Light
    Ricotta Cheese
1¼ cups packed light brown sugar
½ cup half-and-half
⅓ cup unsweetened cocoa powder
¼ cup all-purpose flour
1 teaspoon vanilla
¼ teaspoon salt
3 eggs
½ cup (2 ounces) coarsely chopped
    walnuts
    Confectioners' sugar (optional)

Lightly grease sides of 8- or 9-inch springform
pan. Combine crust ingredients; mix well. Press
evenly over bottom of pan. Chill while preparing
filling. In bowl of electric mixer, combine Ricotta
cheese, brown sugar, half-and-half, cocoa, flour,
vanilla and salt; beat until smooth. Add eggs,
one at a time; beat until smooth. Stir in walnuts.
Pour batter over crust. Bake at 350°F 1 hour
and 10 minutes or until center is just set. Turn
off oven; cool in oven with door propped open
30 minutes. Remove to wire cooling rack;
loosen cake from rim of pan with metal spatula.
Cool completely; chill at least 4 hours. Sift
confectioners' sugar over cheesecake just
before serving, if desired.   *Makes 8 servings*

MINI CHEESECAKES: Line 24 medium
(2½-inch) muffin cups with paper liners.
Sprinkle scant 1 tablespoon crust mixture into
each cup; pat lightly. Pour scant ⅓ cup filling
over each crust. Bake at 350°F 30 minutes or
until set. Remove to wire cooling rack; cool
completely. Cover and chill at least 2 hours.
Garnish as desired just before serving.

Easy Chocolate Cheesecake

INDIVIDUAL ORANGE SOUFFLÉS

Nonstick cooking spray
3 oranges
1 tablespoon plus 1½ teaspoons cornstarch
3 tablespoons orange-flavored liqueur
6 egg whites
⅛ teaspoon salt
6 tablespoons granulated sugar
1½ tablespoons sliced almonds (optional)
1½ tablespoons powdered sugar (optional)

Preheat oven to 450°F. Spray 6 individual soufflé dishes (8 to 10 ounces each) with cooking spray. Place dishes on jelly-roll pan; set aside.

Grate enough orange peel to equal 1½ teaspoons; set aside. Cut peel and membrane from oranges; section oranges over 1-quart saucepan. Dice oranges; add to saucepan. (There will be 1½ cups juice and pulp.) Stir in cornstarch until smooth. Cook and stir over medium heat until mixture comes to a boil and thickens slightly. Remove from heat. Stir in liqueur and reserved orange peel.

Beat egg whites and salt with electric mixer at high speed in large bowl until soft peaks form. Gradually beat in granulated sugar, 1 tablespoon at a time, until stiff peaks form and sugar is dissolved. Fold ¼ of egg white mixture into orange mixture, using rubber spatula or wire whisk. Fold all of orange mixture into remaining egg white mixture. Spoon into prepared dishes. Sprinkle with almonds, if desired. Immediately bake 12 to 15 minutes or until soufflés are puffed and browned. Sprinkle with powdered sugar, if desired. Serve immediately. *Makes 6 servings*

CHOCOLATE MOUSSE

1 teaspoon unflavored gelatin
1 tablespoon cold water
2 tablespoons boiling water
½ cup sugar
¼ cup HERSHEY'S Cocoa
1 cup chilled whipping cream
1 teaspoon vanilla extract

In small bowl sprinkle gelatin over cold water; let stand 1 minute to soften. Add boiling water; stir until gelatin is completely dissolved and mixture is clear. Cool slightly. In small mixer bowl stir together sugar and cocoa; add whipping cream and vanilla. Beat at medium speed, scraping bottom of bowl occasionally, until mixture is stiff; pour in gelatin mixture and beat until well blended. Spoon into serving dishes. Refrigerate about 30 minutes.
Makes four ½-cup servings

TROPICAL RICE PUDDING

1 cup FARMHOUSE® Original Quick Brown Rice
1½ cups water
⅛ teaspoon salt
2 cups milk
1 (8-ounce) can crushed pineapple in juice, undrained
1 (3½-ounce) package instant vanilla pudding mix
1 (3½-ounce) can *or* 1⅓ cups shredded sweetened coconut
⅔ cup coarsely chopped walnuts, toasted
2 tablespoons brown sugar

In medium saucepan, prepare rice according to package directions using water and salt. Meanwhile, combine remaining ingredients; add cooked rice to pudding mixture, stirring to combine. Serve warm or chilled.
Makes 5 cups

Individual Orange Soufflés

PUMPKIN BREAD PUDDING

½ loaf (8 ounces) raisin bread, cut into cubes
1 cup solid-pack canned pumpkin
½ cup packed brown sugar
½ cup liquid egg substitute *or* 2 eggs, beaten
1 teaspoon vanilla extract
½ teaspoon Dilijan Liquid Spice Ginger *or* 1 teaspoon freshly grated gingerroot
1 (12-ounce) can PET® Light Evaporated Skimmed Milk
⅓ cup walnuts, chopped

Preheat oven to 400°F. Place bread cubes in 9-inch pie plate or 9-inch round or square baking dish sprayed with nonstick cooking spray.

Combine pumpkin, brown sugar, egg substitute, vanilla and liquid spice ginger. Stir in evaporated milk and pour over cubed bread, coating all bread cubes with pumpkin mixture.

Sprinkle with walnuts. Bake 25 to 30 minutes or until knife inserted near center comes out clean. Cut into wedges to serve.

Makes 8 servings

TWO GREAT TASTES PUDDING PARFAITS

1 package (4¾ ounces) vanilla pudding and pie filling
3½ cups milk
1 cup REESE'S® Peanut Butter Chips
1 cup HERSHEY'S Semi-Sweet Chocolate Chips
Whipped topping (optional)

In large, heavy saucepan combine pudding mix and 3½ cups milk (rather than amount listed in package directions). Cook over medium heat, stirring constantly, until mixture comes to full boil. Remove from heat; divide hot mixture between 2 heat-proof medium bowls. Immediately stir peanut butter chips into mixture in one bowl and chocolate chips into mixture in second bowl. Stir both mixtures until melted and smooth. Cool slightly, stirring occasionally. Alternately spoon peanut butter and chocolate mixtures into parfait glasses, champagne glasses or dessert dishes. Place plastic wrap directly onto surface of each dessert; refrigerate several hours or overnight. Top with whipped topping and garnish as desired.

Makes 4 to 6 servings

Two Great Tastes Pudding Parfaits

Apple Pumpkin Dessert

Heat oven to 400°F. Spoon apple filling into 8 to 10 custard cups. In large mixer bowl, beat pumpkin, sweetened condensed milk, eggs, cinnamon, nutmeg and salt; spoon over apple filling. Combine crumbs and margarine. Sprinkle over pumpkin mixture. Place cups on 15×10-inch baking pan. Bake 10 minutes. *Reduce oven temperature to 350°F;* bake 15 minutes or until set. Cool. Garnish with whipped cream, if desired. Refrigerate leftovers. *Makes 8 to 10 servings*

PREP TIME: 20 minutes
TOTAL TIME: 1 hour

APPLE PUMPKIN DESSERTS

1 (21-ounce) can COMSTOCK® Brand
   Apple Filling or Topping
1 (16-ounce) can COMSTOCK® Brand
   Pumpkin (about 2 cups)
1 (14-ounce) can EAGLE® Brand
   Sweetened Condensed Milk (NOT
   evaporated milk)
2 eggs
1 teaspoon ground cinnamon
½ teaspoon ground nutmeg
½ teaspoon salt
1 cup gingersnap crumbs (about
   18 cookies)
2 tablespoons margarine or butter,
   melted

CRANBERRY 'N' BARLEY PUDDING

2 cups cooked barley
½ cup chopped dried cranberries
1⅓ cups milk
½ cup packed brown sugar
2 eggs, beaten
1 tablespoon butter or margarine, melted
1 teaspoon vanilla
½ teaspoon ground cinnamon

Combine cooked barley and cranberries; set aside. In large bowl, combine remaining ingredients; beat well. Stir in barley mixture. Pour into greased 2-quart casserole. Bake at 325°F 50 minutes or until set. Serve hot or cold with cream or your favorite topping.
Makes 6 to 8 servings

*Favorite recipe from **North Dakota Barley Council***

RICE PUDDING WITH DRIED FRUITS AND NUTMEG

⅔ cup CAROLINA®, MAHATMA®,
     RIVER®, or WATER MAID® Rice
⅛ teaspoon salt
4 cups water
3 large eggs *or* 3 ounces egg substitute
2 cups whole milk or 2% lowfat milk
¾ cup sugar
2 teaspoons vanilla
½ teaspoon freshly grated nutmeg
1 package unflavored gelatin
¼ cup cold water
1 cup combined raisins and chopped
     dried apricots, peaches and other
     dried fruit
1 cup whipping cream
   Fresh fruit (optional)
   Toasted coconut (optional)

In large saucepan, combine rice and salt with 4 cups water; bring to a boil. Reduce heat; simmer until most of the water has been absorbed, stirring occasionally. In bowl, whisk together eggs, milk, sugar, vanilla and nutmeg. Stir egg mixture into rice mixture and cook on low heat until thickened. *Do not boil.* In small bowl, sprinkle gelatin over ¼ cup cold water and let soften 10 minutes. Add gelatin mixture to rice mixture. Stir. Add dried fruit. Cover and refrigerate, stirring occasionally.

Whip cream until soft peaks form; fold into rice mixture. Refrigerate 2 to 3 hours. Garnish with additional freshly grated nutmeg, fresh fruit and coconut. *Makes 8 servings*

VARIATION: Substitute 1 cup light sour cream or lowfat vanilla yogurt for whipped cream.

Rice Pudding with Dried Fruits and Nutmeg

OLD–FASHIONED BREAD PUDDING

1 package (4-serving size) JELL-O®
   Vanilla Flavor Pudding & Pie Filling
4 tablespoons sugar, divided
3 cups milk, divided
¼ cup raisins
2 tablespoons grated lemon peel
   (optional)
1 tablespoon PARKAY® Spread Sticks
½ teaspoon vanilla
6 slices day-old white bread, cut into
   cubes
¼ teaspoon cinnamon
⅛ teaspoon ground nutmeg

Mix pudding mix and 2 tablespoons of the sugar in large saucepan. Gradually stir in 2 cups of the milk. Add raisins and lemon peel. Stirring constantly, cook on medium heat until mixture comes to full boil. Remove from heat; stir in spread and vanilla.

Pour remaining 1 cup milk over bread cubes in large bowl to moisten. Stir in pudding mixture. Pour into 1-quart baking dish. Combine remaining 2 tablespoons sugar with cinnamon and nutmeg. Sprinkle over pudding. Heat broiler. Broil 2 to 3 inches from heat 4 minutes or until sugar mixture is lightly browned and bubbly. Serve warm or chilled.

Makes about 6 servings

MOCHA PARFAIT

1½ tablespoons margarine
 ⅓ cup unsweetened cocoa powder
 1 cup boiling water
½ cup sugar
 1 tablespoon instant coffee granules
 1 teaspoon vanilla
 1 pint coffee-flavored nonfat frozen
    yogurt
12 whole coffee beans (optional)

Melt margarine in heavy saucepan over low heat. Add cocoa; cook and stir 3 minutes. Add boiling water, sugar and coffee; cook and stir until thickened. Remove from heat; stir in vanilla. Cool.

Place 2 tablespoons frozen yogurt in bottom of each of 4 parfait glasses. Top each with 1 tablespoon sauce. Top sauce with another 2 tablespoons frozen yogurt; top frozen yogurt with 2 tablespoons sauce. Repeat layering of 2 tablespoons frozen yogurt and 2 tablespoons sauce twice more. Top each parfait with 3 coffee beans, if desired. *Makes 4 servings*

Mocha Parfaits

CRÈME CARAMEL

½ cup sugar, divided
1 tablespoon hot water
2 cups skim milk
⅛ teaspoon salt
½ cup cholesterol free egg substitute
½ teaspoon vanilla
⅛ teaspoon maple extract

Heat ¼ cup sugar in heavy saucepan over low heat, stirring constantly until melted and straw colored. Remove from heat; stir in water. Return to heat; stir 5 minutes or until mixture is dark caramel color. Divide melted sugar evenly among 6 custard cups. Set aside.

Preheat oven to 350°F. Combine milk, remaining ¼ cup sugar and salt in medium bowl. Add egg substitute, vanilla and maple extract; mix well. Pour ½ cup mixture into each custard cup. Place cups in heavy baking pan and pour 1 to 2 inches hot water into pan.

Bake 40 to 45 minutes or until knife inserted near edge of each cup comes out clean. Cool on wire rack. Refrigerate 4 hours or overnight. Before serving, run knife around edge of custard cup. Invert custard onto serving plate; remove cup. *Makes 6 servings*

MAPLE SUNDAE

½ gallon DREYER'S or EDY'S GRAND
    Eggnog Ice Cream
½ cup maple syrup
    Ground cinnamon
    Toasted chopped pecans

• Place 1 scoop Dreyer's or Edy's Grand Eggnog Ice Cream in each of 8 dessert dishes.

• Heat maple syrup and drizzle small amount over each scoop.

• Dust lightly with cinnamon and sprinkle with pecans. *Makes 8 servings*

CREAMY CARAMEL SAUCE

1 cup granulated sugar
1 cup whipping cream
½ cup packed light brown sugar
⅓ cup corn syrup
1 teaspoon vanilla extract

Place granulated sugar, cream, brown sugar and corn syrup in heavy 2-quart saucepan. Stir over low heat until mixture boils. Carefully clip candy thermometer to side of pan (do not let bulb touch bottom of pan). Cook, stirring occasionally, about 20 minutes or until thermometer registers 238°F. Immediately remove from heat. Stir in vanilla. Cool about 15 minutes. Serve warm or pour into clean glass jars and seal tightly. Store up to 6 months in refrigerator. Reheat sauce over low heat before serving. *Makes about 2 cups sauce*

Crème Caramel

Honey Turtle Sauce, Honey Caramel Sauce, Honey Chocolate Sauce

HONEY CARAMEL SAUCE

1 cup honey
1 cup evaporated skim milk
½ cup butter or margarine

Combine honey, milk and butter in medium saucepan; mix well. Cook and stir until mixture comes to a boil. Cook over medium heat 8 to 10 minutes longer or until mixture thickens and becomes caramel colored. Pour into sterilized gift jars. Keep refrigerated. *Makes 2 cups*

*Favorite recipe from **National Honey Board***

HONEY CHOCOLATE SAUCE

1½ cups honey
1½ cups unsweetened cocoa
2 tablespoons butter or margarine

Combine all ingredients; mix well. Cover with waxed paper and microwave at HIGH (100% power) 2 to 2½ minutes, stirring after 1 minute. Pour into sterilized gift jars. Keep refrigerated.
Makes 2½ cups

*Favorite recipe from **National Honey Board***

HONEY TURTLE SAUCE

2 cups Honey Caramel Sauce (page 424)
1 cup Honey Chocolate Sauce (page 424)
½ to 1 cup broken pecans

Combine Honey Caramel Sauce, Honey Chocolate Sauce and pecans; mix well. Pour into sterilized gift jars. Keep refrigerated.
Makes 3 cups

Favorite recipe from **National Honey Board**

HOT FUDGE SAUCE

1 (6-ounce) package semi-sweet chocolate chips *or* 4 (1-ounce) squares semi-sweet chocolate
2 tablespoons margarine or butter
1 (14-ounce) can EAGLE® Brand Sweetened Condensed Milk (NOT evaporated milk)
2 tablespoons water
1 teaspoon vanilla extract

In heavy saucepan, over medium heat, melt chips and margarine with sweetened condensed milk and water. Cook and stir constantly until thickened, about 5 minutes. Add vanilla. Serve warm over ice cream or as a fruit dipping sauce. Refrigerate leftovers.
Makes about 2 cups

MICROWAVE DIRECTIONS: In 1-quart glass measure, combine ingredients. Cook on HIGH (100% power) 3 to 3½ minutes, stirring after each minute. Proceed as above.

TO REHEAT: In small heavy saucepan, combine desired amount of sauce with small amount of water. Over low heat, stir constantly until heated through.

VARIATIONS
Mocha: Add 1 teaspoon instant coffee with water. Proceed as directed.

Toasted Almond: Omit vanilla extract. Add ½ teaspoon almond extract. When sauce is thickened, stir in ½ cup chopped toasted almonds.

Choco-Mint: Omit vanilla extract. Add ½ to 1 teaspoon peppermint extract.

Spirited: Add ⅓ cup almond-, coffee-, mint- or orange-flavored liqueur after mixture has thickened.

Mexican: Omit water. Add 2 tablespoons coffee-flavored liqueur *or* 1 teaspoon instant coffee dissolved in 2 tablespoons water and 1 teaspoon ground cinnamon after mixture has thickened.

GOOEY HOT FUDGE SAUCE

2 cups (12 ounces) semisweet chocolate chips
2 tablespoons butter
½ cup half-and-half
1 tablespoon corn syrup
⅛ teaspoon salt
½ teaspoon vanilla extract

Melt chocolate and butter with half-and-half, corn syrup and salt in heavy 2-quart saucepan over low heat, stirring until smooth. Remove from heat; let stand 10 minutes. Stir in vanilla. Serve warm or pour into clean glass jars and seal tightly. Store up to 6 months in refrigerator. Reheat sauce in double-boiler over hot (not boiling) water before serving, if desired.
Makes about 1½ cups sauce

Santa Pleasin'

COOKIES

PINWHEELS

1 package DUNCAN HINES® Golden Sugar
    Cookie Mix
1 egg
¼ cup CRISCO® Oil or CRISCO® PURITAN®
    Canola Oil
4½ teaspoons water
1 egg white, lightly beaten
    Coarse decorating sugar
18 candied maraschino cherries, halved

1. Preheat oven to 375°F.

2. Combine cookie mix, egg, oil and water in large bowl. Stir until thoroughly blended. Roll dough to ⅛-inch thickness on lightly floured surface. Cut into 2½-inch squares. Place squares 1 inch apart on ungreased baking sheets. Cut 1-inch slits diagonally from each corner towards center. Fold every other corner tip towards center. Brush tops with egg white. Sprinkle with sugar. Place cherry half on center of each pinwheel. Bake at 375°F for 8 to 9 minutes or until edges are light golden brown. Remove to cooling racks. Cool completely. Store between layers of waxed paper in airtight containers.

Makes 3 dozen cookies

TIP: You may substitute granulated sugar for coarse decorating sugar, if desired.

CHRISTMAS ORNAMENT COOKIES

2¼ cups all-purpose flour
¼ teaspoon salt
1 cup granulated sugar
¾ cup butter or margarine, softened
1 large egg
1 teaspoon vanilla
1 teaspoon almond extract
Icing (recipe follows)
Assorted candies or decors

Place flour and salt in medium bowl; stir to combine. Beat sugar and butter in large bowl with electric mixer at medium speed until light and fluffy. Beat in egg, vanilla and almond extract. Gradually add flour mixture. Beat at low speed until well blended. Divide dough in half; cover and refrigerate 30 minutes or until firm.

Preheat oven to 350°F. Working with 1 portion at a time, roll out dough on lightly floured surface to ¼-inch thickness. Cut dough into desired shapes with assorted floured cookie cutters. Reroll trimmings and cut out more cookies. Place cutouts on *ungreased* cookie sheets. Using drinking straw or tip of sharp knife, cut a hole near top of each cookie to allow for piece of ribbon or string to be inserted for hanger. Bake 10 to 12 minutes or until edges are golden brown. Let cookies stand on cookie sheets 1 minute. Remove cookies to wire racks; cool completely.

Prepare Icing. Spoon Icing into small resealable plastic food storage bag. Cut off very tiny corner of bag; pipe Icing decoratively onto cookies. Decorate with candies as desired. Let stand at room temperature 40 minutes or until set. Thread ribbon through each cookie hole to hang as Christmas tree ornament.   *Makes about 2 dozen cookies*

ICING

2 cups powdered sugar
2 tablespoons milk or lemon juice
Food coloring (optional)

Place powdered sugar and milk in small bowl; stir with spoon until smooth. (Icing will be very thick. If it is too thick, stir in 1 teaspoon additional milk.) Divide into small bowls and tint with food coloring, if desired.

DUTCH ST. NICHOLAS COOKIES

½ cup whole natural almonds
¾ cup butter or margarine, softened
½ cup packed brown sugar
2 tablespoons milk
1½ teaspoons ground cinnamon
¼ teaspoon ground nutmeg
¼ teaspoon ground ginger
¼ teaspoon ground cloves
2 cups sifted all-purpose flour
1½ teaspoons baking powder
½ teaspoon salt
¼ cup coarsely chopped citron

Spread almonds in single layer on baking sheet. Bake at 375°F, 10 to 12 minutes, stirring occasionally, until lightly toasted. Cool. Chop finely. In large bowl, cream butter, sugar, milk and spices. In small bowl, combine flour, baking powder and salt. Add flour mixture to creamed mixture; blend well. Stir in almonds and citron. Knead dough slightly to make ball. Cover; refrigerate until firm. Roll out dough ¼ inch thick on lightly floured surface. Cut out with cookie cutters. Place 2 inches apart on greased cookie sheets. Bake at 375°F, 7 to 10 minutes, until lightly browned. Remove to wire racks to cool.

Makes about 3½ dozen cookies

*Favorite recipe from **Almond Board of California***

Christmas Ornament Cookies

CREAM CHEESE CUTOUT COOKIES

1 cup butter, softened
1 (8-ounce) package cream cheese,
    softened
1½ cups sugar
1 egg
1 teaspoon vanilla
½ teaspoon almond extract
3½ cups all-purpose flour
1 teaspoon baking powder
Almond Frosting (recipe follows)

In large mixer bowl combine butter and cream cheese. Beat until well combined. Add sugar; beat until fluffy. Add egg, vanilla and almond extract; beat well.

In medium bowl stir together flour and baking powder. Add flour mixture to cream cheese mixture; beat until well mixed. Divide dough in half. Cover and chill in refrigerator about 1½ hours or until dough is easy to handle.

On lightly floured surface roll dough to ⅛-inch thickness. Cut with desired cookie cutters. Place on ungreased cookie sheets. Bake in 375°F oven for 8 to 10 minutes or until done. Remove to wire racks; cool. Pipe or spread Almond Frosting on cooled cookies.

Makes about 90 cookies

ALMOND FROSTING: In small mixer bowl beat 2 cups sifted powdered sugar, 2 tablespoons softened butter and ¼ teaspoon almond extract until smooth. Beat in enough milk (4 to 5 teaspoons) until frosting is of piping consistency. For spreadable frosting, add a little more milk. Stir in a few drops of food coloring, if desired. Garnish with colored sugar, dragées or nuts, if desired.

Favorite recipe from **Wisconsin Milk Marketing Board**

Cream Cheese Cutout Cookies

GINGERBREAD KIDS

**2 ripe, small DOLE® Bananas, peeled
and cut into chunks**
4 cups all-purpose flour
1½ teaspoons ground ginger
1 teaspoon baking soda
1 teaspoon ground cinnamon
½ cup butter, softened
½ cup packed brown sugar
½ cup dark molasses
Prepared icing and candies

• Purée bananas in blender. Combine flour, ginger, baking soda and cinnamon. Cream butter and sugar until light and fluffy. Beat in molasses and bananas until blended. Stir in flour mixture with wooden spoon until completely blended. (Dough will be stiff.) Cover; refrigerate 1 hour.

• Preheat oven to 375°F. Divide dough into 4 parts. Roll out each part to ⅛-inch thickness on lightly floured surface. Cut out cookies using small gingerbread people cutters. Use favorite cookie cutters for any smaller amounts of remaining dough.

• Bake on greased cookie sheets 10 to 15 minutes or until just brown around edges. Cool completely on wire racks. Decorate as desired with favorite icing and candies.

Makes 30 to 35 cookies

Gingerbread Kids

CHRISTMAS STAINED GLASS COOKIES

Colored hard candy
¾ cup butter or margarine, softened
¾ cup granulated sugar
2 eggs
1 teaspoon vanilla extract
3 cups all-purpose flour
1 teaspoon baking powder
Frosting (optional)
Small decorative candies (optional)

Separate colors of hard candy into resealable plastic freezer bags. Crush with mallet or hammer to equal about ⅓ cup crushed candy; set aside. In mixing bowl, cream butter and sugar. Beat in eggs and vanilla. In another bowl, sift together flour and baking powder. Gradually stir flour mixture into butter mixture until dough is very stiff. Wrap in plastic wrap and chill about 3 hours.

Preheat oven to 375°F. Roll out dough to ⅛-inch thickness on lightly floured surface. Additional flour may be added to dough if necessary. Cut out cookies using large Christmas cookie cutters. Transfer cookies to foil-lined baking sheets. Using small Christmas cookie cutter of the same shape as large one, cut out and remove dough from center of each cookie.* Fill cut out sections with crushed candy. If using cookies as hanging ornaments, make holes near tops of cookies for string with drinking straw or chopstick. Bake 7 to 9 minutes or until cookies are lightly browned and candy is melted. Slide foil off baking sheets. When cool, carefully loosen cookies from foil. Use frosting and candy for additional decorations, if desired.
Makes about 2½ dozen medium-sized cookies

*For different designs, other cookie cutter shapes can be used to cut out centers of cookies (i.e., small circle and star-shaped cutters can be used to cut out ornament designs on large Christmas tree cookies).

Favorite recipe from **The Sugar Association, Inc.**

APPLE SAUCE GINGERBREAD COOKIES

4 cups all-purpose flour
2 teaspoons ground ginger
2 teaspoons ground cinnamon
1 teaspoon baking soda
½ teaspoon salt
¼ teaspoon ground nutmeg
½ cup margarine, softened
1 cup sugar
⅓ cup light (gold label) molasses
1 cup MOTT'S® Natural Apple Sauce
Decorator Icing (recipe follows)

Sift together flour, ginger, cinnamon, baking soda, salt and nutmeg; set aside. In bowl, with electric mixer at high speed, beat margarine, sugar and molasses until creamy. Alternately blend in dry ingredients and apple sauce. Cover and chill dough for several hours or overnight.

Preheat oven to 375°F. On floured surface, roll dough out to ⅛-inch thickness with lightly floured rolling pin. Cut with floured gingerbread man cutter or other shapes. Place on greased baking sheet. Bake 12 minutes or until done. Remove from sheet; cool on wire rack. Frost with Decorator Icing as desired. After icing dries, store in airtight container.
Makes 2½ dozen (5½-inch) cookies

DECORATOR ICING: Mix 2 cups confectioners' sugar and 1 tablespoon water. Add more water, 1 teaspoon at a time, until icing holds its shape and can be piped through a decorating tube.

Christmas Stained Glass Cookies, Teddy Bear
Gift Bread (page 288)

Gingerbread Bears

GINGERBREAD BEARS

3½ cups all-purpose flour
2 teaspoons ground cinnamon
1½ teaspoons ground ginger
1 teaspoon salt
1 teaspoon baking soda
1 teaspoon ground allspice
1 cup butter or margarine, softened
1 cup firmly packed brown sugar
1 teaspoon vanilla
⅓ cup molasses
2 eggs
Assorted cookie nonpareils (optional)
Ornamental Frosting (page 435) or
   prepared creamy or gel-type frostings
   in tubes (optional)
Colored sugar, assorted candies and
   grated chocolate (optional)

Place flour, cinnamon, ginger, salt, baking soda and allspice in medium bowl; stir to combine. Set aside. Beat butter, sugar and vanilla in large bowl with electric mixer at medium speed about 5 minutes or until light and fluffy. Beat in molasses and eggs until well blended. Beat in flour mixture at low speed until well blended. Divide dough into 3 equal portions; cover and refrigerate at least 2 hours or up to 24 hours.

Preheat oven to 350°F. Grease large cookie sheets; set aside. Working with 1 portion at a time, roll out dough on lightly floured surface to ⅛-inch thickness. Cut out dough with 3-inch bear-shaped cookie cutters. Place cookies 1 inch apart on prepared cookie sheets. Roll dough scraps into balls and ropes to make eyes and noses and to decorate bears. Decorate bears with nonpareils, if desired. Bake 10 minutes or until bottoms of cookies are golden brown. Let stand on cookie sheets 1 minute. Remove cookies to wire racks; cool completely.

Prepare Ornamental Frosting, if desired. Pipe or spread frosting on cooled cookies to decorate. Decorate with assorted nonpareils, colored sugar, assorted candies and/or grated chocolate, if desired. Store tightly covered at room temperature.

Makes about 3½ dozen cookies

ORNAMENTAL FROSTING

- ½ cup butter or margarine, softened
- 1 teaspoon vanilla
- 1 package (16 ounces) powdered sugar, sifted
- 2 tablespoons milk

Beat butter and vanilla in large bowl with electric mixer at medium speed. Beat in powdered sugar and enough milk at low speed until frosting is of desired spreading consistency. *Makes about 2 cups*

KRINGLE'S CUTOUTS

- 1¼ cups granulated sugar
- 1 BUTTER FLAVOR* CRISCO® Stick *or* 1 cup BUTTER FLAVOR CRISCO all-vegetable shortening
- 2 eggs
- ¼ cup light corn syrup or regular pancake syrup
- 1 teaspoon vanilla
- 3 cups plus 4 tablespoons all-purpose flour, divided
- ¾ teaspoon baking powder
- ½ teaspoon baking soda
- ½ teaspoon salt
- Colored sugar, decors and prepared frosting (optional)

1. Combine sugar and shortening in large bowl. Beat at medium speed of electric mixer until well blended. Add eggs, syrup and vanilla. Beat until well blended and fluffy.

2. Combine 3 cups flour, baking powder, baking soda and salt. Add gradually to creamed mixture at low speed. Mix until well blended.

3. Divide dough into 4 quarters. Cover and refrigerate at least two hours or overnight.

4. Heat oven to 375°F. Place sheets of foil on countertop for cooling cookies.

5. Spread 1 tablespoon flour on large sheet of waxed paper. Place one quarter of dough on floured paper. Flatten slightly with hands. Turn dough over. Cover with another large sheet of waxed paper. Roll dough to ¼-inch thickness. Remove top layer of waxed paper. Cut out dough with seasonal cookie cutters. Place cutouts 2 inches apart on ungreased baking sheets. Roll and cut out remaining dough. Sprinkle with colored sugar and decors or leave plain to frost when cool.

6. Bake at 375°F for 5 to 9 minutes, depending on size of cookies. (Bake small, thin cookies about 5 minutes; larger cookies about 9 minutes.) *Do not overbake.* Cool 2 minutes on baking sheets. Remove cookies to foil sheets to cool completely.

Makes 3 to 4 dozen cookies (depending on size and shape)

*Butter Flavor Crisco® is artificially flavored.

LINZER SANDWICH COOKIES

1⅓ cups all-purpose flour
¼ teaspoon baking powder
¼ teaspoon salt
¾ cup granulated sugar
½ cup butter, softened
1 large egg
1 teaspoon vanilla
    Powdered sugar (optional)
    Seedless raspberry jam

Place flour, baking powder and salt in small bowl; stir to combine. Beat granulated sugar and butter in medium bowl with electric mixer at medium speed until light and fluffy. Beat in egg and vanilla. Gradually add flour mixture. Beat at low speed until dough forms. Divide dough in half; cover and refrigerate 2 hours or until firm.

Preheat oven to 375°F. Working with 1 portion at a time, roll out dough on lightly floured surface to ³⁄₁₆-inch thickness. Cut dough into desired shapes with floured cookie cutters. Cut out equal numbers of each shape. (If dough becomes too soft, refrigerate several minutes before continuing.) Cut 1-inch centers out of half the cookies of each shape. Reroll trimmings and cut out more cookies. Place cookies 1½ to 2 inches apart on *ungreased* cookie sheets. Bake 7 to 9 minutes or until edges are lightly browned. Let cookies stand on cookie sheets 1 to 2 minutes. Remove cookies to wire racks; cool completely.

Sprinkle cookies with holes with powdered sugar, if desired. Spread 1 teaspoon jam on flat side of whole cookies, spreading almost to edges. Place cookies with holes, flat side down, over jam. Store tightly covered at room temperature or freeze up to 3 months.
Makes about 2 dozen cookies

OLD-FASHIONED MOLASSES COOKIES

4 cups sifted all-purpose flour
2 teaspoons ARM & HAMMER® Pure
    Baking Soda
1½ teaspoons ground ginger
½ teaspoon ground cinnamon
⅛ teaspoon salt
1½ cups molasses
½ cup shortening, melted
¼ cup butter or margarine, melted
⅓ cup boiling water
    Sugar

In medium bowl, combine flour, baking soda, spices and salt. In large bowl, mix molasses, shortening, butter and water. Add flour mixture to molasses mixture; blend well. Cover; refrigerate until firm, about 2 hours. Roll out dough ¼ inch thick on well-floured surface. Cut out with 3½-inch cookie cutters; sprinkle with sugar. Place 2 inches apart on ungreased cookie sheets. Bake in preheated 375°F oven about 12 minutes. Remove to wire racks to cool.
Makes about 3 dozen cookies

Linzer Sandwich Cookies

ALMOND BISCOTTI

¼ cup finely chopped almonds
½ cup sugar
2 tablespoons margarine
4 egg whites, lightly beaten
2 teaspoons almond extract
2 cups all-purpose flour
2 teaspoons baking powder
¼ teaspoon salt

Preheat oven to 375°F. Place almonds in small baking pan. Bake 7 to 8 minutes or until golden brown, watching carefully. Set aside.

Beat sugar and margarine in medium bowl with electric mixer until smooth. Add egg whites and almond extract; mix well. Combine flour, baking powder and salt in large bowl; mix well. Stir egg white mixture and almonds into flour mixture until well blended.

Spray two 9×5-inch loaf pans with nonstick cooking spray. Evenly divide dough between prepared pans. With wet fingertips, spread dough evenly over bottoms of pans. Bake 15 minutes or until knife inserted in centers comes out clean. Remove from oven and turn out onto cutting board. As soon as loaves are cool enough to handle, cut each into 16 (½-inch-thick) slices. Place slices on baking sheets covered with parchment paper or sprayed with nonstick cooking spray. Bake 5 minutes; turn over. Bake 5 minutes more or until golden brown. Serve warm or cool completely and store in airtight container.   *Makes 32 cookies*

Almond Biscotti

Lemony Butter Cookies

LEMONY BUTTER COOKIES

  ½ cup butter, softened
  ½ cup sugar
  1 egg
1½ cups all-purpose flour
  2 tablespoons fresh lemon juice
  1 teaspoon grated lemon peel
  ½ teaspoon baking powder
  ⅛ teaspoon salt
    Additional sugar

Beat butter and ½ cup sugar in large bowl with electric mixer until creamy. Beat in egg until light and fluffy. Mix in flour, lemon juice and lemon peel, baking powder and salt. Cover; refrigerate about 2 hours or until firm.

Preheat oven to 350°F. Roll out dough, a small portion at a time, on well-floured surface to ¼-inch thickness. (Keep remaining dough in refrigerator.) Cut with 3-inch round cookie cutter. Transfer to ungreased cookie sheets. Sprinkle with additional sugar.

Bake 8 to 10 minutes or until lightly browned on edges. Cool 1 minute on cookie sheets.
Remove to wire racks; cool completely. Store in airtight container.

Makes about 2½ dozen cookies

SUGAR-DUSTED SNOWFLAKES

½ cup Florida orange juice
⅓ cup milk
1 tablespoon butter or margarine
1 cinnamon stick, 3 inches long
2 cups unsifted all-purpose flour
1½ teaspoons grated orange peel
⅛ teaspoon baking powder
    Vegetable oil for frying
    Confectioners' sugar

In small saucepan, combine orange juice, milk, butter and cinnamon stick. (Mixture will curdle.) Bring to a boil over high heat. Remove from heat; let stand 15 minutes. Remove and discard cinnamon stick.

In large bowl, mix flour, orange peel and baking powder; make well in center. Add warm milk mixture all at once; stir, gradually incorporating flour mixture, until dry ingredients are moistened.

Turn out onto well-floured surface; knead 2 or 3 times until smooth. Cover; let stand 20 minutes to allow dough to cool and become less sticky.

Divide dough in half; roll half on well-floured surface to ⅛-inch thickness. Using floured 3-inch star or round cookie cutter, cut dough into shapes. Place on paper towel and let dry 10 minutes or until top is dry to the touch. Repeat with remaining dough, rolling scraps together. Cut out small designs in each cookie with canapé cutters, so cookie resembles snowflake.

Pour 1 inch of oil in medium skillet; heat to 350°F. Fry cookies, 2 or 3 at a time, turning once until very lightly browned. Drain on paper towels. Cool; sprinkle liberally with confectioners' sugar.   *Makes 3 dozen cookies*

Favorite recipe from **Florida Department of Citrus**

GLAZED SUGAR COOKIES

COOKIES
1 package DUNCAN HINES® Golden
    Sugar Cookie Mix
1 egg
¼ cup CRISCO® Oil or CRISCO®
    PURITAN® Canola Oil
1 teaspoon water
GLAZE
1½ cups sifted confectioners sugar
2 to 3 tablespoons water or milk
¾ teaspoon vanilla extract
    Food coloring (optional)
    Red and green sugar crystals,
        nonpareils or cinnamon candies

1. Preheat oven to 375°F.

2. For Cookies, combine cookie mix, egg, oil and water in large bowl. Stir until thoroughly blended. Roll dough to ¼-inch thickness on lightly floured surface. Cut dough into desired shapes using floured cookie cutters. Place cookies 2 inches apart on ungreased baking sheets. Bake at 375°F for 7 to 8 minutes or until edges are light golden brown. Cool 1 minute on baking sheets. Remove to cooling racks. Cool completely.

3. For Glaze, combine confectioners sugar, water and vanilla extract in medium bowl. Beat until smooth. Tint glaze with food coloring, if desired. Brush glaze on each cookie with clean pastry brush. Sprinkle cookies with sugar crystals, nonpareils or cinnamon candies before glaze sets. Allow glaze to set before storing between layers of waxed paper in airtight containers.   *Makes 4 dozen cookies*

TIP: Use DUNCAN HINES® Creamy Homestyle Vanilla Frosting for a quick glaze. Heat frosting in opened container in microwave oven at HIGH (100% power) for 10 to 15 seconds. Stir well. Spread on cookies and decorate as desired before frosting sets.

Top to bottom: Bavarian Cookie Wreaths (page 449),
Sugar-Dusted Snowflakes

PINWHEELS AND CHECKERBOARDS

2 cups flour
1 teaspoon CALUMET® Baking Powder
½ teaspoon salt
⅔ cup margarine or butter
1 cup sugar
1 egg
1 teaspoon vanilla
2 squares BAKER'S® Unsweetened
    Chocolate, melted

Mix flour, baking powder and salt in medium bowl. Beat margarine in large bowl with electric mixer on medium speed to soften. Gradually add sugar, beating until light and fluffy. Beat in egg and vanilla. Stir in flour mixture until well blended. Divide dough into two equal portions; blend chocolate into one portion. Use prepared doughs to make Pinwheels or Checkerboards.

Makes about 4½ to 5 dozen cookies

PINWHEELS: Roll out chocolate and plain doughs separately between sheets of waxed paper into 12×8-inch rectangles. Remove top sheets of paper. Invert plain dough onto chocolate dough and remove remaining paper. Roll up as for jelly roll; wrap in waxed paper. Refrigerate 3 hours or overnight. (Or, freeze 1 hour.) Heat oven to 375°F. Slice dough into ¼-inch-thick slices. Place on ungreased cookie sheets. Bake 10 minutes or until cookies just begin to brown around edges. Cool on racks.

CHECKERBOARDS: Roll out chocolate and plain doughs separately between sheets of waxed paper into 9×4½-inch rectangles. Brush chocolate dough lightly with milk and top with plain dough. Using a long, sharp knife, cut lengthwise into 3 equal strips, 1½ inches wide. Stack strips, alternating colors and brushing each layer with milk. Cut lengthwise again into 3 equal sections, ½ inch wide. Invert middle section so that colors are alternated; press together lightly. Carefully wrap in waxed paper; refrigerate overnight or freeze until firm enough to slice. Heat oven to 375°F. Slice dough into ⅛-inch-thick slices. Place on ungreased cookie sheets. Bake 8 minutes or just until white portions begin to brown. Cool on racks.

NOTES: If dough softens while handling, refrigerate until firm. To hang on Christmas tree, poke holes in unbaked cookies near edges, using a straw or wooden pick. Insert red string licorice through holes in cooled, baked cookies and tie.

CHOCO-COCO PECAN CRISPS

½ cup butter or margarine, softened
1 cup packed light brown sugar
1 egg
1 teaspoon vanilla
1½ cups all-purpose flour
1 cup chopped pecans
⅓ cup unsweetened cocoa
½ teaspoon baking soda
1 cup flaked coconut

*Left to right: Choco-Coco Pecan Crisps,
Holiday Fruit Drops (page 468)*

Cream butter and sugar in large bowl until light and fluffy. Beat in egg and vanilla. Combine flour, pecans, cocoa and baking soda in small bowl until well blended. Add to creamed mixture, blending until stiff dough is formed. Sprinkle coconut on work surface. Divide dough into 4 parts. Shape each part into a roll about 1½ inches in diameter; roll in coconut until thickly coated. Wrap in plastic wrap; refrigerate until firm, at least 1 hour or up to 2 weeks. (For longer storage, wrap in foil and freeze up to 6 weeks.)

Preheat oven to 350°F. Cut rolls into ⅛-inch-thick slices. Place 2 inches apart on ungreased cookie sheets. Bake 10 to 13 minutes or until firm, but not overly browned. Remove to wire racks to cool.   *Makes about 6 dozen cookies*

AUSTRIAN TEA COOKIES

1½ cups sugar, divided
½ cup (1 stick) butter, softened
½ cup vegetable shortening
1 egg, beaten
½ teaspoon vanilla extract
2 cups all-purpose flour
2 cups ALMOND DELIGHT® brand
    cereal, crushed to 1 cup
½ teaspoon baking powder
¼ teaspoon ground cinnamon
14 ounces almond paste
2 egg whites
5 tablespoons raspberry or apricot jam,
    warmed
¼ cup sliced almonds (optional)

In large bowl cream 1 cup sugar, butter and shortening. Add egg and vanilla; mix well. Stir in flour, cereal, baking powder and cinnamon until well combined. Chill 1 to 2 hours or until firm.

Preheat oven to 350°F. Roll dough on lightly floured surface to ¼-inch thickness. Cut into 2-inch circles and place on ungreased cookie sheet; set aside. In small bowl beat almond paste, egg whites and remaining ½ cup sugar until smooth. With pastry tube, pipe almond paste mixture ½ inch thick on top of each cookie along outside edge. Place ¼ teaspoon jam in center of each cookie, spreading out to paste. Place 1 sliced almond on top of jam. Bake 8 to 10 minutes or until lightly browned. Let stand 1 minute before removing from cookie sheet. Cool on wire rack.
Makes 3½ dozen cookies

BASIC HOLIDAY RAISIN COOKIES

½ cup butter or margarine, softened
⅓ cup sugar
1 egg yolk
⅛ teaspoon salt
1 cup all-purpose flour
½ cup raisins
   Semisweet or white chocolate
   Colored sprinkles, raisins, nuts or
     candied fruit pieces, for decoration

Cream butter and sugar; beat in egg yolk and salt. Add flour just to blend thoroughly. Mix in raisins. On lightly floured surface, roll into 12-inch log. Wrap securely and refrigerate at least 1 hour or up to 1 week.

Preheat oven to 350°F. With sharp knife, slice cookies ⅓ inch thick; place 1 inch apart on ungreased baking sheets. Bake 15 to 20 minutes until cookies are set and bottoms are lightly browned. Remove to racks to cool completely. Decorate as desired with melted semisweet or white chocolate and top with colored sprinkles, raisins, nuts or candied fruit pieces. Cool; store between sheets of waxed paper in airtight container.

Makes 3 dozen cookies

*Favorite recipe from **California Raisin Advisory Board***

CHOCOLATE SPRITZ COOKIES

1 package DUNCAN HINES® Golden
   Sugar Cookie Mix
⅓ cup unsweetened cocoa
1 egg
⅓ cup CRISCO® Oil or CRISCO®
   PURITAN® Canola Oil
2 tablespoons water

1. Preheat oven to 375°F.

2. Combine cookie mix and cocoa in large mixing bowl. Stir until blended. Add egg, oil and water. Stir until thoroughly blended.

3. Fill cookie press with dough. Press desired shapes 2 inches apart onto ungreased cookie sheets. Bake at 375°F for 6 to 8 minutes or until set. Cool 1 minute on cookie sheets. Remove to cooling racks. Cool completely.

Makes 5 to 6 dozen cookies

NOTE: For a delicious, no-cholesterol variation, substitute 2 egg whites for whole egg.

TIP: For festive cookies, decorate before baking with assorted decors or after baking with melted milk chocolate or semi-sweet chocolate, or white chocolate and chopped nuts.

Chocolate Spritz Cookies

CHRISTMAS SPRITZ COOKIES

2¼ cups all-purpose flour
¼ teaspoon salt
1¼ cups powdered sugar
1 cup butter, softened
1 large egg
1 teaspoon vanilla
1 teaspoon almond extract
Green food coloring (optional)
Candied red and green cherries and assorted decorative candies (optional)
Icing (recipe follows), optional

Preheat oven to 375°F. Place flour and salt in medium bowl; stir to combine. Beat powdered sugar and butter in large bowl with electric mixer until light and fluffy. Beat in egg, vanilla and almond extract. Gradually add flour mixture. Beat at low speed until well blended.

Divide dough in half. If desired, tint half of dough with green food coloring. Fit cookie press with desired plate (or change plates for different shapes after first batch). Fill press with dough; press dough 1 inch apart onto *ungreased* cookie sheets. Decorate cookies with cherries and assorted candies, if desired.

Bake 10 to 12 minutes or until just set. Remove cookies to wire racks; cool completely.

Prepare Icing, if desired. Pipe or drizzle onto cooled cookies. Decorate with cherries and assorted candies, if desired. Store tightly covered at room temperature or freeze up to 3 months.   *Makes about 5 dozen cookies*

ICING
1½ cups powdered sugar
2 tablespoons milk plus 1 teaspoon additional, if needed
⅛ teaspoon almond extract

Place all ingredients in medium bowl; stir with spoon until thick, but spreadable. (If Icing is too thick, stir in 1 teaspoon additional milk.)

Christmas Spritz Cookies

CALIFORNIA APRICOT PISTACHIO BISCOTTI

1¼ cups all-purpose flour
½ cup whole-wheat flour
1 cup sugar
½ teaspoon baking powder
¼ teaspoon salt
5 tablespoons cold unsalted butter, cut into pieces
¾ teaspoon vanilla extract
2 eggs, slightly beaten
⅔ cup coarsely chopped California dried apricots
1 cup shelled natural California pistachios
1 teaspoon sugar

Preheat oven to 350°F. Lightly grease large baking sheet.

In food processor or blender, process flours, 1 cup sugar, baking powder and salt until blended. Add butter and vanilla; process until mixture resembles coarse crumbs. Add eggs; process until blended. Add apricots and pistachios; process just until dough is evenly moistened.

Remove dough from food processor; form into 2 balls. On prepared baking sheet, shape each half of dough into a 12-inch log. With hands, flatten each log to a width of 2 inches. Sprinkle each log with ½ teaspoon sugar. Bake 25 minutes or until golden brown. Remove logs to cooling rack; cool 10 minutes. *Do not turn oven off.* With serrated knife, carefully cut logs diagonally into ½-inch slices. Place on baking sheet with cut sides up; return to oven and bake 7 minutes or until very lightly browned. Transfer to wire rack; cool completely.
Makes 4 dozen cookies

*Favorite recipe from **California Apricot Advisory Board***

LEMONY SPRITZ STICKS

1 cup butter or margarine, softened
1 cup confectioners' sugar
¼ cup REALEMON® Lemon Juice from Concentrate
2½ cups unsifted flour
¼ teaspoon salt
Chocolate Glaze (recipe follows)
Finely chopped nuts

Preheat oven to 375°F. In large mixer bowl, beat butter and sugar until fluffy. Add ReaLemon® brand; beat well. Stir in flour and salt; mix well. Place dough in cookie press with star-shaped plate. Press dough onto greased baking sheets into 3-inch strips. Bake 5 to 6 minutes or until lightly browned on edges. Cool 1 to 2 minutes; remove from baking sheets. Cool completely. Dip ends of cookies in Chocolate Glaze, then into nuts.
Makes about 8½ dozen cookies

CHOCOLATE GLAZE: In small saucepan, melt 3 ounces semisweet chocolate and 2 tablespoons margarine or butter. Makes about ⅓ cup.

TIP: When using electric cookie gun, use decorator tip. Press dough onto greased baking sheets into 3×½-inch strips. Bake 8 to 10 minutes or until lightly browned on edges.

447

DANISH COOKIE RINGS
(VANILLEKRANSER)

- ½ cup blanched almonds
- 2 cups all-purpose flour
- ¾ cup sugar
- ¼ teaspoon baking powder
- 1 cup butter, cut into small pieces
- 1 large egg
- 1 tablespoon milk
- 1 tablespoon vanilla
- 8 candied red cherries
- 16 candied green cherries

Grease cookie sheets; set aside. Process almonds in food processor until ground, but not pasty. Place almonds, flour, sugar and baking powder in large bowl. Cut butter into flour mixture with pastry blender or 2 knives until mixture is crumbly.

Beat egg, milk and vanilla in small bowl with fork until well blended. Add egg mixture to flour mixture; stir until soft dough forms.

Spoon dough into pastry bag fitted with medium star tip. Pipe 3-inch rings 2 inches apart onto prepared cookie sheets. Refrigerate 15 minutes or until firm.

Preheat oven to 375°F. Cut cherries into halves. Cut each red cherry half into quarters; cut each green cherry half into 4 slivers. Press red cherry quarter onto each ring where ends meet. Arrange 2 green cherry slivers on either side of red cherry to form leaves. Bake 8 to 10 minutes or until golden. Remove cookies to wire racks; cool completely. Store tightly covered at room temperature or freeze up to 3 months. *Makes about 5 dozen cookies*

Danish Cookie Rings

Golden Kolacky

GOLDEN KOLACKY

　½ cup butter, softened
　4 ounces cream cheese, softened
　1 cup all-purpose flour
　　Fruit preserves

Combine butter and cream cheese in large bowl; beat until smooth and creamy. Gradually add flour to butter mixture, blending until mixture forms soft dough. Divide dough in half; cover and refrigerate until firm.

Preheat oven to 375°F. Roll out dough, ½ at a time, on floured surface to ⅛-inch thickness. Cut into 3-inch squares. Spoon 1 teaspoon preserves in center of each square. Bring two opposite corners to center; pinch together tightly to seal. Fold sealed tip to one side; pinch to seal. Place 1 inch apart on *ungreased* cookie sheets. Bake 10 to 15 minutes or until lightly browned. Remove to cooling racks; cool completely.　*Makes about 2½ dozen cookies*

BAVARIAN COOKIE WREATHS

　3½ cups unsifted all-purpose flour
　　1 cup sugar, divided
　　3 teaspoons grated orange peel, divided
　　¼ teaspoon salt
　1⅓ cups butter or margarine
　　¼ cup Florida orange juice
　　⅓ cup finely chopped blanched almonds
　　1 egg white beaten with 1 teaspoon
　　　water
　　　Prepared frosting (optional)

Preheat oven to 400°F. In large bowl, mix flour, ¾ cup sugar, 2 teaspoons orange peel and salt. Using pastry blender, cut in butter and orange juice until mixture holds together. Knead a few times and press into a ball.

Shape dough into ¾-inch balls. On lightly floured surface, roll each ball into a 6-inch rope. Using two ropes, twist together to form one rope. Pinch ends of rope together to make a wreath; place on lightly greased baking sheets.

In shallow dish, mix almonds, remaining ¼ cup sugar and 1 teaspoon orange peel. Brush top of each wreath with egg white mixture and sprinkle with sugar-almond mixture.

Bake 8 to 10 minutes or until lightly browned. Remove to wire racks; cool completely. Frost if desired.　*Makes 5 dozen cookies*

*Favorite recipe from **Florida Department of Citrus***

SPANISH CHURROS

1 cup water
¼ cup butter or margarine
6 tablespoons sugar, divided
¼ teaspoon salt
1 cup all-purpose flour
2 large eggs
    Vegetable oil for frying
1 teaspoon ground cinnamon

Place water, butter, 2 tablespoons sugar and salt in medium saucepan; bring to a boil over high heat. Remove from heat; add flour. Beat with spoon until dough forms ball and releases from side of pan. Vigorously beat in eggs, 1 at a time, until mixture is smooth. Spoon dough into pastry bag fitted with large star tip. Pipe 3×1-inch strips onto waxed-paper-lined baking sheets. Place baking sheets in freezer; freeze 20 minutes.

Pour vegetable oil into 10-inch skillet to ¾-inch depth. Heat oil to 375°F. Transfer frozen dough to hot oil with large spatula. Fry 4 or 5 cookies at a time until deep golden brown, 3 to 4 minutes, turning once. Remove cookies with spatula to paper towels; drain.

Combine remaining 4 tablespoons sugar with cinnamon. Place in paper bag. Add warm cookies 1 at a time; close bag and shake until cookie is coated with cinnamon mixture. Repeat with remaining cinnamon mixture and cookies. Remove cookies to wire racks; cool completely. Store tightly covered at room temperature or freeze up to 3 months.
Makes about 3 dozen cookies

PINWHEELS

3 to 3¼ cups all-purpose flour, divided
1 package RED STAR® Active Dry Yeast
    or Quick-Rise™ Yeast
⅓ cup granulated sugar
1 teaspoon salt
½ cup water
⅓ cup shortening
2 eggs
    Cherry or raspberry preserves
1 egg, slightly beaten, plus 1 tablespoon
    water, for egg wash mixture
    Candied cherries and confectioners'
    sugar for garnish

In large mixer bowl, combine 1½ cups flour, yeast, granulated sugar and salt; mix well. Heat water and shortening until very warm (120° to 130°F). Add shortening mixture to flour mixture. Blend in 2 eggs at low speed until moistened; beat 3 minutes at medium speed. By hand, gradually stir in enough remaining flour to make soft dough. Cover dough with plastic wrap. Refrigerate 6 to 12 hours. While dough is chilling, punch down several times.

Allow dough to come to room temperature. Divide dough in half. Roll each half into 14×10½-inch rectangle. Cut into 3½-inch squares. Place on greased baking sheets. Cut each square diagonally from each corner to ½ inch from center so that there are 2 points at each corner. Place rounded teaspoonful preserves in center of each square. Lightly brush every other point with egg wash mixture. Bring moistened points toward center; gently twist and pinch to fasten together. Top each center with small piece of dough (about ½ inch in diameter), or use a candied cherry for garnish.

Lightly cover; let rise at room temperature until almost doubled, 15 to 20 minutes (10 to 15 minutes for Quick-Rise™ Yeast). Bake at 350°F for 15 minutes or until golden brown. Remove to wire rack to cool slightly. Sprinkle with confectioners' sugar.
Makes 2 dozen cookies

Spanish Churros

Pfeffernusse

PFEFFERNUSSE

3½ cups all-purpose flour
2 teaspoons baking powder
1½ teaspoons ground cinnamon
1 teaspoon ground ginger
½ teaspoon baking soda
½ teaspoon salt
½ teaspoon ground cloves
½ teaspoon ground cardamom
¼ teaspoon freshly ground black pepper
1 cup butter, softened
1 cup granulated sugar
¼ cup dark molasses
1 large egg
Sifted powdered sugar

Grease cookie sheets; set aside. Place flour, baking powder, cinnamon, ginger, baking soda, salt, cloves, cardamom and pepper in large bowl; stir to combine. Beat butter and granulated sugar in large bowl with electric mixer at medium speed until light and fluffy. Beat in molasses and egg. Gradually add flour mixture. Beat at low speed until dough forms. Cover dough and refrigerate until firm, 30 minutes or up to 3 days.

Preheat oven to 350°F. Roll dough into 1-inch balls. Place balls 2 inches apart on prepared cookie sheets. Bake 12 to 14 minutes or until golden brown. Remove cookies to wire racks; dust with sifted powdered sugar. Cool completely. Store tightly covered at room temperature or freeze up to 3 months.

Makes about 5 dozen cookies

ALMOND CRESCENTS

1 cup butter or margarine, softened
⅓ cup granulated sugar
1¾ cups all-purpose flour
¼ cup cornstarch
1 teaspoon vanilla extract
1½ cups ground almonds, toasted*
Chocolate Glaze (recipe follows) or
powdered sugar

Preheat oven to 325°F. Beat butter and granulated sugar in large bowl until creamy. Mix in flour, cornstarch and vanilla. Stir in almonds. Shape tablespoonfuls of dough into crescents. Place 2 inches apart on *ungreased* cookie sheets. Bake 22 to 25 minutes or until light brown. Cool 1 minute. Remove to wire racks; cool completely. Drizzle with Chocolate Glaze, if desired. Allow chocolate to set, then store cookies in airtight container. Or, before serving, sprinkle with powdered sugar.

Makes about 3 dozen cookies

Top to bottom: Scottish Shortbread (page 474), Almond Crescents

CHOCOLATE GLAZE: Place ½ cup semisweet chocolate chips and 1 tablespoon butter or margarine in small resealable plastic bag. Place bag in bowl of hot water for 2 to 3 minutes or until chocolate is softened. Dry with paper towel. Knead until chocolate mixture is smooth. Cut off very tiny corner of bag. Drizzle chocolate mixture over cookies.

*To toast almonds, spread on cookie sheet. Bake at 325°F for 4 minutes or until almonds are fragrant and golden.

RASPBERRY JEWELS

1 package DUNCAN HINES® Moist
Deluxe Raspberry Cake Mix
¾ cup butter or margarine, softened
2 eggs, separated
Chopped pecans
Seedless raspberry jam

1. Preheat oven to 350°F.

2. Combine cake mix, butter and egg yolks in large bowl. Beat at low speed with electric mixer until dough forms. Shape dough into 1-inch balls. Dip into egg whites, then into chopped pecans. Place, pecan side up, 2 inches apart on ungreased baking sheets. Make indentation in center of each ball with thumb or handle of wooden spoon. Fill with ¼ teaspoon jam.

3. Bake at 350°F for 10 to 12 minutes or until light golden brown. Cool 1 minute on baking sheets. Remove to cooling racks. Cool completely. *Makes 4½ dozen cookies*

CHOCOLATE ALMOND BISCOTTI

2 cups (12-ounce package) NESTLÉ®
　Toll House® Semi-Sweet Chocolate
　Morsels, divided
2 cups all-purpose flour
¼ cup NESTLÉ® Toll House® Baking
　Cocoa
1½ teaspoons baking powder
¼ teaspoon baking soda
¼ teaspoon salt
½ cup granulated sugar
½ cup packed brown sugar
¼ cup (½ stick) butter or margarine,
　softened
½ teaspoon vanilla extract
½ teaspoon almond extract
3 eggs
1 cup slivered almonds, toasted
2 tablespoons shortening

MICROWAVE *1 cup* morsels in medium microwave-safe bowl on HIGH (100% power) for 1 minute; stir. Microwave at additional 10 to 20 second intervals, stirring until smooth; cool to room temperature. Combine flour, cocoa, baking powder, baking soda and salt in medium bowl.

BEAT granulated sugar, brown sugar, butter, vanilla and almond extract until crumbly. Add eggs one at a time, beating well after each addition. Beat in melted chocolate. Gradually beat in flour mixture. Stir in nuts. Chill for 15 minutes until firm.

SHAPE dough into 2 loaves (3 inches wide and 1 inch high) with floured hands on 1 large or 2 small greased baking sheets.

BAKE in preheated 325°F. oven for 40 to 50 minutes or until firm. Let stand for 15 minutes. Cut into ¾-inch-thick slices; turn slices on their sides. Bake for 10 minutes on *each* side until dry. Remove to wire racks to cool completely.

MICROWAVE *remaining* 1 cup morsels and shortening in medium microwave-safe bowl on HIGH (100% power) for 1 minute; stir. Microwave at 10 to 20 second intervals, stirring until smooth. Dip biscotti into chocolate coating, pushing mixture halfway up biscotti with a spatula; shake off excess. Place on waxed-paper-lined tray. Chill for 10 minutes or until chocolate is set. Store in airtight containers in a cool place or in refrigerator. *Makes about 2½ dozen cookies*

PEANUT BUTTER CRACKLES

1½ cups all-purpose flour
1 teaspoon baking soda
⅛ teaspoon salt
½ cup MAZOLA® Margarine, softened
½ cup SKIPPY SUPER CHUNK® or
　Creamy Peanut Butter
½ cup granulated sugar
½ cup packed brown sugar
1 egg
1 teaspoon vanilla
　Granulated sugar
　Chocolate candy stars

In small bowl, combine flour, baking soda and salt. In large bowl, beat margarine and peanut butter until well blended. Beat in sugars until blended. Beat in egg and vanilla. Gradually beat in flour mixture until well mixed. Shape dough into 1-inch balls. Roll in granulated sugar. Place 2 inches apart on ungreased cookie sheets. Bake in preheated 375°F oven 10 minutes or until lightly browned. Remove from oven and quickly press chocolate star firmly into top of each cookie (cookie will crack around edge). Remove to wire racks to cool completely. *Makes about 5 dozen cookies*

MINI CHIP SNOWBALL COOKIES

1½ cups (3 sticks) butter, softened
¾ cup powdered sugar
1 tablespoon vanilla extract
½ teaspoon salt
3 cups all-purpose flour
**2 cups (12-ounce package) NESTLÉ®
    Toll House® Semi-Sweet Chocolate
    Mini Morsels**
**½ cup finely chopped pecans
    Powdered sugar**

Beat butter, ¾ cup powdered sugar, vanilla and salt in large mixer bowl. Gradually beat in flour; stir in morsels and pecans. Shape level tablespoonfuls of dough into 1-inch balls. Place on ungreased baking sheets.

Bake in preheated 375°F. oven for 10 to 12 minutes or until cookies are set and lightly browned. Remove from oven. Sift powdered sugar over hot cookies on baking sheets. Let stand for 10 minutes; remove to wire racks to cool completely. Sprinkle with additional powdered sugar if desired. Store in airtight containers.   *Makes 5 dozen cookies*

SNOWBALLS

**½ cup DOMINO® Confectioners 10-X
    Sugar**
¼ teaspoon salt
1 cup butter or margarine, softened
1 teaspoon vanilla extract
2¼ cups all-purpose flour
**½ cup chopped pecans
    DOMINO® Confectioners 10-X Sugar**

In large bowl, combine ½ cup sugar, salt and butter; mix well. Add extract. Gradually stir in flour. Work nuts into dough. Chill well. Form into 1-inch balls. Place on ungreased cookie sheets. Bake at 400°F for 8 to 10 minutes or until set but not brown. Roll in confectioners sugar immediately. Cool on rack. Roll in sugar again. Store in airtight container.
Makes 5 dozen cookies

Mini Chip Snowball Cookies

SWISS MOCHA TREATS

- 2 ounces imported Swiss bittersweet chocolate candy bar, broken
- ½ cup plus 2 tablespoons butter, softened, divided
- 1 tablespoon instant espresso powder
- 1 teaspoon vanilla
- 1¾ cups all-purpose flour
- ½ teaspoon baking soda
- ½ teaspoon salt
- ¾ cup sugar
- 1 large egg
- 3 ounces imported Swiss white chocolate candy bar, broken

Melt bittersweet chocolate and 2 tablespoons butter in small, heavy saucepan over low heat, stirring often. Add espresso powder; stir until dissolved. Remove mixture from heat; stir in vanilla. Let cool to room temperature.

Place flour, baking soda and salt in medium bowl; stir to combine. Beat ½ cup butter and sugar in large bowl with electric mixer at medium speed until light and fluffy. Beat in bittersweet chocolate mixture and egg. Gradually add flour mixture. Beat at low speed until well blended. Cover; refrigerate 30 minutes or until firm.

Preheat oven to 375°F. Roll tablespoonfuls of dough into 1-inch balls. Place balls 3 inches apart on *ungreased* cookie sheets. Flatten each ball into ½-inch-thick round with fork dipped in sugar. Bake 9 to 10 minutes or until set *(do not overbake)*. Immediately remove cookies to wire racks; cool completely.

Place white chocolate in small resealable plastic freezer bag; seal bag. Microwave at MEDIUM (50% power) 1 minute. Turn bag over; microwave at MEDIUM 1 minute or until melted. Knead bag until chocolate is smooth. Cut off very tiny corner of bag; pipe or drizzle white chocolate decoratively onto cooled cookies. Let stand at room temperature 30 minutes or until set. Store tightly covered at room temperature or freeze up to 3 months.

Makes about 4 dozen cookies

CHOCOLATE ALMOND BUTTONS

- 1⅓ cups flour
- ⅓ cup unsweetened cocoa powder
- ¼ teaspoon salt
- 1 cup BLUE DIAMOND® Blanched Almond Paste
- ½ cup plus 1½ tablespoons softened butter, divided
- ¼ cup corn syrup
- 1 teaspoon vanilla extract
- 3 squares (1 ounce each) semisweet chocolate
- ⅔ cup BLUE DIAMOND® Blanched Whole Almonds, toasted

Sift flour, cocoa powder and salt; reserve. Cream almond paste and ½ cup butter until smooth. Beat in corn syrup and vanilla. Beat in flour mixture, scraping sides of bowl occasionally, until well blended. Shape into ¾-inch balls. Place on lightly greased cookie sheets; indent centers of cookies with finger. Bake at 350°F for 8 to 10 minutes or until done. (Cookies will be soft but will become firm when cooled.) In top of double boiler, stir chocolate and remaining 1½ tablespoons butter over simmering water until melted and smooth. With spoon, drizzle small amount of chocolate into center of each cookie. Press an almond into chocolate on each cookie.

Makes 6 dozen cookies

Swiss Mocha Treats

Honey Nut Rugelach

HONEY NUT RUGELACH

 1 cup butter or margarine, softened
 3 ounces cream cheese, softened
 ½ cup honey, divided
 2 cups flour
 1 teaspoon lemon juice
 1 teaspoon ground cinnamon, divided
 1 cup finely chopped walnuts
 ½ cup dried cherries or cranberries

Cream butter and cream cheese until fluffy. Add 3 tablespoons honey and mix well. Mix in flour until dough holds together. Form into a ball, wrap and refrigerate at least 2 hours. Divide dough into 4 equal portions. On floured surface, roll one portion of dough into 9-inch circle. Combine 2 tablespoons honey and lemon juice; mix well. Brush dough with ¼ of honey mixture; sprinkle with ¼ teaspoon cinnamon. Combine walnuts and cherries in small bowl; drizzle with remaining 3 tablespoons honey and mix well.

Spread ¼ of walnut mixture onto circle of dough, stopping ½ inch from outer edge. Cut circle into 8 triangular pieces. Roll up dough staring at wide outer edge and rolling toward tip. Gently bend both ends to form a crescent. Place on oiled parchment paper-lined baking sheet and refrigerate 20 minutes or longer. Repeat with remaining dough and filling. Bake at 350°F 20 to 25 minutes or until golden brown. Cool on wire racks.   *Makes 32 cookies*

FREEZING TIP: Unbaked cookies can be placed in freezer-safe containers or bags and frozen until ready to bake.

*Favorite recipe from **National Honey Board***

FRUIT BURST COOKIES

 1 cup margarine or butter, softened
 ¼ cup sugar
 1 teaspoon almond extract
 2 cups all-purpose flour
 ½ teaspoon salt
 1 cup finely chopped nuts
   SMUCKER'S® Simply Fruit

Cream margarine and sugar until light and fluffy. Blend in almond extract. Combine flour and salt; add to mixture and blend well. Shape level tablespoonfuls of dough into balls; roll in nuts. Place 2 inches apart on ungreased cookie sheets; flatten slightly. Indent centers; fill with fruit spread. Bake at 400°F for 10 to 12 minutes or just until lightly browned. Cool.
Makes 2½ dozen cookies

FRIED NORWEGIAN COOKIES
(FATTIGMANDBAKKELSE)

2 large eggs, at room temperature
3 tablespoons granulated sugar
¼ cup butter, melted
2 tablespoons milk
1 teaspoon vanilla
1¾ to 2 cups all-purpose flour, divided
    Vegetable oil
    Powdered sugar

Beat eggs and granulated sugar in large bowl with electric mixer at medium speed until thick and lemon colored. Beat in butter, milk and vanilla until well blended. Gradually add 1½ cups flour. Beat at low speed until well blended. Stir in enough remaining flour with spoon to form soft dough. Divided dough into 4 portions; cover and refrigerate until firm, at least 2 hours or overnight.

Working with floured hands, shape 1 portion dough at a time into 1-inch-thick square. Place dough on lightly floured surface. Roll out dough to 11-inch square. Cut dough into 1¼-inch strips; cut strips diagonally at 2-inch intervals. Cut a 1¼-inch slit vertically down center of each strip. Insert one end of strip through cut to form twist; repeat with each strip. Repeat with remaining dough.

Heat oil in large saucepan to 365°F. Place 12 cookies at a time in hot oil. Fry about 1½ minutes or until golden brown, turning cookies once with slotted spoon. Drain on paper towels. Dust cookies with powdered sugar. Cookies are best if served immediately, but can be stored in airtight containers for 1 day.

Makes about 11 dozen cookies

Fried Norwegian Cookies

DANISH LEMON–FILLED SPICE COOKIES (*MEDALJEKAGER*)

2¼ cups all-purpose flour
1 teaspoon ground cinnamon
½ teaspoon ground allspice
½ teaspoon ground ginger
½ teaspoon ground nutmeg
¼ teaspoon salt
1 large egg yolk
¾ cup butter, softened
¾ cup sugar
¼ cup milk
1 teaspoon vanilla
Lemon Filling (recipe follows)

Grease cookie sheets; set aside. Place flour, cinnamon, allspice, ginger, nutmeg and salt in medium bowl; stir to combine. Place egg yolk in large bowl; add butter, sugar, milk and vanilla. Beat butter mixture with electric mixer at medium speed until light and fluffy. Gradually add flour mixture. Beat at low speed until dough forms. Cover dough and refrigerate 30 minutes or until firm.

Preheat oven to 350°F. Roll teaspoonfuls of dough into ½-inch balls; place 2 inches apart on prepared cookie sheets. Flatten each ball to ¼-inch thickness with bottom of glass dipped in sugar. Prick top of each cookie using fork. Bake 10 to 13 minutes or until golden brown. Remove cookies to wire racks; cool completely.

Prepare Lemon Filling. Spread filling on flat side of half the cookies. Top with remaining cookies, pressing flat sides together. Let stand at room temperature until set. Store tightly covered at room temperature or freeze up to 3 months.

Makes about 3 dozen sandwich cookies

LEMON FILLING

2¼ cups sifted powdered sugar
1½ tablespoons butter, softened
3 tablespoons lemon juice
½ teaspoon lemon extract

Beat all ingredients in medium bowl with electric mixer at medium speed until smooth.

Makes about 1 cup filling

FRUITED SHORTBREAD COOKIES

2½ cups unsifted flour
1 teaspoon baking soda
1 teaspoon cream of tartar
1 cup margarine or butter, softened
1½ cups confectioners' sugar
1 egg
1 (9-ounce) package NONE SUCH®
Condensed Mincemeat, crumbled
1 teaspoon vanilla extract
Lemon Frosting (recipe follows),
optional

Preheat oven to 375°F. Stir together flour, baking soda and cream of tartar; set aside. In large mixer bowl, beat margarine and sugar until fluffy. Add egg; beat well. Stir in mincemeat and vanilla. Add flour mixture; mix well (dough will be stiff). Roll into 1¼-inch balls. Place on ungreased baking sheets; flatten slightly. Bake 10 to 12 minutes or until lightly browned. Cool. Frost with Lemon Frosting, if desired. *Makes about 3 dozen cookies*

LEMON FROSTING: In small mixer bowl, beat 2 cups confectioners' sugar, 2 tablespoons softened margarine or butter, 2 tablespoons water and ½ teaspoon grated lemon peel until well blended. Makes about ⅔ cup.

Danish Lemon-Filled Spice Cookies

PEPPERMINT PUFFS

1 cup firmly packed light brown sugar
¾ BUTTER FLAVOR* CRISCO® Stick or
  ¾ cup BUTTER FLAVOR CRISCO
  all-vegetable shortening
2 tablespoons milk
1 tablespoon vanilla
1 egg
1¾ cups all-purpose flour
1 teaspoon salt
¾ teaspoon baking soda
⅔ cup crushed peppermint candy canes**

1. Heat oven to 375°F. Place sheets of foil on countertop for cooling cookies.

2. Combine brown sugar, shortening, milk and vanilla in large bowl. Beat at medium speed of electric mixer until well blended. Beat egg into creamed mixture.

3. Combine flour, salt and baking soda. Mix into creamed mixture at low speed just until blended. Stir in crushed candy.

4. Shape dough into 1-inch balls. Place 2 inches apart on ungreased baking sheet.

5. Bake one baking sheet at a time at 375°F for 8 to 10 minutes for chewy cookies or 11 to 13 minutes for crisp cookies. *Do not overbake.* Cool 2 minutes on baking sheet. Remove cookies to foil to cool completely.
Makes about 3 dozen cookies

*Butter Flavor Crisco® is artificially flavored.

**To crush candy canes, break into small pieces. Place in plastic food storage bag. Secure top. Use rolling pin to break candy into very small pieces.

CHERRY DOT COOKIES

2¼ cups all-purpose flour
2 teaspoons baking powder
½ teaspoon salt
¾ cup margarine, softened
1 cup sugar
2 eggs
2 tablespoons low-fat milk
1 teaspoon vanilla
1 cup chopped nuts
1 cup finely chopped pitted dates
⅓ cup finely chopped maraschino
  cherries
2⅔ cups KELLOGG'S CORN FLAKES®
  cereal, crushed to 1⅓ cups
15 maraschino cherries, cut into quarters

1. Stir together flour, baking powder and salt. Set aside.

2. In large mixing bowl, beat margarine and sugar until light and fluffy. Add eggs; beat well. Stir in milk and vanilla. Add flour mixture; mix well. Stir in nuts, dates and chopped cherries.

3. Shape level measuring tablespoonfuls of dough into balls. Roll in crushed Kellogg's Corn Flakes® cereal. Place on lightly greased baking sheets. Top each with cherry quarter.

4. Bake at 350°F about 12 minutes or until lightly browned. Remove to wire racks to cool.
Makes 5 dozen cookies

CHOCOLATE CRINKLE COOKIES

2 cups granulated sugar
¾ cup vegetable oil
¾ cup HERSHEY'S Cocoa
4 eggs
2 teaspoons vanilla extract
2⅓ cups all-purpose flour
2 teaspoons baking powder
½ teaspoon salt
Powdered sugar

In large mixer bowl, stir together granulated sugar and oil; add cocoa, blending well. Beat in eggs and vanilla. In separate bowl, stir together flour, baking powder and salt; add to cocoa mixture, blending well. Cover; refrigerate at least 6 hours.

Heat oven to 350°F. Shape dough into 1-inch balls; roll in powdered sugar. Place 2 inches apart on greased cookie sheets. Bake 12 to 14 minutes or until almost no indentation remains when touched. Remove from cookie sheets to wire racks. Cool completely.

Makes about 4 dozen cookies

CHOCOLATE DIPPED BRANDY SNAPS

½ cup (1 stick) butter
½ cup granulated sugar
⅓ cup dark corn syrup
½ teaspoon ground cinnamon
¼ teaspoon ground ginger
1 cup all-purpose flour
2 teaspoons brandy
1 cup (6 ounces) NESTLÉ® Toll House® Semi-Sweet Chocolate Morsels
1 tablespoon shortening
⅓ cup finely chopped nuts

Chocolate Dipped Brandy Snaps

HEAT butter, sugar, corn syrup, cinnamon and ginger in medium, heavy saucepan over low heat, stirring until smooth. Remove from heat; stir in flour and brandy. Drop by rounded teaspoonfuls onto ungreased baking sheets about 3 inches apart, baking no more than six at a time.

BAKE in preheated 300°F. oven for 10 to 14 minutes or until deep caramel color. Let stand for a few seconds. Remove from baking sheets and immediately roll around wooden spoon handle; cool.

MICROWAVE morsels and shortening in medium, microwave-safe bowl on HIGH (100% power) for 45 seconds; stir. Microwave at additional 10 to 20 second intervals, stirring until smooth. Dip cookies halfway in melted chocolate; shake off excess. Sprinkle with nuts; set on waxed-paper-lined baking sheets. Chill for 10 minutes or until chocolate is set. Store in airtight container in refrigerator.

Makes about 3 dozen cookies

ARGENTINEAN CARAMEL–FILLED CRESCENTS
(PASTELES)

 3 cups all-purpose flour
½ cup powdered sugar
 1 teaspoon baking powder
¼ teaspoon salt
 1 cup butter, cut into small pieces
 6 to 7 tablespoons ice water
½ package (14 ounces) caramel candies
    (about 25)
 2 tablespoons milk
½ cup flaked coconut
 1 large egg
 1 tablespoon water

Place flour, powdered sugar, baking powder and salt in large bowl; stir to combine. Cut butter into flour mixture with pastry blender or 2 knives until mixture forms pea-sized pieces. Add ice water, 1 tablespoon at a time; toss with fork until mixture holds together. Divide dough in half; cover and refrigerate 30 minutes or until firm.

Meanwhile, melt caramels and milk in medium saucepan over low heat, stirring constantly; stir in coconut. Remove from heat; cool.

Working with 1 portion at a time, roll out dough on lightly floured surface to ⅛-inch thickness. Cut dough with 3-inch round cookie cutter. Reroll trimmings and cut out more cookies.

Preheat oven to 400°F. Grease cookie sheets; set aside. Beat egg and 1 tablespoon water in cup. Place ½ teaspoon caramel mixture in center of each dough round. Moisten edge of dough round with egg mixture. Fold dough in half; press edges firmly to seal in filling. Press edge with fork. Place cookies on prepared cookie sheets; brush with egg mixture. Cut 3 slashes across top of each cookie with tip of utility knife. Bake 15 to 20 minutes or until golden brown. Remove cookies to wire racks; cool completely. Store tightly covered at room temperature.   *Makes about 4 dozen cookies*

NOTE: These cookies do not freeze well.

BANANA CRESCENTS

½ cup DOLE® Chopped Almonds, toasted
 6 tablespoons sugar, divided
½ cup margarine, cut into pieces
1½ cups plus 2 tablespoons all-purpose
    flour
⅛ teaspoon salt
 1 extra-ripe, medium DOLE® Banana,
    peeled and cut into chunks
 2 to 3 ounces semisweet chocolate chips

• Pulverize almonds with 2 tablespoons sugar.

• Beat margarine, almonds, remaining 4 tablespoons sugar, flour and salt.

• Purée banana; add to almond mixture and mix until well blended.

• Roll tablespoonfuls of dough into logs, then shape into crescents. Place on ungreased cookie sheet. Bake in 375°F oven 25 minutes or until golden. Cool on wire rack.

• Melt chocolate in microwavable dish at MEDIUM (50% power) 1½ to 2 minutes, stirring once. Dip ends of cookies in chocolate. Refrigerate until chocolate is set.
    Makes 2 dozen cookies

Argentinean Caramel-Filled Crescents

MINI MINCE LEMON TARTS

1⅓ cups (½ of 27-ounce jar) NONE SUCH® Ready-to-Use Mincemeat (Regular or Brandy & Rum)
1½ teaspoons grated lemon peel
1 (15-ounce) package refrigerated pie crusts

Preheat oven to 375°F. In small bowl, combine mincemeat and peel; mix well. Cut pastry into 24 (2¼-inch) circles; press each circle into 1¾-inch muffin cup. Fill with mincemeat mixture. From pastry scraps, cut out small designs; top tarts with cutouts. Bake 20 to 25 minutes or until lightly browned. Cool. Remove from pans. Store loosely covered at room temperature.   *Makes 2 dozen tarts*

ORANGE–CASHEW COOKIES

½ cup butter or margarine, softened
⅔ cup sugar
1 egg
1 teaspoon grated orange peel
3 tablespoons orange juice
2 cups all-purpose flour
1 teaspoon baking soda
¼ teaspoon salt
1 cup chopped cashews

Preheat oven to 350°F. Beat butter and sugar in large bowl until creamy. Beat in egg, orange peel and juice until light and fluffy. Mix in flour, baking soda and salt until well blended. Stir in cashews. Drop tablespoonfuls of dough 2 inches apart onto ungreased cookie sheets.

Bake 9 minutes or until lightly browned. Remove to wire racks; cool completely. Store in airtight container.
           Makes about 1½ dozen cookies

MILK CHOCOLATE FLORENTINE COOKIES

⅔ cup butter
2 cups quick oats, uncooked
1 cup granulated sugar
⅔ cup all-purpose flour
¼ cup corn syrup
¼ cup milk
1 teaspoon vanilla extract
¼ teaspoon salt
2 cups (11½-ounce package) NESTLÉ® Toll House® Milk Chocolate Morsels

In medium saucepan, melt butter; remove from heat. Stir in oats, sugar, flour, corn syrup, milk, vanilla and salt; mix well. Drop by level teaspoonfuls, about 3 inches apart, onto foil-lined baking sheets. With rubber spatula, spread thinly. Bake in preheated 375°F. oven for 6 to 8 minutes, until golden brown; cool. Peel foil from cookies. Over hot (not boiling) water, melt morsels, stirring until smooth. Spread thin layer of melted chocolate on flat side of half the cookies. Top with remaining cookies.
           Makes about 3½ dozen sandwich cookies

Milk Chocolate Florentine Cookies

ANGEL PILLOWS

½ BUTTER FLAVOR* CRISCO® Stick *or*
   ½ cup BUTTER FLAVOR CRISCO
   all-vegetable shortening
1 package (3 ounces) cream cheese,
   softened
1 tablespoon milk
¼ cup firmly packed brown sugar
½ cup apricot preserves
1¼ cups all-purpose flour
1½ teaspoons baking powder
1½ teaspoons ground cinnamon
¼ teaspoon salt
½ cup coarsely chopped pecans or flake
   coconut
FROSTING
1 cup confectioners' sugar
¼ cup apricot preserves
1 tablespoon BUTTER FLAVOR*
   CRISCO® Stick *or* 1 tablespoon
   BUTTER FLAVOR CRISCO all-
   vegetable shortening
Flake coconut or finely chopped
   pecans (optional)

Heat oven to 350°F. Grease baking sheets with shortening. Place sheets of foil on countertop for cooling cookies. Cream shortening, cream cheese and milk at medium speed of electric mixer until well blended. Beat in brown sugar. Beat in preserves. Combine flour, baking powder, cinnamon and salt. Mix into creamed mixture. Stir in nuts. Drop 2 level measuring tablespoons of dough into a mound to form each cookie. Place 2 inches apart on baking sheets.

Angel Pillow

Bake one baking sheet at a time at 350°F for 14 minutes. *Do not overbake.* Cool on baking sheet one minute. Remove cookies to foil to cool completely.

For frosting, combine confectioners' sugar, preserves and shortening in small mixing bowl. Beat with electric mixer until well blended. Frost cooled cookies. Sprinkle coconut over frosting, if desired.   *Makes 1½ dozen cookies*

TIP: Try peach or pineapple preserves in place of apricot.

*Butter Flavor Crisco® is artificially flavored.

PREP TIME: 25 minutes
BAKE TIME: 14 minutes

HOLIDAY FRUIT DROPS

½ cup butter, softened
¾ cup packed brown sugar
1 egg
1¼ cups all-purpose flour
1 teaspoon vanilla
½ teaspoon baking soda
½ teaspoon ground cinnamon
   Pinch salt
1 cup (8 ounces) diced candied
   pineapple
1 cup (8 ounces) whole red and green
   candied cherries
8 ounces chopped pitted dates
1 cup (6 ounces) semisweet chocolate
   chips
½ cup whole hazelnuts
½ cup pecan halves
½ cup coarsely chopped walnuts

Preheat oven to 325°F. Lightly grease cookie sheets or line with parchment paper. Cream butter and sugar in large bowl. Beat in egg until light and fluffy. Mix in flour, vanilla, baking soda, cinnamon and salt. Stir in pineapple, cherries, dates, chocolate chips, hazelnuts, pecans and walnuts. Drop dough by rounded teaspoonfuls 2 inches apart onto prepared cookie sheets.

Bake 15 to 20 minutes or until firm and lightly browned around edges. Remove to wire racks to cool completely.

Makes about 8 dozen cookies

NOTE: The cherries, hazelnuts and pecan halves are not chopped, but left whole.

CAPPUCCINO BON BONS

1 package DUNCAN HINES® Chocolate
   Lovers' Fudge Brownie Mix, Family
   Size
2 eggs
⅓ cup water
⅓ cup CRISCO® Oil or CRISCO®
   PURITAN® Canola Oil
1½ tablespoons FOLGERS® Instant Coffee
1 teaspoon ground cinnamon
   Whipped topping
   Ground cinnamon

1. Preheat oven to 350°F. Place 40 (2-inch) foil cupcake liners on cookie sheet.

2. Combine brownie mix, eggs, water, oil, instant coffee and 1 teaspoon cinnamon. Stir with spoon until well blended, about 50 strokes. Fill each cupcake liner with 1 measuring tablespoonful batter. Bake at 350°F for 12 to 15 minutes or until toothpick inserted in center comes out clean. Cool completely. Garnish with whipped topping and a dash of cinnamon. Refrigerate until ready to serve.

Makes 40 bon bons

Cappuccino Bon Bons

FROST ON THE PUMPKIN COOKIES

- 2 cups all-purpose flour
- 1 teaspoon baking powder
- 1 teaspoon ground cinnamon
- ½ teaspoon baking soda
- ½ teaspoon ground nutmeg
- 1 cup butter, softened
- ¾ cup JACK FROST® Granulated Sugar
- ¾ cup JACK FROST® Brown Sugar (packed)
- 1 egg
- 1 cup canned pumpkin
- 2 teaspoons vanilla
- ½ cup raisins
- ½ cup chopped walnuts
  Cream Cheese Frosting (recipe follows)

In small mixing bowl combine flour, baking powder, cinnamon, baking soda and nutmeg. Set aside. In large mixer bowl beat butter for 1 minute. Add granulated sugar and brown sugar. Beat until fluffy. Add egg, pumpkin and vanilla; beat well. Add dry ingredients to beaten mixture; mix until well blended. Stir in raisins and walnuts. Drop by teaspoonfuls 2 inches apart onto greased cookie sheet. Bake in 350°F oven for 10 to 12 minutes. Cool on cookie sheet for 2 minutes, then transfer to wire rack to finish cooling. Frost with Cream Cheese Frosting. Garnish with chopped nuts, if desired.

Makes about 48 cookies

CREAM CHEESE FROSTING: In medium mixing bowl, beat 3 ounces softened cream cheese, ¼ cup softened butter and 1 teaspoon vanilla until light and fluffy. Gradually add 2 cups JACK FROST® Powdered Sugar, beating until smooth.

COCONUT MACAROONS

- 2 (7-ounce) packages flaked coconut (5⅓ cups)
- 1 (14-ounce) can EAGLE® Brand Sweetened Condensed Milk (NOT evaporated milk)
- 2 teaspoons vanilla extract
- 1½ teaspoons almond extract

Preheat oven to 350°F. In large bowl, combine coconut, sweetened condensed milk and extracts; mix well. Drop by rounded teaspoonfuls onto baking sheets lined with generously greased aluminum foil. Bake 8 to 10 minutes or until lightly browned around edges. *Immediately* remove from baking sheets (macaroons will stick if allowed to cool). Store loosely covered at room temperature.

Makes about 4 dozen cookies

WALNUT MACAROONS

- 2⅔ cups flaked coconut
- 1¼ cups coarsely chopped California walnuts
- ⅓ cup flour
- ½ teaspoon ground cinnamon
- ¼ teaspoon salt
- 4 egg whites
- 1 teaspoon grated lemon peel
- 2 (1-ounce) squares semisweet chocolate

Combine coconut, walnuts, flour, cinnamon and salt. Add egg whites and lemon peel; mix well.

Drop teaspoonfuls of walnut mixture onto lightly greased baking sheets. Bake in 325°F oven 20 minutes or until golden brown. Remove from baking sheets immediately.

Place chocolate in microwavable bowl. Microwave on HIGH (100% power) until melted, about 2½ minutes; stir. Dip macaroon bottoms in chocolate. Place on waxed paper. Let stand until chocolate is set.

Makes about 3 dozen cookies

*Favorite recipe from **Walnut Marketing Board***

Top to bottom: Walnut Macaroons, Walnut Brandy Shortbread (page 482), Chocolate Walnut Truffles (page 519)

OATMEAL MACAROONS

1¼ cups all-purpose flour
1 teaspoon baking soda
1 cup margarine, softened
1 cup packed brown sugar
2 eggs
½ teaspoon almond extract
3 cups QUAKER® Oats (quick or old-fashioned), uncooked
1 package (4 ounces) flaked or shredded coconut

In medium bowl, combine flour and baking soda. In large bowl, cream margarine and sugar until light and fluffy. Blend in eggs and almond extract. Add flour mixture; mix well. Stir in oats and coconut. Drop dough by rounded teaspoonfuls onto greased cookie sheets. Bake in preheated 350°F oven 10 minutes or until light golden brown. Let cookies cool 1 minute before removing from cookie sheets to wire racks.   *Makes 4½ dozen cookies*

BUTTER DROP-INS

½ BUTTER FLAVOR* CRISCO® Stick *or*
   ½ cup BUTTER FLAVOR CRISCO all-vegetable shortening
¾ cup granulated sugar
1 tablespoon milk
1 egg
½ teaspoon vanilla
1¼ cups all-purpose flour
¼ teaspoon salt
¼ teaspoon baking powder
FROSTING
½ BUTTER FLAVOR CRISCO Stick *or*
   ½ cup BUTTER FLAVOR CRISCO all-vegetable shortening
1 pound (4 cups) confectioners' sugar
⅓ cup milk
1 teaspoon vanilla

Heat oven to 375°F. Grease baking sheets with shortening. Place sheets of foil on countertop for cooling cookies. Combine shortening, granulated sugar and milk in medium bowl at medium speed of electric mixer until well blended. Beat in egg and vanilla. Combine flour, salt and baking powder. Mix into creamed mixture. Drop level measuring tablespoonfuls 2 inches apart onto baking sheet. Bake one baking sheet at a time at 375°F for 7 to 9 minutes. Remove cookies to foil to cool completely.

For frosting, combine shortening, confectioners' sugar, milk and vanilla in small mixing bowl. Beat at low speed of electric mixer for 15 seconds. Scrape bowl. Beat at high speed for 2 minutes, or until smooth and creamy. Frost cookies.   *Makes 1½ to 2 dozen cookies*

*Butter Flavor Crisco® is artificially flavored.

NOTE: Frosting can be tinted with food coloring and piped decoratively onto cookies, if desired.

PREP TIME: 20 minutes
BAKE TIME: 7 to 9 minutes

471

Kahlúa® Kisses

KAHLÚA® KISSES

¾ teaspoon instant coffee powder
⅓ cup water
1 cup plus 2 tablespoons sugar
¼ cup KAHLÚA®
3 egg whites, room temperature
¼ teaspoon cream of tartar
    Dash salt

In heavy 2-quart saucepan, dissolve coffee powder in water. Add 1 cup sugar; stir over low heat until sugar dissolves. Do not allow to boil. Stir in Kahlúa®. Brush down sides of pan with pastry brush frequently dipped in cold water. Bring mixture to a boil over medium heat. *Do not stir.* Boil until candy thermometer registers 240° to 242°F, about 15 minutes, adjusting heat if necessary to prevent boiling over. Mixture will be very thick. Remove from heat (temperature will continue to rise).

Immediately beat egg whites with cream of tartar and salt until soft peaks form. Add remaining 2 tablespoons sugar; continue beating until stiff peaks form. Gradually beat hot Kahlúa® syrup into egg whites, beating after each addition to thoroughly mix. Continue beating 4 to 5 minutes or until meringue is very thick, firm and cooled to lukewarm.

Line baking sheet with foil, shiny side down. Using pastry bag fitted with large star tip, pipe meringue into kisses about 1½ inches wide at base and 1½ inches high onto baking sheet. Bake on center rack of 200°F oven for 4 hours. Without opening door, turn off oven. Let kisses dry in oven 2 more hours or until crisp. Remove from oven; cool completely on baking sheet. Store in airtight container up to 1 week.

Makes 2½ dozen cookies

LOADED OATMEAL COOKIES

¾ cup butter or margarine, softened
1 cup packed brown sugar
1 egg
1 tablespoon milk
1 teaspoon vanilla extract
1½ cups uncooked quick oats
1 cup all-purpose flour
½ teaspoon baking soda
½ teaspoon salt
½ teaspoon ground cinnamon
1 cup (6 ounces) semisweet chocolate chips
1 cup (6 ounces) butterscotch chips
¾ cup raisins
½ cup chopped walnuts

Preheat oven to 350°F. Beat butter and brown sugar in large bowl until creamy. Beat in egg, milk and vanilla until light and fluffy. Mix in oats, flour, baking soda, salt and cinnamon until well blended. Stir in chips, raisins and walnuts. Drop rounded tablespoonfuls of dough 2 inches apart onto *ungreased* cookie sheets.

Bake 12 to 15 minutes or until lightly browned around edges. Cool 2 minutes on cookie sheets. Remove to wire racks; cool completely. Store in airtight container.

Makes about 3 dozen cookies

MERINGUE KISSES

2 egg whites
¼ teaspoon cream of tartar
½ cup sugar
Variation Ingredients* (optional)

In small mixer bowl, beat egg whites with cream of tartar at high speed until foamy. Add sugar, 2 tablespoons at a time, beating constantly until sugar is dissolved and whites are glossy and stand in stiff peaks. If desired, beat or fold in Variation Ingredients. Drop meringue by rounded teaspoonfuls or pipe through pastry tube 1 inch apart onto greased or waxed-paper-lined cookie sheets. Bake in preheated 225°F oven until firm, about 1 hour. Turn off oven. Let cookies stand in oven with door closed until cool, dry and crisp, at least 1 additional hour. Store in tightly sealed containers. *Makes 4 to 5 dozen cookies*

*VARIATION INGREDIENTS: Amounts listed are for one batch of cookies. To make two variations at a time, divide meringue mixture equally between two bowls. Beat or fold into each bowl half of the amounts listed for each variation.

CHOCOLATE: Beat in ¼ cup unsweetened cocoa and 1 teaspoon vanilla.

CITRUS: Beat in 1 tablespoon grated orange peel, ¼ teaspoon lemon extract and a few drops yellow food coloring.

MINT: Beat in ¼ teaspoon mint extract and a few drops green food coloring.

ROCKY ROAD: Beat in 1 teaspoon vanilla. Fold in ½ cup semisweet chocolate chips and ½ cup chopped nuts.

CHERRY–ALMOND: Fold in ½ cup chopped, drained maraschino cherries and ½ cup chopped almonds.

*Favorite recipe from **American Egg Board***

GOOEY CARAMEL CHOCOLATE BARS

    2 cups all-purpose flour
    1 cup granulated sugar
    ¼ teaspoon salt
    2 cups (4 sticks) butter or margarine,
       divided
    1 cup packed light brown sugar
    ⅓ cup light corn syrup
    1 cup (6 ounces) semisweet chocolate
       chips

Preheat oven to 350°F. Line 13×9-inch baking pan with foil. Combine flour, granulated sugar and salt in medium bowl; stir until blended. Cut in 14 tablespoons (1¾ sticks) butter until mixture resembles coarse crumbs. Press into bottom of prepared pan.

Bake 18 to 20 minutes or until lightly browned around edges. Remove pan to wire rack; cool completely.

Combine 1 cup (2 sticks) butter, brown sugar and corn syrup in heavy medium saucepan. Cook over medium heat 5 to 8 minutes or until mixture boils, stirring frequently. Boil gently 2 minutes, without stirring. Immediately pour over cooled base; spread evenly to edges of pan with metal spatula. Cool completely.

Melt chocolate in double boiler over hot (not simmering) water. Stir in remaining 2 tablespoons butter. Pour over cooled caramel layer and spread evenly to edges of pan with metal spatula. Refrigerate 10 to 15 minutes or until chocolate begins to set. Remove pan from refrigerator; cool completely. Cut into bars.

Makes 3 dozen bars

OAT-Y NUT BARS

    ½ cup butter or margarine
    ½ cup honey
    ¼ cup corn syrup
    ¼ cup packed brown sugar
    2¾ cups uncooked quick oats
    ⅔ cup raisins
    ½ cup salted peanuts

Preheat oven to 300°F. Grease 9-inch square baking pan. Melt butter with honey, corn syrup and brown sugar in medium saucepan over medium heat, stirring constantly. Bring to a boil; boil 8 minutes until mixture thickens slightly. Stir in oats, raisins and peanuts until well blended. Press evenly into prepared pan.

Bake 45 to 50 minutes or until golden brown. Place pan on wire rack; score top into approximately 2-inch squares. Cool completely. Cut into bars.   *Makes 16 bars*

SCOTTISH SHORTBREAD

    5 cups all-purpose flour
    1 cup rice flour
    2 cups butter or margarine, softened
    1 cup sugar
    Candied fruit (optional)

Preheat oven to 325°F. Sift together flours. Beat butter and sugar in large bowl with electric mixer until creamy. Blend in ¾ of flour until mixture resembles fine crumbs. Stir in remaining flour by hand. Press dough firmly into ungreased 15½×10½×1-inch jelly-roll pan or two 9-inch fluted tart pans; crimp and flute edges, if desired. Bake 40 to 45 minutes or until light brown. Place pan on wire rack. Cut into bars or wedges while warm. Decorate with candied fruit, if desired. Cool completely. Store in airtight containers.

Makes about 4 dozen bars or 24 wedges

Top to bottom: Oat-y Nut Bars,
Gooey Caramel Chocolate Bars

Santa's Favorite Brownies

SANTA'S FAVORITE BROWNIES

    1 cup (6 ounces) milk chocolate chips
    ½ cup butter or margarine
    ¾ cup granulated sugar
    2 eggs
    1 teaspoon vanilla extract
1¼ cups all-purpose flour
    3 tablespoons unsweetened cocoa
    1 teaspoon baking powder
    ½ teaspoon salt
    ½ cup chopped walnuts
        Buttercream Frosting (recipe follows), optional
        Small jelly beans, icing gels and colored sugar for decoration (optional)

Preheat oven to 350°F. Grease 9-inch square baking pan. Melt chocolate and butter with granulated sugar in medium saucepan over low heat, stirring constantly. Pour into large bowl; add eggs and vanilla. Beat with electric mixer until well blended. Stir in flour, cocoa, baking powder and salt; blend well. Fold in walnuts. Spread into prepared pan.

Bake 25 to 30 minutes or until wooden toothpick inserted in center comes out clean. Place pan on wire rack; cool completely. Frost with Buttercream Frosting, if desired. Cut into squares. Decorate with jelly beans, icing gels and colored sugar, if desired. Store in airtight container.   *Makes 16 brownies*

BUTTERCREAM FROSTING
    3 cups powdered sugar, sifted
    ½ cup butter or margarine, softened
    3 to 4 tablespoons milk, divided
    ½ teaspoon vanilla extract

Combine powdered sugar, butter, 2 tablespoons milk and vanilla in large bowl. Beat with electric mixer on low speed until blended. Beat on high speed until light and fluffy, adding more milk, 1 teaspoon at a time, as needed for good spreading consistency.
   Makes about 1½ cups frosting

SPICED DATE BARS

    ½ cup margarine, softened
    1 cup packed brown sugar
    2 eggs
    ¾ cup light sour cream
    2 cups all-purpose flour
    1 teaspoon baking soda
    1 teaspoon ground cinnamon
    ½ teaspoon ground nutmeg
    1 package (8 or 10 ounces) DOLE® Chopped Dates or Pitted Dates, chopped
        Powdered sugar (optional)

• Beat margarine and brown sugar until light and fluffy. Beat in eggs, one at a time. Stir in sour cream.

• Combine dry ingredients. Beat into sour cream mixture; stir in dates. Spread batter evenly into greased 13×9-inch baking pan.

• Bake at 350°F 25 to 30 minutes or until toothpick inserted in center comes out clean. Cool completely in pan on wire rack. Cut into bars. Dust with powdered sugar.

Makes 24 bars

PREP TIME: 15 minutes
BAKE TIME: 30 minutes

CHOCONUT FINGER COOKIES

  1 package (8 ounces) PHILADELPHIA
     BRAND® Cream Cheese, softened
½ cup PARKAY® Spread Sticks, softened
¾ cup sugar
  1 teaspoon vanilla
  2 cups flour
½ teaspoon CALUMET® Baking Powder
  1 cup BAKER'S® Semi-Sweet Real
     Chocolate Chips
½ cup BAKER'S® ANGEL FLAKE®
     Coconut, toasted
½ cup butterscotch chips
½ cup chopped pecans, toasted

• Heat oven to 375°F.

• Beat cream cheese, spread, sugar and vanilla in large mixing bowl at medium speed with electric mixer until well blended. Add flour and baking powder; mix well. Spread mixture into ungreased 13×9-inch baking pan.

• Bake 15 minutes. Immediately sprinkle chocolate chips over crust; let stand about 5 minutes or until chocolate chips are slightly softened. Spread chocolate over crust. Sprinkle with remaining ingredients. Cool. Cut into bars.

Makes 2 dozen cookies

PREP TIME: 10 minutes
COOK TIME: 15 minutes

CRANBERRY ALMOND SQUARES

  3 cups cranberries
  1 cup raisins
  1 cup chopped peeled apple
  1 cup unsweetened apple juice
  1 tablespoon granulated sugar
1½ cups whole wheat flour
  1 cup regular oats, uncooked
⅓ cup firmly packed brown sugar
  1 teaspoon ground cinnamon
⅛ teaspoon salt
½ cup molasses
¼ cup CRISCO® Oil
  2 tablespoons slivered almonds, toasted,
     chopped

Heat oven to 350°F. Lightly oil 13×9-inch baking pan. Combine cranberries, raisins, apple, apple juice and granulated sugar in saucepan. Bring to a boil. Cook 5 minutes or until cranberry skins pop, stirring occasionally. Reduce heat and simmer, uncovered, 10 minutes. Stir occasionally. Cool.

Combine flour, oats, brown sugar, cinnamon and salt in medium bowl. Combine molasses and Crisco® Oil; add to flour mixture. Toss with fork until mixture resembles coarse meal.

Press 2 cups flour mixture in bottom of prepared pan. Top with cranberry mixture. Spread evenly. Combine remaining flour mixture and almonds. Sprinkle over cranberry mixture. Press lightly.

Bake at 350°F for 35 minutes or until golden. Cool. Cut into squares. Store loosely covered.

Makes 24 servings

ORANGE CREME BROWNIES

¾ cup all-purpose flour
¼ teaspoon baking powder
¼ teaspoon salt
1 package (6 ounces) semi-sweet
   chocolate morsels
½ cup (1 stick) butter, cut into small
   pieces
⅓ cup granulated sugar
3 tablespoons orange juice
1 teaspoon grated orange peel
1 teaspoon vanilla
2 eggs
1⅓ cups (about 6 ounces) chopped
   walnuts
   Orange Creme (recipe follows)
   Chocolate Icing (recipe follows)

Preheat oven to 325°F. Line bottom and sides of 9-inch square baking pan with foil, allowing foil to overhang slightly. Butter foil; set aside. On square of waxed paper, combine flour, baking powder and salt. In small saucepan, combine chocolate morsels, butter, sugar and orange juice. Cook and stir over very low heat until chocolate and butter are melted; remove from heat. Stir in orange peel and vanilla. Using wire whisk, beat in eggs, 1 at a time. Add reserved flour mixture, beating until smooth. Stir in nuts; spread in prepared pan. Bake until wooden toothpick inserted in center comes out clean, 23 to 25 minutes. Cool completely on wire rack.

Spread brownies with Orange Creme. Refrigerate until firm, about 15 minutes, or place in freezer about 5 minutes. Spread warm Chocolate Icing over Orange Creme. Using knife, score Chocolate Icing layer into 36 (1½-inch) squares; refrigerate until Chocolate Icing is firm, about 25 minutes, or place in freezer about 5 minutes.

Remove from pan by lifting foil edges. Cut into squares. Refrigerate up to 4 days or wrap and freeze up to 1 month. *Makes 36 bars*

Left to right: Nutty Caramel Bars, Orange Creme Brownies

ORANGE CREME

½ cup (1 stick) butter, softened
2 cups confectioners' sugar
1 teaspoon grated orange peel
1 teaspoon milk
1 teaspoon vanilla

In small mixer bowl, beat butter and sugar until light and fluffy. Beat in orange peel, milk and vanilla. *Makes 1½ cups*

CHOCOLATE ICING

1 package (6 ounces) semi-sweet
   chocolate morsels
1 tablespoon butter
1 tablespoon vegetable shortening

In small saucepan, combine chocolate morsels, butter and shortening. Stir over very low heat until melted. *Makes about 1 cup*

*Favorite recipe from **National Dairy Board***

NUTTY CARAMEL BARS

1½ cups (3 sticks) butter, divided
½ cup granulated sugar
1 egg
1 teaspoon vanilla
2 cups all-purpose flour
¼ cup honey
¾ cup firmly packed light brown sugar
¼ cup whipping cream
1 can (12 ounces) lightly salted mixed whole nuts

Preheat oven to 350°F. Butter 13×9-inch baking pan; set aside. In large mixer bowl, beat 1 cup (2 sticks) softened butter with granulated sugar until light and fluffy; beat in egg and vanilla. Stir in flour until well mixed; press evenly into prepared pan. Bake until edges are brown and center looks dry, about 15 minutes. Remove to wire rack while preparing topping. Maintain oven temperature. In heavy, medium saucepan over medium heat, heat remaining ½ cup (1 stick) butter with honey until butter is melted. Stir in brown sugar; bring to a boil. Boil without stirring for exactly 2 minutes; remove from heat. Stir in cream and nuts. Immediately spoon caramel nut mixture evenly over crust. Bake until caramel bubbles, about 10 minutes. Cool completely on wire rack; cut into 2×2-inch bars. Store in tightly covered container at room temperature. *Makes about 24 bars*

Favorite recipe from **National Dairy Board**

CRANBERRY–ORANGE MUESLI BARS

FILLING
1 package (12 ounces) OCEAN SPRAY® Cranberries, fresh or frozen
1 cup granulated sugar
1 teaspoon grated orange peel (optional)
1 cup orange juice
BASE/TOPPING
4 cups RALSTON® brand Fruit Muesli with Cranberries, crushed to 3 cups
1½ cups all-purpose flour
¾ cup packed brown sugar
¾ cup (1½ sticks) margarine or butter, softened
1½ teaspoons baking powder
½ teaspoon salt

To prepare Filling: In medium saucepan over medium heat combine cranberries, granulated sugar, orange peel and orange juice. Cook, stirring frequently, until mixture comes to a boil. Reduce heat; simmer 15 to 18 minutes, stirring frequently. Cool.

To prepare Base/Topping: Preheat oven to 350°F. In large bowl combine cereal, flour, brown sugar, margarine, baking powder and salt. Reserve 1½ cups cereal mixture for topping; set aside. Press remaining cereal mixture firmly and evenly into ungreased 13×9×2-inch baking pan. Bake 10 minutes. Spread cranberry filling evenly over base; sprinkle with reserved cereal mixture. Bake an additional 18 to 20 minutes or until lightly browned. Cool; cut into bars.

Makes 24 bars

GERMAN HONEY BARS (LEBKUCHEN)

2¾ cups all-purpose flour
2 teaspoons ground cinnamon
1 teaspoon baking powder
½ teaspoon baking soda
½ teaspoon salt
½ teaspoon ground cardamom
½ teaspoon ground ginger
½ cup honey
½ cup dark molasses
¾ cup packed brown sugar
3 tablespoons butter, melted
1 large egg
½ cup chopped toasted almonds
    (optional)
Glaze (recipe follows)

Preheat oven to 350°F. Grease 15×10-inch jelly-roll pan; set aside. Place flour, cinnamon, baking powder, baking soda, salt, cardamom and ginger in medium bowl; stir to combine. Combine honey and molasses in medium saucepan; bring to a boil over medium heat. Remove from heat; cool 10 minutes. Stir in brown sugar, butter and egg.

Place brown sugar mixture in large bowl. Gradually add flour mixture. Beat at low speed until dough forms. Stir in almonds with spoon. (Dough will be slightly sticky.) Spread evenly into prepared pan. Bake 20 to 22 minutes or until golden brown and set. Remove pan to wire rack; cool completely.

Prepare Glaze. Spread over cooled bar cookies. Let stand until set, about 30 minutes. Cut into 2×1-inch bars. Store tightly covered at room temperature or freeze up to 3 months.
Makes about 6 dozen bars

GLAZE
1¼ cups powdered sugar
1 teaspoon grated lemon peel
3 tablespoons fresh lemon juice

Place all ingredients in medium bowl; stir with spoon until smooth.

KAHLÚA® PUMPKIN SQUARES WITH PRALINE TOPPING

1 cup flour
¼ cup powdered sugar
½ cup unsalted butter
1 cup LIBBY'S® Solid Pack Pumpkin
1 (8-ounce) package cream cheese, cut
    up and softened
2 eggs
¼ cup granulated sugar
¼ cup KAHLÚA®
1 cup chopped walnuts or pecans
¾ cup firmly packed brown sugar
¼ cup unsalted butter, melted

In bowl, combine flour and powdered sugar. Using 2 knives or pastry blender, cut in ½ cup butter until mixture forms fine crumbs. Press mixture into bottom of 8-inch square broilerproof baking dish. Bake at 350°F for 15 to 18 minutes or until golden.

Meanwhile, in food processor or blender, process pumpkin, cream cheese, eggs, granulated sugar and Kahlúa® until smooth. Pour pumpkin filling over warm baked crust; return to oven and bake about 20 minutes or until set. Cool in dish on rack. Cover; refrigerate.

In small bowl, combine nuts, brown sugar and melted butter. Just before serving, sprinkle topping over pumpkin filling.

Broil, watching carefully, just until topping begins to brown. Cut into 2-inch squares.
Makes 16 squares

German Honey Bars

Pear Mince Oatmeal Bars

PEAR MINCE OATMEAL BARS

¾ cup butter or margarine, softened
¾ cup packed brown sugar
1½ cups all-purpose flour
1¼ cups quick-cooking oats
½ cup chopped walnuts
½ teaspoon salt
½ teaspoon baking soda
2 USA Anjou pears, cored and chopped
1 cup prepared mincemeat
1 teaspoon lemon juice
½ teaspoon grated lemon peel

Preheat oven to 375°F. Cream butter and sugar. Stir in flour, oats, nuts, salt and baking soda until crumbly. Press ⅔ of flour mixture into ungreased 13×9-inch baking pan.

Combine pears, mincemeat, lemon juice and peel; spread over crumb crust. Top with remaining crumb mixture; pat lightly. Bake 25 to 30 minutes or until crust is golden. Cut into bars.   *Makes 30 to 35 bars*

Favorite recipe from **Oregon Washington California Pear Bureau**

WALNUT BRANDY SHORTBREAD

1 cup butter, softened
½ cup packed brown sugar
⅛ teaspoon salt
2 tablespoons brandy
1 cup all-purpose flour
1 cup finely chopped toasted California walnuts
Granulated sugar

Cream butter with brown sugar and salt; mix in brandy. Gradually add flour; stir in walnuts. Spread in ungreased 9-inch square baking pan. Refrigerate 30 minutes.

Prick dough all over using fork. Bake at 325°F about 55 minutes or until dark golden brown. If dough puffs up during baking, prick again. Sprinkle lightly with granulated sugar; cool. Cut into fingers or squares with sharp knife.
Makes 36 shortbreads

NOTE: Shortbread may be stored in airtight container at room temperature 1 to 2 months.

Favorite recipe from **Walnut Marketing Board**

YULETIDE TOFFEE SQUARES

4½ cups quick or old-fashioned oats, uncooked
1 cup packed brown sugar
¾ cup (1½ sticks) butter or margarine, melted
½ cup light corn syrup
1 tablespoon vanilla extract
½ teaspoon salt
2 cups (12-ounce package) NESTLÉ® Toll House® Semi-Sweet Chocolate Morsels
⅔ cup chopped nuts

COMBINE oats, brown sugar, butter, corn syrup, vanilla and salt in large bowl; mix well. Firmly press mixture into greased 15×10-inch jelly-roll pan.

BAKE in preheated 400°F. oven for about 18 minutes or until mixture is brown and bubbly. Remove from oven. Immediately sprinkle chocolate morsels evenly over toffee. Let stand for 10 minutes.

SPREAD chocolate evenly over toffee; sprinkle with nuts. Cool completely; cut into squares. Store tightly covered in cool, dry place.

Makes about 6 dozen squares

PEANUT BUTTER PAISLEY BROWNIES

½ cup butter or margarine, softened
¼ cup peanut butter
1 cup granulated sugar
1 cup packed light brown sugar
3 eggs
1 teaspoon vanilla extract
2 cups all-purpose flour
2 teaspoons baking powder
¼ teaspoon salt
½ cup (5.5-ounce can) HERSHEY®S Syrup

Blend butter and peanut butter in large mixer bowl. Add granulated sugar and brown sugar; beat well. Add eggs, one at a time, beating well after each addition. Blend in vanilla. Combine flour, baking powder and salt; add to peanut butter mixture.

Spread half the batter in greased 13×9-inch baking pan. Spoon syrup over top. Carefully spread with remaining batter. Swirl with spatula or knife for marbled effect. Bake at 350°F for 35 to 40 minutes or until lightly browned. Cool; cut into squares.

Makes about 3 dozen brownies

BANANA CARAMEL BARS

2½ cups all-purpose flour
1 cup sugar
1 teaspoon baking powder
1 cup margarine, cut up
1 large egg, beaten
2 extra-ripe, medium DOLE® Bananas, peeled
½ cup caramel topping

• Combine flour, sugar and baking powder in large bowl. Cut in margarine with pastry blender until mixture resembles coarse meal. Slowly stir in egg, mixing with a fork until crumbly. Pat half of mixture into 13×9-inch baking pan to form crust.

• For filling, mash bananas. Blend bananas with caramel topping. Spread evenly over crust.

• Sprinkle remaining crumb mixture over filling. Pat gently. Bake in 375°F oven 35 minutes or until golden brown. Cool pan on wire rack. Cut into bars when cooled. *Makes 24 bars*

Banana Caramel Bars

Left to right: Pecan Pie Bars, Triple Layer Cookie Bars

PECAN PIE BARS

   2 cups unsifted flour
   ½ cup confectioners' sugar
   1 cup cold margarine or butter
   1 (14-ounce) can EAGLE® Brand
      Sweetened Condensed Milk (NOT
      evaporated milk)
   1 egg
   1 teaspoon vanilla extract
   1 (6-ounce) package almond brickle
      chips
   1 cup chopped pecans

Preheat oven to 350°F (325°F for glass dish).
In medium bowl, combine flour and sugar; cut
in margarine until crumbly. Press firmly on
bottom of 13×9-inch baking pan. Bake 15
minutes. Meanwhile, in medium bowl, beat
sweetened condensed milk, egg and vanilla.
Stir in chips and pecans. Spread evenly over
crust. Bake 25 minutes or until golden brown.
Cool. Cut into bars. Store covered in
refrigerator.   *Makes 36 bars*

TRIPLE LAYER COOKIE BARS

   ½ cup margarine or butter
   1½ cups graham cracker crumbs
   1 (7-ounce) package flaked coconut
      (2⅔ cups)
   1 (14-ounce) can EAGLE® Brand
      Sweetened Condensed Milk (NOT
      evaporated milk)
   1 (12-ounce) package semi-sweet
      chocolate chips
   ½ cup creamy peanut butter

Preheat oven to 350°F (325°F for glass dish).
In 13×9-inch baking pan, melt margarine in
oven. Sprinkle crumbs evenly over margarine.
Top evenly with coconut, then sweetened
condensed milk. Bake 25 minutes or until lightly
browned. In small saucepan, over low heat,
melt chips with peanut butter. Spread evenly
over hot coconut layer. Cool 30 minutes. Chill
thoroughly. Cut into bars. Garnish as desired.
Store loosely covered at room temperature.
                              Makes 24 to 36 bars

PEANUT BUTTER RICE SNACKS

   1 cup light corn syrup
   ½ cup granulated sugar
   ½ cup packed brown sugar
   1 cup crunchy peanut butter
   6 cups RICE CHEX® brand cereal

Line tray with waxed paper. Combine corn
syrup and sugars in large saucepan. Cook over
medium heat just until mixture comes to a boil,
stirring frequently. Remove from heat. Stir in
peanut butter; mix well. Gradually add cereal,
stirring until all pieces are evenly coated. Drop
by level tablespoons onto prepared tray. Chill
15 minutes or until firm.
                              Makes 3 dozen snacks

MAGIC COOKIE BARS

½ cup margarine or butter
1½ cups graham cracker or other crumbs
1 (14-ounce) can EAGLE® Brand
    Sweetened Condensed Milk (NOT
    evaporated milk)
1 cup semi-sweet chocolate chips
1 (3½-ounce) can flaked coconut
    (1⅓ cups)
1 cup chopped nuts

Preheat oven to 350°F (325°F for glass dish). In 13×9-inch baking pan, melt margarine in oven. Sprinkle crumbs over margarine; pour sweetened condensed milk evenly over crumbs. Top with remaining ingredients; press down firmly. Bake 25 to 30 minutes or until lightly browned. Cool. Chill if desired. Cut into bars. Store loosely covered at room temperature.

Makes 24 to 36 bars

SEVEN LAYER MAGIC COOKIE BARS: Add 1 cup butterscotch-flavored chips after chocolate chips.

DOUBLE CHOCOLATE MAGIC COOKIE BARS: Increase chocolate chips to 1 (12-ounce) package.

RAINBOW MAGIC COOKIE BARS: Add 1 cup plain candy-coated chocolate pieces after chocolate chips.

MAGIC PEANUT COOKIE BARS: Omit chocolate chips. Add 2 cups (about ¾ pound) chocolate-covered peanuts.

Magic Cookie Bars

MAGIC MINT COOKIE BARS: Combine ½ teaspoon peppermint extract and 4 drops green food coloring if desired with sweetened condensed milk.

MAGIC MOCHA COOKIE BARS: Add 1 tablespoon instant coffee and 1 tablespoon chocolate-flavored syrup with sweetened condensed milk.

MAGIC PEANUT BUTTER COOKIE BARS: Beat ⅓ cup peanut butter with sweetened condensed milk.

MAGIC MAPLE COOKIE BARS: Combine ½ to 1 teaspoon maple flavoring with sweetened condensed milk.

LEMON ICED AMBROSIA BARS

1¾ cups unsifted flour
  ⅓ cup confectioners' sugar
  ¾ cup cold margarine or butter
  2 cups firmly packed light brown sugar
  4 eggs, beaten
  1 cup flaked coconut
  1 cup finely chopped pecans
  ½ teaspoon baking powder
    Lemon Icing (recipe follows)

Preheat oven to 350°F. In medium bowl, combine *1½ cups* flour and confectioners' sugar; cut in margarine until crumbly. Press onto bottom of lightly greased 13×9-inch baking pan; bake 15 minutes. Meanwhile, in large bowl, combine remaining ingredients except Lemon Icing; mix well. Spread evenly over baked crust; bake 20 to 25 minutes. Cool. Spread with Lemon Icing; cover and refrigerate. Cut into bars. Store, covered, in refrigerator.

Makes about 36 bars

LEMON ICING: Mix 2 cups confectioners' sugar, 3 tablespoons REALEMON® Lemon Juice from Concentrate and 2 tablespoons softened margarine until smooth. Makes about ⅔ cup.

SWIRL OF CHOCOLATE CHEESECAKE TRIANGLES

CRUST
- 2 cups graham cracker crumbs
- ½ cup (1 stick) butter or margarine, melted
- ⅓ cup granulated sugar

FILLING
- 2 packages (8 ounces each) cream cheese, softened
- 1 cup granulated sugar
- ¼ cup all-purpose flour
- 1½ cups (12-fluid-ounce can) *undiluted* CARNATION® Evaporated Milk
- 2 eggs
- 1 tablespoon vanilla extract
- 1 cup (6 ounces) NESTLÉ® Toll House® Semi-Sweet Chocolate Morsels

FOR CRUST:
COMBINE crumbs, butter and sugar in medium bowl; press onto bottom of ungreased 13×9-inch baking pan.

FOR FILLING:
BEAT cream cheese, sugar and flour in large mixer bowl until smooth. Gradually beat in evaporated milk, eggs and vanilla.

MICROWAVE morsels in medium, microwave-safe bowl on HIGH (100% power) for 1 minute; stir. Microwave at additional 10 to 20 second intervals, stirring until smooth. Stir 1 cup cream cheese mixture into chocolate. Pour remaining cheese mixture over crust. Pour chocolate mixture over cheese mixture; swirl with spoon to create marble effect.

BAKE in preheated 325°F. oven for 40 to 45 minutes or until set. Cool to room temperature; chill until firm. Cut into triangles.
Makes about 2½ dozen triangles

CINNAMONY APPLE STREUSEL BARS

- 1¼ cups graham cracker crumbs
- 1¼ cups all-purpose flour
- ¾ cup packed brown sugar, divided
- ¼ cup granulated sugar
- 1 teaspoon ground cinnamon
- ¾ cup butter or margarine, melted
- 2 cups chopped apples (2 medium apples, cored and peeled)
- Glaze (recipe follows)

Preheat oven to 350°F. Grease 13×9-inch baking pan. Combine graham cracker crumbs, flour, ½ cup brown sugar, granulated sugar, cinnamon and melted butter in large bowl until well blended; reserve 1 cup. Press remaining crumb mixture into bottom of prepared pan.

Bake 8 minutes. Remove from oven; set aside. Toss apples with remaining ¼ cup brown sugar in medium bowl until brown sugar is dissolved; arrange apples over baked crust. Sprinkle reserved 1 cup crumb mixture over filling. Bake 30 to 35 minutes more or until apples are tender. Remove pan to wire rack; cool completely. Drizzle with Glaze. Cut into bars.
Makes 3 dozen bars

GLAZE: Combine ½ cup powdered sugar and 1 tablespoon milk in small bowl until well blended.

Cinnamony Apple Streusel Bars

Sugarplum
DELIGHTS

GERMAN CHOCOLATE NO-COOK FUDGE

**3 (4-ounce) packages German sweet chocolate,
    broken into pieces
1 cup (6 ounces) semisweet chocolate chips
1 can (14 ounces) sweetened condensed milk
1 cup chopped pecans
2 teaspoons vanilla
36 pecan halves (optional)**

Butter 8-inch square pan; set aside. Melt chocolate and chips in heavy, small saucepan over very low heat, stirring constantly. Remove from heat. Stir in condensed milk, chopped pecans and vanilla until combined. Spread in prepared pan. Arrange pecan halves on fudge. Score fudge into squares with knife. Refrigerate until firm.

Cut into squares. Store in refrigerator. Bring to room temperature before serving. *Makes about 2 pounds*

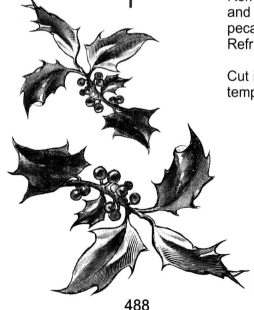

EGGNOG GIFT FUDGE

¾ cup prepared eggnog
2 tablespoons light corn syrup
2 tablespoons butter or margarine
2 cups sugar
1 teaspoon vanilla

Butter 8-inch square pan. Lightly butter inside of heavy, medium saucepan. Combine eggnog, corn syrup, butter and sugar in prepared saucepan. Cook over medium heat, stirring constantly, until sugar dissolves and mixture comes to a boil. Wash down side of pan with pastry brush frequently dipped in hot water to remove sugar crystals. Add candy thermometer. Continue to cook until mixture reaches 238°F (soft-ball stage). Pour into large heatproof bowl. Cool to lukewarm (about 110°F). Add vanilla; beat with heavy-duty electric mixer until thick. Spread in prepared pan. Score fudge into 36 squares with knife. Refrigerate until firm. Cut into squares. Wrap individual pieces in plastic wrap and decorate with fabric or paper bows.

Makes 36 pieces

Left to right: Cherry Merry Christmas Crunch (page 524), Eggnog Gift Fudge

CREAMY WHITE FUDGE

1½ pounds white confectioners' coating*
1 (14-ounce) can EAGLE® Brand Sweetened Condensed Milk (NOT evaporated milk)
⅛ teaspoon salt
¾ to 1 cup chopped nuts
1½ teaspoons vanilla extract

In heavy saucepan, over low heat, melt confectioners' coating with sweetened condensed milk and salt. Remove from heat; stir in nuts and vanilla. Spread evenly into wax paper-lined 8- or 9-inch square pan. Chill 2 hours or until firm. Turn out fudge onto cutting board; peel off paper and cut into squares. Store tightly covered at room temperature.

Makes about 2¼ pounds

MICROWAVE DIRECTIONS: In 2-quart glass measure, combine coating, sweetened condensed milk and salt. Microwave on full power (HIGH) 3 to 5 minutes or until coating melts, stirring after 3 minutes. Stir in nuts and vanilla. Proceed as above.

*If white confectioners' coating is not available at your grocery store it can be purchased in candy specialty stores.

PRALINE FUDGE: Omit vanilla. Add 1 teaspoon maple flavoring and 1 cup chopped pecans. Proceed as above.

CONFETTI FUDGE: Omit nuts. Add 1 cup chopped mixed candied fruit. Proceed as above.

RUM RAISIN FUDGE: Omit vanilla. Add 1½ teaspoons white vinegar, 1 teaspoon rum flavoring and ¾ cup raisins. Proceed as above.

CHERRY FUDGE: Omit nuts. Add 1 cup chopped candied cherries. Proceed as above.

Cherries 'n Chocolate Fudge

CHERRIES 'N CHOCOLATE FUDGE

1 can (14 ounces) sweetened condensed
   milk
2 cups (12-ounce package) HERSHEY'S
   Semi-Sweet Chocolate Chips
½ cup coarsely chopped almonds
½ cup chopped candied cherries
1 teaspoon almond extract
   Candied cherry halves and pecan
   halves

MICROWAVE DIRECTIONS: Line 8-inch
square pan with foil; set aside. In medium
microwave-safe bowl, combine sweetened
condensed milk and chocolate chips; stir lightly.
Microwave at HIGH (100% power) 1½ to 2
minutes or until chips are melted and mixture is
smooth when stirred. Stir in almonds, cherries
and almond extract. Spread evenly in prepared
pan. Place cherry and pecan halves over
fudge. Cover; refrigerate until firm. Cut into
1-inch squares. Cover; store in refrigerator.
Makes about 5 dozen squares

CHRISTMAS FUDGE

3 cups sugar
1 cup PET® Evaporated Milk
½ cup butter
2 cups semisweet chocolate chips
1 jar (7 to 7½ ounces) marshmallow
   creme
1 teaspoon vanilla extract
1 cup crushed peppermint candies

1. Butter 13×9×2-inch pan; set aside.

2. In heavy 3-quart saucepan, combine sugar,
evaporated milk and butter. Bring to a full rolling
boil over high heat, stirring constantly.

3. Reduce heat to medium and boil 6 minutes
(234°F), stirring constantly.

4. Remove from heat and stir in chocolate
chips, marshmallow creme and vanilla.

5. Stir in peppermint candies.

6. Pour into prepared pan. Cool until firm. Cut
into 1-inch squares.
Makes 117 (1-inch) pieces

EASY ROCKY ROAD

2 cups (12-ounce package) HERSHEY'S
   Semi-Sweet Chocolate Chips
¼ cup butter or margarine
2 tablespoons shortening
3 cups miniature marshmallows
½ cup coarsely chopped nuts

Butter 8-inch square pan. In large microwave-
safe bowl, place chocolate chips, butter and
shortening. Microwave at HIGH (100% power)
1 to 1½ minutes or just until chocolate chips
are melted and mixture is smooth when stirred.
Add marshmallows and nuts; blend well.
Spread evenly in prepared pan. Cover;
refrigerate until firm. Cut into 2-inch squares.
Makes 16 squares

TIGER STRIPES

1 package (12 ounces) semisweet chocolate chips
3 tablespoons chunky peanut butter, divided
2 (2-ounce) white chocolate baking bars

Line 8-inch square pan with foil. Grease lightly. Melt semisweet chocolate and 2 tablespoons peanut butter over low heat in small saucepan; stir well. Pour half of chocolate mixture into prepared pan. Let stand 10 to 15 minutes to cool slightly. Melt white baking bars with remaining 1 tablespoon peanut butter over low heat in small saucepan. Spoon half of white chocolate mixture over semisweet chocolate mixture. Drop remaining semisweet and white chocolate mixtures by spoonfuls over mixture in pan. Using small metal spatula or knife, pull through the chocolates to create tiger stripes. Freeze about 1 hour or until firm. Remove from pan; peel off foil. Cut into 36 pieces. Refrigerate until ready to serve.

Makes 36 pieces

OLD FASHIONED FUDGE

3 cups sugar
1 cup PET® Evaporated Milk
½ cup butter
2 cups semisweet chocolate chips
1 jar (7 to 7½ ounces) marshmallow creme
1 cup chopped nuts (optional)
1 teaspoon vanilla extract

1. Butter 13×9×2-inch pan; set aside.

2. In heavy 3-quart saucepan, combine sugar, evaporated milk and butter. Bring to a full rolling boil over high heat, stirring constantly.

3. Reduce heat to medium and boil 5 minutes (approximately 234°F), stirring constantly.

4. Remove from heat and stir in chocolate chips, marshmallow creme, nuts and vanilla.

5. Pour into prepared pan. Cool until firm. Cut into 1-inch squares.

Makes 117 (1-inch) pieces

MICROWAVE FUDGE

½ cup butter
3 cups sugar
¾ cup PET® Evaporated Milk
2 cups semisweet chocolate chips
1 jar (7 to 7½ ounces) marshmallow creme
1 teaspoon vanilla extract

1. Butter 13×9×2-inch pan; set aside.

2. Place butter in microwave-safe 3-quart bowl. Microwave on HIGH (100% power) for 1 minute or until melted.

3. Stir in sugar and evaporated milk. Microwave on HIGH 11 minutes, stirring every 2 minutes (approximately 234°F).

4. Stir in chocolate chips, marshmallow creme and vanilla.

5. Pour into prepared pan. Cool until firm. Cut into 1-inch squares. Store in covered container.

Makes 117 (1-inch) pieces

Clockwise from left: Festive Popcorn Treats (page 527), Good Luck Meringue Mushrooms (page 510), Tiger Stripes

FOOLPROOF DARK CHOCOLATE FUDGE

3 (6-ounce) packages semi-sweet chocolate chips
1 (14-ounce) can EAGLE® Brand Sweetened Condensed Milk (NOT evaporated milk)
Dash salt
½ to 1 cup chopped nuts
1½ teaspoons vanilla extract

In heavy saucepan, over low heat, melt chips with sweetened condensed milk and salt. Remove from heat; stir in nuts and vanilla. Spread evenly into wax paper-lined 8- or 9-inch square pan. Chill 2 hours or until firm. Turn out fudge onto cutting board; peel off paper and cut into squares. Store loosely covered at room temperature. *Makes about 2 pounds*

MICROWAVE DIRECTIONS: In 1-quart glass measure, combine chips with sweetened condensed milk. Microwave on full power (HIGH) 3 minutes. Stir until chips melt and mixture is smooth. Stir in remaining ingredients. Proceed as above.

CREAMY DARK CHOCOLATE FUDGE: Melt 2 cups CAMPFIRE® Miniature Marshmallows with chips and sweetened condensed milk. Proceed as above.

MILK CHOCOLATE FUDGE: Omit 1 (6-ounce) package semi-sweet chocolate chips. Add 1 cup milk chocolate chips. Proceed as above.

CREAMY MILK CHOCOLATE FUDGE: Omit 1 (6-ounce) package semi-sweet chocolate chips. Add 1 cup milk chocolate chips and 2 cups CAMPFIRE® Miniature Marshmallows. Proceed as above.

MEXICAN CHOCOLATE FUDGE: Reduce vanilla to 1 teaspoon. Add 1 tablespoon instant coffee and 1 teaspoon ground cinnamon to sweetened condensed milk. Proceed as above.

BUTTERSCOTCH FUDGE: Omit chocolate chips and vanilla. In heavy saucepan, melt 2 (12-ounce) packages butterscotch flavored chips with sweetened condensed milk. Remove from heat; stir in 2 tablespoons white vinegar, ⅛ teaspoon salt, ½ teaspoon maple flavoring and 1 cup chopped nuts. Proceed as directed.

LAYERED MINT CHOCOLATE CANDY

1 (12-ounce) package semi-sweet chocolate chips
1 (14-ounce) can EAGLE® Brand Sweetened Condensed Milk (NOT evaporated milk)
2 teaspoons vanilla extract
6 ounces white confectioners' coating*
1 tablespoon peppermint extract
Few drops green or red food coloring (optional)

In heavy saucepan, over low heat, melt chips with *1 cup* sweetened condensed milk. Stir in vanilla. Spread half the mixture into wax paper-lined 8- or 9-inch square pan; chill 10 minutes or until firm. Hold remaining chocolate mixture at room temperature. In heavy saucepan, over low heat, melt confectioners' coating with remaining sweetened condensed milk. Stir in peppermint extract and food coloring if desired. Spread on chilled chocolate layer; chill 10 minutes longer or until firm. Spread reserved chocolate mixture on mint layer. Chill 2 hours or until firm. Turn out onto cutting board; peel off paper and cut into squares. Store loosely covered at room temperature. *Makes about 1¾ pounds*

*If white confectioners' coating is not available at your grocery store it can be purchased in candy specialty stores.

CHOCOLATE PECAN CRITTERS

1 (11½-ounce) package milk chocolate chips

1 (6-ounce) package semi-sweet chocolate chips

¼ cup margarine or butter

1 (14-ounce) can EAGLE® Brand Sweetened Condensed Milk (NOT evaporated milk)

⅛ teaspoon salt

2 cups coarsely chopped pecans

2 teaspoons vanilla extract

Pecan halves

In heavy saucepan, over medium heat, melt chips and margarine with sweetened condensed milk and salt. Remove from heat; stir in chopped nuts and vanilla. Drop by teaspoonfuls onto wax paper-lined baking sheets. Top with pecan halves. Chill. Store tightly covered. *Makes about 5 dozen*

MICROWAVE DIRECTIONS: In 2-quart glass measure, microwave chips, margarine, sweetened condensed milk and salt on full power (HIGH) 3 minutes, stirring after 1½ minutes. Stir to melt chips; stir in chopped nuts and vanilla. Proceed as above.

Clockwise from top right: Coconut Rum Balls (page 512), Chocolate Pecan Critters, Fruit Bon Bons (page 512), Milk Chocolate Bourbon Balls (page 512), Buckeyes (page 519), Foolproof Dark Chocolate Fudge, Peanut Butter Logs (page 507), Layered Mint Chocolate Candy, Cherry Fudge (page 490)

Coffee Liqueur Pecan Fudge

COFFEE LIQUEUR PECAN FUDGE

3 cups miniature marshmallows
2 cups (12-ounce package) NESTLÉ®
   Toll House® Semi-Sweet Chocolate
   Morsels
2 ounces NESTLÉ® Unsweetened
   Chocolate Baking Bars, coarsely
   chopped
⅔ cup *undiluted* CARNATION®
   Evaporated Milk
1⅓ cups granulated sugar
¼ cup butter
1 cup coarsely chopped pecans
¼ cup coffee liqueur

In large bowl, combine marshmallows, morsels and unsweetened chocolate. In heavy 2-quart saucepan, combine evaporated milk, sugar and butter. Bring to a boil over medium heat, stirring frequently; boil for 6 minutes, stirring constantly. Pour over marshmallow mixture; stir until marshmallows and chocolate are completely melted and mixture is smooth. Stir in nuts and liqueur. Pour into buttered 8-inch square baking pan; cool. Chill until firm. Cut into 36 squares.

Makes 2½ pounds

TRADITIONAL CHRISTMAS FUDGE

2 tablespoons butter or margarine
⅔ cup *undiluted* CARNATION®
Evaporated Milk
1½ cups granulated sugar
¼ teaspoon salt
2 cups (4 ounces) miniature
marshmallows
1½ cups (9 ounces) NESTLÉ® Toll House®
Semi-Sweet Chocolate Morsels
½ cup chopped pecans or walnuts
1 teaspoon vanilla extract

COMBINE butter, evaporated milk, sugar and salt in medium, heavy saucepan. Bring to a boil over medium heat, stirring constantly. Boil for 4 to 5 minutes, stirring constantly. Remove from heat.

STIR in marshmallows, morsels, nuts and vanilla. Stir vigorously for 1 minute or until marshmallows are melted. Pour into foil-lined 8-inch square baking pan. Sprinkle with additional pecans if desired. Chill until firm. Cut into pieces. *Makes about 2 pounds*

VARIATIONS
Milk Chocolate Fudge: Substitute 2 cups (11½-ounce package) NESTLÉ® Toll House® Milk Chocolate Morsels for Semi-Sweet Morsels.

Butterscotch Fudge: Substitute 2 cups (12-ounce package) NESTLÉ® Toll House® Butterscotch Flavored Morsels for Semi-Sweet Morsels.

Mint Chocolate Fudge: Substitute 1½ cups (10-ounce package) NESTLÉ® Toll House® Mint-Chocolate Morsels for Semi-Sweet Morsels.

HONEY NUT WHITE FUDGE

2 tablespoons butter or margarine
⅔ cup *undiluted* CARNATION®
Evaporated Milk
1½ cups granulated sugar
2 cups (4 ounces) miniature
marshmallows
2 cups (12-ounce package) NESTLÉ®
Toll House® Premier White Morsels
1½ cups honey roasted peanuts, divided
2 teaspoons vanilla extract

COMBINE butter, evaporated milk and sugar in medium, heavy saucepan. Bring to a *full rolling boil* over medium heat, stirring constantly. Boil for 4½ to 5 minutes, stirring constantly. Remove from heat.

STIR in marshmallows, morsels, *1 cup* peanuts and vanilla. Stir vigorously for 1 minute or until marshmallows are melted. Pour into foil-lined 9-inch square baking pan. Coarsely chop *remaining* peanuts; sprinkle over fudge and press lightly. Chill until firm. Remove fudge from pan by lifting edges of foil. Remove foil and cut fudge into squares.

Makes about 1¾ pounds fudge

CHOCOLATE-NUT SQUARES

1 cup (6 ounces) semisweet chocolate
    chips
1 cup milk chocolate chips
1 tablespoon shortening
1 package (14 ounces) caramels
2 tablespoons butter or margarine
3 tablespoons milk
2 cups coarsely chopped pecans

Line 8-inch square pan with buttered foil; set aside. Melt both kinds of chips with shortening in heavy, small saucepan over very low heat, stirring constantly. Spoon half the chocolate mixture into prepared pan, spreading evenly over bottom and ¼ inch up sides of pan. Refrigerate until firm.

Meanwhile, combine caramels, butter and milk in heavy, medium saucepan. Cook over medium heat, stirring constantly. When mixture is smooth, stir in pecans. Cool to lukewarm. Spread caramel mixture evenly over chocolate in pan. Melt remaining chocolate mixture again over very low heat, stirring constantly; spread over caramel layer. Refrigerate until almost firm. Cut into squares. Store in refrigerator.

Makes about 2 pounds

HINT: Squares are easier to cut without breaking if chocolate is not completely firm.

CHOCOLATE PEPPERMINTS

1 cup (6 ounces) semisweet chocolate
    chips
1 cup milk chocolate chips
¼ teaspoon peppermint extract
½ cup crushed peppermint candy

Line baking sheet with buttered waxed paper; set aside. Melt both kinds of chips in heavy, medium saucepan over low heat, stirring constantly. Stir in peppermint extract. Spread mixture in rectangle about ¼ inch thick on prepared baking sheet. Sprinkle with candy; press into chocolate. Refrigerate until almost firm. Cut into squares. Refrigerate until firm before removing from paper.

Makes about 100 mints

HINT: Squares are easier to cut without breaking if chocolate is not completely firm.

TRIPLE CHOCOLATE SQUARES

1½ cups BLUE DIAMOND® Blanched
    Almond Paste, divided
8 ounces semisweet chocolate, melted
¾ cup softened butter, divided
8 ounces milk chocolate, melted
8 ounces white chocolate, melted

Line bottom and sides of 8-inch square pan with aluminum foil. Beat ½ cup almond paste with semisweet chocolate. Beat in ¼ cup butter. Spread evenly in bottom of prepared pan. Chill to harden. Beat ½ cup almond paste with milk chocolate. Beat in ¼ cup butter. Spread mixture evenly over chilled semisweet chocolate layer. Chill to harden. Beat remaining ½ cup almond paste with white chocolate. Beat in remaining ¼ cup butter. Spread mixture evenly over chilled milk chocolate layer. Chill. Remove candy from pan by lifting edges of foil. Peel off foil and cut candy into 1-inch squares.

Makes 64 squares

Chocolate-Nut Squares, Chocolate Peppermints

GERMAN CHOCOLATE FUDGE SWIRL

FILLING
- ¾ cup flaked coconut
- ¾ cup chopped nuts
- 2 tablespoons *undiluted* CARNATION® Evaporated Milk

FUDGE
- 2 tablespoons butter or margarine
- ⅔ cup *undiluted* CARNATION® Evaporated Milk
- 1½ cups granulated sugar
- ¼ teaspoon salt
- 2 cups (4 ounces) miniature marshmallows
- 1½ cups NESTLÉ® Toll House® Semi-Sweet Chocolate Morsels
- 1 teaspoon vanilla extract

FOR FILLING:
MIX coconut, nuts and evaporated milk in small bowl.

FOR FUDGE:
LINE 15×10-inch jelly-roll pan with heavily buttered wax paper.

COMBINE butter, evaporated milk, sugar and salt in medium saucepan. Bring to a boil over medium heat, stirring constantly. Boil for 4 to 5 minutes, stirring constantly; remove from heat.

STIR in marshmallows, morsels and vanilla. Stir vigorously for 1 minute or until marshmallows melt completely.

POUR into prepared pan, spreading evenly (if fudge is difficult to spread, let stand for 1 minute). Sprinkle with filling. Let cool for about 5 minutes. Starting with long side of pan, roll up fudge jelly-roll style, using wax paper to assist, if necessary. Wrap fudge roll in wax paper. Cool and cut into slices.

Makes about 2 pounds

German Chocolate Fudge Swirl

Chocolate Walnut Candy

CHOCOLATE WALNUT CANDY

1½ pounds EAGLE™ Brand Chocolate-
    Flavored Candy Coating
1 (14-ounce) can EAGLE® Brand
    Sweetened Condensed Milk (NOT
    evaporated milk)
⅛ teaspoon salt
1 teaspoon vanilla extract
4 cups coarsely chopped walnuts, toasted
    (about 1 pound)

In heavy saucepan, over low heat, melt candy coating with sweetened condensed milk and salt. Remove from heat; stir in extract and walnuts. Spread evenly into waxed paper-lined 15×10-inch baking pan. Chill 2 hours or until firm. Turn out onto cutting board; peel off paper and cut into triangles or squares. Store tightly covered at room temperature.

Makes 3¼ pounds

CREAMY CARAMELS

½ cup slivered or chopped toasted
    almonds (optional)
1 cup butter or margarine, cut into small
    pieces
1 can (14 ounces) sweetened condensed
    milk
2 cups sugar
1 cup light corn syrup
1½ teaspoons vanilla

Line 8-inch square baking pan with foil, extending edges over sides of pan. Lightly grease foil; sprinkle almonds over bottom of pan, if desired.

Melt butter in heavy 2-quart saucepan over low heat. Add milk, sugar and corn syrup. Stir over low heat until sugar is dissolved and mixture comes to a boil. Carefully clip candy thermometer to side of pan (do not let bulb touch bottom of pan.) Cook over low heat about 30 minutes or until thermometer registers 240°F (soft-ball stage), stirring occasionally. Immediately remove from heat and stir in vanilla. Pour mixture into prepared pan. Cool completely.

Lift caramels out of pan using foil; remove foil. Place candy on cutting board; cut into 1-inch squares with sharp knife. Wrap each square in plastic wrap. Store in airtight container.

Makes about 2½ pounds or 64 caramels

LOUISIANA CREAM PRALINES

2⅓ cups packed brown sugar
¾ cup PET® Evaporated Milk
1 tablespoon butter
⅛ teaspoon salt
2 cups pecan halves
1 teaspoon vanilla extract

1. Grease baking sheet; set aside.

2. In heavy 2-quart saucepan, combine sugar, evaporated milk, butter and salt. Cook and stir over low heat until sugar is dissolved.

3. Add pecans. Cook over medium heat to 234°F (approximately 9 minutes), stirring constantly.

4. Remove from heat; add vanilla. Cool 5 minutes without stirring.

5. Stir vigorously until mixture thickens and loses its gloss; about 5 minutes.

6. Drop quickly by tablespoonfuls onto prepared baking sheet. Cool. Store in covered container. *Makes 2½ to 3 dozen*

PECAN ROLLS

¼ cup corn syrup
¼ cup water
1¼ cups sugar
1 egg white
⅛ teaspoon cream of tartar
1 teaspoon vanilla
1 package (14 ounces) caramels
3 tablespoons water
2 cups coarsely chopped pecans

Line 9×5-inch loaf pan with buttered waxed paper; set aside. Combine corn syrup, ¼ cup water and sugar in heavy, small saucepan. Cook over medium heat, stirring constantly, until sugar dissolves and mixture comes to a boil. Wash down side of pan frequently with pastry brush dipped in hot water to remove sugar crystals. Carefully clip candy thermometer to side of pan (do not let bulb touch bottom of pan). Continue to cook until mixture reaches the hard-ball stage (255°F).

Meanwhile, beat egg white and cream of tartar with heavy-duty electric mixer until stiff but not dry. Slowly pour hot syrup into egg white mixture, beating constantly. Add vanilla; beat until candy forms soft peaks and starts to lose its gloss. Spoon mixture into prepared pan. Cut into 3 strips lengthwise, then crosswise in center. Freeze until firm.

Line baking sheet with waxed paper; set aside. Melt caramels with 3 tablespoons water in heavy, small saucepan over low heat, stirring occasionally. Arrange pecans on waxed paper. Working quickly, drop 1 piece of frozen candy mixture into melted caramels to coat. Roll in pecans to coat completely. Place on prepared baking sheet to set. Repeat with remaining candy pieces, reheating caramels if mixture becomes too thick.

Cut logs into ½-inch slices. Store in refrigerator in airtight container between layers of waxed paper or freeze up to 3 months.
Makes 6 (5-inch) rolls

HINT: For perfect slices, freeze finished rolls before cutting.

Pecan Rolls

HEAVENLY ANGELS

6 tablespoons Marzipan (recipe follows)
3 (2-ounce) white chocolate baking bars
6 ice cream sugar cones
    Assorted colored sugars and sprinkles
6 large pretzel twists
    Assorted food colors
⅓ cup shredded coconut, tinted yellow
6 small round cookies (1½ inch
    diameter)

Prepare Marzipan; set aside. Melt white chocolate in double boiler over hot, not boiling, water. Using spoon, coat 1 ice cream cone at a time with white chocolate. Dip edge of cone in colored sugar and decorate side with sprinkles. Place on waxed-paper-lined baking sheet; refrigerate.

Dip pretzels in white chocolate, turning to coat completely. Remove to waxed-paper-lined baking sheet. Refrigerate. Reserve remaining white chocolate. To form head, roll 1 tablespoon Marzipan into ball; repeat to make 6 heads. Paint features on heads with wooden toothpicks and cotton swabs dipped in food color. Press Marzipan heads onto ends of cones. Attach pretzels to backs of cones with reserved melted white chocolate. (Attach smooth side of pretzels to body.) Attach tinted coconut hair and cookie halos to heads with melted white chocolate. Refrigerate until firm.
Makes 6 angels

MARZIPAN
1 can (8 ounces) almond paste
1 egg white*
3 cups powdered sugar, divided

Combine almond paste and egg white in small bowl. Add 2 cups powdered sugar; mix well. Knead in remaining 1 cup sugar until smooth and pliable.

Wrap tightly in plastic wrap; refrigerate until ready to serve.   *Makes about 2 cups*

*Use only clean, uncracked eggs.

PENUCHE

¼ cup butter
2½ cups packed brown sugar
¾ cup PET® Evaporated Milk
2 tablespoons light corn syrup
1 teaspoon vanilla extract
1 cup chopped pecans (optional)

1. Butter 8-inch square pan; set aside.

2. In heavy 3-quart saucepan, melt butter. Add sugar, evaporated milk and corn syrup; stir well. Bring to a full, rolling boil over medium heat, stirring constantly.

3. Cover pan and continue boiling very gently over low heat 2 minutes. Remove cover and scrape sides of pan with a rubber scraper.

4. Continue boiling, uncovered, over low heat until mixture reaches 236°F. (It is not necessary to stir mixture during cooking time, though gently scraping sides of pan occasionally is desirable. DO NOT SCRAPE BOTTOM OF PAN.)

5. Pour mixture into a heat-proof bowl. Do not scrape sides and bottom of pan. Place candy thermometer in mixture. Place bowl in ½ inch of lukewarm water. Cool mixture to 110°F *without stirring.*

6. Add vanilla. Beat mixture until it thickens and starts to lose its gloss. Stir in pecans, if desired. Pour into buttered pan. Cool until firm. Cut into 1-inch squares. Store in covered container.   *Makes 64 pieces*

Heavenly Angels

ELEGANT CREAM CHEESE MINTS

> **Chocolate Topping (recipe follows), optional**
> **1 package (3 ounces) cream cheese, softened**
> **3 tablespoons butter or margarine, softened**
> **½ teaspoon vanilla extract**
> **¼ to ½ teaspoon desired food coloring**
> **¼ teaspoon peppermint extract**
> **1 pound powdered sugar (3½ to 4 cups)**
> **⅓ cup granulated sugar**

Line large cookie sheet with waxed paper. Prepare Chocolate Topping, if desired; keep warm.

Beat cream cheese, butter, vanilla, food coloring and peppermint extract in large bowl with electric mixer on medium speed until smooth. Gradually beat in powdered sugar on low speed until well combined. (If necessary, stir in remaining powdered sugar with wooden spoon or knead candy on work surface that has been lightly sprinkled with powdered sugar.)

Place granulated sugar in shallow bowl. Roll 2 teaspoons cream cheese mixture into a ball. Roll ball in granulated sugar until coated. Flatten ball with fingers or fork to make a patty. Place patty on prepared cookie sheet. Repeat with remaining cream cheese mixture and granulated sugar. Drizzle patties with topping, if desired. Refrigerate until firm. Store in airtight container in refrigerator.
Makes about 1½ pounds or 40 (1-inch) mints

CHOCOLATE TOPPING: Place ½ cup semisweet chocolate chips and 1 tablespoon shortening in 1-cup glass measuring cup. Microwave on HIGH (100% power) about 2 minutes or until melted, stirring after 1½ minutes.

Citrus Candied Nuts (page 526),
Elegant Cream Cheese Mints

PEANUT BUTTER LOGS

1 (12-ounce) package peanut butter flavored chips
1 (14-ounce) can EAGLE® Brand Sweetened Condensed Milk (NOT evaporated milk)
1 cup CAMPFIRE® Miniature Marshmallows
1 cup chopped peanuts

In heavy saucepan, over low heat, melt chips with sweetened condensed milk. Add marshmallows; stir until melted. Remove from heat; cool 20 minutes. Divide in half; place each portion on a 20-inch piece of wax paper. Shape each portion into 12-inch log. Roll in nuts. Wrap tightly; chill 2 hours or until firm. Remove paper; cut into ¼-inch slices.

Makes 2 (12-inch) logs

MICROWAVE DIRECTIONS: In 2-quart glass measure, microwave chips, sweetened condensed milk and marshmallows on full power (HIGH) 4 minutes or until melted, stirring after 2 minutes. Let stand at room temperature 1 hour. Proceed as above.

PEANUT BUTTER FUDGE: Stir peanuts into hot mixture. Spread into wax paper-lined 8- or 9-inch square pan. Chill 2 hours or until firm. Turn out fudge onto cutting board; peel off paper and cut into squares.

COAL CANDY

2 cups sugar
¾ cup light corn syrup
½ cup water
1 teaspoon anise extract
½ teaspoon black paste food coloring

Line 8-inch square baking pan with foil, extending edges over sides of pan. Lightly grease foil with butter; set aside. Measure sugar, corn syrup and water into heavy 2-quart saucepan. Stir over medium-low heat until sugar is dissolved and mixture comes to a boil, being careful not to splash sugar mixture on side of pan. Carefully clip candy thermometer to side of pan (do not let bulb touch bottom of pan). Cook about 15 minutes, without stirring, until thermometer registers 290°F. Immediately remove from heat. Stir in anise extract and food coloring. Pour mixture into prepared pan. Cool completely.

Lift candy out of pan using foil; remove foil. Place candy between 2 layers of heavy-duty foil. Pound with mallet to break candy into 1- to 2-inch pieces. *Makes about 1½ pounds*

CHIPPER PEANUT CANDY

1 cup semi-sweet chocolate chips or butterscotch-flavored chips
1 (14-ounce) can EAGLE® Brand Sweetened Condensed Milk (NOT evaporated milk)
1 cup peanut butter
2 cups crushed potato chips
1 cup coarsely chopped peanuts

In large heavy saucepan, over low heat, melt chocolate chips with sweetened condensed milk and peanut butter; stir until well blended. Remove from heat. Add potato chips and peanuts; mix well. Press into aluminum foil-lined 8- or 9-inch square pan. Chill 2 hours or until firm. Turn out onto cutting board; peel off foil and cut into squares. Store loosely covered at room temperature.

Makes about 2 pounds

MICROWAVE DIRECTIONS: In 2-quart glass measure, combine chocolate chips, sweetened condensed milk and peanut butter. Cook on 100% power (HIGH) 4 minutes, stirring after each 2 minutes. Proceed as directed.

CARAMELS

> 2 cups sugar
> 2 cups light corn syrup
> ⅛ teaspoon salt
> ½ cup butter
> 2 cups PET® Evaporated Milk
> 1 teaspoon vanilla extract
> 1 cup chopped nuts (optional)

1. Butter 9-inch square baking pan.

2. In heavy 3-quart saucepan, combine sugar, corn syrup and salt. Cook over medium-high heat until mixture reaches firm-ball stage (244°F), stirring constantly.

3. Stir in butter.

4. Very slowly add evaporated milk so that mixture does not stop boiling. Cook rapidly to firm-ball stage again (approximately 30 minutes), stirring constantly.

5. Stir in vanilla and nuts. Pour into prepared pan without scraping side of saucepan. Cool until firm. Cut into 1-inch squares.

Makes 81 (1-inch) caramels

MARBLE CARAMELS: After pouring caramel mixture into baking pan, sprinkle with ⅓ cup semisweet chocolate chips. Let stand until soft enough to spread, 1 to 2 minutes. Swirl chocolate through caramels using a metal spatula or knife. Cool until firm.

MOCHA CARAMELS: Follow caramel recipe as directed, except add 2 tablespoons instant coffee crystals to sugar, corn syrup and salt mixture before cooking.

BUTTERSCOTCH– CHOCOLATE DIVINITY

> 2 cups sugar
> ⅓ cup light corn syrup
> ⅓ cup water
> 2 egg whites
> ⅛ teaspoon cream of tartar
> 1 teaspoon vanilla
> ½ cup milk chocolate chips
> ½ cup butterscotch chips
> ½ cup chopped nuts

Line 2 or 3 baking sheets with buttered waxed paper; set aside. Combine sugar, corn syrup and water in heavy, medium saucepan. Cook over medium heat, stirring constantly, until sugar dissolves and mixture comes to a boil. Wash down side of pan frequently with pastry brush dipped in hot water to remove sugar crystals. Add candy thermometer. Continue to cook until mixture reaches hard-ball stage (255°F).

Meanwhile, beat egg whites and cream of tartar with heavy-duty electric mixer until stiff peaks form. Slowly pour hot syrup into egg white mixture, beating constantly. Add vanilla; beat until candy forms soft peaks and starts to lose its gloss. Stir in both kinds of chips and nuts. Immediately drop tablespoonfuls of candy in mounds on prepared baking sheets. Store in refrigerator in airtight container between layers of waxed paper or freeze up to 3 months.

Makes about 36 pieces

Butterscotch-Chocolate Divinity

GOOD LUCK MERINGUE MUSHROOMS

2 egg whites
Pinch cream of tartar
½ cup sugar
½ cup semisweet chocolate chips, melted
Unsweetened cocoa

Preheat oven to 250°F. Beat egg whites in small bowl until foamy. Add cream of tartar and beat until soft peaks form. Add sugar, 2 tablespoons at a time, beating until stiff and glossy. Line baking sheets with parchment paper. Spoon mixture into pastry bag fitted with large writing tip. Pipe 1-inch rounds to make mushroom caps. Smooth tops with wet fingertips. Pipe 1-inch-high cones to make stems. (Pipe an equal number of caps and cones.) Bake about 30 minutes or until firm. Turn oven off; let stand in oven 1 hour. Remove from oven; cool completely. Make small hole in center of flat side of each cap with sharp knife. Fill hole with melted chocolate. Insert stem into hole. Set aside until chocolate sets. Sift cocoa through fine-mesh sieve over mushroom caps.
Makes about 2½ dozen

NOTE: These confections may be made ahead and stored, loosely covered, at room temperature for up to 1 week. Avoid making on humid days as the candy may become moist and sticky.

DREAMY DIVINITY

3½ cups DOMINO® Granulated Sugar
⅔ cup water
⅔ cup light corn syrup
⅓ teaspoon salt
3 egg whites, beaten until stiff
1½ teaspoons vanilla extract
Food coloring, candied cherries and chopped nuts (optional)

Combine sugar, water, corn syrup and salt in saucepan. Heat, stirring occasionally, until sugar dissolves. Wipe down sugar crystals from side of pan as necessary with pastry brush dipped in water. Boil syrup mixture, without stirring, until mixture reaches 265°F or hard-ball stage on candy thermometer.

Gradually beat hot syrup into beaten egg whites. Add vanilla. Tint with food coloring, if desired. Continue beating until candy holds shape. Drop by teaspoonfuls onto buttered baking sheet or plate. Garnish with cherries and nuts as desired. When firm, store in airtight container. *Makes 50 pieces (1½ pounds)*

CHOCOLATE BRITTLE DROPS

½ package (4 squares) BAKER'S® Semi-Sweet Chocolate
1½ cups (½ pound) coarsely crushed peanut brittle

Place unwrapped chocolate in heavy saucepan on very low heat; stir constantly until just melted. Remove from heat; stir in peanut brittle. Drop by teaspoonfuls onto wax paper-lined cookie sheet. Let stand at room temperature or refrigerate until chocolate is firm.
Makes about 2 dozen

Dreamy Divinity

COCONUT RUM BALLS

- 1 (12-ounce) package vanilla wafer cookies, finely crushed (about 3 cups crumbs)
- 1 (3½-ounce) can flaked coconut (1⅓ cups)
- 1 cup finely chopped nuts
- 1 (14-ounce) can EAGLE® Brand Sweetened Condensed Milk (NOT evaporated milk)
- ¼ cup rum
   Additional flaked coconut or confectioners' sugar

In large mixing bowl, combine crumbs, coconut and nuts. Add sweetened condensed milk and rum; mix well. Chill 4 hours. Shape into 1-inch balls. Roll in coconut. Store tightly covered in refrigerator.   *Makes about 8 dozen*

TIPS: The flavor of these candies improves after 24 hours. They may be made ahead and stored in refrigerator for several weeks.

FRUIT BON BONS

- 1 (14-ounce) can EAGLE® Brand Sweetened Condensed Milk (NOT evaporated milk)
- 2 (7-ounce) packages flaked coconut (5⅓ cups)
- 1 (6-ounce) package fruit flavor gelatin, any flavor
- 1 cup ground blanched almonds
- 1 teaspoon almond extract
   Food coloring (optional)

In large mixing bowl, combine sweetened condensed milk, coconut, ⅓ *cup* gelatin, almonds, extract and enough food coloring to tint mixture desired shade. Chill 1 hour or until firm enough to handle. Using about ½ tablespoon mixture for each, shape into 1-inch balls. Sprinkle remaining gelatin on wax paper; roll each ball in gelatin to coat. Place on wax paper-lined baking sheets; chill. Store covered at room temperature or in refrigerator.
Makes about 5 dozen

MILK CHOCOLATE BOURBON BALLS

- 1 (12-ounce) package vanilla wafer cookies, finely crushed (about 3 cups crumbs)
- 5 tablespoons bourbon or brandy
- 1 (11½-ounce) package milk chocolate chips
- 1 (14-ounce) can EAGLE® Brand Sweetened Condensed Milk (NOT evaporated milk)
   Finely chopped nuts

In medium mixing bowl, combine crumbs and bourbon. In heavy large saucepan, over low heat, melt chips. Remove from heat; add sweetened condensed milk. Gradually add crumb mixture; mix well. Let stand at room temperature 30 minutes or chill. Shape into 1-inch balls; roll in nuts. Store tightly covered.
Makes about 5½ dozen

TIP: The flavor of these candies improves after 24 hours. They may be made ahead and stored in freezer. Thaw before serving.

RICH CHOCOLATE PUMPKIN TRUFFLES

2½ cups crushed vanilla wafers
  1 cup toasted ground almonds
  ¾ cup sifted powdered sugar, divided
  2 teaspoons ground cinnamon
  1 cup (6 ounces) NESTLÉ® Toll House®
    Semi-Sweet Chocolate Morsels,
    melted
  ½ cup LIBBY'S® Solid Pack Pumpkin
  ⅓ cup coffee liqueur or apple juice

In medium bowl, combine vanilla wafer crumbs, ground almonds, *½ cup* powdered sugar and cinnamon. Blend in melted chocolate, pumpkin and coffee liqueur. Form into 1-inch balls. Chill. Dust with *remaining ¼ cup* powdered sugar just before serving. *Makes 4 dozen*

HOLIDAY ALMOND TREATS

2½ cups crushed vanilla wafers
  1¾ cups toasted ground almonds, divided
  ½ cup sifted powdered sugar
  ½ teaspoon ground cinnamon
  1 cup LIBBY'S® Pumpkin Pie Mix
  ⅓ cup almond liqueur or apple juice

In medium bowl, blend vanilla wafer crumbs, *1 cup* ground almonds, powdered sugar and cinnamon. Stir in pumpkin pie mix and almond liqueur. Form into 1-inch balls. Roll in *remaining ¾ cup* ground almonds. Chill.

Makes 4 dozen

Left to right: Rich Chocolate Pumpkin Truffles, Holiday Almond Treats

Mint Truffles

MINT TRUFFLES

1 package (10 ounces) mint chocolate chips
⅓ cup whipping cream
¼ cup butter or margarine
1 container (3½ ounces) chocolate sprinkles

Line baking sheet with waxed paper; set aside. Melt chips with whipping cream and butter in heavy, medium saucepan over low heat, stirring occasionally. Pour into pie pan. Refrigerate until mixture is fudgy, but soft, about 2 hours.

Shape about 1 tablespoonful of mixture into 1¼-inch ball. To shape, roll mixture between palms. Repeat procedure with remaining mixture. Place balls on waxed paper.

Place sprinkles in shallow bowl; roll balls in sprinkles. Place truffles in petit four or candy cups. (If sprinkles won't stick because truffle has set, roll truffle between palms until outside is soft.) Truffles may be refrigerated 2 to 3 days or frozen several weeks.

Makes about 24 truffles

HINT: Truffles can be coated with unsweetened cocoa, powdered sugar, chopped nuts, sprinkles or cookie crumbs to add flavor and prevent the truffle from melting in your fingers.

CHOCOLATE TRUFFLES

3 (6-ounce) packages semi-sweet chocolate chips

1 (14-ounce) can EAGLE® Brand Sweetened Condensed Milk (NOT evaporated milk)

1 tablespoon vanilla extract
  Finely chopped nuts, flaked coconut, chocolate sprinkles, colored sprinkles, unsweetened cocoa, colored sugar or confectioners' sugar

In heavy saucepan, over low heat, melt chips with sweetened condensed milk. Remove from heat; stir in vanilla. Chill 2 hours or until firm. Shape mixture into 1-inch balls; roll in any of the above coatings. Chill 1 hour or until firm. Store covered at room temperature.

Makes about 6 dozen

MICROWAVE DIRECTIONS: In 1-quart glass measure, combine chips and sweetened condensed milk. Microwave on full power (HIGH) 3 minutes, stirring after 1½ minutes. Stir until smooth. Proceed as directed.

AMARETTO: Omit vanilla. Add 3 tablespoons amaretto or other almond-flavored liqueur and ½ teaspoon almond extract. Roll in finely chopped toasted almonds.

ORANGE: Omit vanilla. Add 3 tablespoons orange-flavored liqueur. Roll in finely chopped toasted almonds mixed with finely grated orange peel.

RUM: Omit vanilla. Add ¼ cup dark rum. Roll in flaked coconut.

BOURBON: Omit vanilla. Add 3 tablespoons bourbon. Roll in finely chopped toasted nuts.

Chocolate Truffles

BOURBON FRUIT BALLS

1 (9-ounce) package NONE SUCH®
    Condensed Mincemeat, finely
    crumbled
2 cups vanilla wafer crumbs (about
    56 wafers)
1 cup flaked coconut
1 cup confectioners' sugar
¼ cup bourbon or rum
3 tablespoons light corn syrup
2 tablespoons water
    Additional confectioners' sugar

In large bowl, combine all ingredients except additional confectioners' sugar until well blended. Cover; chill 4 hours or overnight. Dip hands in confectioners' sugar; shape mixture into 1-inch balls. (Chill again if mixture becomes too soft.) Roll balls in additional confectioners' sugar. Place on wax paper-lined baking sheets; chill 2 hours or until firm. Store tightly covered at room temperature. Reroll in additional confectioners' sugar before serving, if desired. Store tightly covered.

Makes 50 to 55 balls

TIP: These candies can be made ahead and frozen for several weeks. Reroll in additional confectioners' sugar before serving, if desired.

CHAMPAGNE COCOA TRUFFLES

¾ cup unsalted butter
¾ cup HERSHEY®'S Cocoa
1 can (14 ounces) sweetened condensed
    milk
1 teaspoon vanilla extract
2 to 3 tablespoons champagne
    Cocoa or powdered sugar

In heavy, medium saucepan over low heat, melt butter. Add cocoa; stir until smooth. Blend in sweetened condensed milk; stir constantly until mixture is thick, smooth and glossy, about 4 minutes. Remove from heat; stir in vanilla. Pour mixture into medium bowl; cool to room temperature. Stir in champagne. Cover and refrigerate until firm, 4 to 5 hours. Taking small amount of mixture at a time, form into 1¼-inch balls; roll in cocoa or powdered sugar. Place balls on wax paper-lined tray; refrigerate until firm, 1 to 2 hours. Store, covered, in refrigerator. *Makes about 2½ dozen candies*

FUDGE RUM BALLS

1 package DUNCAN HINES® Moist
    Deluxe Butter Recipe Fudge
    Cake Mix
1 cup finely chopped pecans or walnuts
1 tablespoon rum extract
2 cups sifted confectioners sugar
¼ cup unsweetened cocoa
    Pecans or walnuts, finely chopped

1. Preheat oven to 375°F. Grease and flour 13×9×2-inch baking pan. Prepare, bake and cool cake following package directions.

2. Crumble cake into large bowl. Stir with fork until crumbs are fine and uniform in size. Add 1 cup nuts, rum extract, confectioners sugar and cocoa. Stir until well blended.

3. Shape heaping tablespoonfuls of mixture into balls. Garnish by rolling balls in finely chopped nuts. Press firmly to adhere nuts to balls. *Makes 6 dozen*

TIP: Substitute rum for rum extract.

Fudge Rum Balls

Chocolate Peanut Butter Balls, Crisp Chocolate Truffles

CHOCOLATE PEANUT BUTTER BALLS

1 cup crunchy peanut butter
¼ cup margarine or butter, softened
2 cups KELLOGG'S® RICE KRISPIES® cereal
1 cup confectioners sugar
1 package (14 ounces) chocolate candy coating
2 tablespoons shortening
  White candy coating, melted (optional)

In large bowl, combine peanut butter and margarine. Add Kellogg's® Rice Krispies® cereal and sugar, mixing until evenly combined. Portion cereal mixture using a rounded measuring teaspoon. Roll into balls; set aside.

In top of double boiler, over hot water, melt chocolate coating and shortening. Dip each peanut butter ball in coating and place on waxed-paper-lined baking sheet. Drizzle with melted white coating, if desired. Refrigerate until firm. Place in small candy paper cups to serve.   *Makes 4½ dozen*

NOTE: One package (12 ounces) semi-sweet chocolate morsels may be used in place of chocolate candy coating.

CRISP CHOCOLATE TRUFFLES

1 jar (7 ounces) marshmallow creme
2 tablespoons margarine or butter
1 package (6 ounces) semi-sweet chocolate morsels (1 cup)
2 cups KELLOGG'S® RICE KRISPIES® cereal
1 package (14 ounces) white candy coating
2 tablespoons shortening
  Multicolored sprinkles (optional)

In heavy 2-quart saucepan, combine marshmallow creme, margarine and chocolate morsels. Cook over low heat, stirring constantly, until chocolate is melted and mixture is smooth; remove from heat. Stir Kellogg's® Rice Krispies® cereal into hot chocolate mixture, mixing until thoroughly combined. Drop by rounded measuring teaspoonfuls onto waxed-paper-lined baking sheet. Refrigerate until firm, about 1 hour.

In top of double boiler, over hot water, melt white coating and shortening. Dip each chocolate ball in coating and place on waxed-paper-lined baking sheet. Decorate with sprinkles, if desired. Refrigerate until firm. Place in small candy paper cups to serve.
                        Makes 4½ dozen

BUCKEYES

> 2 (3-ounce) packages cream cheese, softened
> 1 (14-ounce) can EAGLE® Brand Sweetened Condensed Milk (NOT evaporated milk)
> 2 (12-ounce) packages peanut butter flavored chips
> 1 cup finely chopped peanuts
> ½ pound chocolate confectioners' coating*

In large mixer bowl, beat cheese until fluffy. Gradually beat in sweetened condensed milk until smooth. In heavy saucepan, over low heat, melt peanut butter chips; stir into cheese mixture. Add peanuts. Chill 2 to 3 hours; shape mixture into 1-inch balls. In small heavy saucepan, over low heat, melt confectioners' coating. With wooden pick, dip each peanut ball into melted coating, not covering completely. Place on wax paper-lined baking sheets until firm. Store covered at room temperature or in refrigerator.

Makes about 7 dozen

*If chocolate confectioners' coating is not available at your grocery store it can be purchased in candy specialty stores.

CHOCOLATE WALNUT TRUFFLES

> 1 cup heavy cream
> 16 ounces semisweet chocolate, cut into small pieces
> 2 tablespoons butter
> 1 cup finely chopped California walnuts
> 4 tablespoons coffee liqueur
>   Grated chocolate, shredded coconut and finely chopped California walnuts

Bring cream to a boil in saucepan over medium heat; add chocolate pieces. Stir with wooden spoon until mixture is smooth and thickened. Add butter; stir until melted. Pour mixture into large bowl; cool slightly. Stir in 1 cup walnuts and liqueur. Refrigerate until firm. Form mixture into walnut-sized balls and roll in chocolate, coconut or walnuts. Chill to set. Store in airtight container in refrigerator.

Makes 3½ dozen truffles

*Favorite recipe from **Walnut Marketing Board***

WHITE TRUFFLES

> 2 pounds EAGLE™ Brand Vanilla-Flavored Candy Coating
> 1 (14-ounce) can EAGLE® Brand Sweetened Condensed Milk (NOT evaporated milk)
> 1 tablespoon vanilla extract
> 1 pound EAGLE™ Brand Chocolate-Flavored Candy Coating, melted *or* ¾ cup unsweetened cocoa

In large, heavy saucepan, over low heat, melt vanilla candy coating with sweetened condensed milk, stirring frequently until smooth. Remove from heat; stir in vanilla. Cool. Shape into 1-inch balls. With wooden pick, partially dip each ball into melted chocolate candy coating or roll in cocoa. Place on wax paper-lined baking sheets until firm. Store covered at room temperature or in refrigerator.

Makes about 8 dozen

MICROWAVE DIRECTIONS: In 2-quart glass measure with handle, combine vanilla candy coating and sweetened condensed milk. Cook on 100% power (HIGH) 3 to 3½ minutes or until coating melts, stirring after each 1½ minutes. Proceed as directed.

CANDIED CITRUS PEEL

6 large, thick-skinned oranges
13½ cups water, divided
5 cups sugar, divided

Remove peel from white part of oranges in long strips with sharp paring knife. Reserve fruit for another use. Discard all pithy fruit membranes from peel. Cut peel into 2×½-inch strips. (There will be some oddly shaped pieces.) Place sheet of waxed paper under wire rack. Bring 4 cups water to a boil in heavy 3-quart saucepan over high heat. Add peel; return to a boil. Reduce heat to low. Cover; cook 20 minutes. Drain. Repeat process 2 times.

Bring 4½ cups sugar and 1½ cups water to a boil in same saucepan over medium heat, stirring occasionally. Reduce heat to low. Carefully clip candy thermometer to side of pan (do not let bulb touch bottom of pan). Cook over low heat, without stirring, about 20 minutes or until thermometer registers 230°F. Add drained peel. Cook over low heat about 20 minutes more or until thermometer registers 240°F (soft-ball stage), stirring occasionally. Remove from heat. Remove strips with slotted spoon to wire rack over waxed paper. Discard syrup or save for another use. Cool strips until syrup has dripped off.

Place remaining ½ cup sugar on another sheet of waxed paper. Roll strips, one at a time, in sugar. Set strips on wire rack about 1 hour or until dry. Store in airtight container. Keep in a cool place up to 2 weeks. If strips become slightly sticky, roll again in additional sugar.
Makes about 90 strips

VARIATION: Melt ½ cup semisweet chocolate chips and 1 tablespoon butter in small saucepan over low heat, stirring until smooth. Dip one end of each strip in melted chocolate; set on wire rack over waxed paper to dry. Let chocolate set completely before storing in airtight container.

APRICOT ALMOND CHEWIES

4 cups finely chopped dried apricots (about 1 pound)
4 cups flaked coconut or coconut macaroon crumbs (about 21 macaroons)
2 cups slivered almonds, toasted and finely chopped
1 (14-ounce) can EAGLE® Brand Sweetened Condensed Milk (NOT evaporated milk)
Whole almonds (optional)

In large bowl, combine all ingredients except whole almonds. Chill 2 hours. Shape into 1-inch balls. Top each with whole almond if desired. Store tightly covered in refrigerator.
Makes about 6½ dozen

WHITE CHOCOLATE-DIPPED APRICOTS

3 ounces white chocolate, coarsely chopped
20 dried apricot halves

Line baking sheet with waxed paper; set aside. Melt white chocolate in bowl over hot (not boiling) water; stir constantly.

Dip half of each apricot piece in chocolate, coating both sides. Place on prepared baking sheet. Refrigerate until firm. Store in refrigerator in container between layers of waxed paper.
Makes 20 apricots

White Chocolate-Dipped Apricots,
Stuffed Pecans (page 524)

CHOCOLATE-DIPPED MORSELS

1 package (4 ounces) BAKER'S® GERMAN'S® Sweet Chocolate *or* 6 to 8 squares BAKER'S® Semi-Sweet Chocolate*
Assorted centers (suggestions follow)

Microwave chocolate in small microwavable bowl on HIGH 1½ to 2 minutes, stirring halfway through heating time. Stir until chocolate is completely melted.**

Insert toothpicks into food to be dipped. Dip, 1 at a time, into chocolate, covering at least half; let excess chocolate drip off. (To dip pretzels or nuts, stir into chocolate to coat; then remove with fork.)

Let stand at room temperature or refrigerate on wax paper-lined cookie sheet 30 minutes or until chocolate is firm. Store fresh fruit in refrigerator up to 2 days. Store dried fruit, cookies, nuts and pretzels in airtight container for up to 1 month.   *Makes about 2 dozen*

SUGGESTED CENTERS:
Fruit: Firm strawberries, ½-inch banana slices, fresh pineapple wedges or drained canned pineapple chunks, peeled orange slices or orange sections, well-drained stemmed maraschino cherries, dried figs, dried apricots or dates.
Cake: Cut into 1-inch squares.
Peanut Butter and Jelly Sandwich on White Bread: Cut into 1-inch squares.
Large Marshmallows
Nuts: Walnut or pecan halves, or whole almonds or Brazil nuts.
Fruitcake Fingers: Coat only half of cake.
Pretzels

*Or use 1 package (6 squares) BAKER'S® Premium White Chocolate.

TOP OF STOVE PREPARATION: Melt chocolate in heavy saucepan on very low heat; stir constantly until just melted. Remove from heat. Continue as above.

MARZIPAN FRUITS

1¾ cups BAKER'S® ANGEL FLAKE® Coconut, finely chopped
1 package (4-serving size) JELL-O® Brand Gelatin, any flavor
1 cup ground blanched almonds
⅔ cup sweetened condensed milk
1½ teaspoons sugar
1 teaspoon almond extract
Food coloring (optional)

Mix all ingredients in large bowl until well combined. Shape by hand into small fruits, vegetables, hearts, Easter eggs or other forms. (Or use small candy molds.) If desired, use food coloring to paint details on fruit; add whole cloves and citron or angelica for stems and blossom ends. Refrigerate until dry. Store at room temperature in airtight container.
    Makes about 3 cups or 2 to 3 dozen pieces

FOR FRUITS: Use the appropriate flavors and/or colors: strawberry flavor gelatin for strawberries; lemon flavor gelatin for bananas, grapefruit, lemons and Bartlett pears; lime flavor gelatin for green apples, pears, leaves, stems and limes; orange flavor gelatin for tangerines and oranges; cherry or black cherry flavor gelatin for cherries; grape flavor gelatin for grapes.

WALNUT-GRANOLA CLUSTERS

¼ cup butter
1 (10½-ounce) package miniature marshmallows
½ teaspoon ground cinnamon
3 cups rolled oats
2 cups chopped California walnuts
1 cup flaked coconut
2 (1-ounce) squares semi-sweet chocolate

Microwave butter in large microwavable mixing bowl at HIGH (100% power) 40 seconds or until melted. Stir in marshmallows and cinnamon. Microwave 1½ minutes or until melted, stirring halfway through cooking time. Quickly stir in oats, walnuts and coconut. With wet hands, form mixture into small balls and place on wax paper-lined baking sheets.

Microwave chocolate in glass measuring cup at HIGH 2½ minutes or until melted; stir. Lightly drizzle chocolate over clusters. Clusters may be stored at room temperature, uncovered, 4 to 5 days.   *Makes 5 dozen*

Favorite recipe from **Walnut Marketing Board**

ALMOND BUTTER CRUNCH

1 cup BLUE DIAMOND® Blanched
    Slivered Almonds
½ cup butter
½ cup sugar
1 tablespoon light corn syrup

Line bottom and sides of 8- or 9-inch cake pan with aluminum foil (*not* plastic wrap or wax paper). Butter foil heavily; set aside. Combine almonds, butter, sugar and corn syrup in 10-inch skillet. Bring to a boil over medium heat, stirring constantly. Boil, stirring constantly, until mixture turns golden brown, about 5 to 6 minutes. Working quickly, spread candy in prepared pan. Cool about 15 minutes or until firm. Remove candy from pan by lifting edges of foil. Peel off foil. Cool thoroughly. Break into pieces.   *Makes about ¾ pound*

Almond Butter Crunch

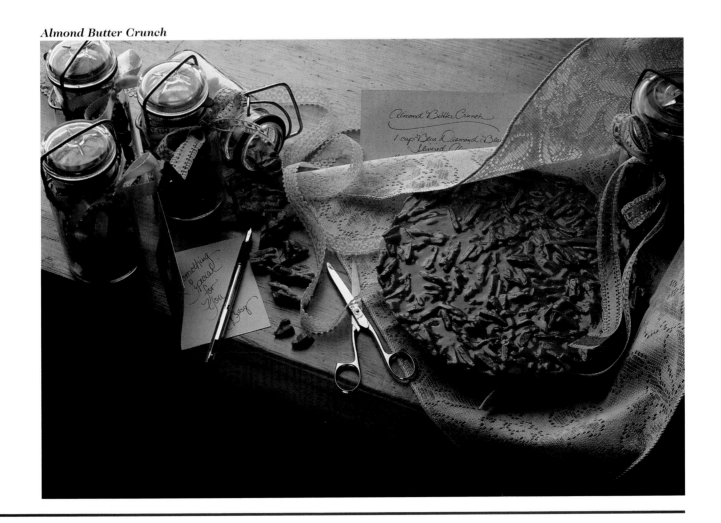

BUTTER ALMOND CRUNCH

1½ cups HERSHEY'S Semi-Sweet
   Chocolate Chips, divided
1¾ cups chopped almonds, divided
1½ cups butter or margarine
1¾ cups sugar
  3 tablespoons light corn syrup
  3 tablespoons water

Heat oven to 350°F. Line 13×9×2-inch pan with foil; butter foil. Sprinkle 1 cup chocolate chips into pan; set aside. In shallow baking pan spread chopped almonds. Bake about 7 minutes or until golden brown; set aside. In heavy 3-quart saucepan melt butter; blend in sugar, corn syrup and water. Cook over medium heat, stirring constantly, to 300°F on a candy thermometer (hard-crack stage) or until mixture separates into hard, brittle threads when dropped into very cold water. (Bulb of candy thermometer should not rest on bottom of saucepan.) Remove from heat; stir in 1½ cups toasted almonds. Immediately spread mixture evenly over chocolate chips in prepared pan; *do not disturb chips.* Sprinkle with remaining ¼ cup toasted almonds and remaining ½ cup chocolate chips; cool slightly. With sharp knife score candy into 1½-inch squares, wiping knife blade after drawing through candy. Cool completely; remove from pan. Remove foil; break candy into pieces. Store in airtight container in cool, dry place.
Makes about 2 pounds candy

STUFFED PECANS

½ cup semisweet chocolate chips
¼ cup sweetened condensed milk
½ teaspoon vanilla
  Powdered sugar (about ½ cup)
80 large pecan halves

Melt chips in very small saucepan over very low heat, stirring constantly. Remove from heat. Stir in sweetened condensed milk and vanilla until smooth. Stir in enough sugar to make stiff mixture. Refrigerate, if needed.

Place 1 rounded teaspoonful chocolate mixture on flat side of 1 pecan half. Top with another pecan half. Repeat with remaining pecans and chocolate mixture. Store in refrigerator.
Makes about 40 candies

CHERRY MERRY CHRISTMAS CRUNCH

2 cups walnut halves
1 cup candied red and green cherries,
   cut in half
2 tablespoons butter or margarine
1 teaspoon salt
1 teaspoon maple extract
¼ teaspoon cherry extract
2 cups sugar
¾ cup light corn syrup
¼ cup maple syrup

Generously grease baking sheet; set aside. Combine walnuts, cherries, butter, salt and extracts in medium bowl; set aside. Combine sugar, corn syrup and maple syrup in heavy, large saucepan. Bring to a boil. Carefully clip candy thermometer to side of pan (do not let bulb touch bottom of pan). Cook over medium heat until thermometer registers 300°F (hard-crack stage). Remove from heat; stir in walnut mixture. Quickly pour onto prepared baking sheet. Cool completely. Break into pieces.
Makes about 2 pounds candy

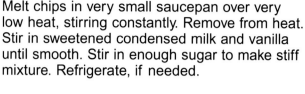

Butter Almond Crunch

CITRUS CANDIED NUTS

　　1 egg white
　1½ cups whole almonds
　1½ cups pecan halves
　　1 cup powdered sugar
　　2 tablespoons lemon juice
　　2 teaspoons grated orange peel
　　1 teaspoon grated lemon peel
　⅛ teaspoon ground nutmeg

Preheat oven to 300°F. Generously grease 15½×10½×1-inch jelly-roll pan. Beat egg white in medium bowl with electric mixer on high speed until soft peaks form. Add almonds and pecans; stir until coated. Stir in powdered sugar, lemon juice, orange peel, lemon peel and nutmeg. Turn out onto prepared pan, spreading nuts in single layer.

Bake 30 minutes, stirring after 20 minutes. *Turn off oven.* Let nuts stand in oven 15 minutes more. Immediately remove nuts from pan to sheet of foil. Cool completely. Store up to 2 weeks in airtight container.

Makes about 3 cups nuts

ORANGE-CANDIED WALNUTS

　1½ cups sugar
　½ cup corn syrup
　2 tablespoons butter
　4 cups California walnuts
　1 teaspoon orange extract

Melt sugar, corn syrup and butter in large, shallow pan over medium-high heat. Add walnuts. Cook and stir about 15 minutes or until sugar mixture begins to caramelize. Stir in extract. Spread walnut mixture evenly onto greased baking sheet, separating walnuts into small clusters. Cool completely.

Makes 4 cups

Favorite recipe from **Walnut Marketing Board**

Clockwise from top left: Easy Caramel Pop Corn Balls, Almond Butter Crunch Pop Corn, Rocky Road Peanut Butter Pop Corn Bars

EASY CARAMEL POP CORN BALLS

　2½ quarts popped JOLLY TIME® Pop Corn
　1 package (14 ounces) light caramels
　¼ cup light corn syrup
　2 tablespoons water

Keep popped pop corn warm in deep pan in oven at 200°F. Melt caramels in heavy saucepan over low heat, stirring occasionally, about 15 minutes. Add corn syrup and water; mix until smooth. Slowly pour over pop corn in pan, mixing well. Shape into balls.

Makes 10 medium-sized pop corn balls

MICROWAVE DIRECTIONS: Microwave caramels and water in large microwave-safe bowl on HIGH for 2 to 3 minutes or until mixture is smooth. Stir every minute. Add corn syrup and mix until smooth. Proceed as directed.

ALMOND BUTTER CRUNCH POP CORN

  ½ cup butter or margarine
  1 cup sugar
  ¼ cup light corn syrup
  ¼ teaspoon salt
  ¼ teaspoon baking soda
  ½ teaspoon vanilla
  ½ teaspoon butter extract
  2½ quarts popped JOLLY TIME® Pop Corn
  1½ cups whole almonds, toasted*

Melt butter in medium saucepan. Stir in sugar, corn syrup and salt. Heat to a boil, stirring constantly. Boil for 8 minutes, stirring only once, over lowest heat possible to maintain a boil. Remove from heat; stir in soda, vanilla and butter extract. Gradually pour over combined popped pop corn and nuts, mixing well. Turn into large, shallow baking pan. Bake at 250°F for 30 minutes, mixing well after 15 minutes. Allow to cool completely. Break apart and store in tightly covered container.

Makes about 3 quarts

*To toast almonds, spread on large cookie sheet and toast at 325°F for 15 to 20 minutes.

ROCKY ROAD PEANUT BUTTER POP CORN BARS

  3 quarts popped JOLLY TIME® Pop Corn
  ½ cup raisins
  1 cup light corn syrup
  1 tablespoon butter or margarine
  ½ cup peanut butter pieces
  ⅓ cup chunky or creamy peanut butter
  ¾ cup miniature marshmallows
  ½ cup peanuts
  ½ cup semisweet chocolate pieces
  1 teaspoon vegetable shortening

Place popped pop corn and raisins in large bowl. In saucepan, heat corn syrup and butter to boiling. Boil 3 minutes. Remove from heat. Stir in peanut butter pieces and peanut butter. Stir until smooth. Pour mixture over pop corn, tossing gently to coat all pieces. Press into buttered 9-inch square baking pan. Sprinkle marshmallows and peanuts over top, pressing lightly into pop corn mixture. Melt combined chocolate pieces and shortening over very low heat. Drizzle over top. Cool several hours before serving. Cut into 2¼×1-inch bars.

Makes 36 bars

FESTIVE POPCORN TREATS

  6 cups popped popcorn
  ½ cup sugar
  ½ cup light corn syrup
  ¼ cup peanut butter
     Green food color
  ¼ cup red cinnamon candies

Line baking sheet with waxed paper. Pour popcorn into large bowl. Combine sugar and corn syrup in medium saucepan. Bring to a boil over medium heat, stirring constantly; boil 1 minute. Remove from heat. Add peanut butter and green food color; stir until peanut butter is completely melted. Pour over popcorn; stir to coat well. Lightly butter hands and shape popcorn mixture into trees. While trees are still warm, press red cinnamon candies into trees. Place on prepared baking sheet; let stand until firm, about 30 minutes.   *Makes 6 servings*

OLD-FASHIONED POP CORN BALLS

  2 quarts popped JOLLY TIME® Pop Corn
  1 cup sugar
  ⅓ cup light or dark corn syrup
  ⅓ cup water
  ¼ cup butter or margarine
  ½ teaspoon salt
  1 teaspoon vanilla

Keep popped pop corn warm in 200°F oven while preparing syrup. In 2-quart saucepan, stir together sugar, corn syrup, water, butter and salt. Cook over medium heat, stirring constantly, until mixture comes to a boil. Continue cooking without stirring until temperature reaches 270°F on candy thermometer or until small amount of syrup dropped into very cold water separates into threads that are hard but not brittle. Remove from heat. Add vanilla; stir just enough to mix through hot syrup. Slowly pour over popped pop corn, stirring to coat well. Cool just enough to handle. With JOLLY TIME® Pop Corn Ball Maker or buttered hands, shape into balls.
Makes 12 medium-sized pop corn balls

BAKED CARAMEL CORN

  6 quarts popped JOLLY TIME® Pop Corn
  1 cup butter or margarine
  2 cups firmly packed brown sugar
  ½ cup light or dark corn syrup
  1 teaspoon salt
  ½ teaspoon baking soda
  1 teaspoon vanilla

Old-Fashioned Pop Corn Balls, Baked Caramel Corn

Preheat oven to 250°F. Coat bottom and sides of large roasting pan with nonstick cooking spray. Place popped pop corn in roasting pan. In heavy saucepan, melt butter over low heat; stir in brown sugar, corn syrup and salt. Bring to a boil, stirring constantly; boil without stirring for 5 minutes. Remove from heat; stir in baking soda and vanilla. (Mixture will froth and foam.) Gradually pour over popped pop corn, mixing well. Bake for 1 hour, stirring every 15 minutes. Remove from oven; cool completely. Break apart and store in tightly covered container.

Makes about 6 quarts

HOLIDAY WREATHS

½ cup margarine or butter
1 package (10 ounces, about 40) regular marshmallows
1 teaspoon green liquid food coloring
6 cups KELLOGG'S CORN FLAKES® cereal
Red cinnamon candies

1. Melt margarine in large saucepan over low heat. Add marshmallows and cook, stirring constantly, until marshmallows melt and mixture is syrupy. Remove from heat. Stir in food coloring.

2. Add Kellogg's Corn Flakes® cereal. Stir until well coated.

3. Portion warm cereal mixture using ¼ cup dry measure onto wax paper-lined baking sheet. Using buttered fingers, quickly shape mixture into individual wreaths. Dot with red cinnamon candies. *Makes 16 wreaths*

VARIATION: Press warm cereal mixture into buttered 5½-cup ring mold or shape into ring on serving plate. Remove from mold and dot with red candies. Slice to serve.

GLAZED POPCORN

8 cups popped popcorn
¼ cup butter or margarine
3 tablespoons light corn syrup
½ cup firmly packed light brown sugar or granulated sugar
1 package (4-serving size) JELL-O® Brand Gelatin, any flavor

Heat oven to 300°F. Line 15×10×1-inch jelly-roll pan with foil.

Place popcorn in large bowl. Heat butter and syrup in saucepan over low heat. Stir in brown sugar and gelatin; bring to a boil over medium heat. Reduce heat to low and gently simmer 5 minutes. Pour syrup immediately over popcorn; toss to coat well. Spread popcorn on prepared pan, using two forks to spread evenly.

Bake 10 minutes. Cool. Remove from pan and break into small pieces. *Makes 2 quarts*

RAINBOW POPCORN: Prepare Glazed Popcorn 3 times, using 3 gelatin flavors with different colors, such as strawberry, lemon and lime. Bake as directed; break into small pieces. Layer 3 cups of each color in 3-quart serving bowl. Store remaining popcorn in airtight container. Makes 6 quarts.

Sparkling
REFRESHERS

SPICED APPLE TEA

2 cups unsweetened apple juice
6 whole cloves
1 cinnamon stick
3 cups water
3 bags cinnamon herbal tea

Combine juice, cloves and cinnamon stick in medium saucepan. Bring to a boil over high heat. Reduce heat to low; simmer 10 minutes. Meanwhile, place water in another medium saucepan. Bring to a boil over high heat. Remove from heat; drop in tea bags and allow to steep for 6 minutes. Remove and discard tea bags.

Strain juice mixture; discard spices. Stir juice mixture into tea. Serve warm with additional cinnamon sticks, if desired *or* refrigerate and serve cold over ice. (Tea may be made ahead and reheated.)   *Makes 4 servings*

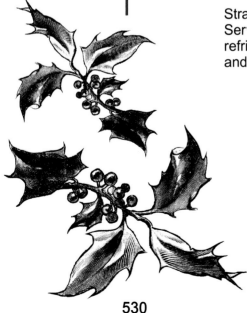

HOT SPICED CIDER

2 quarts apple cider
⅔ cup KARO® Light or Dark Corn Syrup
3 cinnamon sticks
½ teaspoon whole cloves
1 lemon, sliced
  Cinnamon sticks and lemon slices
    (optional)

In medium saucepan combine cider, corn syrup, cinnamon sticks, cloves and lemon slices. Bring to boil over medium-high heat. Reduce heat; simmer 15 minutes. Remove spices. If desired, garnish each serving with a cinnamon stick and lemon slice.

Makes about 10 servings

PREP TIME: 20 minutes

CHRISTMAS CAROL PUNCH

2 medium red apples
2 quarts clear apple cider
½ cup SUN-MAID® Raisins
8 cinnamon sticks
2 teaspoons whole cloves
  Orange slices
  Lemon slices
¼ cup lemon juice

Core apples; slice into ½-inch rings. In Dutch oven, combine cider, apple rings, raisins, cinnamon and cloves. Bring to boil over high heat; reduce heat to low and simmer 5 to 8 minutes or until apples are just tender. Remove cloves; add orange and lemon slices and lemon juice. Pour into punch bowl. Ladle into large mugs, including an apple ring, some raisins and citrus slices in each serving. Serve with spoons.

Makes about 2 quarts

COCONUT SNOWBALL COCOA

1 pint vanilla ice cream
1 cup flaked coconut
½ cup unsweetened cocoa
1 quart milk
½ cup dark rum (optional)
¾ to 1 cup cream of coconut
1 teaspoon coconut extract
½ cup chocolate-flavored ice cream sauce
    (optional)
8 maraschino cherries (optional)

Scoop ice cream into 8 small balls; immediately roll in coconut. Place on waxed-paper-lined baking sheet; freeze until ready to use.

Whisk cocoa into milk in large saucepan. Stir in rum, if desired, cream of coconut and coconut extract. Bring to a simmer over medium-high heat. Pour into 8 large heatproof mugs.

Float ice cream balls in cocoa. If desired, drizzle each ice cream ball with chocolate sauce and top with cherry.   *Makes 8 servings*

Hot Spiced Cider

SPICED MAPLE CIDER

2 quarts apple juice or cider
1 cup CARY'S®, MAPLE ORCHARDS® or MACDONALD'S™ Pure Maple Syrup
⅓ cup REALEMON® Lemon Juice from Concentrate
1 small orange, sliced
3 cinnamon sticks
8 whole cloves
¼ cup Southern Comfort* liqueur (optional)

In large saucepan, combine all ingredients except liqueur; bring to a boil. Reduce heat; simmer, uncovered, 20 minutes. Remove and discard orange slices and spices. Add liqueur, if desired. Serve warm; garnish as desired.
Makes about 9 cups

TIP: Cider can also be served chilled. Or, chill and add 1 (32-ounce) bottle ginger ale just before serving.

*Southern Comfort is a registered trademark of the Southern Comfort Corporation.

HOT APPLE 'N' SPICE LEMONADE

4 scoops or ¾ cup WYLER'S® Sugar Sweetened Lemonade Flavor Crystals
3 cups apple juice
3 cups water
3 cinnamon sticks
6 whole cloves

In 2-quart saucepan, combine all ingredients. Simmer 10 minutes or until heated through. Remove spices. Serve in mugs and garnish, if desired, with apple slices.
Makes about 6 servings

CROCK OF SPICE FOR APPLE CIDER

12 cinnamon sticks, broken into small pieces
¼ cup whole cloves
¼ cup allspice berries
¼ cup juniper berries
1 tablespoon dried orange peel, chopped
1 tablespoon dried lemon peel, chopped
1 teaspoon ground nutmeg

Combine all ingredients in airtight container. To prepare spiced cider, measure 1 heaping teaspoonful spice mixture for each mug of cider into large saucepan. Simmer cider with spices for 5 minutes. Strain before serving.

VARIATION: Pack mixture in muslin bouquet garni bags available at kitchen or specialty stores. Use like tea bags to flavor mugs of hot cider or mulled wine.

HOT MULLED CIDER

½ gallon apple cider
½ cup packed light brown sugar
1½ teaspoons balsamic or cider vinegar
1 teaspoon vanilla
1 cinnamon stick
6 whole cloves
½ cup applejack or bourbon (optional)

Combine all ingredients except applejack in large saucepan; bring to a boil. Reduce heat to low; simmer, uncovered, 10 minutes. Remove from heat; stir in applejack. Pour into punch bowl.
Makes 16 servings

Spiced Maple Cider

HOT HOLIDAY PUNCH

4 cups apple cider
1 cup granulated sugar
½ cup packed brown sugar
1 cinnamon stick
12 whole cloves
2 cups Florida Grapefruit Juice
2 cups Florida Orange Juice
Orange slices (optional)
Maraschino cherry halves (optional)
Whole cloves (optional)

Combine apple cider and sugars in large saucepan. Heat over medium heat, stirring until sugars dissolve. Add cinnamon stick and cloves. Bring to a boil over medium heat. Reduce heat to low; simmer 5 minutes. Add grapefruit and orange juices. Heat, but do not boil. Strain into heatproof punch bowl. Garnish with orange slices decorated with maraschino cherry halves and whole cloves. Serve in heatproof punch cups.

Makes about 8 (8-ounce) servings

Favorite recipe from **Florida Department of Citrus**

KAHLÚA® HOT SPICED APPLE CIDER

1½ ounces KAHLÚA®
1 cup hot apple cider or apple juice
1 cinnamon stick

Pour Kahlúa® into hot cider. Stir with cinnamon stick.　　　*Makes 1 serving*

HOT MULLED PINEAPPLE JUICE

6 cups DOLE® Pineapple Juice
1 DOLE® Apple, cored and cut into chunks
½ cup DOLE® Raisins
½ cup packed brown sugar
Grated peel of 1 DOLE® Orange
2 cinnamon sticks, broken
½ teaspoon whole cloves

• Combine pineapple juice, apple, raisins, brown sugar, peel, cinnamon sticks and cloves in saucepan. Simmer 5 minutes.

• Remove and discard spices before serving.
Makes 6 servings

HOT BUTTERED PINEAPPLE SMOOTHIE

5½ cups DOLE® Pineapple Juice
¼ cup packed brown sugar
2 tablespoons butter or margarine
10 whole cloves
3 cinnamon sticks
1 DOLE® Lemon, sliced

• In large saucepan, combine pineapple juice, brown sugar, butter, cloves and cinnamon sticks. Bring to a boil; simmer 5 minutes.

• Remove spices. Add lemon slices. Serve hot in mugs.　　　*Makes 1½ quarts*

FIRESIDE PUNCH

1½ cups cranberry juice cocktail
1½ cups cold water
4 bags LIPTON® Cinnamon Apple or
   Gentle Orange Herbal Flo-Thru Tea
2 tablespoons brown sugar
   Cinnamon sticks (optional)
   Fresh cranberries (optional)

In medium saucepan, bring cranberry juice and water to a boil. Add cinnamon apple herbal tea bags; cover and brew 5 minutes. Remove tea bags; stir in sugar. Pour into mugs and garnish with cinnamon sticks and fresh cranberries.

Makes about 5 servings

MICROWAVE HOT CHOCOLATE

1 quart milk
1 package (4-serving size) JELL-O®
   Chocolate or Chocolate Fudge Flavor
   Pudding & Pie Filling
   COOL WHIP® Whipped Topping,
   thawed

Pour milk into 2-quart microwavable bowl. Add pudding mix. Beat with wire whisk 20 to 30 seconds. Microwave on HIGH 5 minutes; whisk. Pour into mugs. Top with whipped topping and garnish with shaved chocolate, if desired.

Makes about 4 servings

Hot Pineapple Port Cup

HOT PINEAPPLE PORT CUP

6 cups DOLE® Pineapple Juice
1 bottle (750 mL) port wine
1 cup DOLE® Raisins
½ cup sugar
   Peel of 1 DOLE® Orange*

• Combine pineapple juice, wine, raisins, sugar and peel in Dutch oven. Heat to boiling. Remove from heat and steep 15 minutes.

• Remove and discard peel before serving. Serve warm.   *Makes 12 servings*

* Remove peel from orange with vegetable peeler.

"GLOGG"

3 cups boiling water
1 package (4-serving size) JELL-O®
   Brand Gelatin, any flavor
1 cinnamon stick (optional)
6 whole cloves (optional)
3 orange slices (optional)

Stir boiling water into gelatin in 4-cup measuring cup 2 minutes or until dissolved. Add cinnamon stick, cloves and orange slices. Cover and let stand 5 minutes. Remove spices. Serve with additional cinnamon sticks and clove-studded orange slices, if desired.

Makes about 3 servings

VARIATION: For single serving, use 2 tablespoons gelatin and 1 cup boiling water.

WISCONSIN SPICY APPLE EGGNOG

2 beaten eggs*
3 cups milk
2 cups light cream or half-and-half
⅓ cup sugar
½ teaspoon ground cinnamon
   Dash salt
¾ cup apple brandy
   Ground nutmeg

In large saucepan combine beaten eggs, milk, light cream, sugar, cinnamon and salt. Cook and stir over medium heat until mixture is slightly thickened and heated through, but *do not boil*. Remove from heat; stir in apple brandy. To serve, ladle mixture into 12 heatproof glasses or cups. Sprinkle each serving with nutmeg. Serve warm.

Makes 12 servings

*Use clean, uncracked eggs.

PREP TIME: 25 minutes

*Favorite recipe from **Wisconsin Milk Marketing Board***

PEACHY MEXICAN HOT CHOCOLATE

1 can (16 ounces) California cling peach
   halves or slices, undrained
¼ cup sugar
2 tablespoons unsweetened cocoa
2 cups milk
½ teaspoon ground cinnamon
1 teaspoon vanilla
¼ cup dark rum (optional)
   Whipped cream and additional ground
   cinnamon for garnish

Place peaches with syrup in food processor or blender; process until smooth. Set aside. Combine sugar and cocoa in heavy saucepan. Whisk in enough milk to make a paste, then whisk in remaining milk, peach mixture and ½ teaspoon cinnamon. Cook and stir until mixture comes to a boil. Stir in vanilla and dark rum. To serve, ladle hot chocolate into mugs or glasses. Garnish each with whipped cream and sprinkle with additional cinnamon.

Makes 8 servings

*Favorite recipe from **Canned Fruit Promotion Service, Inc.***

Left to right: "Glogg", Microwave Hot Chocolate (page 537)

EASY COCOA MIX

   2 cups nonfat dry milk powder
   1 cup sugar
   ¾ cup powdered non-dairy creamer
   ½ cup unsweetened cocoa
   ¼ teaspoon salt

Combine all ingredients in 1-quart airtight container.

Makes about 4 cups mix or 16 servings

For single serving: Place rounded ¼ cup Easy Cocoa Mix in mug or cup; add ¾ cup boiling water. Stir until mix is dissolved. Top with sweetened whipped cream and marshmallows, if desired. Serve immediately.

COCOA MARSHMALLOW MIX: Prepare Easy Cocoa Mix in 2-quart airtight container as directed, adding 1 package (10½ ounces) miniature marshmallows.

Makes about 7 cups mix or 14 servings

For single serving: Place rounded ½ cup Cocoa Marshmallow Mix in mug or cup; add ¾ cup boiling water. Stir until mix is dissolved. Serve immediately.

HOT MAPLE TODDY

   1 to 1¼ cups whiskey
   1 cup CARY'S®, MAPLE ORCHARDS® or MACDONALD'S™ Pure Maple Syrup
   ¾ cup REALEMON® Lemon Juice from Concentrate
   Butter and cinnamon sticks (optional)

In medium saucepan, combine all ingredients except butter and cinnamon sticks. Over low heat, simmer to blend flavors. Pour into mugs; dot with butter and stir with cinnamon sticks, if desired.   *Makes about 3 cups*

MICROWAVE DIRECTIONS: In 1-quart glass measure, combine ingredients as above. Microwave on HIGH (100% power) 4 to 5 minutes or until heated through. Serve as above.

HOT COCOA MIX

   1 cup CREMORA® Non-Dairy Creamer*
   1 cup nonfat dry milk
   ¼ to 1 cup sugar
   ½ cup unsweetened cocoa

In medium bowl, combine ingredients; mix well. Store in airtight container. To serve, spoon 3 heaping tablespoons mix into mug; add ¾ cup boiling water. Stir.   *Makes about 3 cups*

MOCHA: Add ¼ cup instant coffee.

MEXICAN: Add 1 teaspoon ground cinnamon.

LOW–CALORIE: Omit sugar. Add 15 envelopes low-calorie sweetener with NutraSweet® or 2 teaspoons (5 envelopes) low-calorie granulated sugar substitute. To serve, spoon 2 heaping tablespoons into mug; add ¾ cup boiling water. Stir.

*Cremora is a coffee whitener and should not be used as a milk replacement.

Easy Cocoa Mix

VIENNESE COFFEE

1 cup heavy cream, divided
1 teaspoon powdered sugar
1 bar (3 ounces) bittersweet or
    semisweet chocolate
3 cups strong freshly brewed hot coffee
¼ cup crème de cacao or Irish cream
    (optional)

Chill bowl, beaters and cream before whipping. Place ⅔ cup cream and sugar in chilled bowl. Beat with electric mixer at high speed until soft peaks form. *Do not overbeat.* Cover and refrigerate up to 8 hours. If mixture has separated slightly after refrigeration, whisk lightly with wire whisk.

To make chocolate shavings for garnish, make short, quick strokes across chocolate with vegetable peeler; set aside. Break remaining chocolate into pieces.

Place remaining ⅓ cup cream in heavy, small saucepan. Bring to a simmer over medium-low heat. Add chocolate pieces; cover and remove from heat. Let stand 5 minutes or until chocolate is melted; stir until smooth. Add hot coffee to chocolate mixture. Heat on low heat just until bubbles form around edge of pan and coffee is heated through, stirring frequently. Remove from heat; stir in crème de cacao. Pour into 4 warmed mugs. Top with whipped cream. Garnish with chocolate shavings.
Makes about 3½ cups, 4 servings

KAHLÚA® PARISIAN COFFEE

1 ounce cognac or brandy
½ ounce KAHLÚA®
½ ounce Grand Marnier
    Hot coffee
    Whipped cream
    Orange peel (optional)

Pour cognac, Kahlúa® and Grand Marnier into steaming cup of coffee. Top with whipped cream. Garnish with orange peel.
Makes 1 serving

SPIRITED COFFEE LOPEZ

4 cups hot coffee
½ cup COCO LOPEZ® Cream of Coconut
½ cup Irish whiskey
1 teaspoon vanilla extract
    Whipped cream

In heatproof pitcher, combine all ingredients except whipped cream; mix well. Pour into mugs; top with whipped cream. Serve immediately. *Makes 5 cups*

KAHLÚA® & COFFEE

1½ ounces KAHLÚA®
    Hot coffee
    Whipped cream (optional)

Pour Kahlúa® into steaming cup of coffee. Top with whipped cream. *Makes 1 serving*

Viennese Coffee

MOCHA COFFEE MIX

1 cup nonfat dry milk powder
¾ cup granulated sugar
⅔ cup powdered non-dairy creamer
½ cup unsweetened cocoa
⅓ cup instant coffee, pressed through
    fine sieve
¼ cup packed brown sugar
1 teaspoon ground cinnamon
¼ teaspoon salt
¼ teaspoon ground nutmeg

Combine all ingredients in 1-quart airtight container.
Makes about 3½ cups mix or 10 to 12 servings

FOR SINGLE SERVING: Place rounded ¼ cup Mocha Coffee Mix in mug or cup; add ¾ cup boiling water. Stir until mix is dissolved. Serve immediately.

MOCHA COOLER

1 quart DREYER'S or EDY'S GRAND
    Light Cafe Au Lait Ice Cream
½ cup chocolate milk or regular lowfat
    milk
    Instant coffee granules or espresso
    powder to taste

• Place 2 scoops Dreyer's or Edy's Grand Light Cafe Au Lait Ice Cream in blender.

• Add chocolate milk and instant coffee granules. Blend until smooth and creamy.

• Pour into large drink glass. Garnish with sprinkle of coffee granules.
Makes 1 serving

NOTE: You may substitute DREYER'S or EDY'S Coffee Fudge Sundae Fat Free Frozen Yogurt for Light Cafe Au Lait Ice Cream.

ICED MOCHA

2 cups strongly brewed coffee
¾ cup skim milk
1 tablespoon packed brown sugar
½ teaspoon unsweetened cocoa powder
    Ice

Add coffee, milk, sugar and cocoa to blender. Process until smooth. Pour over ice and serve immediately, or refrigerate, stir well and serve over ice. *Makes 2 servings*

Favorite recipe from **The Sugar Association, Inc.**

EGGNOG CHILL

½ gallon DREYER'S or EDY'S GRAND
    Eggnog Ice Cream
2 cups skim or lowfat milk
3 vanilla wafer cookies
    Ground nutmeg

• Blend 2 cups Dreyer's or Edy's Grand Eggnog Ice Cream and milk in blender until smooth.

• While mixture is blending, use sharp knife to cut small slit in vanilla wafers so they will sit on side of glass.

• Pour shake into large drink glasses. Sprinkle with nutmeg. Garnish with vanilla wafers.
Makes 3 servings

Iced Mocha

MAPLE EGG NOG

1 (32-ounce) can BORDEN® Egg Nog, chilled
½ cup CARY'S®, MAPLE ORCHARDS® or MACDONALD'S™ Pure Maple Syrup
Ground nutmeg (optional)

In large pitcher, combine egg nog and syrup. Chill. Stir before serving; garnish with nutmeg, if desired. Refrigerate leftovers.

Makes about 1 quart

APPLE SPICE EGG NOG

3 (32-ounce) cans BORDEN® Egg Nog, chilled
3 cups apple cider, chilled
½ teaspoon ground cinnamon

In large bowl, combine ingredients; mix well. Chill. Garnish as desired. Refrigerate leftovers.

Makes about 3½ quarts

Pineapple Raspberry Punch

KAHLÚA® & EGGNOG

1 quart dairy eggnog
¾ cup KAHLÚA®
Whipped cream
Ground nutmeg

Combine eggnog and Kahlúa® in 1½-quart pitcher. Pour into punch cups. Top with whipped cream. Sprinkle with nutmeg.

Makes about 8 servings

PINEAPPLE RASPBERRY PUNCH

5 cups DOLE® Pineapple Juice
1 quart raspberry-cranberry drink
1 pint fresh or frozen raspberries
1 lemon, thinly sliced
Ice

• Chill ingredients. Combine in punch bowl.

Makes 9 cups

CHAMPAGNE PUNCH

1 orange
1 lemon
¼ cup cranberry-flavored liqueur or cognac
¼ cup orange-flavored liqueur or triple sec
1 bottle (750 mL) pink or regular champagne or sparkling white wine, well chilled
Fresh cranberries (optional)
Citrus strips for garnish

Remove colored peel, not white pith, from orange and lemon in long thin strips with citrus peeler. Refrigerate orange and lemon for another use. Combine peels and cranberry- and orange-flavored liqueurs in glass pitcher. Cover and refrigerate 2 to 6 hours.

Just before serving, tilt pitcher to one side and slowly pour in champagne. Leave peels in pitcher for added flavor. Place a cranberry in bottom of each champagne glass. Pour punch into champagne glasses. Garnish with citrus strips tied in knots, if desired.

Makes 4 cups, 6 to 8 servings

NONALCOHOLIC CRANBERRY PUNCH:
Pour 3 cups well-chilled club soda into ⅔ cup (6 ounces) cranberry cocktail concentrate, thawed. Makes 3⅔ cups, 6 servings.

Champagne Punch

DOUBLE BERRY COCO PUNCH

Ice Ring (recipe follows, optional) or
    block of ice
2 (10-ounce) packages frozen
    strawberries in syrup, thawed
1 (15-ounce) can COCO LOPEZ® Cream
    of Coconut
1 (48-ounce) bottle cranberry juice
    cocktail, chilled
2 cups light rum (optional)
1 (32-ounce) bottle club soda, chilled

Prepare Ice Ring in advance if desired. In blender container, purée strawberries with cream of coconut until smooth. In large punch bowl, combine strawberry mixture, cranberry juice and rum. Just before serving, add club soda and Ice Ring.   *Makes about 4 quarts*

ICE RING: Fill ring mold with water to within 1 inch of top rim; freeze. Arrange strawberries, cranberries, mint leaves, lime slices or other fruits on top of ice. Gradually pour small amount of cold water over fruits; freeze.

CITRUS BERRY FROST

4 scoops or ¾ cup WYLER'S® Sugar
    Sweetened Lemonade Flavor Crystals
4 cups chilled cranberry juice cocktail
4 cups water
1 cup chilled orange juice
    Ice

In large pitcher, combine all ingredients except ice. Serve over ice and garnish, if desired, with cranberries and orange slices.
    Makes about 8 servings

CITRUS COOLER

2 cups fresh squeezed orange juice
2 cups unsweetened pineapple juice
1 teaspoon fresh lemon juice
¾ teaspoon vanilla extract
¾ teaspoon coconut extract
2 cups cold sparkling water
    Ice
    Lemon slices (optional)

Combine juices and extracts in large pitcher; refrigerate until cold. Stir in sparkling water; serve over ice. Garnish with lemon slices, if desired.   *Makes 8 servings*

CELEBRATION PUNCH

1 bottle (48 fluid ounces) DEL MONTE®
    Pineapple Orange Blended Juice
    Drink, chilled
1 can (46 fluid ounces) DEL MONTE®
    Apricot Nectar, chilled
1 cup orange juice
1 cup rum (optional)
¼ cup fresh lime juice
2 tablespoons grenadine
    Ice cubes

In punch bowl, combine all ingredients. Garnish with pineapple wedges and lime slices, if desired.   *Makes 16 (6-ounce) servings*

Citrus Cooler

RASPBERRY WINE PUNCH

1 package (10 ounces) frozen red
    raspberries in syrup, thawed
1 bottle (750 mL) white zinfandel or
    blush wine
¼ cup raspberry-flavored liqueur
    Empty ½-gallon milk or juice carton
3 to 4 cups distilled water, divided
    Fresh cranberries
    Sprigs of pine and tinsel

Process raspberries with syrup in food processor or blender until smooth; press through strainer, discarding seeds. Combine wine, raspberry purée and liqueur in pitcher; refrigerate until serving time. Rinse out wine bottle and remove label.

Fully open top of carton. Place wine bottle in center of carton. Tape bottle securely to carton so bottle will not move when adding water. Pour 2 cups distilled water into carton. Carefully push cranberries, pine sprigs and tinsel into water between bottle and carton to form decorative design. Add remaining water to almost fill carton. Freeze until firm, 8 hours or overnight.

Just before serving, peel carton from ice block. Using funnel, pour punch back into wine bottle. Wrap bottom of ice block with white cotton napkin or towel to hold while serving.

Makes 8 servings

NOTE: Punch may also be served in a punch bowl, if desired.

Raspberry Wine Punch

Cranberry Orange Punch

CRANBERRY ORANGE PUNCH

2 (32-ounce) bottles cranberry juice cocktail, chilled
1½ cups REALEMON® Lemon Juice from Concentrate
⅔ cup sugar
2 (12-ounce) cans orange soda, chilled
Ice

In large punch bowl, combine cranberry juice, REALEMON® brand and sugar; stir until sugar dissolves. Just before serving, add orange soda and ice. Garnish as desired.

Makes about 3½ quarts

EASY ORANGE FIZZ

Maraschino cherries
Mint leaves
1 (6-ounce) can frozen Florida Orange Juice Concentrate, thawed
Club soda or tonic water, chilled

Thoroughly drain maraschino cherries. Arrange mint leaves and cherries in compartments of ice cube trays; fill with water and freeze until firm to form decorative ice cubes. Prepare orange juice concentrate according to label directions, *except* substitute club soda or tonic water for the water. Pour into glasses over decorative ice cubes. Serve immediately.

Makes 4 (6-ounce) servings

*Favorite recipe from **Florida Department of Citrus***

CRANBERRY SANGRÍA

- 1 bottle (750 ml) Beaujolais or dry red wine
- 1 cup cranberry juice cocktail
- 1 cup orange juice
- ½ cup cranberry-flavored liqueur (optional)
- 1 orange,* thinly sliced
- 1 lime,* thinly sliced

Combine wine, cranberry juice cocktail, orange juice, liqueur, orange slices and lime slices in large glass pitcher. Chill 2 to 8 hours before serving.

Pour into glasses; add orange and/or lime slices from sangría to each glass.
Makes about 7 cups, 10 to 12 servings

SPARKLING SANGRÍA: Just before serving, tilt pitcher and slowly add 2 cups well-chilled sparkling water or club soda. Pour into glasses; add orange and/or lime slices from sangría to each glass. Makes about 9 cups, 12 to 15 servings.

*Orange and lime may be scored before slicing to add a special touch. To score, make a lengthwise groove in fruit with citrus stripper. Continue to make grooves ¼ to ½ inch apart until entire fruit has been grooved.

KAHLÚA® PARTY PUNCH

- 2 cups KAHLÚA®
- 1 can (12 ounces) frozen apple juice concentrate, undiluted
- ½ cup lemon juice
- 1 small block of ice
- 1 bottle (25.4 ounces) sparkling apple juice
- 1 quart club soda or lemon-lime beverage
- 1 bottle (750 mL) dry champagne
  Thin lemon slices and small orange slices for garnish

Refrigerate ingredients until well chilled. Combine Kahlúa® with undiluted apple juice concentrate and lemon juice. Pour over small block of ice in punch bowl. Add sparkling apple juice, club soda and champagne; stir gently. Add lemon and orange slices.
Makes 30 (½-cup) servings (about 1 gallon)

NOTE: Kahlúa®, undiluted apple juice concentrate and lemon juice may be mixed and refrigerated the day before.

Cranberry Sangría

Peach Fizz

PEACH FIZZ

**3 fresh California peaches, peeled,
halved, pitted and sliced
1 can (6 ounces) pineapple juice
¼ cup frozen limeade or lemonade
concentrate
¼ teaspoon almond extract
Finely crushed ice
3 cups club soda, chilled**

Add peaches to food processor or blender.
Process until smooth to measure 2 cups purée.
Stir in pineapple juice, limeade and almond
extract. Fill 12-ounce glasses ⅔ full with
crushed ice. Add ⅓ cup peach base to each.
Top with club soda. Stir gently. Serve
immediately. *Makes 6 servings*

Favorite recipe from **California Tree Fruit Agreement**

PIÑA COLADA PUNCH

**5 cups DOLE® Pineapple Juice, divided
1 can (15 ounces) cream of coconut
1 liter lemon-lime soda
2 limes, divided
1½ cups light rum (optional)
Ice cubes
Mint sprigs**

• Chill all ingredients.

• Blend 2 cups pineapple juice with cream of
coconut in blender. Combine puréed mixture
with remaining 3 cups pineapple juice, soda,
juice of 1 lime, rum and ice. Garnish with 1
lime, sliced and mint. *Makes 15 servings*

LEMONY LIGHT COOLER

3 cups dry white wine or white grape
   juice, chilled
½ to ¾ cup sugar
½ cup REALEMON® Lemon Juice from
   Concentrate
1 (32-ounce) bottle club soda, chilled
   Strawberries, plum, peach or orange
   slices or other fresh fruit
   Ice

In pitcher, combine wine, sugar and
ReaLemon® brand; stir until sugar dissolves.
Chill. Just before serving, add club soda and
fruit; serve over ice.   *Makes about 7 cups*

APPLE CINNAMON CREAM LIQUEUR

1 (14-ounce) can EAGLE® Brand
   Sweetened Condensed Milk (NOT
   evaporated milk)
1 cup apple schnapps
2 cups (1 pint) BORDEN® or MEADOW
   GOLD® Whipping Cream or Half-
   and-Half
½ teaspoon ground cinnamon
   Ice

In blender container, combine all ingredients
except ice; blend until smooth. Serve over ice.
Garnish as desired. Store covered in
refrigerator. Stir before serving.
                    Makes about 1 quart

FUZZY NAVEL CREAM LIQUEUR: Omit
apple schnapps and cinnamon. Add 1 cup
peach schnapps and ¼ cup frozen orange juice
concentrate, thawed. Proceed as above.

Lemony Light Cooler

SPICED RED WINE

Grape Ice Ring (recipe follows)
½ cup sugar
½ cup water
1 bottle (750 mL) Burgundy wine, chilled
2 cups white grape juice, chilled
1 cup peach schnapps, chilled

Prepare Grape Ice Ring.

Combine sugar and water in small saucepan. Bring to a boil. Boil, stirring constantly, until sugar dissolves. Cool to room temperature. Cover; refrigerate until chilled, about 2 hours.

Combine wine, grape juice, schnapps and sugar syrup in punch bowl. Float Grape Ice Ring in punch.   *Makes 14 servings*

GRAPE ICE RING

2 pounds assorted seedless grapes (Thompson, Red Empress, etc.)
Lemon leaves* (optional)

Fill 4-cup ring mold with water to within ¾ inch of top. Freeze until firm, about 8 hours or overnight. Arrange clusters of grapes and leaves on ice; fill with water to top of mold. Freeze until solid, about 6 hours. To unmold, dip bottom of mold briefly in hot water.

*These nontoxic leaves are available in florist shops.

BLOODY MARY MIX

1 quart vegetable juice cocktail
2 tablespoons HEINZ® Worcestershire Sauce
1 tablespoon fresh lime or lemon juice
¼ teaspoon granulated sugar
¼ teaspoon black pepper
¼ teaspoon hot pepper sauce
⅛ teaspoon garlic powder
Ice

In pitcher, thoroughly combine vegetable juice, Worcestershire sauce, lime juice, sugar, black pepper, hot pepper sauce and garlic powder; cover and chill. Serve over ice. Garnish with celery stalks and lime wedges, if desired.
          Makes about 1 quart

NOTE: To prepare Bloody Mary Cocktail, add 3 or 4 parts Bloody Mary Mix to 1 part vodka.

HOMEMADE CREAM LIQUEURS

1 (14-ounce) can EAGLE® Brand Sweetened Condensed Milk (NOT evaporated milk)
1¼ cups flavored liqueur (almond, coffee, orange or mint)
1 cup (½ pint) BORDEN® or MEADOW GOLD® Whipping Cream or Half-and-Half
Ice

In blender container, combine all ingredients except ice; blend until smooth. Serve over ice. Garnish as desired. Store tightly covered in refrigerator. Stir before serving.
          Makes about 1 quart

Spiced Red Wine with Grape Ice Ring

Acknowledgments

The publishers would like to thank the companies and organizations listed below for the use of their recipes and photographs in this publication.

Alaska Seafood Marketing Institute
Almond Board of California
American Dairy Association
American Egg Board
American Lamb Council
Arm & Hammer Division, Church & Dwight Co., Inc.
American Spice Trade Association
Best Foods, a Division of CPC International Inc.
Bongrain Cheese U.S.A.
Blue Diamond Growers
Bob Evans Farms®
Borden Kitchens, Borden, Inc.
California Apricot Advisory Board
California Beef Council
California Kiwifruit Commission
California Raisin Advisory Board
California Table Grape Commission
California Tree Fruit Agreement
Canned Food Information Council
Canned Fruit Promotion Service, Inc.
Chef Paul Prudhomme's Magic Seasoning Blends®
Chilean Fresh Fruit Association
Clear Springs Foods
Del Monte Corporation
Delmarva Poultry Industry, Inc.
Dole Food Company, Inc.
Domino Sugar Corporation
Dreyer's Grand Ice Cream, Inc.
Farmhouse Foods Company
Filippo Berio Olive Oil

Florida Department of Agriculture and Consumer Services, Bureau of Seafood and Aquaculture
Florida Department of Citrus
Florida Tomato Committee
Grandma's Molasses, a division of Cadbury Beverages, Inc.
Heinz U.S.A.
Hershey Foods Corporation
The HVR Company
Illinois State Fair
Imperial Holly Corporation
Jolly Time® Pop Corn
Jones Dairy Farm
Kahlúa Liqueur
Keebler® Company
Kellogg Company
Kerr Group, Inc.®
Kikkoman International Inc.
Kraft Foods, Inc.
Lawry's® Foods, Inc.
Leaf®, Inc.
Thomas J. Lipton Co.
McIlhenny Company
Michigan Apple Committee
MOTT'S® U.S.A., a division of Cadbury Beverages Inc.
Nabisco Foods Group
National Cherry Foundation
National Dairy Board
National Fisheries Institute
National Honey Board
National Live Stock & Meat Board
National Pasta Association

National Pork Producers Council
National Sunflower Association
National Turkey Federation
Nestlé Food Company
Newman's Own, Inc.
New York Apple Association, Inc.
Norseland, Inc.
North Dakota Barley Council
Ocean Spray Cranberries, Inc.
Oregon Washington California Pear Bureau
Pecan Marketing Board
Perdue® Farms
The Procter & Gamble Company
The Quaker Oats Company
Ralston Foods, Inc.
Reckitt & Colman Inc.
RED STAR® Yeast & Products, A Division of Universal Foods Corporation
Refined Sugars Incorporated
Chocolate Riesen® Caramels
Riviana Foods Inc.
Sargento Foods, Inc.®
The J. M. Smucker Company
StarKist Seafood Company
The Sugar Association, Inc.
Sun-Diamond Growers of California
USA Dry Pea & Lentil Council
USA Rice Council
Walnut Marketing Board
Washington Apple Commission
Wisconsin Milk Marketing Board

Index

METRIC CONVERSION CHART

VOLUME MEASUREMENTS (dry)

⅛ teaspoon = 0.5 mL
¼ teaspoon = 1 mL
½ teaspoon = 2 mL
¾ teaspoon = 4 mL
1 teaspoon = 5 mL
1 tablespoon = 15 mL
2 tablespoons = 30 mL
¼ cup = 60 mL
⅓ cup = 75 mL
½ cup = 125 mL
⅔ cup = 150 mL
¾ cup = 175 mL
1 cup = 250 mL
2 cups = 1 pint = 500 mL
3 cups = 750 mL
4 cups = 1 quart = 1 L

VOLUME MEASUREMENTS (fluid)

1 fluid ounce (2 tablespoons) = 30 mL
4 fluid ounces (½ cup) = 125 mL
8 fluid ounces (1 cup) = 250 mL
12 fluid ounces (1½ cups) = 375 mL
16 fluid ounces (2 cups) = 500 mL

WEIGHTS (mass)

½ ounce = 15 g
1 ounce = 30 g
3 ounces = 90 g
4 ounces = 120 g
8 ounces = 225 g
10 ounces = 285 g
12 ounces = 360 g
16 ounces = 1 pound = 450 g

DIMENSIONS

$\frac{1}{16}$ inch = 2 mm
⅛ inch = 3 mm
¼ inch = 6 mm
½ inch = 1.5 cm
¾ inch = 2 cm
1 inch = 2.5 cm

OVEN TEMPERATURES

250°F = 120°C
275°F = 140°C
300°F = 150°C
325°F = 160°C
350°F = 180°C
375°F = 190°C
400°F = 200°C
425°F = 220°C
450°F = 230°C

BAKING PAN SIZES

Utensil	Size in Inches/Quarts	Metric Volume	Size in Centimeters
Baking or Cake Pan (square or rectangular)	8×8×2	2 L	20×20×5
	9×9×2	2.5 L	22×22×5
	12×8×2	3 L	30×20×5
	13×9×2	3.5 L	33×23×5
Loaf Pan	8×4×3	1.5 L	20×10×7
	9×5×3	2 L	23×13×7
Round Layer Cake Pan	8×1½	1.2 L	20×4
	9×1½	1.5 L	23×4
Pie Plate	8×1¼	750 mL	20×3
	9×1¼	1 L	23×3
Baking Dish or Casserole	1 quart	1 L	—
	1½ quart	1.5 L	—
	2 quart	2 L	—